In the Classroom

- Read all of the directions. Make sure you understand them. When you see ▨, be sure to follow the safety rule.

- Listen to your teacher for special safety directions. If you don't understand something, ask for help.

- Wear safety goggles when your teacher tells you to wear them and whenever you see ▨.

- Wear a safety apron if you work with anything messy or anything that might spill.

- If you spill something, wipe it up right away or ask your teacher for help.

- Tell your teacher if something breaks. If glass breaks do not clean it up yourself.

- Keep your hair and clothes away from open flames. Tie back long hair and roll up long sleeves.

- Be careful around a hot plate. Know when it is on and when it is off. Remember that the plate stays hot for a few minutes after you turn it off.

- Keep your hands dry around electrical equipment.

- Don't eat or drink anything during an experiment.

- Put equipment back the way your teacher tells you.

- Dispose of things the way your teacher tells you.

- Clean up your work area, and wash your hands.

In the Field

- Always be accompanied by a trusted adult—like your teacher or a parent or guardian.

- Never touch animals or plants without the adult's approval. The animal might bite. The plant might be poison ivy or another dangerous plant.

Responsibility

- Treat living things, the environment, and each other with respect.

McGRAW-HILL
SCIENCE

MACMILLAN/McGRAW-HILL EDITION

RICHARD MOYER ■ **LUCY DANIEL** ■ **JAY HACKETT**
PRENTICE BAPTISTE ■ **PAMELA STRYKER** ■ **JOANNE VASQUEZ**

NATIONAL
GEOGRAPHIC
SOCIETY

McGraw-Hill
School Division

New York   Farmington

PROGRAM AUTHORS

Lucy H. Daniel, Ed.D.
*Teacher, Consultant
Rutherford County Schools,
North Carolina*

Dr. Jay Hackett
*Emeritus Professor of Earth
Sciences
University of Northern
Colorado*

Dr. Richard H. Moyer
*Professor of Science
Education
University of Michigan-
Dearborn*

Dr. H. Prentice Baptiste
*Professor of Curriculum and
Instruction
New Mexico State
University*

Pamela Stryker, M.Ed.
*Elementary Educator and
Science Consultant
Eanes Independent School
District
Austin, Texas*

JoAnne Vasquez
*Elementary Science
Education Specialist
Mesa Public Schools,
Arizona
NSTA President 1996–1997*

NATIONAL
GEOGRAPHIC
SOCIETY

Washington, D.C.

CONTRIBUTING AUTHORS

Dr. Thomas Custer
Dr. James Flood
Dr. Diane Lapp
Doug Llewellyn
Dorothy Reid
Dr. Donald M. Silver

CONSULTANTS

Dr. Danny J. Ballard
Dr. Carol Baskin
Dr. Bonnie Buratti
Dr. Suellen Cabe
Dr. Shawn Carlson
Dr. Thomas A. Davies
Dr. Marie DiBerardino
Dr. R. E. Duhrkopf
Dr. Ed Geary
Dr. Susan C. Giarratano-Russell
Dr. Karen Kwitter
Dr. Donna Lloyd-Kolkin
Ericka Lochner, RN
Dr. Dennis L. Nelson
Dr. Fred S. Sack
Dr. Martin VanDyke
Dr. E. Peter Volpe
Dr. Josephine Davis Wallace
Dr. Joe Yelderman

McGraw-Hill School Division

A Division of The McGraw·Hill Companies

Copyright © 2000 McGraw-Hill School Division,
a Division of the Educational and Professional
Publishing Group of The McGraw-Hill Companies, Inc.

McGraw-Hill School Division
Two Penn Plaza
New York, New York 10121

Printed in the United States of America

ISBN 0-02-277437-8 / 5

2 3 4 5 6 7 8 9 027/046 05 04 03 02 01 00 99

CONTENTS

UNIT 1

PLANTS

UNIT 2 WEATHER AND CLIMATE

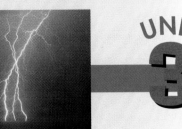

UNIT 3

THE ENERGY OF SOUND AND LIGHT

UNIT 4 MATTER

UNIT 5 EARTH AND ITS RESOURCES

UNIT 6 ECOSYSTEMS AROUND THE WORLD

EXPLORE ACTIVITIES

YOUR TEXTBOOK at a Glance

Begin each topic with an **Explore** ▶ question. Investigate further by doing an **Explore Activity**.

Topic EARTH SCIENCE 3

WHY IT MATTERS

...rain, snow, ...can have ...pact on ...d on us.

...WORDS

...a cloud that ...tlike layer

...a puffy cloud ...up from a

...high-altitude ...rlike shape,

...ms at

...form of ...s from ...eaches

Water cycle the continuous movement of water between Earth's surface and the air, changing from liquid to gas to liquid

---

Geography Link

SCIENCE MAGAZINE

In Tune with the Monsoon

In one part of India, the average winter rainfall is 2.54 centimeters (1 inch) a month. During the summer it gets up to 2.54 meters (100 inches) of rain a month! Farmers depend on the monsoons. When the rain starts, farmers plant rice and other crops. If monsoons come late, nothing grows on the dusty land; however, really heavy rains can wash away the crops!

DISCUSSION STARTER
How do you think the monsoons affect people in monsoon regions who aren't farmers?

In 1997 monsoon killed more than 1,000 people in Pakistan, and ruined nearly 4 million acres of farmland.

To learn more about the monsoons, visit www.mhschool.com/science and enter the keyword MONSOON.

interNET CONNECTION

Life Sciences Link

If you've tried to swim underwater, you know how difficult it is to stay down. Why is it so easy for fish? The answer is built-in—a swim bladder. A fish controls its swim bladder. To float, the fish lets...

Clouds of Water and Ice

How can you predict the weather without using the instruments weather forecasters use? Look at the sky. There are clues up there. They're called clouds. Different kinds of clouds bring different kinds of weather. What is a cloud?

EXPLORE

HYPOTHESIZE Sometimes the sky is full of clouds. Sometimes there are no clouds at all. Why? What makes a cloud form? Do evaporation and condensation have anything to do with it? Write a hypothesis in your *Science Journal*. How might you make a model to test your ideas?

▲ Discuss an exciting **Science Magazine** after each topic. **National Geographic World of Science** is the first magazine in each unit.

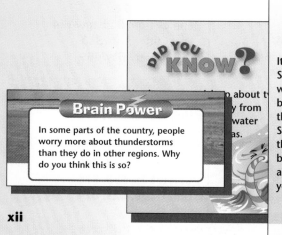

DID YOU KNOW?

Brain Power

In some parts of the country, people worry more about thunderstorms than they do in other regions. Why do you think this is so?

...about t... ...y from ...water ...as.

NATIONAL GEOGRAPHIC

FUNtastic Facts

It's easy to float in Utah's Great Salt Lake. That's because salt water is denser and has greater buoyancy than fresh water—and the lake has 6 billion tons of salt! Swimmers float higher in the lake than in ocean water. The salt has been building up in the lake for about 1 million years. Where can you find another large salty lake?

◀ Flex your brain with questions about real-world facts.

EXPLORE ACTIVITY

Investigate Why Clouds Form

Watch what can happen when you cool off some air.

PROCEDURES

⚠️ **SAFETY** Be careful handling the hot water. Use the handle to hold the mug. Do not burn yourself.

1. Chill container 1 by putting it in a refrigerator or on ice for about ten minutes.

2. Fill a mug with hot tap water.

3. **MAKE A MODEL** Fill container 2 with hot water. Place empty cold container 1 upside down on top of container 2 with the water. Fit the mouths together carefully. Place the ice cubes on top of container 1.

4. **OBSERVE** Write your observations in your *Science Journal*.

CONCLUDE AND APPLY

1. **COMMUNICATE** What did you observe?

2. **COMMUNICATE** Where did this take place?

3. **COMMUNICATE** Where did the water come from?

4. **INFER** Explain what made it happen.

GO FURTHER: Apply

5. **DRAW CONCLUSIONS** Where would you expect to find more clouds—over the ocean or over a desert? Why?

6. **INFER** Why don't all clouds look the same?

MATERIALS
- hot tap water
- 2 identical clear containers
- mug
- 3 ice cubes
- food coloring
- refrigerator or freezer
- *Science Journal*

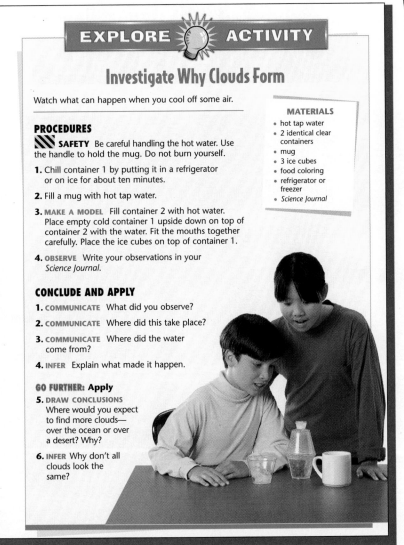

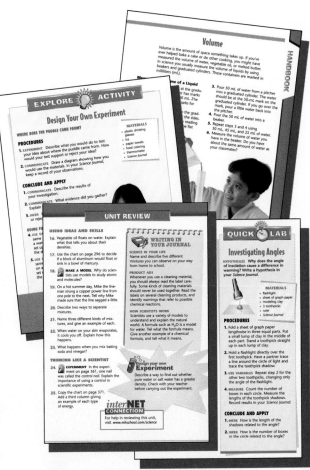

Design Your Own Experiments, do **Quick Labs**, use **Internet Connections**, and try **Writing in Your Journal**. Use the **Handbook** for help.

Reading Graphs, Diagrams, Maps, and **Charts** help you learn by using what you see.

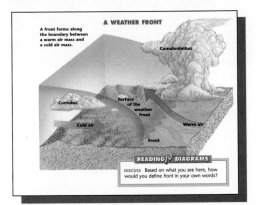

A WEATHER FRONT

A front forms along the boundary between a warm air mass and a cold air mass.

Cumulonimbus

Cumulus

Cold air

Surface of the weather front

Warm air

Front

READING DIAGRAMS

DISCUSS Based on what you see here, how would you define *front* in your own words?

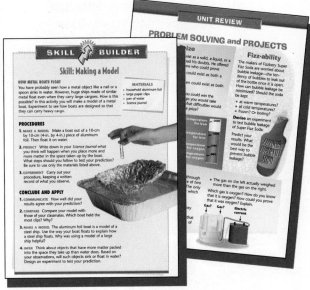

Build your skills with **Skill Builders** and **Problems and Puzzles**.

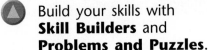

Nurturing strangler fig seedlings is part of Laman's research.

Safely strapped in, Laman works high above the rain forest floor.

Tim Laman

Tim Laman's research takes him up into the sky-high rain forest canopy of Indonesia's Gunung Palung National Park. The Harvard University biologist climbs trees in the rain forest to study strangler figs. The figs sprout high in the trees and send their roots snaking down to the ground. Eventually the roots circle the host tree, cutting off growth.

Laman is a careful observer. Sometimes an observation pays off dramatically. One day when he was collecting samples high in a tree, Laman noticed tiny ants carrying fig seeds. "As I followed the trail of ants to their tree-crotch nest site, I realized I had discovered a new player in the strangler fig's seed dispersal."

Laman had already discovered that birds play a major role in spreading strangler fig seeds. Birds eat the figs and then scatter the seeds throughout the rain forest. The seeds most likely to sprout are the ones that fall in decayed leaves high in the clefts of tree branches.

Measuring the growth of strangler fig seedlings is another part of Laman's work. High above the forest floor, he has planted more than 6,000 strangler fig seeds in the crowns of 45 trees.

Laman calls the pristine Indonesian rain forest a "biological frontier where there is much to discover."

For observing at night, Laman uses an infrared camera.

Birds like this rhinoceros hornbill help spread the fig seeds through the rain forest.

BE A SCIENTIST

Have you ever watched a tree grow from a tiny seed? Trees can grow taller than any other living things. Giant sequoias can grow as tall as a 20-story skyscraper and weigh six times more than the heaviest dinosaur that ever lived! **Mass** (mas) is what scientists use to measure the amount of matter in an object. Giant sequoias started as small seeds. How did they gain so much mass?

Think of a heavy log burning in a fireplace. After several hours there is nothing left but a few ounces of ash. What happened to the rest of the log?

A fully grown giant sequoia can grow 100 meters (300 feet) tall.

EXPLORE

Where do plants get their mass? Write some possible explanations in your *Science Journal*. How might you test your explanations?

EXPLORE ACTIVITY

Investigate Where Plants Get Their Mass

Where do you think the extra mass comes from as a plant grows?

Think of a hypothesis about this question. A hypothesis is a statement in answer to a question. You must be able to test the statement in an experiment.

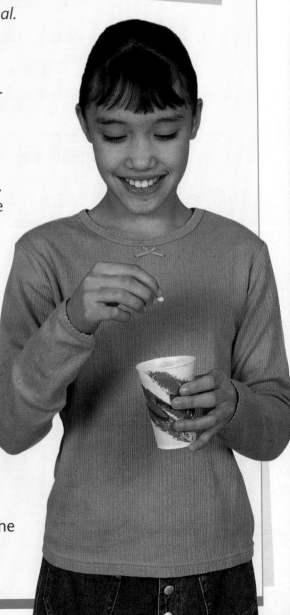

MATERIALS

- package of lima bean seeds
- 4 paper cups
- soil
- balance
- ruler
- water
- *Science Journal*

PROCEDURES

1. Fill the paper cups with a premeasured amount of soil. Use the same amount for each cup. Record the mass of the soil and the date in your *Science Journal.*

2. Find the mass of the seed. Record it and the date. Plant one lima bean seed in each cup.

3. Place the cups where they will get sunlight. Water the soil the same amount each week.

4. OBSERVE After three months, measure the plant height with the ruler and record your findings. Carefully remove the plant and root from the soil. Find the mass of the plant, and record it. Find the mass of the soil again, and record it.

5. INTERPRET DATA Compare the mass of the plant and soil now to the start of the experiment.

Sample data

	September	December
Plant height	7.6 cm (3 in.)	25.4 cm (10 in.)
Mass of plant	2 g	68 g
Mass of soil	225 g	223 g

CONCLUDE AND APPLY

1. DRAW CONCLUSIONS How much mass did the plant gain in three months?

2. Do you think the added mass of the plant came from the soil? Why? Do you think it came from the water you added? Explain.

Where Do Plants Get Their Mass?

All around us things are changing their properties due to chemical changes. A **chemical change** is a change of matter that occurs when atoms link together in a new way, creating a new substance different from the original substances.

The Explore Activity showed that a chemical change took place when the seed was planted in the soil. Plants use energy from the Sun, water, nutrients from the soil, and air to make their own food and grow. The food-making process in green plants that uses sunlight is called **photosynthesis**.

There are many types of chemical changes. Fire (1) causes a chemical change in burning wood. As the wood burns, the chemical energy stored in it is changed to light and heat. Some of the chemicals in the wood produce gas as they burn. Smoke is formed when the gas mixes with tiny particles of the burnt wood. The only solid material left behind is the ash, which has much less mass than the log.

Vinegar and baking soda (2) combine to form a gas. The gas is so light it rises into the air. Metals (3) turn to rust after being exposed to air for a long time.

1

2

3

How Do Scientists Begin?

For hundreds of years, scientists have studied the chemical changes that make green plants grow. At one time it seemed reasonable to think that plants got their food by absorbing soil through their roots. A scientist named Jean Baptiste van Helmont helped change that view nearly 300 years ago.

Scientists are curious about the world around them. This curiosity causes them to ask questions about things they don't understand. Sometimes they question the explanations accepted by others. This was the case with Helmont. He wondered whether plants really absorbed soil as others thought. He wondered whether anyone had ever actually tested the idea. He thought about how he could test this idea himself.

Does the mass of a tree come from absorbing the soil it grows in? He concluded that if a tree uses up soil to get its food, then the soil around it should get lighter. Helmont conducted an experiment to test his hypothesis. His findings changed the way scientists thought about how green plants grow.

Scientists need to think of ways to control as many parts of an experiment as they can. This helps determine what is or what isn't causing the change they are investigating. To investigate whether plants were absorbing the soil around them for food, Helmont decided to measure it.

Jean Baptiste van Helmont was a biologist.

How Do Scientists Learn from the Work of Others?

Helmont planted a young willow tree that weighed 5 pounds in a tub that contained 200 pounds of soil. Then he carefully studied the tree and the soil for five years, recording all the changes that occurred. During this period his measurements showed that the tree grew to a weight of 164 pounds. In all that time, the soil lost only 2 ounces! The evidence showed that the tree had not gained all its mass directly from the soil. In fact it gained very little of its added mass from the soil!

The experiment answered one question, but it raised another question! How did the tree increase its mass?

After his experiment Helmont guessed that water provided everything a plant needed to grow. Now we know he was only partly right. Plants do need water to increase their mass, but most of all, green plants need sunlight. Thanks to the work of many scientists since Helmont's day, we know that few organisms can survive without receiving energy directly or indirectly from the Sun. Green plants use photosynthesis to mix energy from the Sun with water, air, and soil nutrients to make a kind of sugar. The sugar is used by the plant to grow its stems, its roots, its seeds, and all its other parts.

Helmont studied the growth of a willow tree to explore where plants get their mass.

How Do Scientists Know What Questions to Ask?

Scientists today understand much about photosynthesis, but not everything. They still can't make it happen in a laboratory experiment. We *have* learned that the relationship between plants and soil is much more complicated than what was believed in Helmont's time.

One scientist who studies the way trees grow is Roy Renkin. Renkin is a **biologist** (bī ol'ə jist) who works for the National Park Service at Yellowstone National Park in Wyoming. A biologist is a scientist who studies plant and animal life. Thanks to the work of Helmont, Renkin learned that the trees he studies don't absorb much soil to increase their mass. When scientists answer one question, it often leads to more questions. Renkin had two questions. What makes forests grow? When a forest dies, how does it grow back?

In August 1988 a huge forest fire raged at Yellowstone National Park. Winds tore through the park at 112 kilometers (70 miles) per hour. Flames soared 91 meters (700 feet) into the sky. When it was over, more square miles of Yellowstone Park had burned during one

Roy Renkin is a biologist for Yellowstone National Park.

week than during any ten-year period since 1872! The fire burned nearly 1 million acres of forest, an area larger than the entire state of Rhode Island!

The fire was a great tragedy, but for Roy Renkin it was also the chance of a lifetime. It gave him the chance to investigate the questions he had about how forests begin to grow.

Scientists used to believe that forest fires destroyed the roots and soil nutrients that plants need to grow. Renkin helped show that that was not true.

In his investigation Renkin discovered that some trees use a forest fire to help them reproduce. Some of the pine cones dropped by a lodgepole pine evergreen tree open to release

Some lodgepole pine cones open only after a fire.

their seeds only after they have been burned! After the Yellowstone fire, Renkin and other scientists found as many as 150,000 lodgepole pine seeds per acre. Renkin also discovered that the ash from the fire made the soil's nutrient levels increase for the first year or two after the fire. Within five years after the fire, he found the forest ground was covered with new growth.

The 1988 Yellowstone fire destroyed nearly 1 million acres of forest!

Renkin also investigated the park's aspen trees after the fire and made an important discovery. He discovered that a forest fire is one the best things that can happen to aspens.

Aspens grow mostly in the western areas of North America. Scientists know that groups of aspens are connected underground through a large root system. Scientists used to think that new aspen trees grew only as shoots from the underground root system of the older aspens. After the Yellowstone fire, Renkin discovered aspens growing from seedlings. He also discovered they were growing from seeds because the fire changed the forest soil. The change in the soil's nutrients and moisture content because of the fire created the conditions in which the aspen seedlings could grow on their own!

Renkin has helped us understand that fire can be a natural process

Aspen trees often share one huge root system.

that helps a forest. As forests age, dead timber builds up on the ground. Fires become more likely. Careless people cause many forest fires, but lightning can also start one. Lightning striking a new forest may have little effect, but if it strikes the downed, dry timber of an old forest, it can spark a widespread fire. Some trees, like the lodgepole pine and the aspen, have developed ways to use the new conditions to their benefit.

How Can I Be Like a Scientist?

Scientists start with curiosity! They **look carefully** at things around them and **ask questions**. How can trees grow so tall? How can heavy, burning logs turn into lightweight ashes? Do forest fires prevent new young trees from growing, or do they help them? You may have observed things around you that made you wonder.

Thinking like a scientist means trying to find answers to questions like these. Sometimes it means not believing the explanations of others. Helmont conducted his experiment because he did not believe the conclusions of the scientists before him.

Try picking a favorite tree and learning what you can by observing it over the course of a year. See if your observations lead to another hypothesis you might be able to test.

A deciduous tree changes with the seasons.

Now let's go back and look at how you thought like a scientist when you did the Explore Activity on the increase in mass during plant growth.

YOU ASKED YOURSELF QUESTIONS

To be a scientist means asking questions about the world around you.

When you thought about tall trees growing from tiny seeds, you wondered where their mass came from. You asked yourself: How can I test my ideas to answer my questions?

YOU SET UP AN INVESTIGATION

At the beginning of the Explore Activity, you thought about a **hypothesis**. It was an idea or a guess about what would happen that you could test. You then **planned your experiment** and planted your seeds.

You **measured** the materials and **started your observations**. You **recorded** and **organized** the information to help you understand it better. You **shared your observations** with others in the class. Just as later scientists learned from Helmont, you learned by looking at the data of the other students.

YOU USED THE RESULTS OF YOUR INVESTIGATION TO ANSWER QUESTIONS

To be a scientist, you need to observe the process of your experiment closely. You also need to **analyze the results** and **draw conclusions**. After you studied the measurements of the experiment, it was clear the gain

in mass by the plant did not come from the soil. From this you learned whether or not your hypothesis was correct.

Scientists **share the findings** of their experiments. During the Explore Activity, you shared your analysis of the data with your partner. You also recorded your explanations in your *Science Journal*. The data table you put together made the information easier to understand.

Sharing the results of an experiment helps scientists decide how strong or weak their hypothesis is. They can **compare their results** with the results of other scientists doing the same experiment. To be even more certain, scientists often **repeat their experiment**.

Just as Renkin learned from Helmont's experiment, you learned from the experiments of other students. The results of the experiment did show that the mass of the plant did not come from the soil. The results did not tell you where the added plant mass did come from.

How might you improve on the experiment conducted by Helmont? Using what you now know, what other questions about growing plants does your experiment raise? For example: Does water account for all the increase in the mass of the plant? How could you find out?

For scientists a successful experiment often raises more questions than it answers. What are some of the new questions you have about chemical changes that are occurring around you? Can you think of ways to test these questions to learn more about them?

In this book you will be doing many Explore Activities. Complete all the steps you just learned each time. It's called the scientific method. It's what makes you a real scientist! Answers are important. In science it's also important *how* you found the answers.

WHY IT MATTERS

The Smokey Bear campaign changed our ideas about forest fires. It has been telling us for years that we need to prevent forest fires. The campaign has been a success because it's a good message. The carelessness of humans still results in the destruction of too many acres of valuable forest.

Local fire departments warn people about how likely fires can be in their areas.

The work of scientists like Roy Renkin has also changed our ideas about forest fires. It is only now that we are beginning to realize the benefits of burning to some forests. As Renkin discovered, fire allows old forests to be replaced by young ones more quickly. Renkin saw what those before him did not. He discovered that the fire gave the soil more nutrients for new plants to grow in. After a fire he also saw a clear, open area where more rain and sunlight could reach the new growth.

From the work of scientists, we've also learned how beneficial trees are to us. Trees are actually large air conditioners! They cool the air by absorbing water from the ground and releasing moisture through their leaves. A single large tree has the cooling power of five air conditioners. Scientists have also shown that tree leaves filter air pollution. This can be very helpful because a large tree may have 200,000 leaves.

Using this information scientists in Dayton, Ohio, discovered that the temperature in an urban area ecosystem can be reduced by 2°C (4°F) by planting enough trees in the area.

A dozen fifth graders in El Segundo, California, used the information scientists have gathered about trees to help their community. It is an urban environment with very few trees. When the students learned how beneficial trees can be, they decided to start a new organization.

El Segundo is near Los Angeles. It has a huge oil refinery on one side and the enormous Los Angeles Airport on the other. Both the refinery and the airport produce a lot of pollution. Calling themselves the Tree Musketeers, the group decided to try to plant enough trees to create a "pollution barrier" around their town.

In the nine years since they started, the Tree Musketeers have planted more than 700 trees in their community. They have also inspired other young people around the United States to plant thousands more trees.

The Tree Musketeers group is run entirely by kids. The county of Los Angeles and the state government of California both gave awards to the group. Several years ago the Tree Musketeers even received a special volunteer Action Award from the President of the United States!

Tree Musketeers planting a tree.

REVIEW

1. Where do plants get their mass?

2. How do scientists study trees and plants?

3. What discoveries did Roy Renkin make about forest fires?

4. Why do you think the lodgepole pine has cones that open only after a fire?

BE A SCIENTIST Glossary

These are words you can use as a scientist as you use this book and in your life.

A

analyze separate anything into its parts to find out what it is made of and how it is put together

C

classify place materials that share properties together in groups

collect data put together all useful information

communicate share information

D

define put together a description that is based on observations and experience

draw conclusions put together in a statement all the facts you have learned

E

evaluate find out the value or amount of something

evidence clues used to solve a problem

experiment a test that is used to discover or prove something

H

hypothesis a statement in answer to a question; you must be able to test the statement

I

identify patterns find a group of facts that repeat or do not change

infer form an idea from facts or observations

interpret data use the information that has been gathered to answer questions or solve a problem

M

make decisions make up your mind from many choices

measure find the size, volume, area, mass, weight, or temperature of an object or how long an event occurs

model something that represents an object or event

O

observe use one or more of the senses to identify or learn about an object or event

P

plan think out ahead of time how something is to be done or made, including methods and materials

predict state possible results of an event or experiment

T

test the examination of a substance or event to see what it is or why it happens

theory an explanation based on observation and reasoning

U

use numbers ordering, counting, adding, subtracting, multiplying, and dividing to explain data

V

variable a thing in an experiment that can be changed or controlled

These are words that you will use as a thinker whenever you read or study.

cause and effect something (cause) that brings about a change in something else (effect)

compare and contrast find out how things are the same (compare) and how they are different (contrast)

identify name or recognize

reproduce results repeat an experiment to verify findings

revise examine and improve

sequence a series of things that are related in some way

These are new Science Words that you learned in Be a Scientist.

biologist a scientist who studies plant and animal life

chemical change a change of matter that occurs when atoms link together in a new way, creating a new substance different from the original substances

mass a measure of the amount of matter in an object

photosynthesis the food-making process in green plants that uses sunlight

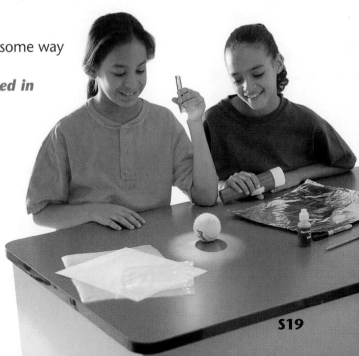

METHODS OF SCIENCE

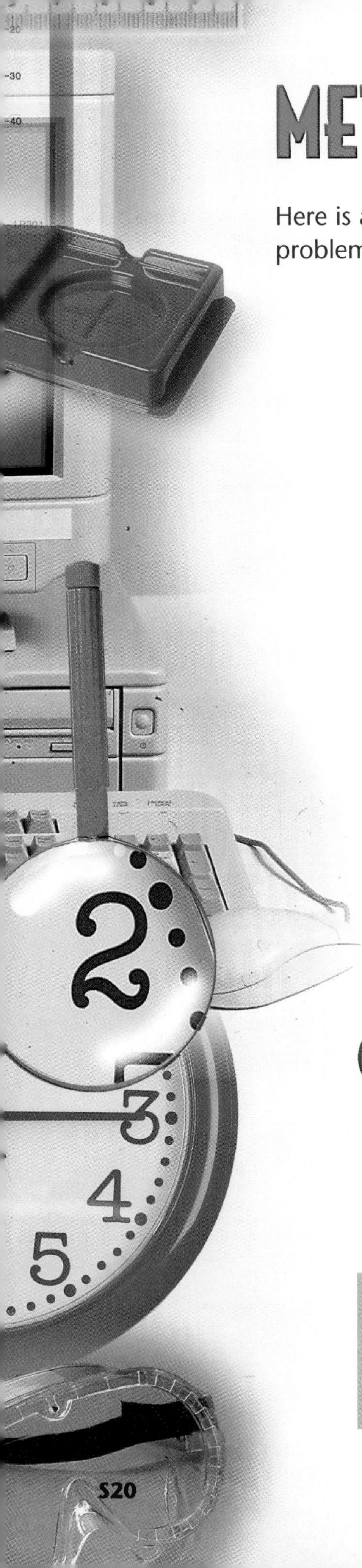

Here is a chart that shows the steps to follow when solving a problem in science.

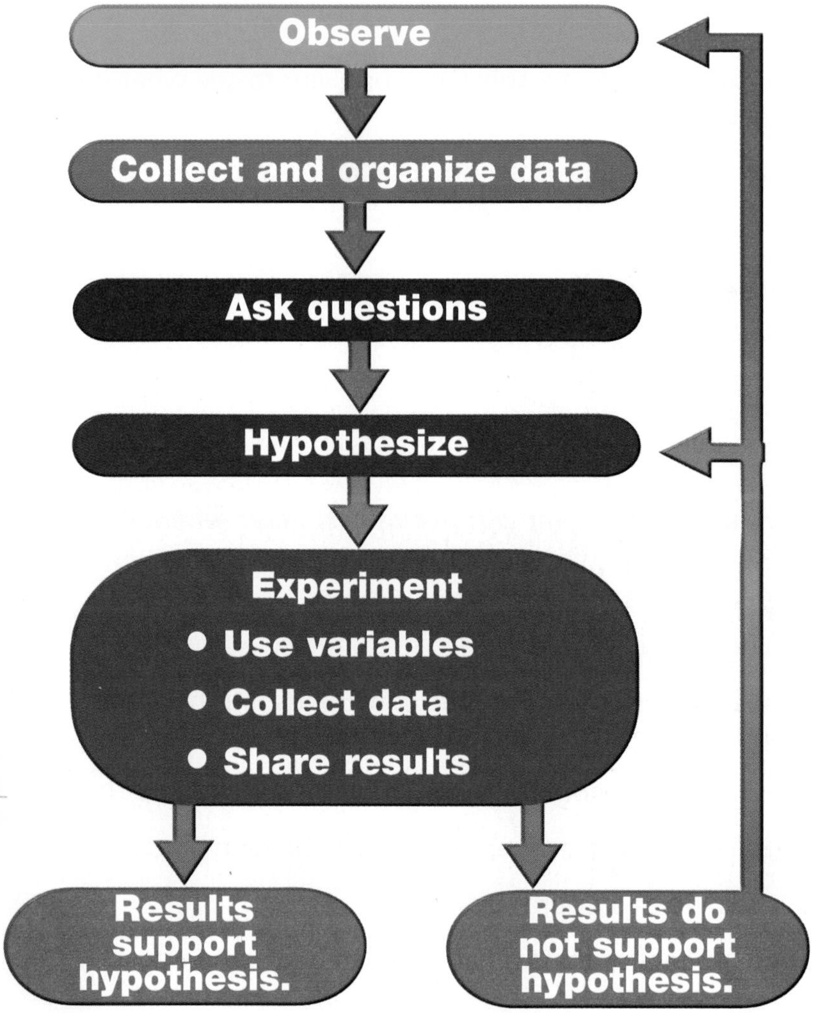

Observe

↓

Collect and organize data

↓

Ask questions

↓

Hypothesize

↓

Experiment
- Use variables
- Collect data
- Share results

↓ ↓

Results support hypothesis.   **Results do not support hypothesis.**

READING /\/ CHARTS

WRITE How would you solve a problem in science? Write a paragraph based on the chart.

CHAPTER 1

THE IMPORTANCE OF PLANTS

Plants give us shade and protect our soil. They give us food, such as fruits and vegetables. They also provide food for animals that people eat.

Plants also give us beautiful flowers we use as gifts and for decoration.

In Chapter 1 you will draw conclusions about things. Drawing conclusions means making reasoned judgments. You will draw conclusions from facts—things you can see and measure.

WHY IT MATTERS

There are many different kinds of plants, and they are used in many different ways.

SCIENCE WORDS

chlorophyll a green chemical in plant cells that allows plants to use the Sun's energy for making food

vascular plants that contain tissue through which water moves up and food moves down

nonvascular plants that do not have tissue through which water and food move

fungus a member of a kingdom that contains one-celled and many-celled living things that absorb food from their environment

protist a member of a kingdom that contains one-celled and many-celled living things, some that make food and some that hunt for food

bacterium a member of either of two kingdoms of one-celled living things that have no nucleus, or center, in their cell body

The Plant Kingdom

What things in a ballpark come from plants? What things that you use every day come from plants? Wood products, cotton clothes, many medicines and foods are from plants. Plants make oxygen! Meats that you eat come from animals that eat plants or from animals that eat animals that eat plants.

Trees, shrubs, grasses, and flowers are familiar and easy to identify as plants. Others may not be so familiar. Are mushrooms plants? Is seaweed a plant?

EXPLORE

HYPOTHESIZE Most plants live on land, but some live in water. Some are tiny, and others grow very large. Do all plants have common traits? Write a hypothesis in your *Science Journal*. Then test your ideas.

Investigate What Plants Have in Common

Define what a plant is by observing four plants and comparing their characteristics.

MATERIALS

- *Elodea* plant
- moss plant
- fern plant
- geranium (or other flowering plant)
- microscope
- microscope slide
- coverslip
- dropper
- water
- *Science Journal*

PROCEDURES

1. OBSERVE Your group will need to get four plants from your teacher. Observe each of the plants.

2. COMMUNICATE As you observe each plant, draw the plant and describe the plant in your *Science Journal*.

3. Make a wet-mount slide of an *Elodea* leaf by placing the leaf in a drop of water in the center of the slide and carefully putting a coverslip on top.

4. OBSERVE View the slide under low power.

5. COMMUNICATE In your *Science Journal*, draw what you see under low power.

CONCLUDE AND APPLY

1. COMMUNICATE What plant traits can you observe without using the microscope?

2. COMMUNICATE What other plant traits can you observe with the microscope?

3. DEFINE Based on what you observed, come up with your own definition of a plant.

GOING FURTHER: Problem Solving

4. HYPOTHESIZE Examine some other kinds of plants with the microscope. Do all the plants seem to have the same traits, or do some plants look quite different from the others? Do plants that look similar under the microscope have the same traits? How would you set up an experiment to find out?

What Do Plants Have in Common?

You don't need a microscope to discover that all of the plants in the Explore Activity are green. That's because their cells contain a green chemical called **chlorophyll** (klôr′ə fil′). It allows plants to use the Sun's energy to make their own food. The other things plants need to make food are water and minerals from the soil and carbon dioxide from the air.

What Are Plants Made Of?

If you looked at the *Elodea* leaf under a microscope, you would see what looked like little boxes. These are the cells, or basic building blocks, of the *Elodea*. All living things are made up of cells. Plants are made up of many different kinds of cells. All plant cells have certain things in common that help plants live and grow.

Let's look at a tree to find out how its cells help it survive. A tree rises up from the ground. Its rigid trunk supports all its weight. Its roots anchor it into the soil. It doesn't walk, run, or swim. In order to live and grow, the tree must be made of rigid building blocks—rigid cells that support it.

What did you discover when you looked at *Elodea* cells under the microscope? You found cells that looked like

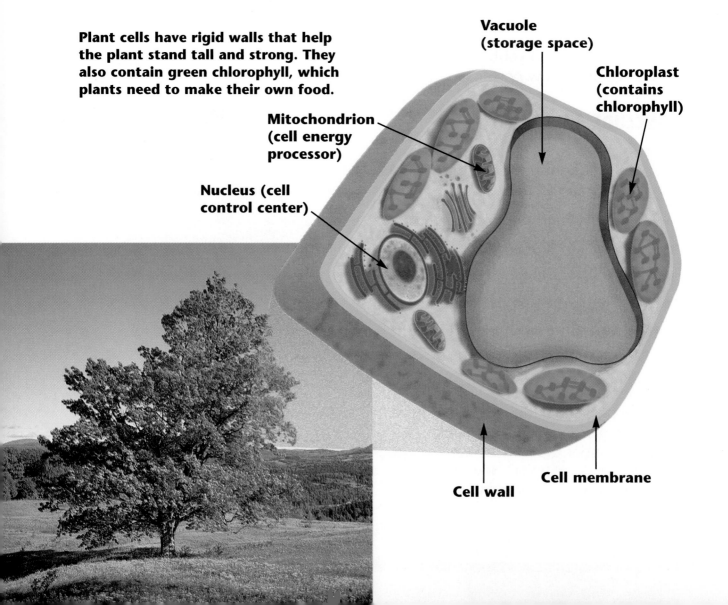

Plant cells have rigid walls that help the plant stand tall and strong. They also contain green chlorophyll, which plants need to make their own food.

Vacuole (storage space)

Chloroplast (contains chlorophyll)

Mitochondrion (cell energy processor)

Nucleus (cell control center)

Cell wall

Cell membrane

boxes. What is one characteristic of boxes? They have walls, which keep them from collapsing into a heap. All plant cells have walls. That's why an oak tree can stand tall and strong.

How Do Cells Work Together?

The cells of all plants work together to keep the plants alive. Different kinds of cells do different kinds of jobs. Each job contributes to the health and survival of the plant. For example, in a tree, cells in leaves make the plant's food. Cells in stems, branches, roots, and the trunk form tubes through which the food or water is moved, or *transported* (trans pôrt'əd). Other cells may form flowers, fruits, and seeds that allow the tree to reproduce.

Cells are organized into *tissues* (tish´üz). The "strings" in celery stalks and the flesh of fruits are examples of plant tissues. Some tissues carry water and minerals to various parts of the plant. Some tissues support the plant.

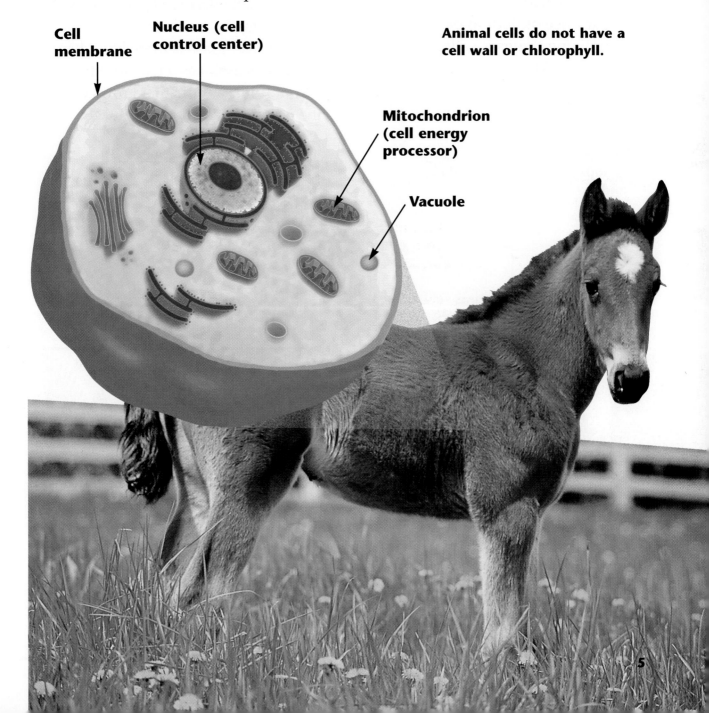

Cell membrane

Nucleus (cell control center)

Animal cells do not have a cell wall or chlorophyll.

Mitochondrion (cell energy processor)

Vacuole

How Can Plants Be Grouped?

People have always tried to make sense of their surroundings. One way to do this is to look for patterns. Finding such patterns among plants can help answer very important questions, such as: What plants are good to eat? What plants are poisonous? What plants contain valuable medicines? What plants produce wood that is strong and hard?

The science of finding patterns among living things is called *classification* (klas´ə fi kā´shæn). Ancient scientists came up with very simple classification systems for plants.

These were based on characteristics that anyone could see. Remember, there were no microscopes or other complex instruments in those days. In 350 b.c. the Greek scientist Aristotle classified plants into three large groups—herbs (little plants), shrubs (bigger plants), and trees (the biggest plants). Aristotle's classification system was based on size.

This made sense at the time. However, as scientists learned more about plants, they realized that size was not a sensible way to classify them.

For example, today we know that a tiny blade of grass is more like a bamboo that is as tall as a ten-story building than it is like a moss that grows close to the ground.

The chart shows the two largest groups in the plant kingdom and examples of each.

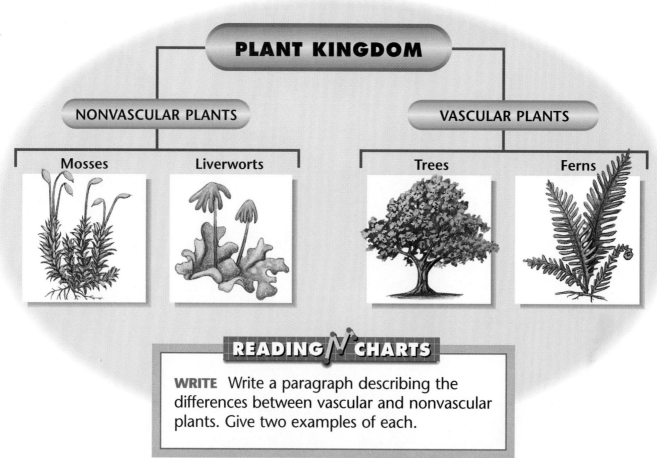

PLANT KINGDOM

NONVASCULAR PLANTS

Mosses   Liverworts

VASCULAR PLANTS

Trees   Ferns

READING N CHARTS

WRITE Write a paragraph describing the differences between vascular and nonvascular plants. Give two examples of each.

What Are Two Major Plant Groups?

By getting a look at what goes on inside plants—not what they look like on the outside—scientists have been able to divide them into two large groups. So let's take a close look inside plants to see what scientists found; something that separates one large group from the other.

First, look inside the stem of a moss. What do you see? You see lots of cells packed together like pieces in a jigsaw puzzle. The cells look very much like one another. Water from outside is passing directly into the cells.

Now, do the same thing with the stem of a corn plant. You see something very different here. Lengths of tubelike cells tunnel up and down the stem. Water taken in by the plant's roots is moving up one set of tubes toward the plant's leaves, flowers, and other parts. At the same time, foods made in the leaves are moving down the other set of tubes, which lead to all of the plant's parts. These tubes are called *vascular tissue*.

Scientists call plants that have this kind of tissue—such as trees and flowering plants—**vascular** (vas′kyə lər) plants. *Vascular* means "composed of or containing vessels," like the veins and arteries in your body. Scientists call plants that don't have this kind of tissue—such as mosses and other simple plants—**nonvascular** plants. All plants fall into one of these two groups.

QUICK LAB

Tubelike Plant Parts

HYPOTHESIZE How does water get to different parts of a plant? Write a hypothesis in your *Science Journal.* Then test your ideas.

MATERIALS
- celery stalk
- bit of moss
- lettuce leaf
- oak or maple leaf
- water
- food coloring
- narrow-mouthed bottle
- hand lens
- knife
- *Science Journal*

PROCEDURES

1. **OBSERVE/COMMUNICATE** Use the hand lens to examine the plant parts. Describe in your *Science Journal* the structures you see.

2. **HYPOTHESIZE** Make a guess about the function of each structure.

3. Add water to the bottle so the water is about an inch deep. Add a few drops of food coloring to the water.

4. Try putting different plant pieces in the colored water. Observe them after a few minutes. Record your observations in your *Science Journal.*

CONCLUDE AND APPLY

1. **INTERPRET DATA** Write an explanation. Include a statement about why your observations support or don't support your guess.

How Are Plant Groups Divided?

As you've discovered, all plants have certain characteristics in common. Every living thing that has these characteristics belongs to the plant kingdom. A kingdom is the largest subdivision of living things.

While all plants have certain characteristics in common, they have their differences, too. As you have seen, plants may be vascular or nonvascular. However, the plants within each of these two groups are far from identical. This observation prompted scientists to divide nonvascular plants into smaller and smaller

The divisions of the plant kingdom and the kinds of plants in each

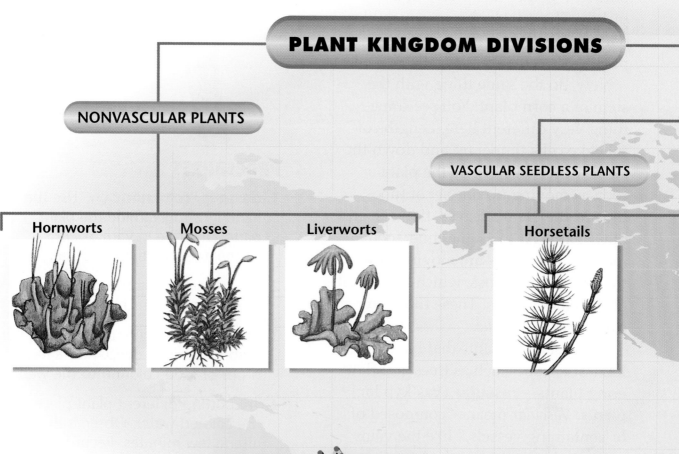

PLANT KINGDOM DIVISIONS

NONVASCULAR PLANTS

VASCULAR SEEDLESS PLANTS

Hornworts   Mosses   Liverworts   Horsetails

READING N CHARTS

1. **DISCUSS** Name two plants you are familiar with and the division you think each belongs to.
2. **WRITE** Pick two plant divisions from the chart. List two ways they are alike. List two ways they are different.

groups. The scientists did the same for vascular plants.

The smallest groups would have plants most like one another. The larger groups would have plants least like one another. This meant that the smaller the group, the more closely related were its members.

The chart on these two pages shows the plants divided into groups called *divisions*. These divisions make up the plant kingdom. You will discover the other kingdoms of living things on the following four pages.

Brain Power

What division of plant is most common where you live? Are there any plants from the other divisions there?

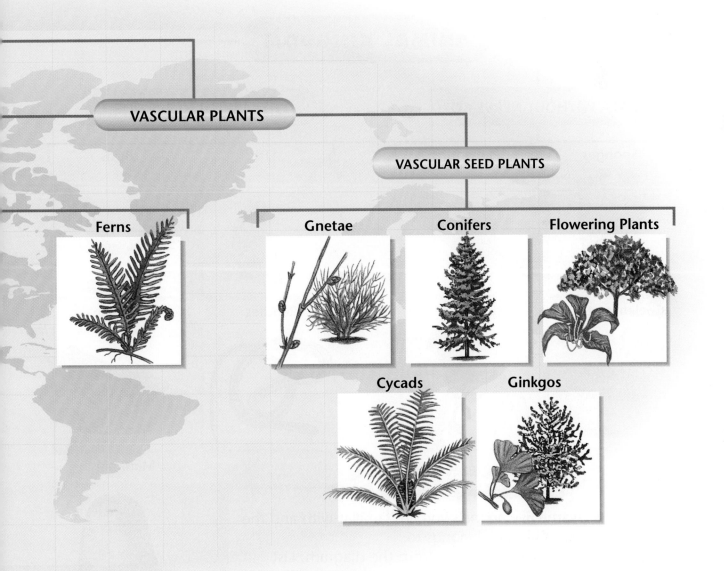

VASCULAR PLANTS

VASCULAR SEED PLANTS

Ferns

Gnetae

Conifers

Flowering Plants

Cycads

Ginkgos

What Makes Animals Different from Plants?

Unlike plants, animals cannot make their own food. Animals also differ from plants because animals can move from one place to another during some parts of their lives.

All animals are grouped into one kingdom, known as the animal kingdom. The animal kingdom is divided into smaller and smaller groups. The chart on this page shows the first two levels of these groups. The first level includes animals that have a nerve cord running down their back and animals that don't. The next level contains groups called *phyla* (fī′lə) (singular, *phylum*). The chart shows examples of some animal phyla and the kinds of living things in each of them.

The phyla in the animal kingdom are like the divisions in the plant kingdom. Not all the phyla are shown in the chart.

ANIMAL KINGDOM

PHYLA WITHOUT NERVE CORD

Sponges   Flatworms

Coelenterates   Arthropods

PHYLA WITH NERVE CORD

Fish   Birds

Reptiles   Amphibians

Mammals

READING CHARTS

1. **DISCUSS** Name five animals you are familiar with and the phylum you think each belongs to.
2. **WRITE** Pick two animal phyla from the diagram. List two ways they are alike. List two ways they are different.

What Is a Fungus?

It may be one celled or many celled. It doesn't make its own food as plants do or take in food as animals do. Instead it simply absorbs (takes in) food from decaying dead organisms and wastes in its environment. What is it? It's a **fungus** (fung′gəs).

Fungi (fun′jī)—the plural of fungus—can be very useful living things. Some of them have great flavors. Others contain chemicals that fight diseases. Still others put the bubbles in your favorite loaf of bread or turn cheeses sharp and tangy. Fungi in soil break down decaying plants and animals so that their chemicals can be used by living things. So you might say that such fungi clean up our environment.

Unfortunately, the fungus kingdom also contains organisms that cause problems for people. Some fungi are poisonous. Some fungi give people itchy diseases, like athlete's foot. Some fungi turn foods bad and ugly. Some fungi coat bathroom tiles and basement walls with smelly black or white fuzz. In the autumn of 1997, one kind of fungus was even responsible for the closing of a library in Staten Island, a part of New York City. The fungus, which grows in damp places like the library's basement, caused people to cough and sneeze as if they had the flu.

The chart on this page shows the groups of the fungus kingdom.

FUNGUS KINGDOM

Yeasts, Morels, Mildews

Molds

Mushrooms, Smuts, Rusts

READING ⋀ CHARTS

1. **DISCUSS** Which fungus can cause problems in your shower?
2. **REPRESENT** Make a chart listing useful fungi. Draw a picture of the fungi. Label each kind of fungus with its name. Write a sentence about how the fungus is used.

What Is a Protist?

What do you see when you look into a lake, pond, river, or ocean? Sometimes it looks like clear water. Yet that "clear" water is home to millions of microscopic living things that belong to the **protist** (prō´tist) kingdom. This kingdom isn't made up of just microscopic living things. It also includes living things you can see without a microscope, such as seaweed and green pond scum. Although most protists live in water, some inhabit the land.

Some protists are single cells that swim in the water in search of smaller living things to eat. Others, like seaweeds, are made up of groups of the same cells that are linked together. Called algae, these protists don't have to hunt for food. They contain chloro-phyll. All they have to do is float on water in the Sun, soak up the Sun's rays, and make their own food. Still other kinds of protists are one celled, swim around, and contain chlorophyll.

Members of the protist kingdom certainly seem very different. Yet if scientists put them in the same kingdom, they must have something in common. You would discover that "something" if you peered at the cells of protists under a microscope. You'd notice a dense, dark structure, called a *nucleus* (nü´klē əs) inside each cell. If you looked very carefully, you'd see that the nucleus was surrounded by a thin envelope. Scientists call this envelope a *membrane* (mem´brān). The nucleus of the *Elodea* plant could also have been seen in the Explore Activity.

The chart shows some of the groups of the protist kingdom.

PROTIST KINGDOM

Slime molds

Diatoms

Dinoflagellates

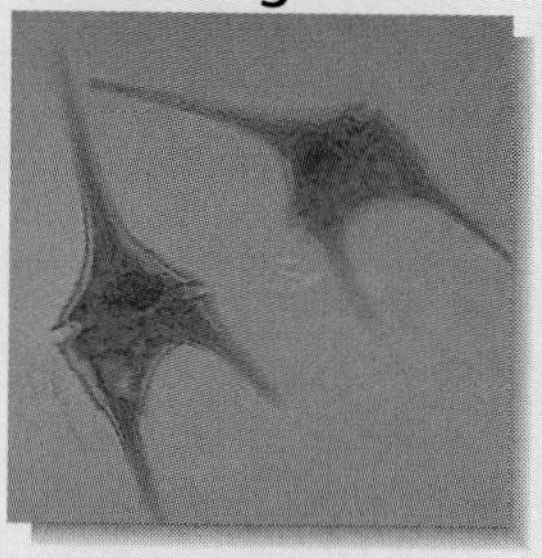

Euglenas

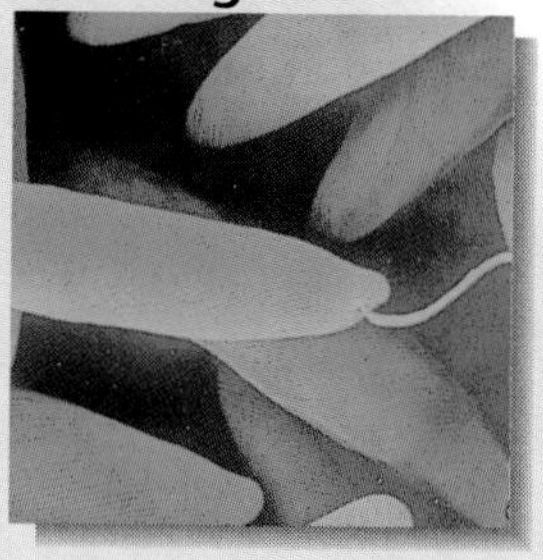

Green algae

READING *N* CHARTS

1. **DISCUSS** What are some of the ways some protists are like animals?
2. **WRITE** What are some of the ways some protists are like plants?

What Are the Tiniest Living Things?

Bacteria (bak tîr′ē ə) are both tiny and very simple. Some can cause a great deal of trouble, like infections. Others are necessary for animals and plants to survive.

Some kinds of bacteria group together in clusters or chains. Other kinds don't. You can only see bacteria under a microscope. Each *bacterium* (bak tîr′ēəm) is a single cell without a nucleus.

The "ancient" bacteria kingdom includes some fascinating organisms. One type lives in the digestive system of cows. It helps the cow by digesting cellulose, the main substance in grass, which the cow eats but can't digest. Still another kind of "ancient" bac-

terium lives deep in the ocean, where lava seeps through cracks in the ocean floor. The red-hot lava heats the water up to 105°C. That's hotter than the temperature of boiling water!

The true bacteria kingdom also contains some unusual members. Have you ever seen a blue-green spot in a polar bear's white fur? If so, you detected *cyanobacteria* (sī′ə nō bak tîr′ē ə). The prefix *cyano-* means "blue".

Some true bacteria cause diseases in plants, animals, and people. A "strep" throat is caused by a true bacterium. If your stomach aches after eating spoiled food, the culprit's likely to be another true bacterium. More serious diseases like tuberculosis and certain kinds of pneumonia are also caused by true bacteria.

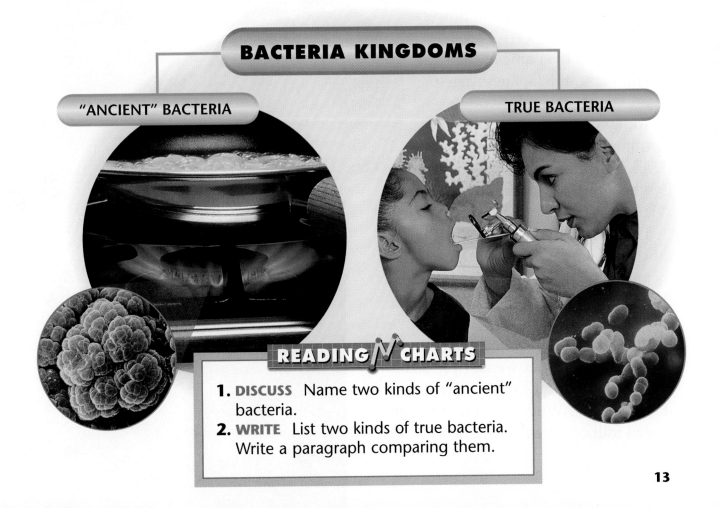

BACTERIA KINGDOMS

"ANCIENT" BACTERIA

TRUE BACTERIA

READING N CHARTS

1. **DISCUSS** Name two kinds of "ancient" bacteria.
2. **WRITE** List two kinds of true bacteria. Write a paragraph comparing them.

13

The Vine That Ate the South

The year was 1876. People all over the United States were celebrating the nation's 100th birthday. In Philadelphia the celebration focused on the exhibits of the Philadelphia Centennial Exposition. Many countries showed off their prized possessions there. The Japanese were known for their fine gardens, and there were many unusual plants at the Japanese exhibit.

One plant undoubtedly caught the eye of many passersby. It was a woody vine. Little hairs sprang from the edges of its 10-centimeter-wide (4-inch-wide) green leaves. However, what stopped viewers in their tracks were the plant's purple flowers. Although each was only $1\frac{1}{4}$ centimeters ($\frac{1}{2}$ inch) long, they hung in long clusters. The flowers also gave off a powerful aroma. When asked the name of the wonderful plant, the Japanese caretaker simply replied, "Kudzu."

Today people in America's southern states call it other things: "Mile-a-Minute Vine," "Foot-a-Night Vine," and more frighteningly, "The Vine That Ate the South."

There is more than some truth in all of these names. "Mile-a-Minute Vine" is an exaggeration, but "Foot-a-Night Vine" is not. The plant can grow that much each day. It can spread out over 60 feet in a single summer and choke the life out of other weaker plants.

How did kudzu escape from Philadelphia? Why does it now cover seven million acres of America's south-land? It was pretty. In the late 1800s, American homeowners used it to decorate gardens and homes. It was tasty to animals. In the 1920s American farmers grew it to feed cows, sheep, and other farm animals. Its huge 6-foot-long roots grew to be 7 inches in diameter and weighed up to 400 pounds. Those roots hung on to soil in a tight grip. In the 1940s American conservation workers planted it all over the South to prevent soil from being washed away by heavy rains.

What nobody counted on was the hardiness of the plant. It grew best

The purple flowers of the kudzu are very beautiful. They smell good, too. Lots of people bought the plants to decorate their properties.

where temperatures rose above 80°F and where 40 inches or more of rain fell. It found an ideal home in the South. There was something else that promoted its rapid growth. Something kept it in check in Japan but not in America—its natural enemies. These were insect pests that lived in Japan but not in the American South.

Today kudzu is labeled a weed by the United States Department of Agriculture. Many people are trying to find ways to control it. Will they succeed, or will the vine continue to gobble up huge chunks of the South? The answer is anyone's guess.

There are many different kinds of plants, but they are all very important. Without plants, life would be impossible on Earth. Almost everything you eat comes from plants, or from animals that ate plants.

Kudzu is a very fast growing plant. It can spread 60 feet in a single summer.

REVIEW

1. What do plants have in common?

2. How are plants similar to animals, protists, fungi, and bacteria? How are plants different?

3. How are vascular plants different from nonvascular plants?

4. **COMMUNICATE** Describe three characteristics of plants.

5. **CRITICAL THINKING** *Analyze* How can plants that are imported from other parts of the world become pests here?

WHY IT MATTERS THINK ABOUT IT
How are plants important to your survival?

WHY IT MATTERS WRITE ABOUT IT
Write a paragraph explaining what plants are important in your life.

READING SKILL
Write a paragraph to describe any conclusions you can draw about plants after reading this lesson.

Analyzing ALGAE

Kelp

Blue-green Algae

History of Science

Sea Lettuce

Aristotle was the first to divide all living things into two kingdoms—plants and animals. He put algae in the plant kingdom because many algae looked like plants, made their own food, and didn't seem able to move on their own.

With the development of microscopes, scientists could examine algae more closely. They discovered that some, such as the tiny green algae in pond water, had just one cell. Other algae had many cells and looked like tiny palm trees, mushrooms, lettuce, or moss. One kind of algae, kelp, can grow to be 61 meters (200 feet) long!

Even the largest algae are still simple organisms. They're collections of nearly identical cells. Algae with many cells have no root, leaf, or seed tissue. Lettuce-shaped algae are just sheets of cells, two cells thick.

Today scientists place most algae in the protist kingdom because of their simple structures. Blue-green algae have no nucleus in their cells, so some scientists place them in the bacteria kingdom.

Most scientists believe that green algae are the ancestors of plants. All algae contain chlorophyll, even brown and red algae. Green algae have cell walls and store starch as food. They're so much like plants that they probably were Earth's first plants!

Scientists today group living things into six different kingdoms, with protists making up their own kingdom, Protista. Scientists continue to study algae. They want to know for sure whether algae are plants, protists, or members of a whole new kingdom of their own!

Discussion Starter

1 Why do you think scientists had trouble placing algae in a kingdom?

2 In what kingdom or kingdoms would you place algae? Why?

*inter*NET CONNECTION To learn more about algae, visit **www.mhschool.com/science** and enter the keyword **ALGAE.**

WHY IT MATTERS

Every part of a plant helps it and us to survive.

SCIENCE WORDS

root cap a thin covering made up of cells that protect the root tip as it grows into the soil

epidermis an outermost layer of parts of a plant, such as roots and leaves

cortex a layer just inside the epidermis of roots and stems

xylem tissue through which water and minerals move up through a plant

phloem tissue through which food from the leaves moves down through a plant

cambium a layer that separates xylem from phloem

chloroplast a part of a plant cell containing chlorophyll, the green substance that enables the plant to produce food

transpiration the loss of water through a plant's leaves, as water rises up through the plant replacing the lost water

Plant Survival

What do you have in common with a plant? Would you believe that you and a plant have similar needs? However, there is a big difference. You can move around to get things. You can change things around you—like your room temperature. Plants stay in one place. However, different kinds of plants can survive in very different places. How?

EXPLORE

HYPOTHESIZE How may plants from different places differ from each other? How do the differences help the plants survive in their surroundings? Write a hypothesis in your *Science Journal.* Then test your ideas.

Investigate How a Plant's Parts Help It Survive

Observe differences in plants that come from different environments.

MATERIALS

- cactus
- water plant, such as an *Elodea* or a duckweed
- flowering plant, such as a geranium
- *Science Journal*

PROCEDURE

1. OBSERVE Look at the physical properties of the leaves of each plant. Note the color, size, and shape of the leaves in your *Science Journal*.

2. ANALYZE List any other plant parts that you see.

3. COMMUNICATE Observe the physical properties of these parts and record your observations in your *Science Journal*.

4. Record any other physical properties that you observe.

CONCLUDE AND APPLY

1. DRAW CONCLUSIONS How do the parts of a cactus help it survive in a hot, dry desert?

2. INFER Would the geranium be able to survive in the desert? Why or why not?

3. INFER Could the water plant survive out of water? Why or why not?

GOING FURTHER: Problem Solving

4. PREDICT Could these plants survive outside where you live? Why or why not? For each plant what conditions would you have to change so that the plant could survive outside where you live?

How Do a Plant's Parts Help It Survive?

Some plant roots help you survive. That's because they are foods. Beets, carrots, sweet potatoes, radishes, and turnips are the roots of different plants. As the Explore Activity showed, plant parts help plants survive. How do roots help a plant survive?

Most plants have roots that hold them in the ground. Some plants, like mosses, don't have true roots. Still, mosses have rootlike structures that anchor them. Roots help keep plants from getting swept away by wind and running water. Roots draw up water and minerals from the soil. Plants must have water and minerals to make their own food. Roots also store food for the plant. That's especially true of sweet potato, sugar beet, and carrot plants.

A root gets its start early in the life of a plant. If you were to look at a lima bean as it sprouted, you would see a tiny piece of the young plant growing straight downward. This is the plant's first root.

This root bores deeper and deeper into the soil. Why don't the rough particles of soil rub away and harm the young root? The tip of the root is protected by a layer of tough cells called the **root cap**

Soon more roots branch out from the sides of the original root. *Taproots* have

PARTS OF A ROOT

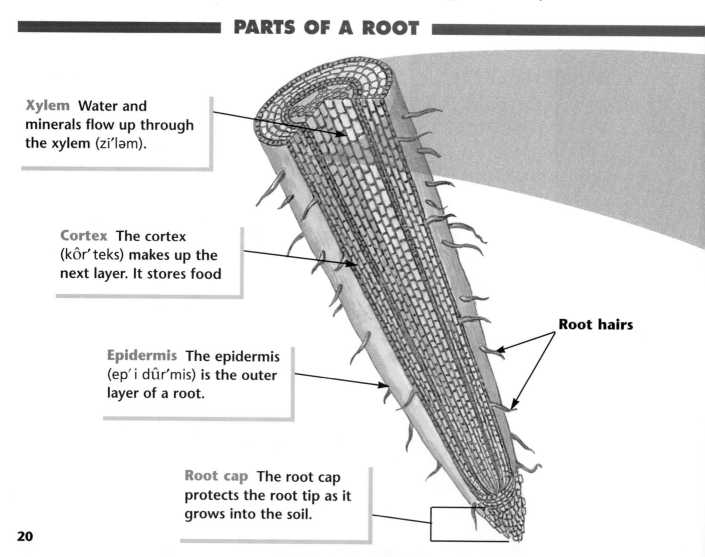

Xylem Water and minerals flow up through the xylem (zī'ləm).

Cortex The cortex (kôr'teks) makes up the next layer. It stores food

Epidermis The epidermis (ep'i dûr'mis) is the outer layer of a root.

Root cap The root cap protects the root tip as it grows into the soil.

Root hairs

one large root with a few hairy branching roots. They look like a carrot or a beet. Other roots, like those of grass or rye plants, are made up of only thin hairy branching roots called *fibrous roots*.

Taproots tend to grow deep into the ground and reach water deep down. Fibrous roots spread out near the soil's surface. They collect water where there is little rain that only soaks into the very top layer of soil.

Fibrous roots can make huge networks. All the fibrous roots and root hairs of a single rye plant put end to end would stretch over 10,000 kilometers (6,200 miles)!

Some plants like orchids, that grow high in the branches of rain forest trees, have *aerial roots*. These roots never touch the ground. They take in moisture from the air. *Prop roots*, like those of a corn plant, grow like fingers out of the bottom of the stem. These roots help prop up the plant.

How Do Roots Work?

The structure of a root helps it absorb water and minerals and send them to other parts of the plant. These drawings show how this happens.

READING N DIAGRAMS

REPRESENT Organize the information in this diagram into a table or map.

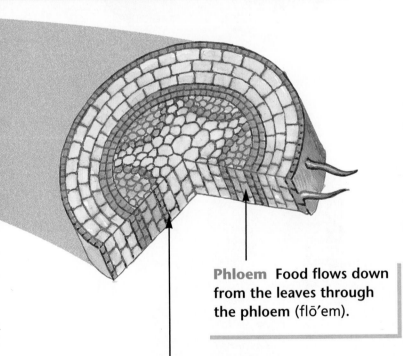

Phloem Food flows down from the leaves through the phloem (flō'em).

Cambium The cambium (kam'bē əm) separates the xylem from the phloem. The cambium is where new xylem and phloem grow.

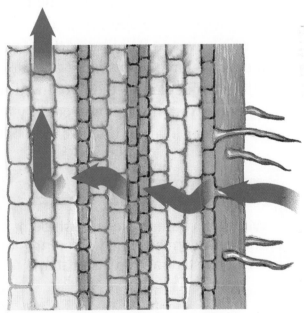

Water and minerals enter the root hairs. They pass through the root's cortex to the xylem. They then move up the xylem, into the plant's stem, and to all parts of the plant.

How Are Stems Similar?

Some stems are soft and delicate, like those of a young corn plant. Others are hard and tough, like those of a giant redwood tree. No matter what they look like, all stems have certain things in common.

All stems support leaves. Some also support flowers. Stems help leaves reach open places, where the leaves can be bathed in sunlight.

Stems also hold the transportation system for plants. This system lets water and minerals move from the roots to all parts of the plant, especially its leaves. It moves foods made in leaves to all other parts of the plant.

The *xylem* makes up the part of the transportation system that moves water and minerals up from the roots. The *phloem* moves food from the plant's leaves to its other parts. Many stems also have a *cambium*—a layer of cells—that separates the two. In addition woody stems are protected by a tough outer layer of tissue, called bark.

READING N DIAGRAMS

WRITE How are the xylem, phloem, and cambium arranged differently in a woody stem and in a soft stem?

PARTS OF A STEM

Soft and woody stems have the same basic parts for transporting water, minerals, and food to all parts of a plant.

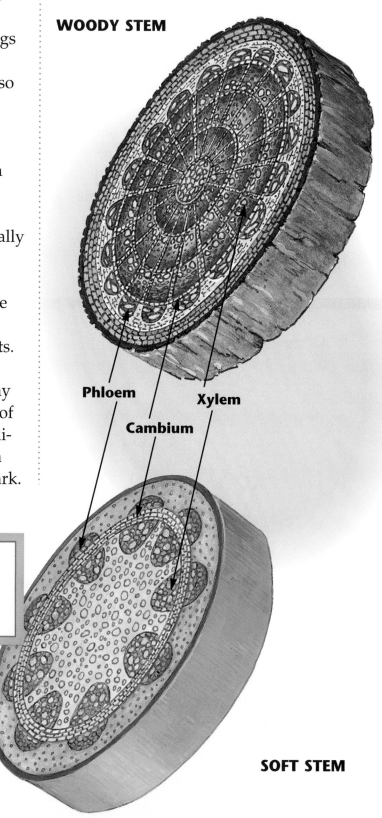

WOODY STEM

Phloem

Cambium

Xylem

SOFT STEM

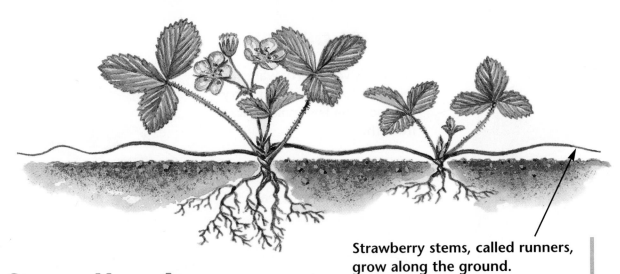

Strawberry stems, called runners, grow along the ground.

Stems: How Are They Different?

Some stems do more than support a plant and give it a transportation system. For example, the stems of plants like potatoes and sugarcane store food for the plants to use later. The potatoes and sugarcane you eat actually are stems. The stems of cactus plants store water, which the plants use during long dry periods in the desert. Still other stems, like those of asparagus, help make the plant's food.

Not all stems grow up into the air. Those of strawberries grow along the ground. That's how a strawberry patch spreads and grows.

The stem of the cactus stores water.

A potato is an underground stem.

23

PARTS OF LEAVES

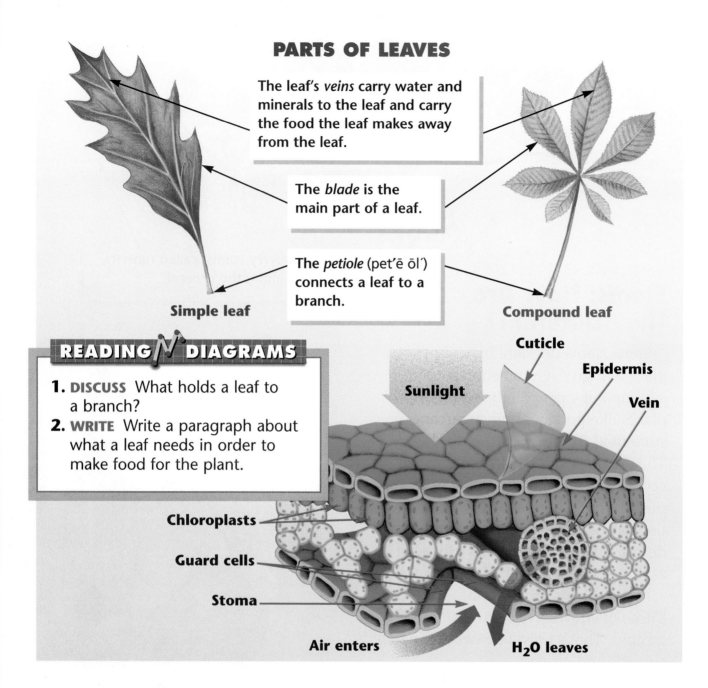

The leaf's *veins* carry water and minerals to the leaf and carry the food the leaf makes away from the leaf.

The *blade* is the main part of a leaf.

The *petiole* (pet'ē ōl') connects a leaf to a branch.

Simple leaf

Compound leaf

Cuticle

Epidermis

Sunlight

Vein

Chloroplasts

Guard cells

Stoma

Air enters

H₂O leaves

READING 🧲 DIAGRAMS

1. **DISCUSS** What holds a leaf to a branch?
2. **WRITE** Write a paragraph about what a leaf needs in order to make food for the plant.

What Are Leaves?

Leaves come in all shapes and sizes. Most of the leaves you see hang from their plants as single leaves or in groups. Maple and oak trees have single leaves. They're called *simple* leaves.

Horse chestnut and locust leaves come in clusters. These are called *compound* leaves.

The parts of a leaf work together to help keep the plant alive.

The outermost layer of a leaf is its *epidermis*. Cells inside the epidermis make a waxy coating, called a *cuticle* (kū'ti kəl). The cuticle helps keep water from leaving the leaf.

The leaf makes food in cells between the layers of the epidermis. These cells contain **chloroplasts** (klôr'ə plasts'), the green food factories of plants. In addition to sunlight, these factories need water, minerals, and the carbon dioxide in air to make food.

The air comes through tiny pores in the bottom of the leaves called *stomata* (stō′mə tə) (singular, *stoma*). When the stomata are open to let in air, water can also evaporate from the leaf. The job of opening and closing each stoma is the job of two *guard cells* that surround it.

When the plant has too much water, the guard cells swell and pull open the stoma. When the plant has too little water, the guard cells shrink and close the stoma.

How Do Leaf Shapes Differ?

Many leaves have green, broad, flat surfaces that help "capture" the sunlight the plant needs to make its food. Other leaves have different shapes for different purposes. The spines on a cactus protect the plant. The needles of a pine tree are covered with a wax that keeps the tree from losing too much water. The crunchy layers of an onion store food. The leaves of the garden pea plant wind around objects to give the plant added support.

The leaves of the Venus's-flytrap are colorful insect traps. They snap shut when an insect flies inside.

Leaves Help Roots Get Water

Leaves are far from roots, yet they help roots take in water from soil. When water evaporates from the leaves, more water moves up through the plant to replace the lost water. This process is called **transpiration** (tran′spə rā′shən).

Leaves as Food

People eat all parts of plants, including leaves such as lettuce, cabbage, parsley, and spinach. Why are leaves important to you?

QUICK LAB

Leaves

HYPOTHESIZE In what ways are the leaves that are important to you alike? In what ways are they different? Write a hypothesis in your *Science Journal.*

MATERIALS
- various plant leaves that you eat
- hand lens
- *Science Journal*

PROCEDURES

1. Collect a variety of different leaves that you eat as food.

2. **OBSERVE** Examine them with a hand lens. Record your observations in your *Science Journal*.

3. **COMPARE** What do the leaves you brought have in common?

4. **COMPARE** In what ways are they different from each other?

CONCLUDE AND APPLY

1. **COMMUNICATE** Write how the leaves you examined are similar and how they are different.

2. **COMPARE AND CONTRAST** Compare the leaves you examined with the leaves your classmates looked at. In what ways are your leaves similar to theirs? In what ways are they different?

Dangling their roots in the air, these orchids cling to trees high in the canopy of a tropical rain forest. Their aerial roots soak up water that trickles along tree trunks and branches.

Rooted Firmly in . . . the Air?

Many kinds of orchids are rooted in the ground. However, in tropical rain forests, certain orchids grow high up in the trees, dangling their roots in the air. The orchids' colors "paint" the trees with flashes of red, purple, pink, and orange.

One kind of orchid looks and smells a lot like a certain kind of female bee. The orchid attracts male bees. As the bees go from flower to flower, they help the orchids reproduce.

A sudden shower drenches the tree where the orchid lives. Tiny streams of water trickle down the tree's bark. The orchid's exposed roots soak up some of the water that washes off the tree trunk and branches above. Along with the water come minerals the orchid needs.

The roots of a nearby orchid are very strange. They are flat, as long as you are tall, and wrapped around the branches of a tree like a huge flat worm. In fact the scientific name of the orchid means "tapeworm leaf."

You might think that this is a strange name for a root. However, in a way, it makes sense. The roots of this plant are green, like leaves! Scientists have discovered that these roots do two jobs for the orchid. They absorb water and minerals that pass by, and like leaves, they make food for the orchid. This orchid needs no leaves, although it has some very little ones covering its stem.

Orchids are rare and beautiful. If you have an older sister, you may know that orchids do more than cling to rain forest trees. That's because orchids are the favorite flowers for girls to wear to a prom.

WHY IT MATTERS

Since plants are needed by all living things, it is important to know how they survive. Part of a plant's ability to survive depends on how well its parts work together to move water and minerals in one direction and food in the other direction. The parts that do this are roots, stems, and leaves.

Brain Power

What part of plants do you use most often? Explain your answer.

FUNtastic Facts

The giant leaves of the royal water lily are strong enough to bear the weight of a small child. A network of air-filled ribs keeps the 2.5-meter-wide (8-foot) leaves floating on the surface of the water. Royal water lilies grow in sluggish streams in the Amazon basin of South America. How do the leaves of the royal water lily help the plant survive?

REVIEW

1. List three things plants need in order to live and grow.

2. **COMPARE AND CONTRAST** Describe two or more different kinds of roots. Explain how they are different and how they are similar. Do the same for stems and leaves.

3. How do roots, stems, and leaves help a plant survive?

4. How can rain forest orchids live high up in the trees?

5. **CRITICAL THINKING** *Analyze* How do you think that having flowers that look like bees can help a plant survive?

WHY IT MATTERS THINK ABOUT IT
What plant parts are especially important to you? Can you think of some plants whose leaves are important to you? Can you think of some plants whose stems are important to you? Can you think of some plants whose roots are important to you?

WHY IT MATTERS WRITE ABOUT IT
Write a paragraph about a plant that is important to you because of its stems, roots, or leaves. Can you think of a plant that is important to you because you use several of its parts? Write about the things you use that plant for.

Plant Power:
MEDICINES

What good are plant parts? Bitter or poisonous chemicals in some plant parts protect them from predators. The chemicals have powerful effects on animals that eat them. They might also be useful in medicines for humans!

Fever Powder of Peru

Missionaries to Peru in the 1600s found natives making a bitter powder. It was ground-up bark from the cinchona, a rare jungle tree. The powder cured the fever of malaria!

Suddenly there was a demand for cinchona bark, and the quinine in it. Most cinchonas were cut down.

Doctors now use artificial quinine and other drugs to treat malaria. However, the parasite that causes malaria is becoming resistant to the drugs. Only cinchona bark still works when modern medicine fails!

Poison to Kill Cancer?

Humans have used yews for thousands of years. Spears and bows were made from the wood. The bark yielded a poison.

In the 1960s the National Cancer Institute began looking for plant chemicals that might kill cancer cells. In 1963 they found such a chemical, taxol, in the bark of the Pacific yew.

Pacific yews weren't valued for their wood, so many were cut down and thrown away!

Quinine is a bitter chemical found in the bark of the cinchona tree.

Science, Technology, and Society

By the time cancer scientists proved that taxol works against cancer, the Pacific yew was rapidly disappearing. Today scientists make taxol from needles and twigs of all kinds of yews, not just the bark of the Pacific yew.

Many plants may be in danger of extinction. People are destroying Earth's rain forests. If plants die off before they're found, we'll never know if their chemicals could have cured diseases.

MEDICINES FROM PLANTS
Here are a few medicines made from plant parts.

PLANT	PARTS	MEDICINE	USED FOR
Belladonna	leaves/roots	atropine	breathing problems
Foxglove	leaves	digitalis	heart problems
Periwinkle	leaves	vinblastine	lukemia
Rauwolfia	roots	reserpine	high blood pressure
Willow	bark	aspirin	reducing pain and fever
Wild Mexican yam	tuberous roots	cortisone	curbing inflammation

DISCUSSION STARTER

1. If we can make imitation chemicals, is it still important to protect wild plants? Why or why not?

2. Why do plant chemicals that stop predators also kill malaria parasites or cancer cells?

To learn more about medicines from plants, visit *www.mhschool.com/science* and enter the keyword MEDICINE.

*inter*NET
CONNECTION

29

Topic 3
LIFE SCIENCE

WHY IT MATTERS

Plants and animals need each other to survive.

SCIENCE WORDS

photosynthesis a food-making process that uses sunlight

respiration the release of energy from food (sugar)

Making Food

Did you ever wonder why crops are planted in open fields, not in the shade? Do plants need light? If so, why? What happens to plants that are kept in a dark corner of the room? Do they do as well as plants that get more light?

EXPLORE

HYPOTHESIZE How will a plant change if it does not get sunlight for several days? Why does it change? Write a hypothesis in your *Science Journal.* Then test your ideas.

Investigate What Light Does for a Plant

Observe how plant leaves are affected when they don't get light.

PROCEDURES

SAFETY Be sure to wash your hands after handling plants.

1. Cover part of a leaf of a growing plant.

2. USE VARIABLES Cover at least four different leaves of the plant in the same way.

3. Place the whole plant in a window that gets lots of light.

4. COLLECT DATA Remove the foil from one leaf after one class period. How is that leaf different from the uncovered leaves? Record your observations in your *Science Journal*. Then cover the leaf again.

5. COLLECT DATA Continue your observations. Remove the foil from another leaf after one day, another after two days, and another after a week. Record your observations in your *Science Journal*. Replace the foil each time.

CONCLUDE AND APPLY

1. OBSERVE After one class period, how was the leaf you had just uncovered different from the uncovered leaves?

2. IDENTIFY PATTERNS How did the difference you noticed change after a day, two days, and a week?

3. DRAW CONCLUSIONS How do light and darkness affect the growth of leaves?

GOING FURTHER: Problem Solving

4. USE VARIABLES Remove the coverings from the four leaves, and observe them for another week. How do they respond to being uncovered? Do their differences from the other leaves remain or disappear?

MATERIALS

- growing plant (window plants from home or plants from an aquarium)
- opaque paper or aluminum foil
- *Science Journal*

What Does Light Do for a Plant?

When you walk to a grocery store to buy food, you are really doing two things. You are using energy to get to the store, and you are buying energy at the store. Walking uses energy. Food provides you with energy.

All living things need energy to survive. Where do they get energy? Animals eat food to get energy. Plants make their own food. Yet the very process of making food uses up energy. Where does the plant get this energy? It comes from light, especially sunlight.

Light is a form of energy that plants use to make their food. Plants capture the energy of light and trap it in the foods they make. Later, when they need this energy, they get it back out of the food. The food-making process is called **photosynthesis** (fō′ tə sin′ thə sis). This term comes from Greek words that mean "putting together by light." The process is very complex, but basically here's how it happens.

First, sunlight strikes a green part of a plant, such as a leaf. The leaf is green because it has a green chemical called chlorophyll. Chlorophyll helps the plant make its food. The

Carbon dioxide + Water	Light Chlorophyll $\longrightarrow$	Sugar + Oxygen

light

carbon dioxide

sugars

cells with chlorophyll

oxygen

water

In photosynthesis hydrogen (from water) and carbon dioxide join in the presence of sunlight to form sugars and oxygen.

The water and carbon dioxide that form are released into the air.

chlorophyll is found in plant parts called chloroplasts. The chloroplasts act like tiny chemical factories. Inside them water and carbon dioxide from the air combine to make sugar and oxygen. However, as the Explore Activity showed, this reaction could not happen without the help of light energy.

The sugars that the Sun's energy helps the leaf to make then go into the leaf's veins and off to all parts of the plant. If you've ever eaten maple syrup, you've tasted sugars made by a plant.

The oxygen the plant makes goes into the air. All animals must breathe in oxygen to stay alive. At the same time, you breathe out carbon dioxide, which the plants need. You might think of this as a kind of special partnership between animals and plants.

Now that the Sun's energy is trapped in the sugars that the plant made, how does the plant get the energy back out? Its cells use oxygen to break apart the sugar. When the sugar breaks apart, it gives out energy that the plant uses. This process is called **respiration** (res′ pə rā′ shən). This is the same process that releases energy in animals.

READING N DIAGRAMS

REPRESENT Draw a circle with labels to show the main points of this diagram.

The oxygen is released into the air.

The sugars that form are stored in green plants.

In respiration, which occurs in plants and animals, sugars and oxygen join to produce water, carbon dioxide, and energy.

In autumn cooling temperatures signal trees to stop making green chlorophyll. The chlorophyll disappears, uncovering other colors.

How Do Leaves Change Color?

Do you live in an area where the leaves change color in the autumn? If so, you may have noticed that the leaves of all plants, except evergreens, change color in the fall. You wake up one morning in September or October and the trees near where you live are speckled with flashes of yellow, orange, and maybe red.

All the yellows and oranges were inside the leaves ever since summer. However, you couldn't see them because there was too much green chlorophyll there.

It's as if you put some yellow and orange objects in the bottom of a bucket of green paint. The yellow and orange objects would be in there. Yet all you would see is green.

However, if you could take out all the green paint, what would you see? The answer is what you see in the fall.

But how is the greenness taken out of leaves in the fall?

As temperatures begin to drop, the leaves of trees other than evergreens stop making chlorophyll. Slowly the chlorophyll that remains begins to break down and vanishes. Now you can see the yellow and orange colors. If the weather is especially cool and the sky is clear most of the time, you may see another color—red. This color wasn't in the leaves to begin with. It's made by them in places where the fall climate is cool and clear. Where the climate is warmer and the sky is cloudy a lot of the time, the colors will be mostly yellows and oranges.

Brain Power

Let's say you thought the amount of rainfall was the reason leaves changed color. Make a set of drawings showing an experiment that would test this hypothesis.

Skill: Experimenting

WHY DO LEAVES CHANGE COLOR?

To find an answer to this question, the first thing you might do is figure out what changes occur in the fall that *might* cause leaves to change color. Scientists call such changes *variables*. You might identify two of these variables as the amount of daylight and the temperature, both of which go down in the fall.

Next you would make a guess that *seems* to make sense about which variable causes leaves to change color. This guess is called a *hypothesis*. It is often made in the form of an *if ...then...* statement. For example, "*If* the plant doesn't get water, *then* it won't grow." To see if your hypothesis is a good idea, you would perform an experiment. That experiment has to be set up so that it gives a clear answer.

MATERIALS
- *Science Journal*

PROCEDURES

1. Look at the drawings. They show three experiments—A, B, C. Study the setups.

2. **OBSERVE** What variable or variables are being tested in the first experiment? Write your answer in your *Science Journal*. What variable or variables are being tested in the other two experiments?

CONCLUDE AND APPLY

1. **INFER** Which experiment is testing to see whether light causes leaves to change color? Explain why in your *Science Journal*.

2. **INFER** Which experiment is testing to see whether temperature causes leaves to change color? Explain why.

3. **INFER** Which experiment will not give a clear answer? Explain why not.

35

How Do Water and Minerals Get from Roots to Leaves?

If you were to dry 1,000 grams of leaves, you would end up with between 50 and 300 grams of crumbly matter. That's because plants are made up of 70–95 percent water.

Cells in all parts of a plant need water to live and grow. They need water to carry out many vital chemical reactions, including photosynthesis. They also need water to stay firm and not wilt.

Plants constantly lose water through *transpiration*. Over its lifetime an average plant in a mild climate area will lose more than 100 times its weight in water!

It is very important for a plant to efficiently move water from its roots to all its other parts. The drawing shows how this is done.

If a normal plant (left) gets too little water, it will lose firmness and wilt (below).

Brain Power

Plants need water in order to survive, but how much water is too much? What happens to plants in flooded areas? How would you find out?

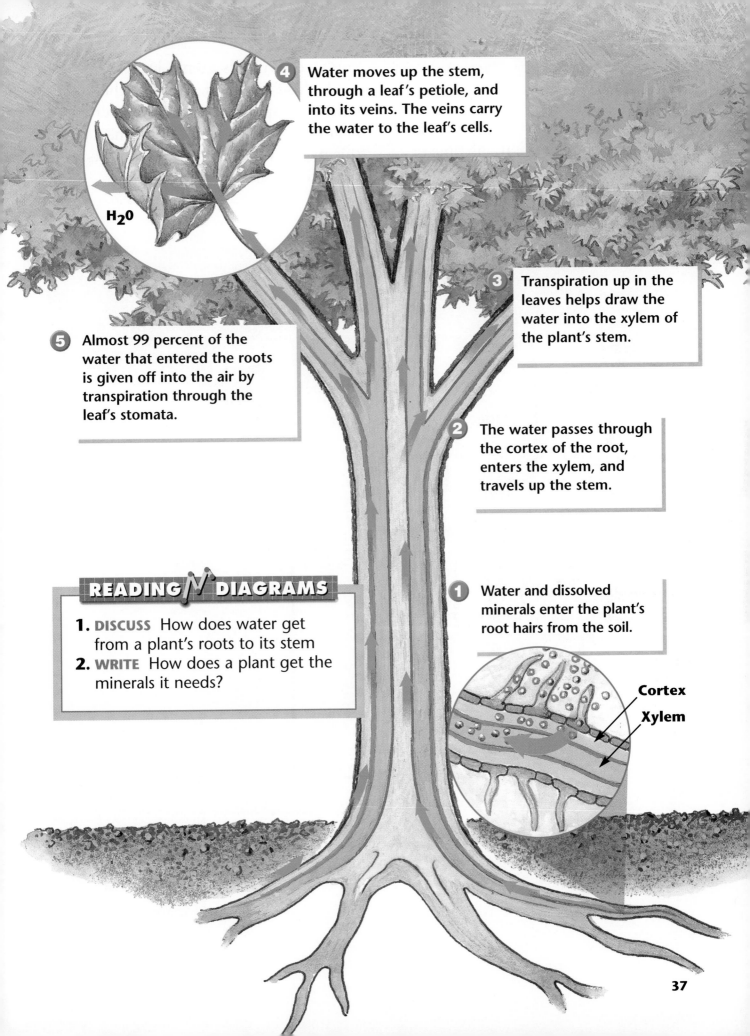

4 Water moves up the stem, through a leaf's petiole, and into its veins. The veins carry the water to the leaf's cells.

H_2O

3 Transpiration up in the leaves helps draw the water into the xylem of the plant's stem.

5 Almost 99 percent of the water that entered the roots is given off into the air by transpiration through the leaf's stomata.

2 The water passes through the cortex of the root, enters the xylem, and travels up the stem.

READING IN DIAGRAMS

1. DISCUSS How does water get from a plant's roots to its stem

2. WRITE How does a plant get the minerals it needs?

1 Water and dissolved minerals enter the plant's root hairs from the soil.

Cortex

Xylem

What Parts of Plants Do You Eat?

There probably isn't a part of a plant that you haven't eaten at one time or another. Whether you know it or not, you've eaten roots, stems, leaves, seeds, fruits, flowers, and even the bark and sap of plants. If you don't believe this is true, look at the chart on this page. Which of these plant parts have you eaten?

HEALTH LINK

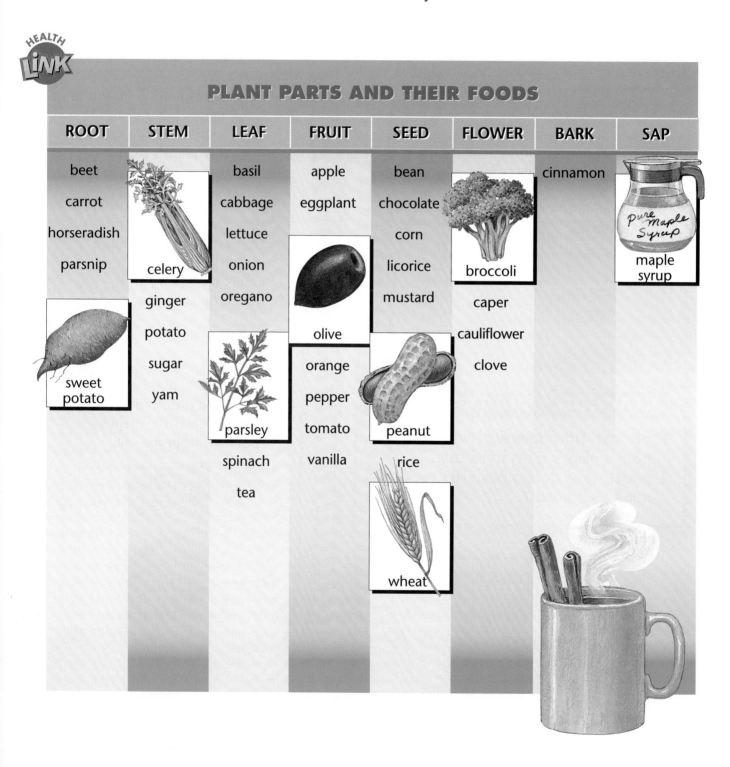

PLANT PARTS AND THEIR FOODS

ROOT	STEM	LEAF	FRUIT	SEED	FLOWER	BARK	SAP
beet		basil	apple	bean		cinnamon	
carrot		cabbage	eggplant	chocolate			
horseradish		lettuce		corn			maple syrup
parsnip	celery	onion		licorice	broccoli		
	ginger	oregano	olive	mustard	caper		
sweet potato	potato		orange		cauliflower		
	sugar		pepper		clove		
	yam	parsley	tomato	peanut			
		spinach	vanilla	rice			
		tea		wheat			

38

How Do Plants Enrich the Air?

About 21 percent of the air you breathe is oxygen. You use this oxygen to release energy from the foods you eat. Then you use the energy to keep warm, to move, to think, to keep your heart beating, to do all the things that keep you alive.

Most of the oxygen in air comes from plants and other green living things, like algae, that carry on photosynthesis. That's because oxygen is a product of photosynthesis. The evolution of living things that carry on photosynthesis created the conditions that allowed animals to evolve, since animals cannot survive without oxygen.

Plants provide the foods you eat and the oxygen you need to get energy out of those foods.

Tropical rain forests pump great amounts of oxygen into the air.

REVIEW

1. Describe the process of photosynthesis.

2. **EXPERIMENT** How would you design an experiment to see if the changing temperature or the changing amount of daylight plays a bigger part in why leaves change color in autumn?

3. Trace the path of water from the soil, through a plant, and into the air.

4. Describe the process of respiration in plants.

5. **CRITICAL THINKING** *Apply* If there were no plants, would animals be able to survive? Explain your answer.

WHY IT MATTERS THINK ABOUT IT
How are you important to plants?

WHY IT MATTERS WRITE ABOUT IT
Write a paragraph explaining ways you help plants survive.

Air to Breathe

Where do we get the oxygen we breathe? Much of it comes from plants, trees, and other organisms that give off oxygen during photosynthesis.

The first living things on Earth were one-celled, plantlike organisms in the oceans. They gave off oxygen during photosynthesis, and some of it got into the air. Finally, there was enough oxygen for animals to survive.

Did you know that 90 percent of all photosynthesis still takes place in the oceans? Simple, one-celled algae still live there. Some blue-green algae fossils are 3.4 billion years old!

Some ocean algae aren't green, but they still contain chlorophyll. Algae may be golden brown, red, or even pink-orange.

Most algae live in water. That green scum you see on ponds is floating algae! Some algae live on dry land. They also get their energy through photosynthesis.

About 600 million years ago, the atmosphere was only 1 percent oxygen. Today, thanks mostly to photosynthetic organisms, the air we breathe is about 21 percent oxygen!

Epiphyte algae

Earth Science Link

Some green algae live with fungi to form lichens (lī′kənz). Fungi cells enter the algae and absorb food made by photosynthesis.

DISCUSSION STARTER

1. Why are organisms such as algae, which are not plants, able to produce oxygen?

2. How did algae help animals on Earth develop?

Euglena (ū glē′nə) is classified as an algae, but it can move by whipping a tail-like form. Therefore, it's a transition between plantlike and animal-like organisms.

To learn more about oxygen, visit *www.mhschool.com/science* and enter the keyword OXYGEN.

*inter*NET
CONNECTION

CHAPTER 1 REVIEW

SCIENCE WORDS

cambium p.21

chlorophyll p.4

chloroplast p.24

cortex p.20

epidermis p.20

fungus p.11

nonvascular p.7

phloem p.21

photosynthesis p.32

respiration p.33

root cap p.20

xylem p.20

USING SCIENCE WORDS

Number a paper from 1 to 10. Fill in 1 to 5 with words from the list above.

1. The outer layer of a root is the ___?___.

2. Water and minerals flow up through the ___?___.

3. Foods flow down from the leaves through the ___?___.

4. Water and minerals then pass through the root's ___?___ to the xylem.

5. A green chemical called ___?___ allows plants to use the Sun's energy to make their own foods.

6–10. Pick five words from the list above that were not used in 1 to 5 and use each in a sentence.

UNDERSTANDING SCIENCE IDEAS

11. What is the difference between the way plants make food and the way plants use food?

12. Discuss why vascular plants can be taller than nonvascular plants.

13. Discuss how food travels through a plant.

14. Discuss how water travels through a plant.

15. Describe the "food factory" inside a plant.

USING IDEAS AND SKILLS

16. READING SKILL: DRAW CONCLUSIONS What is there about ferns that allows them to grow taller than mosses?

17. How does photosynthesis contribute to the life of animals?

18. In what ways do mosses contribute to the environment?

19. **EXPERIMENT** Design an experiment to determine how much mosses, ferns, and grasses depend on water for survival. Write how you would set up the experiment. Write down your hypothesis. Tell what variables you would test.

20. THINKING LIKE A SCIENTIST You dig in the ground and find a fossil of a fern. You then dig deeper and find a fossil of a club moss. What reasoning might let you conclude that club mosses evolved earlier than ferns?

PROBLEMS and PUZZLES

Why Is It Green? Why do plants look green? Hold a sheet of green paper about 10 cm above a sheet of white paper. Aim a flashlight up to hit the underside of the green paper. What do you see on the white paper? Repeat with other colors of paper. Explain what is happening.

CHAPTER 2

PLANT REPRODUCTION AND RESPONSE

There are plants that have seeds and plants that don't have seeds. How do all these different kinds of plants produce new plants?

Flowers aren't just nice to look at. Flowers serve a purpose for a plant. What role do flowers play in plants' lives?

How do plants respond to changes in their world?

 In Chapter 2 you will compare and contrast ways different kinds of plants produce new plants. To compare means to find ways two things are alike. To contrast means to find ways two things are different.

WHY IT MATTERS

Mosses help make the soil needed by other plants.

SCIENCE WORDS

rhizoid hairlike fiber that anchors a moss to the soil and takes in water from the soil

spore cells in seedless plants that grow into new organisms

frond the leaf of a fern

rhizome the underground stem of a fern

asexual reproduction the production of a new organism from only one cell

fertilization the joining of a female sex cell and a male sex cell into one cell, a fertilized egg

sexual reproduction the production of a new organism from a female sex cell and a male sex cell

Plants Without Seeds

Have you ever seen plants like these? If so, probably there were none as tall as these. You are looking at ferns in Costa Rica's Monteverde rain forest, one of Earth's dampest places. This fern grows taller than an eight-story building. Its leaves are more than three times longer than you are tall.

You may have seen mosses growing on trees, on rocks, or on damp ground. Mosses and ferns grow best in warm, wet places. Why do you think this is so?

EXPLORE

HYPOTHESIZE Why do ferns grow tall while mosses grow only very close to the ground? How do the parts of mosses help them live where they do? Write a hypothesis in your *Science Journal*. Test your ideas.

EXPLORE ACTIVITY

Investigate How Mosses Get Water

Examine a moss plant to find out how its parts allow the plant to live where it does.

MATERIALS

- hand lens
- forceps
- dropper
- 3 microscope slides
- coverslip
- microscope
- moss plant
- *Science Journal*

PROCEDURES

1. **OBSERVE** Place a moss on a paper towel. Examine it with a hand lens. Find its rootlike cells. Use the hand lens to view the stemlike and leaflike parts. Record your observations in your *Science Journal*.

2. **MEASURE** Use the forceps to remove a leaflike part. Make a wet-mount slide of the part. Observe its cells using the microscope on low power. Determine how thick the leaflike part is by moving the focus up and down.

3. **OBSERVE** Find a capsule-shaped object at the end of the brownish stalk. Observe it with the hand lens. Place the capsule on a slide. Add a drop of water. Place a second slide on top of the capsule. Press down on the top slide with your thumb, and crush the capsule. Carefully remove the top slide and place a coverslip over the crushed capsule.

4. **OBSERVE** Examine the released structures under low power. Draw what you see.

CONCLUDE AND APPLY

1. **OBSERVE** Which parts of the moss are green? Explain why they are green.

2. **OBSERVE** How many cell layers make up the leaflike structure?

3. **INTERPRET DATA** What structures anchor the moss plant? What was the capsule?

GOING FURTHER: Problem Solving

4. **PREDICT** What do you think the objects inside the capsule do? How would you set up an experiment to test your prediction?

45

How Do Mosses Get Water?

Mosses and their close relatives the liverworts are nonvascular plants. They don't have the long tubelike structures vascular plants have. They cling to damp soil, sheltered rocks, and the shady side of trees. Mosses and liverworts are tiny plants, only 2 to 5 centimeters tall. Mosses' leaves are only one or two cells thick.

Mosses and liverworts don't have roots. However, they stay anchored in one place. That's because they have hairlike fibers that do a job much like roots. The fibers are called **rhizoids** (rī′zoidz). Rhizoids can take in water from their surroundings. The water then travels directly from one cell to the next.

Most of the plants you see every day grow from seeds. However, mosses and liverworts are seedless plants. They grow from **spores**. Spores are cells that can develop into new organisms. Those tiny structures inside the capsule on the moss were spores. The capsule seen in the Explore Activity is called a *spore capsule*.

Many mosses look like green, fuzzy pillows. Liverworts look more like flat leaves. Ancient people thought that the shape of these plants resembled a liver. That's how they got their name.

Mosses and liverworts (above) grow in damp places. They are tiny plants, growing only 2 to 5 centimeters tall.

Club mosses produce spores at the ends of stems in structures that look like tiny pine cones.

Seedless Vascular Plants

True mosses and liverworts are seedless plants. So are their more distant relatives club mosses, spike mosses, horsetails, and ferns. All of them use spores to reproduce. However, mosses and liverworts are different from the other four in a very important way. Mosses and liverworts don't have a vascular system. Club mosses, spike mosses, horsetails, and ferns do.

The vascular tissue in these plants is made up of long tubelike cells. These cells let water and food move easily over long distances. That is why vascular plants can grow very tall and thick. That is also why nonvascular plants like true mosses and liverworts are so short and delicate. The trunks of the largest ferns can be as thick as your body.

Ferns come in all sizes and shapes and live in different kinds of climates.

The stems of horsetails are hollow, have a ring of vascular tissue and joints, and contain a gritty, sandy substance called silica.

Spike mosses, such as this "resurrection plant," live in the desert. Resurrection plants can dry out when there is no rain, but they do not die. They revive when water becomes available again.

QUICK LAB

Ferns

HYPOTHESIZE In what ways are ferns and mosses alike and different? Write a hypothesis in your *Science Journal.* Then examine a fern, and compare the results with those from the Explore Activity.

MATERIALS
- fern plant
- fern leaf with spore cases
- microscope
- microscope slide
- toothpick
- water
- *Science Journal*

PROCEDURES

1. OBSERVE
Carefully examine the whole fern plant. Look at the stem. Observe how the leaves grow from the stem. Find the veins in the leaves. Record your observations in your *Science Journal.*

2. OBSERVE Find a leaf whose bottom is covered with brownish spots. These are spore cases.

3. EXPERIMENT Place a drop of water on a clean slide. Use a toothpick to scrape one of the spore cases into the drop of water. Observe the spore case under the low power of a microscope.

CONCLUDE AND APPLY

1. OBSERVE What do the spore cases contain?

2. INFER What do ferns and mosses have in common?

What Are Ferns

Ferns once formed huge forests on Earth. You can still find them today in many wooded areas. Many people also grow ferns at home. What are ferns like?

1

Finding spore cases on the bottom of a fern leaf

2

Preparing a slide for viewing one spore case

More About Ferns

The whole fern plant you examined in the activity is at the stage of its life cycle when it forms spores. As you'll soon discover, there are other stages in the life cycle of a fern.

The leaves you saw are called **fronds** (frondz). They grow above the ground from an underground stem called a **rhizome** (rī′zōm). Roots, which anchor the plant to the soil or to a tree, branch out from the rhizome.

As you found out, the bottom sides of some fronds are covered with rows of brownish or rust-colored spore cases that contain spores. Under the right conditions, the spore cases pop open and spray spores as far away as a few meters. If the spores land in a place where conditions are right for fern growth, the spores will develop into the first stage in a new fern's life cycle.

Spore cases arranged on the bottom of a fern frond will pop open, spraying spores all around. If conditions are right where the spores fall, the spores will produce new fern plants.

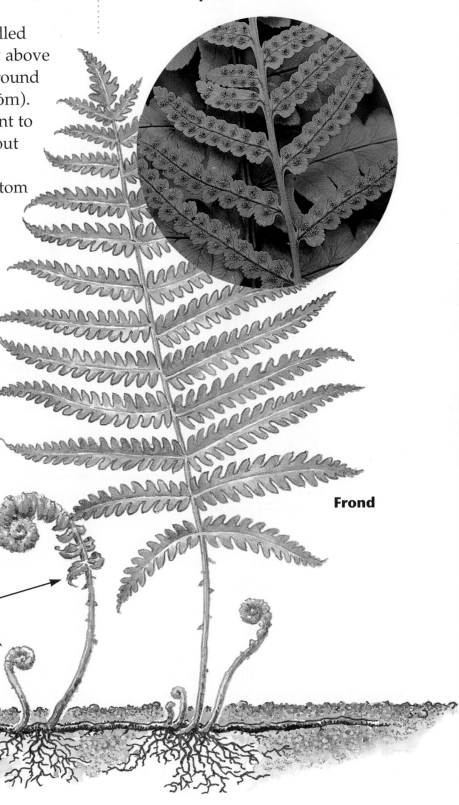

Frond

Young ferns (fiddleheads)

Rhizome

Roots

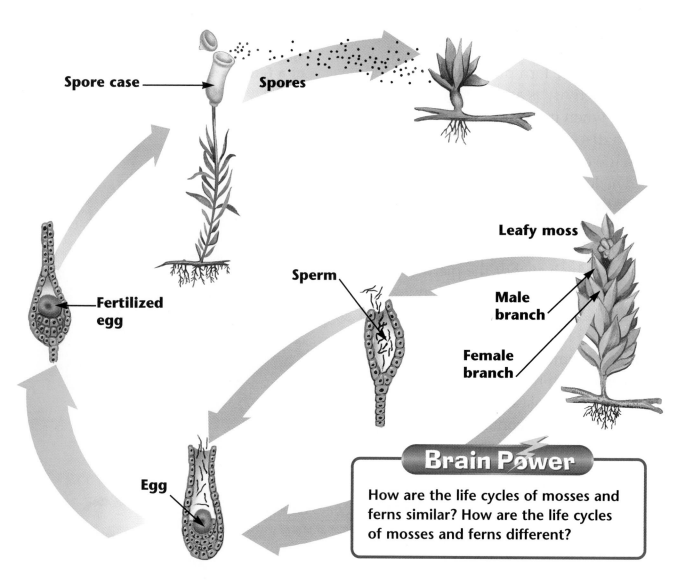

Spore case → **Spores**

Fertilized egg

Sperm

Leafy moss

Male branch

Female branch

Egg

Brain Power

How are the life cycles of mosses and ferns similar? How are the life cycles of mosses and ferns different?

How Do the Life Cycles of Mosses and Ferns Differ?

Since mosses and ferns use spores to reproduce, you might guess that their life cycles are similar. That guess would be correct. But there are differences, too.

Look at the drawings on these two pages as you read on. They will help you compare and contrast the life cycles of mosses and ferns.

The Life Cycle of a Moss

Both mosses and ferns have two separate stages to their life cycles, and both have a stage when they produce spores.

This stage in its life cycle is called **asexual reproduction** (ā sek′shü əl rē′prə duk′shən). That's because the plant needs only one type of cell—the spore—in order to *reproduce* (rē′prə düs′).

Moss spores grow into leafy moss plants that have male branches and female branches. The male branches produce *sperm*—male sex cells. The female branches produce eggs—female sex cells. When a male sex cell meets a female sex cell, the two may join together. When this happens, the egg is **fertilized** (fûr′tə līzd′).

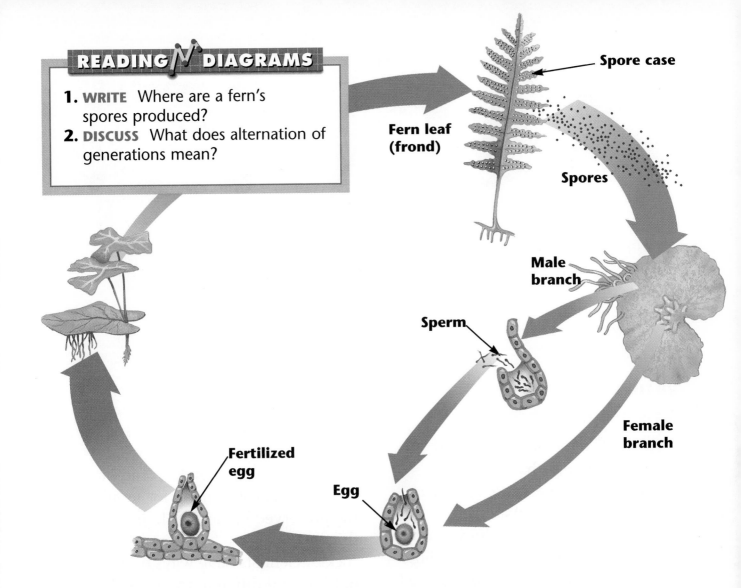

Spore case

Fern leaf (frond)

Spores

Male branch

Sperm

Female branch

Egg

Fertilized egg

This stage in the cycle is called **sexual reproduction** (sek′shü əl rē′prə duk′shən). That's because the plant needs both male sex cells and female sex cells in order to reproduce.

The fertilized egg eventually becomes a thin stalk with a spore case on top. When the spore case opens, the spores are released. Spores that land on damp ground may grow into new moss plants, and the cycle begins again.

This process of going from sexual reproduction to asexual reproduction to sexual reproduction again is called *alternation of generations* (ôl′tər nā′shən uv jen′ə rā′shənz).

The Life Cycle of a Fern

Ferns also reproduce by alternation of generations. Leafy fern plants produce spores on the undersides of their fronds.

Spores landing in shady, moist soil are most likely to grow. The spores grow into small, heart-shaped plants. These plants produce male and female sex cells.

If a male sex cell fertilizes a female sex cell, the fertilized egg starts to form a new plant. The new plant develops into a leafy fern plant. Spore cases on the fern's fronds produce spores, and the cycle begins again.

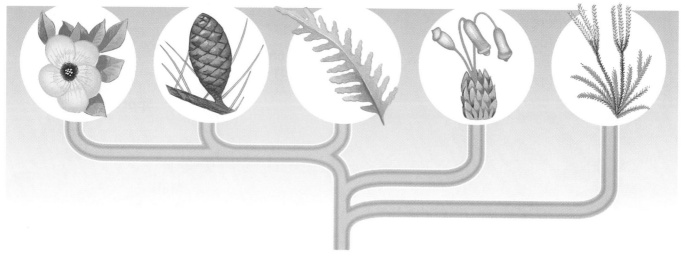

Angiosperms   Gymnosperms   Ferns   Mosses   Club mosses

Green algae

What Were the Ancestors of Plants?

The first land plants developed from living things that lived in the water. Which living things were the ancestors of land plants?

Scientists searched for clues linking organisms that lived in water to those that first grew on land. A good place to start was with photosynthetic organisms. These were living things that made their own food.

To narrow the search, the scientific detectives compared the chlorophyll of various simple organisms living today with that of plants. They found the closest match was with green algae.

Scientists found other clues. The cell walls of both green algae and plants contain cellulose. Cellulose can help plants survive on land, since a strong cell wall helps plants stay upright and holds in water.

There was another clue. Both green algae and plants store food as starch.

Finally, scientists found that some algae that live on land had a waterproof waxy cuticle just like land plants.

Next, scientists hunted for fossils—the preserved remains of living things. Fossils are found mostly in rocks. Scientists have ways of finding out how old different rocks are. If you know the age of a rock, you also know the age of the fossil in it.

Putting all the pieces of this puzzle together, scientists concluded that club mosses were the first land plants to evolve, or develop, from algae. They first appeared about 420 million years ago. Mosses and liverworts began living on land some 340 million years ago. Ferns did not emerge till about 310 million years ago.

This fernlike plant was found in rock that is over 340 million years old.

How Do Mosses Help the Environment?

After a forest fire or the eruption of a volcano, the land can be stripped of all plants. Nothing may remain except ashes. As time passes, plants return. The first ones are often mosses, which prepare the way for other plants.

Mosses do this in three important ways. First, their rhizoids grasp rocks and break off tiny pieces of them. These pieces contain minerals that all plants need to stay healthy.

Mosses also soak up water during rain showers and help keep the soil moist. In addition, their clinging rhizoids hold the top, most fertile layer of soil from being washed aw the wind blows a seed of a sl tree onto the soil, the seed fir good conditions for it to sprc Soon the mosses find them-selves sharing the land with all sorts of plants.

WHY IT MATTERS

Mosses and ferns were among the first plants to live on land. Today mosses are often the first plants to return to an area where plant life has been destroyed. Mosses help break down rocks into soil. Mosses also help hold on to the soil, making it easier for other plants to survive in the area. Without mosses, perhaps your favorite plants would never have had a chance to grow where they do.

A volcanic eruption or forest fire leaves the land empty of plants. The first to return are often mosses, which create the conditions for other plants to grow.

REVIEW

1. Why do mosses grow close to the ground?

2. **INFER** Why do people sometimes add moss to a garden?

3. How do mosses change rocky areas so other plants can grow?

4. List two differences between mosses and ferns.

5. **CRITICAL THINKING** *Analyze* How do cell walls help plants survive on land?

WHY IT MATTERS **THINK ABOUT IT**
Think about your lawn or a park you have gone to. What might it be like if the rocks had never been turned into soil?

WHY IT MATTERS **WRITE ABOUT IT**
Write a paragraph about why what mosses do for the soil is important to you.

ANIMAL LIFE CYCLES

What if you saw a tadpole but had never seen a frog? Would people have a hard time convincing you a frog was a grown-up tadpole?

When you see seedlings, you can predict that the fully grown plants will be on stems and have leaves. However, some baby animals look nothing like the adults. They change shape by going through metamorphosis.

Frogs lay eggs in ponds and lakes. The eggs hatch into tadpoles. They must live in water because they have gills, like fish, not lungs.

The tadpoles begin to change. They grow legs. Their tails disappear. They develop lungs and lose their gills. Now they can live on land and in the water!

Insects have two kinds of metamorphosis—complete and incomplete. In the complete metamorphosis, an egg hatches into a wormlike larva. It eats a lot and grows quickly to become a pupa. This is a resting phase. Many body changes take place. Some pupae spin protective cocoons. Finally, the adult winged insect emerges.

Adult frog

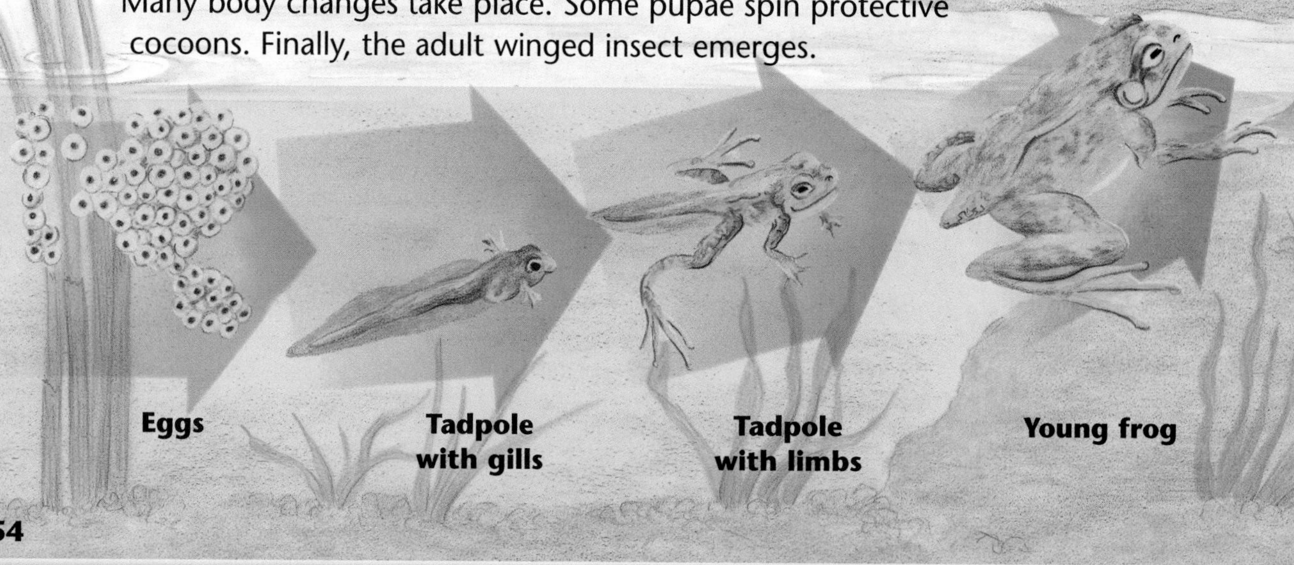

Eggs

Tadpole with gills

Tadpole with limbs

Young frog

Egg **Larva** **Pupa** **Adult butterfly**

During incomplete metamorphosis the insect changes shape gradually as it grows. An egg hatches into a nymph. It looks like a small adult, but without wings. As a nymph the insect grows and slowly changes. Finally, it grows wings and becomes an adult.

Changes in metamorphosis allow animals to move and get food in different ways. For example, a caterpillar has jaws to help it eat plants. A butterfly, however, has no teeth. Instead it has a long, hollow tongue that helps it suck nectar from flowers.

Egg **Nymph** **Adult grasshopper**

DISCUSSION STARTER

1. Compare complete and incomplete metamorphosis.

2. What advantages do you think animals that go through metamorphosis have?

To learn more about metamorphosis, visit *www.mhschool.com/science* and enter the keyword CHANGING.

inter**NET**
CONNECTION

WHY IT MATTERS

Seed plants are used as food, clothing, and many other important things.

SCIENCE WORDS

seed an undeveloped plant with stored food sealed in a protective covering

angiosperm a seed plant that produces flowers

gymnosperm a seed plant that does not produce flowers

conifer any of a group of gymnosperms that produce seeds in cones and have needle-like leaves

cotyledon a tiny leaflike structure inside a seed of an angiosperm

monocot an angiosperm with one cotelydon in each seed

dicot an angiosperm with two cotelydons in each seed

Plants With Seeds

How many plants do you munch on? When you munch on an apple, a watermelon, a grape, an orange, a peanut, or a banana, you are munching on a member of one main group of plants.

Have you ever picked up a pine cone? If so, you were holding a part of a plant from another main plant group.

Just about all the plants you are most familiar with can be grouped together with one or the other of the plants shown here. How are the two plants here different? How are they alike? One way they are alike is they produce seeds. They are seed plants.

EXPLORE

HYPOTHESIZE Have you ever noticed the differences in plant leaves? Are some leaves larger than others? How do these differences help the plant survive? Write a hypothesis in your *Science Journal*. How would you test your ideas?

Investigate How Seed Plants Differ

Compare the leaves of three kinds of plants to find how they enable each plant to survive in its environment.

MATERIALS

- small pine seedling or other conifer
- grass plant
- garden plant or houseplant, such as a geranium
- hand lens
- microscope slide
- coverslip
- microscope
- *Science Journal*

PROCEDURES

1. **OBSERVE** Examine each plant. Use the hand lens to examine a leaf from each one. In your *Science Journal*, draw each leaf and label it with the name of the plant it came from.

2. **OBSERVE** Remove a part of the lower epidermis from the grass leaf. Make a wet-mount slide. Examine the slide under low power.

3. **COMMUNICATE** In your *Science Journal*, draw what you observe.

4. **OBSERVE** Repeat step 2 with a pine needle and a houseplant leaf (such as a geranium). In your *Science Journal*, draw what you observe.

CONCLUDE AND APPLY

1. **COMPARE AND CONTRAST** How are the leaves of the three plants alike? How are the leaves of the three plants different from one another?

2. **INFER** Which one of the plants do you think is least like the other two? Explain your reasoning in your *Science Journal*.

GOING FURTHER: Problem Solving

3. **EXPERIMENT** Predict which of the plants you examined could survive best in a dry environment. How do you think the plant's leaves would help it do this? Design an experiment that would test your prediction.

How Do Seed Plants Differ?

The Explore Activity showed the leaves of three seed plants. Two leaves came from one major group of seed plants, while the other came from a different group.

Both groups are vascular plants. Both groups reproduce from **seeds**. A seed contains an undeveloped plant and stored food for the young plant.

Most of the plants that you see every day are seed plants. They include grasses, trees, shrubs, and bushes. They all have roots, stems, and leaves. Some, called **angiosperms** (an'jē ə spûrmz´), produce flowers. The others, called **gymnosperms** (jim'nə spûrmz´), do not produce flowers. These are the two major groups of seed plants.

The gymnosperms are the oldest seed plants. They include such evergreen trees as pine, fir, cedar, juniper, yew, larch, and spruce.

Gymnosperms first appeared on Earth about 250 million years ago. One hundred million years would pass before the first angiosperms appeared.

The fruits, vegetables, grains, and almost all of the nuts you eat are produced by angiosperms. However, one tasty nut—the pine nut, or pignoli—is a gymnosperm seed. It is the seed of certain pine trees.

What Kinds of Gymnosperms Are There?

The gymnosperms are divided into four divisions. They are the **conifers** (kon'ə fərz), *cycads* (sī'kadz), *ginkgoes* (ging'kōz), and *gnetophytes* (ne'tō fīts´).

Gymnosperms include some of the largest and oldest living things. The giant redwood (left) can grow as tall as a 30-story building.

The seed for this bristlecone pine (above) sprouted about 5,000 years ago.

Look at the photographs on this page. You'll notice that these plants look different. Yet they all have certain things in common.

Their seeds are produced on the scales of female cones. The seeds are not surrounded by a fruit. The leaves of most gymnosperms look like needles or scales. Most gymnosperms are *evergreens*. Evergreens lose only a few leaves at a time and constantly replace the leaves they have lost.

Some conifers, such as the larch, dawn redwood, and bald cypress, lose their leaves each fall. Plants that do this are called *deciduous* (di sij'ü əs).

When gymnosperms evolved, most of Earth was cold and dry. These plants are well adapted to cold, dry climates. For example, the needles of conifers have a very small surface area and are covered with a thicker cuticle. They lose less water than the wider leaves of flowering plants.

Brain Power

How do gymnosperms and angiosperms differ from mosses and ferns?

The maidenhair tree is the only member of the ginkgo division. It lives where the climate is neither too hot nor too cold.

Cycads live in warm climates. The red strawberry-shaped structures are not fruits but female cones.

Gnetophytes are more closely related to flowering plants than any other gymnosperm.

Conifers are found mostly in the northern parts of the world.

What Kinds of Angiosperms Are There?

Angiosperms are the most recently evolved and best-adapted division of seed plants. There are about 235,000 different kinds of angiosperms, which makes them the largest division in the plant kingdom.

Some, like duckweeds, float on water and are about the size of a large bee's eye. Duckweed is the smallest flowering plant. The largest flowering plant is the giant eucalyptus tree, which can be 100 meters tall and 20 meters in circumference.

Flowering trees (top) produce the fruits you eat. Wheat (bottom), an angiosperm, is a grass that produces one of the world's most important food crops.

Angiosperms are adapted to every environment on Earth.

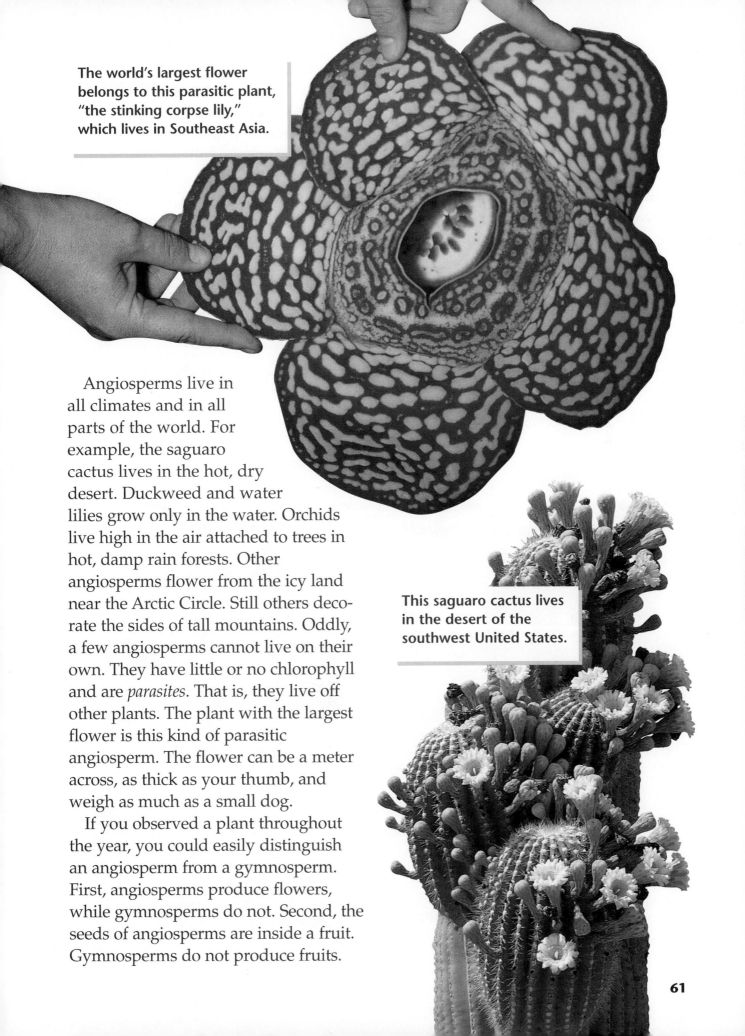

The world's largest flower belongs to this parasitic plant, "the stinking corpse lily," which lives in Southeast Asia.

Angiosperms live in all climates and in all parts of the world. For example, the saguaro cactus lives in the hot, dry desert. Duckweed and water lilies grow only in the water. Orchids live high in the air attached to trees in hot, damp rain forests. Other angiosperms flower from the icy land near the Arctic Circle. Still others decorate the sides of tall mountains. Oddly, a few angiosperms cannot live on their own. They have little or no chlorophyll and are *parasites*. That is, they live off other plants. The plant with the largest flower is this kind of parasitic angiosperm. The flower can be a meter across, as thick as your thumb, and weigh as much as a small dog.

If you observed a plant throughout the year, you could easily distinguish an angiosperm from a gymnosperm. First, angiosperms produce flowers, while gymnosperms do not. Second, the seeds of angiosperms are inside a fruit. Gymnosperms do not produce fruits.

This saguaro cactus lives in the desert of the southwest United States.

How Many Leaves Are Inside a Seed?

Scientists divide the angiosperms into two classes. As you might guess, scientists are able to do this because of some particular characteristic that sets the two classes apart. That characteristic turns out to be the number of an angiosperm's **cotyledons** (kot´ə lē´dənz). A cotyledon is a tiny leaflike structure inside a seed.

Some angiosperm seeds contain only one cotyledon. Plants whose seeds contain only one cotyledon are called *monocotyledons*, or **monocots** (mon´ə kots´) for short. (The prefix *mono-* comes from a Greek word meaning "one.") There are over 60,000 different kinds of monocots.

Angiosperms whose seeds contain two cotyledons are called *dicotyledons*, or **dicots** (dī´kots) for short. (The prefix *di-* comes from a Greek word meaning "two.") There are over 170,000 kinds of dicots. Corn, rice, wheat, grasses, orchids, and coconut palms are examples of monocots. Bean plants, maple trees, rose plants, and cactuses are some of the dicots.

READING /\/ CHARTS

DISCUSS Describe three differences between monocots and dicots.

MATH LINK

Main Differences Between Monocots and Dicots

Characteristics	Monocots	Dicots
Cotyledons	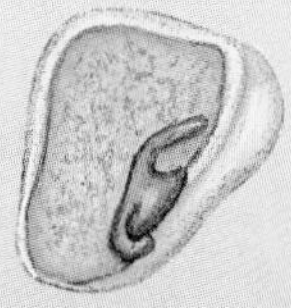 One	Two 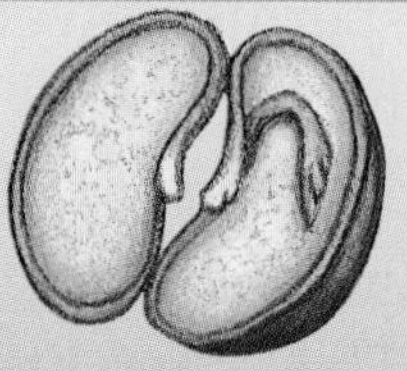
Leaf veins	Parallel 	 Branched
Flower parts	 Multiples of three	Multiples of four or five 
Vascular system	Scattered in bundles 	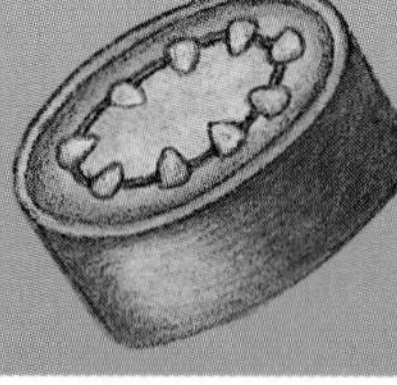 In rings

SKILL BUILDER

Skill: Classifying

FLOWERING PLANTS

In this activity you will classify flowering plants. That is, you will examine several plants and try to determine whether each is a monocot or a dicot. As you examine each plant sample, refer to the chart on page 62 to help you classify each sample.

PROCEDURES

1. OBSERVE Get together with a few of your classmates and go on a leaf- and flower-collecting field trip. (Make sure to avoid poison ivy, poison oak, and poison sumac leaves. Your teacher can tell you how to spot them.)

2. OBSERVE Find a number of different angiosperms. Try to get a sample of a leaf and flower from each plant. If you can't get a flower, a leaf will do.

3. INTERPRET DATA Look at the chart of Main Differences Between Monocots and Dicots. It will give you clues on how to tell if the sample leaves and flowers you chose are monocots or dicots.

CONCLUDE AND APPLY

1. OBSERVE Examine the plant parts you have chosen. For each sample leaf, describe how the leaf veins look. For each sample flower, tell how many parts each flower has. Record your answers in your *Science Journal*.

2. CLASSIFY Mount the leaves and flowers on a heavy sheet of cardboard, and indicate whether each came from a monocot or a dicot.

The awful-smelling jack-in-the-pulpit flower attracts insects that help the plant reproduce.

Why Do Flowers Have Aromas?

The characteristics of living things help them survive in their environment. It would make sense to expect that the aromas of flowers do the same for their plants.

To your nose some of these aromas are very pleasing. That's why chemicals that produce the aromas of such flowers as roses and jasmines are used in perfumes. However, some flowers, like those of the jack-in-the-pulpit plant, smell awful. Yet, surprisingly, both beautiful and awful aromas serve the same purpose for these plants. They attract insects! What's the advantage of this?

When the insect enters the flower, it brushes against a part of the flower that holds tiny grains of dust, called *pollen*. These grains contain the plant's male sex cells.

The pollen sticks to the insect. As the insect moves around the flower—or moves to another flower on the plant—some of the pollen rubs off on parts of the flower that hold female sex cells. The two sex cells join, and the reproduction of a new plant has begun.

However, why should the awful smell of a plant attract insects? First, many plants attract one particular kind of insect. In the case of the awful-smelling jack-in-the-pulpit, the insects are dung beetles and flies. These insects generally feed on dead or decaying animals or animal wastes, which smell awful. The insects mistake the aroma of the plant for that of a good meal.

Once inside the flower, the insects discover that its sides are so smooth that they can't climb out. But they try. As they rush around the inside of the flower, they keep transferring pollen to the part of the flower that holds female sex cells.

After about 24 hours, something strange happens. The inside of the flower changes from smooth to wrinkled. Their job done, the insects can now get a foothold and escape. They will live to make the same "mistake" again and give a new life to the awful-smelling jack-in-the-pulpit.

Almost all of the food you eat that comes from plants is produced by flowering plants. Flowering plants also decorate the landscape and homes with beautiful colors. Some produce chemicals that are used in perfumes and other cosmetics. Others, such as plants used as spices, flavor the foods you eat. Like all plants, flowering plants help keep the balance of gases in the air by using up carbon dioxide and producing oxygen.

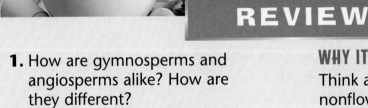

REVIEW

1. How are gymnosperms and angiosperms alike? How are they different?

2. How are flowers important to a plant?

3. **CLASSIFY** List five plants that are angiosperms and five plants that are gymnosperms. Explain what characteristics helped you determine which was which.

4. What are the differences between monocots and dicots?

5. **CRITICAL THINKING** *Apply* How have seed plants become adapted to the environment?

WHY IT MATTERS THINK ABOUT IT
Think about the flowering and nonflowering plants you are familiar with. Which ones are most important in your life?

WHY IT MATTERS WRITE ABOUT IT
Write a paragraph about a day in your life and all the plants that are important to you. Classify the plants as angiosperms or gymnosperms and as monocots or dicots.

READING SKILL
Write a paragraph to compare and contrast some of the plants you read about in this lesson.

65

A Wildflower Crusade

Growing up in the woods of east Texas, Lady Bird Johnson loved wildflowers. When Lady Bird was young, most people didn't think about the environment. Years later, as the wife of President Lyndon B. Johnson, Lady Bird helped to change that!

As First Lady, Lady Bird promoted the nation's parks. She worked to ban billboards along America's roads. The Highway Beautification Act of 1965 that banned billboards on rural highways was called Lady Bird's Bill.

In 1968 Lady Bird and her husband left the White House. In 1982 she founded the National Wildflower Research Center, now known as the Lady Bird Johnson Wildlife Center, in Austin, Texas. The center tells people about plants unique to different parts of our country.

One of Lady Bird's goals was to "provide a sense of place. California would look like California, Pennsylvania like Pennsylvania, and Texas like Texas."

Lady Bird Johnson helped to make people aware of the beauty and importance of wildflowers.

Making a Difference

To do that the center gave people information about plants native to different areas. It told people how to get them and how to grow them.

Lady Bird pointed out many good reasons to grow native plants. They have adapted to the land. They need less watering. They use less fertilizer. They use fewer pesticides. They do well with what nature provides!

Another reason to grow them is one that Lady Bird called "dear to my heart." They bring "beauty, regionalism, and seasonal color."

Interest in the center has grown. It now has one of the largest collections of information about North America's native plants. Like her wildflowers Lady Bird's idea has taken root and done well!

DISCUSSION STARTER

1. How would having a wildflower center help maintain the diversity of plant life in this country?

2. Why would people use less water, fewer pesticides, and less fertilizer if they planted native plants?

To learn more about wildflowers, visit *www.mhschool.com/science* and enter the keyword WILDFLOWER.

*inter*NET
CONNECTION

WHY IT MATTERS

People eat all of the parts of flowering plants.

SCIENCE WORDS

ovary a structure containing egg cells

pollination the transfer of a pollen grain to the egg-producing part of a plant

embryo the immature plant inside a seed

seed coat the outer covering of a seed

fruit the ripened ovary of a flowering seed plant

From Plant to Seed to Plant

What do people use flowers for? What do bees use them for? Have you ever seen bees buzzing around? Don't disturb them if you ever do see them. From a distance you might watch as a bee goes from flower to flower, as if it is collecting or giving out something. What do you think it is doing?

Not just bees, but other insects—and other animals—hover around flowers as well. A hummingbird is one example. What do you think the hummingbird is doing?

EXPLORE

HYPOTHESIZE Are all flowers alike? If not, how are flowers different? How are they alike? What do you think plants use their flowers for? Write your ideas in your *Science Journal*. Test your ideas.

Design Your Own Experiment

HOW DO FLOWERS DIFFER?

PROCEDURES

1. PLAN Decide on how you will compare the flowers you look at. You may choose to look for parts that they seem to have in common. Describe what the parts are and how they differ from plant to plant.

2. Begin by removing the outer leaflike parts. Examine them. Draw what they look like in your *Science Journal*.

3. Remove the petals. Examine them. Draw what they look like in your *Science Journal*.

4. OBSERVE Examine the rest of the flower as you decide.

5. COMMUNICATE In your *Science Journal,* draw the parts you examined.

MATERIALS

- several large flowers from different plants
- hand lens
- forceps
- dropper
- toothpick
- black paper
- *Science Journal*

CONCLUDE AND APPLY

1. COMMUNICATE What color is each flower? What do you think the job of the petals is? How would you design an experiment to find out?

2. INFER What do you think the various parts of each flower are for? Do you think the same parts of different flowers do the same kinds of jobs for their plants?

GOING FURTHER: Apply

3. INFER Why do you think a plant has flowers? Make a hypothesis. Design an experiment to test your ideas.

How Do Flowers Differ?

Not all flowers are alike. Some flowers, like the one in the Explore Activity, are *complete flowers*. Complete flowers have sepals, petals, stamens, and pistils. *Incomplete flowers* are missing one of these parts. Some flowers are called perfect. *Perfect flowers* have both female and male parts, that is, both pistils (female parts) and stamens (male parts).

Imperfect flowers have either pistils or stamens but not both. You might think of these flowers as "female" or "male." Some plants, like corn and oak trees, have separate male and female flowers on the same plant. Other plants, like willow trees and holly trees, have only male flowers or female flowers.

PARTS OF A FLOWER

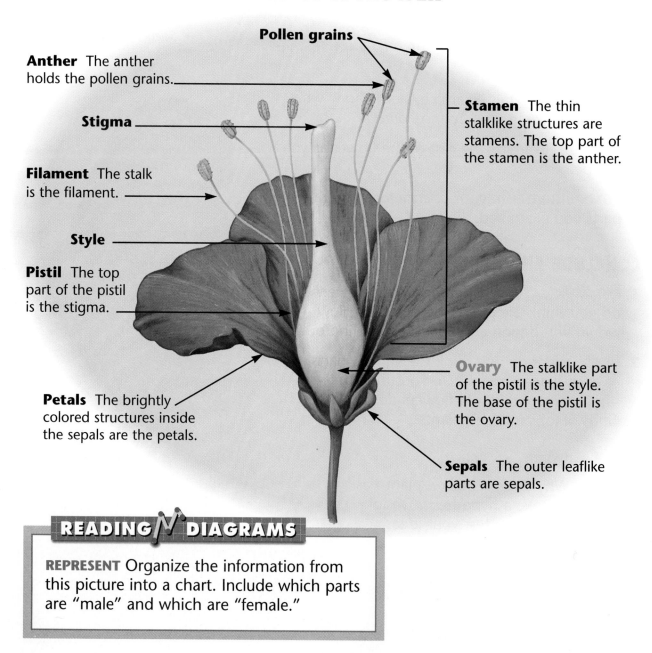

Pollen grains

Anther The anther holds the pollen grains.

Stigma

Filament The stalk is the filament.

Style

Pistil The top part of the pistil is the stigma.

Petals The brightly colored structures inside the sepals are the petals.

Stamen The thin stalklike structures are stamens. The top part of the stamen is the anther.

Ovary The stalklike part of the pistil is the style. The base of the pistil is the ovary.

Sepals The outer leaflike parts are sepals.

READING ∕∖ DIAGRAMS

REPRESENT Organize the information from this picture into a chart. Include which parts are "male" and which are "female."

The red holly berries that you see on holly trees in the late fall appear only on holly trees with female flowers. In order to produce the berries (the holly's fruit), the tree with female flowers needs to be fertilized by pollen from a holly tree with male flowers.

Brain Power

A fruit will only develop if male and female sex cells join. Based on this information, suggest why a person who wants to grow fruit may be advised to buy at least two trees.

Did this holly tree have male flowers or female flowers? How can you tell?

An oak tree has both male and female flowers on the same tree.

Seeds

Some seeds are very tiny, while others are really large. The largest is produced by the double-coconut tree, whose seeds can be about half your weight. Some of the smallest seeds belong to orchid plants. You could put thousands of them in a teaspoon.

But no matter how large or small, all seeds develop the same way. As you read on, pause every now and then to look at the drawings on this page. They will help you follow what you are reading.

First, a pollen grain must be transferred from a flower's anther to its stigma, or to another flower's stigma. Pollen grains contain sperm, which are male sex cells. This transfer is called **pollination** (pol'ə nā'shən).

POLLINATION

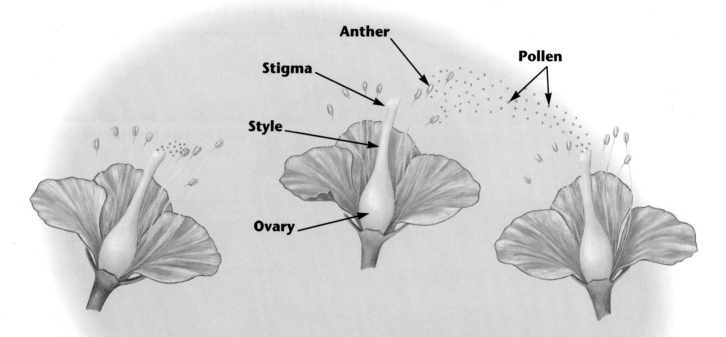

Anther

Stigma

Pollen

Style

Ovary

SELF-POLLINATION
Pollination occurs when a pollen grain from an anther reaches the stigma. Since this flower has both anthers and a stigma, it is pollinating itself.

CROSS-POLLINATION
Pollination can occur between two or more flowers on separate plants.

READING ✍ DIAGRAMS

1. DISCUSS How are self-pollination and cross-pollination alike? How are they different?
2. WRITE Write a paragraph describing the steps in fertilization.

If the pollen is transferred from an anther to a stigma in the same flower, the process is called *self-pollination*. If the transfer is from one flower to another flower, the process is called *cross-pollination*.

On the stigma a tube forms from the pollen grain. The tube grows down the stigma and into the flower's ovary. Sperm travel down the tube, through the style, and into the ovary. There a sperm cell combines with, or fertilizes, an egg cell. This combining is called *fertilization* (fûr´tə lə zā'shən).

A seed develops from a fertilized egg cell. Under the right conditions, a new plant will develop from the seed. The process of making a new plant from the joining of a sperm and an egg cell is called *sexual reproduction*.

AND FERTILIZATION

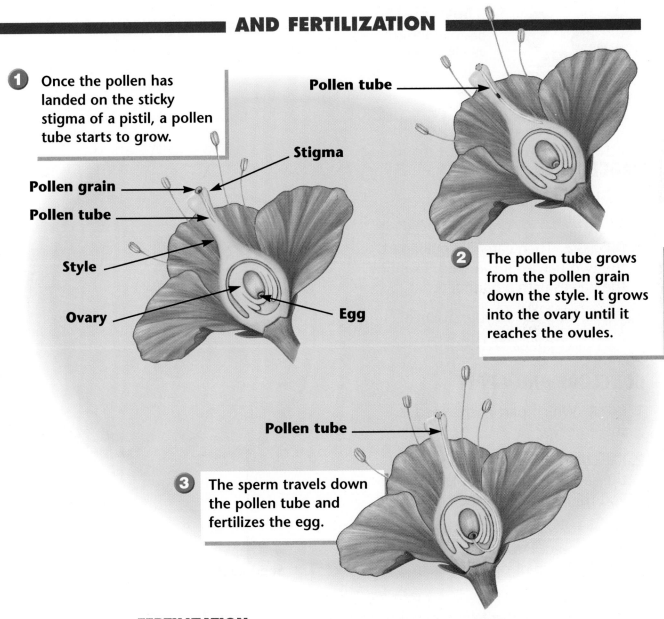

1 Once the pollen has landed on the sticky stigma of a pistil, a pollen tube starts to grow.

Stigma

Pollen grain

Pollen tube

Style

Ovary

Egg

Pollen tube

2 The pollen tube grows from the pollen grain down the style. It grows into the ovary until it reaches the ovules.

Pollen tube

3 The sperm travels down the pollen tube and fertilizes the egg.

FERTILIZATION
Fertilization occurs when sperm from the pollen grains travel down the style and combine with eggs in the ovary.

73

Inside a Seed

HYPOTHESIZE What does a seed do? Where does it store its food? How do different seeds compare? Write a hypothesis in your *Science Journal*.

MATERIALS
- bean seed (such as a lima bean)
- corn seed
- water
- hand lens
- *Science Journal*

PROCEDURES

1. Soak the bean seed in water overnight.

2. **OBSERVE** Then carefully pull apart the two halves of the seed. Examine the halves with a hand lens.

3. **COMMUNICATE** In your *Science Journal*, draw what you see.

CONCLUDE AND APPLY

1. **INFER** Which part of the seed is the embryo?

2. **IDENTIFY** On your drawing, label the seed coat and the place where you think food is stored.

3. **COMPARE AND CONTRAST** Look at a corn seed. Describe how its parts are similar to or different from a bean seed.

4. **COMMUNICATE** Explain why you think one is the seed of a dicot and the other is the seed of a monocot. Which is which?

What's in a Seed?

A seed is made up of three main parts. One part is an **embryo** (em′brē ō′). An embryo is an immature plant. Another part is where food is stored in the form of starch. The third part is the **seed coat**. The seed coat encases the whole seed in a tough, protective covering.

PARTS OF A SEED

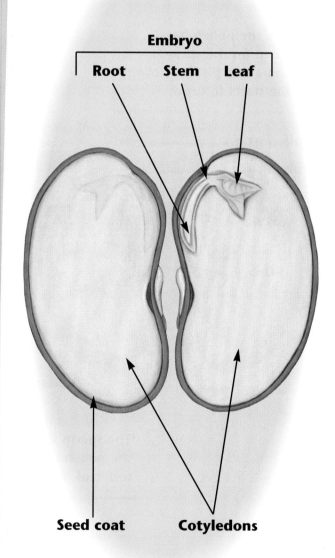

Embryo — Root · Stem · Leaf

Seed coat · Cotyledons

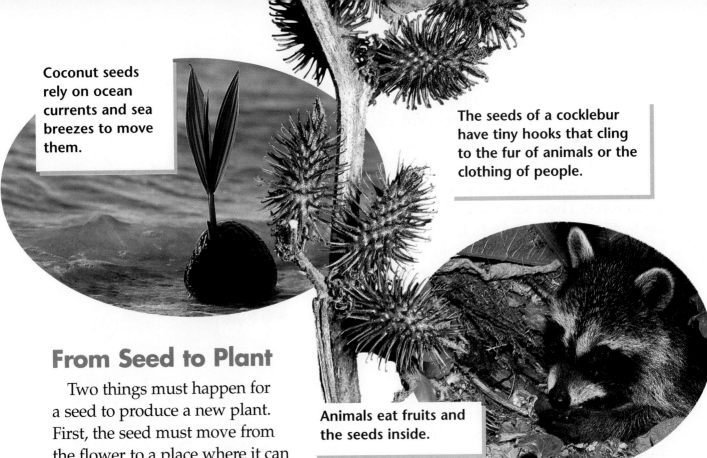

Coconut seeds rely on ocean currents and sea breezes to move them.

The seeds of a cocklebur have tiny hooks that cling to the fur of animals or the clothing of people.

Animals eat fruits and the seeds inside.

From Seed to Plant

Two things must happen for a seed to produce a new plant. First, the seed must move from the flower to a place where it can sprout. This is called *seed dispersal* (sēd di spûr′səl). Second, the place must provide everything that is needed for sprouting, which is called *germination* (jûr′mə nā′shən). A warm temperature and water are the two most important needs for germination. Food is not needed because the seed has its own supply of stored food.

Usually the seed must move a relatively long distance from its parent plant. Why? Competition from its parent, and plants like it, may make the development of a new plant difficult. For example, nearby plants may block sunlight from reaching the young plant. They may soak up the water or minerals from the soil that the new plant needs.

Seeds have evolved all sorts of adaptations for dispersal. For example, dandelion fruits and cottonwood seeds have feathery "parachutes." These parachutes can be blown great distances by the wind. Animals also help move plant seeds.

Animals eat **fruits**. A fruit is a mature ripened ovary of a plant. The animals digest the soft parts of the fruits but not the hard seeds inside. As the animals move from place to place, they deposit the seeds in their wastes.

Scientists have discovered that animals tend to eat only ripe fruits. Only the seeds of ripe fruits are ready for dispersal. How do the fruits reveal that they are ripe? They change color and flavor. For example, a Macintosh apple will turn from green to red. Its flesh will turn from sour to sweet. Both of these changes signal animals that the fruit is ready to eat. These changes help ensure that the apple tree will have successful offspring.

Flying Seeds

Some seeds, like those of the witch hazel and the dwarf mistletoe, explode from their fruits under special conditions. In the witch hazel, when its fruits dry out, they split open with great force. Their seeds are propelled up to 45 meters (148 feet). In the dwarf mistletoe, fluids build up in the fruits. When the pressure gets too great, the fruits burst, sending their seeds flying at 100 kilometers (62 miles) an hour.

How Do Gymnosperms Spread Their Seeds?

Gymnosperms don't produce fruits. They disperse their seeds in other ways. For example, the cones of the balsam fir tree shatter. When they do this, they release winglike seeds that ride on the wind. Animals move cones from place to place. Heavy rains, floods, and streams can disperse them also.

READING ⁄Ν⁄ DIAGRAMS

REPRESENT Use the picture to write an outline of the steps in the life cycle of a conifer.

Mature tree

76

Life Cycle of a Conifer

Since gymnosperms don't produce flowers or fruits, their life cycle is not the same as angiosperms. However, there are similarities. As you read on and look at the drawings on this page, make a list of the similarities and differences.

Let's examine the life cycle of a pine tree. A pine tree belongs to a group of gymnosperms called conifers. Pines produce male and female cones on a mature tree. The scales that form the cones carry spore cases that produce the plant's sperm and egg cells. Male cones produce pollen grains, which contain sperm cells.

When pollen grains fall away from a male cone, the wind carries them through the air. If a pollen grain happens to land on a female cone, a sperm cell from the pollen may fertilize an egg cell in the female cone.

The fertilized cell eventually becomes a seed. As autumn and winter come, the female pine cones fall from the trees. Their seeds scatter on the ground. Sometimes wind or water will carry the seeds far from the tree. If they end up in a place where conditions are right for germination, the seeds will sprout, and a new pine tree will start growing.

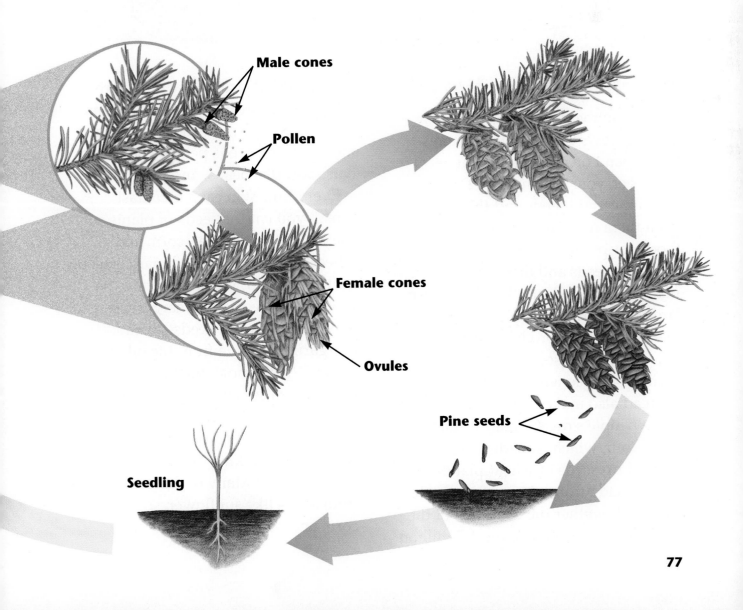

Male cones

Pollen

Female cones

Ovules

Pine seeds

Seedling

Breakfast cereals are made from the seeds of plants such as rice, wheat, corn, and oats.

Which Seeds Do We Eat?

Although you eat seeds and their products every day, your life may not depend on eating such things. However, your health does. That's because certain seeds and things made from them make up one of the major food groups—grains. For many people on Earth, seeds and their products *are* a matter of life or death. That's because a large part of these people's diets is made up of seed products. For example, rice—which is a seed—is the main food of many people who live in Asia.

Bread also makes up a large part of some people's diets. Bread is made from flour, which is made mostly from ground up seeds of wheat plants. Flour is also made from corn, rye, and other seeds. Altogether the countries of the world produce an amazing 1.5 million metric tons of rice, wheat, and corn. (A metric ton equals 1,000 kilograms, or 2,205 pounds.) This figure does not include other seeds people eat, like oats, peanuts, beans, and peas.

Every time you eat a breakfast cereal, you eat the seeds of plants such as rye, barley, rice, oat, corn, and wheat. When you spread margarine on a slice of bread, you are putting the product of seeds—the margarine—on another product of seeds—bread. Margarine is made from the oils of seeds. What's more, the bread may be dotted with sesame, poppy, or caraway seeds to give it more flavor.

Do you like salad oil, or do your parents use cooking oils to prepare certain foods? Many of these oils come from seeds like sunflower, soybean, corn, and sesame.

Can You Start New Plants Without Seeds?

Some plants can be grown from pieces of the plant—such as stems, leaves, and roots—rather than from seeds. This is called *vegetative propagation*. It is also called *asexual reproduction* because it happens without sperm and egg cells joining. For example, strawberry plants send shoots into the soil from stems that grow along the ground. Each shoot will make a new strawberry plant.

Flowering plants produce almost all of the plants you eat. People eat all of the parts of these plants. The parts include the flowers themselves, fruits, seeds, leaves, stems, and roots. Flowering plants are also eaten by animals that we, in turn, eat.

New African violet plants can be grown from a cutting of a leaf that has a small bit of stem attached to it.

REVIEW

1. Identify the different parts of a flower and tell what each part does.

2. Explain how seeds are produced.

3. Give at least three examples of how seeds are dispersed.

4. **COMPARE AND CONTRAST** Describe the difference between fertilization and germination.

5. **CRITICAL THINKING** *Analyze* How do you think trees that produce seedless oranges are grown? Write down your prediction. Then do library research to see if your prediction was correct.

WHY IT MATTERS THINK ABOUT IT
Flowers, fruits, seeds, leaves, stems, and roots all play important roles in your life. Which plant parts do you use most often?

WHY IT MATTERS WRITE ABOUT IT
Write a paragraph that describes the plants and plant parts that are most important to you. Be sure to explain why they are important.

Timing Trees

How do you know a tree's age? Look at its rings! Not the kind you wear on your fingers, but the kind you see in the cross section of a log!

A tree forms a layer of wood each year. In spring large thin-walled cells form below the bark. As summer ends, new cells become smaller, and the walls are thicker. In winter growth stops.

This process continues for as long as the tree lives. You can see the layers in a cross section from a tree. Scientists use those layers, or rings, to tell the age of a tree.

Rings not only tell a tree's age, they give clues about weather in the area. A year with warm temperatures and lots of rain produces a thick ring. A year with cold temperatures and little rain produces a thin ring. Trees in the same area have similar ring patterns.

A warm and wet year

A cool and dry year

Math Link

Because of this, tree rings help scientists date wood found in ancient ruins. They find a cross section from a living tree nearby. Then they compare its rings to the wood from the ruins. This has been very helpful in the southwestern United States, where the dry climate helps to preserve trees.

In ancient Native American villages there, scientists found wooden beams used to hold up roofs centuries ago. Some beams were so old, they showed the marks of stone axes!

The beams were compared with wood from many sources. Using wood cut on a known date, scientists dated beams with similar ring patterns. The scientists were able to date Native American villages 1,500 years old. The people who lived there left no written records, but the trees they cut told their story for them!

DISCUSSION STARTER

1. Explain why the pattern of a tree's cross section looks the way it does.

2. What was the weather like if a tree ring for that year is thin?

Mesa Verde, a Native American village, is about 1,500 years old!

To learn more about tree rings, visit **www.mhschool.com/science** and enter the keyword TIMING.

*inter*NET
CONNECTION

Topic 7
LIFE SCIENCE

WHY IT MATTERS

Some behaviors are inherited. Others have to be learned.

SCIENCE WORDS

response what a living thing does as a result of a stimulus

stimulus something in the environment (such as light or heat) that causes a living thing to react

tropism a growth response of a plant toward or away from a stimulus

adaptation a characteristic that enables a living thing to survive in its environment

Plant Responses

What happens when you jump up? What happens to skateboard jumpers when they reach the top of the slope? Why don't they just fly up and away from Earth's surface?

There is a pull between Earth and everything on it. This pull is called gravity. It never stops. How does gravity affect what you do?

How do you think gravity affects what a plant does—for example, how it grows? Gravity pulls things downward. However, as plants grow, do their parts—roots, stems, and leaves—grow downward?

EXPLORE

HYPOTHESIZE Do roots always grow "down" no matter how you plant a seed? Write a hypothesis in your *Science Journal.* Then test your ideas.

EXPLORE ⚡ ACTIVITY

Investigate How Roots Grow

Place seeds in many positions to observe how roots grow from them.

PROCEDURES

1. Soak two paper towels. Wrinkle the paper towels and place them in the bottom half of the petri dish.

2. Place the four seeds on top of the wet paper towels as shown in diagram 1. Place the seeds so that the curved part is turned toward the center of the dish.

3. Place the top on the petri dish. The top will hold the seeds in the wet paper towels. Seal the top with transparent tape. Draw an arrow on the petri dish with the glass-marking pen as shown in diagram 2. This will show which direction is down. Write the number or name of your group on the petri dish.

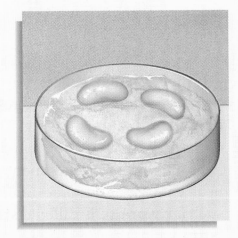

4. In a place your teacher provides, stand the petri dish on its edge so the arrow is pointing downward. Tape the petri dish so that it will remain standing. Do not lay the dish down flat.

5. PREDICT In your *Science Journal*, make a prediction about the direction you think the roots will grow.

6. COMMUNICATE Examine the seeds for the next four days. Record the direction of root growth.

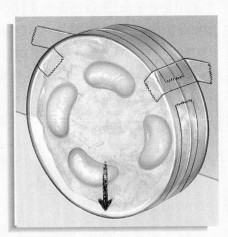

CONCLUDE AND APPLY

1. OBSERVE In what direction were the roots growing on day 1? On day 4?

2. INFER Is your prediction supported by your data?

GOING FURTHER: Problem Solving

3. PREDICT What would happen if a seedling were not able to grow its roots down into the soil? Design an experiment to test your prediction.

If a plant bends toward a stimulus, its change is called a positive tropism. If it bends away, the change is called a negative tropism.

How Do Roots Grow?

If the flash of a camera goes off near your eyes, you are likely to respond to the bright light by blinking. The flash of light stimulated your blinking. Anything in the environment—light, heat, gravity, and more—that produces such a **response** is called a **stimulus** (stim′yə ləs).

Plants also respond to a stimulus, but they tend to respond more slowly than animals do. Plants slowly bend or curve toward or away from a stimulus. Scientists call this kind of response a **tropism** (trō′piz əm). Tropisms help a plant survive in its environment. The Explore Activity showed that as seeds sprout, their roots grow downward. Why do you think the seeds' roots grow downward?

There are several major kinds of tropisms. You already explored one of

these—gravitropism. The plant's roots were responding to a stimulus. That stimulus was gravity.

The roots of a plant show positive gravitropism. No matter how the plant is tilted, its roots will always grow downward into the soil. The roots grow in the direction Earth's gravity is pulling them. Stems show negative gravitropism. They grow away from the force of gravity. They grow into the air, where their leaves can get the most sunlight.

Light, of course, is very important to plants' survival. Plants respond to changes in light. These responses are called *phototropisms*. (*Photo* comes from a Greek word meaning "light.") If a plant is exposed to light coming from only one direction, its stem will bend in that direction. That is positive phototropism.

What Makes a Plant's Parts Move?

If you examine the roots of a willow tree growing near a stream, you will discover *hydrotropism*. *Hydro* means "water." The willow's roots show positive hydrotropism. They grow toward a source of water.

Some plants, like squash and grape plants, show a response to touch. Grape vines grow around posts farmers stick in the ground. The vines send out threadlike tendrils. The tendrils coil toward whatever they touch.

People long knew about plant tropisms. Yet they didn't always know the process inside a plant that made a plant's parts move. The first clue was discovered by Charles Darwin and his son Francis in the 1850s. Charles Darwin cut off the tips of some very young plant shoots. He left other plants alone. The plants with tips bent toward light. The plants without tips did not. Darwin concluded that something in the tips was causing the bending, but what?

The tendrils of this plant respond to touch as they coil around other objects.

The second clue was found in the 1920s by Dutch scientist Fritz Went. Went guessed that a chemical made only in the shoot's tip was responsible for the bending. He separated many chemicals from shoot tips. One by one he placed them on the cutoff tops of plant shoots. Finally, he found the chemical that let the cut shoots bend toward light.

The chemical is called an *auxin*. Auxins are chemicals that stimulate plant growth. Auxins work on stems, roots, tendrils, and all other parts of the plant. Auxins cause tropisms of all kinds. How do auxins cause plant parts to bend? When one side of a stem is exposed to light, for example, auxins move to the other side and down. The auxins cause more cells to grow on the dark side. The dark side begins to grow longer, but not the side facing the light. This unequal growth causes the stem to bend toward the light.

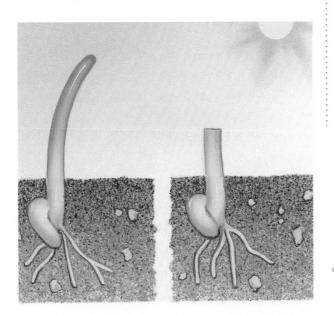

Charles Darwin showed that when the tip of a plant shoot is cut off, the plant will not bend toward light.

Adaptations for Survival

Plants survive in deserts, rain forests, and the arctic. They survive in all these places because they have adapted to their environment. An **adaptation** (ad´əp tā′shən) helps an organism survive in its environment.

Water Shortages

Desert plants have adaptations for collecting, storing, and saving water. Cactus plants have roots that absorb water very quickly. The water is stored in the center of the plant. A thick, waterproof, waxy coating helps stop water loss. Finally, the plant's stomata only open at night, when temperatures are cooler. Less water is lost through transpiration.

Carnivorous (meat-eating) plants can't get enough nutrients from the soil. These plants trap and digest insects to get some of the nutrients they need.

Changes in Light

Plants like spinach, lettuce, and wheat bloom in late spring and early summer. They are called *long-day* plants. That's because when they bloom, there is much more daylight than darkness. By contrast, *short-day* plants, like strawberries, soybeans, and ragweed, bloom in early spring or in the fall. Short-day plants bloom when there is more darkness and less daylight. This flowering response is called *photoperiodism*.

SHORT-DAY, LONG-DAY PLANTS

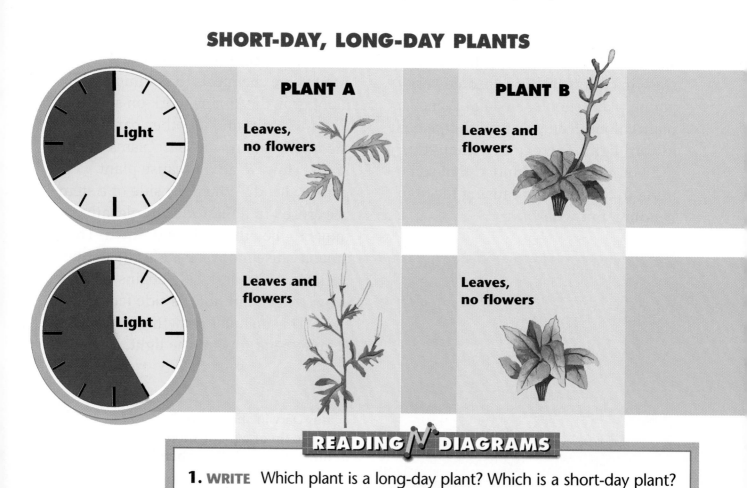

PLANT A

Light

Leaves, no flowers

PLANT B

Leaves and flowers

Light

Leaves and flowers

Leaves, no flowers

READING DIAGRAMS

1. WRITE Which plant is a long-day plant? Which is a short-day plant?

2. DISCUSS In what season would plant A bloom?

Why Do Plants Compete?

Like all organisms, plants compete with one another for what they need to survive and grow—sunlight, water, and nutrients.

Each plant has its own strategy for winning its battle with other plants. Vines, like ivy and honeysuckle, climb the trunks of trees to get a greater share of sunlight. The trees themselves rise to great heights. They spread their branches to form leafy canopies above the forest. That's why in a forest, trees like oaks and maples have more leaves at their tops.

Have you ever been in a forest full of giant redwoods or other conifers? If so, you probably felt as if you were in a huge building filled with soaring columns. Only when you look high up do you see branches covered with green needles. Trees like these also preserve the nutrients and water in the soil for themselves. They do this by blocking sunlight from reaching the ground. Without sunlight few plants can grow in the soil and soak up nutrients and water near great trees.

QUICK LAB

Plants Compete for Light

HYPOTHESIZE Do some plants need more light than others? Can some plants survive in shady areas? Write a hypothesis in your *Science Journal*.

MATERIALS
- grass seed
- ivy plant
- various houseplants
- paper cup
- soil
- *Science Journal*

PROCEDURES

1. Collect samples of various houseplants that grow to different widths and heights.

2. Plant them, with some grass seed, in your cup. Record in your *Science Journal* the types of plants you used.

3. **OBSERVE** Examine your plants over the next few days.

CONCLUDE AND APPLY

1. **OBSERVE** Which plants are being shaded by others? Are the plants in the shade doing as well as the plants that are getting more light?

2. **HYPOTHESIZE** How would you design an experiment to test which plants need more light to grow? How could you determine if these plants have anything else in common?

How Else Do Plants Fight for Survival?

Some plants use another strategy for keeping other plants at a distance. They produce chemicals that are poisons to other plants. Creosote bushes, which live in dry areas, release such a poison from their roots. The poison keeps the seeds of other plants from germinating. It may even kill other plants that are already growing.

Plants also make chemicals that discourage insects and animals from feeding on or infecting them. The most powerful insect-fighting plant chemical is made by the neem tree of Africa and Asia. This chemical is so strong that if you dissolved a teaspoon of it in a medium-sized swimming pool and sprayed the water on a plant, insects would not feed on it. Some plants, like the hemlock, even make poisons that can kill a person.

Unlike the plant below, which is being eaten by an insect, other plants such as the poison ivy above, produce chemicals that keep insects away or make them sick.

How Do Animals Adapt?

If you've ever smelled the spray of a skunk, you unpleasantly discovered an adaptation of animals. It's one that protects an animal from harm.

Animals have many adaptations that help them survive in their environment. Some are able to run or swim fast to escape from a predator. Others have sharp claws or teeth to hunt or fight with. Plants rely mostly on adaptations like color, aroma, poisonous chemicals, and structures like thorns.

How Does Looking Like Something Else Protect an Animal?

Looking like something else—especially something unpleasant—is called *mimicry*. Mimicry can be a powerful protector. For example, the viceroy butterfly tastes good to birds. Yet birds tend to avoid eating viceroys. Why? Viceroys look like the bad-tasting monarch. Predators also avoid some perfectly harmless flies and bugs because they look like stinging wasps or bees.

Some animals mimic plants or their parts. For example, the *kallima* butterfly of Asia looks just like a dead leaf. It also has markings that look very much like the fungus that grows on dead leaves. A stick insect looks just like the twig of a plant on which it is resting.

Animals avoid this harmless fly because it mimics a stinging wasp.

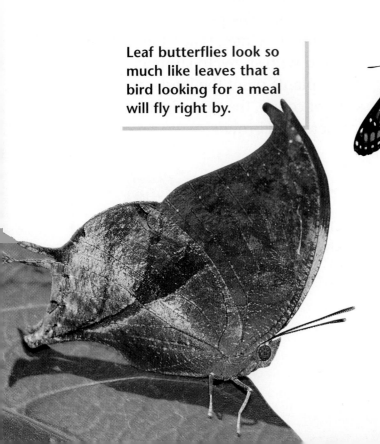

Leaf butterflies look so much like leaves that a bird looking for a meal will fly right by.

The good-tasting viceroy butterfly (top) mimics the bad-tasting monarch butterfly (bottom). Birds leave the viceroy alone because they've learned that insects with the same color patterns taste bad.

Ptarmigan in winter Ptarmigan in summer

Camouflage helps hide this lion from its prey, an unsuspecting zebra.

How Does Camouflage Help Animals?

An animal that does not move, or moves very, very slowly, and looks like its surroundings is *camouflaged*. In this way a tan-colored lion poised on a sandy African plain can surprise a zebra. However, if the zebra is standing in a thicket of bushes, its stripes may blend in with the pattern of twigs and branches. This hides the zebra from the lion. This kind of camouflage is called *protective coloration*.

Some animals—like chameleons, which are lizards—change color to match the background. Chameleons don't decide to do this. It happens automatically. Other animals change color with the seasons. This is true of an arctic bird known as the *ptarmigan* (tär′mi gən). The ptarmigan's feathers are white in winter, when the arctic is covered with snow. In summer, when many plants paint the landscape all sorts of colors, the ptarmigan's feathers turn brown.

Brain Power

When do people camouflage themselves? Why?

Inherited or Learned?

What behaviors do you inherit? What behaviors do you learn? Many traits animals have are automatic responses. These are inherited from their parents. However, some animal behaviors are learned. Birds that avoid eating viceroy butterflies have learned butterflies that look like viceroys taste awful. Your cat may come to the kitchen every time she hears you opening a can. She has learned that the sound could mean dinner is coming.

Some things you do are automatic responses. You pull your hand away from a hot stove before you have a chance to think about what you are doing. You avoid moving cars when you cross the street. Other things you do are learned. You learn how to cook a good meal. You learn to safely cross a street by waiting for the light to turn green.

WHY IT MATTERS

All living things respond to changes in their environment. They do these things in order to survive. Many of their behaviors are traits inherited from their parents. However, some behaviors are learned. Your pet learns to come when you call. You learn important skills at home and in school that will help you now and in the future.

REVIEW

1. What are tropisms? Give an example of one.

2. Where does a cactus store water?

3. How do auxins help plants grow toward the light?

4. **COMPARE AND CONTRAST** In what ways are plant behaviors like certain animal behaviors? In what ways are some animal behaviors different from plant behaviors?

5. **CRITICAL THINKING** *Analyze* What do you think might happen if all the plants bloomed at the same time?

WHY IT MATTERS THINK ABOUT IT
Think about your favorite animal. What are some of its inherited responses? What are some of its learned behaviors?

WHY IT MATTERS WRITE ABOUT IT
Write a paragraph about some of your favorite animal's behaviors. Which of its behaviors are automatic? Which of its behaviors are learned? Write another paragraph about some of your automatic responses. Compare them to some of the things you have learned to do.

Science, Technology, and Society

Cut Trees, Save Forests?

In Greece 2,000 years ago, people told of a "Golden Age" when hills were covered with trees. Then the forests were gone, and the Greeks discovered that when trees go, soil washes away. Greece has never recovered from the loss of its trees.

Lots of rainfall west of the Rocky Mountains helps trees grow larger than anywhere in the world. Lumber companies built roads into the forests. All the trees were cut down, but only the biggest logs were used. That's called clear cutting, and it leaves large bare patches. Forest animals lose their homes. Soil washes into streams, and the fishes' environment is changed!

Today helicopters fly in workers and tools. A tree is cut and lifted away. The other trees, the animals, and the soil all remain in the forest.

DISCUSSION STARTER

1. Where does soil go if it washes away?

2. Write or act out a scene in which people who fish for a living and a home builder discuss clear cutting. How might their views differ?

To learn more about saving forests, visit *www.mhschool.com/science* and enter the keyword FORESTS.

*inter*NET
CONNECTION

SCIENCE WORDS

adaptation p.86   gymnosperm p.58

angiosperm p.58   pollination p.72

cotyledon p.62   seed p.58

dicot p.62   spore p.46

fertilization p.50 stimulus p.84

frond p.49   tropism p.84

fruit p.75

USING SCIENCE WORDS

Number a paper from 1 to 10. Fill in 1 to 5 with words from the list above.

1. A seed plant that does not produce fruits is a(n) ___?___.

2. A new moss plant is produced by a(n) ___?___.

3. The leaflike structure of a fern is a(n) ___?___.

4. A tiny lifelike structure inside a seed is a(n) ___?___.

5. Something in the environment that produces a response in an organism is a(n) ___?___.

6–10. Pick five words from the list above that were not used in 1 to 5, and use each in a sentence.

UNDERSTANDING SCIENCE IDEAS

11. What causes sunflowers to bend toward the sunlight?

12. When a bee travels from flower to flower, how does it help the plants produce seeds?

13. Give an example of asexual reproduction.

14. Describe how fruits help plants spread their seeds.

15. Describe the part of the seed that protects the embryo.

USING IDEAS AND SKILLS

16. **READING SKILL: COMPARE AND CONTRAST** What is the difference between a monocot and a dicot?

17. What would happen if a tree sprouted from the side of a cliff?

18. Describe two ways that adaptations can help plants survive.

19. **CLASSIFY** Tell which of these plants are angiosperms and which are gymnosperms—bristlecone pine, rose, wheat, oat, fir, cedar, lily, juniper, yew, larch, violet, tomato, spruce, giant redwood tree.

20. **THINKING LIKE A SCIENTIST** If you were lost in the woods in the United States, had no compass, and could not see the sky, how might plants help you infer direction?

PROBLEMS and PUZZLES

Turning Food Into Plants Place a sweet potato at the top of a glass of water, so that water is soaking into the sweet potato. However, it should not sink in the water.

Observe what happens over time. Keep the water level the same.

SCIENCE WORDS

adaptation p.86   fungus p.11

angiosperm p.58   photosynthesis p.32

chlorophyll p.4   spore p.46

embryo p.74   tropism p.84

epidermis p.20   xylem p.20

USING SCIENCE WORDS

Number a paper from 1 to 10. Beside each number write the word or words that best completes the sentence.

1. The chemical that makes plant leaves green is __?__ .

2. Yeast and mushrooms are members of the __?__ kingdom.

3. The outer layer of a root is the __?__ .

4. Water moves up the part of a root or stem called the __?__ .

5. Plants make food by a process called __?__ .

6. Ferns do not reproduce with seeds, but with __?__ .

7. Plants with flowers are members of the __?__ division of the plant kingdom.

8. The immature plant within a seed is called a(n) __?__ .

9. The movement of a leaf toward light is an example of a(n) __?__ .

10. A cactus's special features that allow it to live in a desert are examples of __?__ .

UNDERSTANDING SCIENCE IDEAS

Write 11–15. For each number write the letter for the best answer. You may wish to use the hints provided.

11. Which of the following is a fungus?
    a. mold
    b. moss
    c. fern
    d. conifer
    (Hint: Read page 11.)

12. In the process of making food, plants give off
    a. sugar
    b. carbon dioxide
    c. oxygen
    d. chloroplasts
    (Hint: Read pages 32–33.)

13. What kinds of plants do very well in hot, damp climates?
    a. apple trees
    b. ferns
    c. fir trees
    d. grains
    (Hint: Read page 44.)

14. Which of the following are gymnosperms?
    a. apple trees
    b. ferns
    c. fir trees
    d. grains
    (Hint: Read page 58.)

15. Tropism is the process of
    a. movement of a plant toward or away from a stimulus
    b. making sugar from sunlight
    c. transporting water along a stem
    d. adaptation to a hot climate
    (Hint: Read page 84.)

USING IDEAS AND SKILLS

16. Describe what makes plants different from fungi and algae.

17. Make a simple diagram that shows how water moves from the ground to a leaf in a plant.

18. Explain why having a needle-shaped leaf is important to a pine tree's survival.

19. **EXPERIMENTING** Bo grew two tomato plants. One grew well but the other barely grew at all. Write three questions that you would ask Bo to find out why they grew so differently.

20. Diagram the life cycle of a fern. Use labels as appropriate.

21. How are monocot and dicot seeds different from each other?

22. Is this leaf from a monocot or a dicot? Explain how you can tell.

23. Explain why bees are important to many farmers.

THINKING LIKE A SCIENTIST

24. **CLASSIFYING** Classify angiosperms according to how we use them. See how many categories you can think of.

25. Explain how a gardener helps vegetable plants compete with each other and with weeds.

WRITING IN YOUR JOURNAL

SCIENCE IN YOUR LIFE
Describe how people use wood. List what kinds of plants produce wood, and explain what parts of those plants the wood comes from. Present some of your information in a chart.

PRODUCT ADS
Look at the ingredients listed on boxes of breakfast foods. What kinds of plants are most commonly used to make breakfast foods? Explain why.

HOW SCIENTISTS WORK
Classifying is one of the most valuable methods of studying living things. Give two different examples from this unit that show how scientists have classified living things to understand them better.

Design your own Experiment

Plan a method to determine how the amount of water a bean seed gets affects how fast it produces sprouts. Review your experiment with your teacher before trying it out.

interNET CONNECTION

For help in reviewing this unit, visit *www.mhschool.com/science*

PROBLEMS and PUZZLES

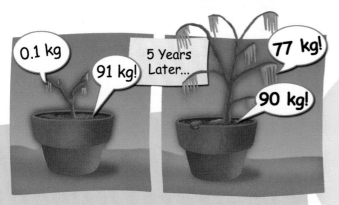

Van Helmont's Experiment

A 17th-century Belgian doctor named Jean-Baptiste van Helmont planted a tiny seedling in a large pot. The pot contained 91 kilograms of soil. Van Helmont watered the plant for five years. During that time he did not add or take away soil from the pot. After five years had passed, van Helmont found that the plant weighed 77 kilograms.

How do you explain van Helmont's results? How did the plant gain so much weight? What materials did it use to gain this weight?

Planet Hollyhocks

Which of these planets would be best for growing plants? Choose one of the three planets shown. Support your choice with a list of reasons.

Planet	Muton-4	Vungus-A	Yerth
Atmosphere	100% oxygen	carbon dioxide, oxygen	hydrogen, oxygen, sulfur
Sunlight	Strong	Low	Medium
Water	Lakes, rivers, oceans	Puddles	Oceans
Soil	Mineral-rich	Some minerals	Mineral-rich

Bright Green Thumb Top Ten

Scientists for the Bright Green Thumb Plant Company made a list of experimental future projects. Rank the projects below from 1 to 10. Which project do you think has the greatest chance of success? Which project would be the most useful to people?

- Rootless plants
- Plants with square fruits
- Leafless plants
- Plants that move
- Plants that grow in complete darkness
- Seedless flowering plants
- Soilless plants
- Nongreen plants
- Waterless plants
- Talking plants

WEATHER AND CLIMATE

CHAPTER 3
WEATHER

Weather is all around you. It affects you every day. Weather can affect how you feel. It can also affect the plans you've made.

In Chapter 3 you'll explore what makes up the weather. For example, why do some clouds give us rain or snow, while others just float overhead? Why do clouds form?

 In Chapter 3 you will read to find the main idea and details that support the main idea.

WHY IT MATTERS

Many things affect how hot it can get.

SCIENCE WORDS

insolation the amount of the Sun's energy that reaches Earth at a given time and place

atmosphere the blanket of gases that surrounds Earth

troposphere the layer of the atmosphere closest to Earth's surface

air pressure the force put on a given area by the weight of the air above it

weather what the lower atmosphere is like at any given place and time

barometer a device for measuring air pressure

Atmosphere and Air Temperature

Is it always hot everywhere in summer? Vacationers in the heart of Africa on a July day might see lions snoozing in the afternoon heat. On the same day, tourists huddled on a cruise ship in Alaska might be watching seals play near icy glaciers. How can two places on Earth have such different temperatures?

EXPLORE

HYPOTHESIZE How does the angle at which the Sun's energy hits Earth affect the warming of Earth? Write a hypothesis in your *Science Journal*. Set up an experiment to test your ideas.

Investigate if the Sun's Angle Matters

Test what factors might affect how warm an area gets.

PROCEDURES

SAFETY Do not look into the lamplight. Prop up a foam bowl, using a plate or clay, to shield your eyes from the light.

1. Place a thermometer onto each of the three blocks, as shown. Cover each with black paper. Put blocks 20 cm from the bulb, level with its filament (curly wire).

2. OBSERVE Measure the starting temperature of each block. Record the temperatures in your *Science Journal*.

3. PREDICT What will happen when the lamp is turned on? Turn the lamp on. Record the temperature of each block every two minutes, for ten minutes.

4. COMMUNICATE Make a line graph showing the change in temperature of each block over time.

5. USE VARIABLES Repeat the activity with white paper.

CONCLUDE AND APPLY

1. COMMUNICATE Which block's surface was warmed most by the lamplight? Which block's surface was warmed the least?

2. INFER How does the angle at which light hits a surface affect how much the surface is heated? How does the surface color affect how much it is heated?

GOING FURTHER: Problem Solving

3. EXPERIMENT What other factors might affect how much a surface is warmed by sunlight? How would you test your ideas?

MATERIALS

- 3 thermometers
- triangular blocks
- black paper
- white paper
- centimeter ruler
- scissors
- tape
- 150-W clear bulb lamp
- stopwatch
- foam bowl
- clay
- *Science Journal*

Does the Angle Matter?

Where do you think you might find warm temperatures all year long? Where would you find very cold weather? As the Explore Activity shows, angles make a difference in how much the Sun warms an area. The areas around the equator are hottest. That's because the Sun's path is directly overhead at midday. In those areas the Sun's rays hit Earth at their strongest.

The areas around the North and South Poles are coldest. That's because in those areas, the Sun is lower at midday. The Sun's rays hit Earth's surface at a low angle. The strength of the rays is much weaker at this angle.

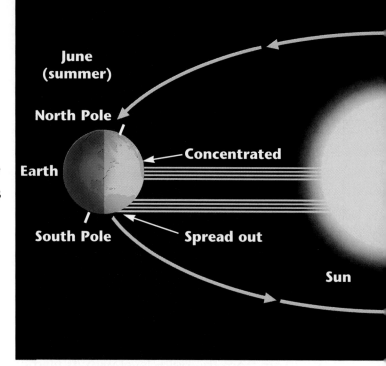

The Sun's rays strike the surface at different angles as the Earth travels around the Sun.

 MONTHLY MEAN TEMPERATURE

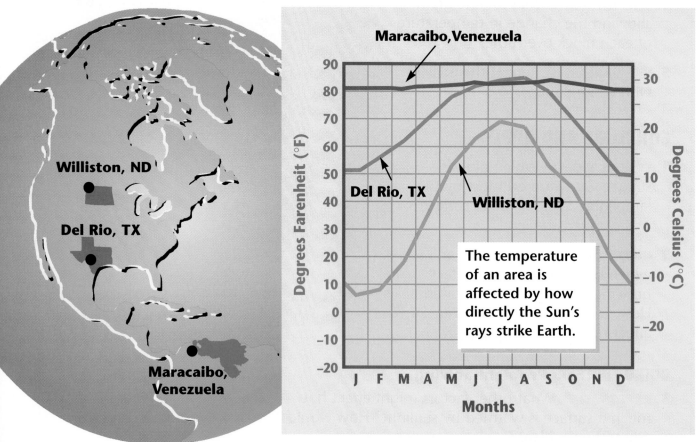

The temperature of an area is affected by how directly the Sun's rays strike Earth.

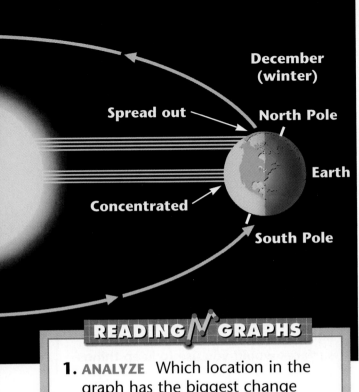

December (winter)

Spread out

North Pole

Earth

Concentrated

South Pole

1. **ANALYZE** Which location in the graph has the biggest change between winter and summer? Which has the smallest change?
2. **WRITE** How can you describe the pattern of temperatures using what you know about the Sun's rays?

Angles and Light

The angle at which sunlight strikes Earth's surface is so important, it is given a specific name. It is called the angle of **insolation**. *Insolation* is short for *in*coming *sol*ar radi*ation.* It means the amount of the Sun's energy that reaches Earth at a given place and time.

The diagram shows how sunlight warms Earth in summer and winter. The amount of warming depends on the angle of insolation. The greater the angle, the warmer it gets. The angle of insolation is always smaller near the poles than near the equator. That means while it's freezing cold in one part of the world, it's hot and humid in another part of the world. How does Earth's position in its path around the Sun affect the angle of insolation where you live?

QUICK LAB

Investigating Angles

HYPOTHESIZE Why does the angle of insolation cause a difference in warming? Write a hypothesis in your *Science Journal.*

MATERIALS
- flashlight
- sheet of graph paper
- modeling clay
- 3 toothpicks
- ruler
- *Science Journal*

PROCEDURES

1. Fold a sheet of graph paper lengthwise in three equal parts. Put a small lump of clay in the middle of each part. Stand a toothpick straight up in each lump of clay.

2. Hold a flashlight directly over the first toothpick. Have a partner trace a line around the circle of light and trace the toothpick shadow.

3. **USE VARIABLES** Repeat step 2 for the other two toothpicks, changing only the angle of the flashlight.

4. **MEASURE** Count the number of boxes in each circle. Measure the lengths of the toothpick shadows. Record results in your *Science Journal.*

CONCLUDE AND APPLY

1. **INFER** How is the length of the shadows related to the angle?

2. **INFER** How is the number of boxes in the circle related to the angle?

What Has the Time Got to Do with It?

In the morning the Sun is close to the horizon. What happens as time goes by? By noon the Sun is high up in the sky, as high as it gets during the day. After noon the Sun is lower and lower in the sky.

How does this affect the angle of insolation? How do we measure it? In an earlier illustration, you saw that both location and time of year affect this angle. This illustration shows how the time of day affects the angle of insolation.

Measuring the angle of insolation is a challenge. It is not easy to see indi-vidual light rays. How can you tell if they are hitting a surface directly? Look at the shadows cast by objects they strike! The less direct the light rays, the longer the shadows. As you can see in the chart, the angle of insolation is the same as the angle between the tip of a shadow and the top of the object that casts it.

Brain Power

Why do many coolers have smooth, light-colored surfaces? What kinds of surfaces would you use to keep things warm?

MATH LINK ANGLE OF INSOLATION

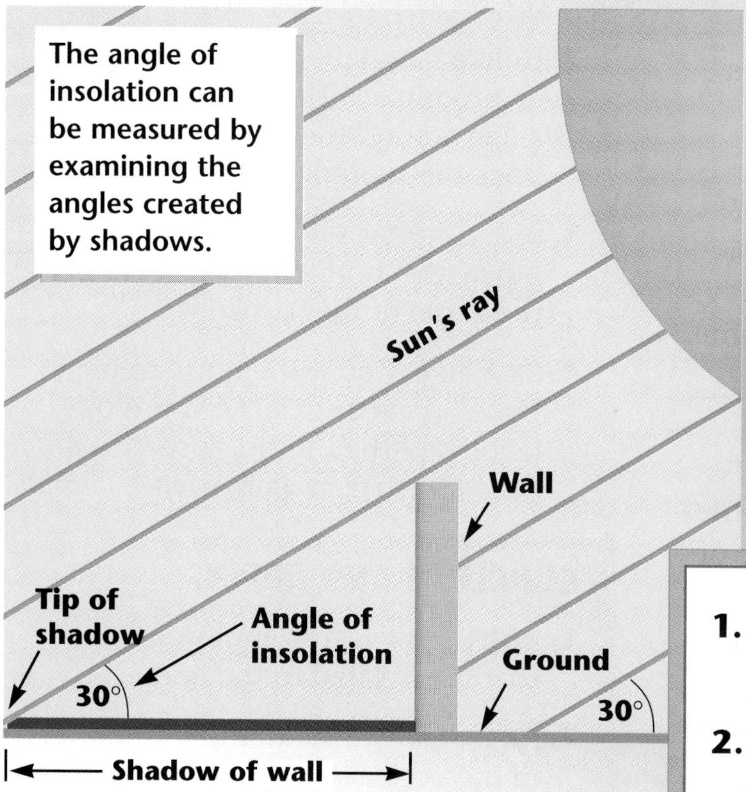

The angle of insolation can be measured by examining the angles created by shadows.

Sun's ray

Wall

Tip of shadow

Angle of insolation

Ground

30°

30°

|← Shadow of wall →|

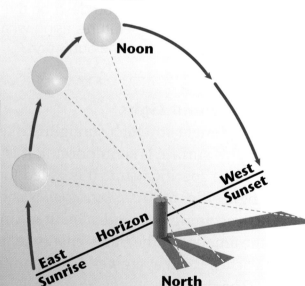

Path of sun

Noon

West
Sunset

Horizon

East
Sunrise

North

The higher the Sun is in the sky, the shorter the shadow.

READING DIAGRAMS

1. **DISCUSS** How can you measure the angle of insolation without being able to see the Sun's rays individually?
2. **WRITE** What will happen to the angle as the Sun gets higher in the sky? How will this affect the temperature?

Do Some Things Get Hotter than Others?

The Explore Activity showed that dark colors get hotter than light colors in the same light. This is why black asphalt roads get so hot in the sunlight. Dark soils and rocks also get very hot. White sand and light-colored soils do not get as hot in sunlight. Plants can also help keep an area cooler in sunlight than surrounding rocks and soil, or black asphalt.

Texture is how smooth or rough a surface is. Look at the drawing on the right. See how rough textures cause light to bounce around at many angles. Each time a little more energy is absorbed by the surface. Rough surfaces tend to get hotter in sunlight than smooth surfaces.

Why do you go swimming when it is hot and you want to cool off? Because the water is cooler than the air. The water and the land next to it are

Rough texture   Smooth texture

More impacts = more heat energy absorbed
Less impacts = less heat energy absorbed

receiving identical Sun's rays. You would expect them to be the same temperature. Why is the water cooler? Water reacts differently to light energy. As you can see in the drawing below, the same amount of light energy will heat land to a higher temperature than it will heat water.

READING GRAPHS

1. **DISCUSS** Which material is warmer after being placed near the light?
2. **DISCUSS** How can you use the graph to tell which substance heats faster?

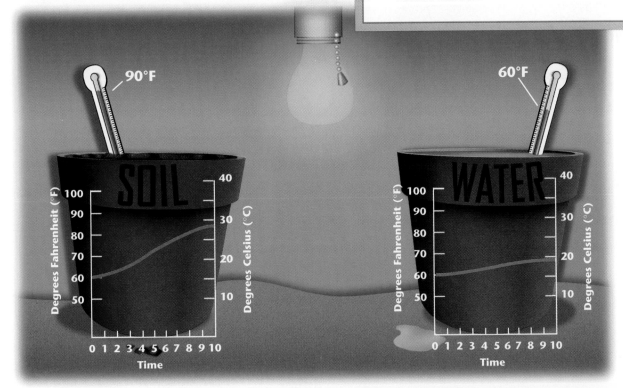

Why Do You Cool Down as You Go Up?

Did you ever climb a high mountain? As you go higher and higher above sea level, air temperatures drop. The natural drop in air temperature with altitude is about 2°C (3.5°F) for every 305 meters (1,000 ft). On a recent day in June, the air temperature in Lewiston, Maine (elevation: 34 meters (110 ft), was a pleasant 21°C (70°F). Two hours away the air temperature at Mount Washington, New Hampshire elevation: 1,917 meters (6,288 ft), was a frosty 1°C (34°F).

Driving up a mountain is really a journey up into the **atmosphere**, the air that surrounds Earth. The atmosphere reaches from Earth's surface to the edge of space. What if you could travel to the top part of the atmosphere? The diagram of the atmosphere shows what you would find.

You would find that the temperature does not fall steadily with altitude. It changes abruptly several times. These changes mark the boundaries of four main layers. These layers surround Earth like huge shells.

The layer closest to Earth's surface is the **troposphere** (trop'ə sfîr'). It's the narrowest layer—between 8 and 18 kilometers (5–11 miles) thick—but it contains most of the air in the atmosphere. All life on Earth exists here. In this layer all moisture is found and all clouds, rain, snow, and thunderstorms occur. Above this layer the air gradually thins out to the near-emptiness of space, with no exact upper boundary.

THE LAYERS OF THE ATMOSPHERE

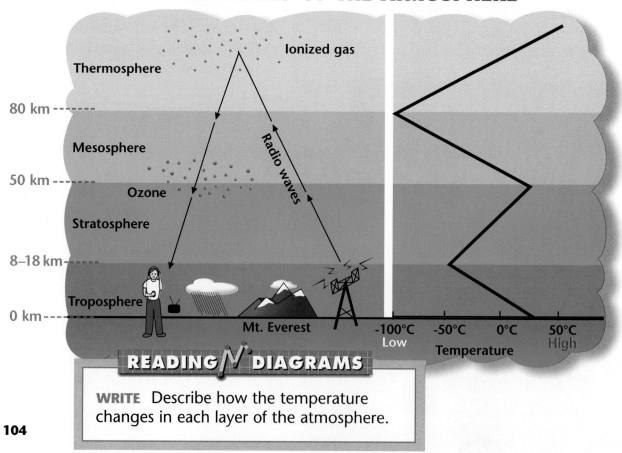

READING /V DIAGRAMS

WRITE Describe how the temperature changes in each layer of the atmosphere.

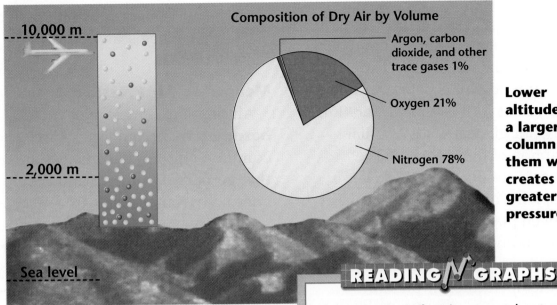

Composition of Dry Air by Volume

Argon, carbon dioxide, and other trace gases 1%

Oxygen 21%

Nitrogen 78%

10,000 m

2,000 m

Sea level

Lower altitudes have a larger air column above them which creates greater air pressure.

READING N GRAPHS

1. **DISCUSS** What is meant by *trace*?
2. **WRITE** Which gas is the most abundant in the atmosphere?

What Else Happens?

As you go higher in altitude, **air pressure** decreases steadily. Air pressure is the force put on a given area by the weight of the air above it. Air is a mixture of gases. It is made up mostly of *molecules* of nitrogen and oxygen. Molecules are the smallest pieces that a substance can be broken into without changing what the substance is.

The molecules have mass. They are attracted to Earth by gravity, so they have weight.

Normal air pressure is greatest at sea level. There the column of air extending above the surface to the top of the atmosphere is tallest. Sea level air pressure is about 1.04 kilograms per square centimeter (14.7 pounds per square inch). As you go higher in altitude, the height of the air column above you becomes shorter. Therefore the weight of that column—or air pressure—becomes less.

In the lower atmosphere, the composition of air varies very little. Up to an elevation of about 100 kilometers (621 miles), air consists of a mixture of gases, water vapor, and dust particles. The gases found in pure, dry air are shown in the circle graph. Nitrogen and oxygen make up 99 percent of the gases in dry air.

Water vapor is water in the gas phase. It should not be confused with clouds or fog, which are made of liquid or solid water. The amount of water vapor in air varies from $\frac{1}{10,000}$ of air in dry arctic regions to $\frac{1}{25}$ of air in moist equatorial regions.

The dust in air is made of particles so tiny that 100,000 lined up would only form a row 1 centimeter long. Some of it comes from Earth's surface, from fires and volcanic eruptions, or from tiny crystals of salt.

What Is Weather?

When you say, "It sure is hot today!" the *it* is the air. You really mean that the air around you is hot. The same is true if you say, "It is windy, " or "It is cloudy," or give any other similar description of the **weather**. The weather is simply what the lower atmosphere, or troposphere, is like at any given place and time.

The conditions that make up weather are the characteristics that change. They are air temperature, air pressure, amount of moisture in the air, wind, clouds, and rain or snow.

Measuring Temperature

You can measure temperature with a thermometer. Thermometers can use two different temperature scales. The Celsius scale is marked with the letter *C*. The Fahrenheit scale is shown by the letter *F*.

Measuring Air Pressure

Air pressure is measured with a **barometer** (bə rom′i tər). Two common types of barometers are the mercury barometer and the aneroid barometer.

Mercury barometers use a glass tube with one closed end. The open end is submerged in liquid mercury. Air pressure on the mercury pushes it up into the tube. When the weight of the mercury column equals the air pressure, the mercury stops rising.

An *aneroid* (an′ə roid′) barometer is an accordion-like metal can with most of the air removed. Inside, a spring balances the outside air pressure. When outside air pressure increases, the can squeezes the spring. When air pressure decreases, the spring pushes outward. A needle inside indicates the changes in air pressure.

Room temperature

Freezing point

Thermometer

Aneroid barometer

These are two common types of barometers

Mercury barometer

How Can You Start a Weather Station?

You can monitor and record weather conditions for your own weather station. Measure and record the air temperature on both scales several times each day. If you have a barometer, you can measure and record the daily air pressure. You might also record the daily air pressure by listening to the weather reports. They often say, "The barometer reads . . . and is falling." They may say it "is rising." You will learn more about air pressure later in this chapter.

In the next few topics, you will add instruments to your weather station. Each instrument can be used to measure a different property of your local weather. By the end of the chapter, you will have a real working weather station.

Have you ever heard a day called a "scorcher"? That means a really hot day. On really hot days, your body can lose a lot of moisture. Your body gives off sweat gradually most of the time. On a hot day, your body tends to give off more and more. That's why you might consider having a bottle of water handy on a hot day.

On really cold days, many people have other problems—such as frostbite. You have to cover your face and hands to avoid contact with air at extremely low temperatures.

REVIEW

1. How do temperatures on Earth depend on angles?

2. List factors that affect temperatures of places on Earth.

3. What is air pressure? How does it change in the atmosphere?

4. COMPARE AND CONTRAST How are the *troposphere* and *atmosphere* alike? Different?

5. CRITICAL THINKING *Analyze* Is the weather one or more than just one thing? Defend your answer.

WHY IT MATTERS THINK ABOUT IT
Why is the atmosphere so important for Earth?

WHY IT MATTERS WRITE ABOUT IT
How do you depend on the weather?

NATIONAL GEOGRAPHIC

World of SCIENCE

What's UP?

LAYERS OF THE ATMOSPHERE

Thermosphere
From 90–700 km (56–435 mi)

Ionosphere
From 60–400 km (36–240 mi)

Mesosphere
From 50–90 km (31–56 mi)

Stratosphere
From 11–50 km (7–31 mi)

Troposphere
From 0–11 km (0–7 mi)

Take a deep breath. Chances are you can breathe easily. That's because Earth's atmosphere contains oxygen. At sea level breathing's easy. On a mountain-top, the breathing's more difficult. Why?

In the 1600s the newly invented barometer, a device for measuring air pressure, was taken high in the mountains. There the barometer registered a lower air pressure than at sea level. The lower the air pressure, the harder it is to breathe.

Over the centuries scientists have gone even higher to investigate the layers of Earth's atmosphere. The troposphere is the layer where all life and weather occur. The troposphere begins at sea level and rises 11 kilometers (7 miles).

In the late 1800s, a scientist launched a balloon carrying a thermometer and a barometer. He discovered a warm atmospheric layer we call the stratosphere. There sunlight changes oxygen into ozone, which is why we call it the ozone layer. Ozone absorbs the Sun's radiation and keeps it from reaching Earth.

In 1901 Gugliemo Marconi sent the first radio signal across the Atlantic Ocean. The radio waves couldn't bend to follow the curvature of the Earth. Instead they were reflected back by particles, or ions, in the ionosphere.

Scientists later identified the mesosphere and thermosphere. They also discovered that some chemicals used on Earth caused a thinning of the ozone layer. Because the ozone layer protects Earth from harmful radiation, the world's nations agreed to ban the chemicals.

Air in the thermosphere is so thin that a special spacesuit is needed.

Discussion Starter

1 TV signals bounce off satellites. What does this tell you about the waves that carry TV signals?

2 When we protect the ozone layer, we protect ourselves. Why?

*inter*NET CONNECTION To learn more about atmosphere, visit www.mhschool.com/science and enter the keyword **SKY.**

WHY IT MATTERS

The amount of water in the air can affect how you feel.

SCIENCE WORDS

water vapor water in the form of a gas

humidity the amount of water vapor in the air

evaporation the changing of a liquid into a gas

relative humidity a comparison between the actual amount of water vapor in the air and the amount the air can hold at a given temperature

condensation the changing of a gas into a liquid

Water in the Air

What if you are walking on this bridge? What do you see and feel all around you? Here's a hint. Put a cold glass of lemonade outside on a table on a hot, humid day. What do you see and feel on the outside of the glass?

What is a humid day like? You can feel a humid day. The word *humid* may make you think of moisture—fine droplets of water. Where is the moisture on a humid day?

EXPLORE

HYPOTHESIZE The lemonade glass has moisture on the side and in a puddle around the bottom. Where does the moisture come from? Is it from inside the glass? Write a hypothesis in your *Science Journal*. How might you design an experiment to test your ideas?

Design Your Own Experiment

WHERE DOES THE PUDDLE COME FROM?

PROCEDURES

1. EXPERIMENT Describe what you would do to test your idea about where the puddle came from. How would your test support or reject your idea?

2. COMMUNICATE Draw a diagram showing how you would use the materials. In your *Science Journal,* keep a record of your observations.

MATERIALS

- plastic drinking glasses
- ice
- paper towels
- food coloring
- thermometer
- *Science Journal*

CONCLUDE AND APPLY

1. COMMUNICATE Describe the results of your investigation.

2. COMMUNICATE What evidence did you gather? Explain what happened.

3. INFER How does this evidence support or reject your explanation?

GOING FURTHER: Problem Solving

4. USE VARIABLES Do you get the same results on a cool day as on a warm day? How might you set up an investigation to show the difference?

5. USE VARIABLES Do you get the same results on a humid day as on a dry day? How might you set up an investigation to show the difference?

111

Where Does the Puddle Come From?

The Explore Activity showed the water in the puddle on the table did not come from inside the glass! The water level in the glass did not drop as the puddle formed. The water in the puddle isn't lemonade. It didn't have the same color or smell.

The water in the puddle came from the air around the glass. When the warm air touched the cold glass, the air cooled. Droplets of water formed, ran down the side of the glass, and made a puddle on the table.

The water in the air is **water vapor**. Water vapor is water in the form of a gas. Water vapor is invisible, colorless, odorless, and tasteless. The amount of water vapor in the air is called **humidity**. Do not confuse humidity with droplets of liquid water you see in rain, fog, or clouds.

How does water vapor get into the air in the first place? Think about planet Earth. More than two-thirds of this planet is covered with liquid water—mostly oceans. Much of the rest—the land—has rivers, lakes, and water in the ground. The land is covered with plants. Plants also contain water. To get into the air, this liquid water must be changed into water vapor.

The changing of a liquid into a gas is called **evaporation**. This takes lots of energy. The main energy source for Earth is the Sun. Each day the Sun turns trillions of tons of ocean water into water vapor.

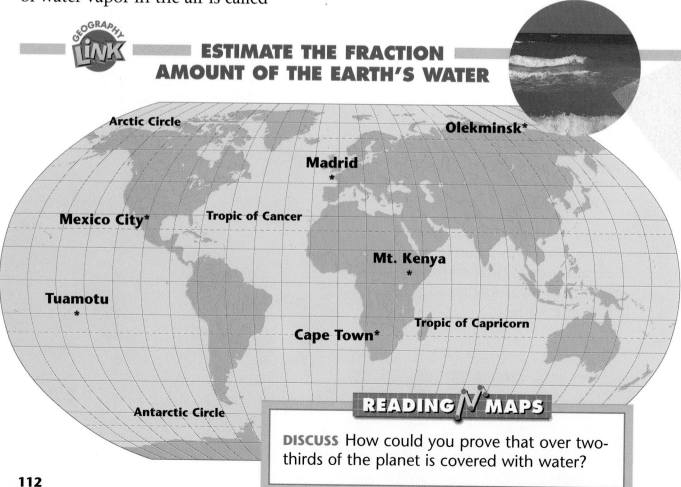

GEOGRAPHY LINK

ESTIMATE THE FRACTION AMOUNT OF THE EARTH'S WATER

Arctic Circle

Olekminsk*

Madrid *

Mexico City*

Tropic of Cancer

Mt. Kenya *

Tuamotu *

Tropic of Capricorn

Cape Town*

Antarctic Circle

READING MAPS

DISCUSS How could you prove that over two-thirds of the planet is covered with water?

112

The Sun's energy gives molecules of water a "lift." Water molecules near the surface of the liquid "escape" into the atmosphere as water vapor.

They move about in all directions. They may hit molecules of gas in the air and get knocked back to the liquid and become trapped again.

Plants' roots absorb water that has seeped into the ground. Plants transport the liquid water through their roots and stems to their leaves.

The leaves then give off water in the process called transpiration. This is the second-largest source of water vapor in the atmosphere.

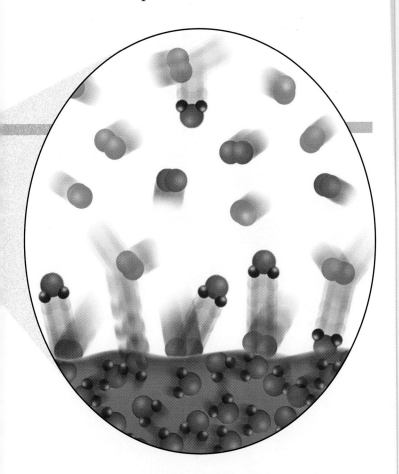

Water molecules fit between moving molecules of gas in the air. Some water molecules are knocked back into the liquid water.

QUICK LAB

Transpiration

HYPOTHESIZE What evidence can you find for transpiration? Write a hypothesis in your *Science Journal.*

MATERIALS

- potted houseplant (geraniums work well)
- transparent plastic bag
- *Science Journal*

PROCEDURES

1. Place the plastic bag completely over the plant, and secure it tightly around the base of the stem. Do not put the soil-filled pot into the bag.

2. **OBSERVE** Place the plant in a sunny location, and observe it several times a day. Record your observations.

3. When you are done, remove the plastic bag from the plant.

CONCLUDE AND APPLY

1. **COMMUNICATE** Describe what you see on the inside of the bag. Explain what happened?

2. **DRAW CONCLUSIONS** *Transpiration* sounds like *perspiration*—sweating. How might the two processes be alike?

3. **PREDICT** How would your results vary if you put the plant in the shade?

Can Air Fill Up with Water?

Does water just keep evaporating? For example, a puddle may evaporate in minutes until all the water from the puddle has gone into the air. What about water from a lake, a river, the ocean? Does all water keep evaporating, or is there a limit to how much water the air can "hold"?

Any amount of air can hold only so much water. Eventually all the spaces between air molecules are filled up with water vapor. At that point just as many water molecules are entering the air as are leaving it. The air is filled.

In warm air gas molecules are spread out and moving fast. A "box" of warm air can hold more water vapor than colder air. In cooler air gas molecules are moving slower and are more crowded together. Water vapor entering cool air is more likely to drop back into the water.

Relative humidity is a comparison between how much water vapor is in the air and how much the air can hold at a given temperature. Relative humidity is given in percents. "100%" means the air is filled at that temperature. "50%" means the air is half-filled. Water can still keep evaporating into the air.

 MATH LINK **RELATIVE HUMIDITY**

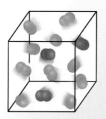 

Cold air   **Warm air**

Water Vapor and Temperature

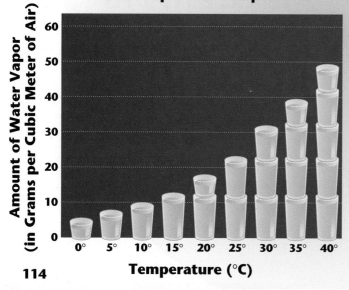

Amount of Water Vapor (in Grams per Cubic Meter of Air)

Temperature (°C): 0° 5° 10° 15° 20° 25° 30° 35° 40°

READING GRAPHS

1. **DISCUSS** How does the amount of water vapor that air can hold compare at 25°C and 40°C?
2. **WRITE** How does the little van stand for 100% relative humidity?

$\dfrac{6 \text{ people}}{6 \text{ seats}} = 1 = 100\%$ **relative humidity**

$\dfrac{6 \text{ people}}{12 \text{ seats}} = \dfrac{1}{2} = 50\%$ **relative humidity**

people = water vapor
little van = cooler air
bigger van = warm air

114

Why Can Air Feel "Sticky"?

Relative humidity can be used to predict how the air will feel to a person. The higher the relative humidity, the less water can evaporate into the air. The less water, such as sweat, can evaporate from our skin, the wetter and "stickier" the air feels.

Relative humidity can also be used to predict when **condensation** will occur. Condensation, like the drops of water on the lemonade glass, is the changing of a gas into a liquid. In the atmosphere condensation is usually the result of warm air being cooled.

When warm air is cooled, its ability to hold water vapor shrinks. The water vapor already there occupies more of the available space. We say the air is becoming more moist. When the air cools enough so that it can no longer hold any more water vapor, condensation occurs.

Condensation explains what happened to the glass of lemonade. The cold glass cooled the air that touched it. The cooled air could no longer hold as much water vapor as when it was warm. Water vapor condensed, forming liquid droplets on the outside of the glass.

Can you see condensation happening? Have you ever seen frozen food held over hot water? What do you notice? You see a mist forming. When this happens in the air, a cloud forms. The greater the relative humidity the more likely condensation will occur, and the greater the chance of clouds—and rain.

Brain Power

You may have heard people complain on a hot day, "It's not the heat, it's the humidity!" Why do you think the humidity is so important, especially when the weather is hot? Why doesn't a cold day with 70 percent humidity feel as uncomfortable as a hot day with 70 percent humidity?

1

2

What Happens Next?

How can warm, moist air cool off? You have learned that in the lower atmosphere, the air gets colder with increasing altitude.

- One way that air cools is by being pushed upward over mountains by winds.

- Heating of air also causes it to rise. When the ground is strongly heated by the Sun, air above the ground gets warmed and rises. It expands as it rises. As the air expands, it cools.

- Air can also be pushed upward when cooler air and warmer air meet. When the two meet, they don't mix. The lighter, warm air is pushed up over the heavier, cold air. The result is that the warm air is pushed up higher into the atmosphere, where it cools.

Whatever causes air to rise and cool, the end result is the same. As the air

The process that forms droplets of water on the lemonade glass is also the process that forms clouds—condensation.

rises and cools, the water vapor in it condenses into tiny water droplets, forming clouds.

If the temperature falls below the freezing point of water, its water vapor will form a cloud of tiny ice crystals.

In order for water vapor to condense, it must have a surface on which the liquid droplet or ice crystal will form. This surface is provided by the tiny dust particles that are part of the air. You will learn more about clouds in the next topic.

The glass of lemonade helped you see how several processes work. One process is evaporation. Evaporation occurs when liquid water from Earth's surface changes into a gas—water vapor. The water vapor rises and cools. Condensation takes place. Tiny droplets of water form on the glass— just as tiny droplets of water can form up in the sky and become a cloud.

Cloud forms

Warm air

Cool air

③

Have you ever had sweat trickle down your face on a hot day? People sweat every day. Sweating is a way our bodies release wastes. We don't always feel the sweat because we sweat gradually and it evaporates.

As sweat evaporates, the water droplets absorb heat from the surface of the skin. This cools the skin. It is a way your body controls surface temperature.

On very hot days and when you are physically active, you may sweat a lot. The sweat builds up and does not evaporate fast enough to keep it from collecting.

On a low-humidity day, the sweat evaporates more quickly. You might think you're not sweating—but you are.

READING ∿ DIAGRAMS

1. **DISCUSS** What can cause air to rise?
2. **WRITE** What happens to the air temperature as air rises?

REVIEW

1. Where does water vapor in the air come from? What produces it?

2. **COMPARE AND CONTRAST** How is relative humidity different from humidity? How are the two terms alike?

3. What causes water vapor to change into droplets of liquid water?

4. How does water vapor get cooled in the atmosphere?

5. **CRITICAL THINKING** *Apply* Would you say that the Sun is a cause of clouds? Defend your answer.

WHY IT MATTERS THINK ABOUT IT
How do the two processes evaporation and condensation depend on each other? Why can't there be one without the other?

WHY IT MATTERS WRITE ABOUT IT
Why are you more comfortable when the relative humidity is low than when it is high?

SCIENCE MAGAZINE

Comparing Quantities

When weather forecasters point out the relative humidity, what do they mean? The humidity relative to what? Do this activity, and you'll better understand the concept.

WHAT YOU NEED

▶ 3 plastic glasses (small, medium, large)

▶ graduated cylinder

▶ water

WHAT TO DO

1. Fill the small glass with water. Pour it in the cylinder to determine how much water the glass holds. Record this number. Repeat with the medium and large glasses.

2. Fill the small glass with water again. What percent of its volume is filled? Record this percent.

3. Pour the water from the small glass into the medium glass. Divide the amount of water in the medium glass by the amount of water it could hold. Multiply this number by 100. This is the percent of the medium glass that's filled with water. Record this percent.

4. Refill the small glass. Now pour the water into the large glass. Find the percent of the large glass that's now filled with water. (Follow the procedure in step 3.) Record this percent.

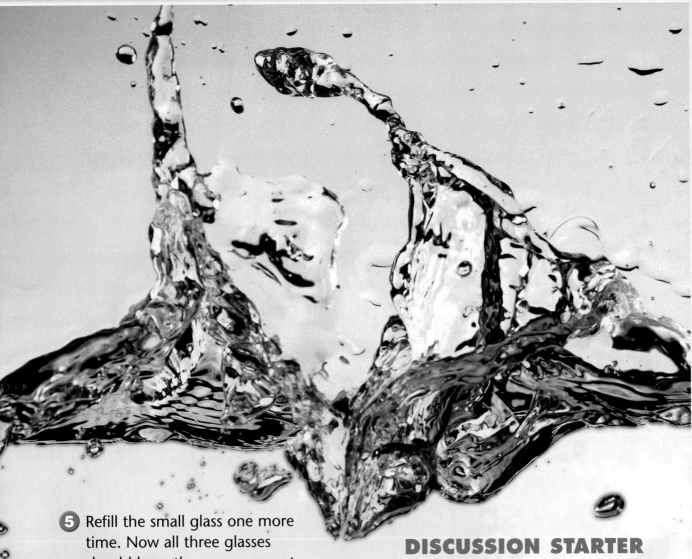

5. Refill the small glass one more time. Now all three glasses should have the same amount of water in them.

6. Compare the sizes of the glasses to the air's ability to hold water by answering these questions.

   a. Which glass represents the warmest air? Why?

   b. Which glass represents the coolest air? Why?

DISCUSSION STARTER

If the amount of water vapor in the air stays the same:

1. What will happen to the relative humidity if the temperature rises? Why?

2. How will the relative humidity be affected if the temperature drops? Why?

To learn more about humidity, visit *www.mhschool.com/science* and enter the keyword HUMIDITY.

*inter*NET
CONNECTION

119

WHY IT MATTERS

Clouds, rain, snow, and hail can have great impact on crops and on us.

SCIENCE WORDS

stratus cloud a cloud that forms in a blanketlike layer

cumulus cloud a puffy cloud that appears to rise up from a flat bottom

cirrus cloud a high-altitude cloud with a featherlike shape, made of ice crystals

fog a cloud that forms at ground level

precipitation any form of water particles that falls from the atmosphere and reaches the ground

water cycle the continuous movement of water between Earth's surface and the air, changing from liquid to gas to liquid

Clouds of Water and Ice

How can you predict the weather without using the instruments weather forecasters use? Look at the sky. There are clues up there. They're called clouds. Different kinds of clouds bring different kinds of weather. What is a cloud?

EXPLORE

HYPOTHESIZE Sometimes the sky is full of clouds. Sometimes there are no clouds at all. Why? What makes a cloud form? Do evaporation and condensation have anything to do with it? Write a hypothesis in your *Science Journal*. How might you make a model to test your ideas?

120

EXPLORE ACTIVITY

Investigate Why Clouds Form

Watch what can happen when you cool off some air.

MATERIALS

- hot tap water
- 2 identical clear containers
- mug
- 3 ice cubes
- food coloring
- refrigerator or freezer
- *Science Journal*

PROCEDURES

SAFETY Be careful handling the hot water. Use the handle to hold the mug. Do not burn yourself.

1. Chill container 1 by putting it in a refrigerator or on ice for about ten minutes.

2. Fill a mug with hot tap water.

3. **MAKE A MODEL** Fill container 2 with hot water. Place empty cold container 1 upside down on top of container 2 with the water. Fit the mouths together carefully. Place the ice cubes on top of container 1.

4. **OBSERVE** Write your observations in your *Science Journal*.

CONCLUDE AND APPLY

1. **COMMUNICATE** What did you observe?

2. **COMMUNICATE** Where did this take place?

3. **COMMUNICATE** Where did the water come from?

4. **INFER** Explain what made it happen.

GO FURTHER: Apply

5. **DRAW CONCLUSIONS** Where would you expect to find more clouds— over the ocean or over a desert? Why?

6. **INFER** Why don't all clouds look the same?

121

Stratus clouds

Cumulus clouds

Cirrus clouds

Why Do Clouds Form?

What has to happen for a cloud to form? The Explore Activity was a model of how clouds form. Clouds are made up of tiny water droplets or ice crystals. The air is filled with water vapor. When the air is cooled, the water vapor condenses. That is, the water molecules clump together around dust and other particles in the air. They form droplets of water.

Clouds look different depending on what they are made of. Water-droplet clouds tend to have sharp, well-defined edges. If the cloud is very thick, it may look gray, or even black. That's because sunlight is unable to pass through. Ice-crystal clouds tend to have fuzzy, less distinct edges. They also look whiter.

Clouds are found only in the troposphere. There are three basic cloud forms. **Stratus clouds** form in blanketlike layers. **Cumulus clouds** are puffy clouds that appear to rise up from a flat bottom. **Cirrus clouds** form at very high altitudes out of ice crystals and have a wispy, featherlike shape. If rain or snow falls from a cloud, the term *nimbo*—for "rain"—is added to the cloud's name.

Clouds are further grouped into families by height and form. They are low clouds, middle clouds, high clouds, and clouds that develop upward–clouds of vertical development. Cumulonimbus clouds develop upward. These clouds bring thunderstorms. They can start as low clouds and reach up to the highest clouds.

If moist air at ground level cools, a cloud can form right there. A cloud at ground level is called **fog**.

TYPES OF CLOUDS

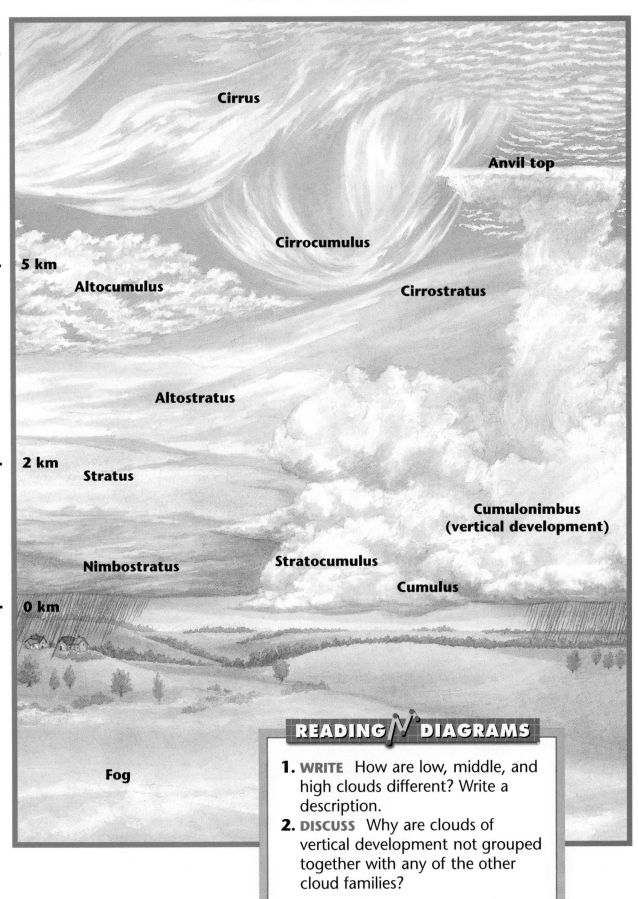

High clouds

Middle clouds

Low clouds

Clouds of vertical development

Cirrus

Anvil top

Cirrocumulus

5 km

Altocumulus

Cirrostratus

Altostratus

2 km

Stratus

Cumulonimbus
(vertical development)

Nimbostratus

Stratocumulus

Cumulus

0 km

Fog

READING 🖊 DIAGRAMS

1. **WRITE** How are low, middle, and high clouds different? Write a description.
2. **DISCUSS** Why are clouds of vertical development not grouped together with any of the other cloud families?

How Do Rain and Snow Happen?

How do rain and snow form and fall? **Precipitation** is any form of water particles that falls from the atmosphere and reaches the ground. Precipitation can be liquid (rain) or solid (such as snow).

Clouds are made up of tiny water droplets or ice crystals. They are only about $\frac{1}{50}$ of a millimeter. These tiny particles are so light that they remain "hanging" in the air. This is why many clouds do not form precipitation.

Precipitation occurs when cloud droplets or ice crystals join together and become heavy enough to fall. They clump around particles of dust in the air. Each particle is like a *nucleus* that the water molecules condense around. The chart shows the different types of precipitation and how they form.

READING N CHARTS

1. **DISCUSS** Classify the types of precipitation into two groups—solids and liquids. Explain.
2. **WRITE** Which types of precipitation form in similar ways? Explain.

TYPES OF PRECIPITATION

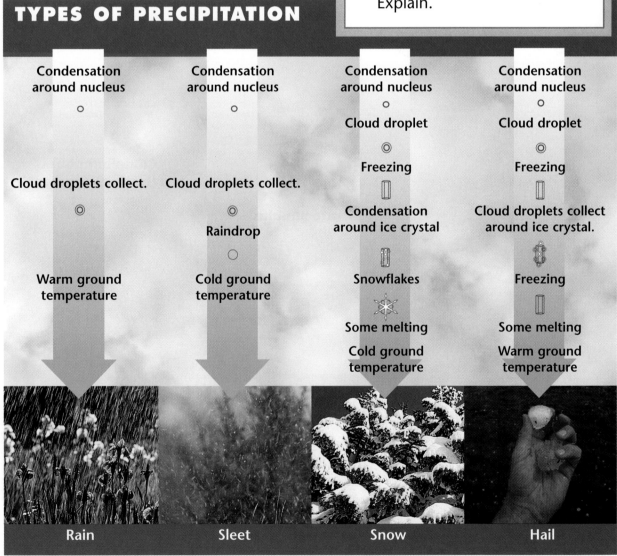

Condensation around nucleus	Condensation around nucleus	Condensation around nucleus	Condensation around nucleus
		Cloud droplet	Cloud droplet
		Freezing	Freezing
Cloud droplets collect.	Cloud droplets collect.	Condensation around ice crystal	Cloud droplets collect around ice crystal.
	Raindrop	Snowflakes	Freezing
Warm ground temperature	Cold ground temperature	Some melting	Some melting
		Cold ground temperature	Warm ground temperature
Rain	Sleet	Snow	Hail

How Are Cloud Type and Precipitation Related?

Do certain kinds of clouds give certain kinds of precipitation? Yes.

- In tall clouds there is more chance for droplets to run into one another and combine, making larger raindrops.

- Precipitation from large cumulus clouds is often heavy rain or snow showers. However, it usually doesn't last too long.

- Precipitation from stratus clouds is usually long lasting, with smaller drops of rain or snowflakes.

- Clouds with great vertical development hold a lot of water. These clouds are very *turbulent,* or violent. Their tops often reach heights where it is below freezing. They often produce great downpours. They also sometimes produce *hail.* Hail is pellets made of ice and snow.

These clouds have updrafts—strong winds move up inside. Hail forms when updrafts in these huge clouds hurl ice crystals upward again and again. As the crystals fall, they become coated with water. As they rise the water freezes into an icy outer shell. This process usually happens over and over, adding more and more layers to the hailstones. The more violent the updrafts, the bigger the hailstone can get before it falls to the ground.

Path of Growing Hailstone

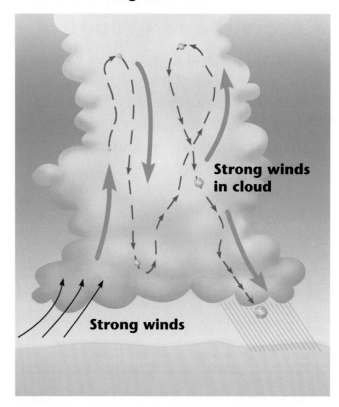

Strong winds in cloud

Strong winds

NATIONAL GEOGRAPHIC

FUNtastic Facts

In March 1952 the island of Réunion in the Indian Ocean was drenched with 74 inches of rain in just 24 hours! That's more than 6 feet of water! How many inches of precipitation did your state receive this month?

How Does Water Go Around and Around?

When precipitation reaches Earth's surface, it doesn't just disappear. Some of it evaporates right back into the atmosphere. Some of it runs off the surface into rivers and streams. We call this water *runoff*.

Much of it seeps into the ground. We call this water *groundwater*.

Groundwater collects in tiny holes, or pores, in soil and rocks. Groundwater can often seep down through soil and rocks when the pores are interconnected. It can fill up all the pores in a layer of rock below the surface. Much of this water eventually moves back to the rivers and then to lakes or oceans.

Brain Power

What kind of precipitation is most common in your area? Where does the run off go?

THE WATER CYCLE

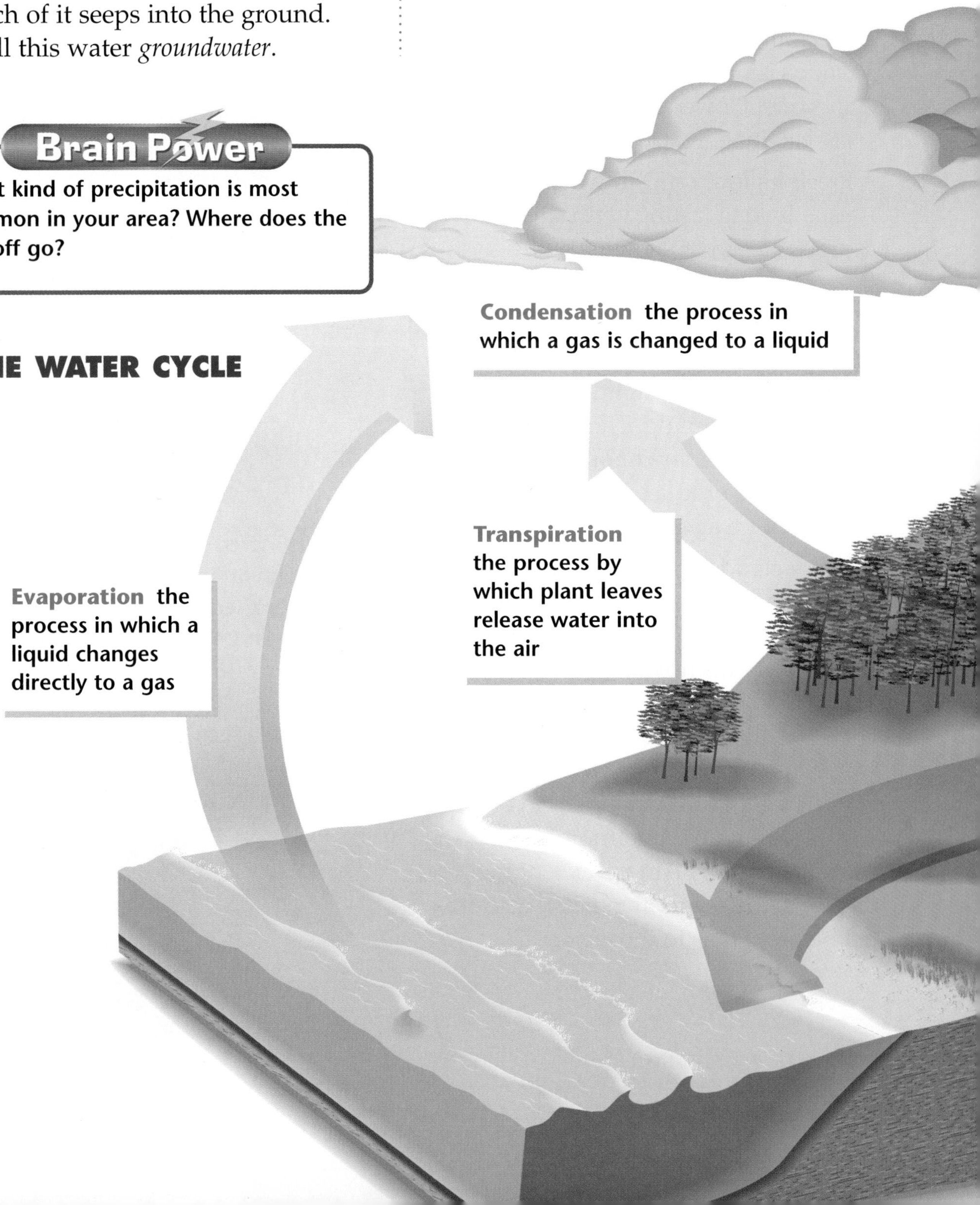

Condensation the process in which a gas is changed to a liquid

Transpiration the process by which plant leaves release water into the air

Evaporation the process in which a liquid changes directly to a gas

Earth's water moves from place to place through the processes of evaporation, condensation, and precipitation. Condensation and precipitation take water out of Earth's atmosphere. Evaporation puts water back into the atmosphere. This complex web of changes is called the **water cycle**.

The water cycle is the continuous movement of water between Earth's surface and the air, changing from liquid to gas to liquid. The diagram shows the many different paths water can take into and out of the atmosphere in the water cycle.

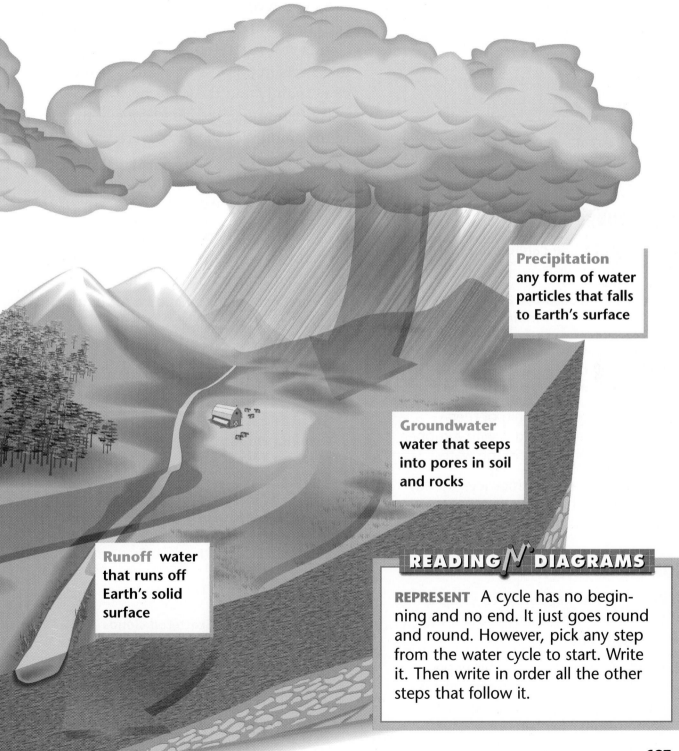

Precipitation
any form of water particles that falls to Earth's surface

Groundwater
water that seeps into pores in soil and rocks

Runoff water that runs off Earth's solid surface

READING N' DIAGRAMS

REPRESENT A cycle has no beginning and no end. It just goes round and round. However, pick any step from the water cycle to start. Write it. Then write in order all the other steps that follow it.

QUICK LAB

Feel the Humidity

HYPOTHESIZE Why do you feel warmer on a high humidity day? Write a hypothesis in your *Science Journal.*

MATERIALS

- 2-in.-square piece of old cotton cloth
- rubber band
- thermometer
- $\frac{1}{2}$ c of cold water
- 1 c of warm water
- Science Journal

PROCEDURES

SAFETY Be careful handling warm water.

1. **OBSERVE** Record the air temperature in your *Science Journal.*

2. Put thermometer in cold water. Add warm water slowly until water temperature matches air temperature.

3. Wrap cloth around bulb of thermometer. Gently hold it with a rubber band. Dampen cloth in the water.

4. **OBSERVE** Wave thermometer gently in air. Record temperatures every 30 seconds for three minutes.

CONCLUDE AND APPLY

1. **INFER** What happened to temperature of wet cloth? How does cloth feel? Explain.

2. **INFER** Suppose you try this experiment on a day that is humid and on a day that is dry. Will you get the same results? Explain.

How Do You Record the Amount of Clouds?

In Topic 1 you started your weather station. Now that you have learned about humidity and precipitation, let's add observations of these weather conditions to your weather station.

As you record weather information each day, you might record the types of clouds you see in the sky. You can use the charts in this lesson to indicate the cloud family and the types of clouds.

Try to estimate the cloud cover—that is, the amount of the sky covered by clouds. Use the terms *clear, scattered clouds, partly cloudy, mostly cloudy,* or *overcast* to describe cloud cover.

A Weather Station Model

One way to record cloud cover is to make a weather station model. Start by drawing a circle for each day. An empty circle means "clear skies." A fully shaded circle means "completely overcast." Portions of a circle are shaded to show different amounts of cloud cover.

Showing cloud cover on a weather station model.

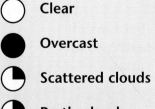
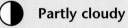
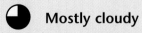

○ Clear

● Overcast

◔ Scattered clouds

◑ Partly cloudy

◕ Mostly cloudy

How Do You Measure Rainfall?

Precipitation is measured with a rain gauge. You can make a simple rain gauge from an empty coffee can. Just place it outside, open end up. Keep it out in the open, away from buildings or trees. When the precipitation stops, measure its depth in the can. You may measure in inches with a standard ruler. If you have a metric ruler, use millimeters (the smallest unit). Keep track of the type of precipitation and how much falls.

You should also record the relative humidity. Listen to weather reports or refer to your local newspaper to obtain the relative humidity.

WHY IT MATTERS

If you ever had a baseball game rained out, you know how rain can ruin your day.

Rain may ruin your plans for a day, but rain is vital for life on Earth. Rain helps crops grow. That means food for you and others! Rain helps build the amount of water in wells and water-collecting areas, such as reservoirs. If you ever had a drought in your area, a time when there was little or no precipitation, you know how scarce water can be.

Hail on the other hand, can ruin entire crops. It can also damage cars and buildings.

REVIEW

1. How do clouds form?

2. What are some different types of precipitation? Why are there different types?

3. SEQUENCE OF EVENTS What are the main processes that show how liquid water changes in the water cycle? List the parts in order to show the changes.

4. How can you measure and describe the amount of precipitation and cloud cover on a given day?

5. CRITICAL THINKING *Apply* "Sun showers" are sudden rainfalls on a sunny day. How can a sun shower happen?

WHY IT MATTERS THINK ABOUT IT
What are some things you do that need a sunny day—or at least a day without precipitation? What do you do if it rains or snows?

WHY IT MATTERS WRITE ABOUT IT
If there was a drought in your area, what would you do to cut back on using water?

Flood: Good News or Bad?

Can you imagine a flood being good news? It was to many ancient Egyptians living near the Nile River. They looked forward to its annual summer flood. Land that was flooded was better for crops!

The flood wasn't all good news. Buildings and fences were swept away. Landowners had to hire "rope stretchers" to mark their property lines again.

No one knew for sure why the flood came. People believed that great rains fell near the source of the Nile to start the flood. It actually started in the mountains of Ethiopia!

Ethiopia has many mountains over 4,000 meters (13,000 feet) tall. In June the monsoons blow from the South Atlantic over the rain forests of Africa. When the winds reach the mountains of Ethiopia, giant rain clouds let loose their water in great thunderstorms. Rain-filled mountain streams join to form a great river. It carries the water to the Nile. By July the water reaches Egypt and produces the flood.

Summer winds

MEDITERRANEAN SEA

EGYPT

SAUDI ARABIA

RED SEA

SUDAN

ETHIOPIA

Science, Technology, and Society

Today the flood waters are stopped soon after they reach Egypt. A high dam holds back the water to form a great lake. The good news is that buildings on the shore are no longer swept away. Fences mark boundaries, and instead of one crop a year, farmers plant two.

Stopping the flood has changed the environment, and that's bad news. The flood kept the fields fertile; but now farmers must use fertilizer. The Mediterranean was nourished by mud from the Nile. Now fish that were common are gone, and a serious disease is spread by snails thriving in the Nile's slow waters.

DISCUSSION STARTER

1. A dry canyon has a FLOOD DANGER sign. How could the canyon flood when no rain is falling near the sign?

2. Straightening a river can stop flooding. Why? What are the disadvantages of doing it?

To learn more about floods, visit **www.mhschool.com/science** and enter the keyword OVERFLOW.

inter**NET**
CONNECTION

WHY IT MATTERS

Wind results from differences in air pressure. Wind can be destructive but is often quite useful.

SCIENCE WORDS

wind air that moves horizontally

convection cell a circular pattern of air rising, air sinking, and wind

sea breeze wind that blows from sea to land

land breeze wind that blows from land to sea

Coriolis effect the curving of the path of a moving object caused by Earth's rotating

isobar a line on a weather map connecting places with equal air pressure

wind vane a device that indicates wind direction

anemometer a device that measures wind speed

Air Pressure and Wind

What makes the air move? Air is almost always on the move. Sometimes it's huge country-sized masses of air that are moving. Sometimes it's small patches. You've felt moving air. It's called wind. Some winds move so fast and powerfully, they can knock down trees or even lift trucks into the air. Winds move these balloons. Winds can be so gentle, they hardly ruffle your hair. Strong or weak, what makes winds blow?

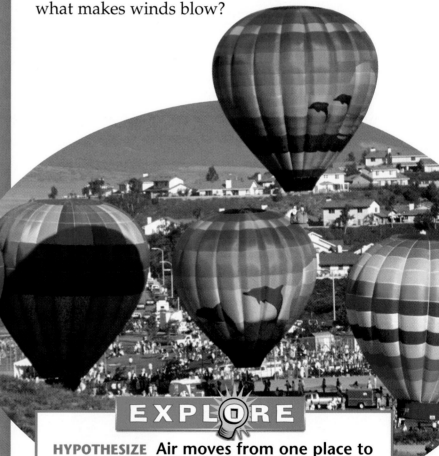

EXPLORE

HYPOTHESIZE Air moves from one place to another because of differences in air pressure. What causes these differences? Write a hypothesis in your *Science Journal*. Make a model to test your ideas.

EXPLORE ACTIVITY

Investigate What Can Change Air Pressure

Put the atmosphere in a jar to explore air pressure.

MATERIALS

- plastic jar with hole in bottom
- plastic sandwich bag
- rubber band
- masking tape
- *Science Journal*

PROCEDURES

1. **MAKE A MODEL** Set up a jar-and-bag system as shown. Make sure the masking tape covers the hole in the jar. Have a partner place both hands on the jar and hold it firmly. Reach in and slowly pull up on the bottom of the bag. In your *Science Journal*, describe what happens.

2. **EXPERIMENT** Pull the small piece of tape off the hole in the bottom of the jar. Repeat step 1. Push in on the bag. Record results in your *Science Journal*.

3. **OBSERVE** Place some small bits of paper on the table. Hold the jar close to the table. Point the hole toward the bits of paper. Pull up on the bag, and observe and record what happens.

4. **EXPERIMENT** Do just the opposite. Push the bag back into the jar, and observe. What happened?

Step 1

Plastic sandwich bag

Rubber band

Plastic jar

Hole

CONCLUDE AND APPLY

1. **COMPARE AND CONTRAST** What differences did you observe with the hole taped and with the tape removed?

2. **INFER** Explain what happened each time you pushed the bag back into the jar. Why did it happen?

3. **DRAW CONCLUSIONS** How does this model show air pressure changes?

GOING FURTHER: Problem Solving

4. **USE VARIABLES** Will the model work the same with paper clips? Bits of cotton? Rubber pads? Make a prediction, and test it.

133

How Can Air Pressure Change?

Many factors can affect the air pressure of a region. Here are some of those factors.

Volume

Pulling up on the bag in the Explore Activity increases the volume inside the bag-jar system. The amount of air inside stays the same. The air inside the jar spreads out into the larger volume. The air pressure inside the bag-jar becomes less. The outside air pushes in harder than the inside air pushes out. That extra force pushing in is what you pull against as you pull up on the bag.

Height Above Earth's Surface

Air pressure depends on the weight of its molecules pressing down on a given area. Molecules are closer together, or more dense, at sea level than high in the atmosphere. Denser air weighs more than an equal volume of less dense air and pushes down harder. That is why air pressure is higher at sea level than high in the atmosphere.

Temperature

Air pressure also depends on temperature. When air is heated, its molecules speed up. The faster-moving molecules move around more. They spread out into a larger space. Thus the same volume of air weighs less, and the pressure decreases. What do you think happens when air is cooled?

AN AIR PRESSURE MODEL

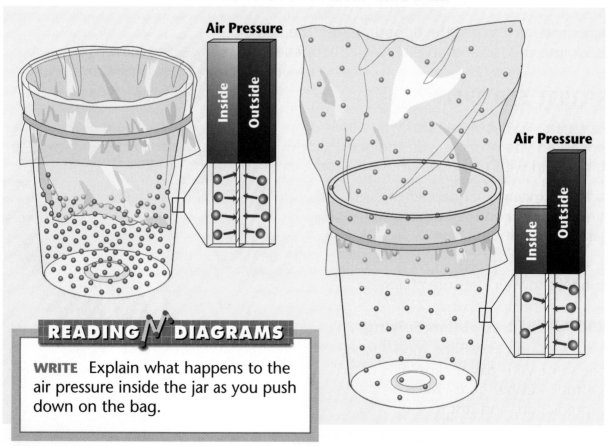

Air Pressure

Inside | Outside

Air Pressure

Inside | Outside

READING DIAGRAMS

WRITE Explain what happens to the air pressure inside the jar as you push down on the bag.

134

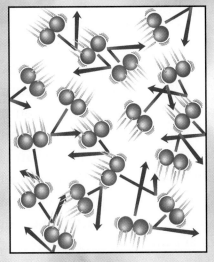

Even though the molecules are moving slower and collide with less force, the cold air on the left exerts more pressure because its closely spaced molecules collide much more frequently.

Cold air

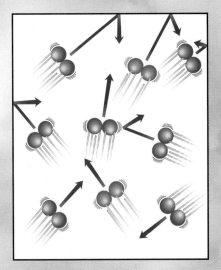

Warm air

READING ✎ DIAGRAMS

WRITE What differences do you see between the pictures for cold air and warm air?

Amount of Water Vapor

Air is a mixture of nitrogen, oxygen, and other gases. Adding water vapor to air also affects air pressure. Molecules of oxygen or nitrogen are heavier than molecules of water vapor. Light molecules exert less pressure because they weigh less. In moist air lighter water vapor molecules take the place of heavier oxygen and nitrogen molecules. Thus moist air exerts less pressure than dry air.

Air Pressure on a Station Model

You can now enter two more bits of information on your weather station model. To the upper right, place the air pressure reading in millibars. Right below this number, you may wish to put a short line. This line tells how air pressure is changing at that station.

- A line slanting to the upper right indicates the air pressure is rising (a rising

barometer). A rising barometer may be a sign that fair weather is approaching.

- A line slanting to the lower right tells the air pressure is falling (a falling barometer). A falling barometer may be a sign that a storm is on its way.

- A horizontal line indicates the air pressure is not changing. In the station model, the air pressure is 980 millibars and is rising.

Showing Air Pressure on a Station Model

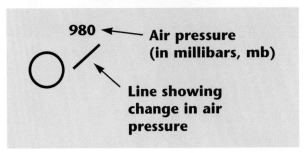

980 ← Air pressure (in millibars, mb)

Line showing change in air pressure

Why Do Winds Blow from High to Low?

Think of what happens if you put a blob of soft clay on a table and push down on it, using a flat hand. The putty squishes out from under your fingers, where the pressure is high. It moves to the spaces between your fingers, where the pressure is lower.

Air acts in a similar way. Denser air exerts a higher pressure than less dense air. Like the putty, denser air flows toward less dense air. This flow of air is wind. Air that moves horizontally is called **wind**. Air that rises or sinks is an *updraft* or a *downdraft*.

Convection Cells

How can air become more or less dense? As the Sun's rays hit an area, it transfers energy to the air. The air heats up. Because it is warmer, the heated air is less dense. Then, just like a cork in water, the warm air rises above the surrounding cooler, denser air. On the other hand, if a region of air is cooled, it becomes denser and sinks.

This unequal heating and cooling of the air often makes a pattern of rising air, sinking air, and winds, called a **convection** (kən vek'shən) **cell**. A convection cell is a part of the atmosphere where air moves in a circular pattern because of unequal heating and cooling.

The drawing shows how a convection cell forms. Cities A and B have the same air pressure. Then direct sunlight heats city A. The air above it warms and expands. It becomes less dense and rises, forming an updraft. The air pressure goes down. The unheated air on either side has a higher pressure. This air moves in toward the low-pressure area, making a surface wind.

READING DIAGRAMS

DISCUSS Use the diagram to explain what happens to city B during the formation of the convection cell.

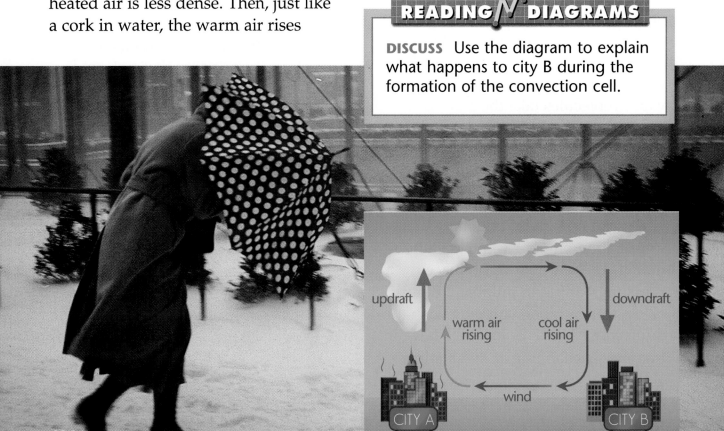

Warm air

Cold air

Sea breeze

Warm air

Cold air

Valley breeze

What Are Sea and Land Breezes?

An example of convection is a breeze that occurs along a coastline. In Topic 1 you learned that land warms faster than water. On sunny days air over land warms faster than air next to it over the sea. The warm air expands and rises. Cooler air from over the ocean replaces the rising warm air. A wind blows onto the land. A wind that blows from the sea toward the land is called a **sea breeze**.

At night the reverse happens. The air over the land cools more rapidly than the air over the water. A **land breeze** blows from land toward the water.

Convection cells also occur along mountains. As the Sun shines on a mountain during the day, the slope heats up faster than the valley below. Air over the mountain slope warms

READING ✎ DIAGRAMS

REPRESENT These pictures show what happens during the day. How would you show what happens at night?

and rises. Cooler air over the valley replaces the rising warm air. This causes a wind called a *valley breeze* to blow up the slope. At night the mountain slope cools rapidly. The air over the mountain slope is colder than the air over the valley. This causes a wind called a *mountain breeze* to blow down the slope.

What Is the Coriolis Effect?

Earth's rotation affects winds blowing across its surface. As Earth rotates, every spot on its surface moves with it. However, in the same 24-hour period, places near the poles travel a shorter distance than places near the equator. This means that places near the poles are moving slower!

Now what if you are in an airplane flying in a straight line from the North Pole to Chicago? While you are in the air, Earth is *rotating*, or spinning, underneath you. Earth rotates counterclockwise as seen from the North Pole. As Earth rotates, Chicago is moving west to east. To someone in Chicago, though, the plane's flight path seems to curve to the southwest.

The same thing happens with winds blowing from the North Pole. Because Earth spins, the winds seem to curve to the right as they head southward.

No matter which way the wind blows, it will curve to the right in the Northern Hemisphere. This curving is called the **Coriolis effect**. In the Southern Hemisphere, the Coriolis effect causes winds to curve to the left. This is because, as viewed from the South Pole, Earth rotates clockwise. The effect works on other moving objects as well, such as missiles and rockets.

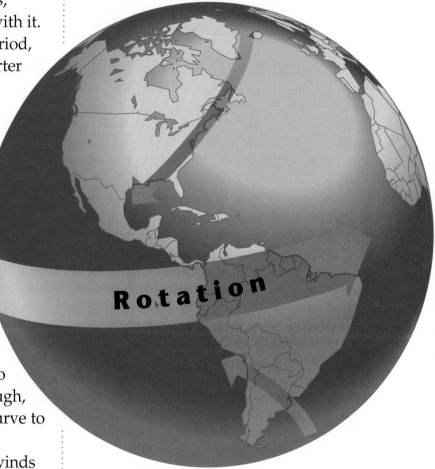

If you were standing at the North Pole looking south, this arrow would appear to curve to the right.

Rotation

If you were standing at the South Pole looking north, this arrow would appear to curve to the left.

Brain Power

Have you ever watched as you let the water out of a sink or tub? How does it move as it goes down the drain? Hint: The answer has to do with the Coriolis effect.

How Are Wind Patterns Produced Globally?

Year round the equator is heated strongly by sunlight. The air becomes very warm. Heat also causes evaporation, so the air becomes moist. Warm, moist air over the equator creates a zone of low pressure that circles the globe.

As the air at the equator warms, it becomes less dense and rises. It rises to the top of the troposphere and spreads out, moving north and south. As the air moves away from the equator, it cools and becomes denser. At about 30° north and south latitudes, the cold air begins to sink toward the surface. This sinking air creates a high-pressure zone on both sides of the equator at these latitudes. A belt of winds is set in motion around Earth by air moving from these high-pressure zones toward the low pressure at the equator. These are the *trade winds*. The Coriolis effect curves these winds as you see in the diagram.

The poles get very indirect sunlight, and the air there is very cold. Cold, dense air can hold very little water vapor. Cold, dry air over the poles has high pressure. Air at the poles moves toward 60° latitude, forming winds. Because of the Coriolis effect, the winds curve. These are the polar *easterly winds. Easterly* means the wind blows "from the east."

Other winds occur between 60° latitude and the poles as well as between 30° and 60° latitudes. Between 30° and 60° latitudes is the zone of *westerly winds.* The continental United States is in the zone of westerly winds.

GEOGRAPHY LINK GLOBAL WIND ZONES

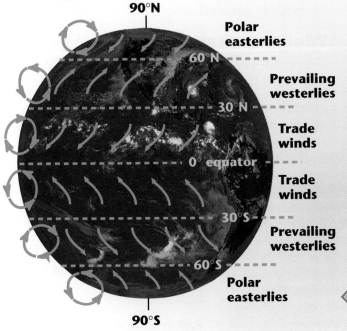

90°N

Polar easterlies

60°N

Prevailing westerlies

30°N

Trade winds

0° equator

Trade winds

30°S

Prevailing westerlies

60°S

Polar easterlies

90°S

READING DIAGRAMS

REPRESENT Make a table listing different global wind zones and a description of the directions in which winds move in each zone.

Can You Predict How Air Will Move?

Why is it important to know about air pressure? Knowing where the air pressure is high or low allows you to predict which way air will move. This is why weather scientists make maps showing air pressure. They start by plotting the air pressure at many different locations on a map. Then they connect all places with the same air pressure with a line. A line on a map connecting places with equal air pressure is called an **isobar**. Isobars make pressure patterns easier to see.

Do you see the series of circular isobars in the west, surrounding a region of high pressure? This pattern is called a *high-pressure system*. Since the center has higher pressure than its surroundings, winds blow outward from the center in a clockwise pattern.

A similar set of isobars in the east marks a *low-pressure system*. In a low-pressure system, the central region is surrounded by higher pressure. The

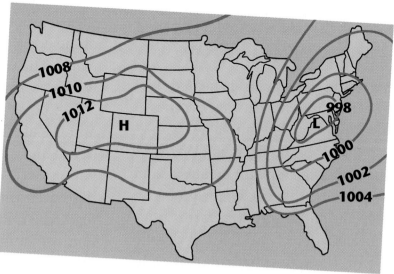

The pressure on each isobar is labeled in millibars (mb).

winds blow in toward the center. This time the winds blow in a counterclockwise pattern.

Isobars also help scientists predict how fast air will move. Big differences in air pressure over short distances cause strong winds. This is shown on a map by drawing closely spaced isobars. Small differences in air pressure cause gentle winds. This is shown by widely spaced isobars.

Wind on a Station Model

You show wind on a station model by a straight line touching the circle. The line tells where the wind is blowing from. "Feathers" are used to show speed.

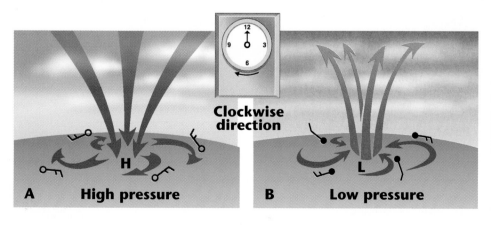

Clockwise direction

A   High pressure

B   Low pressure

Showing Wind on a Station Model

NE

NE = Northeast wind

Half feather = 5 – 13 km/h (3 – 7 knots)

Full feather = 14 – 22 km/h (8 – 12 knots)

SKILL BUILDER

Skills: Using Numbers and Interpreting Data

A WEATHER STATION MODEL

A weather station model shows the weather at one weather station. A station model includes temperature, cloud cover, air pressure, pressure tendency, wind speed, and wind direction. The circle is at the location of the station. The temperature may be recorded.

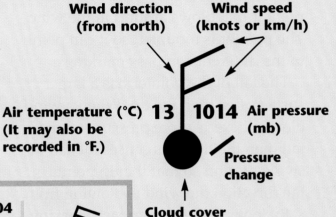

Wind direction (from north)   Wind speed (knots or km/h)

Air temperature (°C) **13** | **1014** Air pressure (mb)
(It may also be recorded in °F.)

Pressure change

Cloud cover

PROCEDURES

1. **USE NUMBERS** Look carefully at the first weather station model. How fast is the wind blowing? What is the wind direction? Record your answers in your *Science Journal*.

2. **USE NUMBERS** What other information does the first weather station model give you?

3. Look at the weather station models of the other cities. Make a table in your *Science Journal*. In your table record the weather conditions for each city.

34 | **1004**
Dallas

28 | **980**
Charlotte

14 | **1012**
Oakland

30 | **996**
Tampa

CONCLUDE AND APPLY

1. **EVALUATE** Compare the information in the table you made with these station models. Which way is the information easier to interpret?

2. **COMPARE AND CONTRAST** Where was wind the fastest? The slowest? Which tells you this information more quickly, the chart or your models?

3. **COMPARE AND CONTRAST** Compare and contrast other weather conditions in the cities. Tell which is the "most" or "least" for each condition.

How Do We Determine Wind Direction and Speed?

What do all of the buildings in the photograph have in common? Each has a curious-looking device on the roof. Did you know that each of these is a **wind vane**? A wind vane is used to tell wind direction. A wind vane has a pointer that blows around in the wind. The pointer is mounted so it can point to the different compass markings.

The tail of the pointer has a larger surface area than the tip. When a wind blows, it exerts more pressure on the tail than the tip. This causes the tail to swing around so that the tip points in the direction the wind is blowing from.

By looking at the compass markings, you can tell which direction the wind is blowing from. Can you tell the tip from the tail in each of the wind vanes shown?

An anemometer gives the speed of a wind.

Wind speed is measured with a device called an **anemometer** (anʹə momʹi tər). An anemometer is a series of cups mounted on a shaft that can spin freely. When the wind blows against the cups, they spin like a pinwheel. The faster the wind blows, the faster the cups spin the shaft. A speedometer is attached to the shaft and calibrated to measure wind speed. Can you pick out the anemometer in the array of instruments at this weather station?

What Is the Beaufort Scale?

In 1806 Admiral Francis Beaufort of the British Navy devised a system for measuring wind speed by observing its effect on the surface of the sea. He assigned a number from 0 to 12 to each effect. This is the Beaufort scale.

Wind can be very useful. It is often used as a source of power. Winds turn special machinery—windmills—that produce electricity. It runs the machinery that grinds grain. It is still used today to pump water.

Wind also carries pollen to flowers. Seeds form as a result. Many kinds of seeds, in turn, are carried by wind to new places.

BEAUFORT WIND SCALE

Type of Wind	Kilometers per Hour	Miles per Hour	Observations
0 Calm	less than 1	less than 0.6	Calm; smoke rises straight up
1 Light air	1–5	0.6–3	Weather vanes don't move
2 Light breeze	6–11	4–7	Weather vanes move slightly
3 Gentle breeze	12–19	8–12	Leaves move; flags stretch out
4 Moderate breeze	20–28	13–18	Small branches sway
5 Fresh breeze	29–38	19–24	Trees sway; white caps on ponds
6 Strong breeze	39–49	25–31	Large branches sway
7 Moderate gale	50–61	32–38	Hard to walk into the wind
8 Fresh gale	62–74	39–46	Branches break off trees
9 Strong gale	75–88	47–54	Shingles blow off roofs
10 Whole gale	89–102	55–63	Trees are uprooted
11 Storm	103–117	64–73	Extensive damage
12 Hurricane	118+	74+	Violent destruction

REVIEW

1. What makes air pressure change?

2. What causes wind to blow in a particular direction?

3. Why are there zones of winds around the world?

4. **USE NUMBERS/INTERPRET DATA** On a weather map, how can you compare the speed and direction of winds?

5. **CRITICAL THINKING** *Apply* How might you make a simple device to tell wind direction?

WHY IT MATTERS THINK ABOUT IT
How would you use simple observation to get an idea of how fast the wind is moving?

WHY IT MATTERS WRITE ABOUT IT
What are some ways people can actually make use of the wind?

READING SKILL
Write a paragraph describing the main idea and supporting details of this lesson.

In Tune with the Monsoon

Who's in tune with the monsoon winds? Nearly half of Earth's population! The word *monsoon* is Arabic for "season." Aptly named, monsoons change direction with the seasons. Winds blow in one direction for about six months, then in the opposite direction for about six months.

We often hear about monsoons in India and Pakistan, but did you know that other places also have them? Places include Africa, South America, Australia, and even the southern United States!

Why do monsoons change direction? In summer the Sun heats dry air over tropical land, while nearby oceans stay cooler. The warm air rises above the land, and cooler air from the ocean blows in to take its place. The wind blowing from the ocean brings heavy rain from June to October.

In winter the land cools off. Then as warm air rises over the ocean, cool air from the land rushes in to take its place. From November until May, a dry wind blows from the land out to the ocean.

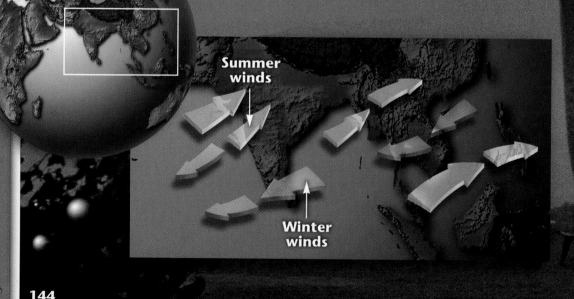

Summer winds

Winter winds

Geography Link

In one part of India, the average winter rainfall is 2.54 centimeters (1 inch) a month. During the summer it gets up to 2.54 meters (100 inches) of rain a month!

Farmers depend on the monsoons. When the rain starts, farmers plant rice and other crops. If monsoons come late, nothing grows on the dusty land. However, really heavy rains can wash away the crops!

In 1997 monsoons killed more than 1,000 people in India and Pakistan, and ruined nearly 4 million acres of farmland.

DISCUSSION STARTER

How do you think the monsoons affect people in monsoon regions who aren't farmers?

To learn more about the monsoons, visit *www.mhschool.com/science* and enter the keyword MONSOON.

*inter*NET
CONNECTION

SCIENCE WORDS

air pressure p.105   evaporation p.113

cirrus cloud p.122   humidity p.112

condensation p.115   precipitation p.124

Coriolis effect p.138   stratus cloud p.122

cumulus cloud p.122   water vapor p.112

USING SCIENCE WORDS

Number a paper from 1to 10. Fill in 1 to 5 with words from the list above.

1. Rain, snow, and sleet are kinds of __?__.

2. The __?__ causes winds to follow a curved path over Earth's surface.

3. A(n) __?__ forms in blanketlike layers.

4. Liquid changes directly to a gas by the process called __?__.

5. The amount of water vapor in the air is called __?__.

6–10. **Pick five words from the list above that were not used in 1 to 5, and use each in a sentence.**

UNDERSTANDING SCIENCE IDEAS

11. Describe three kinds of clouds.

12. Where does weather take place?

13. How do water droplets form on the outside of a cold glass on a warm, humid day?

14. What are isobars?

15. What determines the amount of sunlight a region gets during the summer?

USING IDEAS AND SKILLS

16. **READING SKILL: MAIN IDEA AND SUPPORTING DETAILS** Explain why north winds blow to the southwest.

17. Explain why hot days when the relative humidity is high are more uncomfortable than hot days when the relative humidity is low.

18. Why must both evaporation and condensation occur to have rain?

19. **USE NUMBERS/INTERPRET DATA** What kind of weather is city A having? City B?

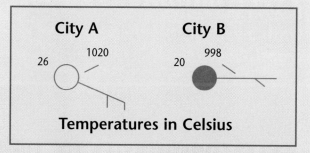

City A   City B

26   1020   20   998

Temperatures in Celsius

20. **THINKING LIKE A SCIENTIST** What if there were no plants? Do you think Earth would still get as much rain as it does now? State and explain a hypothesis. Describe how you might test your ideas.

PROBLEMS and PUZZLES

Draft Drift Observe updrafts and downdrafts in your classroom. Make a sketch of the room. Use a compass to determine north, south, east, and west. Drop a feather, and watch its drift. Mark the "wind direction" on your map. Repeat in many parts of the room. Explain your results.

CHAPTER 4

WEATHER PATTERNS AND CLIMATE

Changes in the weather help scientists predict the weather. They can help you plan activities over a few days.

You may also plan activities over a year. When does your area have the highest temperatures? The lowest? Do you get tornadoes? Hurricanes? Heavy rainfall? When? Temperatures and rainfall are part of a weather pattern in an area that repeats year after year.

In Chapter 4 you'll learn about how weather is predicted. You learn more about patterns that repeat each year.

In Chapter 4 you will read for sequence of events. You will read the events that lead up to a thunderstorm and tornado.

Topic 5
EARTH SCIENCE

WHY IT MATTERS

By studying air masses and fronts, we can predict changes in the weather.

SCIENCE WORDS

air mass a large region of the atmosphere where the air has similar properties throughout

front a boundary between air masses with different temperatures

cold front a front where cold air moves in under a warm front

warm front a front where warm air moves in over a cold front

occluded front a front formed where a warm front and cold front meet

stationary front an unmoving front where a cold air mass and a warm air mass meet

Air Masses and Fronts

Should you plan a trip to the beach tomorrow? Or would it be wiser to locate your umbrella? The answer depends on knowing what kind of weather is on the way. To predict this, both you and weather forecasters can turn to weather maps. The maps show conditions at different weather stations across the country. They also show how weather is changing. This map is a simple kind of weather map you might see in a newspaper.

HYPOTHESIZE How can you tell where the weather may change? Write a hypothesis in your *Science Journal*. Test your ideas. How would you use a weather map to give a weather report of the country?

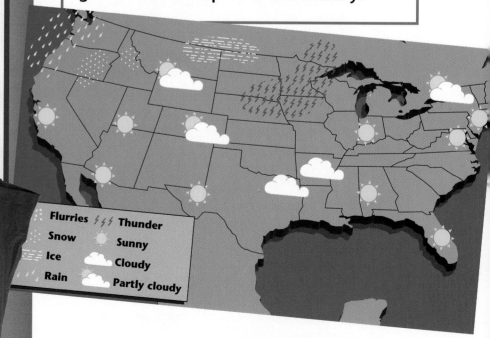

Flurries	⚡⚡ Thunder
Snow	Sunny
Ice	Cloudy
Rain	Partly cloudy

148

EXPLORE ACTIVITY

Investigate How to Compare Weather

Use a map and key to predict the weather.

PROCEDURES

COMMUNICATE Think of the country in large regions—the Northeast, the Southwest, and so on. Think of regions like the Pacific Coast, the Atlantic Coast, and the Gulf Coast. In your *Science Journal,* write a report for the weather in each region based on the map you see here.

CONCLUDE AND APPLY

1. INFER Which areas are having warm, rainy weather?

2. INFER Where is the weather cool and dry?

GOING FURTHER: Problem Solving

3. INFER How do you think weather in any part of the country may change, based on the data in this map? Give reasons for your answer. How would you check your predictions?

4. INTERPRET DATA Using weather maps in a newspaper, or the one on page 148, describe the weather.

MATERIALS

- station model key
- newspaper weather map (optional)
- pencil
- crayons
- newspaper
- *Science Journal*

W   E

San Francisco

Lines are drawn to show wind direction, not speed. This is a wind coming from the east, going west—an eastwind.

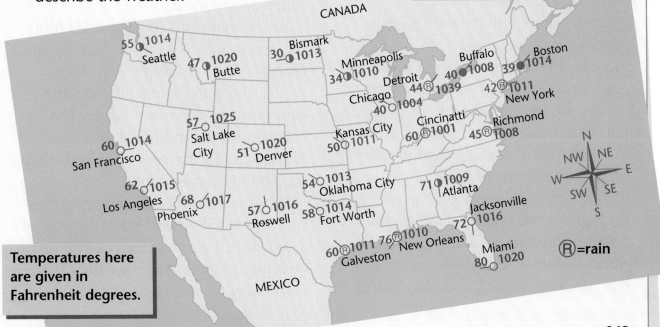

Temperatures here are given in Fahrenheit degrees.

AIR MASSES

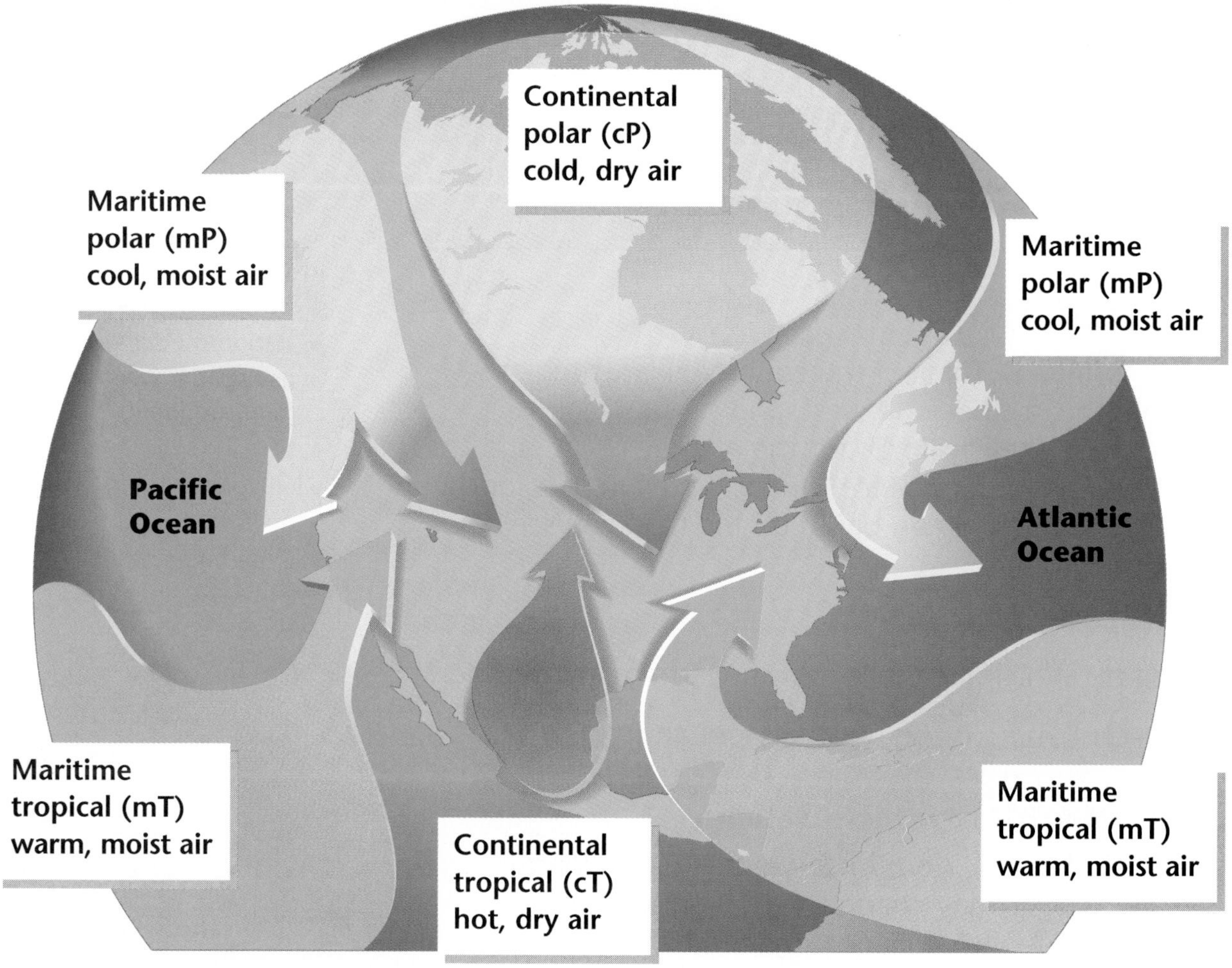

Continental polar (cP) cold, dry air

Maritime polar (mP) cool, moist air

Maritime polar (mP) cool, moist air

Pacific Ocean

Atlantic Ocean

Maritime tropical (mT) warm, moist air

Continental tropical (cT) hot, dry air

Maritime tropical (mT) warm, moist air

How Can We Compare Weather?

The Explore Activity showed that cities across a large region can share the same weather. It also showed how the weather in different areas can differ.

Why are weather conditions in one part of a country different from those in another part? Look back at the map on page 149. Some of the cities are having clear, cool weather. The air throughout this region is cool and dry.

Other cities are having warmer, cloudy weather. The air throughout this region is warm and moist. A large region of the atmosphere where the air has similar properties throughout is called an **air mass**.

An air mass gets its properties from the region where it forms. Air over the Gulf of Mexico is above very warm water. The water warms the air, and evaporation adds water vapor. The air becomes warm and moist, like the Gulf of Mexico. Air masses are named for the region they come from.

As air masses move, they bring these conditions with them. What happens if a cool, moist air mass moves over an area that has warm, dry weather? The warm, dry weather will change.

Once an air mass is formed, it is moved by global winds. In the United States, global winds tend to move air masses from west to east.

Air masses with different conditions can "meet." That is, one runs into another. What happens when air masses with different temperatures meet? They don't mix together. Instead, a narrow boundary forms between them. This boundary is called a **front**. It marks the leading edge, or front, of an air mass that is moving into an area where another air mass is moving out. Weather changes rapidly at fronts. That's because you pass from one kind of air mass into another. Fronts often cause rainy, unsettled weather. There are several types of fronts that can form.

Brain Power

When air masses meet, they form fronts. What do you think happens when two fronts meet?

A WEATHER FRONT

A front forms along the boundary between a warm air mass and a cold air mass.

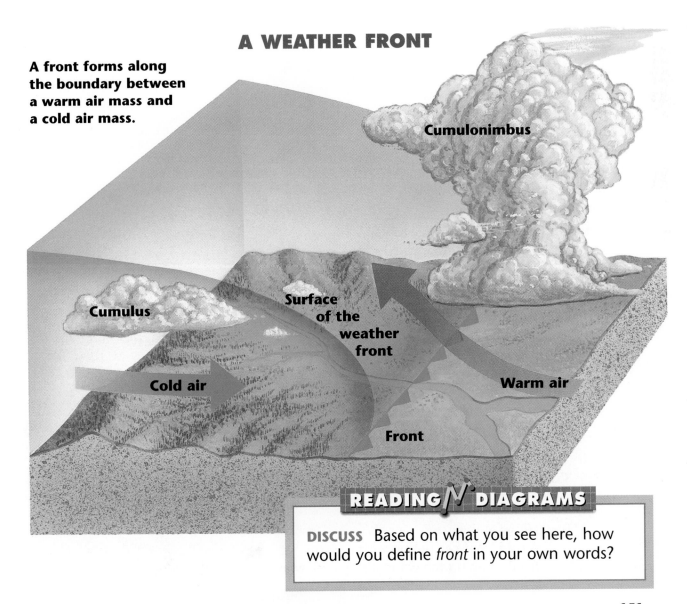

Cumulonimbus

Cumulus

Surface of the weather front

Cold air

Warm air

Front

READING IN DIAGRAMS

DISCUSS Based on what you see here, how would you define *front* in your own words?

151

What Kinds of Fronts Are There?

There are several kinds of fronts. How do fronts make the weather change?

- In a cold front, cold air moves in under a warm air mass. Cold fronts often bring brief, heavy storms. There may be thunderstorms and strong winds. After the storm the skies are usually clearer, and the weather is usually cooler and drier.

- In a warm front, warm air moves in over a cold air mass. Warm fronts often bring light, steady rain or snow. The precipitation may last for days. Winds are usually light. Warm fronts may also bring fog—stratus clouds that form near the ground. Afterward the weather is usually warmer and more humid.

- An **occluded** (ə klüd'əd) **front** occurs when a cold front and a warm front meet. A fast-moving cold front

WEATHER PRODUCED BY FRONTS

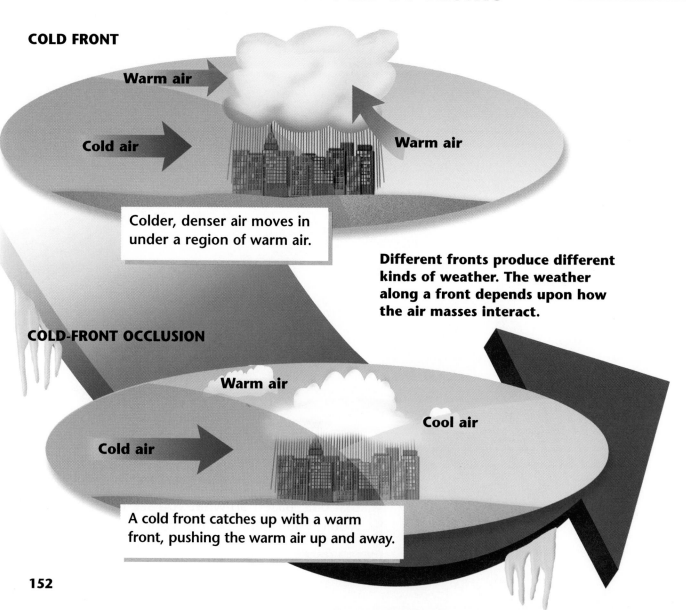

COLD FRONT

Warm air

Cold air

Warm air

Colder, denser air moves in under a region of warm air.

Different fronts produce different kinds of weather. The weather along a front depends upon how the air masses interact.

COLD-FRONT OCCLUSION

Warm air

Cool air

Cold air

A cold front catches up with a warm front, pushing the warm air up and away.

moves in on a warm front. There are two ways this can happen:

In a cold-front occlusion, the air behind the front is cold. The air ahead of the warm front is cool. What is happening is that cold air is moving in on cool air and warm air is pushed up between them. The weather along this front will be like that produced by a cold front.

In a warm-front occlusion, the air behind the incoming cold front is just cool, not cold. The air in front of the warm front, however, might be cold. Then the weather will be more like that produced by a warm front.

• A cold air mass and a warm air mass may meet and remain over an area for days without moving. This is called a **stationary front**. Stationary fronts usually have calm weather.

READING N' DIAGRAMS

1. **WRITE** Write a paragraph comparing a warm front with a cold front.
2. **DISCUSS** Write an explanation of what an occluded front is.

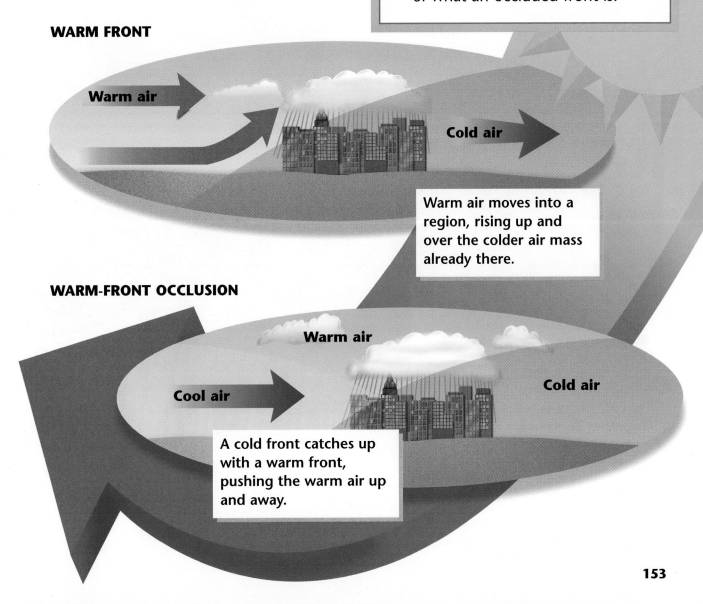

WARM FRONT

Warm air

Cold air

Warm air moves into a region, rising up and over the colder air mass already there.

WARM-FRONT OCCLUSION

Warm air

Cool air

Cold air

A cold front catches up with a warm front, pushing the warm air up and away.

What Do Fronts Look Like from Space?

Pictures taken from space are great tools for seeing large weather patterns, such as fronts and storms. Scientists send up satellites in orbit around Earth. Some of these satellites are equipped to take pictures of weather patterns. These satellites move in orbit in a way that allows them to follow a weather pattern as it moves slowly across Earth's surface.

To find fronts on a satellite map, look for swirling lines of clouds. The curved lines often mark the movement of fronts.

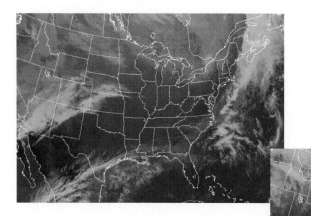

Weather satellites are located above the equator. They are more than 36,000 km (20,000 miles) above Earth's surface. Several of these satellites work together to produce a nearly complete picture of the globe every half-hour.

Why Are Fronts Important?

Fronts are an important clue to how weather will change. As a front moves, areas just ahead of the front are about to have a change in weather. The weather may be cool and dry before a front approaches. The weather then becomes rainy and hot as the front passes by.

When fronts collide, scientists can locate places where the weather may change quickly, even dangerously. Sudden storms may break out. Knowing about fronts helps scientists to stay on the alert!

READING MAPS

1. **DISCUSS** Where do you see low pressure systems in the satellite picture? What do the clouds appear to be doing?
2. **WRITE** What kind of weather is happening in different parts of the country in each map? Explain.

QUICK LAB

Weather Prediction

HYPOTHESIZE How can you use a weather map to predict the weather? Write a hypothesis in your *Science Journal.*

MATERIALS
• *Science Journal*

PROCEDURES

1. ANALYZE The map shows weather in the United States at 6 P.M. on October 29. In your *Science Journal*, describe the weather in Washington, D.C. The temperatures are in degrees Celsius.

2. ANALYZE In your *Science Journal*, describe the weather in the northwest part of the country and the southeast.

CONCLUDE AND APPLY

INFER Weather patterns move from west to east across the United States. How do you think the weather in Washington, D.C., will change in the next day or so? Explain your answer.

How Is Weather Forecasting Done?

Scientists usually forecast the weather using a *synoptic weather map.* This type of map shows a summary of the weather using station models. By comparing maps made every six hours, scientists can tell how weather systems are moving. They then use this information to predict what the weather will be like hours later.

If you look at weather records to see what happened in the past, you can find patterns. *Statistical forecasting* is based on findings patterns.

For example, suppose you notice that the wind has just started blowing from the west. Past records show that 75 out of the last 100 times the wind blew from the west, your weather became clearer and colder. What weather prediction would you make?

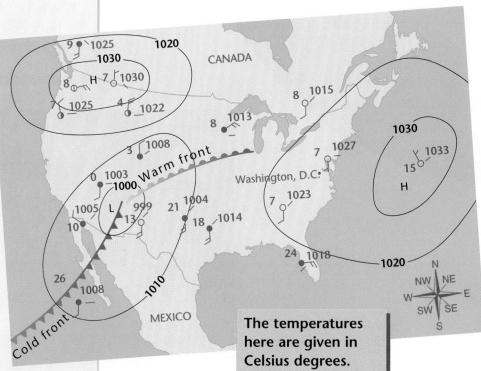

The temperatures here are given in Celsius degrees.

How Else Is Forecasting Done?

Spaceships going to the Moon aren't aimed directly at the Moon. The Moon is always moving. The spaceship aims at where the Moon will be when the ship arrives. Scientists use the spaceship's speed and direction to calculate where this spot is. In the same way, knowing how the atmosphere is moving lets you predict the weather.

The problem is that the atmosphere is huge and complex. Even simple predictions require millions of calculations. This couldn't be done without computers. Computers do high-speed calculations to predict the atmosphere's motion. Predictions are compared with forecasts to account for any differences. Two-day forecasts are calculated every 12 hours. A five-day forecast is calculated daily.

No one can be sure about how the weather will change. A weather forecaster might give a clear prediction of tomorrow's weather. However, another air mass might move in. Everything can change.

Still many people and industries rely on accurate forecasts. Farmers need to know if heavy rains or frosts are coming. Ski slopes must be aware of how much snow is expected. Vacationers use forecasts to plan trips.

REVIEW

1. What are four different kinds of air masses? How are they different?

2. CAUSE AND EFFECT What kind of weather is produced by a cold front? A warm front?

3. How can satellites help predict the weather?

4. How can weather maps help predict the weather?

5. CRITICAL THINKING *Apply* How can you tell what kind of front is passing by just by observing the weather?

WHY IT MATTERS THINK ABOUT IT
Why do you think people listen to the weather report?

WHY IT MATTERS WRITE ABOUT IT
How can changes in the weather affect how you spend your day?

SCIENCE MAGAZINE

Weather Watch: Then and Now

The barometer is invented. Changes in air pressure help modern scientists predict the weather.

The telegraph is invented. Forecasters begin talking to one another and sharing information.

| 400 B.C. | A.D. 1643 | 1732 | 1840 | 1870 |

Aristotle writes one of the first books about weather. He tries to explain rain, snow, and other "meteors" from the sky!

Benjamin Franklin writes *Poor Richard's Almanac,* in which he predicts the next year's weather. He bases his forecasts on what he sees and a few measurements.

A telegraph system is set up across the nation. The system is used to collect weather data and warn people about storms.

Poor Richard, 1733.
AN
Almanack
For the Year of Christ
I 7 3 3,
Being the First after LEAP YEAR.

And makes since the Creation	Years
By the Account of the Eastern Greeks	7241
By the Latin Church, when ☉ ent. ♈	6932
By the Computation of W.W.	5742
By the Roman Chronology	5682
	5494

History of Science

Four scientists in Norway use math and physics to explain weather and identify weather patterns.

Doppler radar is developed. It compares radio waves sent out with those that bounce back. The greater the difference, the faster a storm is moving.

Two kinds of satellites track weather patterns. One orbits about 36,000 kilometers (22,000 miles) above Earth, monitoring changes in storm systems. The other orbits only 850 kilometers (530 miles) above Earth to provide details about cloud systems.

1918   **1940**   **1954**   **1960**   **Today**

During World War II, radar is used to locate storms by bouncing radio waves off raindrops in clouds.

NASA sends up its first weather satellite.

DISCUSSION STARTER

How do you think computers have helped make weather predictions more accurate?

To learn more about weather watching, visit *www.mhschool.com/science* and enter the keyword WATCH.

*inter*NET
CONNECTION

159

Topic
EARTH SCIENCE
6

WHY IT MATTERS

Knowing about severe storms can save lives.

SCIENCE WORDS

thunderstorm the most common severe storm, formed in cumulonimbus clouds

tornado a violent whirling wind that moves across the ground in a narrow path

hurricane a very large, swirling storm with very low pressure at the center

storm surge a great rise of the sea along a shore caused by low pressure

Severe Storms

What's it like to be in the path of a tornado? People have reported a sound like the rumble of an approaching freight train. A tornado packs a windy wallop far more powerful than any train, however. Tornadoes are the most powerful storms on Earth. Although most tornadoes are not very wide and they don't last too long, when they touch down *watch out!* Like deadly whirling brooms, they can sweep away anything in their paths.

EXPLORE

HYPOTHESIZE Tornadoes strike all parts of the United States. However, they are more frequent in some regions than in others. Where in the U.S. is "tornado country"? Write a hypothesis in your *Science Journal.* How might you test your hypothesis?

Investigate What Severe Storms Are

To investigate what severe storms are, begin by plotting tornadoes on a map to tell where they are most likely to happen.

MATERIALS

- map of U.S., including Alaska and Hawaii
- blue marker
- red marker
- *Science Journal*

PROCEDURES

1. INFER The table shown here lists how many tornadoes occurred in each state over a 30-year period. It also shows about how many tornadoes occur in each state each year. Look at the data in the table for two minutes. Now write in your *Science Journal* what part of the country you think gets the most tornadoes.

2. COLLECT DATA Use the red marker to record the number of tornadoes that occurred in each state over the 30-year period. Use the blue marker to record the average number of tornadoes that occurred in a year in each state.

CONCLUDE AND APPLY

1. USE NUMBERS Which states had fewer than 10 tornadoes a year? Which states had more than 20 tornadoes a year?

2. INTERPRET DATA Which six states had the most tornadoes during the 30-year period?

3. INTERPRET DATA Which part of the country had the most tornadoes?

GOING FURTHER: Problem Solving

4. DRAW CONCLUSIONS Many people refer to a certain part of the country as "Tornado Alley." Which part of the country do you think that is? Why do you think people call it that? What else might these states have in common? Describe how you would go about finding the answer to that question.

State	Total	Average per year
AL	668	22
AK	0	0
AZ	106	4
AR	596	20
CA	148	5
CO	781	26
CT	37	1
DE	31	1
FL	1,590	53
GA	615	21
HI	25	1
ID	80	3
IL	798	27
IN	604	20
IA	1,079	36
KS	1,198	40
KY	296	10
LA	831	28
ME	50	2
MD	86	3
MA	89	3
MI	567	19
MN	607	20
MS	775	26
MO	781	26
MT	175	6
NE	1,118	37
NV	41	1
NH	56	2
NJ	78	3
NM	276	9
NY	169	6
NC	435	15
ND	621	21
OH	463	15
OK	1,412	47
OR	34	1
PA	310	10
RI	7	0
SC	307	10
SD	864	29
TN	360	12
TX	4,174	139
UT	58	2
VT	21	1
VA	188	6
WA	45	2
WV	69	2
WI	625	21
WY	356	12

What Are Severe Storms?

The Explore Activity was about a violent kind of storm. It does not happen all the time. It forms under special conditions. Often this storm grows out of another, more common kind of storm—a **thunderstorm**.

Thunderstorms are the most common kind of severe storm. They form in clouds called *thunderheads*—cumulonimbus clouds. The storms cause huge electric sparks called *lightning*. The lightning heats the air and causes the noise called *thunder*. Thunderstorms usually have heavy rains and strong winds. Some thunderstorms also produce hail.

First Stage

A thunderstorm starts when intense heating causes air to rise very quickly. A cloud forms where there is an upward rush of heated air, an *updraft*. As more and more warm, moist air is carried upward, the cloud grows larger and larger. Strong updrafts keep droplets of water and ice crystals in the cloud, so they grow in size, too. When the updrafts can't support them anymore, they fall as heavy rain or even hail. Look at the downpour falling from this thunderstorm.

Second Stage

Once the rain falls, it causes downdrafts in the cloud. That is, air moves downward. When the air going up rubs against air going down, static electricity builds up. When enough builds up, there's a huge spark—lightning.

Lightning is unpredictable. It may jump from the cloud to the ground or from the ground to the cloud. It may jump between two thunderclouds. It may also jump from one spot to

HOW A THUNDERSTORM FORMS

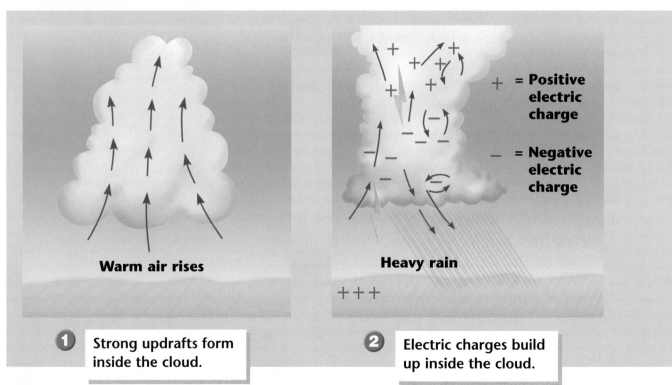

Warm air rises

Heavy rain

+ = Positive electric charge

− = Negative electric charge

1 Strong updrafts form inside the cloud.

2 Electric charges build up inside the cloud.

Brain Power

In some parts of the country, people worry more about thunderstorms than they do in other regions. Why do you think this is so?

another within the cloud. Lightning superheats the air so the air suddenly expands. It slams into the air around it with such force that it makes a mighty sound—thunder.

Third Stage

The storm dies when a downdraft becomes stronger than the updraft. Heavy rain lightens up and stops.

Thunderstorms form in the warm air just ahead of a cold front. The cold, dense air wedges under the warm, moist air and causes the warm air to rise rapidly. Be on the lookout for thunderstorms. They are likely when the weather is hot and humid and a cold front is approaching.

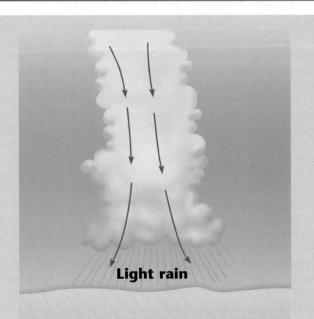

Light rain

READING IN DIAGRAMS

WRITE Write a description of how a thunderstorm forms. Identify what happens during each stage of formation.

3 A thunderstorm dies when a downdraft becomes stronger than the updraft. Heavy rain lightens up and stops.

Tornado in a Bottle

HYPOTHESIZE How does a tornado form? Write a hypothesis in your *Science Journal*.

MATERIALS
- two 2-L plastic bottles
- duct tape
- water
- paper towel
- pencil
- *Science Journal*

PROCEDURES

1. MAKE A MODEL Fill one bottle one-third full of water. Dry the neck of the bottle, and tape over the top. Use the pencil to poke a hole in the tape.

2. Place the other bottle upside down over the mouth of the first bottle. Tape the two bottles together.

3. OBSERVE Hold the bottles by the necks so the one with the water is on top. Swirl them around while your partner gently squeezes on the empty bottle. Then place the bottles on a desk with the water bottle on top. Describe in your *Science Journal* what you see.

CONCLUDE AND APPLY

INFER How is this like what happens when a tornado forms? Explain.

How and Where Do Tornadoes Happen?

The most violent thunderstorms often spin off even more dangerous storms—**tornadoes**. A tornado is a violent whirling wind that moves across the ground in a narrow path.

How They Happen

Late in the day, when Earth's surface is very warm, convection can get very strong. This can lead to a tornado. A tornado is sort of a runaway convection cell.

- When the updraft in a convection cell is really strong, the air rushes in from all sides at high speeds.

- The Coriolis effect makes the air curve into a spin. This lowers the pressure even more. Air rushes in even faster, and the pressure gets even lower, and so on. Like a spinning skater who pulls her arms in close to her sides, the spinning tornado gets faster and faster.

- As the tornado gets stronger, a funnel forms that eventually touches the ground. In the center of a tornado, winds can reach speeds of 500 kilometers per hour (about 300 miles per hour) or more. At such high speeds, winds can destroy anything in their path.

The speed of the wind in the tornado is not the speed with which the tornado moves across the ground. It moves across the ground very fast but can change its direction continually.

Where They Happen

As the Explore Activity shows, most tornadoes in the United States seem to occur in the Midwest and in the South.

Tornadoes form where dry, cold air masses mix with warm, moist air masses. In the United States, this is most likely to happen in the Great Plains region and the Mississippi Valley. Florida also gets lots of tornadoes.

Tornadoes are most likely to occur when there are big differences in the air masses. This happens most often in early spring and summer. Tornadoes can also form over water. Such tornadoes are called *waterspouts*.

More tornadoes occur in the United States than in any other country, especially in the area known as Tornado Alley.

GEOGRAPHY
LiNK

Tornado Alley

READING N MAPS

WRITE What states are included in Tornado Alley?

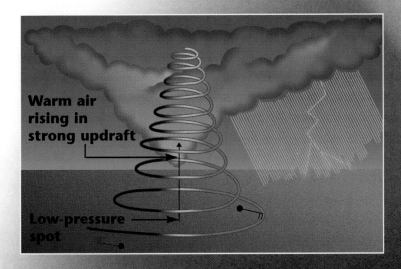

Warm air rising in strong updraft

Low-pressure spot

A tornado has a characteristic funnel-shaped cloud.

READING N DIAGRAMS

1. **DISCUSS** Where is the pressure lowest in the tornado?
2. **DISCUSS** In what direction is the wind spinning—clockwise (like the hands of a clock) counter-clockwise (the opposite)?

165

How Do Hurricanes Form?

If you live near an ocean or the Gulf Coast, you may have experienced a **hurricane**. Hurricanes are very large, swirling storms with very low pressure at their center. They form over tropical oceans—near the equator.

Air masses near the equator tend to be very much alike. They don't form the fronts that you learned about in Topic 5. Instead, they form lots of thunderstorms.

- As global winds push these thunderstorms along, they line up in rows. Strong heating and lots of evaporation over the ocean can cause a large low-pressure center to form. If this happens winds begin to blow in toward the low.

- The Coriolis effect causes winds to spiral counterclockwise in the Northern Hemisphere. Clusters of thunderstorms are pulled into the spiral. The thunderstorms merge, forming a single large storm.

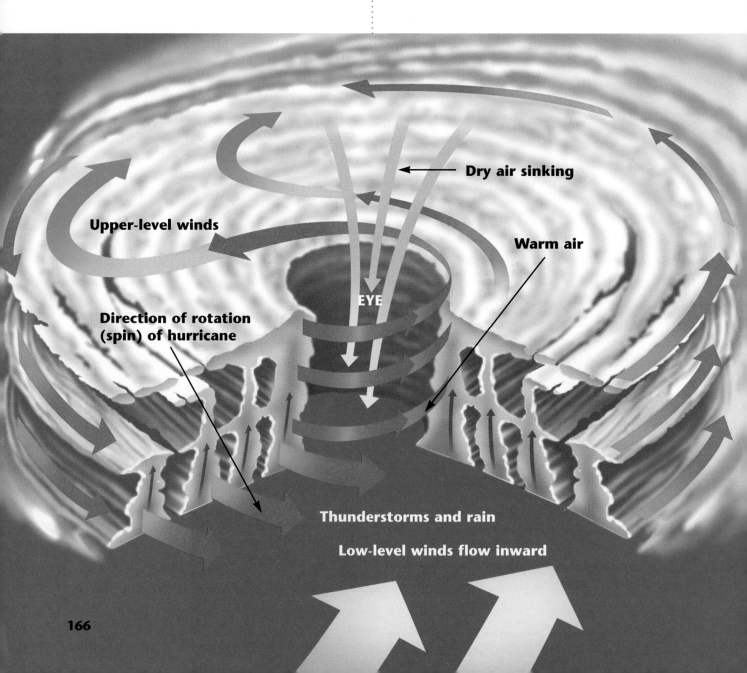

Dry air sinking

Upper-level winds

Warm air

EYE

Direction of rotation (spin) of hurricane

Thunderstorms and rain

Low-level winds flow inward

- As water vapor in the storms condenses, heat is released. The air is warmed. This decreases the air's density and pressure. Moisture evaporating into the air decreases the air's density and pressure even more. Low air pressure favors more evaporation. This lowers the pressure even more.

- The lower the air pressure, the faster are the winds that blow in toward the center of the storm. When the winds reach speeds of 120 kilometers per hour (about 75 miles per hour) or higher, the storm is a hurricane.

DID YOU KNOW?

Hurricanes can pick up about two billion tons of water a day from the oceans. Much of this water falls as rain over land areas. What do you think happens to hurricanes that stay overland for a long time?

- As the moist air in the storm rises and cools, condensation takes place. The clouds thicken. Heavy rains fall through the high winds. When fully formed a hurricane has an eye at its center. The eye is an area of light winds and skies that are nearly clear.

Hurricanes can easily grow to more than 700 kilometers (about 400 miles) in diameter. As you can see from the drawing, the image of Hurricane Fran shows it to be almost as large as the entire state of Florida!

Satellite photograph of a hurricane and its eye

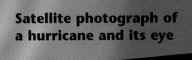
Direction of wind
Eye

READING DIAGRAMS

1. **DISCUSS** In which direction do winds turn in a hurricane—clockwise (the direction of the hands of a clock) or counter clockwise (the opposite)?
2. **DISCUSS** Where is the pressure the lowest?
3. **DISCUSS** Where is rain happening?

How Do Hurricanes Affect Ocean Waves?

Just north of the equator, gentle global winds move hurricanes west to northwest at 10 to 20 kilometers per hour (6 to 12 miles per hour). As they move north, away from the equator, their speed tends to increase.

Hurricane winds whip up large waves in the ocean. These waves move outward from the storm and pound against a shore for days before the storm arrives. However, it is the **storm surge** that causes the most destruction. Storm surge is a great rise of the sea along a shore. Its main cause is low air pressure!

Air pressure normally presses down on the surface of the sea like a giant hand. When the pressure drops in a hurricane, it is like lifting the hand slightly. The surface of the sea rises, forming a bulge beneath a hurricane.

When the hurricane moves over a coast, the bulge can cause water levels to suddenly rise several feet, or surge.

Hurricane winds also push water ahead of the storm, forcing water onshore and adding to the storm surge. If the storm surge comes at high tide, it is even worse. Great storms have surges that raise the water level by 7 meters (about 20 feet) or more.

During a great storm, the surge, large waves, high winds, and torrential rain of the storm all happen at the same time. Low-lying coastal areas are flooded. Beachfront homes are destroyed. Beaches can get worn away.

A Real Hurricane—Fran

On August 22, 1996, a storm formed off the coast of Africa and began moving west-northwest at about 10 miles per hour. By August 29 it had become more concentrated. Winds reached hurricane strength. Hurricane Fran was born. Fran continued moving west and was even stronger by the time it skirted the Bahamas. By September 5, 1996, Fran had 105-knot winds and was 400 km (250 miles) off the Florida coast.

A large low-pressure system over Tennessee steered it westward, and it struck North Carolina and Virginia on September 6. Winds of 120 knots were clocked off Cape Fear as Fran came ashore. Sea level surged to 3.6 m (12 feet) above normal. As much as 40 cm (12 inches) of rain fell in parts of North Carolina. Thirty-four people died. Flash flooding caused most deaths. A storm surge on the North Carolina coast destroyed many beachfront houses.

High winds damaged trees and roofs. They also downed power lines, leaving 4.5 million people without power. Nearly half a million tourists were ordered to evacuate the coast. Altogether it is estimated that Fran caused 3.2 billion dollars of damage.

Hurricanes begin to die out when they move over land. Cut off from the warm ocean, the hurricane has no water to replace what falls as rain. Friction between the winds and the land decreases wind speed. When it has been over land long enough, it will completely die out.

Once Hurricane Fran moved ashore, it steadily weakened. By the time it reached central North Carolina, it was no longer a hurricane. By the time it reached the Great Lakes on September 9, it was no longer even a storm. The remains of Fran disappeared on September 10.

GEOGRAPHY LINK

North America
Atlantic Ocean
Bahamas
Africa
South America

READING MAPS

1. **WRITE** What ocean does a hurricane have to cross as it approaches North America from Africa?
2. **WRITE** What part of North America did Hurricane Fran reach?

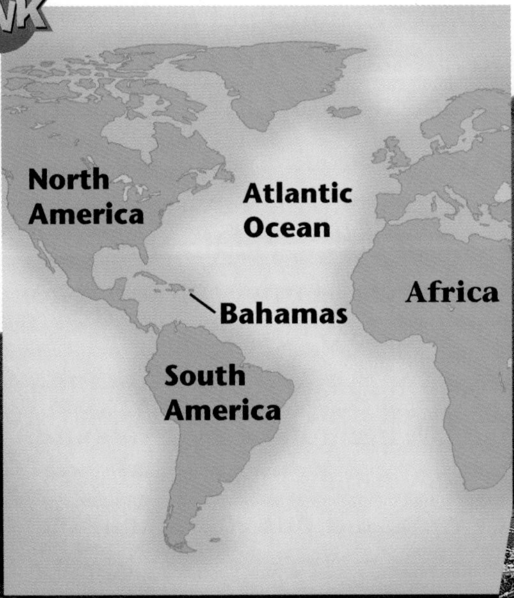

Severe storms can cause damage.

What Can You Do to Be Safe in a Storm?

Hurricanes, tornadoes, and thunderstorms can be very dangerous. In order to stay safe in these storms, you need to follow certain safety rules.

IF YOU HEAR STORM WATCHES OR WARNINGS ON TV OR RADIO, FOLLOW THEIR DIRECTIONS CAREFULLY!

A storm watch means that conditions are right for a storm to form. A storm warning means that a storm has been spotted and is heading your way.

Thunderstorm Safety Rules

1. Go inside a house or large building, but don't go into a small building that stands off by itself. It is also safe to stay inside a closed car or truck (not a convertible!). Be sure the doors and windows are closed. Do not touch any metal inside the car.

2. Stay away from pipes, faucets, electrical outlets, and open windows.

3. Don't use the telephone, except in an emergency. Electricity can travel through phone lines.

4. Stay away from the water. If you are in the water, GET OUT. Do not go out in a boat. Lightning is attracted to water.

5. If you are outside, be sure you are not the tallest thing around. Be sure, also, that you are not standing near or under the tallest thing around. Do not stand up on a beach, in an open field, or on a hilltop. Do not stand under a tree. Do not stand under an object that is standing alone in an open area.

6. If you are stuck in an open area, crouch down. Stay away from metal objects, including bicycles, motorcycles, farm equipment, golf clubs, and golf carts.

7. If your hair feels like it's standing on end, lightning may be about to strike. Crouch down. Lean forward, and put your hands on your knees. Try to make yourself as low to the ground as possible while touching as little of the ground as you can.

Tornado Safety Rules

The National Weather Service issues a tornado watch when conditions for a tornado exist. Be on the alert. If a tornado is spotted, a tornado warning is given. Take action immediately.

1. At home open the windows slightly, then seek shelter. Stay away from windows and doors.

2. The safest place is in a storm cellar. The next safest is a basement. Stay under a table, staircase, or mattress. If you have no storm cellar or basement, seek shelter in a strong building. Stay on the ground floor. Stay under a table or bed, or in a closet.

3. Do not stay in a mobile home.

4. Outdoors lie facedown in a ditch. Cover your head to protect yourself from flying debris.

5. At school go to an inside hallway on the lowest floor. If your school has a tornado shelter, go there. Follow your teacher's or principal's directions.

Hurricane Safety Rules

1. People living in coastal areas may be warned to board up their homes and head for safer, inland areas. If you live in an area connected to the mainland by a bridge, be sure you allow plenty of time to leave. Traffic on the bridge may be very heavy. People who live in low-lying areas that flood in heavy rains may also be warned to go to shelters.

2. Board or tape up windows and glass doors. Bring outdoor objects—such as furniture, bikes, potted plants—indoors.

3. Be sure you stock up on bottled water, canned and packaged foods, and first-aid supplies and medicines for the family and pets. Don't forget flashlights and fresh batteries. Test the flashlights ahead of time to be sure the bulbs are working. You may be without power for several days. Be sure the food you have can be eaten without cooking.

4. If your home is on sturdy, high ground, stay there. Otherwise go to a shelter.

5. Don't be fooled by the eye of the hurricane. Everything may be calm. Skies may be fair for a short time, but the rest of the hurricane's fury is right behind the eye.

How Can We Find Storms?

Storms are hard to predict because they form so quickly. Scientists use the best methods possible to identify conditions before a storm "brews." They look for clues, like the movement of fronts and the formation of very low pressure areas. Once these conditions are located, scientists keep a "weather eye" on them to see how they develop.

Special methods are used to find storms as they form. One such method is Doppler radar. The word *radar* stands for *ra*dio *d*etection *a*nd *r*anging. Radar works by sending out radio waves and recording their echo. The change in the radio signal from the original to the echo tells us something about where it reflected.

Doppler radar looks at how the echoes have changed in frequency from the original signals. This information gives clues about the movement of the reflective surface. Doppler radar is a very good tool for scientists to track storms. The radio waves reflect off storm clouds and are picked back up again at the radar stations.

With Doppler radar scientists can tell if raindrops are moving toward or away from them. Doppler radar can also spot spinning motions of clouds. These motions help warn scientists that tornadoes or hurricanes may be forming. Scientists use Doppler radar to find and track thunderstorms, tornadoes, and hurricanes. Doppler radar helps forecasters predict which way the storms will travel.

Scientists have used radar systems to track storms since the 1950s. More recently they have begun to use NEXRAD. *NEXRAD* stands for "*NEX*t generation of weather *RAD*ar." NEXRAD is a new form of Doppler radar that is replacing older radar systems. NEXRAD can spot small particles such as blowing dust, very light snow, and even drizzle. NEXRAD is also more accurate than conventional radar at predicting floods and flash floods. It can show the exact locations of different fronts. It also shows changes in wind speed and direction. All of this information helps scientists make more and more accurate weather predictions.

Forecasters can warn people when dangerous storms are headed their way.

The more you know about severe storms, the more you can be safe. The dangers of a thunderstorm can be avoided by following simple rules. When a thunderstorm approaches, think "safety first." Even if you are playing an important ball game, the game has to stop, and you have to take cover. Hurricanes may mean that you and your family may have to leave your home until the storm passes.

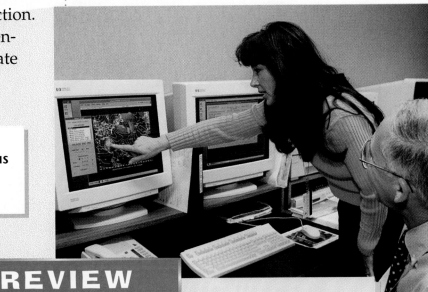

REVIEW

1. **SEQUENCE OF EVENTS** How does a thunderstorm form?

2. How is a tornado related to a thunderstorm?

3. What causes a hurricane to form? What moves it in a certain direction?

4. Why can hurricanes cause so much damage?

5. **CRITICAL THINKING** *Analyze* Why do you think predicting a severe storm is so difficult?

WHY IT MATTERS THINK ABOUT IT
What would you have to do to prepare for a severe storm that might hit your area?

WHY IT MATTERS WRITE ABOUT IT
What are the two or three most important rules for staying safe in a severe storm? Explain your answer.

READING SKILL

Write a paragraph to explain the sequence of events involved when a tornado forms.

Storm Tracking

It's easy for meteorologists to predict a storm that's part of a giant weather system; it's been reported by people experiencing it! Wind direction and changes in air pressure also signal a storm is near.

Smaller storm systems are harder to predict, but computers help. They are fed data about a storm's present location; current wind direction, air pressure, and rainfall; and how similar storms have behaved. The computer plots the path the storm will likely follow.

The use of radar has advanced hurricane prediction. Radar bounces radio waves off raindrops to discover where the storm is heading. Today, thanks to radar tracking, damage from hurricanes has been greatly reduced.

Tornadoes, or twisters, are the most violent windstorms. Because the right conditions for developing tornadoes occur quite often, they're hard to predict. The United States had more "killer tornadoes" during the first half of 1998 than in all of 1996 or 1997!

Doppler radar helps meteorologists predict tornadoes. It doesn't just spot a tornado's heavy rains, it tells the speed and direction of the funnel. With Doppler, people can be warned to seek cover before a twister hits!

There will be heavy rain all up the West Coast. Ships in the Pacific report storm conditions.

A tornado warning is in effect for Mills County. A tornado watch covers the rest of the region.

Science, Technology, and Society

DISCUSSION STARTER

1. How did people predict storms before the inventions of radio, computers, and radar?

2. Why does Doppler radar track storms better?

A large winter storm is in the North Atlantic. Computer projections show it will track inland and strike Boston early Friday, bringing gale winds and up to a foot of snow.

Hurricane Clyde is predicted to make landfall before dawn. People in coastal regions should secure their homes and head inland.

To learn more about tracking storms, visit *www.mhschool.com/science* and enter the keyword TRACKING.

*inter*NET
CONNECTION

175

Topic 7
EARTH SCIENCE

WHY IT MATTERS

All places on Earth have patterns of changes in weather that repeat over time.

Climate

What if you could live in each of these places? What would summers be like? What would winters be like? Which place do you think is wet and warm? Which is dry and cold? Which is hot and dry? Which place do you think has year-round weather most like yours? What evidence in the pictures did you use to answer these questions?

EXPLORE

HYPOTHESIZE What factors are used to describe the average weather pattern of a region? Write a hypothesis in your *Science Journal*. How might you use graphs of year-round weather in different places to test your ideas?

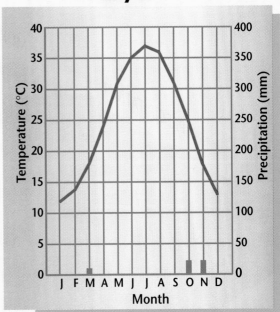
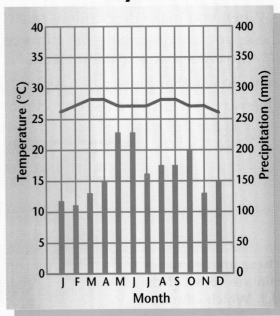

EXPLORE ⚡ ACTIVITY

Investigate What Weather Patterns Tell You ⚡ MATH LINK

Compare weather patterns in two cities.

MATERIALS
• *Science Journal*

PROCEDURES

1. USE NUMBERS Look at the graph for city 1. The bottom is labeled with the months of the year. The left side is labeled with the temperature in degrees Celsius. Use this scale to read the temperature line. What is the average temperature in city 1 during July?

2. USE NUMBERS The right side of the graph is labeled with millimeters of precipitation. Use this scale when reading the precipitation bars. What is the average precipitation in city 1 during July?

3. Repeat steps 1 and 2 for city 2.

CONCLUDE AND APPLY

1. COMPARE AND CONTRAST How do the annual amounts of precipitation compare for the two cities? Record your answer in your *Science Journal*.

2. INTERPRET DATA When is the average temperature highest for each city? Lowest?

3. INTERPRET DATA Describe the average weather pattern for each city. Be sure to include temperature and precipitation, and their relationship to the seasons.

GOING FURTHER: Problem Solving

4. ANALYZE How would you go about making a graph of the weather patterns for your town?

City 1

City 2

— Temperature (in Celsius)
■ Precipitation (in millimeters)

177

What Do Weather Patterns Tell You?

Weather changes from day to day. However, the weather in any area tends to follow a pattern throughout the year. For example, Fairbanks, Alaska, tends to have long, cold winters and short, cool summers. Miami, Florida, tends to have long, hot summers and short, cool winters.

When you make descriptions such as these, you are describing the **climate** (klī′mit) of a region. Climate is the average weather pattern of a region. One way to describe a region's climate is with a temperature-precipitation graph, as in the Explore Activity.

The climate of a region can also be described by some other factors, such as winds, distance from a coast, mountain ranges, and ocean currents. The *climatic zones* shown here take all these factors into account.

Another way to describe the climate of a region is by the plants that grow there, such as, grasslands or coniferous forests. Each kind of plant requires its own conditions for growth, such as amount of sunlight, precipitation and temperature.

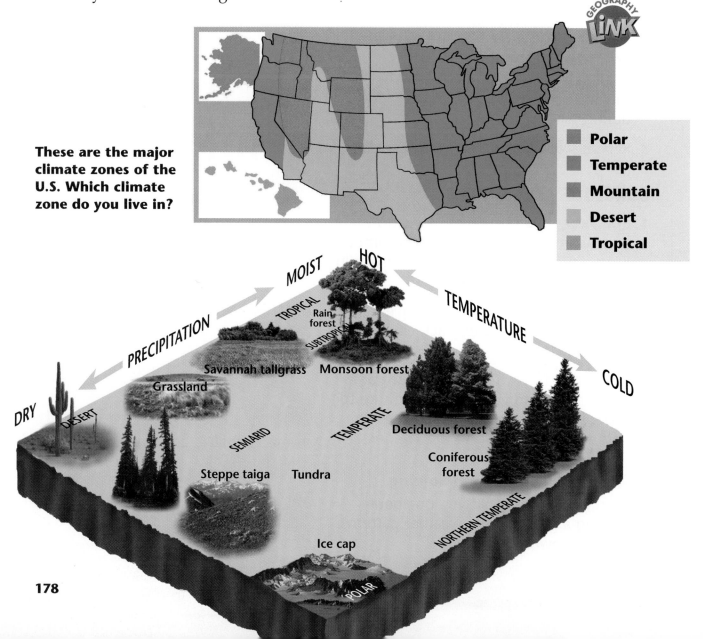

These are the major climate zones of the U.S. Which climate zone do you live in?

Polar
Temperate
Mountain
Desert
Tropical

MOIST HOT

PRECIPITATION

TROPICAL

Rain forest

SUBTROPICAL

TEMPERATURE

Savannah tallgrass

Monsoon forest

Grassland

COLD

DRY

DESERT

SEMIARID

TEMPERATE

Deciduous forest

Steppe taiga

Tundra

Coniferous forest

NORTHERN TEMPERATE

Ice cap

POLAR

Skill: Making a Model

CLIMATES IN TWO AREAS

In this activity you will make a model of the soil conditions in the two cities on page 177. Use the information in the graph from the Explore Activity on page 177. The soil conditions you set up will model—or represent—the climates of the two cities.

MATERIALS

- stick-on notepaper
- marking pencil or pen
- 2 trays of dry soil
- spray bottle of water (like a plant mister)
- lamp
- thermometer
- *Science Journal*

PROCEDURES

1. **MAKE A MODEL** Put 3 cm of dry soil into each tray. Label one tray City 1 and the other tray City 2.

2. **USE NUMBERS** What do the bars on each graph in the Explore Activity represent? Make a list of the amounts given by the bars for each month for each city.

3. **USE VARIABLES** Model the yearly precipitation and temperature like this: Let 5 minutes equal 1 month. One squeeze of water sprayed on the tray equals 10 millimeters of precipitation. Every minute the lamp is on equals 20 degrees of temperature. That means that from 0 to 5 minutes is January. During January the City 2 tray gets no water and the lamp shines on it for $\frac{3}{4}$ minute. The City 1 tray gets 12 squeezes of water and the lamp shines on it for $2\frac{1}{4}$ minutes.

4. Model the two cities for all 12 months. Record your observations in your *Science Journal*.

CONCLUDE AND APPLY

1. **COMPARE AND CONTRAST** Examine the soil in the trays. Compare them at the same points in each year, for example, June and December. How do they differ?

2. **EVALUATE** How does your model show climates?

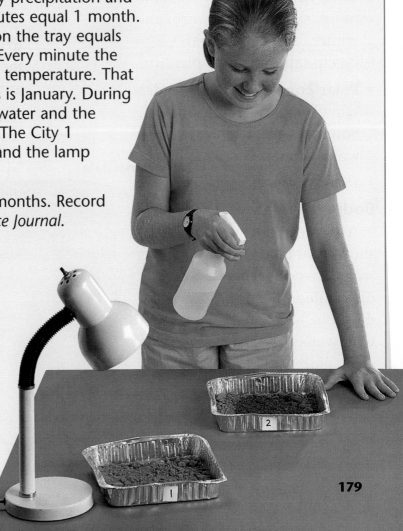

What Affects Climate?

Several things affect temperature and precipitation over a long period of time.

Latitude

One way to describe location is to tell the latitude of a place. Latitude is a measure of how far north or south a place is from the equator. The angle of insolation is different at different latitudes. As a result the temperatures are different at different latitudes.

- **Tropical Zone** Near the equator, temperatures are high all year. Rainfall is plentiful. At about 30° latitude in each hemisphere are deserts, areas of high temperatures and low precipitation.

- **Temperate Zones** In the middle latitudes, summers are warm and winters are cool or cold. Precipitation may be plentiful.

- **Polar Zones** At high latitudes, winters are long and cold. Summers are short and warm. Precipitation all year is low.

Bodies of Water

A glance at any globe shows that land and water are not evenly distributed. Most of the globe is covered with water. However, some places on a continent can be more than 1,000 miles from any large body of water.

Land and water heat and cool at different rates. Land heats up faster in the sunlight than water does. Land also cools off faster than water. As a result air temperatures over land are warmer in summer and cooler in winter than they are over oceans at the same latitude.

Winds and Ocean Currents

In Topic 4 you learned that wind patterns circle the globe. These patterns are not the day-to-day winds. Instead they are winds that blow continually above Earth's surface.

- **Wind Patterns** For example, just above and below the equator, the trade winds blow continually. In the middle latitudes are the westerlies. In the polar areas are the easterlies. Westerlies blow across the continental United States from west (the Pacific) to east. They bring warm, moist air to the west coast. They push air masses and fronts across the country.

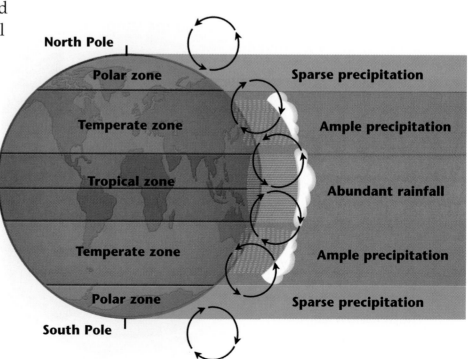

North Pole

Polar zone — Sparse precipitation

Temperate zone — Ample precipitation

Tropical zone — Abundant rainfall

Temperate zone — Ample precipitation

Polar zone — Sparse precipitation

South Pole

HOW ALTITUDE AFFECTS CLIMATE

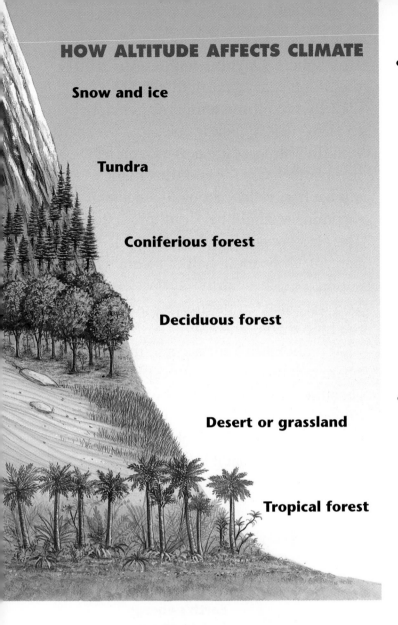

Snow and ice

Tundra

Coniferious forest

Deciduous forest

Desert or grassland

Tropical forest

- **Mountains** Along the base of a high mountain, you may find tropical plants growing. Halfway up you may find pine forests. At the mountain peaks, you will find permanent ice and snow. Mountain ranges affect climate, too. The Alps protect the Mediterranean coast from cold polar air. The Himalayas protect the lowlands of India from cold Siberian air. Mountain ranges also affect rain patterns. Often one side of the mountain gets lots of rain while the other side gets very little. Can you explain why?

- **Winds and Mountains** Global wind patterns can force air up along the side of a mountain. For example, warm moist air from the Pacific Ocean is blown up the side of the Sierra Nevada and the Cascades. As the air moves up, there is precipitation on the windward side. Having lost the moisture, dry air descends down the leeward side of the mountain.

- **Currents** These winds also move water across the surface of the ocean. As ocean water moves, it brings along warm or cool air from where it comes from to where it goes. A warm current, the Gulf Stream, flows up along the east coast. The California Current, a cool current, moves down along the west coast.

Altitude

Altitude is a measure of how high above sea level a place is. The higher a place is above sea level, the cooler its climate is.

Air passing over a mountain cools. Rain clouds may form and drop their moisture on that side of the mountain. Air reaching the other side is often dry.

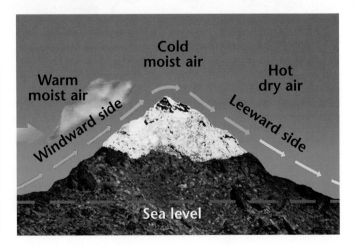

Cold moist air

Warm moist air

Hot dry air

Windward side

Leeward side

Sea level

How Does Earth Gain and Lose Energy?

Earth's climates depend a great deal on the Sun's energy. Earth absorbs heat from sunlight. It also gives out, or *radiates,* heat into space. Earth gains and loses.

If the amount of energy gained balances the energy lost, Earth is in **radiative** (rā'dē ā'tiv) **balance**. Then Earth's average temperature remains about the same. Earth's average temperature is about 14°C (59°F). A tip of the balance will cause Earth's average temperature to rise or fall.

The atmosphere plays an important role in Earth's radiative balance. If Earth had no atmosphere, it would be a lot like the Moon, which has no atmosphere. Daytime temperatures on the Moon soar to more than 100°C (212°F). Nighttime temperatures drop to 115°C (240°F) below zero.

Earth's atmosphere acts as a protective blanket. Clouds and dust in the atmosphere reflect about 30 percent of incoming sunlight back out into space. The atmosphere absorbs another 15–20 percent. Only about half of incoming sunlight reaches Earth's surface. This keeps surface temperatures from rising too high during the day.

At night Earth's surface and the atmosphere radiate heat. The atmosphere absorbs most of this heat. The atmosphere, in turn, radiates this heat, together with its own heat. Earth absorbs back almost half of what it lost. This keeps Earth from getting too cold at night.

EARTH'S ENERGY BUDGET

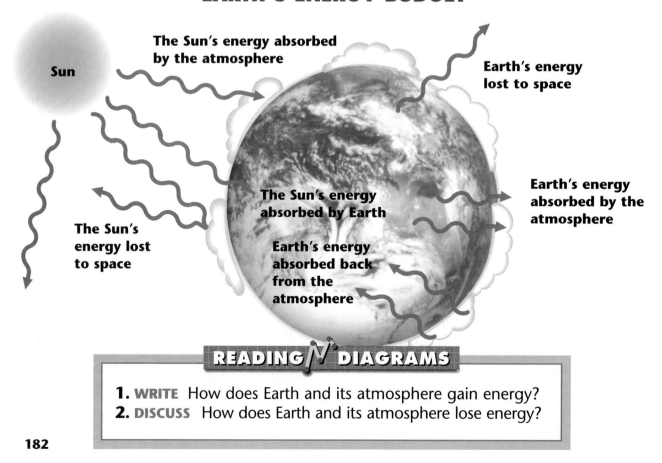

Sun

The Sun's energy absorbed by the atmosphere

Earth's energy lost to space

The Sun's energy absorbed by Earth

Earth's energy absorbed by the atmosphere

The Sun's energy lost to space

Earth's energy absorbed back from the atmosphere

READING DIAGRAMS

1. **WRITE** How does Earth and its atmosphere gain energy?
2. **DISCUSS** How does Earth and its atmosphere lose energy?

182

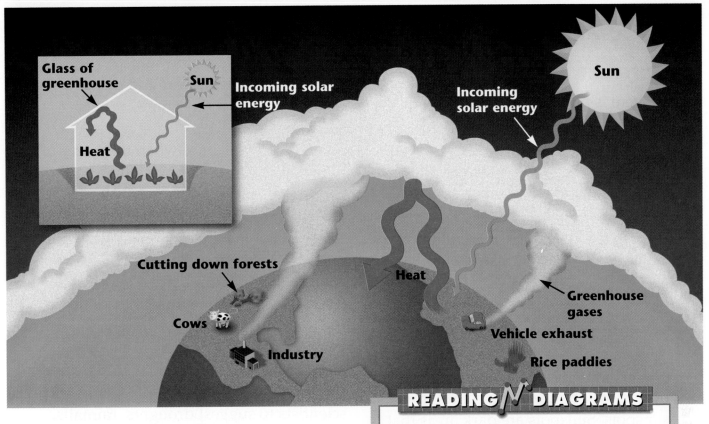

Glass of greenhouse
Sun
Incoming solar energy
Heat
Sun
Incoming solar energy
Cutting down forests
Heat
Greenhouse gases
Cows
Vehicle exhaust
Industry
Rice paddies

READING DIAGRAMS

DISCUSS Write a description from this diagram of what causes the greenhouse effect.

How Is Earth Like a Greenhouse?

Why doesn't all of Earth's heat just go out into space? The atmosphere keeps Earth warmer than it would otherwise be. This is called the **greenhouse effect**. Earth's atmosphere acts somewhat like the glass in a greenhouse. In a greenhouse the glass lets sunlight in but does not let heat escape. This helps create a warm environment in which plants can flourish.

Earth's greenhouse effect is caused by just a few gases. These greenhouse gases make up only a tiny part of the air. The main greenhouse gases are *water vapor, carbon dioxide,* and *ozone.* Other gases also have an effect. These gases are *methane, nitrous oxide, chlorofluorocarbons (CFCs),* and *sulfur dioxide.*

Human activities are putting more and more greenhouse gases into the

atmosphere. Many scientists are worried that these gases may change Earth's climate. Even a small increase in these gases adds to the greenhouse effect, making our planet warmer.

Scientists are still examining and interpreting data in order to understand the greenhouse effect better.

Brain Power

Cans of items under pressure (hair sprays, paint sprays) indicate that they do not contain chlorofluorocarbons. Why is this an important statement to list on a label?

Does Climate Change with Time?

There is much evidence that over long periods of time, Earth goes through warming and cooling trends. Warming and cooling are signs that Earth's radiative balance has shifted. What causes such shifts?

The shifts are caused by changes in sunlight. They are also caused by changes in the movements of air, water, landmasses, and Earth itself.

The Sun's Output

The amount of energy the Sun sends out changes. One clue to how the Sun's output may be changing comes from sunspots. Sunspots are dark areas that appear on the surface of the Sun. They appear dark because they are cooler than the surrounding regions. They appear to be "storms" on the Sun.

Sunspots have been observed for centuries. However, they are not permanent. They appear and disappear over several days time, or over several months.

Also there are times when there are many large sunspots. Such a high count is called a sunspot maximum. The last sunspot maximum was in 1989.

A sunspot maximum appears to happen about every 11 years. Scientists also date changes in Earth's temperatures about the same times. Around the time of a sunspot maximum, Earth's average temperatures have gone up. The pattern is not exact or complete. However, it has led some scientists to suggest droughts, rainfalls, and very cold winters might be related to times when sunspots are very numerous or very few.

The Sun's surface

Brain Power

When might the next sunspot maximum occur?

Sunspot

When they appear sunspots can affect radio and TV broadcasts on Earth. Can they also affect temperatures?

Ocean Currents

How do the oceans help move Earth's heat around? Ocean currents act like huge conveyor belts, carrying heat from the equator to the poles. Changes in the speed and direction of these currents could explain sudden and long-term climate changes.

The continents have changed their positions over time. In fact the continents and ocean bottoms are still moving very gradually. Their climates are likely to change with their locations.

Volcanoes

When volcanoes erupt they send dust and gases into the atmosphere. Atmospheric dust can block sunlight, causing cooling. In the past, eruptions were more frequent. The dust from all of those eruptions may have caused enough cooling to trigger ice ages. Volcanic eruptions are not as common today as they were in the past. While eruptions still cause cooling, they probably don't affect long-term climate as much as in the past.

300 Million Years Ago

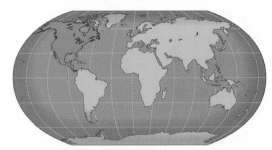

Present

Do you think the ocean currents were the same 300 million years ago as they are today? Changes in ocean currents would profoundly affect climates.

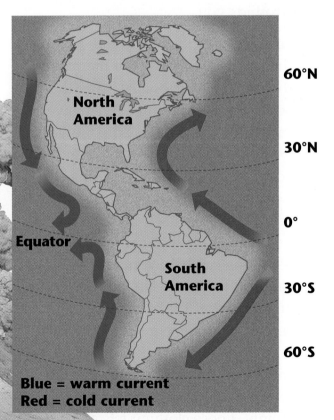

Blue = warm current
Red = cold current

Some currents affecting the Western Hemisphere today

Brain Power

What difference does it make if Earth's climate gets just a couple of degrees warmer or cooler than it is today?

How Can Climate Affect You?

How do you deal with cold weather? Cold weather cools the surface of the body. The body responds by circulating warm blood faster to counteract the cooling. The heart pumps faster. Blood pressure increases and puts a strain on the heart.

Cold Climates

How can you stay warm in cold weather? Use proper clothing and shelter. Clothing traps body heat to warm the air close to your body. Cold-weather clothes are often made with materials that trap air between loose fibers. Your body heats the trapped air, and soon a thin, warm layer of air surrounds you.

Hot Climates

In hot, dry climates, the main health problem is water loss. Heating the body triggers sweating. When sweat evaporates it cools the skin. However, if you don't drink enough water, your body eventually stops sweating. No sweat, no cooling. Body temperature rises. This can cause *hyperthermia* (overheating), which can be fatal.

Clothing can help you deal with the heat. Leaving your skin bare can make you feel hotter. That's because your skin absorbs the full energy of sunlight. It also increases your risk of getting skin cancer. Light-colored fabric protects the skin and reflects a lot of the sunlight. Loose clothing lets air circulate so sweat can evaporate and cool the body.

How to Dress in Hot Weather

Light-colored, loose clothing that protects you from the Sun and lets your skin breathe

●

Sun hat

●

Sunscreen

How to Dress in Cold Weather

Protect nose and ears on blustery, cold days

●

Keep hands, head, and feet warm

●

Dress in layers to trap body heat

Crops in the Past

Climate has been affecting how food is produced, since farming began, about 6,000 years ago. At that time average temperatures were about 2°C (4°F) warmer than today. There was also more rainfall. Crops thrived in the warm, moist climate. About A.D. 200 the climate started to cool. Crops failed.

By A.D. 900–1100, temperatures had warmed up again. However, by 1300 the climate had started to cool again. Between 1450 and 1850, there was a cold period called the Little Ice Age. There were many harsh winters. Stretches of cold, wet summers in the 1590s, the 1690s, and the 1810s caused crops to fail and led to famines.

Crops Since 1900

Since 1900 the average temperature has increased by about 0.5°C (1°F). A drought during the 1920s–1940s led to the Dust Bowl days. Millions of acres of United States farmland dried out. Crops failed. Farmers went broke trying to pay their bills.

WHY IT MATTERS

You may experience several climates in your lifetime. You may travel to faraway places with climates different from your own. In large states like Texas or California, you can experience many climates in different parts of the state.

When you become an adult, your job may bring you to climates different from your present climate. You may enjoy one climate more than another. You may choose to live in a climate different from the one you are used to.

Winter fairs were held on the Thames River in London during the Little Ice Age.

REVIEW

1. What is climate? What are the main factors that are used to describe the climate of an area?

2. **MAKE A MODEL** How can you make models to show a dry climate and a moist climate?

3. Why are climates different at different places on Earth?

4. What is the greenhouse effect?

5. **CRITICAL THINKING** *Analyze* Do you think people can live in all climates? Explain your answer.

WHY IT MATTERS THINK ABOUT IT
What is the climate like in your area?

WHY IT MATTERS WRITE ABOUT IT
Choose a climate that is different from your own. How do people in that climate live differently from you?

SCIENCE MAGAZINE

A Closer Look

A WARMER WORLD?

"Our climate is definitely warming up," says Tom Karl, Senior Scientist at the National Climatic Data Center in North Carolina. It's the world's largest collector of weather data—its computers have more than 150 years of information. Every day 18 million more pages of weather data come in!

Karl and his team studied worldwide temperatures between 1900 and 1997. They discovered that 1997 was the warmest year since 1900 and that 9 of the past 11 years have been warmer than average!

Karl believes the cause is probably an increase in greenhouse gases. Not everyone agrees. In 1997 most state climate experts said global warming is natural, caused by changes in the Sun and in Earth's orbit. They added that Earth's climate would change even if no one lived on the planet!

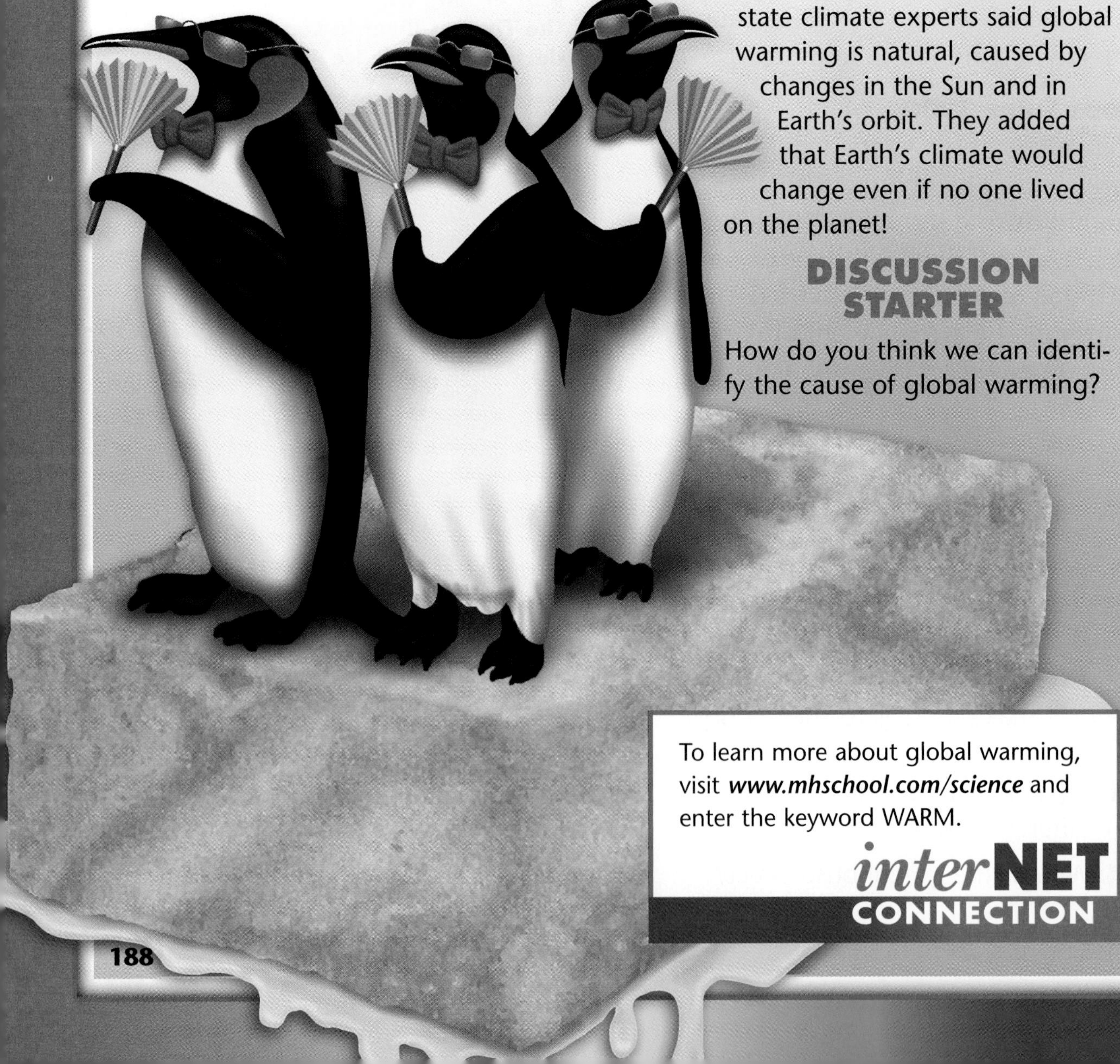

DISCUSSION STARTER

How do you think we can identify the cause of global warming?

To learn more about global warming, visit *www.mhschool.com/science* and enter the keyword WARM.

interNET CONNECTION

SCIENCE WORDS

air mass p.150

climate p.178

cold front p.152

front p.151

greenhouse
 effect p.183

hurricane p.166

radiative
 balance p.182

storm surge p.168

tornado p.164

warm front p.152

USING SCIENCE WORDS

**Number a paper from 1 to 10. Fill in
1 to 5 with words from the list above.**

1. The __?__ may be making Earth warmer.

2. A great rise of sea level at a shore due to a hurricane is a(n)__?__.

3. A dangerous storm that forms over warm ocean waters is a(n) __?__.

4. A(n) __?__ forms when cold air moves in under a warm air mass.

5. The average weather pattern of a region is its __?__.

6–10. Pick five words from the list above that were not used in 1 to 5, and use each in a sentence.

UNDERSTANDING SCIENCE IDEAS

11. What is the difference between a cold front and a warm front?

12. How is the weather a warm front brings different from the weather a cold front brings?

13. What are two things that can affect climate?

14. What happens when a front stays over a region for a long time?

15. How are tornadoes and hurricanes different?

USING IDEAS AND SKILLS

16. **READING SKILL: SEQUENCE OF EVENTS** Pick a severe storm. Describe how it forms.

17. Why is the severe storm you described in number 16 dangerous?

18. How are tornadoes often related to thunderstorms?

19. **MAKE A MODEL** What if your area was to get twice as much rain as usual for the next ten years? How would you make a model of your climate as it is now? How would you adjust it to study the effect of the extra rainfall?

20. **THINKING LIKE A SCIENTIST** Do you think that Earth is getting warmer? State and explain your hypothesis. Describe what you might do to test your ideas.

PROBLEMS and PUZZLES

Forecast Accuracy Write down a weather forecaster's five-day forecast. Check the weather each day over the five days. Determine a way to rate how accurate the forecast turned out to be. Repeat several times. Why isn't it ever competely accurate?

UNIT 2 REVIEW

USING SCIENCE WORDS

air pressure p.105
atmosphere p.104
climate p.178
condensation p.115
convection
  cell p.136
Coriolis effect p.138
evaporation p.112
front p.151

greenhouse
  effect p.183
humidity p.112
hurricane p.166
precipitation p.124
thunderstorm
  p.162
tornado p.164
troposphere p.104

Number a paper from 1 to 10. Beside each number write the word or term that best completes the sentence.

1. The blanket of gases that surrounds Earth is the __?__.

2. Evaporation increases the __?__ in the air.

3. Evaporation is the opposite of __?__.

4. Rain, sleet, and snow are all forms of __?__.

5. Air rises and sinks in a(n) __?__.

6. The curved paths of winds are caused by __?__.

7. The boundary between two masses of air with different temperatures is call a(n) __?__.

8. A violent spinning wind that moves in a narrow path is a __?__.

9. The normal weather pattern of a place is called its __?__.

10. Earth's atmosphere tends to trap heat because of the __?__.

UNDERSTANDING SCIENCE IDEAS

Write 11–15. For each number write the letter for the best answer. You may wish to use the hints provided.

11. On a hot day, a lake is likely to be
    a. cooler than nearby land
    b. hotter than nearby land
    c. the same temperature as the land
    d. the cause of the heat
    (Hint: Read page 103.)

12. Water drops that collect on a cold glass of lemonade come from
    a. the lemonade
    b. the air
    c. a puddle
    d. the glass itself
    (Hint: Read page 112.)

13. The water cycle describes how water
    a. flows upstream
    b. spins in a tornado
    c. changes form
    d. heats up the atmosphere
    (Hint: Read pages 126–127.)

14. Statistical weather forecasts are based on
    a. the kinds of fronts moving out of an area
    b. severe storms
    c. the chance of a weather pattern repeating itself
    d. weather station symbols
    (Hint: Read pages 148–149.)

15. Earth gets its heat from
    a. trees
    b. convection
    c. greenhouses
    d. the Sun
    (Hint: Read page 182.)

USING IDEAS AND SKILLS

16. The troposphere is different from other layers of the atmosphere. What takes place there as a result of this difference?

17. Why does the air temperature usually increase between sunrise and noon?

18. How does water vapor get into the air?

19. What is fog, and how does it form?

20. How is air pressure related to air temperature?

21. USE NUMBERS What does a weather station model tell you?

22. What is the purpose of a weather station?

23. What causes thunderstorms?

THINKING LIKE A SCIENTIST

24. MAKE A MODEL You use sand in a tray to model climates. Why would you build a model using simple things that do not seem to have anything to do with a topic?

25. What is the climate like where you live?

WRITING IN YOUR JOURNAL

SCIENCE IN YOUR LIFE
How does the weather affect your daily activities? Is there a difference between what you do on rainy days and what you do on clear, sunny days?

PRODUCT ADS
What products are advertised to protect you from the weather in the winter? In the summer? What is each product supposed to do? Are the products as good as the ads say? Explain.

HOW SCIENTISTS WORK
In this unit you learned about how weather data is collected. How do you think scientists decide what is the best kind of data to collect?

Design your own Experiment

How much does humidity change over the course of a day? To find out, design an experiment using a glass of cold water, a thermometer, and a timer. Check your experiment with your teacher before you perform it.

inter**NET** CONNECTION

For more help in reviewing this unit, visit
www.mhschool.com/science

PROBLEMS and PUZZLES

Heat Index

When the temperature and the relative humidity are both high, the air temperature may "feel" greater than what the thermometer reads. The temperature that you feel is called the *heat index*.

Find 90°F on the graph. Move your finger across the 90°F line to where it meets the 70% relative humidity line. At the point where the two lines meet, the heat index is 105°F. As you move your finger right to higher relative humidities, the heat index gets higher.

Find the heat index for any temperatures 80°F and over at relative humidities over 40% on the graph. The greater the heat index, the darker the shaded portions of the graph, the greater the chance of the heat affecting your health. How can knowing the heat index help you?

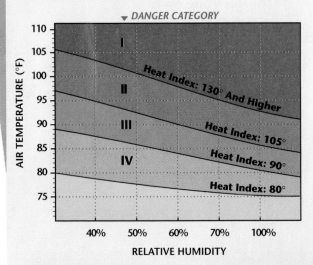

Wind and Clouds

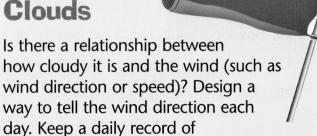

Is there a relationship between how cloudy it is and the wind (such as wind direction or speed)? Design a way to tell the wind direction each day. Keep a daily record of

- cloud cover
- wind direction
- wind speed (using the Beauford scale)
- fronts moving through your area (by listening to local weather reports)

Put this information together over a period of several weeks to try to find a relationship.

Soggy Cereal Caper

Tanya left a box of Corn Roasties cereal open on an 80°F July day when the relative humidity was 80%. The cereal got soggy overnight. In December Tanya did the same thing when the temperature was 20°F and the relative humidity was also 80%. This time the cereal did not get soggy. Can you explain what made the cereal soggy in July but not in December? How could you test your answer?

THE ENERGY OF SOUND AND LIGHT

CHAPTER 5

SOUND

Sound and light are both forms of energy. In Chapter 5 you'll explore sound, energy on the go. You can't see it but it goes out from its source in all directions. You hear sound when the energy reaches your ear. Can you think of some sounds we can't hear?

In Chapter 5 you will read for cause and effect. For example, beating a drum is a cause. The sound is the effect.

SCIENCE WORDS

vibration a back-and-forth movement

matter anything that has mass and takes up space

sound wave a vibration that spreads away from a vibrating object

compression the part of a sound wave where molecules are crowded together

rarefaction the part of a sound wave where molecules are spread apart

Sound and Hearing

Do you know that without earphones you could not hear your radio on the Moon? Why do you think this is true? If you place your hand over the speaker of a radio, you can feel the sound. Try it. Why does it happen? Would you be able to feel the sound on the Moon?

A bell shaking rapidly, a drumhead moving up and down, a string bouncing back and forth—these are all examples of things that make sound. What do they have in common? What do you think all sounds have in common?

EXPLORE

HYPOTHESIZE What causes sound? Write a hypothesis in your *Science Journal*. Remember, sounds can be different. How could you build an instrument to test your ideas?

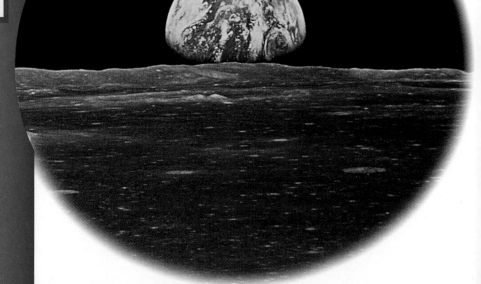

Investigate What Makes Sound

Test what makes sound by building a simple musical instrument.

PROCEDURES

 SAFETY Wear goggles.

1. Use a pen point to poke a hole in the bottom of the cup. Cut the rubber band. Insert one end into the hole. Tie two or three knots to keep the rubber band in place.

2. Tape the cup to the end of the ruler. Stretch the rubber band to the other end of the ruler. Tape it securely.

3. **OBSERVE** Hold the cup next to your ear. Pluck the rubber band. Watch a partner do the same thing. In your *Science Journal*, describe what you hear and see.

4. **EXPERIMENT** Put one finger on the rubber band, hold it against the ruler, and then pluck it again. What happens to the sound?

CONCLUDE AND APPLY

1. **DRAW CONCLUSIONS** What did you observe that made your instrument work? How can you explain what makes sound?

2. **COMPARE AND CONTRAST** What happened to the sound when you changed the rubber band with your finger? Explain why based on your observations.

GOING FURTHER: Problem Solving

3. **PREDICT/EXPERIMENT** What do you think will happen to the sound if you stretch the rubber band tighter? Untape the end of the rubber band and pull it a bit tighter. Retape the end to the ruler. Repeat steps 3 and 4. How do the results compare with your prediction? Give reasons for what happened.

MATERIALS

- 30-cm (12-in.) wood or plastic ruler
- long rubber band (about 20-cm long before cutting)
- 210–270-mL (7–9-oz) plastic or foam cup
- clear tape
- ballpoint pen
- scissors
- goggles
- *Science Journal*

What Makes Sound?

The Explore Activity showed that a sound is provided by making something move back and forth. It shows you can't produce a sound without making something move. If you pluck a rubber band, the rubber band moving back and forth produces twanging sounds. This back-and-forth motion is called a **vibration**. Unless something vibrates, there can be no sound.

Vibrations

How do you know that vibrations make sound? What are some examples? An air hammer drills through the pavement with a deafening "putt-putt." A ball snaps against a baseball bat. Often you can see the vibration that causes a sound. You can see an air hammer rattle up and down. You can also feel vibrations. You can feel the sidewalk shake if you are near the air hammer. Many vibrations are too fast for you to see. You may not see the bat vibrating when the ball hits it, but you can still feel it.

Energy Transfer

If you pluck a guitar string, you can see it moving back and forth. You provide the energy necessary for this vibration when you pluck it. This energy is transferred to the rubber band and causes it to vibrate. When you touch the rubber band, you can feel it vibrating.

What can you notice if you place your fingers gently against your throat while you talk or hum? You can feel a vibration. You feel the vibration of your vocal cords. Vocal cords in your throat vibrate when air moves past them, allowing you to speak.

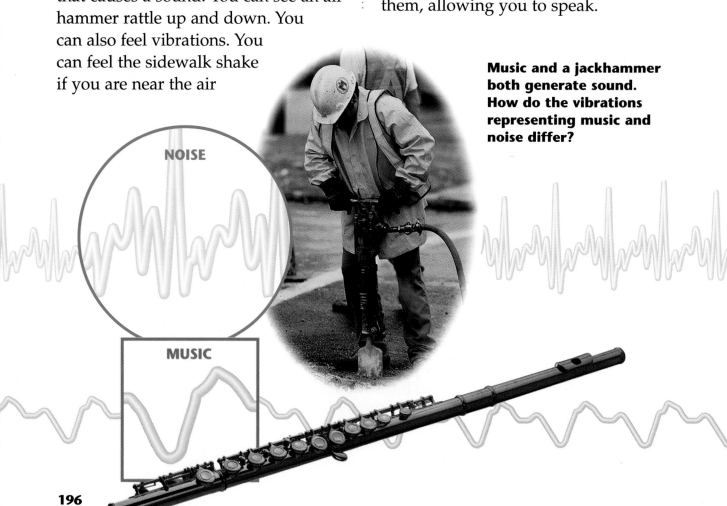

Music and a jackhammer both generate sound. How do the vibrations representing music and noise differ?

NOISE

MUSIC

How Do Instruments Make Sounds?

What vibrates when you play a guitar? When the strings of a guitar or violin are bowed or plucked, they begin to vibrate. They produce sounds. However, not all instruments rely on strings. Sounds can also be produced by vibrating surfaces and by vibrating columns of air. The instruments in each section of the orchestra have their own characteristic ways of producing sounds. In each section different materials vibrate.

NATIONAL GEOGRAPHIC

FUNtastic Facts

A male cricket fiddles his songs. Using one wing like a violinist's bow, the cricket rubs that wing against ridges on the other wing. Males play several songs. What purposes do you think they might serve?

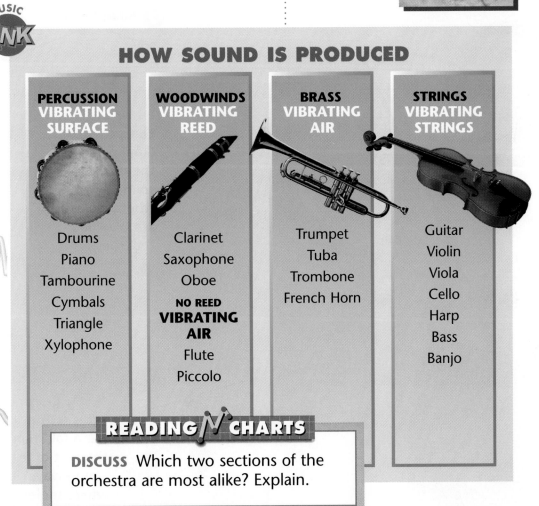

MUSIC LINK

HOW SOUND IS PRODUCED

PERCUSSION VIBRATING SURFACE	WOODWINDS VIBRATING REED	BRASS VIBRATING AIR	STRINGS VIBRATING STRINGS
Drums	Clarinet	Trumpet	Guitar
Piano	Saxophone	Tuba	Violin
Tambourine	Oboe	Trombone	Viola
Cymbals	**NO REED VIBRATING AIR**	French Horn	Cello
Triangle	Flute		Harp
Xylophone	Piccolo		Bass
			Banjo

READING CHARTS

DISCUSS Which two sections of the orchestra are most alike? Explain.

How Does Sound Travel?

Sound is a vibration that travels through **matter**. Matter is anything that has mass and takes up space. Matter can be a solid, liquid, or gas. Some types of matter are made of pieces too small to be seen, called *molecules*. Molecules are the smallest pieces that matter can be broken into without changing the kind of matter.

How does the sound made by a vibrating string travel?

- **Vibrating String** When a string vibrates, it makes molecules of gases in the air next to it vibrate. The molecules squeeze together, then spread apart.

  The vibrating molecules near the string then make the molecules next to them start to vibrate.

- **Sound Wave**s The vibration continues to spread. A vibration that spreads away from a vibrating object is a **sound wave**. It carries the energy from the vibrating object outward in all directions.

LIFE **LINK** SCIENCE

SOUND WAVES FROM STRING TO EAR

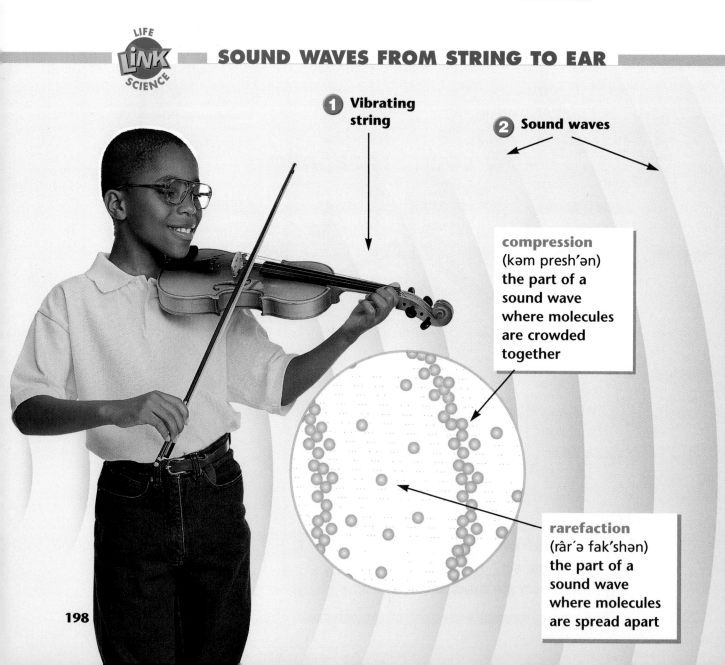

1 Vibrating string

2 Sound waves

compression
(kəm presh'ən)
the part of a sound wave where molecules are crowded together

rarefaction
(râr´ə fak'shən)
the part of a sound wave where molecules are spread apart

How Do You Hear Sound?

When something vibrates, it pushes back and forth against the air next to it, creating sound waves. What happens to sound waves when they reach your ear? How do the waves result in a sound?

- **Outer Ear** Sound waves are collected by the outer ear. The outer ear acts like a funnel to direct sound waves into the ear. The sound waves cause the *eardrum* to vibrate, like a struck drumhead.

- **Middle Ear** The vibrating eardrum makes three tiny bones in the middle ear vibrate. They are the *hammer*, *anvil*, and *stirrup*.

- **Inner Ear** These vibrating bones pass the sound vibrations along to a fluid-filled tube in the inner ear. The vibrations make the fluid in this tube vibrate. This stimulates tiny hair cells in the tube.

- **Nerve to Brain** The hair cell vibrations are passed on to the *auditory* (ô′di tôr′ē) nerve and on to the brain. The brain interprets them as sound.

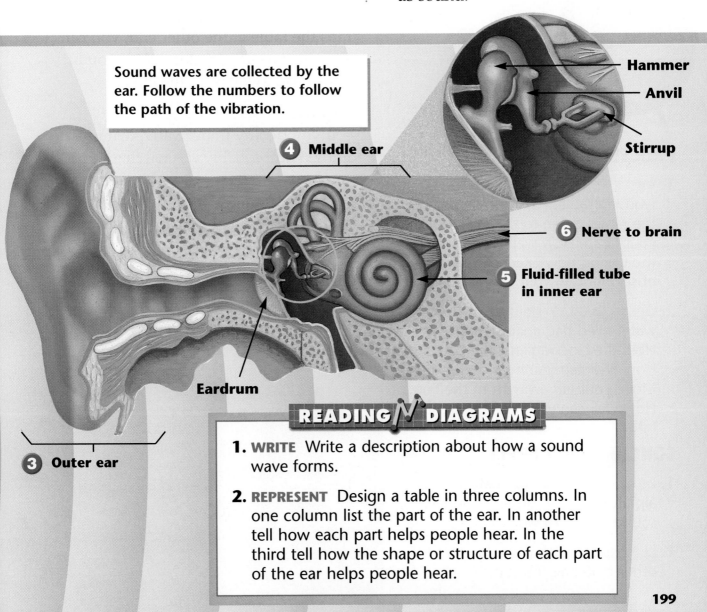

Sound waves are collected by the ear. Follow the numbers to follow the path of the vibration.

Hammer

Anvil

Stirrup

4 **Middle ear**

6 **Nerve to brain**

5 **Fluid-filled tube in inner ear**

Eardrum

3 **Outer ear**

READING DIAGRAMS

1. **WRITE** Write a description about how a sound wave forms.

2. **REPRESENT** Design a table in three columns. In one column list the part of the ear. In another tell how each part helps people hear. In the third tell how the shape or structure of each part of the ear helps people hear.

QUICK LAB

Sound Carriers

HYPOTHESIZE Can sound travel through solids? Liquids? Write a hypothesis in your *Science Journal*.

MATERIALS
- sealable pint-sized plastic food bag filled with water
- wind-up clock
- wooden table or desk
- *Science Journal*

PROCEDURES

1. **OBSERVE** Put the clock on the wooden table. Put your ear against the table. Listen to the ticking. Lift your head. How well can you hear the ticking now? Record your observation in your *Science Journal*.

2. **USE VARIABLES** Hold the water-filled bag against your ear. Hold the clock against the bag. How well can you hear the ticking? Move your ear away from the bag. How well can you hear the ticking?

CONCLUDE AND APPLY

1. **DRAW CONCLUSIONS** Rate wood, air, and water in order from best sound carrier to worst.

2. **EXPERIMENT** How would you test other materials, like sand?

What Else Can Sound Go Through?

When you hear sounds, what is usually around you? Air! You can hear sounds in the air. When sound waves reach your ear, they make parts inside the ear vibrate. Since air is a mixture of gases, you may conclude that sound can travel through gases. It travels as sound waves.

Solids

Can sound also travel through solids and liquids? You can tell that sound travels through solids just by putting your ear onto a tabletop. If someone taps the table at the other end, you can hear the tapping louder than if you lift your head away from the table.

Liquids

If you do any underwater swimming, you probably can tell that you can hear sounds in water. You can hear someone calling you from above the surface. You can also hear sounds in the water around you.

Think about how you can hear when your head is underwater.

Is All Matter Alike?

Sound waves can travel through all forms of matter. In fact sound waves depend on matter in order to travel away from the vibrating object that produces them. Without matter, sound waves could not travel.

Sound waves travel through any substance because the molecules collide and then spread apart. Sound waves travel faster through some substances than through others. How fast they travel depends on

- how close the molecules of the substance are to each other
- how easily the molecules can collide with each other

Can you hear sounds in a vacuum? A vacuum is a place where there is no matter. Outer space is nearly a vacuum. If an astronaut is floating near a space vehicle, there is almost no matter around the astronaut. If the astronaut claps his hands, will there be a sound? No. There is no matter—no air, for example—to carry the vibration of the clap anywhere.

A dolphin communicates underwater by making a series of whistles and clicks. A dolphin does not have outer ears to collect sound waves. Instead, sounds travel through the dolphin's jaw or the sides of its head to its inner ears.

Brain Power

What if you put a ticking clock inside a box and you pumped all the air out of the box? The clock is hanging on a thin string attached to the inside top of the box so that it is not touching the walls of the box. Would you hear the clock ticking?

What Causes Hearing Loss?

Some people cannot hear very well. Loud and clear sounds are soft or muffled, and soft sounds cannot be heard at all. This is known as deafness. People who are totally deaf cannot hear any sounds.

Slight deafness can happen if the tube in the outer ear gets blocked with wax. A doctor can easily clear the tube, and hearing will return to normal. A blow on the ear or a very loud sound can permanently damage the eardrum and ear bones, and diseases may affect parts of the middle ear or inner ear, and cause deafness.

What Is Sign Language?

Sign language is a way for the deaf and hearing impaired to communicate using their hands. This is also a way for people with normal hearing to communicate with the deaf and hearing impaired. Sign language consists of signs for many words and an alphabet to "finger spell" others. How would you finger spell your name?

What is her favorite animal? Can you read the word she is signing?

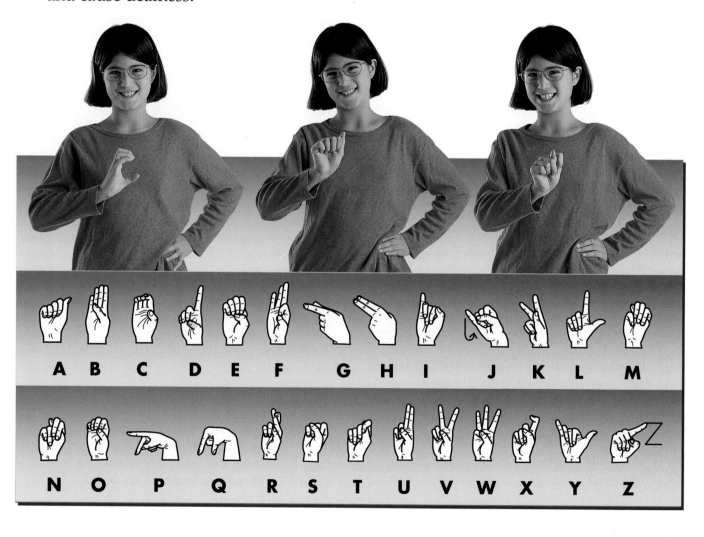

202

How Can Technology Help?

Placing a hearing aid in the outer ear makes sounds louder and may help to overcome deafness. In serious cases an operation may provide a cure. New technology, combined with our knowledge of how we hear, has also led to many other devices that assist deaf people in their daily lives.

Closed-captioned television enables deaf people to watch television and know what is being said. Flashing lights connected to alarm systems and alarm clocks that vibrate the bed are other aids. Computers and electronic devices that can code sounds and words help them communicate to the world.

A hearing aid fits comfortably into the ear. It works like an electronic earphone to make sounds louder.

Sounds are an important part of your life. Sounds bring enjoyment. You use sounds to share information. You learn by listening and speaking with others. Information includes warnings. Think about how important sounds are during a fire drill or when you hear a car horn from an approaching car.

REVIEW

1. What is needed to make a sound?

2. What can sounds travel through?

3. How does sign language help a person who cannot hear communicate?

4. **COMPARE AND CONTRAST** Pick any two musical instruments. How do they make sounds?

5. **CRITICAL THINKING** *Analyze* How are humans structured to hear sounds from their surroundings? Why is it important for humans to do so?

WHY IT MATTERS **THINK ABOUT IT**
Sounds help us communicate, learn, and have fun. What are some sounds that are important to you?

WHY IT MATTERS **WRITE ABOUT IT**
Why are the sounds you chose important to you? What are the things that make these sounds?

READING SKILL
Write a paragraph to describe any causes and effects you read about in this lesson.

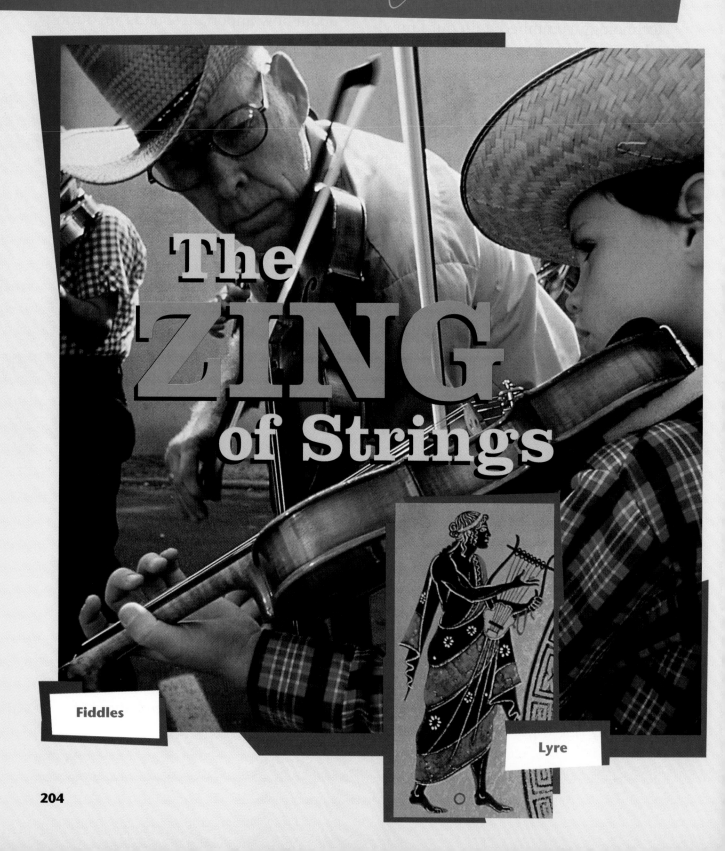

The ZING of Strings

Fiddles

Lyre

Zither

F or thousands of years, humans have plucked, hammered, rubbed, and strummed strings.

Prehistoric Times Prehistoric hunters produced sounds by plucking bowstrings.

4000 B.C. Harps Ancient harps have been found in Egyptian tombs. Harpists pluck strings held in a partly hollow frame, which makes sounds louder.

2500 B.C. Lutes Babylonians were the first to play the lute by pressing strings stretched over a hollow box.

1200–200 B.C. Zithers Zither strings are hit with a soft hammer, or plucked. Some zithers have more than 30 strings. Others can be held in one hand.

1000–400 B.C. Lyres The word *lyric* comes from the harplike lyre, the ancient Greeks' favorite instrument.

A.D. 900–1000 Fiddles The fiddle developed in Europe during the Middle Ages. Fiddlers press and tighten the strings as they rub the bow over them.

1000–1700 Violin Family The violin family includes the progressively larger violin, viola, cello, and double bass. All are played with a bow.

1500s Guitars Guitars are descended from lutes. Unchanged for centuries, the guitar was electrified in the 1930s.

1700–1800 Banjos The banjo was invented by Africans in North America. The base is made of stiff paper stretched over a metal hoop. The wire strings are plucked.

Discussion
Starter

1 What are some of the ways stringed instruments can be played?

2 How would you update this time line?

*inter*NET **CONNECTION** To learn more about stringed instruments, visit *www.mhschool.com/science* and enter the keyword **STRINGS.**

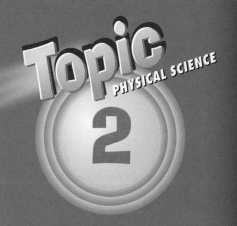
WHY IT MATTERS

Some sounds are higher or louder than others.

SCIENCE WORDS

pitch how high or low a sound is

frequency the number of times an object vibrates per second

hertz a unit for measuring frequency

decibel a unit for measuring loudness

High and Low, Loud and Soft

How have people made music since ancient times? Shepherds have used instruments like this simple one for centuries. They use the instruments to call their flocks or keep them quiet.

How can such a simple instrument be used to communicate with animals? The instrument must be made to make different sounds. It has to make high and low sounds. How can the player use it to make loud and soft sounds?

EXPLORE

HYPOTHESIZE Each musical instrument has a sound all its own. As you play an instrument, you make the sound change. What causes the sound to change? Write a hypothesis in your *Science Journal.* Test it by building a homemade instrument from simple items like straws.

EXPLORE ACTIVITY

Design Your Own Experiment

HOW CAN YOU CHANGE A SOUND?

PROCEDURES

1. **PREDICT** Work in pairs to make a homemade instrument. Try straws for starters. Blow over one end of a straw. Will there be a difference if you seal the other end with tape? Write a prediction in your *Science Journal*.

2. **OBSERVE** Tape one end and blow over the open end. Describe what you hear.

3. **CLASSIFY** Repeat with different lengths cut from a straw. Try at least four lengths. How are the sounds different? Arrange the straws in order to hear the difference.

4. **EXPERIMENT** Flatten one end of a straw. Cut the end to a point. Wet it. With your lips stretched across your teeth, blow into that end of the straw. Try to make different sounds with the straw.

CONCLUDE AND APPLY

1. **COMPARE AND CONTRAST** Why do you think the sounds changed when you cut different lengths of straw? Hint: What is inside the straw—even if it looks empty?

2. **REPRODUCE RESULTS** Write a description of your instruments for a partner to build them exactly as you did. Include measurements taken with a ruler.

GOING FURTHER: Problem Solving

3. **EXPERIMENT** Try other materials to make other instruments. Try such things as bottles with water, craft sticks, and so forth. Tell what causes the sound to change in each case.

MATERIALS
- 12 plastic drinking straws
- scissors
- metric ruler
- masking tape
- *Science Journal*

STEP 3

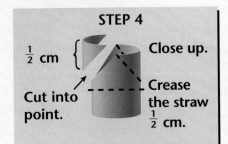

STEP 4

$\frac{1}{2}$ cm {

Cut into point.

Close up.

Crease the straw $\frac{1}{2}$ cm.

207

How Can You Change a Sound?

Pitch

The Explore Activity showed that some sounds are "higher" than others. *High* and *low* are words that describe the **pitch** of a sound. In the sixth century B.C., the Greek mathematician Pythagoras (pi thag′ər əs) observed that a longer string produces a sound with a lower pitch than a shorter string.

Changes in Pitch

What can you do to a rubber band to make different sounds? If you pluck a rubber band to make sounds, you can change the pitch by shortening the rubber band. You make it shorter by pressing a thumb over part of it so less of it vibrates. A shorter string vibrates faster and produces a higher pitch.

A second way you can change the pitch is to stretch the rubber band tighter. This causes the rubber band to vibrate faster and, therefore, to produce a higher-pitched sound.

The pitch of a vibrating string is also related to its thickness. Compare the strings of this guitar.

Pitch of Voices

Did you know that the length and thickness of your vocal cords, and how you tighten or relax them, affects the pitch of your voice?

Singers can sing a range from high to lower notes by tightening and relaxing their vocal cords. Men usually have longer and thicker vocal cords than women, so men's voices tend to be lower pitched than women's voices.

Tuning pegs **are turned to tighten or loosen the strings.**

When you press the frets, you change the length of the vibrating portions of the strings.

A thicker string vibrates slower and produces a lower-pitched sound than a thinner string.

A thinner string vibrates faster and produces a higher-pitched sound than a thicker string.

What Causes Pitch?

Sound Waves

You can't see sound waves, but scientists study them with an oscilloscope. This device makes a "picture" of sound waves. An oscilloscope allows you to compare the waves of sounds that have different pitches.

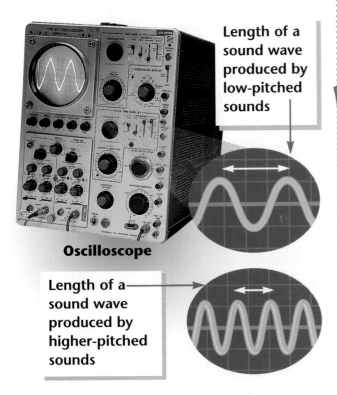

Length of a sound wave produced by low-pitched sounds

Oscilloscope

Length of a sound wave produced by higher-pitched sounds

Frequency

The higher the pitch, the more "squeezed together" the waves are. Higher-pitched waves have a greater **frequency**. Frequency is the number of times an object vibrates per second.

Frequency describes vibrations and sound waves. Pitch describes how your brain interprets a sound. A flute has a high pitch. A bass guitar has a low pitch. Frequency and pitch are related: the higher the frequency, the higher the pitch; the lower the frequency, the lower the pitch.

Frequency is measured in units called **hertz**. A frequency of one vibration per second is one hertz (Hz). *Hertz* comes from the name of Heinrich Hertz (1857–1894), a German physicist who studied sound and radio waves.

Humans hear from about 20 Hz to about 20,000 Hz. Sounds with a frequency higher than 20,000 Hz are *ultrasonic*—too high to be heard by humans, but not by some animals.

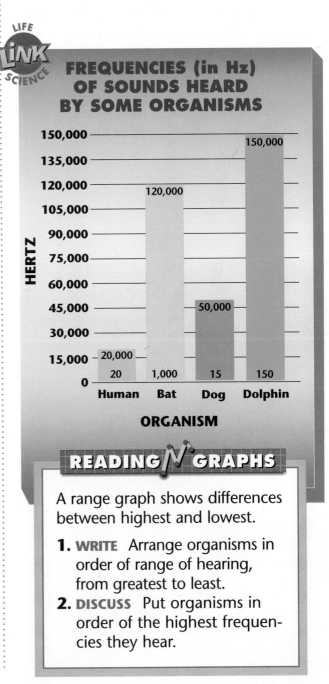

FREQUENCIES (in Hz) OF SOUNDS HEARD BY SOME ORGANISMS

Organism	Hertz (low)	Hertz (high)
Human	20	20,000
Bat	1,000	120,000
Dog	15	50,000
Dolphin	150	150,000

ORGANISM

READING GRAPHS

A range graph shows differences between highest and lowest.

1. **WRITE** Arrange organisms in order of range of hearing, from greatest to least.
2. **DISCUSS** Put organisms in order of the highest frequencies they hear.

209

What Makes Sounds Loud?

Energy of Sound Waves

A sound wave makes the molecules of gases in air vibrate. The back-and-forth distance they vibrate is based on how much energy the sound wave carries. The more the energy, the greater the distance. The more the energy, the greater the height of the wave as it appears on an oscilloscope. Which of these waves is carrying more energy?

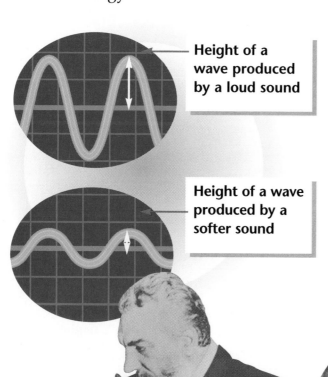

Height of a wave produced by a loud sound

Height of a wave produced by a softer sound

What is the difference between a yell and a whisper? How loud or how soft a sound is depends on the amount of energy in a sound wave. To make a louder sound with a rubber band, pluck it harder. A loud sound has more energy than a soft sound and produces a taller wave on an oscilloscope.

You can also make a sound louder by increasing the amount of surface that vibrates. For example, when a cup is attached to a rubber band, the cup and rubber band vibrate together. Together they make a louder sound than just a rubber band alone.

Loudness

Loudness is measured in units called **decibels** (dB) with an instrument called a decibel meter. On the decibel scale, a sound that measures 50 dB is 10 times louder than one that measures 40 dB. The same 50-dB sound is 100 times louder than a 30-dB sound—that is, 10×10 times louder. The 50-dB sound is 1,000 times louder than a 20-dB sound—$10 \times 10 \times 10$ times louder.

HISTORY LINK

Today's telephones date back to Alexander Graham Bell, who invented the telephone in 1875.

Skill: Communicating

MAKING TABLES AND GRAPHS

In this activity you will interpret data, classify sounds, and create your own table. Tables are helpful tools that organize information. The table shown gives the loudness of some common sounds in decibels (dB). Sounds below 30 dB can barely be heard. Quiet sounds are between 30 dB and 50 dB. Moderate sounds begin at 50 dB. At 70 dB, sounds are considered noisy. At 110 dB and above, sounds are unbearable.

MATERIALS
- *Science Journal*

PROCEDURES

1. **CLASSIFY** Determine which sounds are audible (can barely be heard), quiet, moderate, noisy, or unbearable.

2. **COMMUNICATE: MAKE A TABLE** Make your own table to show how you classified the sounds.

3. **COMMUNICATE: MAKE A GRAPH** Make a data table to record how many quiet, moderate, noisy, or unbearable sounds you hear in one hour. Make a graph to show your results. "Number" is the vertical axis. "Kind of Sound" is the horizontal axis.

CONCLUDE AND APPLY

1. **COMPARE AND CONTRAST** How much louder is a soft radio than your house at night? A classroom than a house at night?

2. **COMPARE AND CONTRAST** How much softer is normal conversation than thunder?

3. **COMMUNICATE** Make a chart listing loud sounds in the environment. What can you do to protect your ears from harm done by each loud noise?

Loudness of Some Sounds

Sound	Loudness (in decibels)
Hearing limit	0
Rustling leaves	10
Whisper	20
Nighttime noises in house	30
Soft radio	40
Classroom/office	50
Normal conversation	60
Inside car on highway	70
Busy city street	80
Subway	90
Siren (30 meters away)	100
Thunder	110
Pain threshold	**120**
Loud indoor rock concert	120
Jet plane (30 meters away)	140

What Is a Musical Scale?

Have you ever sung the musical scale *do-re-mi-fa-so-la-ti-do*? It is a simple, eight-note musical scale. The difference between the *do* at the bottom of the scale and the *do* at the top of the scale is called an octave. The word *octave* is based on the Latin word that means "eight."

C Major Scale

The diagram below shows the *do-re-mi* scale known in music as the C Major scale. The notes of the scale are named with the letters of the alphabet.

Piano Keys

On a piano eight white keys from C to C are in one octave of the C Major scale. When you tap the white key of *do* (middle C), you are making a string inside the piano vibrate at 262 Hz. A black key produces a sound with a frequency halfway between the surrounding white keys. What is the frequency of the black key between middle C and D at 294 Hz?

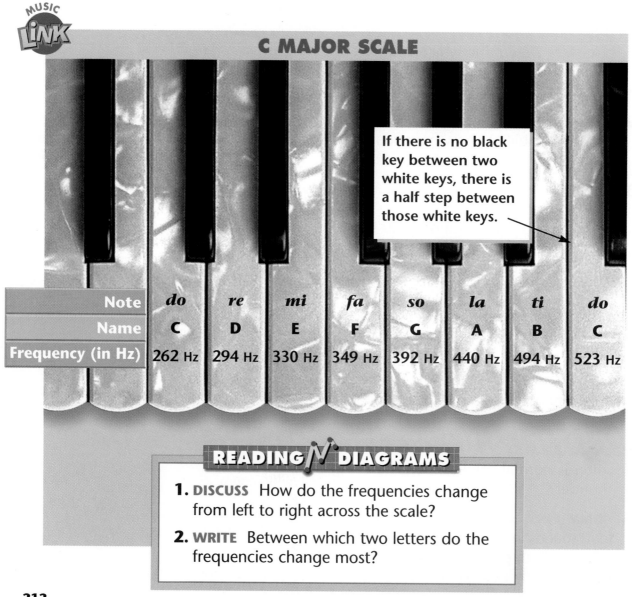

MUSIC LINK

C MAJOR SCALE

If there is no black key between two white keys, there is a half step between those white keys.

Note	*do*	*re*	*mi*	*fa*	*so*	*la*	*ti*	*do*
Name	C	D	E	F	G	A	B	C
Frequency (in Hz)	262 Hz	294 Hz	330 Hz	349 Hz	392 Hz	440 Hz	494 Hz	523 Hz

READING /\/ DIAGRAMS

1. **DISCUSS** How do the frequencies change from left to right across the scale?

2. **WRITE** Between which two letters do the frequencies change most?

Does All Music Sound the Same?

If you start with C, you hit 12 keys, or steps, to get to the note before the next C. That means there are 12 steps to this scale.

In America and Europe, the musical scale has eight notes and 12 steps between octaves. However, the music of some other cultures has a different number of steps between octaves. That is, their scale may have a different number of notes between the bottom of the scale and the top. For example, the Arab scale has 17 steps to our octave. In India the scale has 22 steps! This is one reason that some music may sound quite different from what you are used to hearing.

Music and Noise

Both music and noise are collections of sounds, but in a work of music, the sounds are arranged to make a pattern that can include rhythm, melody, and harmony. On the other hand, noise is just a jumble of sounds that don't make a pattern and haven't been arranged by anyone for others to enjoy. Compare the pleasure of listening to a march played by the school band with the screech of a subway, trolley, or train.

Some noises can be quite pleasing—such as the chirping of crickets on an overnight camping trip—but more often we think of noise as something unpleasant that makes us wince and put our fingers in our ears.

Brain Power

How were the instruments in this photograph built to make many different sounds?

How Is Sound Recorded?

What if there were no favorite recordings of music? Fortunately, Thomas Alva Edison first recorded sound back in 1877. Today sound is recorded using these steps.

Step 1: Change Sound into Electric Current

A microphone includes a diaphragm, a coil of fine wire, and a magnet. When you sing, speak, or play music into the microphone, sound waves make the diaphragm vibrate. The pitch of the sound determines how fast the diaphragm vibrates. The loudness of the sound determines how far the diaphragm moves with each vibration.

The vibration of the diaphragm makes the coil of wire vibrate near the magnet. Each vibration produces a tiny current of electricity. The coil sends this electric pattern to an amplifier.

Let's say a musical note has a frequency of 700 vibrations per second. When that note reaches the microphone, the microphone sends 700 bursts of electricity per second to the amplifier. Louder notes have more electricity in each burst. In this way the microphone translates the frequency and loudness of the sound wave into an electric current.

Step 2: Make the Current Stronger

The tiny pulses of electricity coming from the coil are very weak. The amplifier makes them up to 50,000 times stronger.

Step 3: Change Current to Magnetic Pattern

Blank tapes are coated with scrambled magnetic particles. During recording the electric current from the amplifier arranges the particles on the tape into a pattern—a "code" for the sounds.

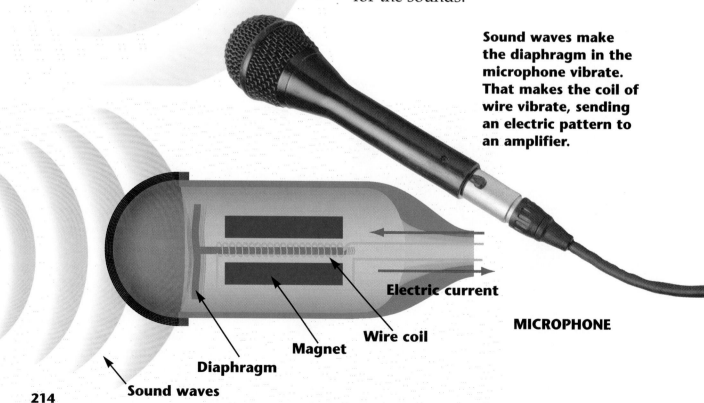

Sound waves make the diaphragm in the microphone vibrate. That makes the coil of wire vibrate, sending an electric pattern to an amplifier.

Electric current

MICROPHONE

Wire coil

Magnet

Diaphragm

Sound waves

What Happens when You Play a Recording?

When you push "play," the process reverses. The magnetic particles on the tape create a current in the coil. This current vibrates a stiff paper cone in the speaker. This creates the sound waves you hear.

Compact discs do not store sound in magnetic patterns. Instead a computer in CD-recording equipment translates the sound waves into a code. The code is a combination of 1s and 0s.

Then a laser beam uses the code to cut millions of tiny pits into a blank compact disc. About 85,000 pits cover only 1 inch of the disc.

When you play a CD, a laser beam shines on it. The flat parts of the CD reflect light back to a small computer. The computer changes the pattern of these reflections back into sound.

Next time you strum a guitar, pound a drum, or sing a tune, keep in mind what you learned in this topic. The different musical sounds you make are different pitches. They are higher or lower than each other. You can play an instrument to make sounds louder or softer. You sing louder when you take a deeper breath and breathe out harder. You use loudness and pitch to express different emotions, too.

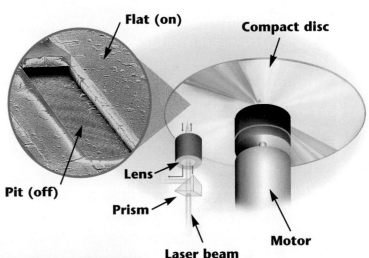

Flat (on)

Compact disc

Pit (off)

Lens

Prism

Laser beam

Motor

REVIEW

1. On a stringed instrument, why are some sounds higher than others?

2. How is pitch related to frequency?

3. How can sounds be changed into an electric current?

4. COMMUNICATE How is loudness measured? How would you set up a table showing the loudness of different sounds?

5. CRITICAL THINKING *Analyze* Why do the notes of a musical instrument have different sounds?

WHY IT MATTERS THINK ABOUT IT
Think about your favorite instruments and the sounds they make.

WHY IT MATTERS WRITE ABOUT IT
Describe some favorite instruments. How are they built to make different pitches? What do you have to do to make sounds louder or softer?

Hit That Note!

Ever think of yourself as a musician? Well you are one. When you sing you play an instrument—your voice!

Musical instruments vary in the pitches, or tones, they can produce. It all depends on the frequencies of vibrating parts. Singers produce different tones, too.

You've probably noticed differences in the sounds of some of your favorite singers. The tones they use depend on the vibrations of their vocal cords. Thicker, longer cords vibrate more slowly and have lower tones. Ever wonder why your voice sounds lower when you have a sore throat? It's because your vocal cords are swollen, so they vibrate more slowly!

Here are pitch categories for most human singing voices. Try classifying some of your favorite singers.

	FEMALE	MALE
High pitch	Soprano	Tenor
Medium pitch	Mezzo-soprano	Baritone
Low pitch	Alto (contralto)	Bass

A baritone usually can't hit the high notes a tenor can because of the size and shape of his vocal cords. Likewise a tenor usually can't hit the low notes a baritone can.

When composers write music, they think about the notes that each instrument and voice can produce.

216

Music and Math Link

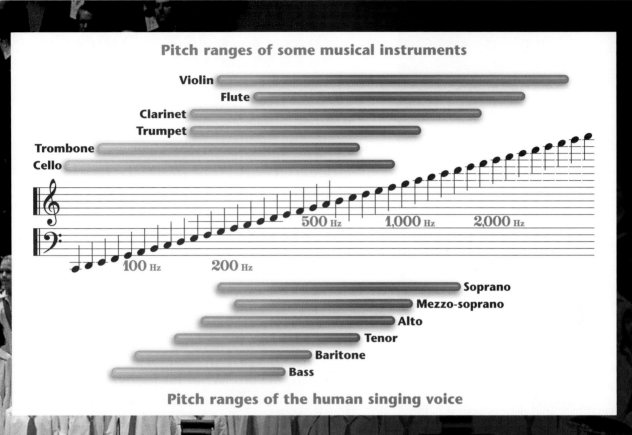

Pitch ranges of some musical instruments

Violin
Flute
Clarinet
Trumpet
Trombone
Cello

500 Hz   1,000 Hz   2,000 Hz

100 Hz   200 Hz

Soprano
Mezzo-soprano
Alto
Tenor
Baritone
Bass

Pitch ranges of the human singing voice

This diagram shows the lowest to the highest notes for each instrument and singing voice. The difference between the highest and lowest is called a range.

DISCUSSION STARTER

1. Which instrument shown can reach the highest pitch? About what frequency is that?

2. Which instrument has the greatest range? The smallest range?

Sounds and Surfaces

What makes a car race at a racetrack so exciting? Is it the speed, the swerves? Is it the roar of the crowd? What would the race be like if it were totally quiet? Would it still be as exciting?

What makes the race so noisy? Describe the racetrack from the photograph. How does the way the racetrack is built contribute to the loud sounds?

WHY IT MATTERS

Sounds can bounce when they hit a surface.

SCIENCE WORDS

reflection the bouncing of a sound wave off a surface

absorption the disappearance of a sound wave into a surface

echo a reflected sound wave

echolocation the finding of an object by using reflected sound

Doppler effect the change in frequency (and pitch) as a source of sound moves toward or away from you

quality the difference you hear in two sounds of the same loudness and pitch

fundamental frequency the lowest frequency at which an object vibrates

overtone one of a series of pitches that blend to give a sound its quality

EXPLORE

HYPOTHESIZE What happens when sound "hits" a surface? Does the kind of surface make a difference? Write a hypothesis in your *Science Journal.* Test your ideas.

EXPLORE ACTIVITY

Investigate if Sounds Bounce

Find out the effect different kinds of materials have on sound.

PROCEDURES

1. Collect a variety of hard, smooth materials and soft, textured materials. Place one of the objects on a table. Set up your tubes in a V-shaped pattern on a table, as shown. The V should meet at the object you are testing. Record the name of the object in your *Science Journal.*

2. **OBSERVE/COMPARE** Place a sound maker (clicker or timer) at one end of the V. Listen for ticking at the other end of the V. Rank the loudness of the ticking on a scale of 1 (lowest) to 5 (highest). Record the number.

3. **EXPERIMENT** Repeat steps 1 and 2 with the different materials you collected.

CONCLUDE AND APPLY

1. **CLASSIFY** What kinds of materials are the best reflectors—hard, smooth materials or soft, textured materials? What kinds of materials are the best absorbers?

2. **MAKE A MODEL** Draw a diagram of the path of sound from the sound maker to your ear. On your diagram mark the point in the path where the sound wave bounced.

GOING FURTHER: Apply

3. **DRAW CONCLUSIONS** Theaters often have soft velvet curtains, thick carpets, and cushioned seats. How do you think these objects affect the sound in a theater?

MATERIALS

- 2 long cardboard tubes (can be taped, rolled-up newspapers)
- sound maker, such as a clicker or timer
- hard and soft test materials, such as book, wood block, cloth, metal sheet, sponge, towel
- *Science Journal*

Do Sounds Bounce?

You may have guessed that a sound hitting a towel will sound different from the same sound hitting a metal sheet. Why? A sound wave does not act the same way when it hits a hard, smooth surface as when it hits a soft, textured surface.

The pictures below show what happens when sound waves come into contact with a surface. When a sound wave hits a surface, some of its energy bounces off the surface. The bouncing of a sound wave off a surface is called **reflection**. But not all of the sound wave reflects off the surface. Some of the wave's energy enters the surface and disappears. The disappearance of a sound wave into a surface is called **absorption**.

When a sound wave is absorbed, its energy is changed into heat energy. Sometimes not all of the energy that enters a surface is absorbed. Part of the energy of the sound wave may also travel through a surface and come out the other side—when you hear a sound through a wall.

How much of the sound wave's energy is reflected or absorbed depends on the kind of material of the surface. When sound waves hit a hard, smooth surface such as the wall around the racetrack, much of the sound wave's energy is reflected. But when sound waves hit a soft, textured surface such as the towel in the Explore Activity, less of the sound wave's energy is reflected and more is absorbed.

Compare (1) the crack of the bat when the ball and bat meet with (2) the sound when the ball hits the glove.

CRACK

THUD

This group is dressed in a style common in the mid- to late 1800s. The billowy gowns and long coats had an effect on sound in a closed space.

Can You Solve the Mystery?

Designing concert halls has always been a tricky business. To get the "right" sound, engineers try to get a good balance of reflection and absorption. Too much reflection results in an empty, hollow sound. Too much absorption deadens the music.

Mystery

These ideas were put to the test in the London Music Hall. When it was built in 1871, the hall was considered to be one of the great places in the world to hear music. By the 1930s listeners complained that the music did not sound good anymore. Sound engineers were baffled. Nothing in the concert hall had changed since it was built, over 60 years earlier.

Solution

Finally, an explanation was found. The concert hall may have stayed the same. But its audience had changed. Most importantly, women were no longer wearing the billowing, layered, sound-absorbing gowns that had been popular earlier. The new styles were shorter and simpler, and didn't absorb sound as well. Overall they changed the balance of reflection and absorption of sound in the room.

221

QUICK LAB

Clap! Clap!

HYPOTHESIZE Can you cause a clear time lag between a sound and its echo? Write a hypothesis in your *Science Journal.*

MATERIALS
- meterstick
- *Science Journal*

PROCEDURES

1. **OBSERVE** Stand about 8 meters away from a large wall, such as the side of your school building. Make sure there is plenty of open space between you and the wall. Clap your hands, and listen for an echo. Notice how much time there is between your clap and the echo.

2. **OBSERVE** Move closer to the wall, and clap again. Listen for an echo.

3. **REPEAT** Try this several times.

CONCLUDE AND APPLY

1. **OBSERVE** As you got closer to the wall, how did the time between the clap and the echo change? Did you always hear an echo? Explain.

2. **EXPERIMENT** Repeat at different distances. What happens?

What Is an Echo?

Have you ever made an echo? When you yell "hello!" your vocal cords make sound waves that travel away from you in all directions. If the sound wave hits a surface, some of the sound wave's energy will reflect off the surface and travel back to you. A reflected sound wave is called an **echo**. If the echo is strong enough, you will hear yourself yelling "hello!" after you said it! If there is more than one reflecting surface near you, you may hear "hello!" several more times.

If you sing in the shower, you may notice how rich your voice sounds. The hard, smooth walls of the bathroom are often great for making echoes. The echoes reflect back and forth off the walls many times. They make your voice sound rich and mellow, as if background singers were repeating each note you sing.

You hear sound as soon as you make it. After it reaches a reflecting surface, you hear the echo when the waves return.

How Fast Is Sound?

It takes almost no time for an echo to bounce back to you after you yell "hello!" Sound waves travel fast. In air at room temperature (20°C), sound waves travel 343 meters per second, faster than most jet planes. In general, sound waves have a greater speed in a solid than in a liquid, and a greater speed in a liquid than in a gas.

The speed of sound waves depends largely on the molecules of the material—on how tightly packed molecules are and how easily they spread apart and move together. Temperature affects the speed of sound. In general, temperature affects the speed of sound more in gases than in liquids and solids.

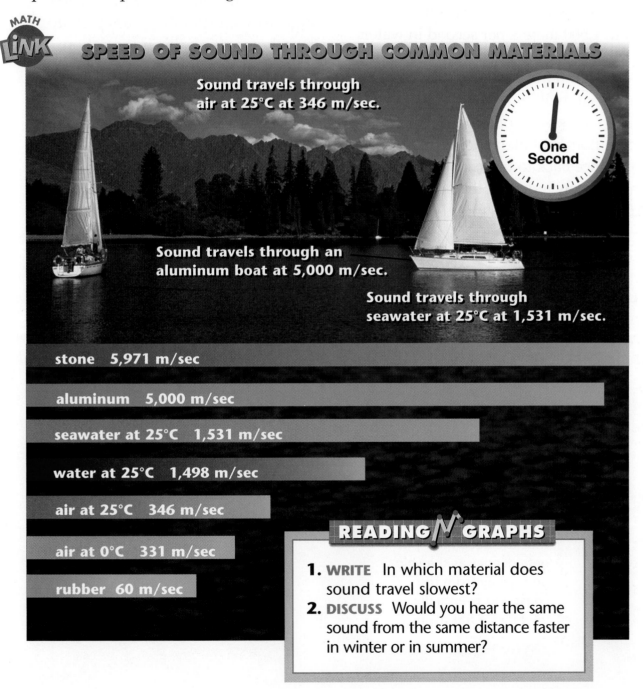

MATH LINK

SPEED OF SOUND THROUGH COMMON MATERIALS

Sound travels through air at 25°C at 346 m/sec.

One Second

Sound travels through an aluminum boat at 5,000 m/sec.

Sound travels through seawater at 25°C at 1,531 m/sec.

stone   5,971 m/sec

aluminum   5,000 m/sec

seawater at 25°C   1,531 m/sec

water at 25°C   1,498 m/sec

air at 25°C   346 m/sec

air at 0°C   331 m/sec

rubber   60 m/sec

READING GRAPHS

1. **WRITE** In which material does sound travel slowest?
2. **DISCUSS** Would you hear the same sound from the same distance faster in winter or in summer?

What Can Echoes Do?

Technology

Sonar, or *so*und *na*vigation and *r*anging, uses sound waves to detect objects far away. A sonar technician sends out sound waves and then times how long those sound waves take to bounce off distant objects and return.

What if a sonar technician on a ship sends out a sound wave toward the ocean bottom? Sound waves travel about 1,500 meters per second in water.

What if the sound wave takes two seconds to return to the ship? The technician will know that the sound wave took one second to reach the ocean floor and then one second more to bounce back to the surface. He or she will conclude that the ocean is 1,500 meters deep.

Animals

Many animals find things around them with a form of sonar called **echolocation**. Whales and dolphins bounce sound waves off objects to find out how far away they are.

Bats are able to live in dark caves because they use a form of echolocation rather than sight to navigate. Bats send out high-pitched squeals and clicks into the air at their prey. Their large, forward-pointing ears pick up the echoes. Using this information, bats can close in on their prey.

Brain Power

If the sound wave takes four seconds to return, how deep is the ocean at that point? How deep is the ocean at a point where it takes three seconds for the sound wave to return?

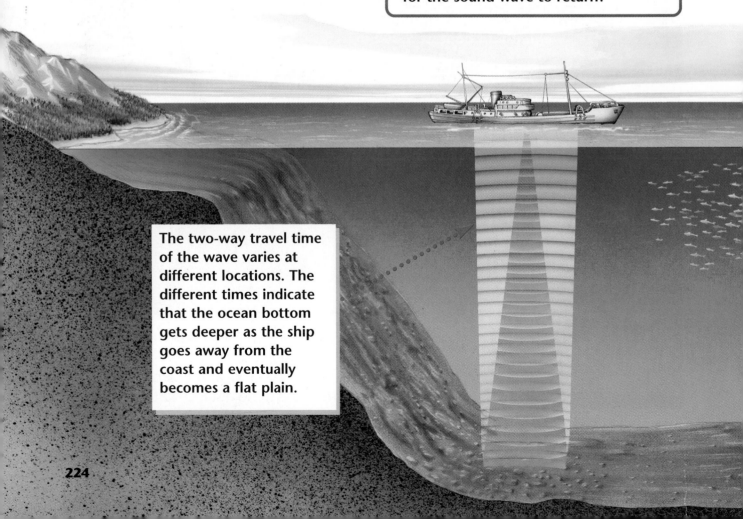

The two-way travel time of the wave varies at different locations. The different times indicate that the ocean bottom gets deeper as the ship goes away from the coast and eventually becomes a flat plain.

How Do Moving Sounds Change?

An echo is a copy of the original sound. Both the original sound and the echo sound alike—they have the same pitch. However, have you ever heard a police car siren blaring as the police car sped past you? Did you notice anything special about the sound?

If you listened carefully, you may have noticed that the pitch of the siren changed as the police car sped by. As the police car came toward you, the siren was higher in pitch. As it sped away from you, the siren was lower in pitch.

Approaching Sound

As the blaring siren approaches, its sound waves crowd together. There are more sound waves reaching your ear each second than there would be if the police car were standing still. The frequency of the sound increases. The pitch of the siren moving toward you is higher.

1

2

Sound waves from the moving police car bunch together (1) as the car approaches the listener. They spread apart (2) as the police car moves away from the listener.

Departing Sound

As the siren moves away from you, its sound waves spread apart. There are fewer sound waves reaching your ear each second than there would be if the police car were standing still. The frequency of the sound decreases. The pitch of the siren moving away from you is lower.

Change of Frequency

This change in frequency (and pitch) as a source of sound moves toward or away from you is known as the **Doppler effect**. It is named for the 19th century Austrian scientist Christian Johann Doppler, who first described it.

Many radar (radio detection and ranging) devices use the effect to find the speed of objects. Patrol cars detect changes in frequency as a way of detecting speeding vehicles.

Whales use a form of sonar to locate things in their environment.

What's the Difference?

How can you tell the difference in voices? What if two people sing the same note—the same pitch—at the same loudness? You can still hear a difference between the two voices. The **quality** of a sound is what makes it different from another sound of the same loudness and pitch. Quality makes a sound unique.

The quality of a sound depends on the vibrations that produce the sound. When a string vibrates, for example, it vibrates at more than one frequency at a time. The whole string vibrates at the **fundamental frequency**, the lowest frequency at which it vibrates.

At the same time, sections of the string are vibrating at higher frequencies, called **overtones**. Each overtone is a different pitch. It is the blend of the fundamental frequency and the overtones produced that gives each sound its own quality.

All sounds—whether it's a voice or a musical instrument, whether produced by a vibrating string or column of air—are different in the same way. Each sound has its own blend of fundamental frequency and overtones that allows you to identify it.

MUSIC
LINK

If these instruments play the same note at the same loudness, the sound waves differ because the blend of overtones differs.

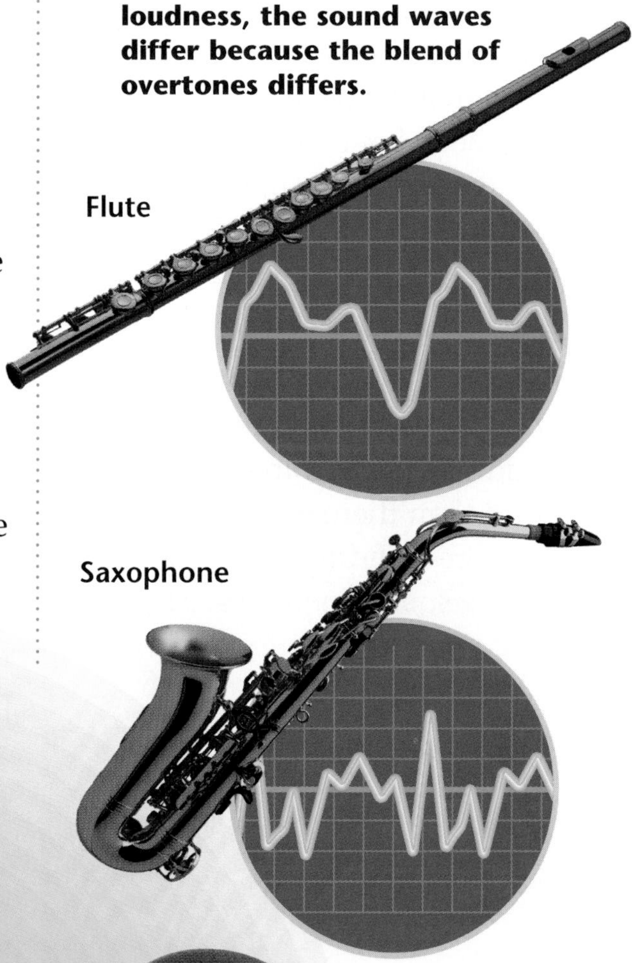

Flute

Saxophone

Trumpet

What Happens on the Road?

A car suspension tends to vibrate naturally at a fundamental frequency. If the car runs over road bumps at a frequency equal to the fundamental frequency of the suspension, then the car may start to vibrate. In order to avoid this problem, car engineers "tune" the car's suspension to make sure its fundamental frequency does not equal the bump frequency the car is likely to meet.

The suspension in Monster Cars allows them to climb over obstacles.

WHY IT MATTERS

When a sound wave hits a surface, its energy can be reflected or absorbed. Different kinds of surfaces are better for reflecting or absorbing.

Knowing how different materials reflect and absorb sound waves can be helpful at school or home. Your school library probably has stacks of books and other sound-absorbing materials. They help keep the library quiet so you can read and study. Whether you are a student deciding what furniture to put in a room to make it quiet or an architect deciding how to design a building, you must know how different materials affect sound waves.

REVIEW

1. What is an echo? What is necessary in order to hear an echo?

2. How can sound be used to find the depth of the ocean?

3. Why does the same note played on two different instruments at about the same loudness sound different?

4. **CLASSIFY** What kinds of materials reflect sound best? What kinds of materials absorb sound best?

5. **CRITICAL THINKING** *Synthesize* Does sound travel with the same speed through all materials? Write a paragraph explaining your answer.

WHY IT MATTERS THINK ABOUT IT
What kinds of materials can make a room louder by reflecting sounds or quieter by absorbing sounds?

WHY IT MATTERS WRITE ABOUT IT
Describe a room at school. Then explain how you might change the room to reflect sounds better. Or explain how you might change it to absorb sounds better.

The Sounds of Earthquakes

The ground begins vibrating wildly. Rising from Earth are seismic (sīz'mik) waves—they're like huge sound waves. It's an earthquake!

A seismograph has a pen held delicately against a rolling drum with graph paper on it. The pen records the seismic waves.

As soon as an earthquake begins, seismic waves travel out in all directions from the focus—where the quake began. They also travel inside Earth. Scientists used seismic waves to piece together a model of the inside of Earth.

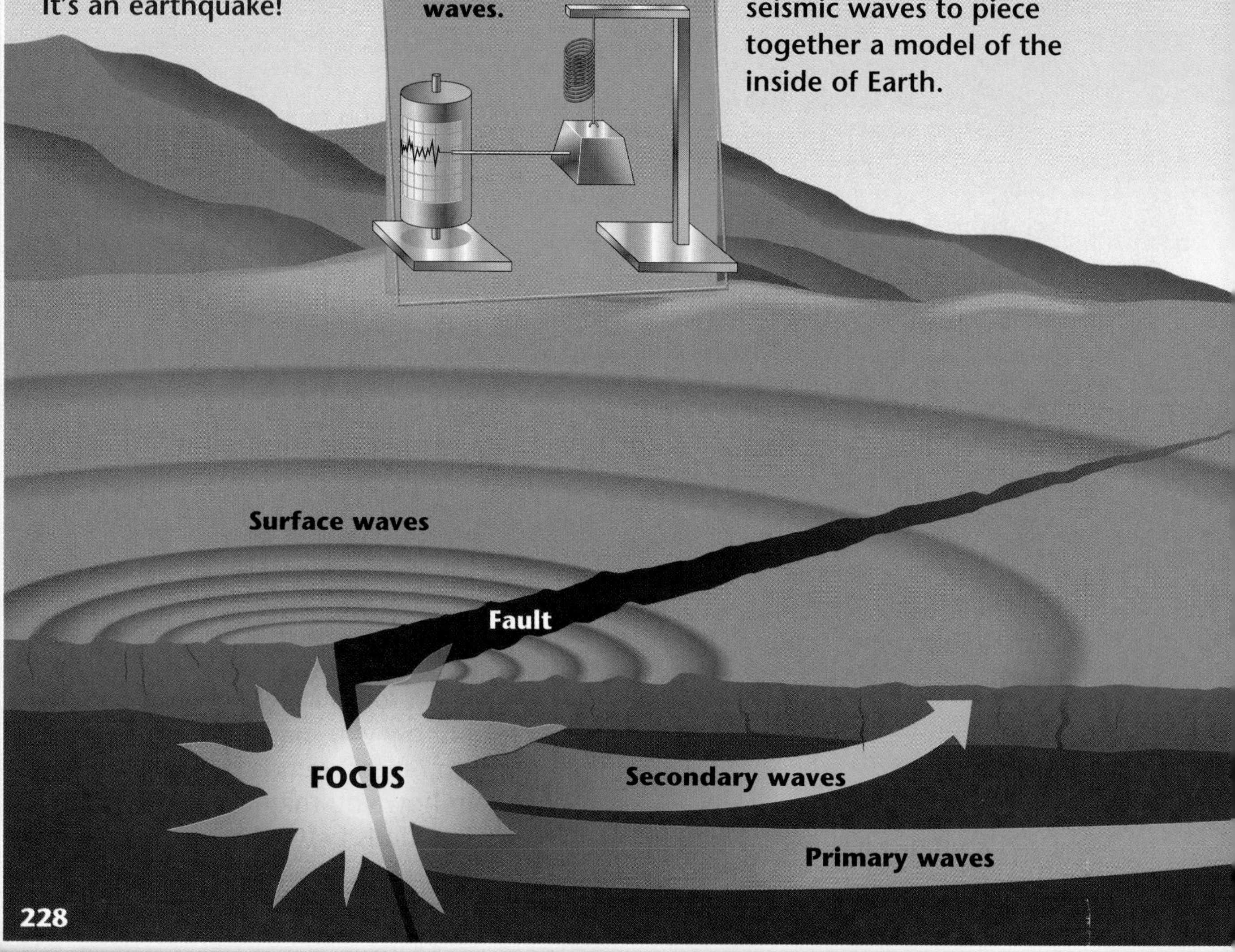

Surface waves

Fault

FOCUS

Secondary waves

Primary waves

Earth Science Link

Seismic waves get weaker the farther they get from the focus. Even so they can still be detected by very sensitive devices called seismographs (sĭz′mə grafs′).

The fastest, or primary, waves are recorded soon after an earthquake occurs. Slower, secondary waves come later. Surface waves, the slowest, come even later.

Scientists found that seismic waves change speeds at certain depths below Earth's surface. They speed up when they reach 30–60 kilometers (19–37 miles) below the surface. Why? This depth, called the Moho (after its discoverer), is a boundary between two of Earth's layers—the outer layer, or thin crust, and the inner layer, or thick mantle.

The primary waves slow down when they reach Earth's outer core, a layer of thick liquid. Secondary waves completely stop there. The primary waves speed up again as they reach Earth's solid, inner core!

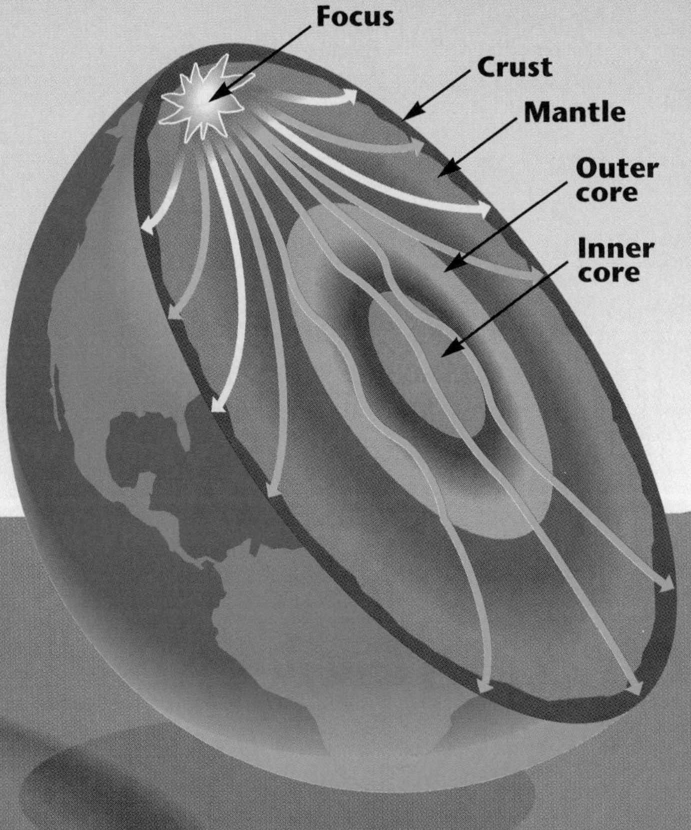

- Focus
- Crust
- Mantle
- Outer core
- Inner core

■ **Primary waves**

☐ **Secondary waves**

DISCUSSION STARTER

1. How many layers are inside Earth? Name them in order, from the outside to the center.

2. Why do you think seismic waves speed up or slow down at certain depths?

To learn more about seismic waves, visit *www.mhschool.com/science* and enter the keyword SEISMIC.

*inter*NET
CONNECTION

229

SCIENCE WORDS

absorption p.220

compression p.198

decibel p.210

Doppler effect p.225

frequency p.209

hertz p.209

pitch p.208

rarefaction p.198

reflection p.220

sound wave p.198

quality p.226

vibration p.196

USING SCIENCE WORDS

Number a paper from 1 to 10. FIll in 1 to 5 with words from the list above.

1. The unit for measuring frequency is a(n) __?__.

2. An echo is caused by a(n) __?__.

3. A sound starts with a(n) __?__.

4. Loudness is measured in a unit called a(n) __?__.

5. Overtones affect the __?__ of a sound.

6–10. Pick five words from the list above that were not used in 1 to 5, and use each in a sentence.

UNDERSTANDING SCIENCE IDEAS

11. Describe two differences we hear in sounds.

12. How are the two parts of a sound wave different?

13. What is one way a sound wave reacts when it hits a surface?

14. Explain how sound waves differ for loud and soft sounds.

15. Describe how the pitch changes as a sound source approaches and passes by.

USING IDEAS AND SKILLS

16. **READING SKILL: CAUSE AND EFFECT** An air hammer drills into a road. How does the sound reach your ear?

17. Pick an instrument. How is it built to make high sounds and lower sounds?

18. All sounds bounce off surfaces. Is this true or false? Explain your answer.

19. **COMMUNICATE** How would you correct this table and add information to show a complete octave?

Name	Note	
	F	352
mi	E	330
so	G	396
la	A	440

20. **THINKING LIKE A SCIENTIST** Do you think louder sounds travel faster than softer ones? State and explain a hypothesis. Describe how you might test your idea.

PROBLEMS and PUZZLES

Noises Off Determine where and what are the loudest, most irritating noises in your school. What can you and your class do to help solve the problem? Make a chart of the noises, causes, and possible solutions.

Which solutions can you actually carry out? How can you make the school a quieter place to learn and to have fun?

CHAPTER 6
LIGHT

Light helps you "see" the world around you. However, forms of light also cook your food, let doctors see inside a person's body, help predict the weather, and allow people to communicate around the world instantly. What produces light? How can light do all these things?

In Chapter 6 you will compare and contrast many things. Compare means "to tell how things are alike." Contrast means "to tell how things are different."

231

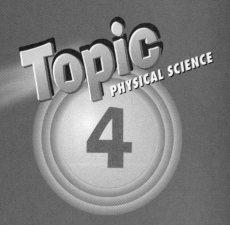

Topic
PHYSICAL SCIENCE
4

WHY IT MATTERS

Light bounces off surfaces.

SCIENCE WORDS

bioluminescence light produced by living organisms

light ray a straight-line beam of light as it travels outward from its source

Law of Reflection the angle of an incoming light ray equals the angle of the reflected ray

concave mirror a mirror that curves in on the shiny side

convex mirror a mirror that curves out on the shiny side

Light and Mirrors

What happens in any city or town when the Sun sets? What if you were in a plane as the Sun was setting and you could look down at a big city? What would you notice as time went by?

What if you are in a room, sitting near a window and reading? The Sun sets. How does everything in the room seem to change? What do you need to do if you want to keep reading?

EXPLORE

HYPOTHESIZE Is it possible to see objects if there is no light? Write a hypothesis in your *Science Journal.* Test your ideas.

EXPLORE · ACTIVITY

Investigate If You Can See Without Light

Experiment with a shoe-box viewer.

PROCEDURES

▨ **SAFETY** Be careful using scissors. Do not put any sharp objects in the box.

1. Cut a hole about the size of a dime in the small end of the box as shown. Put an object inside the box and close the lid.

2. **EXPERIMENT** Look in the box through the hole. What do you see? Describe it in your *Science Journal*.

3. Now cut a small hole in the top of the box.

4. **OBSERVE/COMPARE** Shine the flashlight through the top hole while you look into the box again. Can you see the object this time?

CONCLUDE AND APPLY

1. **OBSERVE/EXPLAIN** Could you see the object inside the box in step 2? In step 4? Explain any difference in your answers.

2. **INFER** Is it possible to see an object in the dark? Explain.

GO FURTHER: Problem Solving

3. **PREDICT/EXPERIMENT** Do any characteristics of the object in the box affect the results? Try different kinds of objects. Predict any differences in your results. Test your ideas.

4. **PREDICT/EXPERIMENT** How much extra lighting would you need on a dark, cloudy day in order to safely walk around your room at home or your classroom? Would a night-light work? Would a lamp with a single light bulb work? How would you test your ideas safely?

Can You See Without Light?

The Moon looks very bright in the evening sky. Yet the Moon does not give off any light of its own. It would not shine if we could place it in a very large, dark box, as in the Explore Activity.

We are able to see the Moon only because sunlight bounces off the Moon's surface and into our eyes. The dark half of the Moon in the photo is actually a part of the side of the Moon that is not being lit by the Sun. Since sunlight does not reach the Moon there, we cannot see this part of the Moon's surface.

What is light? Scientists know that light, like sound, is not matter. We could never observe a "piece" of light

You see the Moon (right) because it is lit by the Sun. A beam of light (below) from a laser carries enough energy to melt the hardest metals.

at rest, taking up space and having mass. Light and sound are both means of transferring energy between points.

The photograph below clearly shows that light carries energy. In fact light is a form of energy.

How Have Scientists Explained Light Through the Ages?

Light is one of the most exciting mysteries scientists have ever studied. About 24 centuries ago, the Greek philosopher Plato thought that the eye gave off light particles that could bounce back from objects, making them visible.

In 1666 Francesco Grimaldi, an Italian mathematician, challenged this theory. Grimaldi thought light acted like waves in water. For the next two centuries, scientists debated whether light was a stream of particles or some kind of wave, as in the diagram.

Today we know that light can act in two ways—either as a wave or as a stream of particles. Look at the rainbow of colors created by the compact disc shown below. This rainbow effect can only be explained if light travels in waves.

Yet we also know that light always delivers its energy in tiny bundles of particles, not in smoothly spread-out waves. There is no simple everyday explanation for light's ability to behave both as a particle and as a wave.

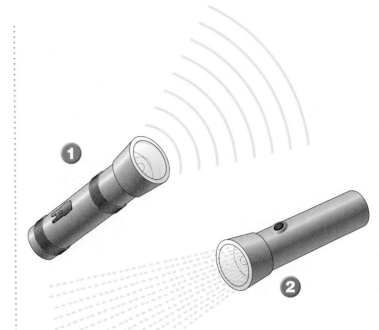

Is light more like a series of waves (1) or a stream of countless tiny particles (2)?

The rainbow effect on the CD occurs because light travels as waves.

How Is Light Produced?

All the objects we can see either give off their own light or, more often, reflect the light from a source such as a light bulb or the Sun. The photos show objects that produce light. As you can see, heat is involved in all three cases. **1:** Nuclear reactions heat the Sun. **2:** Chemical reactions heat the burner flame. **3:** Electricity heats the glowing wire of the light bulb.

In a very hot material, the molecules move swiftly. At times when these molecules collide, some energy from the collision may be given off as light. At other times the molecules themselves vibrate and give off light waves.

Any light source converts energy of one kind into light energy. For example, the Sun makes light from nuclear energy, a burner makes light from chemical energy, and an electric light bulb makes light from electrical energy. The light waves given off by these sources carry the energy away at great speed.

1 The Sun

2 A burner flame

3 An electric light bulb

Can Light Be Cool?

As you've seen, hot objects can give off light. The surface temperatures of stars in this photograph range from about 3,000°C to 40,000°C, while temperatures at their cores reach tens of millions of degrees Celsius! Yet a light source can also convert energy into light without being hot. The photos below show how light can be produced at ordinary temperatures.

In the light sticks, a chemical reaction produces molecules with extra energy. The molecules shed some of this energy as "cool" light. In a similar way, both fireflies and bacteria create a chemical reaction to produce light at an ordinary temperature. We call cool light produced by living organisms **bioluminescence** (bī´ō lü´mə nes´əns).

By standing in a dark room and crushing certain hard candies with pliers, you can create "sparks" of light. Wintergreen candies and maple-sugar candies are especially good for this. (If you try this yourself, be sure to wear safety goggles, and be careful not to pinch your fingers!)

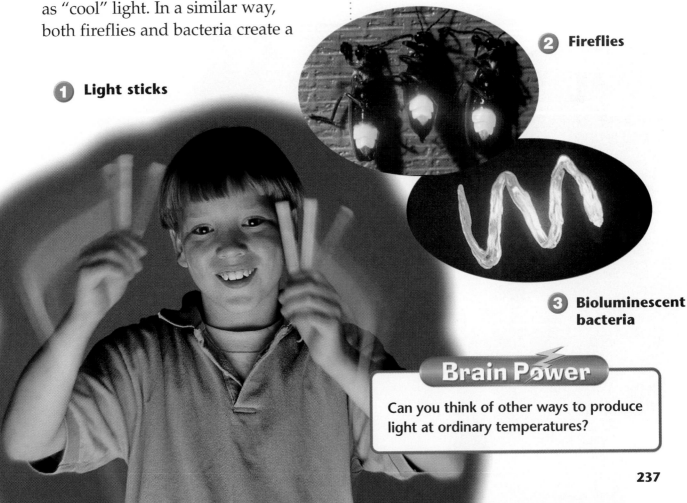

1 Light sticks

2 Fireflies

3 Bioluminescent bacteria

Brain Power

Can you think of other ways to produce light at ordinary temperatures?

237

How Does Light Travel?

Take a look at the drawings shown here. Which path do you think shows how light travels to your eyes?

In this illustration a light bulb casts the shadow of a microscope on a wall. If we draw a straight line from the light bulb to any part of the microscope, we can follow the line directly to that part of the microscope's shadow. This might suggest that light always travels in straight lines. However, this is true only when a substance like air or water remains the same along the whole pathway of light.

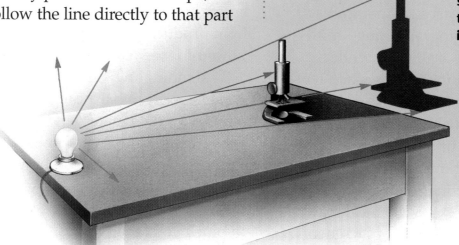

Light casting a shadow suggests that light travels in straight lines.

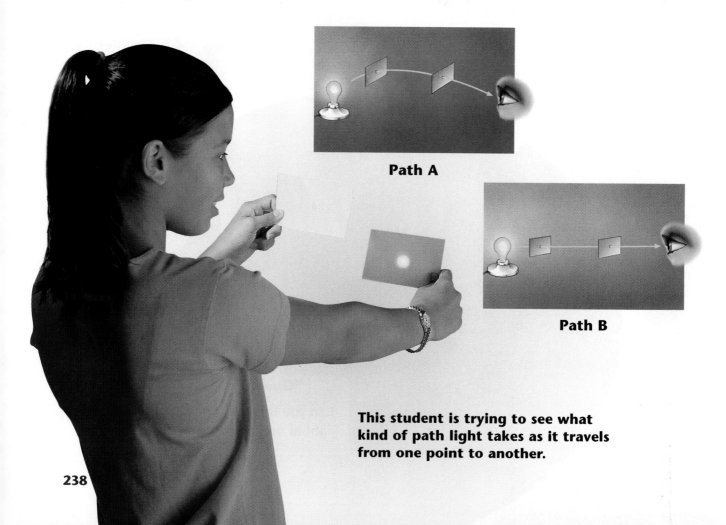

Path A

Path B

This student is trying to see what kind of path light takes as it travels from one point to another.

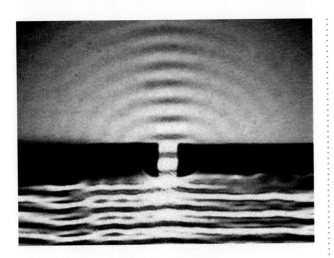

Light waves bend as they travel past very thin objects or pass through very tiny holes.

In fact light usually changes direction when it passes from one substance into another. Otherwise, as long as light travels through air or water, it follows a straight line.

Actually, light travels as a series of waves. These waves can be disturbed or bent when they travel past the edge of a thin object or flow through a very narrow opening.

When free of snags, however, light waves move as shown below. If we could follow a point on a light wave as it ripples outward from its source, we would trace a straight line. This beam of light is called a **light ray**.

Each small section of a light wave follows a straight path, creating a ray of light.

Follow the Bouncing Light

HYPOTHESIZE How does light travel when it bounces off a mirror? Write a hypothesis in your *Science Journal*.

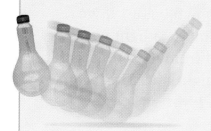

MATERIALS
- mirror
- string
- *Science Journal*

PROCEDURES

1. Sit close together. Hold the mirror as shown. Adjust it so your partner can see your face in the middle of the mirror.

2. Have you and your partner hold a piece of string as shown. In your *Science Journal*, note the angles formed between the string and the mirror.

3. **OBSERVE** Move a little farther apart. Repeat the procedure. How does the mirror have to be moved in order for your partner to see your face? Try at several other positions

CONCLUDE AND APPLY

DRAW CONCLUSIONS Were both of you able to see each other in the mirror? What did you observe about the angles the string made with the mirror?

How Does Light Bounce Off Objects?

Review how any visible object must either give off its own light or reflect light from another light source. We can picture how light reflects (bounces) off objects using light rays as in the diagram.

How is light reflected by a mirror? When a ray of light reaches your eye from a mirror, where did the light come from before it struck the mirror?

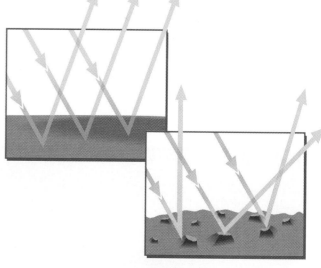

Light rays reflecting off flat, polished surfaces create mirror images. Light rays reflecting off rough surfaces scatter in all directions.

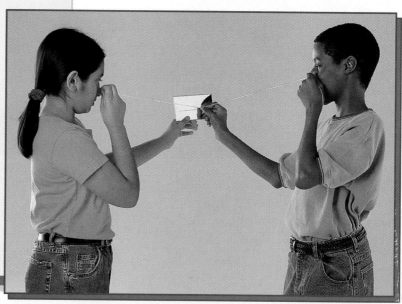

Are the Angles Equal?

As the activity shows, the angle between an incoming light ray and a surface equals the angle between the reflected light ray and the surface. This is called the **Law of Reflection**. The illustration below helps to demonstrate this idea.

Whom does each student see when he or she looks in the mirror?

The path taken by the basketball shows what a light ray does when it reflects off a surface. The angles between the path of the ball and the floor are equal on either side of the bounce.

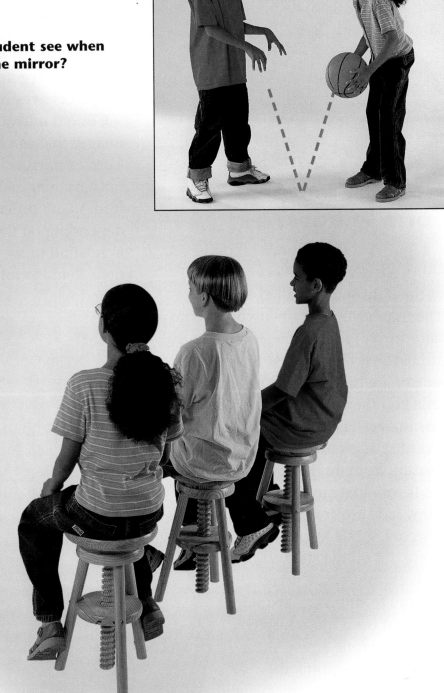

How Do Mirrors Form Images?

Light rays that bounce off polished, shiny surfaces can reflect a "picture" of the light source, called an *image*. The things you see when you look in a flat mirror, for example, look very real, almost as if they existed on the other side of a window. But your experience tells you they are not real—they are just images of the real things in your world. The picture shows how flat mirrors form images.

Mirrors that curve in on the shiny side are **concave mirrors**, while mirrors that curve out on the shiny side are **convex mirrors**. Curved mirrors form images that are different from those formed by flat mirrors.

How do you think the images formed by concave and convex mirrors will differ from one another? From the image formed by a flat mirror?

Have you ever looked at your reflection in a soupspoon? You may have found that your image looked different depending on whether you were looking at the inside or the outside of the spoon's bowl. You may also have found your image changed, depending on how far away you held the spoon.

The inside of the soupspoon behaves like a concave mirror. The outside of the spoon behaves like a convex mirror.

Curved mirrors create a variety of images that can be of practical use. Convex mirrors always form reduced, upright images. Yet concave mirrors can form many different types of images, depending on the position of the object in relation to the mirror. The illustrations demonstrate how curved mirrors form images.

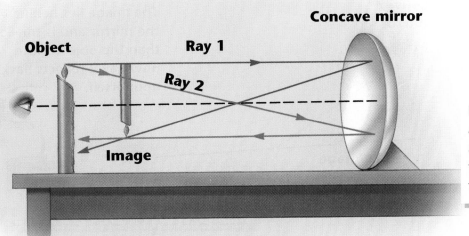

Concave mirror

Object

Ray 1

Ray 2

Image

Images formed by a concave mirror are different from those formed by a flat mirror.

READING ✏ DIAGRAMS

1. **DISCUSS** What happens to the light rays reflected by the concave mirror?
2. **WRITE** Look at the image produced by the concave mirror. How do the image and object compare?

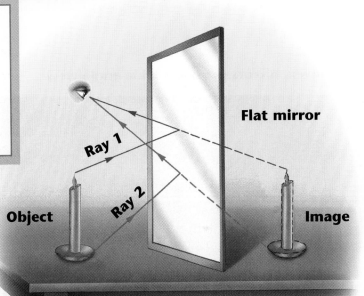

Flat mirror

Ray 1

Ray 2

Object

Image

Light rays coming from the candle bounce off the flat mirror and create an image on the other side of the mirror. The image in a flat mirror is always upright, life sized, and left-to-right reversed.

Concave mirrors are often used in telescopes. The images they form can be cast on film or light detectors for study.

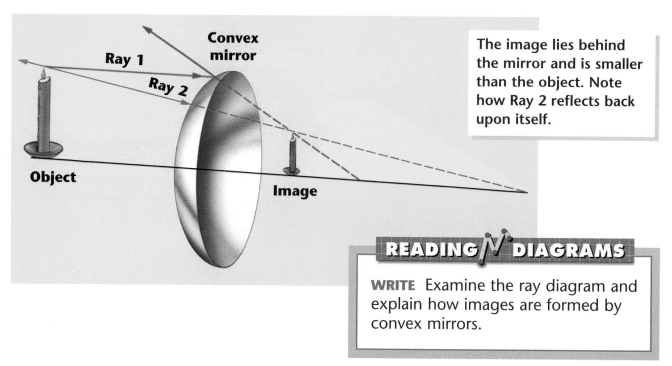

Ray 1

Ray 2

Convex mirror

Object

Image

The image lies behind the mirror and is smaller than the object. Note how Ray 2 reflects back upon itself.

Convex mirrors provide a wide-angle view.

Light rays bouncing off mirrors create useful images. The images made by a flat mirror look real, but are reversed from right to left. Ambulance signs are often done in "mirror writing" so that they read correctly when seen in a rearview mirror. Convex mirrors may be part of a store's security system. Concave mirrors used in telescopes form upside-down images that can be easily photographed. Concave mirrors used as magnifying mirrors give users a real close-up, right-side-up view.

REVIEW

1. Is it possible to see in the dark? Explain.

2. What evidence can you give that light travels in straight lines?

3. How are the images formed by concave mirrors different from those formed by convex mirrors?

4. DRAW CONCLUSIONS The rearview mirror on the right side of a car is usually a convex mirror. Explain why a convex mirror is best for this purpose.

5. CRITICAL THINKING *Analyze* Describe a demonstration that would show how light carries energy.

WHY IT MATTERS **THINK ABOUT IT**
Amusement parks often have "fun house" mirrors that make you look tall and skinny or short and chunky. The fun houses may also have mirrors that make it harder for you to find the exit because you aren't sure if what you are looking at is real or only an image in a mirror.

WHY IT MATTERS **WRITE ABOUT IT**
How would you design your own "fun house of mirrors"? Tell what sorts of mirrors you would use where and why you would use them.

READING SKILL
Write a paragraph that compares and contrasts the images formed by plane, concave, and convex mirrors.

BULBS: The Bright Idea!

This has been the typical light bulb for more than 60 years. It has a tightly coiled tungsten filament in a frosted bulb that's filled with an inert gas.

Whose bright idea was the light bulb? No one person can take all the credit because you need electricity to light the bulb!

It began in 1800, when Alessandro Volta produced the first steady electric current. In 1820 an inventor put a current through a metal wire, saw a glow, and put it in a closed glass container, creating the first light bulb.

In 1841 someone built the first light with glowing carbon. Other inventors used other kinds of filaments—thin materials that glow when electrified.

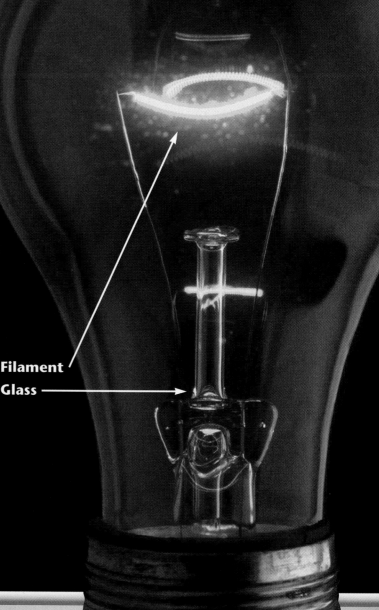

Filament

Glass

Alessandro Volta

Thomas Edison

Science, Technology, and Society

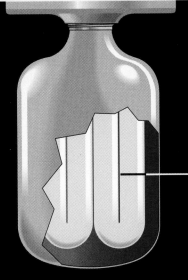

The first popular light bulb in the United States was a carbon-filament bulb invented by Thomas Edison in 1879. Two years later Lewis Howard Latimer patented an improved bulb with a carbon filament he invented. Latimer was later hired by Edison.

By 1902 metal-filament light bulbs were for sale, but they were very expensive. The General Electric Corporation set up a laboratory to create new bulbs. By 1910 lab workers discovered how to make inexpensive, bright bulbs with tungsten filaments. Sadly, black material coated the inside of the bulbs, dimming the light.

Lab scientist Irving Langmuir found that by filling the bulbs with a special gas, they didn't turn black. By 1934 he'd learned that coiling the filament made the light brighter. Our modern light bulb had arrived!

In the 1980s small fluorescent bulbs that screw into ordinary sockets were introduced. These use much less electricity than ordinary light bulbs.

Fluorescent light bulbs were also produced in the 1930s. They use light from a glowing gas to make a coating inside the bulbs glow. Fluorescent lights use less electricity and are cooler than ordinary bulbs.

DISCUSSION STARTER

1. What's the difference between a light bulb and a fluorescent light?

2. How has the invention of the light bulb affected the space shuttle? The camera? The automobile?

Lewis Howard Latimer

Irving Langmuir

To learn more about electricity, visit *www.mhschool.com/science* and enter the keyword BRIGHT.

*inter*NET
CONNECTION

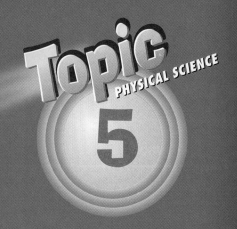

WHY IT MATTERS

Light can only pass through certain kinds of materials.

SCIENCE WORDS

opaque completely blocking light from passing through

transparent letting all light through, so that objects on the other side can be seen clearly

translucent letting only some light through, so that objects on the other side appear blurry

polarization allowing light vibrations to pass through in only one direction

refraction the bending of light rays as they pass from one substance into another

convex lens a lens that curves outward (is thicker at the middle than at the edges) and brings light rays together

concave lens a lens that curves inward (is thicker at the edges than at the middle) and spreads light rays apart

Light and Lenses

What are shadows? What kinds of materials cast shadows? Can a window glass cast a shadow? Are shadows always black?

What if you turn off the lights in your room? Then you flick on a flashlight on various objects in your room. You look for shadows. Do the shadows differ? Are some sharper than others? If so, why?

EXPLORE

HYPOTHESIZE How do objects cast shadows? Do all objects cast shadows the same way? Are all shadows alike? Write a hypothesis in your *Science Journal.* How would you test your ideas?

EXPLORE ACTIVITY

Investigate What Light Can Pass Through

Test materials to see if they all cast the same kind of shadows, if any at all.

PROCEDURES

1. PREDICT/CLASSIFY Sort the test materials into those that you think light can pass through and those that light cannot pass through.

2. EXPERIMENT Use the flashlight to test if light can pass through each of the solid materials. Record your observations in your *Science Journal*. Test if light will pass through water. What about water colored with food dye?

3. PLAN How can you test if light passes through gases? Explain. What materials would you need?

MATERIALS

- plastic sandwich bag
- paper
- waxed paper
- aluminum foil
- other assorted materials to test
- flashlight
- clear plastic cup
- water (other liquids, optional)
- food dye
- *Science Journal*

CONCLUDE AND APPLY

1. OBSERVE Did all the materials allow light to pass through?

2. INTERPRET DATA Can light pass through all the materials equally well?

3. INTERPRET DATA Can light pass through solids, liquids, and gases?

GOING FURTHER: Problem Solving

4. EXPERIMENT Design a room in which shadows of objects are always soft and fuzzy, never sharp. What sorts of materials would you use?

5. PREDICT/EXPERIMENT What else might you add to water to see if light gets through—sand, ink, instant coffee? Predict if each lets light through. How would you test your ideas?

What Can Light Pass Through?

The Explore Activity showed that sometimes when light strikes matter, almost all the light gets through. Sometimes only some light gets through. Sometimes none of it gets through.

- **Opaque** materials completely block light from passing through.

- **Transparent** materials allow light to pass through with almost no disturbance. Transparent materials may or may not color the light, but you can clearly see objects through them.

- **Translucent** materials allow only part of the light to pass through, while also ouncing it in many new directions. Since translucent materials give only a blurry view, they are often used in shower doors. They let some light in, but provide privacy.

You might think empty space is opaque to light. After all, light and sound are both waves, and sound waves do need some kind of matter to travel through. Yet as the starry night sky shows, light *can* travel through empty space. We'll learn why in Topic 6.

Light from celestial objects, such as this galaxy, passes through empty space to reach us.

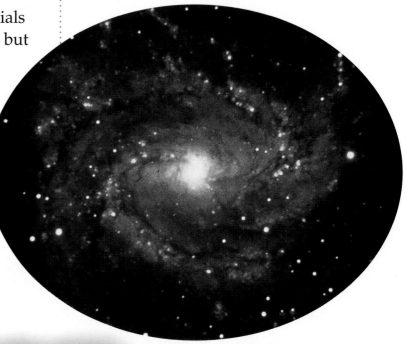

Which objects in this scene are transparent? Translucent? Opaque?

How Can We Control Light?

In our daily lives, we use many products to control light. You may be familiar with some of the products shown here.

One of the most interesting ways for controlling light depends on **polarization** (pōʹlər ə zāʹshən). Light travels in waves. Normally these waves vibrate in all directions. Yet light can be *polarized* by some materials. That is, only one direction of light vibrations can pass through them.

Polarized sunglasses use one kind of polarizing material to help us see better on a bright day. On bright days much of the glare we see comes from light reflecting off water and other surfaces.

This reflected light is often naturally polarized to vibrate sideways. Polarizing materials in sunglasses, however, let through only the light that is vibrating up and down. This blocks glare and all other kinds of light that vibrates sideways.

Scientists have also developed sunglasses that change color by themselves! They turn dark in the sunlight but lighten indoors. The lenses of self-tinting glasses contain very small amounts of a transparent, silver-containing chemical. When struck by bright light, this chemical turns into tiny silver particles. These particles block light and darken the glass.

When taken indoors, the silver particles become transparent again. So the lenses automatically lighten.

Self-tinting glasses indoors

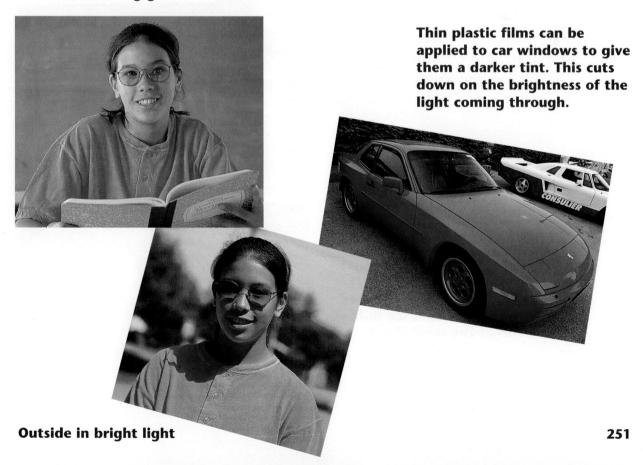

Thin plastic films can be applied to car windows to give them a darker tint. This cuts down on the brightness of the light coming through.

Outside in bright light

How Can Light Rays Be Bent?

The pencil in the photograph certainly appears to be bent. Yet the bend is actually just a "trick" that light rays play on our eyes. The illusion is caused when light rays from the lower part of the pencil change direction as they go from water into air. The bending of light rays as they pass from one substance into another is called **refraction** (ri frak′shən). The photographs below illustrate the refraction of a light beam.

How does light affect what you see when it passes through water?

You've seen that light rays may bend as they move from one substance into another. Can light rays move from one substance into another without bending?

A light beam going from air into water

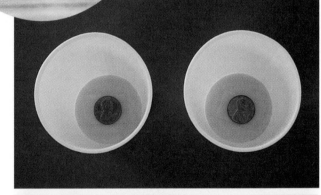

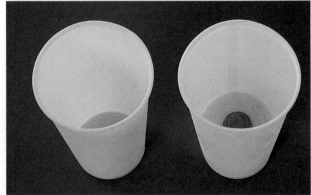

Put a penny in each cup. Fill only one cup with water. Stand away from the table. Can you see both pennies? What would you have to do so that you could see both coins at the same time?

How Does Refraction Work?

Imagine skating onto grass from a sidewalk. If you skate straight onto the grass at a 90° angle, you will slow down, but your direction will remain the same. If you skate onto the grass at any other angle, though, one skate will slow before the other. This will cause you to turn in a new direction. The shallower the angle between your original path and the grass, the more your direction will change.

Like a skater, light traveling from one substance into a *denser* substance slows down. (The *denser substance* is made of material that is *more tightly packed together* than the material that makes up the less-dense substance.)

If light strikes the new material head-on, its direction is unchanged. Yet if it strikes at any other angle, it gets refracted into a new direction. The amount of refraction increases as the incoming angle gets shallower.

Look at the photos of the skaters. The first skater skates onto the grass at a 90° angle. Both skates hit the grass at the same time. The second skater's skates don't hit the grass at the same time. Why not? How will the path the second skater takes differ from the path the first skater takes? How do the paths the skaters take compare with the paths the light beams take?

READING IN DIAGRAMS

1. **DISCUSS** What happens as the light beams enter the glass? Compare the paths of the two light beams. Why are they different?
2. **WRITE** How do the paths the light beams take compare with the paths the skaters take? Why do you think this is so?

Seeing Through a Lens

HYPOTHESIZE What happens when you view the room through a lens? How does it change the way things look? Form a hypothesis.

MATERIALS
- convex lens (magnifying glass)
- index card or piece of paper
- *Science Journal*

PROCEDURES

1. **OBSERVE** Hold the lens about a foot from your eye. View the image of the room around you. Record what you see.

2. Repeat with the lens quite close to the page of a book.

3. **EXPERIMENT** Aim the lens at a light bulb or window. Move the index card back and forth on the other side of the lens until you see an image of the light source cast sharply on the card. Record what you see.

CONCLUDE AND APPLY

1. **OBSERVE** When the image was upright, was it enlarged or reduced?

2. **OBSERVE/COMPARE** When you cast an image on the card, was it upright or inverted?

3. **CLASSIFY** Summarize your observations in a table.

How Do Lenses Work?

Lenses are pieces of transparent materials with curved surfaces that use the refraction of light to make images. **Convex lenses** curve outward, while **concave lenses** curve inward. The diagrams show how these lenses form images.

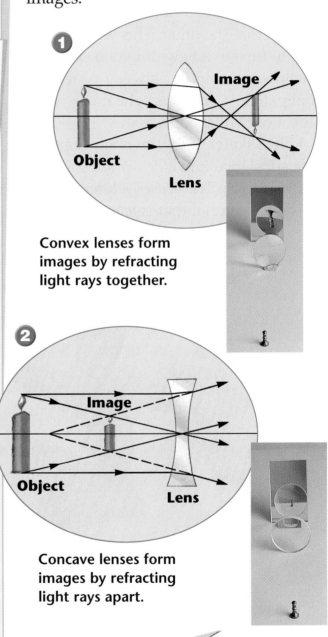

Convex lenses form images by refracting light rays together.

Concave lenses form images by refracting light rays apart.

Brain Power

Which type of lens forms the same kind of images as convex mirrors? As concave mirrors?

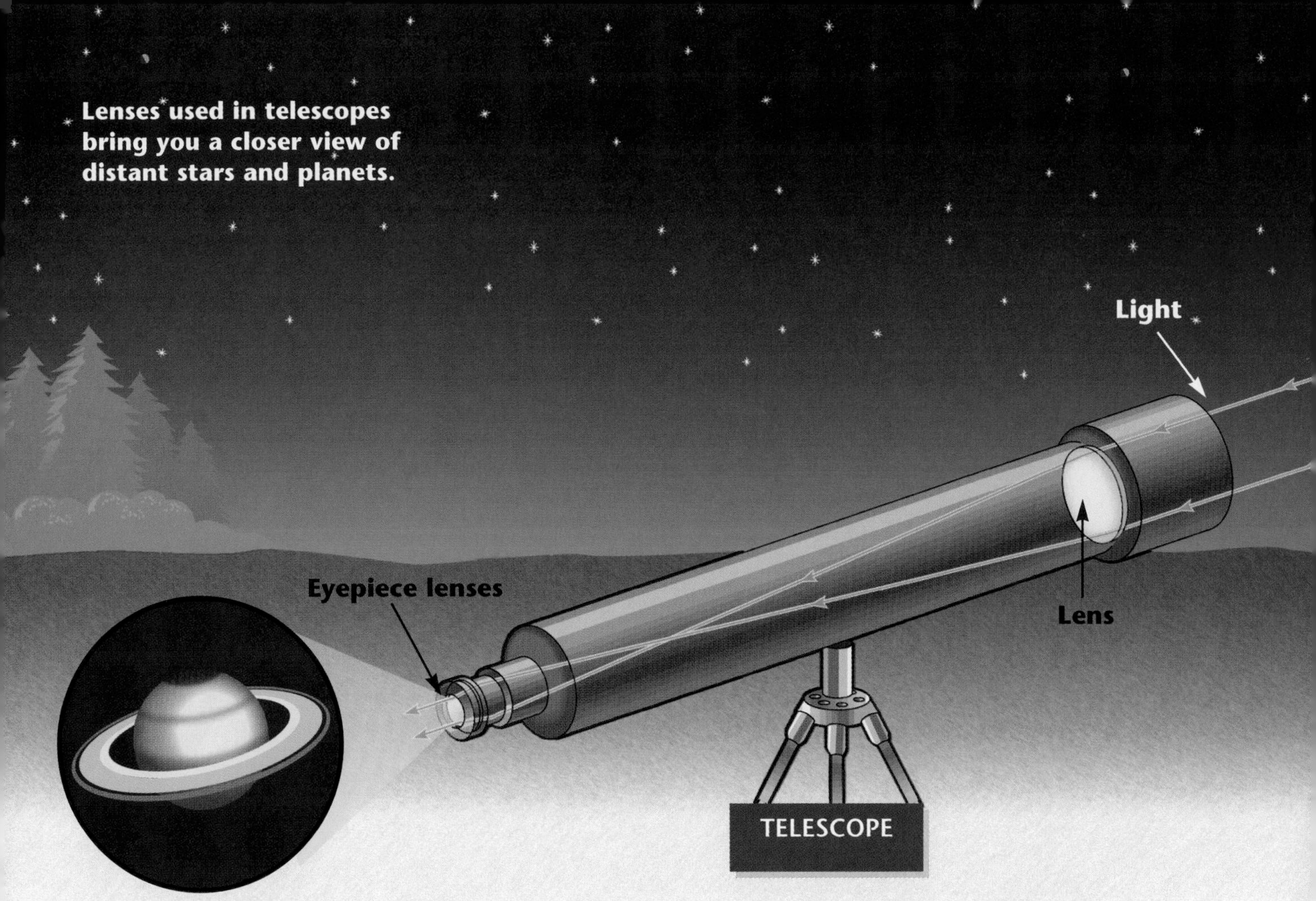

Lenses used in telescopes bring you a closer view of distant stars and planets.

Light

Lens

Eyepiece lenses

TELESCOPE

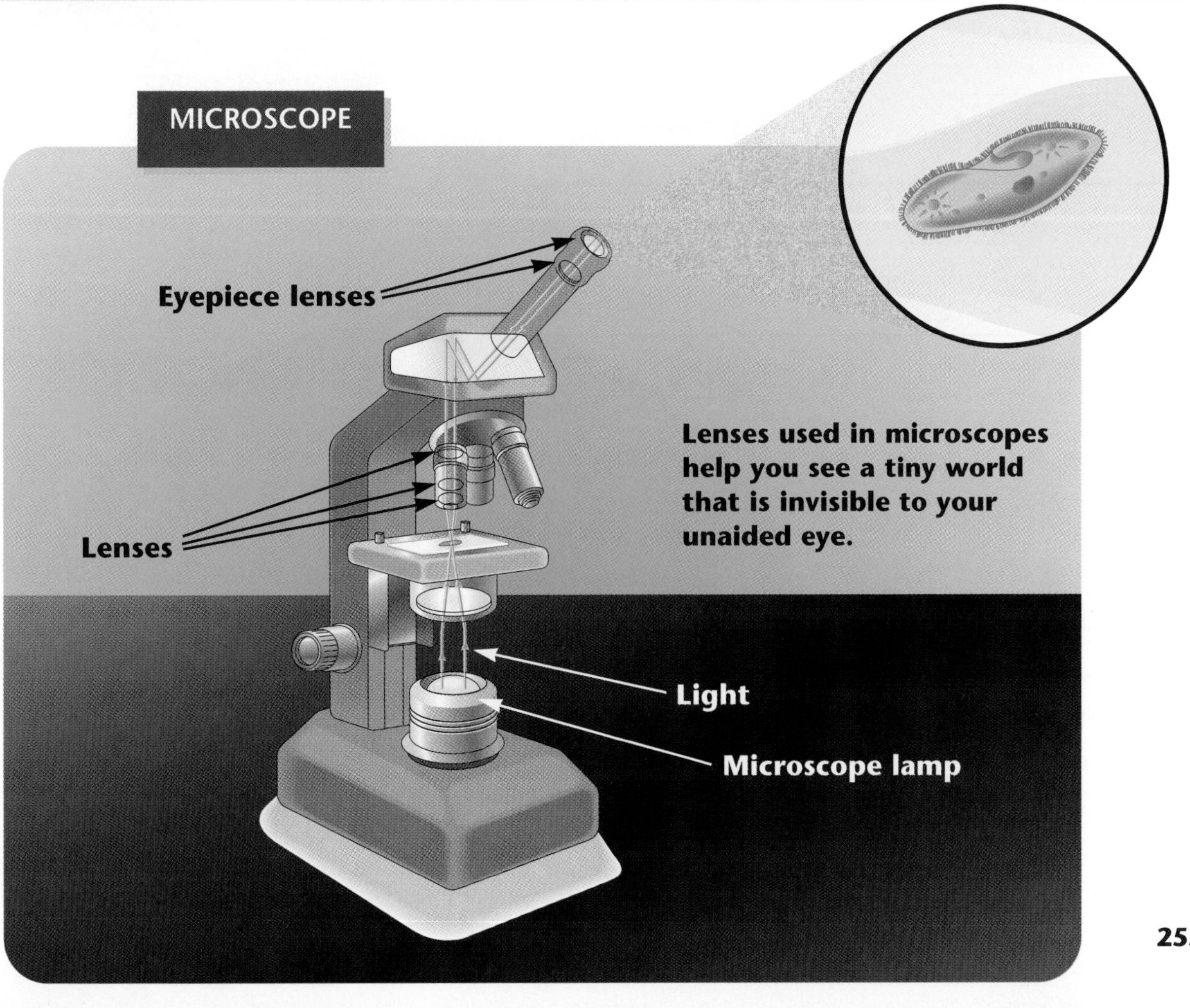

MICROSCOPE

Eyepiece lenses

Lenses

Lenses used in microscopes help you see a tiny world that is invisible to your unaided eye.

Light

Microscope lamp

How Do You See Images?

Your eyes each have a convex lens that casts an image onto the back of the eye. Here a sheet of tissue called the retina converts the light into signals that nerves carry to the brain. Your brain then turns the nerve signals into your view of the world. The diagram shows how your eyes work.

Light from an object reaches the eye and is refracted by the cornea.

The refracted light then enters the eye through the pupil and travels to the lens.

The lens of the eye bends the light even more so that it forms an image on the retina.

Images that form on the retina are sent on by the optic nerve to the brain. The brain then turns these images into your view of the world.

LIFE LINK SCIENCE

HOW THE EYE WORKS

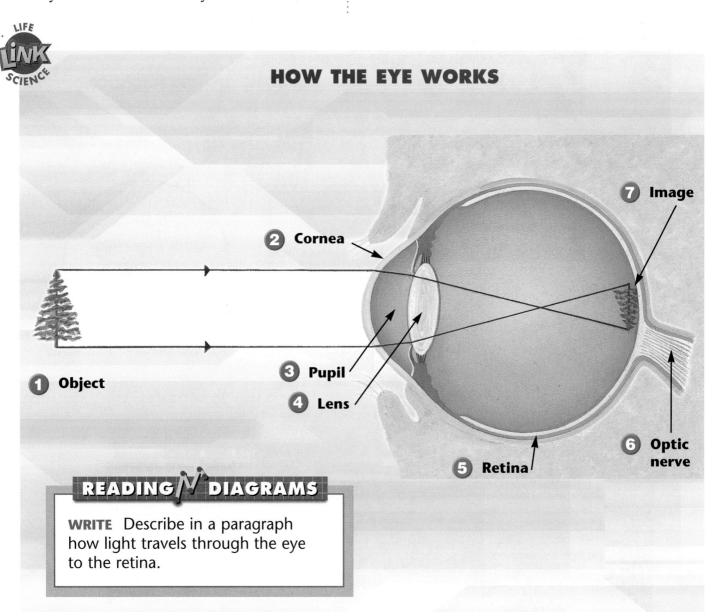

7 **Image**

2 **Cornea**

1 **Object**

3 **Pupil**

4 **Lens**

5 **Retina**

6 **Optic nerve**

READING DIAGRAMS

WRITE Describe in a paragraph how light travels through the eye to the retina.

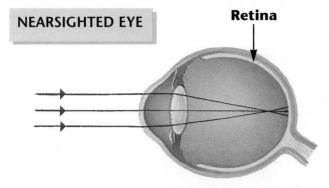

NEARSIGHTED EYE

Retina

IMAGE FALLS SHORT OF RETINA

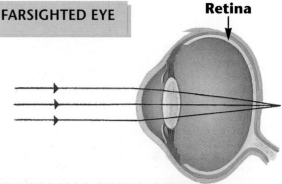

FARSIGHTED EYE

Retina

IMAGE FALLS BEHIND RETINA

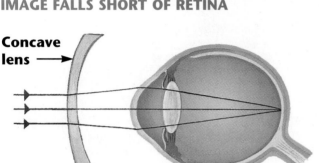

Concave lens →

Lens allows image to fall on retina.

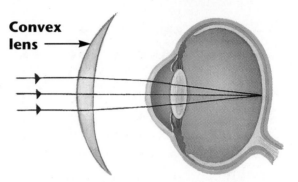

Convex lens →

Lens allows image to fall on retina.

Lenses correct vision problems by bending light rays so that the image formed falls on the retina.

How Do Glasses and Contact Lenses Work?

The lens of the eye should focus the light on the retina. Yet this doesn't always happen properly. Sometimes the lenses of the eyes do not completely focus the light. Sometimes the lenses of the eyes cast the image somewhat in the wrong place. Sometimes the muscles controlling the lens do not work perfectly. Sometimes the eye has the wrong shape. Any of those things can cause blurry vision. For example, a nearsighted person can see things close up but has trouble seeing things that are faraway. That's because images of close-up objects fall

READING DIAGRAMS

1. **DISCUSS** What happens to the light that enters a nearsighted eye? What happens to the light that enters a farsighted eye?
2. **WRITE** What kind of lens is used to correct nearsightedness? Farsightedness?

on the retina, but images of distant objects fall short of the retina. A farsighted person can see things that are faraway but has trouble seeing things that are close up. That's because images of distant objects fall on the retina, but images of close-up objects fall behind the retina. The illustration shows how glasses and contact lenses use lenses to correct nearsightedness and farsightedness.

BRAILLE ALPHABET

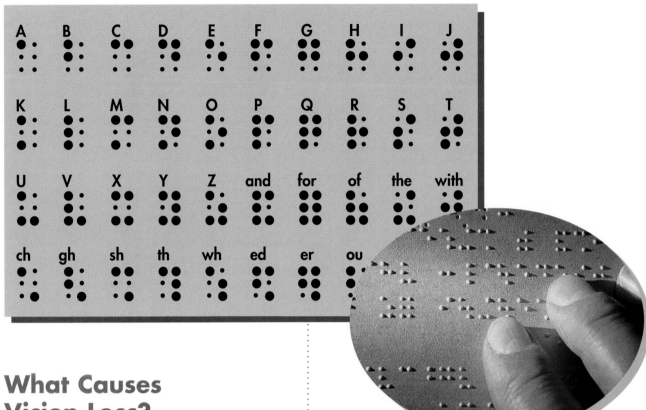

What Causes Vision Loss?

Unfortunately eyeglasses and contact lenses cannot help everyone with vision problems. Some people are born blind or with very poor vision. Some people lose their eyesight through illness or injury. That's why it is very important to have regular checkups with the eye doctor. That's why you need to wear safety goggles when you work with materials that might accidentally hit or splash into your eyes.

What can be done to help people with poor vision? Sometimes an operation can improve their sight. Other times people need low-vision aids, such as glasses with lenses that act like tiny telescopes. People who are blind often use *braille* to read. Braille is a code of patterns of raised dots that can

be read by touch. It was invented in 1824 by Louis Braille, a 15-year-old blind French student. A machine called a *braillewriter* lets people type in braille. There are computers with braille dots on the keys. There are even computer programs that speak what you type and write what you speak.

Guide Dogs

Guide dogs are specially trained to assist visually impaired people. By law these dogs are not considered pets. They accompany their owners everywhere—on public transportation and in restaurants, stores, and theaters. The owners must go through special training with their dogs to be sure they work well together.

Light bends as it travels from one kind of substance to another. You can use lenses to focus light and form various kinds of images. The cornea and lens of your eye act as lenses to focus light rays on the retina of your eye. Without this focusing ability, you would not be able to see things clearly.

This guide dog helps its owner safely travel from place to place.

REVIEW

1. Give two examples each of
   a. an opaque material
   b. a transparent material
   c. a translucent material

2. How can light rays enter a new material without being refracted?

3. Why are lenses curved?

4. **INFER** If it weren't for your brain, you might see the world upside down. Why?

5. **CRITICAL THINKING** *Analyze* The Sun is visible at sunrise a few minutes before its disk actually rises above the horizon. How is this possible?

WHY IT MATTERS THINK ABOUT IT
Lenses are important because they help people with poor eyesight to see better. Yet lenses also give people with normal vision a better view of their world.

WHY IT MATTERS WRITE ABOUT IT
What are some of the ways lenses are important to you?

Cameras—Say "Cheese"!

Even in ancient times, people knew how to make glass. Later they found that curved-glass lenses made an object appear larger or smaller.

One of the earliest devices with a lens was the *camera obscura*. (That's Latin for "dark room.") It was a closed box with a lens on the front, a tilted mirror inside, and glass on the top. The lens brought light from an object into the box. The light hit the mirror and reflected an image of the object onto the glass.

A "bull's-eye" lantern was also an enclosed box with a lens. When a light was placed inside the box, a narrow, bright beam shone through the lens. The lantern was used in lighthouses.

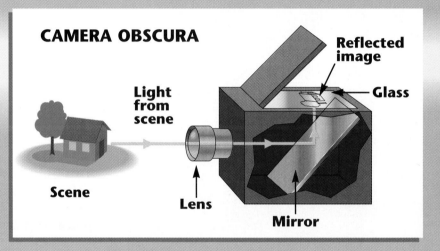

CAMERA OBSCURA

Light from scene

Scene

Lens

Mirror

Reflected image

Glass

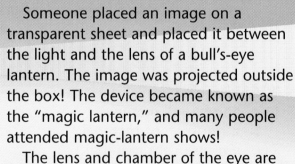

Like the bull's-eye lantern, lenses have also been used in lighthouses. They create beams of light that can even cut through fog.

Someone placed an image on a transparent sheet and placed it between the light and the lens of a bull's-eye lantern. The image was projected outside the box! The device became known as the "magic lantern," and many people attended magic-lantern shows!

The lens and chamber of the eye are like a small camera obscura. Sometimes an image is formed either too far in front or too far in back of the eye. This can be corrected by adding other lenses in front of the eyes—glasses or contacts!

Science, Technology, and Society

Some chemicals change color when light shines on them. Inventors put a surface coated with such chemicals at the back of a camera obscura. After many improvements this became the most common way of taking pictures. No one called it a camera obscura anymore. They just called it a "camera"!

MAGIC LANTERN

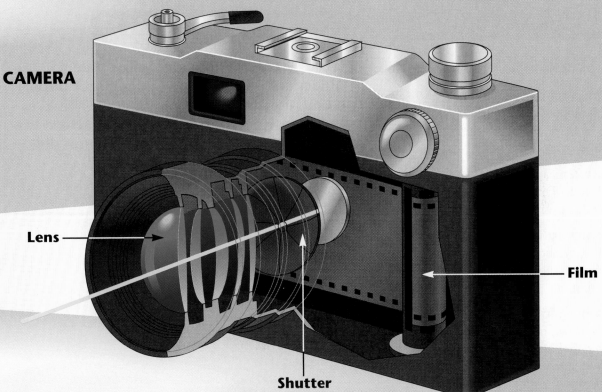

CAMERA

Lens

Film

Shutter

DISCUSSION STARTER

1. What inventions used the idea of the camera obscura?

2. How would life be different today if there were no devices with lenses?

To learn more about cameras, visit *www.mhschool.com/science* and enter the keyword CHEESE.

*inter*NET
CONNECTION

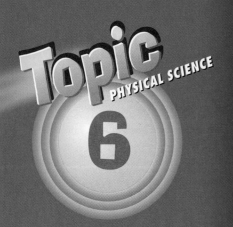

WHY IT MATTERS

Objects seem to change color when viewed in different colored lights.

SCIENCE WORDS

prism a cut piece of clear glass (or plastic) with two opposite sides in the shape of a triangle or other geometric shape

spectrum a band of colors produced when light goes through a prism

primary color red, green, or blue; mixing these colors can produce all the colors of the spectrum

primary pigment magenta, cyan, yellow; material with any of these colors absorbs one primary color of light and reflects the other two

Colors of Light

Is a tomato always red? If you have white, red, and green light bulbs, you can try this. Look at a plump, ripe tomato sitting on white paper under each light, one at a time.

Why do you see different colors of the same tomato? What might objects in your room at home look like if the light bulb in your room was green? Red? Orange? Blue?

Why do you see color at all? Why do objects seem to have a color?

HYPOTHESIZE What color will a blue object appear to be if you look at it under a blue light? Under a red light? Write a hypothesis in your *Science Journal*. How could you test your ideas even if you did not have a red or blue light bulb?

EXPLORE ACTIVITY

Investigate What Color Is

Investigate how colored lights affect colors of objects by shining white light through different-colored cellophanes.

MATERIALS

- red, yellow, blue, and green cellophane sheets
- white paper
- crayons
- red, yellow, blue, green, and black squares of construction paper
- flashlight
- *Science Journal*

PROCEDURES

1. **OBSERVE** Shine a flashlight at a sheet of white paper through each of the cellophane sheets. In your *Science Journal*, record what you see.

2. **PREDICT** What color will each of the colored squares appear to be through each of the cellophane sheets?

3. **OBSERVE/EVALUATE** After you have made your predictions, look at the colored squares through the cellophane sheets. Check your predictions.

4. **MAKE A MODEL** Use the crayons to make additional colored squares to view through the cellophane sheets.

5. **COMMUNICATE** Make a table that shows what color each square appears to be through each of the cellophane sheets.

CONCLUDE AND APPLY

1. **COMMUNICATE** What color does the red square appear to be when viewed through the red cellophane sheet? Why?

2. **COMMUNICATE** What color does the blue square appear to be when viewed through the red cellophane sheet? Why?

GOING FURTHER: Problem Solving

3. **PREDICT** What do you think would happen if you looked at the red square through both the red and blue cellophane sheets at the same time? Try it to test your prediction.

What Is Color?

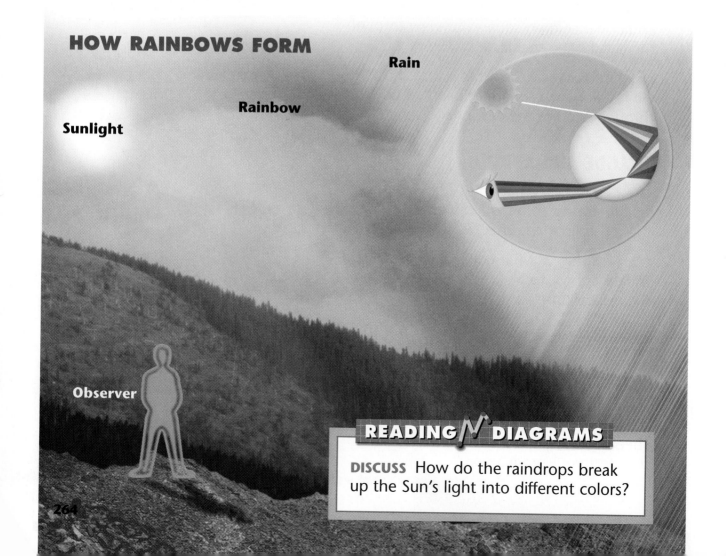

The Explore Activity showed that the color of an object can be changed. When Sir Isaac Newton passed a beam of white sunlight through a **prism**—a triangular piece of cut and polished glass—in a dark room, he was startled to see a band of rainbow colors. He called the color band a **spectrum** after a word meaning "ghostly vision."

Newton wanted to know more about the colors cast by the prism. Where did they come from? He believed that white sunlight was actually a mixture of all the colors. The prism simply spread the colors out by refracting each one at a different angle. Red is refracted the least, violet the most.

Later Newton predicted that if the spectral colors cast by one prism were passed through a second prism, the colors would recombine into white light.

The result proved his prediction was right. White light is really made up of many colors, including red, orange, yellow, green, blue, and violet.

Rainbows

The rainbow colors you see after a storm result from water drops that act both as prisms and mirrors. The drops bend rays of sunlight at different angles, causing the colors to spread out. Then the various colors reflect off the back of the drops into your eye. As the drawing shows, that is how rainbows form in the sky.

HOW RAINBOWS FORM

Rain

Rainbow

Sunlight

Observer

READING DIAGRAMS

DISCUSS How do the raindrops break up the Sun's light into different colors?

Can You Make a Rainbow?

Can you make a rainbow with a garden hose? If you've stood with your back to the Sun and looked at the fine mist from a hose, fountain, or waterfall, you've probably seen a rainbow form.

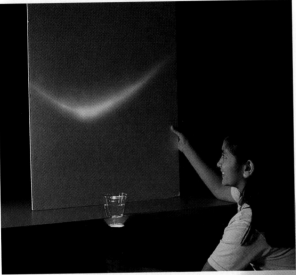

Can you make a rainbow indoors?

You can also make a rainbow indoors, as this student is doing. Fill a clear-plastic cup about halfway with water. Carefully place it on the edge of a table. A third of it should extend over the edge. Hold a piece of white paper directly behind the cup. Shine a flash-light vertically through the bottom of the cup. You should see a rainbow on the paper.

A Recipe for White Light

You've learned that white light is a mixture of an entire spectrum of colors. In the picture the girl is using a color spinner she made from cardboard. She pushed a pencil through the center so that when she twirls it between her palms, others can see the colors mix. She is trying to make the right mix of colors so that others will see white light when she spins the spinner.

What colors would you put on your spinner to try to produce white light?

When the spinner is twirled at the right speed, you can see all the colors turn into white.

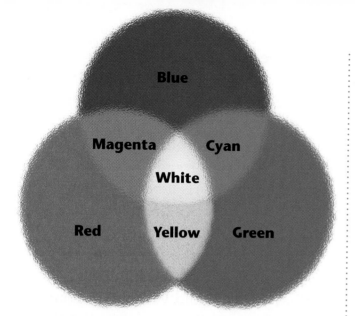

Mixing red, green, and blue light. Note that white is formed in the middle.

How Do Colors Look in Colored Light?

A color filter is a material that absorbs certain colors of light and allows others to pass through. The Explore Activity on page 263 showed that the color of an object depends on the color of the light hitting it. The activity used colored cellophane sheets as color filters. For example, the red cellophane allowed red light to pass through it but blocked other colors.

Try shining a flashlight on a red tomato. Use a sheet of red cellophane as your filter. The tomato still looks red. Now try a green sheet as your filter. Since the tomato can only reflect red light, it now looks black. Try other filters to see how they work.

If you mixed equal amounts of red, green, and blue light, you would get white light and the tomato would look red. In fact all of the colors of the spectrum can be created by mixing proper amounts of red, green, and blue light. For this reason we call red, green, and blue the **primary colors** of light.

How We See Color

Our eyes have cells in the retina that react to colors of light. Some cells react only to red, others only to green, and still others only to blue. If the retina is struck with equal amounts of red, green, and blue light, we see white.

Yet if the retina is struck with only red and green light, we see yellow. The drawing above shows some of the different colors that various mixtures of red, green, and blue light can cause us to see.

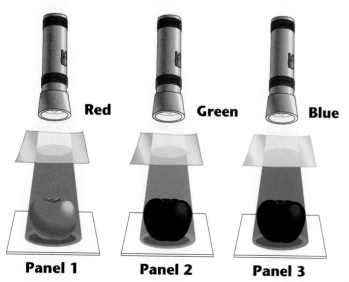

Red   **Green**   **Blue**

Panel 1   **Panel 2**   **Panel 3**

Brain Power

Stare steadily at the blue square below. This tires the cells in your eye that react to blue light. After a full minute, quickly look at a piece of white paper. What color do you see? Why?

Skill: Predicting and Observing

MIXING COLORS

You will use pigments—colored substances—in this activity to see the way pigments blend to make other colors.

In this activity you will make a prediction before you do the activity. That is, you will make a reasonable guess about what you expect the results to be. Predict what colors will result when you mix certain colors of food dyes together.

MATERIALS

- red, yellow, blue and green food dyes
- water
- plastic cups
- *Science Journal*

PROCEDURES

1. Place four cups on a piece of paper. Add enough water to each cup to cover the bottom.

2. PREDICT What color will be made by mixing one drop of red food dye and one drop of yellow food dye in the water? Mix well. In your *Science Journal*, describe the result.

3. EXPERIMENT Do step 2 with red and blue dyes. Be sure to make a prediction before you mix the colors.

4. EXPERIMENT Do step 2 again with yellow and blue, and then with all four colors. Again, be sure to make your predictions before you mix the colors.

CONCLUDE AND APPLY

1. COMMUNICATE What color resulted when you mixed red and yellow? Why?

2. COMMUNICATE What color resulted when you mixed red and blue? Blue and yellow? When you mixed all four colors?

3. CAUSE AND EFFECT What would happen if you used different amounts of each dye? Experiment to find out. Make predictions about the final color before you mix the dyes.

267

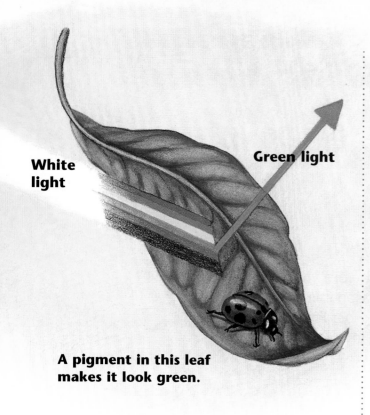

White light

Green light

A pigment in this leaf makes it look green.

Can Color Be Reflected?

When light strikes an object, pigments—colored substances—in the object reflect some colors but absorb other colors. The absorbed colors are missing in the reflected light. The reflected colors mix to produce the color of the object, as shown above.

The leaf in the drawing looks green because it has a pigment that absorbs red and blue light but reflects green light. Some materials reflect all colors and so appear white. Other materials absorb all colors and so appear black.

Colors Made by Blending Paints

Remember that the colors that result when you blend paints are different from the colors that result when you blend colored lights. As you mix colored lights, you keep adding light until you get white.

As you mix pigments, such as food dyes or markers or paints, you keep subtracting colors until you get black. That is how black is formed at the center of the color wheel below.

Magenta, cyan, and yellow are called the **primary pigments**. Each absorbs one primary color of light and reflects the other two. When properly mixed these pigments can create any desired color by reflecting a blend of primary colors of light.

Under white light, for example, equal amounts of magenta and cyan would produce the color blue. The cyan would absorb the red out of the white light and the magenta would absorb the green out of the light. Only blue would be reflected.

THE COLOR WHEEL

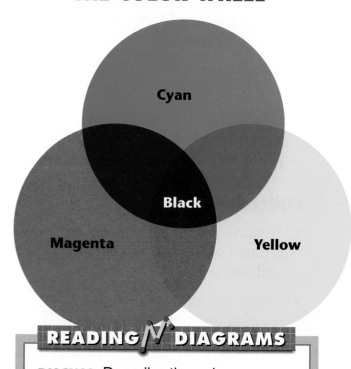

Cyan

Black

Magenta

Yellow

READING DIAGRAMS

DISCUSS Describe the colors you would see if you mixed equal amounts of magenta and yellow, cyan and yellow.

How Does Four-Color Printing Work?

The color pictures shown here should help you realize that most of the colors you see are combinations of two or more colors.

For example, the bright red at the top of the sail in the final print is a combination of different amounts of yellow and magenta. The blue section on the sail contains cyan and a little magenta. The green part is a blend of four colors—yellow, cyan, magenta, and black.

Your world is filled with color. By learning about and using colored lights and pigments, you can understand that color is a matter of what you see and the light you see it by.

Did you ever notice that colors don't look the same under the light of an ordinary light bulb as they do under fluorescent light? They also look different in bright sunlight from the way they look in a dim room.

Four-Color Printing Process

Plate 1 (yellow) + **Plate 2 (cyan)** + **Plate 3 (magenta)** + **Plate 4 (black)** = **Final Print**

 +  +

REVIEW

1. Why do objects appear to be different colors when seen under different-colored lights? When seen through different-colored filters?

2. What happens when white light passes through a prism?

3. What are the primary colors of light? The primary colors of pigments? Why are they different?

4. **PREDICT/OBSERVE** What color would be created by mixing red and green light? What color would be created by mixing cyan and yellow pigments?

5. **CRITICAL THINKING** *Analyze* Where in nature can you see a spectrum? Explain.

WHY IT MATTERS THINK ABOUT IT
Some people are color-blind. They cannot tell the difference between certain colors, such as red and green. Or they may not be able to tell the difference between a certain color (such as green) and the color gray.

WHY IT MATTERS WRITE ABOUT IT
What are some of the ways color is important to your life? What do you think life would be like if you could not see in color?

SCIENCE MAGAZINE

That COLOR-ful TV!

Does one of Isaac Newton's 17th-century discoveries really influence color TV? Yes, he's the one who discovered that combining the colors of the rainbow creates white light! In 1802 Thomas Young mixed the three basic colors of light—blue, red, and green—to create white light. These same principles are used to put color in a TV picture!

Your eyes have cones that react to color. One-third react to red, one-third to blue, and one-third to green. When all three react together, you see white.

A color TV has a special camera that separates the light from images into the main colors of light. Here's how:

The images combine to create one radio-wave signal. When it gets to the TV receiver, it's decoded. Each image goes to a separate electron gun at the back of the picture tube. The gun shoots tiny, electrically charged particles of matter at your TV screen!

White light

Green light **Red light** **Blue light**

❸ Each color goes into its own tube.

❹ Each tube produces a signal.

❷ Mirrors separate the light into the three main colors.

❶ Light from an image comes through the lens

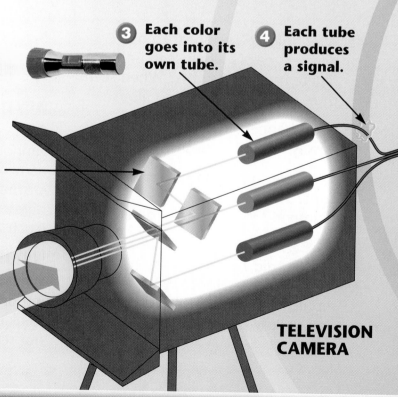

TELEVISION CAMERA

Science, Technology and Society

On the front of the picture tube, tiny dots are arranged in red, blue, and green triangles. Each triangle is one picture element, or *pixel*. When a dot is hit with electrons, it glows briefly. If all three dots glow, the pixel looks white. If none glow the pixel looks black. Other sequences create the colors in between.

There are over 200,000 pixels on a color TV screen. That's more than six times the number of cones in your eyes!

DISCUSSION STARTER

1. What does a TV camera do to the light from an image?

2. Why was Newton's light experiment important to the invention of color TV?

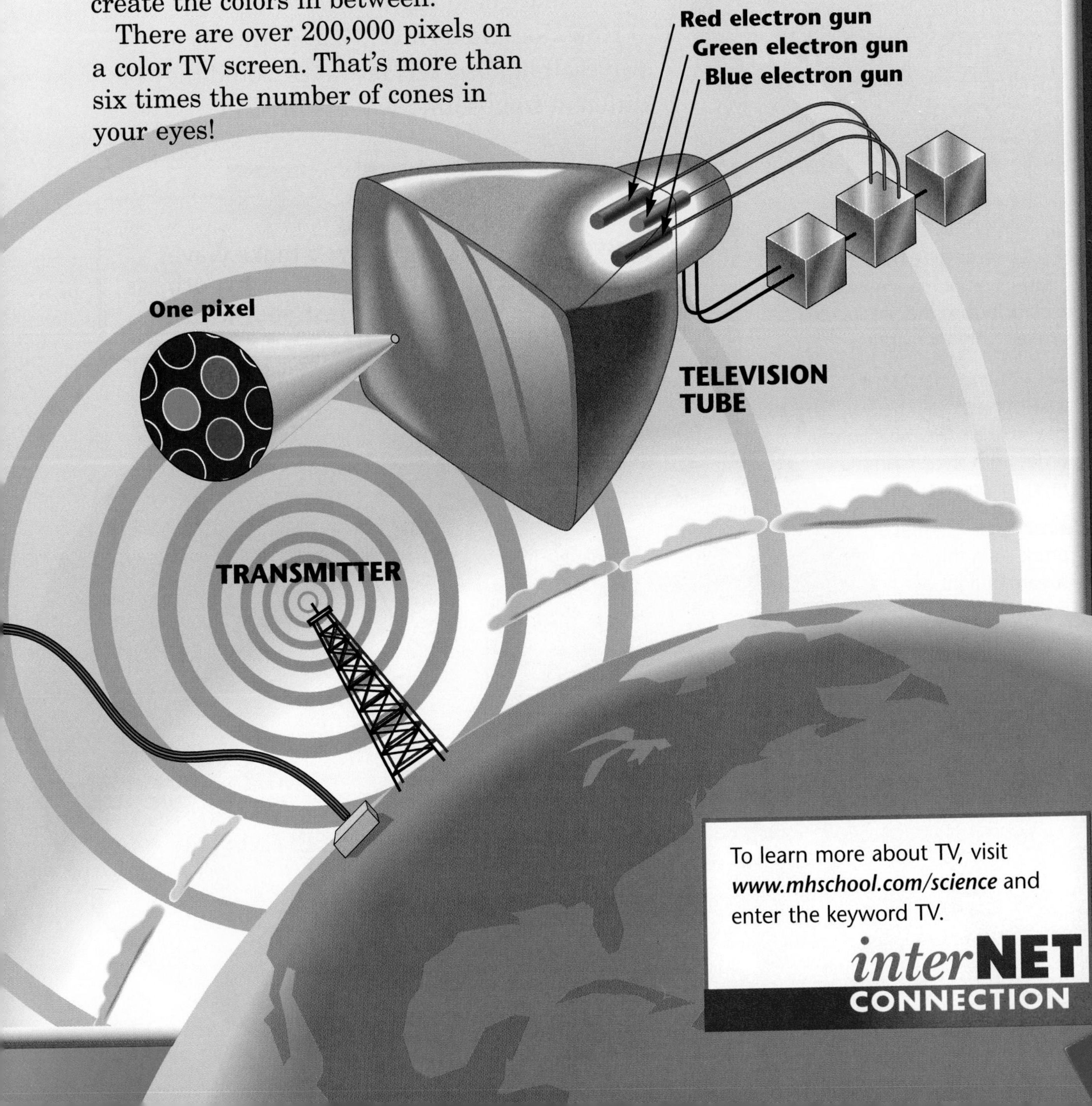

Red electron gun
Green electron gun
Blue electron gun

One pixel

TELEVISION TUBE

TRANSMITTER

To learn more about TV, visit *www.mhschool.com/science* and enter the keyword TV.

inter**NET** CONNECTION

WHY IT MATTERS

Light can be visible or invisible. You use invisible light in many ways each day.

SCIENCE WORDS

electromagnetism the production of magnetism by electricity and the production of electricity by magnets

electromagnetic spectrum all the wavelengths of visible and invisible light in order from short (gamma rays) to long (radio)

laser a device that produces a thin stream of light of just a few close wavelengths

Invisible Light

How long does it take to see light when you turn on a lamp in a darkened room? How long does it take for light from a lamp at the end of a long hallway to reach the other end?

How long do you think it takes light from the Sun to reach Earth? How long does it take sunlight to reach the Moon, reflect off the Moon, and get to Earth?

How does light travel? Sound travels in waves. If light travels in waves, could they be different from sound waves? Explain.

EXPLORE

HYPOTHESIZE How can you make waves move faster or slower? Write a hypothesis in your *Science Journal.* Test your ideas.

Investigate How Waves Move

Build a wave maker to explore what makes waves move faster or slower.

PROCEDURES

1. Work in groups of four. Starting 10 cm from one end, press 20 straws onto the sticky surface of a strip of tape. Be sure the straws are 4 cm apart, centered, and parallel. Secure them with the second strip.

2. **OBSERVE** Have two members of your group each take one end of the model, so it spreads out lengthwise. Have a third person tap a straw at one end. Have the fourth person time how long the wave takes to travel across from one end of the model to the other. In your *Science Journal*, record the time it takes.

3. **EXPERIMENT** Repeat step 2 several times, sometimes with the model tightly stretched, other times with it loosely stretched. Record your results.

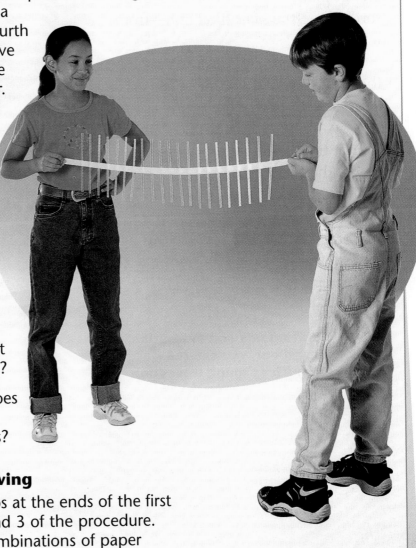

CONCLUDE AND APPLY

1. **OBSERVE** In what direction does the wave move? In what direction do the straws move?

2. **DRAW CONCLUSIONS** How does holding it tighter or looser change how the wave moves?

GOING FURTHER: Problem Solving

3. **EXPERIMENT** Place paper clips at the ends of the first ten straws. Repeat steps 2 and 3 of the procedure. What happens? Try other combinations of paper clips. What happens?

How Do Waves Move?

All waves carry energy from place to place. Yet the way a wave carries energy depends on the kind of wave motion.

Remember that sound waves are produced by vibrations. As a string or bar or some other object vibrates, it causes molecules of gas in the air to move back and forth. The energy of the vibration is carried through the air to your ear. In a similar way, sound waves travel through solids, liquids, and gases.

The wave in the model here moves from left to right. Notice that the particles of matter also vibrate back and forth along the *same* direction—from left to right.

Without particles vibrating back and forth in the direction the sound is traveling, the energy of the sound vibration could not travel. Sound waves cannot travel in a *vacuum*, a space where there is no matter.

The Explore Activity showed a way to study one kind of wave motion. Tapping a straw sent a wave through the length of the tape, but not like the wave you see here.

By vibrating one end of a spring toy in and out, you can see waves travel much as sound waves do.

As the wave moves from left to right, how do the water and the ball move?

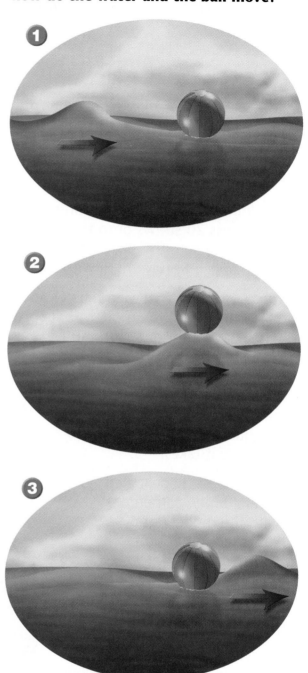

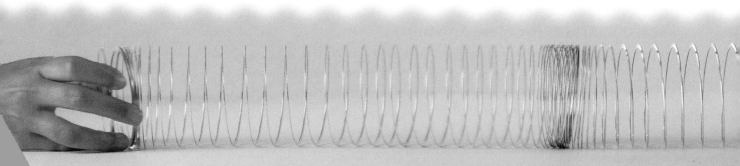

How Do Water Waves Travel?

If you toss a pebble into a quiet pond, you can see waves travel across the surface. They are like sound waves in one way. Without the water, the energy of the wave cannot travel.

However, notice how matter moves as the wave travels from left to right. The water and the ball floating on it go up and down. As energy travels in one direction, matter moves in a *different* direction. That difference means that water waves are not the same type of waves as sound waves.

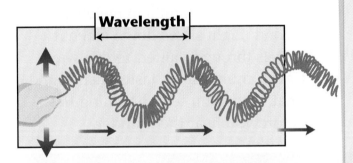

By vibrating one end of a spring toy up and down, you can see waves travel much as waves do on a watery surface.

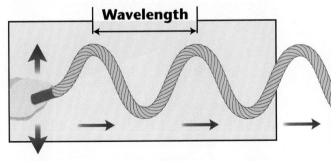

How do the waves made by a jump rope behave?

Brain Power

Now think about light. If light travels as a wave, is a light wave more like a sound wave or more like a water wave?

QUICK LAB

Water Waves

HYPOTHESIZE How do water waves affect the motion of floating objects? Write a hypothesis in your *Science Journal.* Test your ideas.

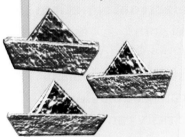

MATERIALS
- aluminum foil
- shallow pan at least 8 x 11 in.
- water
- pencil
- *Science Journal*

PROCEDURES

1. Fill the tray half full of water. Fold small squares of foil (1 cm by 1 cm) into tiny "boats." Place several of these boats on the surface of the water.

2. At one end of the tray, make waves on the water's surface. Do this by moving your pencil horizontally up and down in the water.

3. **PREDICT** What do you think will happen to the boats after two minutes? After five minutes? Record your predictions in your *Science Journal.*

CONCLUDE AND APPLY

1. **OBSERVE** What happened to the boats? How did they move? How far did they move? Were your predictions correct?

2. **EXPERIMENT** What happens if you change how fast you make the waves? What happens if you change the number of boats you use?

275

How Do Light Waves Travel?

Have you ever seen bits of paper pulled onto a comb or balloon that has been rubbed with a cloth? Have you ever picked up a paper clip with a magnet? In both cases the attraction is caused by static electricity, a form of **electromagnetism** (i lek′trō mag′ni tiz′əm).

Electromagnetism refers to forces that come from electricity and magnetism. Namely, magnets can set up a flow of electricity, and electricity can produce a kind of magnet.

In the 1850s James Clerk Maxwell concluded from his work that light is electromagnetic energy. The electrical and magnetic parts of the energy can carry themselves as a wave moving through space. Electromagnetic waves can travel without matter or through matter.

Electromagnetic waves vibrate back and forth across (*perpendicular to*) the direction in which light travels. Water waves are usually used as models for light waves. The wavelength is the distance from crest to crest. Yet light is not just one wavelength. It is many wavelengths. The colors of light are different wavelengths. A prism refracts the different wavelengths different amounts.

However, all the wavelengths of light travel through empty space at the same speed—over 300 million meters per second. Light slows down when it travels through matter. Yet it always travels much, much faster than sound. That's why you see a lightning flash before you hear the thunder.

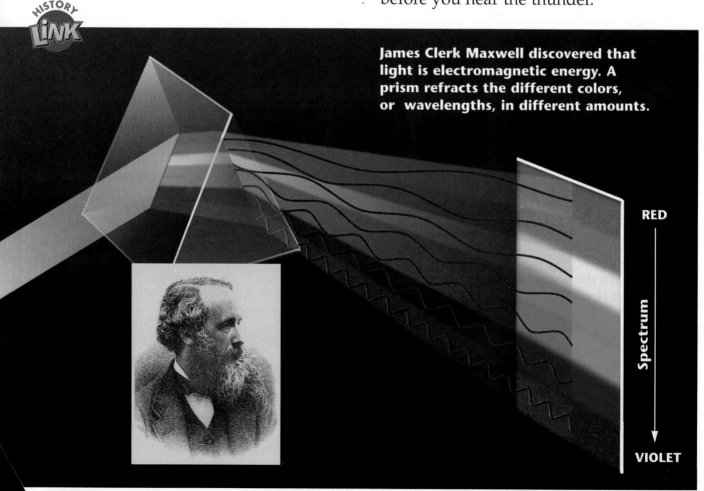

HISTORY LINK

James Clerk Maxwell discovered that light is electromagnetic energy. A prism refracts the different colors, or wavelengths, in different amounts.

RED

Spectrum

VIOLET

ELECTROMAGNETIC SPECTRUM

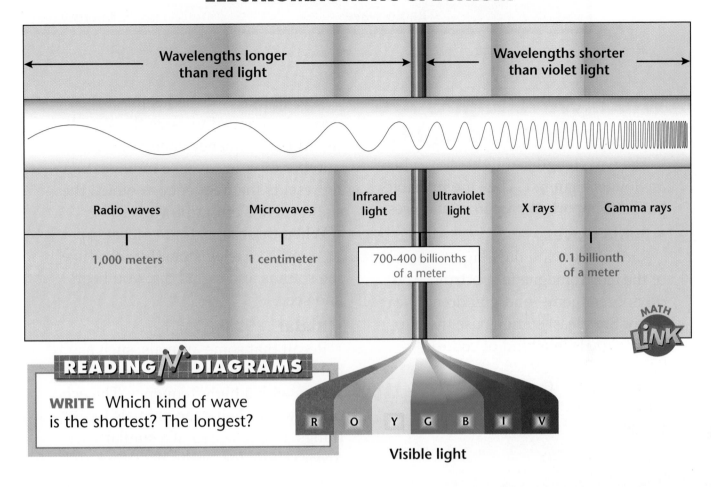

Wavelengths longer than red light

Wavelengths shorter than violet light

Radio waves	Microwaves	Infrared light	Ultraviolet light	X rays	Gamma rays
1,000 meters	1 centimeter	700-400 billionths of a meter		0.1 billionth of a meter	

R O Y G B I V

Visible light

READING ⁄ DIAGRAMS

WRITE Which kind of wave is the shortest? The longest?

What Is "Invisible Light"?

Since Maxwell's work, scientists have formed another idea of how light travels. Rather than as a smooth vibrating wave, perhaps light travels as tiny bundles of energy. Scientists call the bundles *photons*.

Waves or photons? Scientists use both models to explain light. For example, your eye picks up only so many photons of light at any instant. We can see the wavelengths of light that make up the colors of light.

Yet can we see all wavelengths of light? Based on the work of Heinrich Hertz from the 1880s, we now know that there are wavelengths of light that we do *not* see.

When light passes through a prism, there are wavelengths longer than the color red. We cannot see them. There are also wavelengths shorter than violet. We cannot see these wavelengths, either. Together all these wavelengths of light, the ones we see and the ones we cannot see, are called the **electromagnetic spectrum**.

Although we cannot see wavelengths longer than red or shorter than violet, we can detect them, and we can use them in many ways.

Which Wavelengths Are Longer than Red Light?

The wavelengths of light shown here are longer than red. They are invisible but have important properties and uses.

• Radio waves

Radio waves are the longest waves of the electromagnetic spectrum. You do not see them—and you do not hear them. Broadcast stations use them to carry signals in a kind of code—

AM or FM. In AM the height of the waves is changed to carry the signal. In FM the frequency changes. The number of your favorite radio station represents the frequency at which the station sends out radio waves.

When these signals are picked up by a radio or television, they produce the sounds and sights that you hear and see.

• Radar

Recall that some animals, such as bats and whales, send out sound waves with a high frequency. The echo of the waves helps the animals locate things. Radar works in a similar way. *Radar* stands for "**ra**dio **d**etecting **a**nd **r**anging." Radar uses radio waves that reflect off many objects. The waves can help weather forecasters detect rain and thick fog.

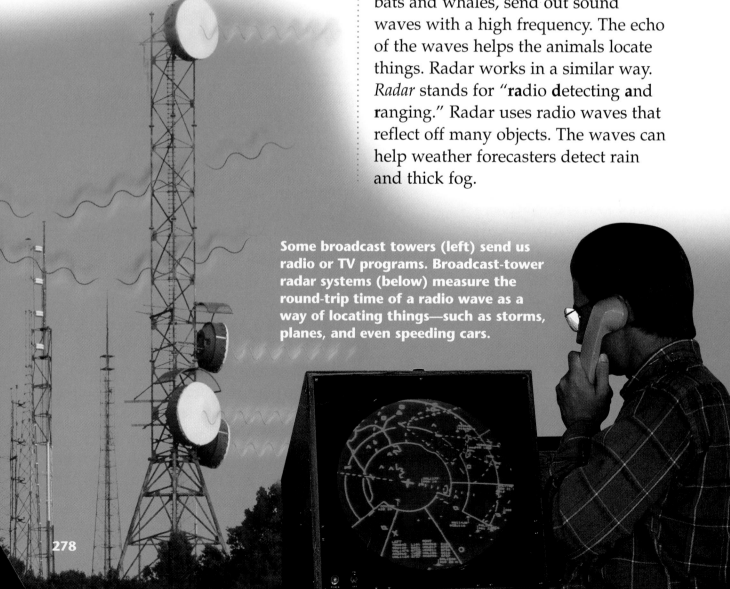

Some broadcast towers (left) send us radio or TV programs. Broadcast-tower radar systems (below) measure the round-trip time of a radio wave as a way of locating things—such as storms, planes, and even speeding cars.

| Infrared light | Ultraviolet light | X rays | Gamma rays |

Visible light

• Microwaves

A microwave oven uses electromagnetic waves, too. Microwaves are shortwave radio waves. Water in foods absorbs microwaves very readily. The energy from the absorbed microwaves speeds up the water molecules inside the food. As the water molecules move faster, the food gets hotter. Microwave ovens can heat many foods faster, using less energy than a regular oven.

• Infrared light

Infrared means "just beyond red." Infrared waves are next to visible red waves in the spectrum. When you stand in sunlight, it is the Sun's infrared waves that warm you. All objects give off infrared waves, depending on their temperature. Warmer objects give off more infrared waves than cooler objects do. Special photographic film and electronic sensors can be used to detect infrared light.

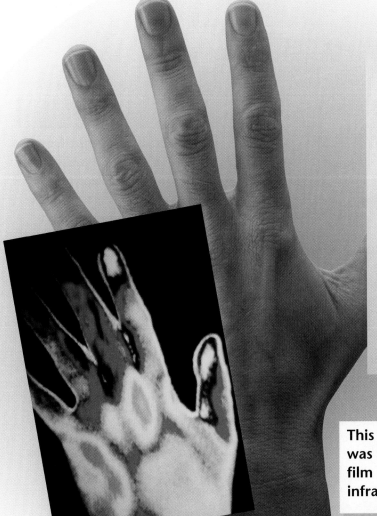

DID YOU KNOW?

You can talk using microwaves. Many long-distance telephone calls are sent using microwaves. They are turned into a special code for security. Then they are sent between antennas, via satellites, or through special cables. How do you think the message is coded?

This photograph was taken with film that picks up infrared light.

279

Which Are Shorter than Violet Light?

The wavelengths of light shown here are shorter than violet. They are invisible but have important properties and uses.

• Ultraviolet light

Ultraviolet (UV) light is made up of waves just shorter than visible violet light on the spectrum. UV light causes chemical changes. It can produce vitamin D in your body. You need vitamin D for healthy bones and teeth. Ultraviolet light produces vitamin D in milk. Hospitals use ultraviolet light to kill harmful bacteria in equipment used in operating rooms. However, UV light can cause harm. UV light from the Sun causes a sunburn. Scientists have found that UV light can also cause some forms of cancer on the skin. Cancer is a disease in which cells multiply rapidly with harmful effects.

Earth is protected from much of the Sun's UV light by the ozone layer. The ozone layer is a part of the upper atmos-phere that screens out UV light. However, some chemicals produced by factories are eating away at the ozone layer. Thus more of the Sun's UV light will pass through to Earth's surface. Care is being taken to prohibit the chemicals from being manufactured.

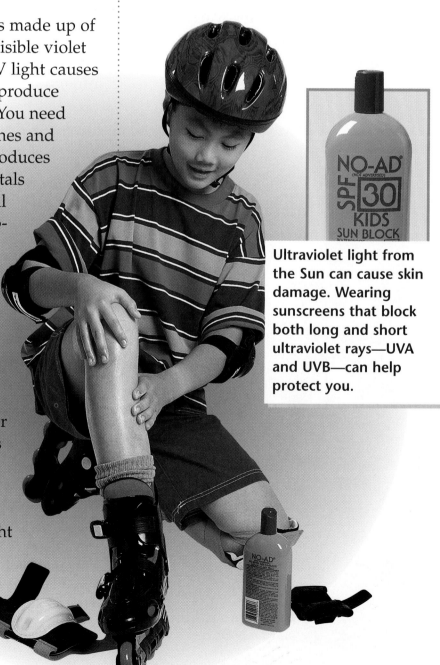

Ultraviolet light from the Sun can cause skin damage. Wearing sunscreens that block both long and short ultraviolet rays—UVA and UVB—can help protect you.

| Infrared light | Ultraviolet light | X rays | Gamma rays |

Visible light

• X rays and Gamma Rays

The shortest wavelengths of the spectrum—X rays and gamma rays—have great penetrating power. X rays can pass right through most objects. Thicker or denser objects tend to absorb X rays. This means that X rays can produce a picture when they pass through an arm or leg, or your jaw. The denser objects, such as bones and teeth, can show up very clearly on the finished picture.

A special "gamma camera" detects the rays and produces images of activity in the person's brain.

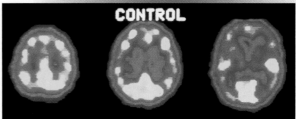

CONTROL

Ever wonder why a dentist makes you wear a heavy vest when you get your teeth x-rayed? The vest protects you from X rays passing into your body.

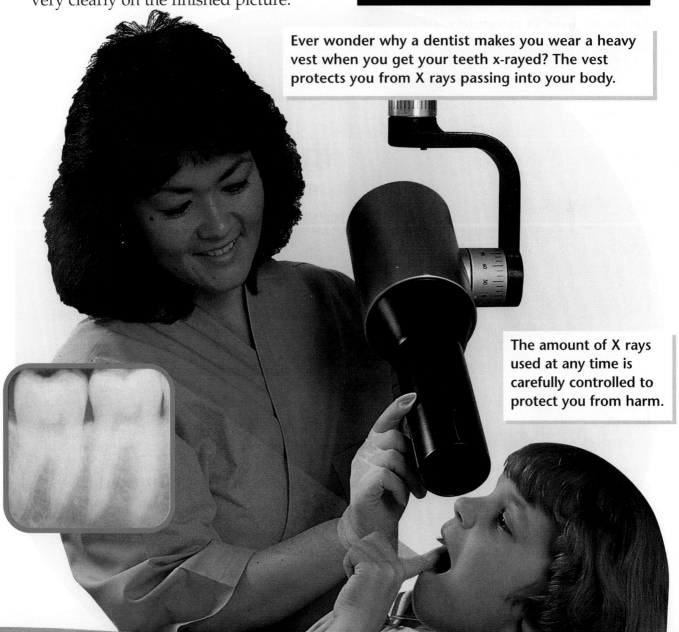

The amount of X rays used at any time is carefully controlled to protect you from harm.

What Are Lasers?

You've seen lasers in many places—such as at music events and even the checkout counter at the supermarket. Lasers are devices that produce thin streams of light. What makes light from a laser special?

Regular light from a bulb or a candle has many wavelengths all mixed together. As the light travels away from the bulb or candle, it spreads out and gets less noticeable. It gets weaker and weaker the farther it travels.

Lasers produce light that does not spread out or become weaker. Lasers, such as this device using a red ruby, produce light by absorbing flashes of light from a coiled tube. Inside the ruby the absorbed light bounces back and forth between mirrors at the ends of the ruby. As a result the ruby gives off a light of just a few close wavelengths. The wavelengths are all one color and line up "in step." The beam that comes out of the ruby is narrow and direct.

Lasers are used in astronomy.

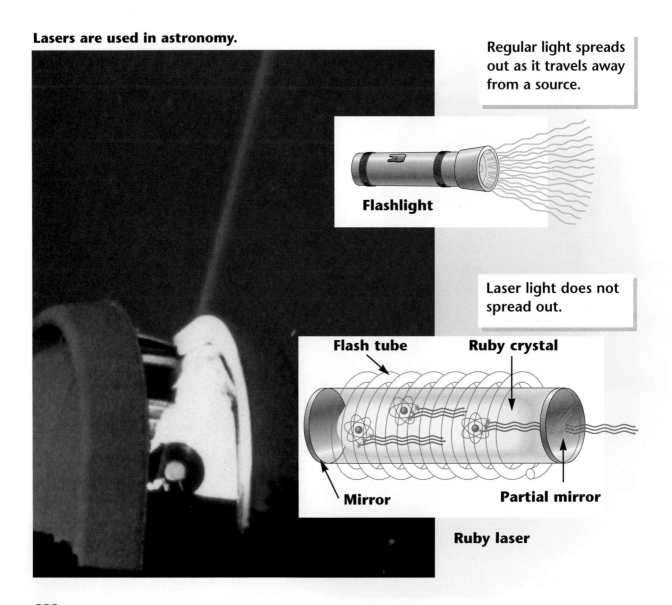

Regular light spreads out as it travels away from a source.

Flashlight

Laser light does not spread out.

Flash tube   **Ruby crystal**

Mirror   **Partial mirror**

Ruby laser

How Do We Use Lasers?

Powerful laser beams can melt even the hardest metals. Weaker ones can stay in narrow beams without causing harm to a person's body. The uses of lasers vary from heavy-duty industry to medicine to entertainment.

Laser beams are used to melt metals and "crack open" granite. Doctors use lasers to repair torn blood vessels in the eye. More and more, lasers are being used in place of surgery that used to require a cut.

There are weak laser beams in CD players. A laser beam penetrates the disk and "reads" the delicately grained code of signals. The beam passes the code into a device that translates it into sounds.

WHY IT MATTERS

We think of light as something "visible." Yet it is more accurate to think of light as a form of energy that travels in waves and also has some properties of particles. Light has many wavelengths. Some of them—the colors of light—are visible. Put all the colors together, and you see white light. Yet there are many wavelengths that we do not see, and yet they are extremely useful. Radar waves help forecasters tell us what the weather will be X rays help dentists and doctors check for cavities and broken bones. Every time you turn on a radio or TV, you are picking up invisible waves of "light."

REVIEW

1. How does light travel? Does it travel the same way sound does?

2. What is radar? How is it used in weather forecasting?

3. How is ultraviolet light harmful? How is it helpful?

4. **USE NUMBERS** If a spacecraft were 900 million meters from Earth, how long would it take to send a radio signal from Earth to the spacecraft?

5. **CRITICAL THINKING** *Synthesize* What's the difference between a beam of light from a flashlight and a beam of light from a laser?

WHY IT MATTERS **THINK ABOUT IT**
Think of three or four forms of electro-magnetic radiation that affect your life every day.

WHY IT MATTERS **WRITE ABOUT IT**
Write a paragraph about how these forms of electromagnetic energy affect you. Which ones do you use the most? Why?

A SPARK-ling Discovery

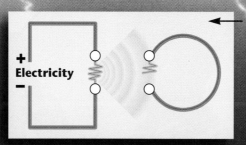

You can't see electromagnetic energy, but it's all around you. Who discovered these invisible forces?

It happened in the mid-1800s. James Clerk Maxwell hypothesized that light was a form of electromagnetic energy. Heinrich Hertz set out to prove Maxwell's theory. In 1887 Hertz built an electric circuit that made an electric spark jump across a gap of space!

Hertz realized that the first spark created a burst of invisible electromagnetic waves. They reached the gap almost immediately, and their energy caused the second spark!

Hertz had discovered what we now call radio waves. They travel at the speed of light but have much

A spark in the circuit at the left sends electromagnetic waves toward the other circuit, causing a spark!

longer wavelengths than visible light. Today scientists measure frequency in special units called hertz!

DISCUSSION STARTER

1. How did Hertz prove that electromagnetic waves exist?

2. How do the lengths of radio waves compare with the wavelengths of visible light?

To learn more about Hertz's discovery, visit **www.mhschool.com/science** and enter the keyword SPARK.

inter**NET** CONNECTION

SCIENCE WORDS

bioluminescence
  p.237

concave lens p.254

concave mirror
  p.242

convex lens p.254

convex mirror p.242

electromagnetic
  spectrum p.277

opaque p.250

primary color p.266

primary pigment
  p.268

transparent p.250

USING SCIENCE WORDS

Number a paper from 1 to 10. Fill in 1 to 5 with words from the list above.

1. Fireflies make cool light through a process called ___?___.

2. A material that light cannot pass through is called ___?___.

3. A material that light can easily pass through is called ___?___.

4. Microwaves and X-rays are part of the ___?___.

5. Security mirrors used in stores are ___?___.

6–10. Pick five words from the list above that were not used in 1 to 5, and use each in a sentence.

UNDERSTANDING SCIENCE IDEAS

11. Describe the difference between transparent objects and opaque ones.

12. Describe how sunglasses can be made so that they reduce glare.

13. What is one way a light wave reacts when it hits a surface?

14. Describe how your eyes see color.

15. Name one form of invisible light. Describe how it is used.

USING IDEAS AND SKILLS

16. You see a friend's reflection in a mirror. How does the light travel to your eye?

17. **READING SKILL: COMPARE AND CONTRAST** What is the difference between the primary colors of light and the primary colors of pigments?

18. You are looking at your friend through a telescope that uses lenses. She appears to be upside down. Why do you think this happened? Explain your answer.

19. **PREDICT** How many different colors do you think you could make using two flashlights, a piece of white paper, and one piece of red and one piece of green cellophane?

20. **THINKING LIKE A SCIENTIST** How might you make a simple camera without a lens to focus the light onto the film? What kind of mirror might you use? State a hypothesis. How would you test your idea?

PROBLEMS and PUZZLES

Pinhole Camera Cut a large square out of one end of an oatmeal container. Tape wax paper over the opening. Cut a smaller square out of the other end. Tape aluminum foil over it. In the center of the foil, poke a hole with a push-pin. Aim the hole at a light bulb 30 centimeters away. Darken the room. What do you see? Why?

SCIENCE WORDS

absorption p.220

decibel p.210

echo p.221

electromagnetic
   spectrum p.277

hertz p.209

opaque p.251

prism p.264

reflection p.220

refraction p.252

vibration p.196

USING SCIENCE WORDS

Number a paper from 1 to 10. Beside each number write the word or words that best complete the sentence.

1. Sound is produced by a back-and-forth motion called a(n) __?__ .

2. The loudness of sound is measured in units called __?__ .

3. The frequency of a sound is measured in units called __?__ .

4. A reflected sound is called a(n) __?__ .

5. Sound tends not to bounce off carpets because of __?__ .

6. A material that completely blocks light is called a(n) __?__ .

7. The property called __?__ explains how lenses can bend light.

8. A(n) __?__ breaks up white light into many different colors.

9. The bouncing of a wave off a surface is called __?__ .

10. Invisible and visible light make up the __?__ .

UNDERSTANDING SCIENCE IDEAS

Write 11 to 15. For each number write the letter for the best answer. You may wish to use the hints provided.

11. If the frequency of a musical note is increased,
    a. the note gets louder
    b. the note gets softer
    c. the note gets higher
    d. the note gets lower
    (Hint: Read page 209.)

12. Echoes are the result of
    a. the Doppler effect
    b. reflection
    c. refraction
    d. absorption
    (Hint: Read page 222.)

13. Light is a form of
    a. heat
    b. electricity
    c. energy
    d. sound
    (Hint: Read page 234.)

14. Which of the following is translucent?
    a. a car windshield
    b. a convex mirror
    c. a frosted light bulb
    d. a concrete block
    (Hint: Read page 250.)

15. Which is *not* found in the electromagnetic spectrum?
    a. X rays
    b. infrared light
    c. FM radio waves
    d. sound waves
    (Hint: Read pages 276–277.)

USING IDEAS AND SKILLS

16. Describe how you can use a rubber band to make a sound. How can you change the pitch of the sound?

17. Explain how pressing the frets on a guitar changes the sound produced.

18. Describe what happens when a sound wave hits a padded surface.

19. Why do the very hot wires in a toaster glow?

20. Copy and complete the diagram to show what happens to the light ray as it passes through the lens.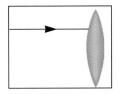

21.  **COMMUNICATE** Make a diagram that shows what the Law of Reflection means. Use labels.

22. Explain what happens when an object absorbs infrared light.

THINKING LIKE A SCIENTIST

23.  **PREDICT/OBSERVE** If you had a job mixing paints, explain how you would use the skill of predicting to do your work well.

24. Explain how sound and light are alike and different.

25. Does a loud sound carry more energy than a soft one? How could you test your idea?

interNET
CONNECTION

For help in reviewing this unit, visit
www.mhschool.com/science

WRITING IN YOUR JOURNAL

SCIENCE IN YOUR LIFE
List ways that color and sound are used to warn you of danger. Explain why some seem to be more effective than others.

PRODUCT ADS
How does TV advertising use light and color to capture your attention? Give examples.

HOW SCIENTISTS WORK
In this unit you have learned about the discoveries of Maxwell and Hertz. Do you think scientists who study invisible things need different skills from those who study things they can see? Describe the skills you think scientists like Maxwell and Hertz need.

Design your own Experiment

People are said to learn better if they listen to Mozart's music than if they listen to rock music. Design an experiment to test this statement. Check with your teacher before trying it out.

PROBLEM SOLVING and PROJECTS

A Light Maze

Build a light maze. Use scissors, a flashlight, a box with a lid, heavy tape, strips of cardboard, mirrors, or just aluminum foil taped to cardboard squares. Start by drawing a plan of the maze to show the path of light. Then build the maze. Find what happens as you add turns into the maze. Have a contest to see who can build a maze with the most turns that doesn't lose a beam of light from the flashlight.

Consumer Testing: Tapes and Recorders

You want to find the best tape recorder you can afford and the best tapes to use in it. Tell how you would design a series of experiments to test various tapes and recorders. Remember to test only one variable at a time. Describe what sorts of things you would look for in determining tape and recorder quality. What other things should you take into consideration?

The Puppy Package Problem

THE PROBLEM

The Puppy Toy Company sends its puppy barking dolls in the mail. They bark in response to movement or noise. They use computer chips that cannot be turned off without destroying the toys. The toys sound so real that postal workers are opening the boxes to see if real puppies are inside.

THE PLAN

Write a hypothesis to describe a kind of design and packing materials for a soundproof box.

TEST

Test your hypothesis. Use a box and gather materials you'll need. Pack the box to make it as soundproof as possible. For sounds, use an item such as an alarm clock.

EVALUATE/PUBLISH

How well did your design work? Could you improve it? If so, how? Write a report to summarize your results. What recommendations would you make to the toy company about packing its toys?

UNIT 4

MATTER

CHAPTER 7

PROPERTIES OF MATTER

Every 65 minutes Old Faithful erupts. It's just water ... but what a sight! It is caused by a complicated series of events, but it all "boils" down to heat. The rocks beneath Old Faithful are very hot. They heat water in the ground. Think of what can happen to water heated in a pot over the stove. Water boils!

Any substance can boil, given the right temperature—even lead. At what temperature does lead boil? Read all about it in Chapter 7.

In Chapter 7 you will get many chances to read for the main idea of pages that have lots of details and facts.

Topic 1

WHY IT MATTERS

There are many ways to measure matter.

SCIENCE WORDS

mass the amount of matter in an object

volume the amount of space an object takes up

weight (on Earth) a measure of the force of gravity between Earth and an object

density a measure of how tightly packed matter is; the amount of mass contained in a given volume

buoyancy the upward push on an object by the liquid (or gas) the object is placed in

conduct allow heat or electricity to flow through readily

insulate not allow heat or electricity to flow through readily

What Matter Is

When you say something is "bigger" than something else, what does "bigger" mean? What is bigger than a circus tent? What is smaller? Is a car from the circus train bigger than the tent?

If the circus tent is taken down and folded up, are the same things bigger or smaller?

Bigger or smaller. More or less. In what ways can things be "more" or "less" than other things? How might a circus tent, folded or not, always be less than an elephant? Than a train car?

EXPLORE

HYPOTHESIZE **What properties do you use to compare things? Are there different ways something can be "more" than other things? Write a hypothesis in your** *Science Journal.* **Test your ideas.**

Design Your Own Experiment

WHICH IS MORE?

PROCEDURES

1. OBSERVE Look at the golf ball (or wooden block) and blown-up balloon. Which is "more"? Think of how one object could be "more":
- more when you use a balance
- more when you put it in water and see how much the water level goes up, and so on

Record your observations in your *Science Journal*.

2. PLAN Use the equipment to verify one way that one object is more than another. Decide which of the three objects is "more" and which one is "less."

3. Repeat your measurements to verify your answer.

4. COMPARE AND CONTRAST Now use different equipment to compare the two objects. Is the same object still "more"? Explain.

5. Repeat your measurements to verify your answer.

CONCLUDE AND APPLY

1. COMMUNICATE Identify the equipment you used. Report your results.

2. COMPARE AND CONTRAST For each test, which object was more? In what way was it more than the other object?

GOING FURTHER: Problem Solving

3. EXPERIMENT What if you were given a large box of puffed oats and a small box of oatmeal? Which do you think would be more? Design an experiment to test your hypothesis. Tell what equipment you would use.

MATERIALS
- golf ball or wooden block
- blown-up balloon
- equal-pan balance
- ruler
- string
- box, such as a shoe box, big enough for the balloon to fit in
- pail of water
- *Science Journal*

Which Is More?

What is matter? All of the gases, liquids, and solids in the world around you—the air you breathe, the water you drink, and the chair you sit on—are made of matter. Testing to see whether a golf ball or a balloon was "more" in the Explore Activity measured *properties* of the matter in these objects.

The golf ball had more **mass** because it tipped the balance more. However, the balloon had more volume because it filled up a greater portion of a box.

Mass is a measure of the amount of matter in an object. Diagram 1 shows how a balance is used to measure mass. Known masses are placed on one side until they balance the unknown mass.

Mass is often reported in kilograms. The camera in the diagram has a mass of 1 kilogram because it comes into balance with this much known mass.

Volume measures how much space a sample of matter takes up. Volumes are often reported in cubic centimeters (cm³). As diagram 2 shows, the volume of a sample of matter can be measured by seeing how many cubes of a chosen size it can fill.

The cough medicine in the dropper has a volume of 2 cm³ because it can just fill two cubes that are 1 centimeter on a side.

Matter is defined using the properties of mass and volume. *Matter is anything that has mass and takes up space.*

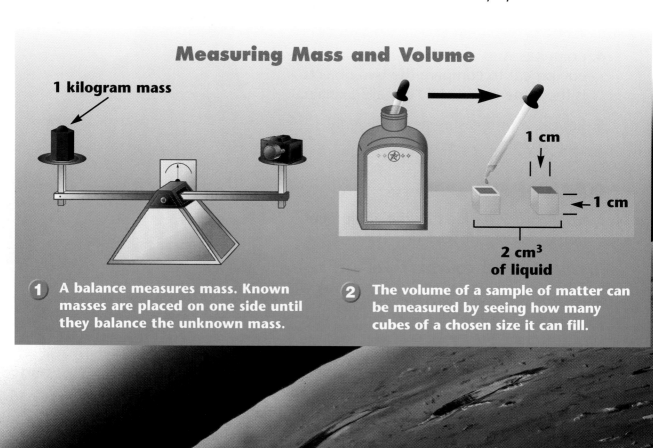

Measuring Mass and Volume

1 kilogram mass

1 A balance measures mass. Known masses are placed on one side until they balance the unknown mass.

1 cm

1 cm

2 cm³ of liquid

2 The volume of a sample of matter can be measured by seeing how many cubes of a chosen size it can fill.

How Are Mass and Weight Different?

Suppose you find the mass of a certain book to be 1 kilogram. You might be tempted to say, "This book weighs 1 kilogram." However, this is incorrect. The book's **weight** is actually the force of gravity between Earth and the book. The book's mass, on the other hand, is a measure of the amount of matter in the book compared to known masses.

As you know, we can use kilograms to measure an object's mass. Yet to measure weight, we must use a quantity that describes the force of gravity between two masses. Scientists prefer to use a quantity called the *newton* (N) to measure force. One newton is the same as 0.22 pound. (Or 1 pound is 4.45 newtons.) Newtons and pounds both describe the amount of pull or push a force produces. In this case the force is the pull of gravity.

An object's weight depends on its location in the universe. If you were to travel to the Moon, for example, you would have less weight. The Moon has less mass than Earth, so the force of gravity between your body and the Moon would be less. However, your mass would remain unchanged, as in the diagram.

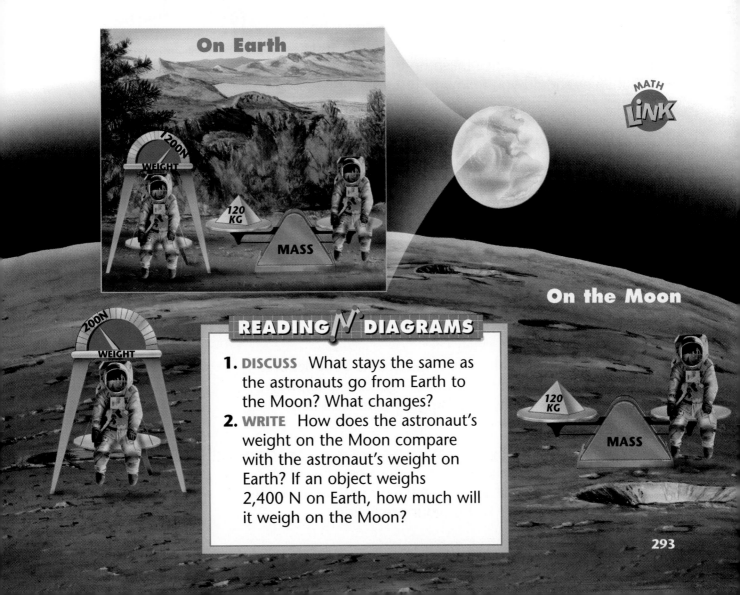

On Earth

1200N
WEIGHT

120 KG

MASS

MATH
LiNK

On the Moon

200N
WEIGHT

120 KG

MASS

READING N DIAGRAMS

1. **DISCUSS** What stays the same as the astronauts go from Earth to the Moon? What changes?
2. **WRITE** How does the astronaut's weight on the Moon compare with the astronaut's weight on Earth? If an object weighs 2,400 N on Earth, how much will it weigh on the Moon?

293

Skill: Making a Model

HOW METAL BOATS FLOAT

You have probably seen how a metal object like a nail or a spoon sinks in water. However, huge ships made of similar metal float even when they carry large cargoes. How is this possible? In this activity you will make a model of a metal boat. Experiment to see how boats are designed so that they can carry heavy cargo.

MATERIALS
- household aluminum foil
- large paper clips
- pan of water
- *Science Journal*

PROCEDURES

1. **MAKE A MODEL** Make a boat out of a 10-cm by 10-cm (4-in. by 4-in.) piece of aluminum foil. Then float it on water.

2. **PREDICT** Write down in your *Science Journal* what you think will happen when you place more and more matter in the space taken up by the boat. What steps should you follow to test your prediction? Be sure to use only the materials listed above.

3. **EXPERIMENT** Carry out your procedure, keeping a written record of what you observe.

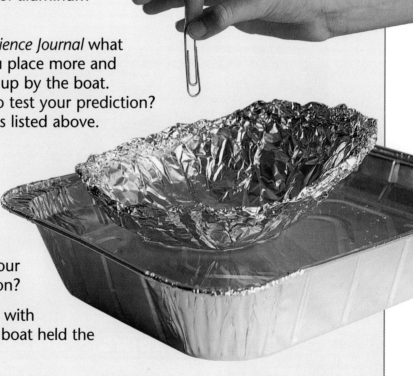

CONCLUDE AND APPLY

1. **COMMUNICATE** How well did your results agree with your prediction?

2. **COMPARE** Compare your model with those of your classmates. Which boat held the most clips? Why?

3. **MAKE A MODEL** The aluminum foil boat is a model of a steel ship. Use the way your boat floats to explain how a steel ship floats. Why was using a model of a large ship helpful?

4. **INFER** Think about objects that have more matter packed into the space they take up than water does. Based on your observations, will such objects sink or float in water? Design an experiment to test your prediction.

How Tightly Packed Is Matter?

In the Skill Builder, the boat sank when the boat and cargo weighed more than an equal volume of water. What makes things sink or float? A material will sink in water when its matter is packed together more tightly than the matter in water. If we divide the mass of a sample of material by its volume, we get a measure of how tightly packed its matter is. This measure is called the material's **density**.

As more matter gets packed into the same amount of space, the material's density increases. Density really tells us how massive something is for its volume. When a material's density is greater than water's density, the material will sink in water. The material will float in water if its density is less than water's density.

The diagram below explains how steel ships can float even though steel sinks in water. The ship is like the hollow ball. The air inside has very little mass. Both the ship and the hollow ball have a large volume in comparison to the total mass. Both are less dense than water, so they float despite their steel shells!

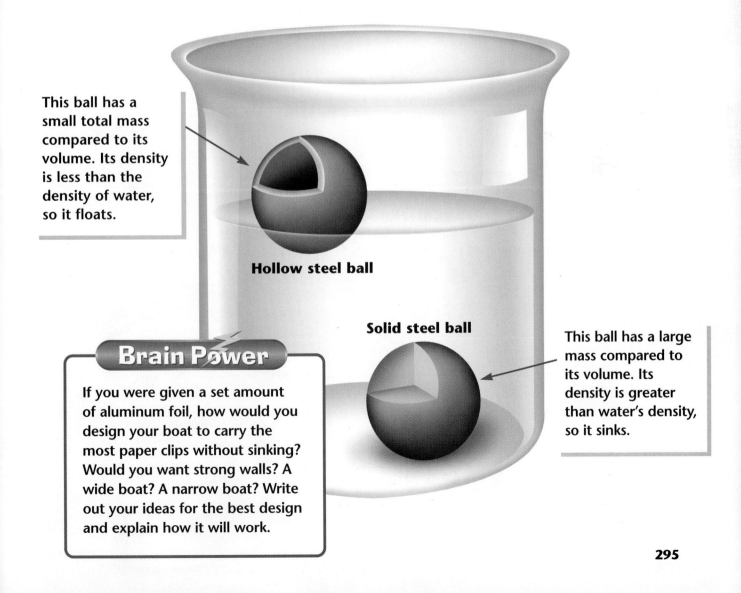

This ball has a small total mass compared to its volume. Its density is less than the density of water, so it floats.

Hollow steel ball

Solid steel ball

This ball has a large mass compared to its volume. Its density is greater than water's density, so it sinks.

Brain Power

If you were given a set amount of aluminum foil, how would you design your boat to carry the most paper clips without sinking? Would you want strong walls? A wide boat? A narrow boat? Write out your ideas for the best design and explain how it will work.

How Dense Are Solids, Liquids, and Gases?

Imagine cutting a piece of aluminum foil into smaller and smaller pieces. Eventually, you would find that aluminum is made of very tiny particles. All matter—solids, liquids, and gases—is made of similar tiny particles. As the diagram shows, gases are much less dense than liquids and solids because the tiny particles in gases are so spread out.

Density is a measure of how massive something is for its size. Therefore, density is found by dividing the mass of a sample by its volume. What if the mass of 10 cm³ of a certain metal is 80 grams (1,000 grams = 1 kilogram)? The density of the metal would be 80 grams divided by 10 cm³, which is 8 g/cm³.

Now imagine that we have another piece of the same metal with twice as much volume, 20 cm³. We would also have twice the mass—160 g. The density would be 160 g divided by 20 cm³, which is still 8 g/cm³. As long as conditions such as temperature do not change, the density of a substance does not depend on how much we measure!

The table shows the densities of some common substances. Look over the values given to see how the densities of various solids, liquids, and gases compare.

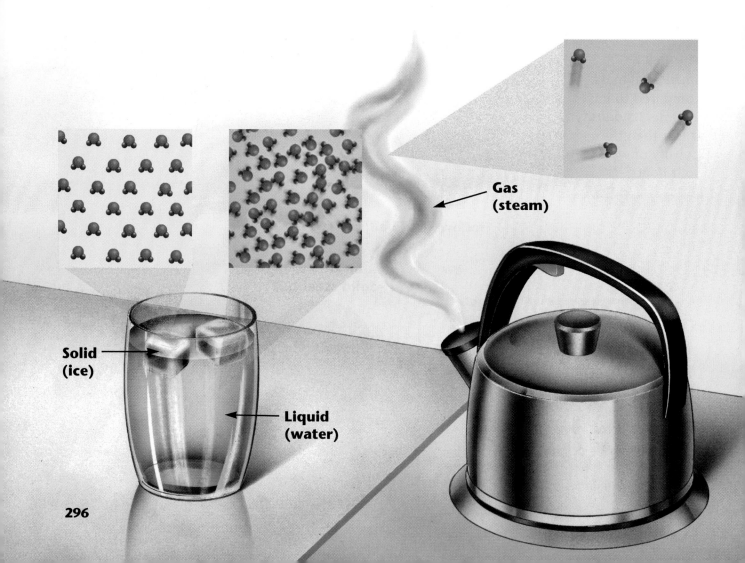

Gas (steam)

Solid (ice)

Liquid (water)

DENSITIES OF COMMON SUBSTANCES

State	Substance		Density (g/cm³)
SOLID	 1	 2	1 ALUMINUM, 2.7 2 GOLD, 18.9
LIQUID	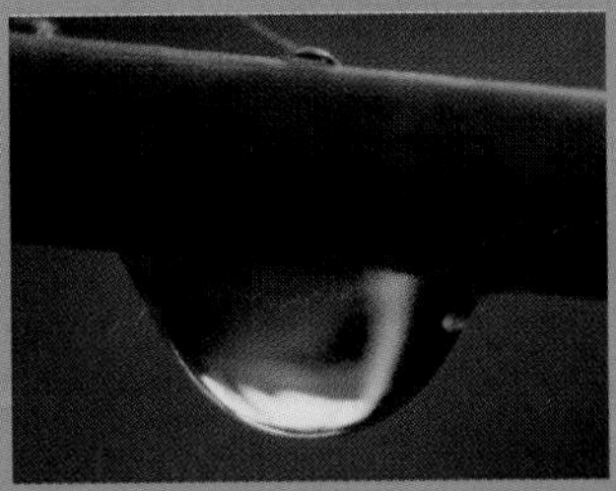 1	 2	1 WATER, 1.0 2 MERCURY, 13.5
GAS	 1	 2	1 HELIUM, 0.00018 2 AIR AT SEA LEVEL, 0.0012

READING N' CHARTS

1. **DISCUSS** Which is denser—aluminum or gold? Mercury or gold?
2. **WRITE** Organize the substances in the chart from the least dense to the densest. Can you explain why helium balloons rise in the air? Would a solid piece of gold float in water?

What Makes Things Sink or Float?

When any object is placed in water, the water actually pushes up on the object. If the upward push is strong enough compared to the object's weight, the object will float.

This happens when the object is less dense than the water. Yet if the object is more dense than the water, the upward push is not strong enough to hold the object up, and it sinks.

Any liquid will push up on an object that is placed in it, just as water does. This push is called **buoyancy**

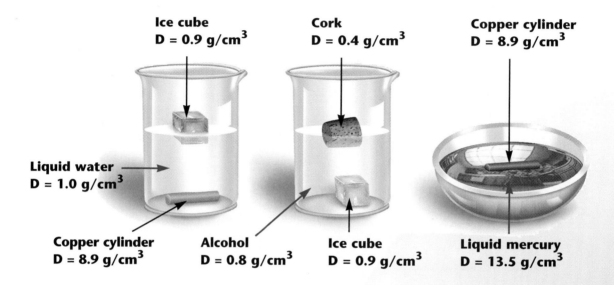

Ice cube
D = 0.9 g/cm³

Cork
D = 0.4 g/cm³

Copper cylinder
D = 8.9 g/cm³

Liquid water
D = 1.0 g/cm³

Copper cylinder
D = 8.9 g/cm³

Alcohol
D = 0.8 g/cm³

Ice cube
D = 0.9 g/cm³

Liquid mercury
D = 13.5 g/cm³

In order to float in a liquid, an object must be less dense than the liquid. Why does ice float in water? Why does it sink in alcohol? The copper cylinder floats in mercury but sinks in water. Do you think it will sink or float in alcohol?

SUBMARINE

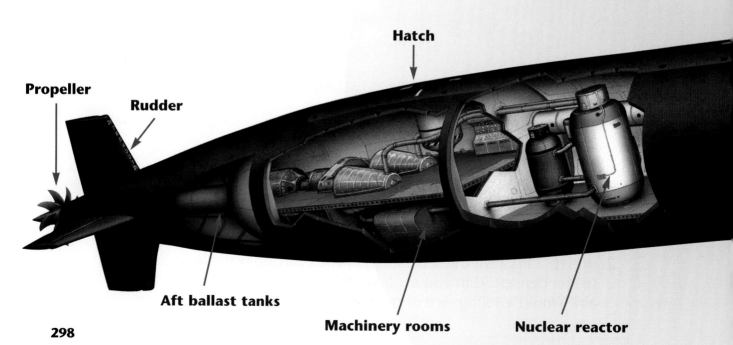

Hatch

Propeller

Rudder

Aft ballast tanks

Machinery rooms

Nuclear reactor

(boi'ən sē). If the buoyancy is great enough, the object will float. Objects have enough buoyancy to float when they are less dense than the liquid in which they are placed.

As the difference in density between a liquid and a floating object gets greater, the object floats higher. The diagrams show examples of sinking and floating that can be explained by buoyancy.

It's easy to float in Utah's Great Salt Lake. That's because salt water is denser and has greater buoyancy than fresh water—and the lake has 6 billion tons of salt! Swimmers float higher in the lake than in ocean water. The salt has been building up in the lake for about 1 million years. Where can you find another large salty lake?

Sailors pump seawater into ballast tanks on a submarine to bring its average density close to the density of the surrounding water. This makes the sub have little tendency to rise or sink.

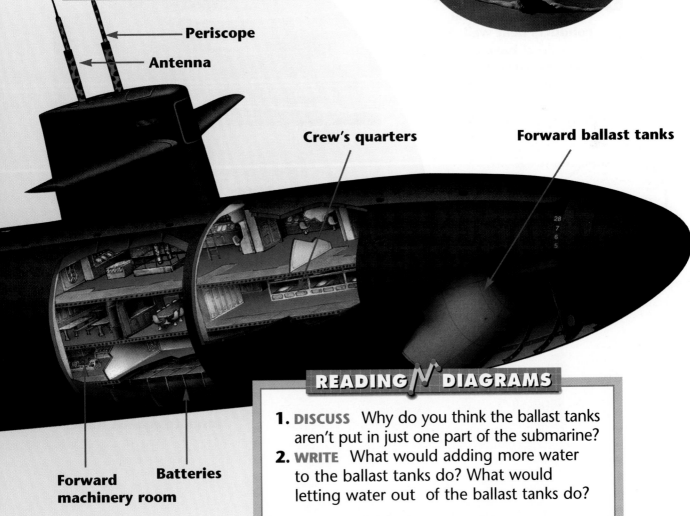

Periscope

Antenna

Crew's quarters

Forward ballast tanks

Forward machinery room

Batteries

READING DIAGRAMS

1. **DISCUSS** Why do you think the ballast tanks aren't put in just one part of the submarine?
2. **WRITE** What would adding more water to the ballast tanks do? What would letting water out of the ballast tanks do?

299

What Other Properties Does Matter Have?

Matter has many important properties besides density. For example, some materials **conduct** heat very well. These materials allow heat to flow through them easily. However, other materials **insulate** against the passage of heat. They do not readily permit heat to flow. Look carefully at the photographs to learn about materials that conduct or insulate.

Cooking pots and pans are made of metal because metal conducts heat well. However, they should have wooden or ceramic handles. Such handles insulate against heat so you don't get burned when you touch the handles.

Metals like the copper in the wire are also good conductors of electricity. The electricity flows from the battery to the light bulb through the wire, producing light and heat. The plastic that coats the wire is an insulator. Anyone who touches the plastic coating will not be shocked, because the electricity cannot pass through it.

Special ceiling tiles help soften noises in a room and insulate the room above from noise.

① Cooking pans are made of metal because metal conducts heat well. Yet the pans must have a handle that insulates against heat. Pans often have wooden or ceramic handles cooks can hold without being burned.

② The wire is a good conductor of electricity. The plastic that coats the wire is an insulator. Why must electrical wire be insulated?

③ Special ceiling tiles insulate against noise.

What Materials Are Magnetic?

Certain objects push or pull on each other because they are *magnetic*. Magnetism is another property of some kinds of matter. A magnet has a north and a south pole. North poles and south poles of magnets attract, but two poles that are alike push apart. Magnets can also attract certain materials that are made of iron metal.

The photograph shows how electricity can be used to make a magnet. Note how the electromagnet attracts the metal paper clips but not the cork or the wooden toothpicks.

We can use properties such as density, ability to conduct electricity,

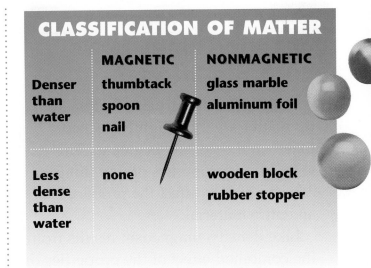

CLASSIFICATION OF MATTER

	MAGNETIC	NONMAGNETIC
Denser than water	thumbtack spoon nail	glass marble aluminum foil
Less dense than water	none	wooden block rubber stopper

and magnetism to *classify* matter. We place materials that share properties together in groups. Look again at the objects in the photograph. The table above shows one way these objects could be classified.

Electricity can be used to make a magnet.

Wrapping wire coils around a nail and connecting the ends of the wire to a battery creates an electromagnet.

What objects does the electromagnet attract? What objects doesn't it attract?

301

How Can Properties of Little Things Have Such Big Effects?

When the tiny particles that make up matter are more tightly packed together, the density is greater. This shows how properties of tiny things can combine to affect the properties of an entire material.

Like density, magnetism results from the combined effect of the properties of tiny particles. In iron metal, for example, each tiny particle of iron is itself a magnet.

Scientists have discovered that some materials become perfect conductors of electricity when they are very cold. The diagram shows a ceramic, glasslike material that conducts perfectly when cooled to 196° below 0°C (that is, −196°C).

Magnet

Ceramic disk

The magnet causes electricity to flow in the ceramic. This causes a reverse magnetic push that holds the magnet up. This effect can lift trains above the rails, so that they can travel faster.

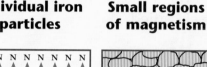

Individual iron particles **Small regions of magnetism**

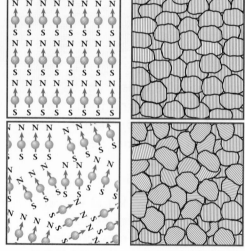

Magnetized iron bar

Demagnetized iron bar

When iron particles in small areas of the metal line up a permanent magnet is formed.

How Do We Use Properties of Matter?

Engineers and scientists use properties of matter when they design and build things. Aerogels are new materials with very low density and relatively great strength. Made of tiny pockets of air surrounded by thin walls of silica, aerogels are nearly transparent. Aerogels are very good insulators against heat. Insulated windows containing aerogel would be from 10 to 20 times better at holding in heat than ordinary glass windows!

You use many different properties of matter every day. Matter that conducts electricity lets you read at night or listen to your favorite CDs. Buoyancy allows you to float boats on a lake or helps you in swimming class. Magnets help you pick up metals or find your way home with the help of a compass.

REVIEW

1. List four properties of matter.

2. If a rock were taken from Earth to the Moon, how would its mass and weight be affected? Why?

3. What if you had paper clips, rubber bands, wood chips, straight pins, strips of aluminum foil, and glass beads? Using a property of matter you've learned, classify these objects. Show your results in a table.

4. **MAKE A MODEL** How does the density of warm water compare with the density of cold water? How would you design a model to test your ideas?

5. **CRITICAL THINKING** *Analyze* The density of corn oil is 0.92 g/cm³. What happens when corn oil is poured into water? Why does this happen?

WHY IT MATTERS **THINK ABOUT IT**
Think of the properties of matter you use every day. In what ways are they important to you?

WHY IT MATTERS **WRITE ABOUT IT**
Write a paragraph about a typical school day from the time you wake up until the time you go to sleep. What properties of matter do you rely on to get to school, do your homework, play with your friends?

READING SKILL
Reread pages 300–301. Look at the pictures and list facts. Write the main idea of these pages.

FISH: Sink or Swim

Swim Bladder

Stomach

Location of a fish's swim bladder

This diver has to add weights to sink; fish just deflate their swim bladders.

If you've ever tried to swim underwater, you know how difficult it is to stay down. Why is it so easy for fish? The answer is built-in— a swim bladder. A fish controls its swim bladder. To dive, the fish lets air out. The fish becomes less buoyant and sinks. Then the fish adds air to its swim bladder. The bladder makes the fish buoyant and it rises!

Ocean fish may have smaller swim bladders than fresh-water fish. Why? Salt water is denser than fresh water so less air is needed to float. Sharks don't have swim bladders. Instead they have large, oily livers. Oil is lighter than water, so the livers keep sharks afloat.

A fish's swim bladder works like the ballast tanks inside a submarine, which allow it to surface or dive. When the ballast tanks are full of air, the submarine floats in the water. To make the sub dive, water is pumped into the ballast tanks. To resurface, air is used to push the water out of the tanks.

A fish's sleek body also helps it dive. Sailfish move at about 109 kilometers per hour (68 miles per hour)! Compare that with the cheetah, the fastest land animal. It runs 96 kilometers per hour (60 miles per hour).

Sharks have oily livers that keep them afloat.

Discussion
Starter

1 How does a fish's swim bladder work?

2 What do sharks have instead of swim bladders?

interNET CONNECTION To learn more about swim bladders, visit **www.mhschool.com/science** and enter the keyword **SWIM.**

WHY IT MATTERS

All substances are made of tiny building blocks of matter.

SCIENCE WORDS

element a basic building block of matter; a pure substance that cannot be broken down into anything simpler

compound a chemical combination of two or more elements into a single substance

atom the smallest unit of an element that still has the properties of the element

proton a particle with a positive charge in the nucleus of an atom

neutron an uncharged particle in the nucleus of an atom

electron a particle with a negative charge moving around the nucleus of an atom

nucleus the dense center part of an atom

molecule a group of more than one atom joined together that acts like a single particle

What Matter Is Made Of

How is Jupiter like Earth? How are they alike on the outside?

Both planets have atmospheres. What are the atmospheres made of? Are they similar? What are the planets made of "beneath" the atmospheres?

Here's a similar question. What is matter made of? If you cannot "look inside" something—a planet or a piece of matter—how can scientists tell what a planet or any piece of matter is made of?

EXPLORE

HYPOTHESIZE How can you tell what is inside a sealed opaque box—without opening it? What sorts of tests would you perform to try to identify its contents? Write a hypothesis in your *Science Journal*. Test your ideas.

Investigate How We Know What's "Inside" Matter

You will examine three boxes to tell how one box has something in common with each of the other two.

PROCEDURES

1. OBSERVE Examine the three boxes, but do not open them. You can lift them, shake them, listen to the noises they make, feel the way their contents shift as you move them, and so on. Record your observations in your *Science Journal*.

2. INFER Try to determine what is in each box.

MATERIALS

- 3 identical, sealed, opaque boxes
- *Science Journal*

CONCLUDE AND APPLY

1. COMMUNICATE Describe in your *Science Journal* what you think is in each box.

2. How did you make your decision?

3. COMPARE AND CONTRAST Do these boxes have anything in common? In what ways are they similar? In what ways are they different?

GOING FURTHER: Problem Solving

4. EXPERIMENT What if you had a can of peanuts and a can of stewed tomatoes? The cans looked the same except for the labels. Now what if your baby brother took the labels off? You wanted the peanuts, but you didn't want to open the tomatoes by mistake. What experiments could you do to find out what was inside— before you opened a can?

How Do We Know What's "Inside" Matter?

In the Explore Activity, the boxes were sealed. Tests had to be done from the outside to infer what each box contained. In studying matter scientists face the same kind of challenge. The basic particles that make up matter are too small to be seen directly. In the past the tests scientists performed on matter gave only hints about how matter is put together. That's because particles of matter cannot be observed.

People have experimented with matter for thousands of years. In ancient times the goal was often a practical product like a colorful dye, a metal sword, or a plow. In recent centuries matter has also been studied with carefully planned scientific experiments.

The ancient Greek philosopher Aristotle believed that all matter was composed of four **elements**—earth, air, fire, and water. However, during the last three centuries, scientists have identified the true chemical elements. These substances are the basic building blocks of all matter. One of the most interesting elements is shown in the photograph at the bottom of the page. It expands very evenly when warmed and makes a good liquid for thermometers. What is it?

HISTORY LINK

1 This bronze coin was made about 2,500 years ago. Bronze is made by mixing the metals copper and tin.

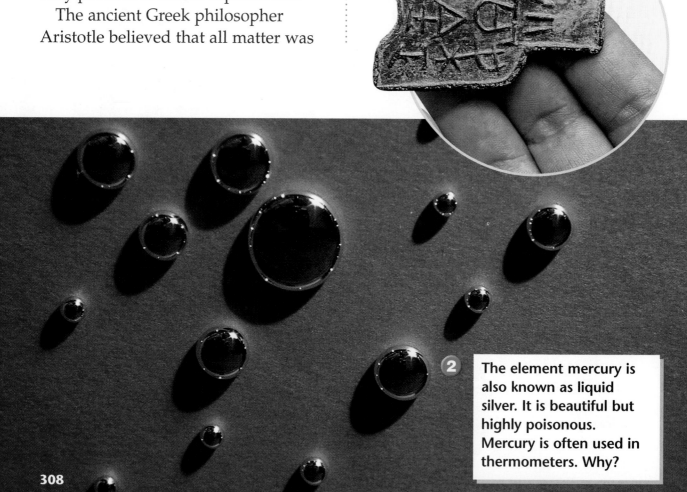

2 The element mercury is also known as liquid silver. It is beautiful but highly poisonous. Mercury is often used in thermometers. Why?

What Are the Elements?

Elements are pure substances that cannot be broken down into any simpler substances. You are probably familiar with many of them. Several are shown in the photographs. How many do you recognize?

Many elements have been known since ancient times but were not truly recognized as elements until the last few centuries. Other elements were found for the first time only recently. For example, germanium was not discovered until 1885. Also, some elements are not even found in nature. They have been made by scientists in nuclear reactors and huge machines called particle accelerators. Yet, even though there are many different elements, living organisms and most materials are made up of just a few elements.

Each element is given a special symbol of one or two letters. The first letter is always a capital. The second letter, if there is one, is never a capital. Sometimes the letters match the English name, such as Ni for nickel or Zn for zinc. In other cases the symbol comes from an ancient name. Gold, for instance, is given the symbol Au from its Latin name, *aurum*.

A few elements are pictured here. How many other elements can you name?

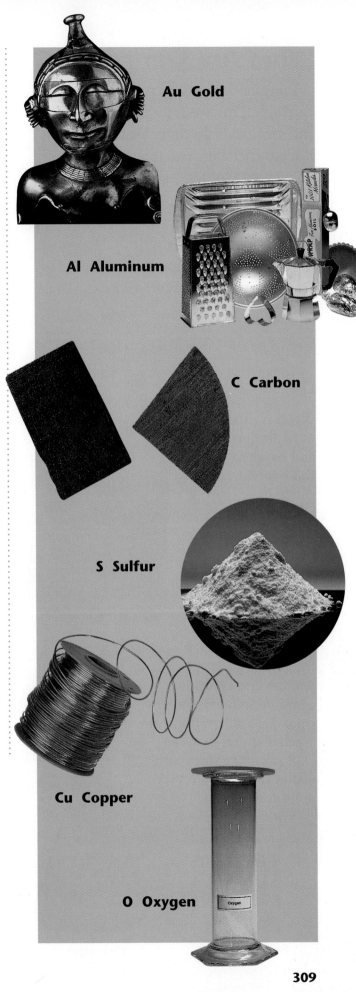

Au Gold

Al Aluminum

C Carbon

S Sulfur

Cu Copper

O Oxygen

What Are Compounds?

Imagine looking at pure water through a microscope. It would look the same everywhere. Water has this appearance because it is a single substance. Yet the photograph below shows how passing electricity through water breaks it apart into two elements, hydrogen and oxygen. If water is a single substance, how could it contain the elements hydrogen and oxygen?

Actually, the hydrogen and oxygen in water are *chemically* combined. This makes them act like a single substance. Any substance that is formed by the chemical combination of two or more elements is called a **compound**.

All compounds are single substances that can only be broken apart into simpler substances by chemical reactions. Compounds have different properties than the elements that make them up, as the lower photographs show.

1 Water is made of hydrogen and oxygen, as this experiment shows.

+ −

BATTERY

The compound sodium chloride is a solid at room temperature. We know it as table salt and use it on our foods to give them more flavor.

2 Sodium and chlorine combine to make sodium chloride. Sodium is a soft, reactive metal that can explode on contact with water. Chlorine is a very poisonous gas.

Sodium   **+**   **Chlorine**   **=**   **Sodium Chloride (table salt)**

310

How Do You Write a Compound's Name?

As you know, each element has a one- or two-letter symbol. Scientists also write symbols for compounds called *chemical formulas*. A compound's chemical formula contains the symbols for the elements that make it up.

The formula also contains numbers below the element symbols called *subscripts*. The table shows chemical formulas for some familiar compounds.

The subscripts in a chemical formula tell us the number of particles that combine together in a compound. For example, water is made up of two elements—hydrogen and oxygen. For every oxygen particle, there are two hydrogen particles. The formula for water is written H_2O.

Table sugar is made up of the elements carbon, hydrogen, and oxygen. For every 12 carbon particles, there are 22 hydrogen particles and 11 oxygen particles. We write $C_{12}H_{22}O_{11}$ for table sugar's chemical formula. The photo shows what happens to table sugar when it is treated with strong sulfuric acid. **(Warning: Sulfuric acid is a dangerous substance.)** The acid takes out all the hydrogen and oxygen, leaving a black mass.

TABLE OF COMPOUNDS

Compound	Chemical Formula
Water	H_2O
Carbon dioxide	CO_2
Baking soda (bicarbonate of soda)	$NaHCO_3$
Table salt	$NaCl$
Table sugar	$C_{12}H_{22}O_{11}$
Glucose (a sugar)	$C_6H_{12}O_6$

Brain Power

What is this black mass made of? How could it have been in the sugar without turning the sugar black? Write out your ideas.

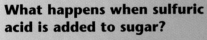
What happens when sulfuric acid is added to sugar?

What Are Elements Made Of?

In 1803 an English scientist named John Dalton stated an important theory: Matter is made up of tiny particles that cannot be cut apart into smaller pieces. Today we call Dalton's tiny particles **atoms**.

According to Dalton, the atoms of one element were all alike. Each element is made up of one kind of atom. However, the atoms of one element were different from the atoms of any other element. While many parts of Dalton's theory have been improved since 1803, the basic idea of atoms is correct. *An atom is the smallest unit of an element that retains the properties of the element.*

Many experiments since Dalton's day have shown us what atoms are like. Yet atoms are so small that we cannot see them directly, even through a microscope. Scientists have had to observe atoms indirectly, in much the same way as you would observe matter inside "mystery" boxes. A special microscope called a *scanning tunneling microscope* uses a very sharp needle that can trace the bumps in a surface made by individual atoms. The photographs below show some of what such special microscopes can "see."

The images of atoms were made with a scanning tunneling microscope.

Dalton drew the symbols (left) for atoms. He believed that each element's atoms weighed a different amount from the atoms of other elements.

Hydrogen (H)

Carbon (C)

Nitrogen (N)

Sulpher (S)

Oxygen (O)

What's Inside Atoms?

John Dalton imagined that atoms were like tiny steel marbles—solid and unbreakable. Yet we now know that atoms are made of still smaller particles. Atoms are far from being solid—they are mostly empty space!

Atoms contain three kinds of particles called **protons** (prō'tonz), **neutrons** (nü'tronz), and **electrons** (i lek'tronz). The protons and neutrons are located in a tiny, very dense body in the atom's center, called the atomic **nucleus** (nü'klē əs). The electrons are in the space outside the nucleus.

Protons and neutrons have nearly the same mass, but electrons are about 2,000 times less massive than protons and neutrons. Protons carry one unit of positive electric charge, while electrons carry one unit of negative electric charge.

Neutrons have no electric charge. All atoms have equal numbers of electrons and protons, so they have no overall electric charge.

The number of protons in an atom determines what element it is. For example, any atom with six protons is a carbon atom. Any atom with eight protons is an oxygen atom.

Look carefully at the diagrams on this page to see how atoms are put together.

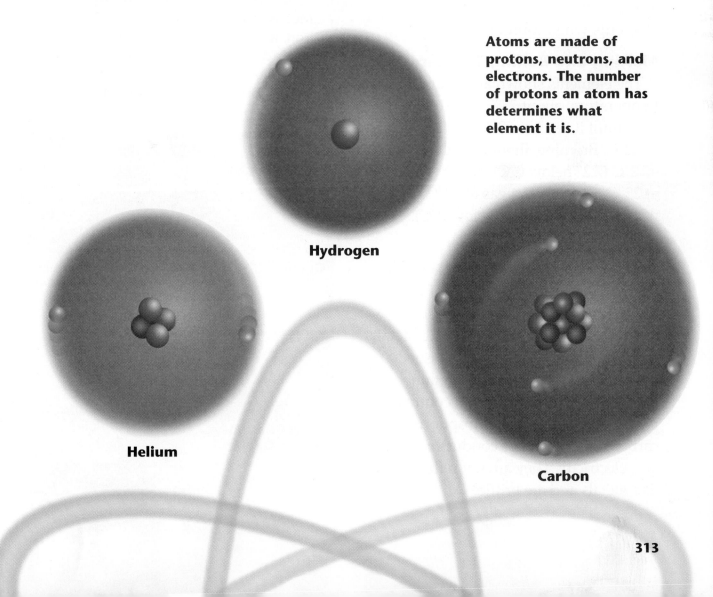

Atoms are made of protons, neutrons, and electrons. The number of protons an atom has determines what element it is.

Hydrogen

Helium

Carbon

What Properties Do Elements Have?

We now know of 112 elements. These substances have many different properties. Yet there are patterns in the properties of the elements. Study the photographs on this page to learn about properties that can demonstrate these patterns.

Chemical Reactivity

Some elements take part in chemical reactions much more easily than others. The magnesium reacts rapidly with the acid. Yet the copper does not react at all. Reactive elements, like magnesium, are usually combined with other elements when found in nature.

Melting and Boiling Temperatures

The elements shown are all at room temperature, about 22°C. Lead does not melt until it reaches 328°C, so it is a solid at 22°C. Bromine, though, melts at –7.2°C (7.2° below 0°C), and it is a liquid at 22°C. Fluorine is a gas at 22°C because it boils at –188°C (188° below 0°C).

Metal Versus Nonmetal

About three-fourths of the elements are metallic, like copper, gold, silver, aluminum, iron, and nickel. Metals conduct electricity and heat well. Metals are also shiny when freshly polished, and many can be worked into thin sheets or different shapes. In contrast nonmetals, like iodine, phosphorus, and carbon, are often poor conductors of heat and electricity. They are not reflective like metals and are brittle.

1 Property: **Chemical Reactivity** Magnesium takes part in chemical reactions much more easily than copper. Here the magnesium reacts rapidly with the acid. Yet the copper does not react at all.

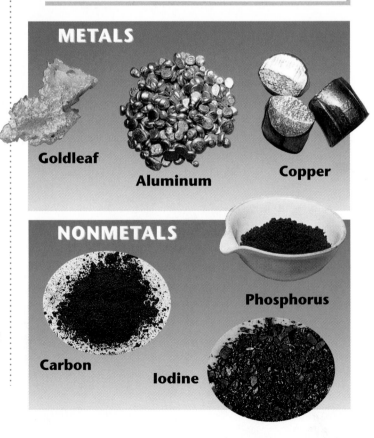

Magnesium

Copper

Hydrochloric acid

2 Property: **Metal Versus Nonmetal** Metals, like copper, gold, silver, aluminum, iron, and nickel, are good conductors of electricity and heat. Nonmetals, like iodine, phosphorus, and carbon, are often poor conductors of heat and electricity.

METALS

Goldleaf

Aluminum

Copper

NONMETALS

Carbon

Phosphorus

Iodine

How Can the Elements Be Grouped?

In 1869 a Russian scientist named Dmitri Mendeleyev found that the properties of the elements went through repeating cycles. Mendeleyev created a table of elements based on these cycles. To Mendeleyev's surprise, groups in his table contained elements with similar chemical properties. For example, one group contained lithium (Li), sodium (Na), potassium (K), rubidium (Rb), and cesium (Cs).

All of these elements combine with chlorine in the same way. The formulas for their chlorine compounds are LiCl, NaCl, KCl, RbCl, and CsCl.

We call Mendeleyev's table the periodic table after the "periodic" changes he found in the elements' properties. The elements are arranged in the Periodic Table by their chemical properties.

1. The metals lie on the left, and the nonmetals lie mainly on the right, with elements called metalloids in between.

2. Most of the elements are solids at room temperature, and all metals are solids except mercury.

3. The most reactive metals are at the lower left, and the most reactive nonmetals are in the second column from the right.

THE MODERN PERIODIC TABLE

The number in each box is the number of protons an atom of that element has.

H 1																	He 2
Li 3	Be 4											B 5	C 6	N 7	O 8	F 9	Ne 10
Na 11	Mg 12											Al 13	Si 14	P 15	S 16	Cl 17	Ar 18
K 19	Ca 20	Sc 21	Ti 22	V 23	Cr 24	Mn 25	Fe 26	Co 27	Ni 28	Cu 29	Zn 30	Ga 31	Ge 32	As 33	Se 34	Br 35	Kr 36
Rb 37	Sr 38	Y 39	Zr 40	Nb 41	Mo 42	Tc 43	Ru 44	Rh 45	Pd 46	Ag 47	Cd 48	In 49	Sn 50	Sb 51	Te 52	I 53	Xe 54
Cs 55	Ba 56	La 57	Hf 72	Ta 73	W 74	Re 75	Os 76	Ir 77	Pt 78	Au 79	Hg 80	Tl 81	Pb 82	Bi 83	Po 84	At 85	Rn 86
Fr 87	Ra 88	Ac 89	Rf 104	Ha 105	Sg 106	Ns 107	Hs 108	Mt 109	Uun 110	Uuu 111	Uub 112						

metals ☐
metaloids ☐
nonmetals ☐

Ce 58	Pr 59	Nd 60	Pm 61	Sm 62	Eu 63	Gd 64	Tb 65	Dy 66	Ho 67	Er 68	Tm 69	Yb 70	Lu 71
Th 90	Pa 91	U 92	Np 93	Pu 94	Am 95	Cm 96	Bk 97	Cf 98	Es 99	Fm 100	Md 101	No 102	Lr 103

READING N CHARTS

1. **WRITE** Is sodium a metal or a nonmetal? Is chlorine a metal or a nonmetal?

2. **DISCUSS** Give an example of a substance that forms when a reactive metal and a reactive nonmetal combine.

Can Atoms Join?

Some elements, such as neon, are made up of single atoms that do not attach to any partners. Yet other elements have atoms that attach to one or more additional atoms. Particles that contain more than one atom joined together are called **molecules**. All matter is made of atoms which may combine to form molecules.

Nitrogen is an example of an element that is made up of molecules. Its molecules have two atoms joined together. Some elements even exist in more than one form, such as oxygen.

Oxygen is usually made up of two-atom molecules, much like nitrogen. Yet oxygen can also exist as three-atom molecules. The three-atom form of oxygen is known as ozone. The three-atom ozone has properties different from the two-atom oxygen.

Molecules of elements always contain only one kind of atom. Yet compounds are made up of molecules that have different kinds of atoms joined together, as the lower diagram shows.

Note how the chemical formulas in both diagrams tell you the number of atoms in the molecules.

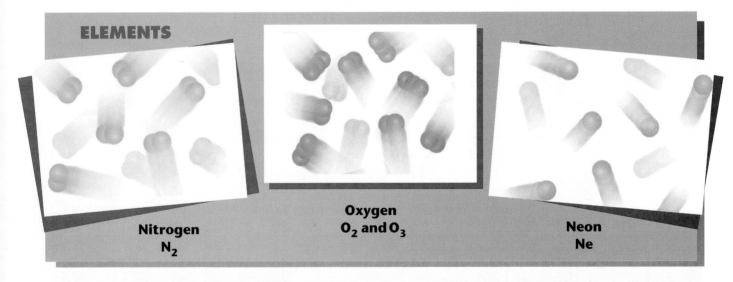

ELEMENTS

Nitrogen
N_2

Oxygen
O_2 and O_3

Neon
Ne

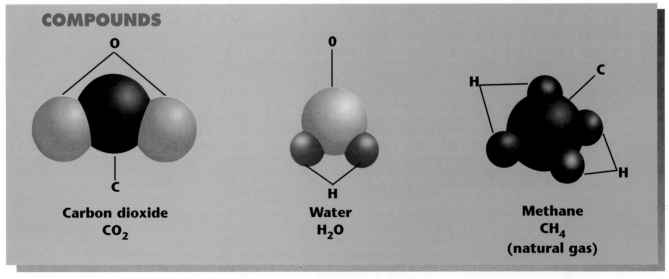

COMPOUNDS

O

C

Carbon dioxide
CO_2

O

H

Water
H_2O

H

C

H

Methane
CH_4
(natural gas)

When a compound forms from elements, changes occur in the way that atoms are linked together. This causes the compound to have properties different from the elements. For example, water is a liquid, yet it is formed from two gases, hydrogen and oxygen. The diagram shows why water has properties different from hydrogen and oxygen gas—the atoms are linked in a new way when water forms.

Hydrogen Plus Oxygen Makes Water

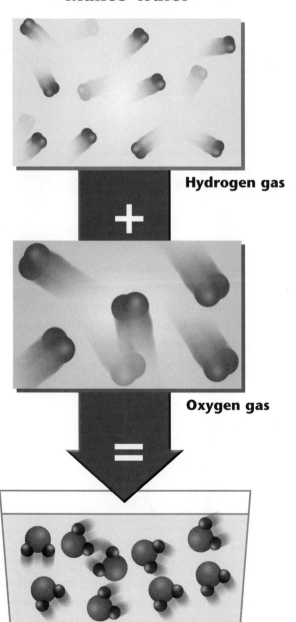

Hydrogen gas

+

Oxygen gas

=

Liquid water

Modeling Molecules

HYPOTHESIZE How do different elements combine to form molecules? Write a hypothesis in your *Science Journal*. Then try building your own molecules.

MATERIALS
- large and small marshmallows
- toothpicks
- *Science Journal*

PROCEDURES

1. Using small marshmallows for hydrogen atoms and large marshmallows for oxygen atoms, make two H_2 molecules and one O_2 molecule. Join the "atoms" with toothpicks.

2. Count the number of "atoms" of each type you have in your molecules. Record these numbers in your *Science Journal*. Take this many more marshmallows and make as many water molecules as you can, using toothpicks to join the atoms.

CONCLUDE AND APPLY

1. OBSERVE How many water molecules did you make?

2. INFER Why would real water molecules have properties different from real hydrogen and oxygen molecules?

317

How Do We Use Compounds?

By studying matter scientists have learned how to prepare compounds that are very useful. Many things are made from the atoms of just a small number of elements. The photographs on this page show several compounds that we depend on a great deal in modern life.

Take petroleum, for example. Petroleum is a complex mixture of *hydrocarbons*—compounds made of hydrogen and carbon atoms. Gasoline comes from petroleum. Its molecules usually have from 5 to 12 carbon atoms in chains. Gasoline gives off a lot of energy when it is burned, so we use it as a fuel in cars.

Many kinds of plastics are also made from hydrocarbons in petroleum or natural gas. Because they are made of molecules that have very long chains of atoms, plastics are called *polymers*.

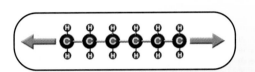

1 The bottle is made of polyethylene, a flexible plastic made from hydrocarbons.

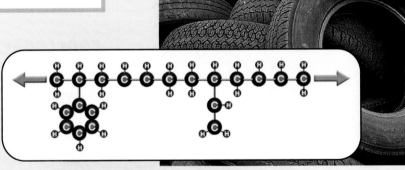

2 Compounds from petroleum are used to make the rubber in this tire's tread. The rubber is treated to make it hard and durable.

3 The dark fluid in the beaker is crude oil, or petroleum. The petroleum was pumped from the ground by an oil well. Petroleum is a complex mixture of hydrocarbons—compounds made of hydrogen and carbon atoms.

Imagine what the world would be like if there were no compounds. You wouldn't be here! Neither would most of the things around you. There would be oxygen, but no carbon dioxide that plants need for survival. Of course, there wouldn't be any plants anyway. There wouldn't be any water or food or animals or things people build. There would be only the elements of the periodic table, floating around separately in space.

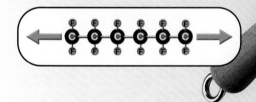

This pan is coated with Teflon, a special polymer made of carbon and fluorine atoms. Teflon is very slippery and makes a good, tough, nonstick coating. Teflon doesn't melt at high temperatures as many other plastics do.

REVIEW

1. Why must some element symbols have two letters instead of just one?

2. A beryllium atom is made of four protons, five neutrons, and four electrons. Draw a model of this type of atom. Label each part.

3. Give an example of a compound whose properties are much different from the elements it is made of. Describe how it is different.

4. **INFER** Gold is often found in nature as pure nuggets. How does gold's location in the periodic table explain why it can be found in this way?

5. **CRITICAL THINKING** *Analyze* Look at the periodic table. List some other elements, besides neon, that are made up of single atoms that do not attach to any partners. Explain why you listed the elements you did.

WHY IT MATTERS **THINK ABOUT IT**
Think of ways elements and compounds are important in your life.

WHY IT MATTERS **WRITE ABOUT IT**
Write a paragraph about the compounds you use every day. Go to the library and find out more about some of these compounds. Then write another paragraph telling about what you learned from your research.

It's ELEMENT-ary!

Air

Earth

If you were in charge, how would you organize the world? In the fourth century B.C., a Greek named Empedocles came up with an idea that the world followed for centuries.

He decided that everything was made up of four elements—earth, air, fire, and water. Some things had more of one element than another. People thought bones were four parts fire, two parts water, and two parts earth!

Empedocles did, however, make one discovery that moved science forward. People had always thought that air was nothing. He showed that air could keep water out of a container. If water could only get in when the air got out, then air must be something!

Love and hate were the two forces Empedocles thought acted on the four elements. Love united the elements, then hate separated them into different forms. That's how everything, from aardvarks to zithers, was created!

Empedocles's theories were accepted for hundreds of years. People believed that they became ill because their bodies were out of balance. To cure people, doctors had to bring the elements back into harmony.

History of Science

The first element—as we know the term—was discovered by Hennig Brand. He extracted phosphorus in 1669. Before the 18th century, there were only about ten known elements. During the next two centuries, most elements that occur in nature were discovered. Scientists also created about 20 synthetic elements.

Fire

Water

DISCUSSION STARTER

1. Explain Empedocles's theory of the elements.

2. How did belief in the elements affect how people were treated for illnesses?

To learn more about the elements, visit *www.mhschool.com/science* and enter the keyword ELEMENTS.

*inter*NET
CONNECTION

WHY IT MATTERS

Matter comes in three basic forms—solid, liquid, and gas.

SCIENCE WORDS

state of matter any of the forms matter can exist in

melting point the temperature at which a solid changes state into a liquid

boiling point the temperature at which a liquid changes state into a gas

freezing point the temperature at which a liquid changes state into a solid

Solids, Liquids, and Gases

What is happening here? How many different kinds of matter do you see here? How are they changing?

Glaciers are huge sheets of moving ice and snow. At a shoreline, chunks of ice fall off and float away as icebergs.

Ice is solid water. You are looking at solid and liquid water. What does it take for solid ice to become liquid—to melt, that is. If all the ice trapped in glaciers melted, what would happen to sea levels around the world?

EXPLORE

HYPOTHESIZE How does the temperature change as a block of ice melts? Does it increase? Write a hypothesis in your *Science Journal*. Test your ideas.

EXPLORE ACTIVITY

Investigate What Happens When Ice Melts

Take temperature readings to see what happens as ice melts.

MATERIALS

- ice cubes
- water
- graduated cylinder
- plastic or paper cup
- thermometer
- heat source (lamp or sunlight)
- watch or clock
- *Science Journal*

PROCEDURES

1. **MEASURE** Put ice cubes in the cup. Add 50 mL of water to the cup. Swirl the ice-and-water mixture together for 15 seconds.

2. **MEASURE** Place the thermometer in the cup. Wait 15 seconds. Then read the temperature. Record your observation in your *Science Journal*.

3. **MEASURE** Put the cup under a heat source (lamp or sunlight). Take temperature readings every 3 minutes as the ice melts.

4. **MEASURE** After all the ice has melted, continue taking temperature readings every 3 minutes for another 15 minutes.

CONCLUDE AND APPLY

1. **OBSERVE** What happened to the temperature as the ice melted?

2. **HYPOTHESIZE** Why do you think you got the results described in question 1?

3. **INFER** What does ice become when it melts?

GOING FURTHER: Problem Solving

4. **PREDICT** What do you think would happen if you didn't add any water to the ice? What do you think will happen if you add more water to the ice? Design an experiment to test each of your predictions. What do you think happens as you freeze water? How would you design an experiment to test your prediction?

What Happens when Ice Melts?

The Explore Activity showed how water turns from a solid to a liquid when it absorbs enough heat. If even more heat is supplied, the water will turn to a gas called steam. Most substances exist in one of three **states of matter**—*solid*, *liquid*, or *gas*. Adding or removing heat can make substances change from one state to another.

When a change of state occurs, the identity of the substance remains the same. However, the substance gains new properties because the molecules are arranged in a different way.

The molecules of any substance are attracted to each other. The attraction is just a weaker form of the force that links the atoms in each of the molecules. When the molecules are linked in organized positions, a solid results.

When heat is absorbed by a solid, the molecules vibrate faster and faster. At some point the molecules separate from one another. This causes the solid to become a liquid. When even more heat is absorbed, the molecules move fast enough to escape the liquid and form a gas.

CHANGE OF STATE

Molecules moving faster and faster
More and more heat absorbed

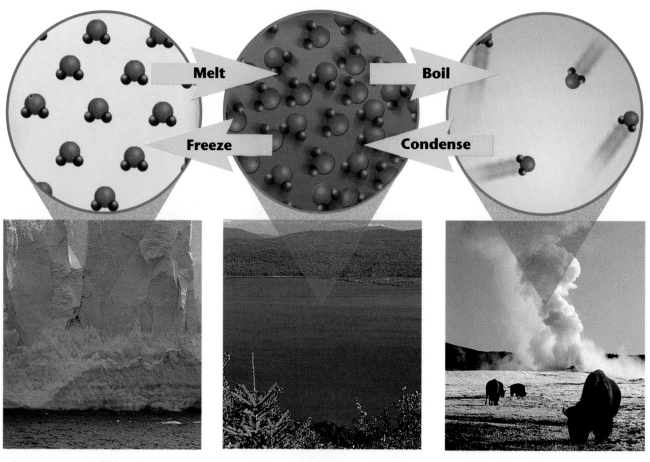

Melt
Boil
Freeze
Condense

Solid
Liquid
Gas

What Temperatures Cause Changes of State?

The graph shows how the temperatures of two different compounds change as they are being heated. As you can see, these substances melt at different temperatures. In fact every pure substance has its own particular **melting point**. Every substance also has a particular boiling temperature, called the **boiling point**.

While a substance is melting or boiling, its temperature stays the same. It warms up only before or after the change of state.

What happens when heat is removed from the substance? It *condenses*—turns from a gas to a liquid—at the boiling temperature. It freezes—turns from a liquid to a solid—at the melting temperature. For this reason the melting point is also known as the **freezing point**.

Instead of boiling, a liquid can also slowly change to a gas. This process is called *evaporation*.

How Long Does It Take Water and PDCB to Melt?

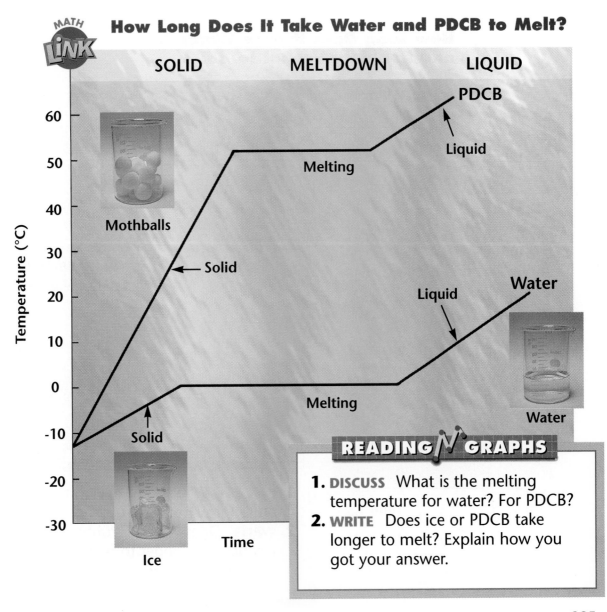

SOLID   MELTDOWN   LIQUID

PDCB

Liquid

Melting

Mothballs

Solid

Liquid

Water

Solid

Melting

Water

Ice

Time

Temperature (°C)

READING GRAPHS

1. **DISCUSS** What is the melting temperature for water? For PDCB?
2. **WRITE** Does ice or PDCB take longer to melt? Explain how you got your answer.

How Do Evaporation and Boiling Differ?

You have probably seen water boiling on the stove. You have probably also observed that water evaporates out of wet clothes. When a liquid evaporates, it gradually changes to a gas. Yet when a liquid boils, it changes to a gas rapidly. The diagram explains how boiling and evaporation occur.

When Something Boils

Remember what happened when the ice melted? The temperature of the melting ice didn't change until all the ice had turned to water. Then the water began to get warmer. In the same way, a substance remains at the same temperature while it boils. This happens because all the heat energy goes into turning the liquid into steam. Once all the liquid becomes steam, the temperature also goes up. The graph below shows what happens to two common liquids when they are heated. Note how their boiling points differ.

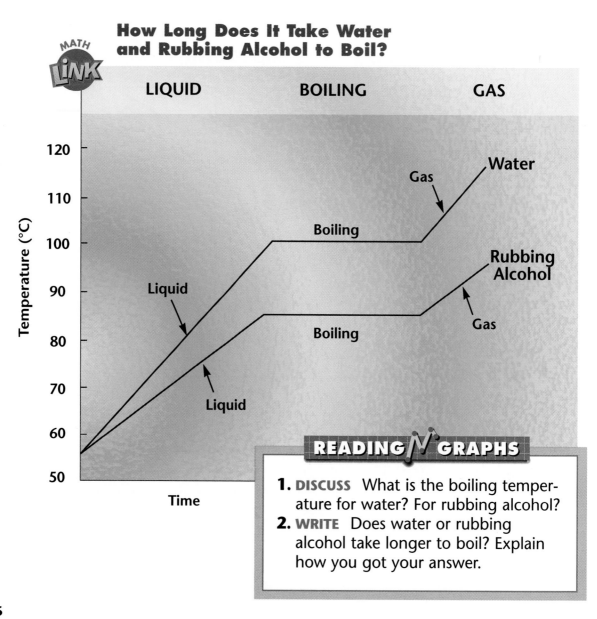

How Long Does It Take Water and Rubbing Alcohol to Boil?

LIQUID   BOILING   GAS

READING GRAPHS

1. **DISCUSS** What is the boiling temperature for water? For rubbing alcohol?
2. **WRITE** Does water or rubbing alcohol take longer to boil? Explain how you got your answer.

EVAPORATION AND BOILING

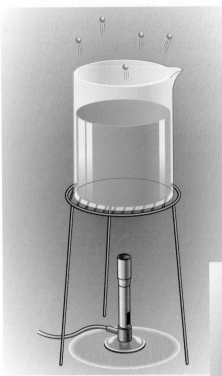

1 Liquid at room temperature. A few molecules escape into the air, causing evaporation.

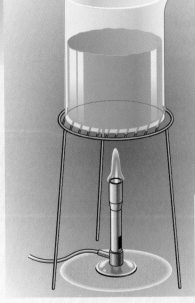

2 The liquid is heated. More molecules escape, so the liquid evaporates faster.

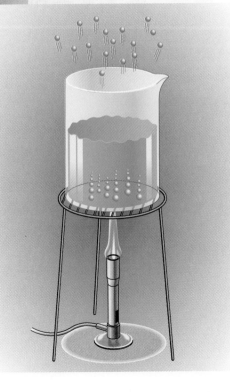

3 Hot spots develop at the bottom of the container. The liquid turns into bubbles of gas at the hot spots. Boiling begins.

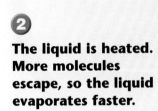 **Brain Power**

If you have ever put rubbing alcohol on your skin, you know that the alcohol evaporates faster than water. Can you suggest why this would happen?

Where Does Dew Come From?

The photograph shows a leaf covered with dewdrops on a cool, clear morning. There was no rain, and water did not leak out of the leaf. Where did the dewdrops come from?

Actually, the dewdrops are water that was first present in the air as a gas. The leaf surface became cold enough to cause water in the air near the leaf to condense into a liquid. The condensed water formed the dewdrops on the leaf's surface.

That's not rain on the flowers, it's dew. Do you think you'd find dew on a hot morning? Explain.

As the temperature of the environment changes, substances may change from one state of matter to another. Yet, since different substances have different melting points and boiling points, they do not all change at the same time. The chart compares the solid and liquid ranges of some familiar substances.

SOLID AND LIQUID RANGES OF COMMON SUBSTANCES
(in degrees Celsius)

NAME	FORMULA	MELT/FREEZE	BOIL/CONDENSE
Oxygen	O_2	218° below 0°C	183° below 0°C
Nitrogen	N_2	210° below 0°C	196° below 0°C
Butane	C_4H_{10}	138° below 0°C	0.5° below 0°C
Rubbing alcohol	C_3H_8O	90° below 0°C	82.4°
Water	H_2O	0°	100°
Lead	Pb	327°	1,740°
Mercury	Hg	39 below 0°C	357°

READING N GRAPHS

1. DISCUSS Which is easier to melt—water or lead?

2. WRITE The temperature of the planet Venus is about 455°C. What state would each of these substances be in if it were on Venus?

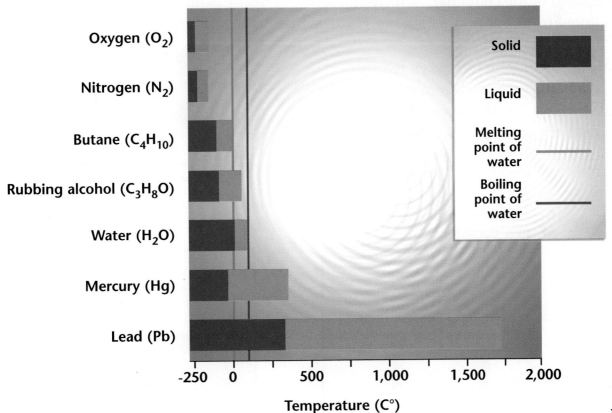

329

What Are the Properties of Solids, Liquids, and Gases?

The aluminum cube in the first photo is a typical solid. It shows that solids retain their shape. Solids have the same volume no matter what container they are placed in. Also, solids cannot be poured, so they are not fluid.

Most solids form crystals, as in the second photograph. A gemlike crystal of alum is shown. The shape of such crystals results from the way the particles are arranged. The particles link together in an organized pattern. They form a solid with a regular shape.

In the third photograph, the same volume of a colored liquid has been placed in two different containers. This shows that liquids take on the shape of their containers. However, liquids do have a definite volume—they settle to the bottom of the container. Also, as you know from pouring water, liquids are fluid.

The last photograph shows a reddish gas in a bottle separated from a second bottle by a glass plate. When the plate is removed, the gas expands to fill both bottles. This shows that gases always fill the full volume of their containers. Also, gases are fluid—they can be pumped through pipelines just like liquids.

1 Solids keep their shape.

2 Most solids form crystals.

3 Liquids take the shape of their containers.

Gases fill the volume of their containers.

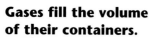

4

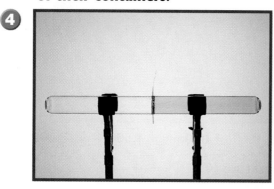

5

What Makes Matter Expand and Contract?

When the temperature of a material increases, its particles move faster. On average these particles tend to spread out more. This causes materials to *expand*—spread out—as they get hotter or *contract*—shrink—as they get cooler. Gases expand or contract the most with changing temperature, but liquids and solids are also affected.

Collapsing Bottles

HYPOTHESIZE How does heat affect an empty plastic bottle? How does cold affect it? Write a hypothesis in your *Science Journal*.

MATERIALS

- flexible plastic bottle with screw cap
- pails of hot and ice-cold water
- *Science Journal*

PROCEDURES

1. **PREDICT** What do you think will happen to the empty plastic bottle when it is warmed? What do you think will happen to it when it is cooled? Record your predictions in your *Science Journal*.

2. With the cap off, hold the bottle for a minute or two in a pail of hot tap water. Then screw the cap on tightly while the bottle is still sitting in the hot water.

3. **EXPERIMENT** Now hold the bottle in a pail of ice water for a few minutes.

CONCLUDE AND APPLY

1. **COMMUNICATE** Write down your observations of what happens next.

2. **INFER** Write out an explanation of why the bottle changed as it did. Be sure to use the idea of how molecules move at different temperatures.

331

How Can Expansion and Contraction Be Used?

Thermometers have liquid mercury or colored alcohol in a bulb connected to a very thin tube. The liquid expands or contracts with changes in temperature and moves up or down in the tube. The position of the liquid in the tube gives the temperature.

1 This thermostat turns on a furnace in a home when the temperature gets too cold. The diagram shows how the thermostat works. The coiled strip is made of two different metal layers. As the temperature falls, the two different metals contract at different rates. This causes the coil to unwind and press on a switch, turning on the furnace.

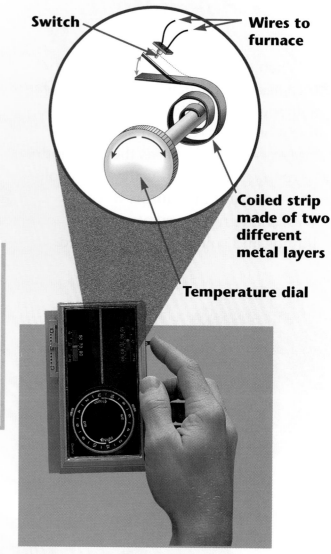

Switch

Wires to furnace

Coiled strip made of two different metal layers

Temperature dial

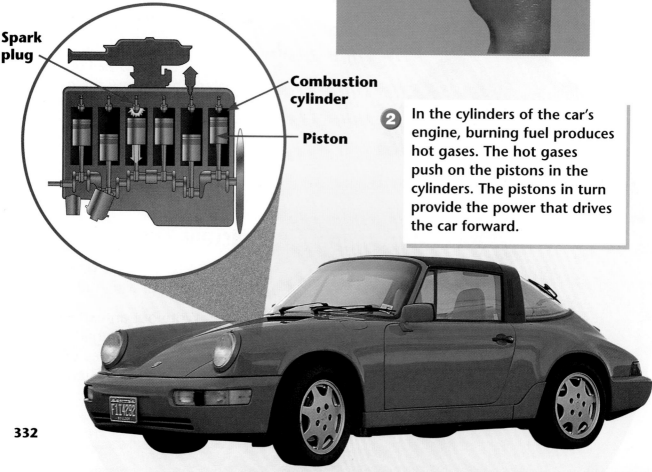

Spark plug

Combustion cylinder

Piston

2 In the cylinders of the car's engine, burning fuel produces hot gases. The hot gases push on the pistons in the cylinders. The pistons in turn provide the power that drives the car forward.

Can Expansion and Contraction Be a Problem?

The solid materials that make up a bridge or sidewalk expand when warmed. If the sections are assembled tightly on a normal day, they will expand against each other on very hot days. This expansion can cause cracks to form. To guard against this problem, engineers leave some space between the sections and fill it with a flexible material. Look for these "expansion joints" in the photograph.

Many of the objects around you are solids. You bathe in, swim in, float on, and drink liquids. Gases are what you breathe and what allow you to smell odors at a distance. You learned that gases always fill the full volume of their containers. Did you realize that you notice this property of gases every time you are in your room and smell food cooking in the kitchen? Changes of state allow you to cook your food and enjoy cold drinks and ice cream in the summer.

REVIEW

1. Explain what happens to the temperature of ice as it melts.

2. Acetone freezes at 95.35° below 0°C and boils at 56.2°C. At 42°C what state of matter would acetone be in? At 84°C?

3. Gases can be easily squeezed into a smaller volume. Why is this so?

4. **INFER** On a hot, damp summer day, drops of water will form on the outside of a glass containing an ice-cold drink. Explain how this happens.

5. **CRITICAL THINKING** *Analyze* Water boils at 100°C at sea level. High up in the mountains, water boils at a lower temperature. Why does it take longer to cook potatoes high up in the mountains than it does to cook potatoes at sea level?

WHY IT MATTERS THINK ABOUT IT
Why are changes of state important to you?

WHY IT MATTERS WRITE ABOUT IT
Describe how matter changing from solid to liquid to gas is important in your life.

ANIMALS: icy SURVIVAL

imagine a world where water's like most other substances—it becomes denser as it freezes. Ice, now heavier than water, sinks to the bottoms of ponds. The water quickly freezes from the bottom up into solid blocks of ice. Fish in the ponds freeze, too. That's the end of most freshwater fish.

In summer the ice near the top of the ponds melts, but not the ice at the bottom. That ice never melts. Each summer things get worse. Before long there's no liquid water left on Earth!

Luckily that scenario is science fiction, but real water is stranger than science fiction! Why doesn't it become denser when it turns solid? The answer lies in what happens when water molecules get cold enough to freeze.

As you know, water molecules are made of two hydrogen atoms and one oxygen atom. When water freezes, the molecules are kept farther apart than they are in liquid water.

Ice is only nine-tenths as dense as liquid water, so when water freezes, it expands. A given volume of ice weighs less than the same volume of water. That's why ice floats in your lemonade!

Life/Earth Science Link

Ice forms a protective covering for ponds. Under the ice the water stays liquid, allowing plants and animals to survive the winter. Because ice floats, oceans have icebergs. They can mean trouble for ships, because most of an iceberg is underwater. Look at the ice cube in your lemonade. How much of it is under the surface?

DISCUSSION STARTER

1. How is the solid form of water different from most other solids?

2. Why don't ponds freeze from the bottom up in winter?

To learn more about survival in cold, visit **www.mhschool.com/science** and enter the keyword COLD.

*inter***NET**
CONNECTION

SCIENCE WORDS

atom p.312

compound p.310

electron p.313

element p.308

evaporation p.325

insulate p.300

mass p.292

molecule p.316

proton p.313

state of

matter p.324

weight p.293

USING SCIENCE WORDS

Number a paper from 1 to 10. Fill in 1 to 5 with words from the list above.

1. Particles in atoms that have a positive charge are called ___?___.

2. Particles made of more than one atom linked together are called ___?___.

3. The force of gravity between a planet and an object is measured as ___?___.

4. The process of going from a liquid to a gas is ___?___.

5. Solid is one ___?___.

6–10. **Pick five words from the list above that were not used in 1 to 5, and use each in a sentence.**

UNDERSTANDING SCIENCE IDEAS

11. Describe two different ways water can turn from liquid to gas.

12. What is the difference between an object's mass and an object's weight?

13. What does an object's buoyancy depend on?

14. What are molecules made of?

15. Are all molecules compounds? Explain your answer.

USING IDEAS AND SKILLS

16. Will cube of aluminum metal will sink in any liquid? Explain your answer.

17. **READING SKILL: MAIN IDEA/ SUPPORTING DETAILS** What is the main difference between mass and weight? Support your answer with any facts or details necessary.

18. If you leave a pan of water on a warm stove for too long, you might find that the water is gone. Where would the water go? Why would the temperature of the stove burner matter?

19. **MAKE A MODEL** A boat is on a canal. It is going from a region of lower water to a region of higher water. The captain wants to know if throwing the cargo overboard will raise the water level. Explain how you could use a model to answer his question.

20. **THINKING LIKE A SCIENTIST** Which do you think would evaporate faster— pure water or salt water? Why? Describe an experiment that would test your idea.

PROBLEMS and PUZZLES

Chill Out Why do people sprinkle salt on ice to melt it? Fill two glasses with ice, and add a thermo–meter to each. Pour a small amount of water in each. Wait for the thermometers to reach the melting point (0°C). Then add a table-spoon of salt to one glass, and shake gently. What happens? How does this help you answer the first question?

CHAPTER 8
PUTTING
IT ALL
TOGETHER

What does it take to launch a space shuttle. It takes a lot of people knowing what to do, for one thing. It also takes a lot of fuel.

The fuel is burned. Burning is a kind of change. After the change happens, the fuel is not fuel anymore. What's left is a waste. Think of what happens when logs are burned in a campfire. What's left after the logs are burned?

In Chapter 8 you will look at many ways that matter can change.

In Chapter 8 you will read about many examples of cause and effect. One event—

WHY IT MATTERS

Mixtures can be separated, but it isn't always easy to do.

SCIENCE WORDS

mixture two or more parts blended together yet keeping their own properties and not turning into a new substance

solution a mixture in which substances are completely blended so that the properties are the same throughout and the substances stay blended

suspension a mixture of substances that separate upon standing

colloid particles (or droplets) large enough to block out light spread throughout another substance

emulsion a liquid spread through another liquid

aerosol liquid drops or solid particles spread through a gas

gel a solid spread through a liquid

foam a gas spread through a liquid or solid

Mixtures and Solutions

Why do people call the Mississippi River the "muddy Mississippi"? What happens when the muddy Mississippi flows into the Gulf of Mexico?

The flowing water of the river meets up with standing water in the gulf. The river drops out much of what it is carrying. The "dropped out" materials build up in the Mississippi Delta.

The Mississippi is made of things mixed together. How many other examples can you give of things that are mixed together?

EXPLORE

HYPOTHESIZE How can you separate substances that are mixed together in a way that they keep their properties? Write a hypothesis in your *Science Journal*. Design an experiment to test it.

EXPLORE ACTIVITY

Design Your Own Experiment

HOW CAN YOU TAKE APART THINGS THAT ARE MIXED TOGETHER?

PROCEDURES

SAFETY Wear goggles. Do not taste your sample.

1. **OBSERVE** Examine the sample your teacher gives you. It is made of different substances. One of the substances is table salt. What else does it seem to be made of? Record your observations in your *Science Journal*.

2. Design an experiment to separate the various ingredients in your sample.

3. Carry out your experiment.

MATERIALS

- sample of substances mixed together
- hand lens
- toothpicks
- magnet
- paper (coffee) filters
- 2 cups or beakers
- water
- goggles
- *Science Journal*

CONCLUDE AND APPLY

1. **INFER** How many parts or substances were mixed into your sample? How did you reach that conclusion?

2. **EXPLAIN** You knew one substance was salt. What properties of salt might help you separate it from the rest? Could you separate salt first? Why or why not?

3. **EXPLAIN** How did you separate out the substances? How did you use the properties of these substances to separate them?

GOING FURTHER: Problem Solving

4. **EXPERIMENT** What if you were given white sand and sugar mixed together? How would you separate the two ingredients?

339

How Can You Take Mixtures Apart?

The Explore Activity dealt with separating sand, salt, and iron filings that had been stirred together. The sand, salt, and iron filings were *physically* combined, so the material you started with was a **mixture**. The first photograph shows another such mixture—iron filings and yellow sulfur powder that have been stirred together.

The substance shown in the second photograph, iron disulfide, also contains both iron and sulfur. However, now the iron and sulfur are *chemically* combined and a new substance is formed.

How do mixtures and compounds differ? Compounds are produced by chemically combining substances. Yet mixtures are created by a physical combination of substances. In mixtures the parts simply blend together without forming new substances. Differences in chemical and physical properties of substances are used to separate mixtures and identify compounds.

A compound has different properties from the substances it contains. For example, iron disulfide is not magnetic, while pure iron is. In contrast, the parts of a mixture keep their original properties. Even though the iron has been mixed with sulfur in the first picture, it remains magnetic. You could pull a magnet through the mixture to remove the iron filings.

Iron filings   **Sulfur powder**

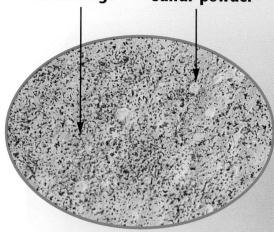

Iron disulfide ("fool's gold")

1 When iron filings and yellow sulfur powder are stirred together to make a *mixture*, the substances keep their original properties. The iron remains magnetic. You could use a magnet to remove the iron filings.

2 A magnet won't work here. This is *iron disulfide*, a mineral known as iron pyrite, or "fool's gold." Iron disulfide is a compound of iron and sulfur. When a *compound* forms, it has different properties from the substances it contains. Unlike iron, iron disulfide is not magnetic.

Are All Mixtures Put Together the Same Way?

What if you stir one spoonful of sugar into a glass of water to make a sugar-water mixture? A friend could stir two spoonfuls of sugar into the same amount of water. You would both have the same kind of mixture. However, your friend's drink would have a much sweeter taste.

Like the sugar water, any type of mixture can contain varying amounts of the parts that make it up. Salt water could be barely salty or very salty. Granola cereal could have many or few raisins. Tea could be strong or weak, and so on.

On the other hand, compounds are *always* made up in the same way. For example, two-fifths of the weight of *any* sample of table salt is sodium, and three-fifths is chlorine.

Brain Power

Here are a number of household materials. Which are mixtures? Which are either elements or compounds? Write out why you placed each material in a particular group. Can you name additional household materials that are examples of elements, compounds, or mixtures?

Orange seltzer

Aluminum foil

Sugar

Raisin bread

Salad dressing

How Can Mixtures Be Separated?

We can separate the parts of mixtures using methods called physical separations. A physical separation gets the parts of a mixture away from one another without changing their identities.

Compounds can also be broken down into simpler parts, but not by physical separations. Chemical reactions are needed to separate compounds into their components.

The illustrations on these pages show examples of physical separation methods. Study them to see the steps and equipment needed.

The mud particles cannot pass through the pores in the paper, but the water molecules can. The mud collects in the paper, while the water drips through.

Muddy water

Filter

Funnel

Mud particles

Water

1 To separate a mixture of sand and salt, pour in water and stir. The salt dissolves, but the sand doesn't.

2 Use a filter to separate the sand from the salt water.

3 Then let the water evaporate to get back the salt.

342

SEPARATING SAND AND WOOD CHIPS

To separate sand and wood chips, first pour in water. Stir briefly.

The wood chips float to the top, while the sand settles to the bottom. The wood chips can be skimmed off and dried. The water can be poured off, and the sand dried.

SEPARATING ALCOHOL AND WATER

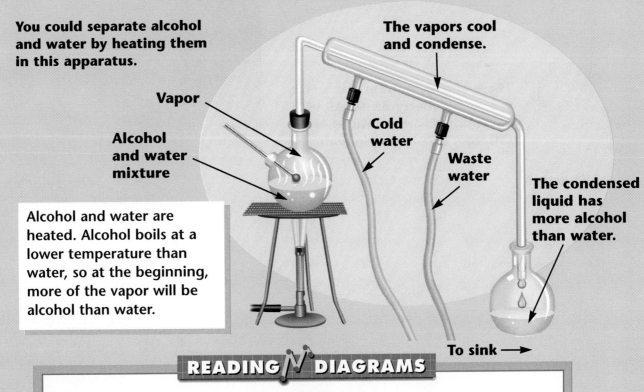

You could separate alcohol and water by heating them in this apparatus.

The vapors cool and condense.

Vapor

Alcohol and water mixture

Cold water

Waste water

The condensed liquid has more alcohol than water.

Alcohol and water are heated. Alcohol boils at a lower temperature than water, so at the beginning, more of the vapor will be alcohol than water.

To sink →

READING ℕ DIAGRAMS

1. **DISCUSS** What is one way to separate two substances in a mixture?
2. **DISCUSS** Could you separate sand and wood chips the same way you separate sand and salt? Explain.
3. **WRITE** Make a list of three ways to separate parts of a mixture.

How Can Mixtures Be Classified?

Mixtures are not pure because they contain more than one element or compound. If the substances in a mixture are blended completely, the mixture looks the same everywhere, even under a microscope. We call such mixtures **solutions**.

On the other hand, the parts of a mixture may be only partly blended. The mixture may look "speckled," either to your eye or through a microscope. This type of mixture is said to be *heterogeneous* (het´ər ə jē'nē əs).

Solutions are usually transparent, or are evenly colored. They never settle into layers. Heterogeneous mixtures do settle into layers in a fluid.

Heterogeneous mixtures are either cloudy or opaque. The photographs on these pages show examples of solutions and heterogeneous mixtures.

Not all solutions are liquid. The tube contains a solution of two gaseous compounds, NO_2 and N_2O_4. NO_2 is red-brown, while N_2O_4 is colorless.

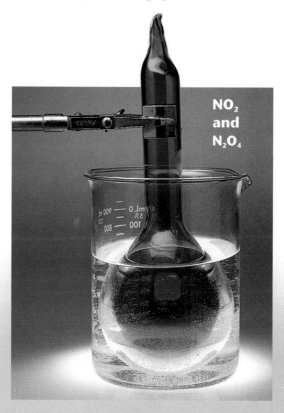

NO_2 and N_2O_4

These glasses contain salt water, tea, and a cherry drink. All of these liquids are solutions of different substances in water.

Salt water   **Tea**   **Cherry drink**

Heterogeneous Mixtures Can Settle Into Layers

Clay and water   Oil and water

1 Freshly shaken mixtures of clay and water, and oil and water

Water
Clay

Oil

Water

2 The mixtures after they were allowed to stand for a length of time. Mixtures like clay and water, with suspended particles that are easily seen, are called suspensions.

This piece of granite is a heterogeneous mixture. It is composed of pieces of several different minerals. Each type of mineral has its own appearance, making the rock look speckled.

This trumpet is made of brass, a solid solution of copper and zinc. Solid metal solutions are called alloys. The properties of an alloy can be varied by changing the amounts of the pure metals it contains.

READING ✎ DIAGRAMS

1. **DISCUSS** What is the difference between a solution and a heterogeneous mixture?
2. **WRITE** Are solutions always liquids? Give two examples to justify your answer.

Are There Other Kinds of Mixtures?

Milk is not transparent, so it cannot be a solution. Yet it does not settle out into layers, so it is not a heterogeneous mixture. Actually, milk is a special type of mixture called a **colloid**. Like milk, all colloids have properties between those of solutions and heterogeneous mixtures.

The first photograph shows what milk looks like under a microscope—droplets of fat spread throughout water. Other colloids are similar. They have particles of one material scattered through another. The particles are big enough to block or cloud light but not big enough to settle out.

There are many types of colloids. Milk is an example of an **emulsion**, a liquid (fat) spread through another liquid (water). The photographs show examples of other types of colloids.

Fat

Water

The fog in this scene is a colloid called an aerosol. Aerosols have either liquid drops or solid particles spread through a gas. Fog is made of tiny drops of water suspended in air.

Many food products are colloids. Gelatin dessert is a **gel**. A gel is a solid spread through a liquid. The solid in the gelatin is protein. The liquid in the gelatin is water. Whipped cream is a **foam**. A foam is a gas spread through a liquid. The gas in the whipped cream is air. The liquid in the whipped cream is water and fat. Marshmallows are a solid foam—a gas spread through a solid. The gas in the marshmallows is air. The solid in the marshmallows is a sweetened gelatin.

Kitchen Colloids

HYPOTHESIZE What happens to cream when you whip it? Write a hypothesis in your *Science Journal*. Test your ideas.

PROCEDURE

1. Pour some whipping cream into a bowl. Set this bowl in a bed of ice in another bowl. Let the cream and bowl chill.

MATERIALS
• whipping cream
• 2 bowls
• wire whisk
• ice
• *Science Journal*

2. EXPERIMENT Use the whisk to whip the cream until it becomes a fluffy texture.

3. OBSERVE Let the cream warm and continue beating it. Observe how it changes. Record your observations in your *Science Journal*.

CONCLUDE AND APPLY

1. DEFINE What kind of colloid is the whipped cream from step 2?

2. INTERPRET DATA What is it made of?

3. INFER In step 3 you made a colloid called a solid emulsion. What is this colloid commonly known as? What do you think it is made of?

347

How Else Can You Separate Important Mixtures?

The photograph below shows a tower that uses a process called *distillation*. It uses this process to separate important chemicals out of crude oil.

First, the crude oil is heated until it becomes a gas. Then, the vapors are sent to the tower. There they rise and cool. As they cool they condense to form liquids.

The substances with large molecules and high boiling points quickly cool into a liquid. The substances with small molecules and low boiling points rise higher in the tower before condensing. The condensed liquids are drawn off as shown.

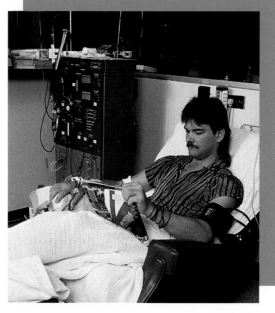

This patient's kidneys can no longer clean waste products from his blood. Doctors pass his blood through a *dialysis* (dīal'ə sis) machine. The blood flows past a material that allows the waste products to leave but not the blood cells. After being filtered the blood is returned to the patient's body.

How Crude Oil Is Turned into Many Useful Products

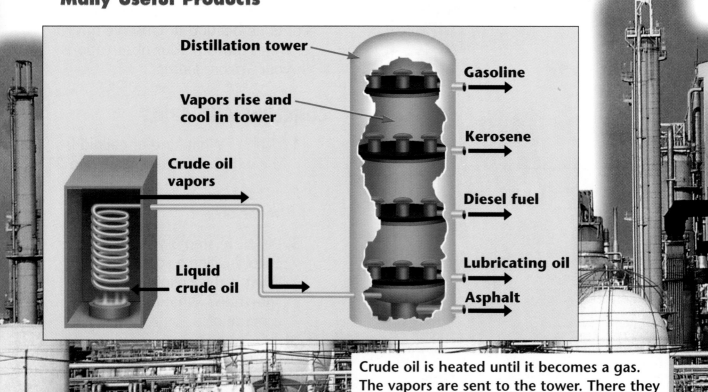

Distillation tower

Vapors rise and cool in tower

Crude oil vapors

Liquid crude oil

Gasoline

Kerosene

Diesel fuel

Lubricating oil

Asphalt

Crude oil is heated until it becomes a gas. The vapors are sent to the tower. There they rise, cool, and condense to form liquids. Substances with smaller molecules and lower boiling points rise higher in the tower before condensing.

Many things you use every day—from the air you breathe to the milk or soda you drink—are mixtures. Many of those mixtures can vary slightly. For example, one day you may want mushrooms on your pizza. The next day you may not. Some mixtures need to blend just the right amounts of their ingredients each time. For example, you need a certain amount of oxygen in the air you breathe. As you go through your day, think of all the mixtures you use and why they are important to you.

REVIEW

1. How do the properties of sugar and water alone compare to the properties of a sugar-water solution?

2. How are mixtures different from compounds?

3. Air is a mixture of oxygen and nitrogen gas. What type of mixture is air? Why?

4. **INFER** Oil paints are made of colored particles suspended in oil. Are oil paints solutions, heterogeneous mixtures, or colloids? How do you know?

5. **CRITICAL THINKING** *Apply* Describe the steps you could follow to separate a mixture of sawdust and salt.

WHY IT MATTERS **THINK ABOUT IT**
Many of the mixtures you are familiar with are mixtures of water and another substance. What are some of these mixtures?

WHY IT MATTERS **WRITE ABOUT IT**
List the mixtures you think should always be blended the same way—with just the right amount of water and other substances. Explain why. List the mixtures you think are still okay if they are blended slightly differently each time. Explain why.

READING SKILL
What are some examples of cause and effect on pages 342–343? Write about them. Identify the cause and the effect.

Got Milk?
Got Butter?

The success of mammals on Earth is helped by what they feed their newborns: milk produced by their mothers. Humans also raise other large mammals to produce milk for them.

A mammal's milk is seven-eighths water, but the other eighth has nearly everything needed for good health! Some food value comes from the lactose, or milk sugar, dissolved in it.

Part of milk is tiny particles suspended as colloids. They're too small to see with a microscope, but they reflect all colors equally. That's why colloidal suspensions are "milky" white!

Milk has a lot of fat globs. Because they're lighter than water, the globs rise to the top of a container. Gravity pulls the heavier liquid down. The fat globs merge to become cream. Milk

← Cream

← Milk

with little or no fat is skim milk.

Many people prefer skim or low-fat milk. The fat in milk contributes to weight problems, heart disease, and possibly other diseases.

Milk you buy has vitamins D and A added to make it an even more perfect food. It's been pasteurized—heated to kill disease-causing bacteria. The

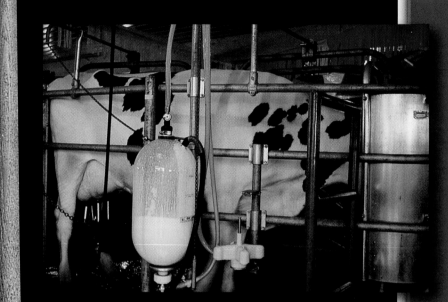

heating also makes some milk proteins inactive and slows down the spoiling.

Milk is homogenized by putting it through a fine screen to break fat globs into tiny specks. They're so small that the movement of the other molecules in milk keeps them from rising. For that reason cream doesn't form at the top of homogenized milk.

By constantly moving cream in a closed container, you cause the fat globs to merge. Drain off the thin, watery stuff and you've got . . . butter!

DISCUSSION STARTER

1. Cream is yellower than milk. What does this show about the yellow part of milk?

2. Fat is used to make cells' outer membranes. How does this explain why mammals' milk is high in fat?

Milk ⟶

Butter ⟶

To learn more about milk products, visit **www.mhschool.com/science** and enter the keyword DAIRY.

*inter***NET** **CONNECTION**

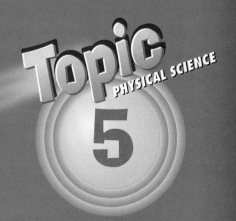

WHY IT MATTERS

Changes in matter can be useful to you.

SCIENCE WORDS

physical change a change in size, shape, or state, without forming a new substance

chemical change a change in matter that produces a new substance with different properties from the original

chemical reaction a chemical change of original substances into one or more new substances

reactant one of the original substances before a chemical reaction takes place

product one of the new substances produced when a chemical reaction takes place

Chemical Changes

What does it take for the space shuttle to blast off and travel into space? One thing is fuel. What happens to the fuel?

When any fuel is used, it is changed. What are the signs that a fuel, like logs, is changing when it is burned? What is left of the fuel after it is burned?

How can you tell changes occur? Milk sours. Bread dough rises when baking powder is mixed into it. A runny egg hardens when it is cooked. What are other changes going on around you?

EXPLORE

HYPOTHESIZE How can you tell if a substance changes into something else? What signs would you look for? Write a hypothesis in your *Science Journal*. Test your ideas.

Investigate How You Can Recognize a Change

Experiment to find signs that a substance has changed.

MATERIALS

- liquids labeled A, B, C, and D
- baking soda
- blueberry juice
- lemon juice
- wax paper
- permanent marker
- 6 small paper drinking cups
- 4 toothpicks
- 6 eyedroppers
- plastic spoon
- *Science Journal*

PROCEDURES

1. Make this grid on wax paper with a marking pen. Copy it into your *Science Journal*. In the first column, make a puddle of ten drops of liquid A in each box.

2. OBSERVE Use a spoon to place a pea-sized amount of baking soda into the puddle in the first box. Stir with a toothpick. Record your observations in your *Science Journal*.

3. EXPERIMENT Add several drops of blueberry juice to the puddle in the next box down. Add several drops of lemon juice to the bottom box. Stir each with a new toothpick. Record what you see.

4. EXPERIMENT Repeat steps 1–3 for liquids B, C, and D.

5. OBSERVE Put a small amount of each liquid into separate cups labeled A, B, C, and D. Put the cups aside until the liquids evaporate. Record your observations of what remains in each cup.

CONCLUDE AND APPLY

1. INFER In which boxes of the grid do you think substances changed into new substances? Explain your answers.

2. INFER Your teacher will give you samples of two unknown liquids. Use what you have learned to carry out tests to identify these liquids. Report on your findings.

GOING FURTHER: Problem Solving

3. EXPERIMENT What if you were given other mystery liquids—or mystery powders—to identify? How might you use the materials from this experiment to help you? Describe how you would set up your experiment.

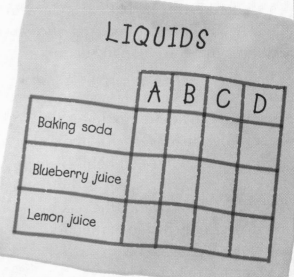

LIQUIDS

	A	B	C	D
Baking soda				
Blueberry juice				
Lemon juice				

How Can You Recognize a Change?

Different kinds of changes are going on all the time. In a **physical change**, matter changes in size, shape, or state without also changing identity. Physical changes include separating matter into different parts or mixing matter with new parts as long as no new substances are made.

The photograph below shows why a change of state is a physical change. The student is holding a small glass dish in the steam that is boiling out of a teakettle. When the steam—which is gaseous water—hits the dish, it cools and turns back into liquid water. When boiling water turns into steam, its state simply changes, not its chemical identity. We know that boiling is a physical change.

The photo above shows another example of a physical change. Here a student is mixing baking soda with water, as in the Explore Activity. He notices that the baking soda mixes with the water so thoroughly that it seems to disappear. However, when some of the liquid mixture is left in a shallow dish overnight, the water evaporates away. Left behind are crystals of baking soda, as the close-up view shows. Since the baking soda did not change in identity when it was mixed with water, the mixing was a physical change.

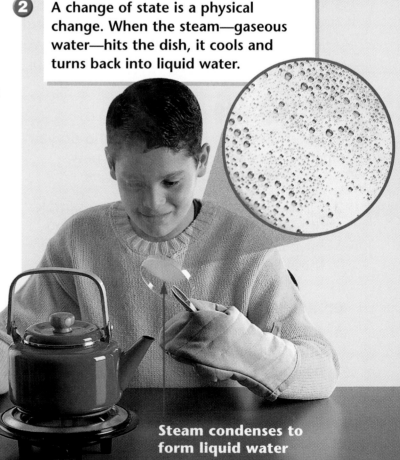

1 When baking soda mixes with water, the baking soda seems to disappear. Yet when the water evaporates, baking soda is left behind. This is a physical change.

Baking soda

Baking soda and water mixture

2 A change of state is a physical change. When the steam—gaseous water—hits the dish, it cools and turns back into liquid water.

Steam condenses to form liquid water

PHYSICAL CHANGES

3 A student is shaking oil and vinegar to get them to mix thoroughly for her salad dressing. However, if the mixture stands too long, the oil and vinegar layer out. Since shaking oil and vinegar only temporarily mixes them, they have undergone a physical change.

4 A pharmacist is dissolving a few crystals of iodine in some alcohol mixed with water to make *tincture of iodine*. Tincture of iodine is used as an antiseptic to help protect cuts from germs. If the alcohol and water evaporate, iodine crystals remain. Making a tincture of iodine involves physical changes.

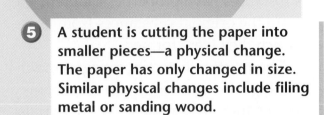

5 A student is cutting the paper into smaller pieces—a physical change. The paper has only changed in size. Similar physical changes include filing metal or sanding wood.

6 The craftsman is working the metal into a new shape—a physical change. The metal takes on a new form but is the same substance as before.

Brain Power

The photographs on this page show more examples of physical changes. How does a change of size, shape, or state happen without making any new substances?

How Else Can You Recognize a Change?

The Explore Activity on page 353 showed several **chemical changes**. Chemical changes occur when atoms link together in new ways. The changes in the linking patterns of the atoms create new substances. The new substances have properties different from the original substances from which they were formed.

The reaction between vinegar and baking soda is an example of a chemical change. When these two materials are mixed, gas bubbles form. A change in the linking pattern of the atoms in the vinegar and baking soda caused a new substance—carbon dioxide to form. Other new products formed, too. However, you could not see them because they remained in the liquid.

Chemical changes are often referred to as **chemical reactions**. The original substances are called the **reactants**. The new substances produced by the chemical change are called the **products**. During chemical reactions, the atoms in the reactants rearrange to form products with different properties. In the reaction between baking soda and vinegar, the baking soda and the vinegar are the reactants. The carbon dioxide, water, and a chemical called sodium acetate are the products.

What Happens when Baking Soda and Vinegar Mix?

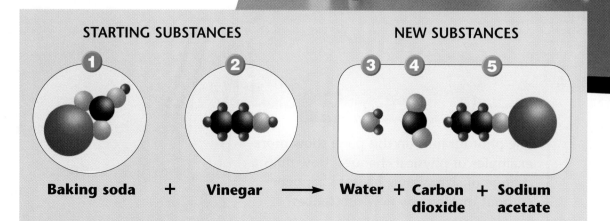

STARTING SUBSTANCES

1 2

Baking soda   +   Vinegar   ⟶

NEW SUBSTANCES

3 4 5

Water + Carbon dioxide + Sodium acetate

Which Are Easier to Reverse—Chemical or Physical Changes?

You'd probably agree that turning carbon dioxide gas, water, and sodium acetate back into baking soda and vinegar would be difficult. Simply stirring the three ingredients together wouldn't give you baking soda and vinegar. In general, chemical changes are difficult to reverse. Imagine trying to "unburn" toast or "unspoil" milk!

On the other hand, physical changes can sometimes be easily reversed. Yet this is not always true. For example, melting an ice cube can easily be reversed by cooling it until it freezes again. Stirring sugar into water can be reversed by letting the water evaporate. However, it would not be so easy to put pieces of paper back together after cutting them from a single page. Still, if a change seems very easy to reverse, it is more likely to be a physical change.

The photograph of a burning candle shows many changes are happening. Wax melts, runs down the side, and turns solid again. However, some of the wax turns into carbon dioxide gas and steam when it combines with oxygen in the air. This change releases enough heat to make the candle flame you see.

What changes occur when toast burns? What happens when a candle burns?

Brain Power

Which changes are physical? Which changes are chemical? How do you know?

What Are the Signs of a Chemical Change?

Chemical reactions often show one or more signs that a chemical change has occurred. These signs include a color change, formation of a gas, and heat changes. The investigation of the mystery liquids in the Explore Activity would show some of these signs.

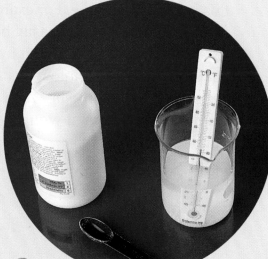

1 When the reddish blueberry juice is mixed with a solution of baking soda, it turns to a greenish color. The green color results from a chemical change in the molecules of the blueberry juice. This reaction shows how a change of color indicates that a chemical change has occurred.

2 In the first photograph, the student is about to add calcium chloride to some water. To start, both the water and the calcium chloride are at room temperature. Yet when they are mixed, the temperature rises.

3 The heat given off by mixing water and calcium chloride is a sign of a chemical change.

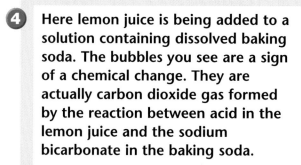

4 Here lemon juice is being added to a solution containing dissolved baking soda. The bubbles you see are a sign of a chemical change. They are actually carbon dioxide gas formed by the reaction between acid in the lemon juice and the sodium bicarbonate in the baking soda.

5

Have you ever put hydrogen peroxide on a cut to kill germs? The bubbles tell you that a chemical change is occurring. The hydrogen peroxide is made of hydrogen and oxygen. When it comes into contact with bodily fluids, it reacts and gives off pure oxygen gas. The oxygen gas, in turn, kills germs in the cut and guards against infection.

6 When you light a match, it gives off light and heat all on its own. This tells you that a chemical change is occurring. The color of the match also changes as it burns. The match head contains phosphorus. When the match is drawn over a rough surface, the friction ignites the phosphorus.

7

Eggs contain a lot of protein. Protein molecules are very long and threadlike. Normally protein molecules are folded into very specific shapes. However, when heated they unravel into random shapes. Egg protein begins to unravel at about 57°C. This chemical change causes it to turn white.

READING ✓ DIAGRAMS

1. **DISCUSS** Does cooking an egg cause a physical change or a chemical change?
2. **WRITE** List three signs of a chemical change, and give an example of each.

What Are Some Familiar Chemical Changes?

As a cake bakes, several chemical changes occur. Heat turns the baking soda (sodium bicarbonate) in the cake dough into sodium carbonate, steam, and carbon dioxide gas. The sodium carbonate is a harmless solid that remains in the cake. The steam helps make the cake moist. The bubbles of carbon dioxide help the dough expand and make the cake light and fluffy. The heat of the oven also triggers other chemical reactions in the cake batter. These strengthen the cake and keep it from collapsing after it is baked.

The red powder covering this wheelbarrow is iron oxide. Iron oxide is commonly known as rust. Rust forms when iron atoms in steel react with oxygen from the air. The reaction is very complex and needs moisture to occur. Steel objects are most likely to rust if they get wet and are not dried right away.

Rocket engines use chemical reactions that produce lots of heat. This space shuttle's main engines are powered by liquid hydrogen and liquid oxygen. When the two react together, they make water vapor and the energy the shuttle needs. The shuttle is also equipped with launch boosters that use a solid fuel. When the solid fuel burns, aluminum powder is converted to aluminum oxide.

This silver object is partly covered with a tarnish of silver sulfide. The silver sulfide forms when silver in the object reacts with sulfur or hydrogen sulfide in foods or the air. Several foods contain sulfur, particularly eggs. Mineral springs can produce small amounts of hydrogen sulfide, which smells like rotten eggs. You can even tarnish silver by wrapping it with a rubber band. Sulfur added to strengthen the rubber causes the tarnish to form. Polishes can be used to remove the tarnish and restore the silver's shiny appearance.

Chemical Reaction That Produces Heat

Rust

Tarnish

Skill: Experimenting

PREVENTING RUST

You've learned that steel forms rust when it is exposed to oxygen and moisture. Rusting can ruin metal objects such as tools, car bodies, and ship hulls. Can you find a way to stop or slow rusting? In this activity you will experiment to try to find the answer. In order to experiment, you need to do the following things. Form a hypothesis. Design a control. Carry out your experiment. Analyze and communicate your results.

MATERIALS

- steel nails and sandpaper
- paper cups
- dilute salt water
- *Science Journal*

PROCEDURES

1. HYPOTHESIZE The photograph shows a method for making a steel nail rust. Think of a way to protect a steel nail from rusting under such conditions. In your *Science Journal*, write down an explanation of why you think your method will work.

2. EXPERIMENT To test your method of rust protection, you need a control nail kept under normal conditions. Each experimental nail will have just one condition (variable) change. For example, suppose you wanted to make a nail rust. You might leave one nail in a clean, empty jar (the control). You might put another in water. You might put a third in lemon juice. Write out how you will set up the experimental and control nails for your experiment.

3. EXPERIMENT Carry out your experiment, and record your observations.

CONCLUDE AND APPLY

1. INFER Write out a description of how well your hypothesis agreed with your results. Be sure to compare the experimental nail to the control nail.

2. COMMUNICATE Why did you need a control in this experiment?

How Do We Fight Rusting?

The car in the photo has been badly rusted. Since rusting continues to eat its way through iron-containing metals, it can weaken the metal. In some cases repairs are possible. In others the metal object is destroyed and must be discarded.

Scientists and engineers have worked very hard to find ways to prevent rusting. Painting or oiling steel surfaces can slow rusting, but more complex methods also exist.

Over the years a car's paint may get chipped. Rusting can start in these spots. Sometimes rust spots can be sanded and repainted to repair them. Other times the rusting may continue despite painting. This can be especially true if rusting starts from the inside out.

In galvanizing baths, steel objects are given a thin coating of zinc. In moist air zinc forms a self-protecting coating of zinc oxide. Zinc does not "rust" like steel. A coating of zinc on steel objects protects the steel underneath from rusting. Perhaps you have seen galvanized buckets or rain gutters.

One common rust-prevention method is shown here. This car body is painted with enamel paint that is baked on. The coating of paint prevents moisture and air from coming into contact with the metal underneath.

How Can Cookware Be Protected from Rusting?

Cookware in the kitchen is often exposed to moisture. If it were made of ordinary steel, it would rust fairly rapidly. Yet scientists have discovered a way to make a special type of steel that is rust resistant. Cooking pots are often made of a special alloy called stainless steel. In this type of steel, chromium and nickel are mixed with the iron, carbon, manganese, and silicon normally found in steel. The resulting alloy is very rust resistant.

Chemical changes bake your cakes and let your bread rise. They turn fuels into heat to warm your home. They also make your bicycle rust and turn old pennies brown. Chemical changes even turn the food you eat into energy to keep you going. In what other ways are chemical changes important to you?

REVIEW

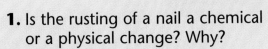

1. Is the rusting of a nail a chemical or a physical change? Why?

2. Is the melting of ice a chemical or a physical change? Why?

3. When a match burns, what evidence is there that a chemical change occurs?

4. **EXPERIMENT** Suppose you wanted to find out if a cake bakes better with baking soda or baking powder. How do you think it would turn out? Design an experiment to test your ideas. Why might you want to use a *control*?

5. **CRITICAL THINKING** *Apply* What if a friend was just given a new bicycle? What advice could you give him or her about protecting the bike from rusting?

WHY IT MATTERS THINK ABOUT IT
In what other ways are chemical changes important in your everyday life?

WHY IT MATTERS WRITE ABOUT IT
Write a paragraph about an average school day. Describe all the chemical changes that you can think of that affect your day.

Checking Acids and Bases

What do you think of when you hear the word *acid?* Did you know that lots of things you eat are acids? It's true. Oranges and lemons have citric acid!

Acids are usually sour to the taste. Bases, like milk, taste better. Bleach, soap, and ammonia are bases that break down grease and wash it away!

How can you tell an acid from a base? Not by tasting them, that could be very dangerous. You can scientifically check it out with litmus paper. Touch a substance with this special paper, and it tells if it's an acid, a base, or neutral—neither acid nor base. How? The paper turns red in an acid solution and blue in a base solution!

Juice from red cabbage or hydrangeas is a acid natural and base

indicator, or marker! Add acid to red cabbage juice, and the juice turns maroon. If there's a lot of acid, the juice turns pink. A neutral substance doesn't change the color. A base turns it green. A very base substance turns it yellow.

If you mix an acid and a base, you get a salt and water! Lye (base) and hydrochloric acid mixed together produce table salt (sodium chloride) and water!

Red cabbage juice indicates which things are acid and which are base.

A Closer Look

Hydrangeas turn blue in acid soil and pink in base soil.

DISCUSSION STARTER

1. Is water an acid or a base? How could you find out?

2. How might acid and base indicators be used to save lives?

A very strong acid that dissolves metal also helps you digest food! Your stomach produces the acid during digestion. If it makes too much, you get "heartburn" or "acid indigestion." You may take an antacid, or base, to make you feel better!

To learn more about acids and bases, visit *www.mhschool.com/science* and enter the keyword PROPERTY.

*inter***NET** **CONNECTION**

WHY IT MATTERS

You depend on many kinds of energy from many different sources.

SCIENCE WORDS

kinetic energy the energy of a moving object

potential energy energy stored in an object or material

conduction movement of energy from a hot object that comes into contact with a cooler object; the material remains in place

convection movement of energy by the flow of matter from place to place

radiation movement of energy in the form of waves that can travel through empty space

wet cell battery a battery containing liquid solution that produces the electric current

dry cell battery a battery that uses "dry chemicals" to produce an electric current

Matter and Energy

If you were scuba diving off the coast of New England and saw this animal, what would you do? Swim the other way! It is an electric ray. It produces enough electricity to power a small motor. How does this feature help the animal survive?

Luckily you don't need an electric ray to run appliances for you. Batteries let you carry electricity with you wherever you go. A chemical reaction takes place inside a battery that produces electricity. Rays don't run out of electricity, however. Do batteries run out?

EXPLORE

HYPOTHESIZE Is it better to buy heavy-duty batteries or less expensive ones? Which last longer? Which ones are really the least expensive to use? Write a hypothesis in your *Science Journal.* Test your ideas.

EXPLORE ACTIVITY

Investigate How Well Batteries Provide Energy

Test different batteries to see which is most economical.

MATERIALS

for each circuit to be tested:
- battery
- flashlight light bulb
- 2 wires
- *Science Journal*

PROCEDURES

1. Connect one end of a wire to the light bulb. Connect the other end of the wire to the battery. Do the same for the other wire. Record in your *Science Journal* what time the light bulb went on. Record the type, size, and brand of battery you used.

2. **OBSERVE** Examine the light bulb every 15 minutes to see if it is still lit.

3. **COMMUNICATE** Record the time the light bulb goes off.

4. Repeat the experiment using another type or brand of battery.

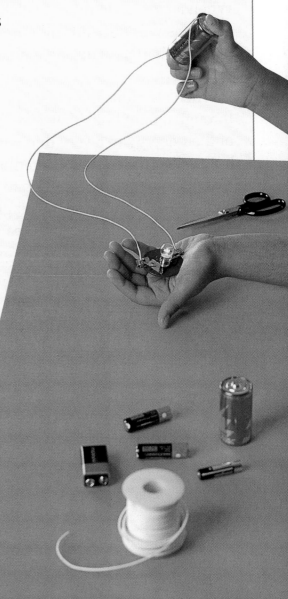

CONCLUDE AND APPLY

1. **USE NUMBERS** Divide the time each battery lasted by the cost of that type of battery.

2. **COMMUNICATE** Share your results with your classmates. Were all the batteries you used made of the same chemicals?

3. **COMPARE** Make a graph of the class's results. Which batteries lasted the longest? Which batteries cost the least per hour of use? Were some brands longer lasting? Were some brands cheaper to use than others?

4. **INFER** Are the cheapest batteries the best buy? Are the longest lasting batteries the best buy?

GOING FURTHER: Problem Solving

5. **APPLY** When might you choose the longest lasting batteries? The least expensive batteries? The batteries that cost the least per hour of use? Explain.

How Well Do Batteries Provide Energy?

As the Explore Activity showed, a battery can produce heat and light when it is connected to a light bulb. Actually, the battery causes electricity to flow through the light bulb. The light bulb changes electrical energy into heat and light.

Chemical reactions are the source of the electrical energy a battery can provide. The reactions produce electrons, and each electron carries energy. When a closed circuit is available, the electrons will flow through the circuit from the battery's negative pole to its positive pole.

When electrons in a circuit pass through a light bulb, they give up some of their energy to a very thin wire in the bulb called the *filament* (fil'ə mənt). The filament gets hot enough to glow and give off light, as in the diagram.

After a time the chemical reactions that power a battery may use up the chemicals. This causes the battery to go dead. Sometimes the chemicals may even begin leaking out of old or dead

Leaking battery

batteries. Leaking batteries can be dangerous. Do not touch them. Find out from your community recycling office what you should do to get rid of them properly.

READING ⌁ DIAGRAMS

DISCUSS Describe the path electrons take in a closed circuit.

Electrical Energy Becomes Light and Heat

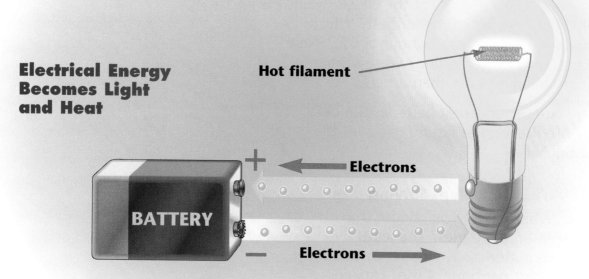

Hot filament

Electrons

BATTERY

Electrons

368

What Are Two Main Kinds of Energy?

Look at the toy truck being driven. Its motion gives it a type of energy called **kinetic energy** (ki net'ik en'ər jē). Any object that is moving has kinetic energy.

When the toy truck is stopped, it appears to have no kinetic energy. Yet it has energy stored in its batteries waiting to be used. We refer to stored energy as **potential energy** (pə ten'shəl en'ər jē).

Forces between atoms create the potential energy in a battery. When a battery is used, chemical changes inside convert, or change, the potential energy into electrical energy. The electrical energy is carried by electrons moving through a circuit.

The electrical energy in a circuit can be converted into motion with motors like the one shown in the photograph. An electric motor changes electrical energy into useful kinetic energy, such as the kinetic energy of the toy truck below.

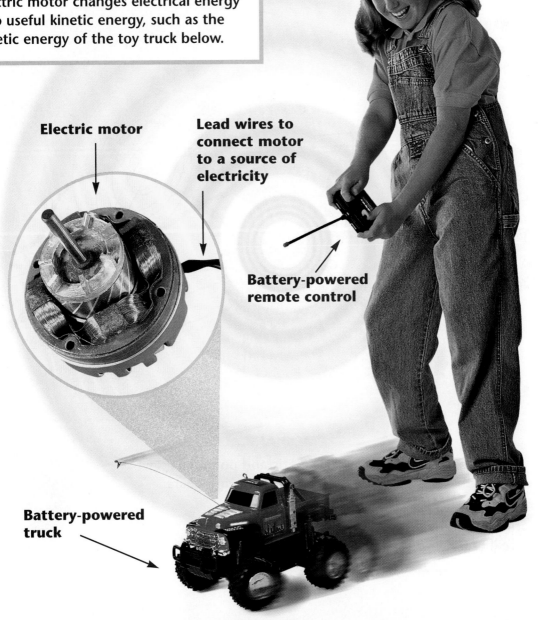

Electric motor

Lead wires to connect motor to a source of electricity

Battery-powered remote control

Battery-powered truck

What Is Energy?

You've seen how chemical changes in a battery can produce electrical energy. You've also seen how that electrical energy can produce light, heat, or motion. All of these things are forms of energy. Yet what exactly is energy? We know energy has many forms. Yet defining energy can be a little difficult.

A good place to start in talking about energy is to look at what energy can do. Energy is a measure of how much work something can produce. To scientists work means moving matter around with forces. The energy something has is how much motion it can give to other matter.

Energy is not a type of matter—it is the ability to move matter around. Unlike matter, pure energy cannot be observed standing still, taking up space, and having a definite mass.

Battery-powered toys show us how electricity must be a form of energy. The electricity can move them around. Light is also a form of energy, as you have learned. Yet how could light move matter around? Think about what lasers can do.

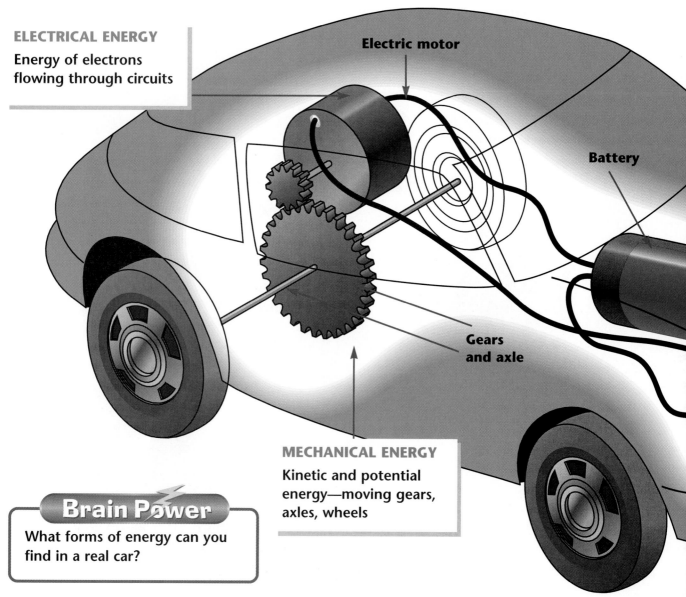

ELECTRICAL ENERGY
Energy of electrons flowing through circuits

Electric motor

Battery

Gears and axle

MECHANICAL ENERGY
Kinetic and potential energy—moving gears, axles, wheels

Brain Power

What forms of energy can you find in a real car?

What Forms Does Energy Take?

Any form of energy can be classified as kinetic or potential. Yet we also describe energy by its source or by how it is carried. For example, the energy produced by a chemical reaction is called chemical energy. Some typical forms of energy are shown in the table.

A laser—an intense, narrow beam of light—can cut like a knife through concrete or steel. Lasers are also used in surgery and can even be used to repair wounds.

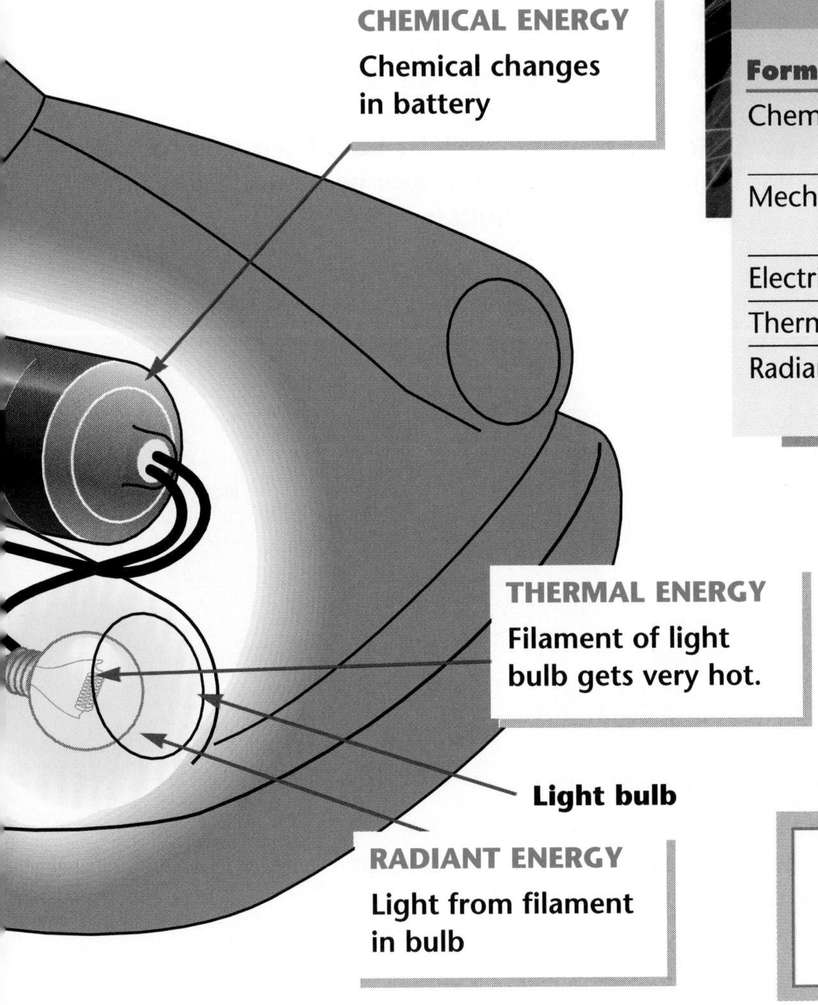

CHEMICAL ENERGY
Chemical changes in battery

Energy Forms and Sources

Form of Energy	Source of Energy
Chemical	Stored in links between atoms
Mechanical	Sum of the kinetic and potential energy of a system
Electrical	Carried by electrons in circuits
Thermal	Carried by heat
Radiant	Carried by light

THERMAL ENERGY
Filament of light bulb gets very hot.

Light bulb

RADIANT ENERGY
Light from filament in bulb

READING ⋀ DIAGRAMS

WRITE List the energy changes that take place in the toy car.

How Can Electricity Be Measured?

When a battery is connected to a circuit, electrons are freed from some of the atoms in the battery's chemicals. The electrons move through the circuit, carrying energy. If we multiply the energy of each electron by the number of electrons moving through the circuit, we can find the total energy.

Electricity can be measured in a number of ways. The circuit with two batteries has twice as many electrons flowing as the circuit with one battery. The bulb is also brighter when two batteries are present. This shows how the brightness of the bulb can measure the amount of electricity.

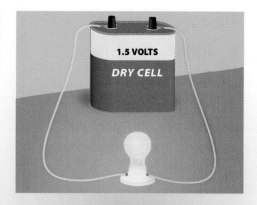

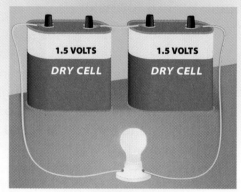

In some cases the amount of electrical energy in a circuit may not be great enough to light certain bulbs. For example, a flashlight battery could not light up a 60-watt light bulb from a lamp. Electrical energy can also be measured by the size of the bulb it can light.

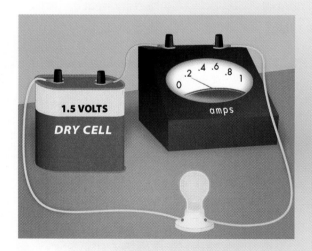

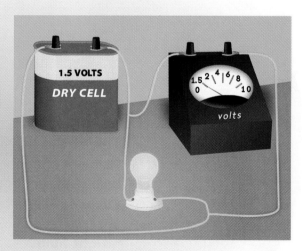

We can also use different kinds of meters to measure electricity. The *ammeter*, above, measures *amps*. It tells us how many electrons flow each second. The *voltmeter* measures *volts*. It indicates the energy each electron carries.

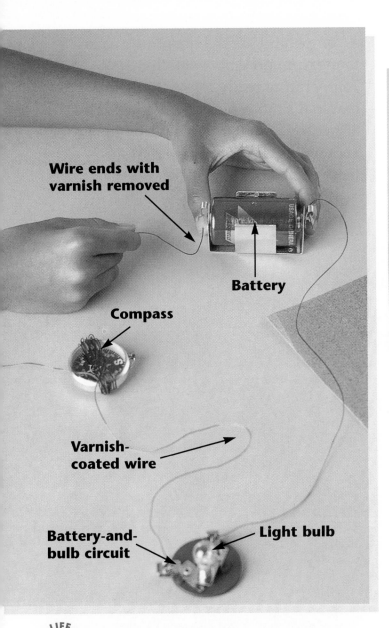

Wire ends with varnish removed

Battery

Compass

Varnish-coated wire

Battery-and-bulb circuit

Light bulb

Measuring Electricity

HYPOTHESIZE Can electricity affect a magnet? Can a magnet be used to measure electricity? Write a hypothesis in your *Science Journal*. Test your ideas.

MATERIALS

- compass
- 5 m of fine varnish-coated wire
- sandpaper
- 1.5-V battery and bulb circuit
- *Science Journal*

PROCEDURES

1. Wrap fine varnished wire around a compass. Use sandpaper to remove the coating from the ends of the wire.

2. Turn the compass until the needle is lined up with the coils of wire.

3. Keeping the compass this way, connect the ends of the wire to a circuit of a battery and small light bulb. See the photograph.

4. **OBSERVE** What happens to the compass needle as you connect and disconnect the circuit? Record your observations in your *Science Journal*.

CONCLUDE AND APPLY

1. **EXPLAIN** How did you know when electricity was flowing in the circuit?

2. **OBSERVE** When electricity was flowing, what did the compass needle do?

3. **INFER** How do you think the needle would move if you used a less powerful battery?

LIFE LINK SCIENCE

DID YOU KNOW?

Animals such as sharks, rays, honeybees, homing pigeons, some migratory birds, tuna, and salmon are all able to detect Earth's magnetic field.

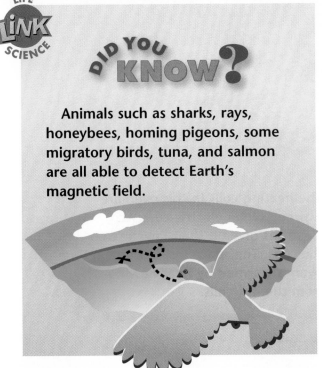

What Are Sources of Heat?

When you cup your hands around a mug of hot chocolate, you feel warmth. This happens because heat flows from the warmer mug into your skin. Heat is the energy that flows out of objects because they are hotter than their surroundings. The photographs show several sources of heat.

Temperature is the quantity we use to measure how hot something is. Temperature really tells us how fast a material's molecules are moving. If one object has a higher temperature than another, heat will flow from the warmer object to the cooler one.

The Sun is the most important source of heat for life on our planet. Nuclear reactions at the core of the Sun heat it to very high temperatures.

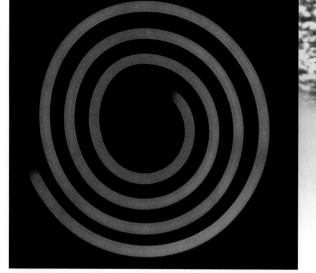

The heating coils in this oven are warmed by an electric current. Electrons give up their energy to the coils. The space inside the oven is warmed by heat flowing from the hot coils.

How Does Heat Move?

Heat always flows from hotter materials to cooler materials, never the other way. In fact, the direction of heat flow between two objects tells us which one is hotter.

When heat flows, it can move through matter in two different ways—**conduction** (kən duk'shən) and **convection** (kən vek'shən). In conduction the heat passes through a material while the material itself stays in place. In convection hot parts of a material rise while cooler parts sink. In convection there is a flow of material and heat.

Heat can also move in a third way, by **radiation**. Any warm object always gives off infrared, or heat, radiation. The infrared rays travel through space and carry energy away from the warm object as heat. This type of heat flow is how the Sun warms Earth.

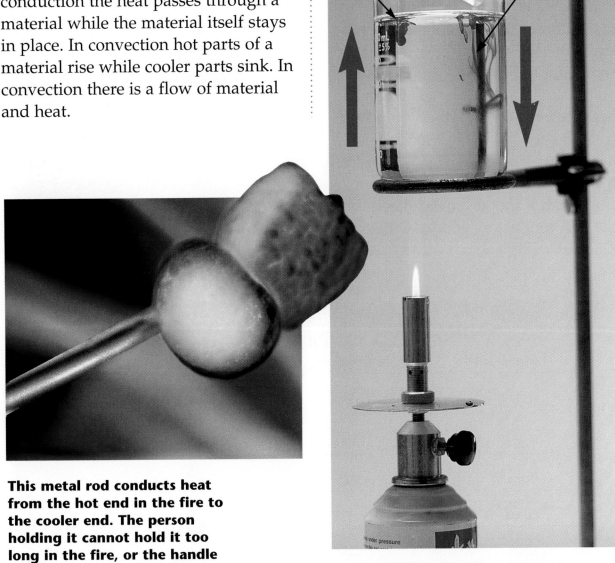

Drop of dye

Drop of dye

This metal rod conducts heat from the hot end in the fire to the cooler end. The person holding it cannot hold it too long in the fire, or the handle will get uncomfortably hot.

Drops of dye were placed at the spots indicated by the arrows. Convection in the water has moved the dye up on the heated side and down on the unheated side.

What Materials Conduct Heat Well?

The photograph shows very hot tea in a Styrofoam cup. A metal spoon has been sitting in the tea for some time. The outside of the cup is slightly warm. Yet the spoon's handle is almost too hot to hold. Why has more heat flowed into the handle of the spoon than into the walls of the cup?

As you learned in Topic 1, some materials are better at conducting heat than others. The metal spoon is a good conductor of heat. However, the Styrofoam cup is a poor conductor of heat. As a result, heat flows quickly from the hot bowl of the spoon to its handle. Yet heat flows very slowly from the tea into the Styrofoam.

As the hot spoon shows, metals are the best conductors of heat. Other kinds of solids, such as wood or glass, usually conduct much less heat than metals. Materials like wood and glass can be used to insulate heat.

Water, alcohol, and similar liquids also conduct heat more poorly than metals. Gases are the poorest thermal conductors of all. Look at the table to see how well common materials conduct heat.

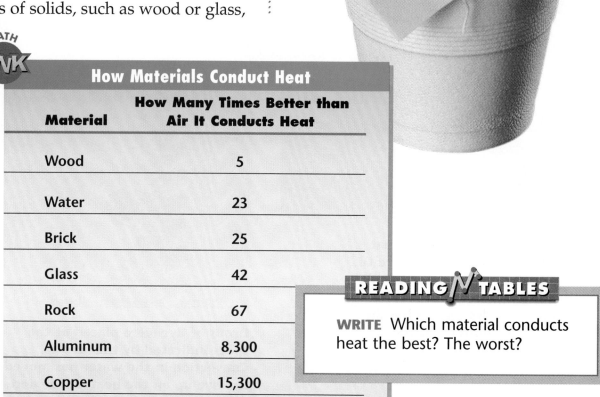

MATH LINK

How Materials Conduct Heat

Material	How Many Times Better than Air It Conducts Heat
Wood	5
Water	23
Brick	25
Glass	42
Rock	67
Aluminum	8,300
Copper	15,300

READING TABLES

WRITE Which material conducts heat the best? The worst?

376

Why Are Some Materials Better Conductors than Others?

As shown in the diagram, heat is carried through a material by the motion of molecules. At the hot end, the molecules move about rapidly. They collide with their neighbors, spreading the motion through the material. The spreading of the motion warms up other parts of the material.

In gases the molecules are widely separated. They cannot transfer heat between one another as easily as in liquids or solids. This explains why air is such a poor conductor of heat.

Why do metals conduct heat so well? Metals have electrons that are unusually free to move. When a metal is heated at one end, the free-moving electrons there can pick up kinetic energy. The electrons quickly carry the energy to other parts of the metal. That's what makes them warm up fast.

The free-moving electrons in metals also make them good conductors of electricity. In contrast, materials like glass or wood do not have free-moving electrons. So these materials are poorer conductors of heat and electricity.

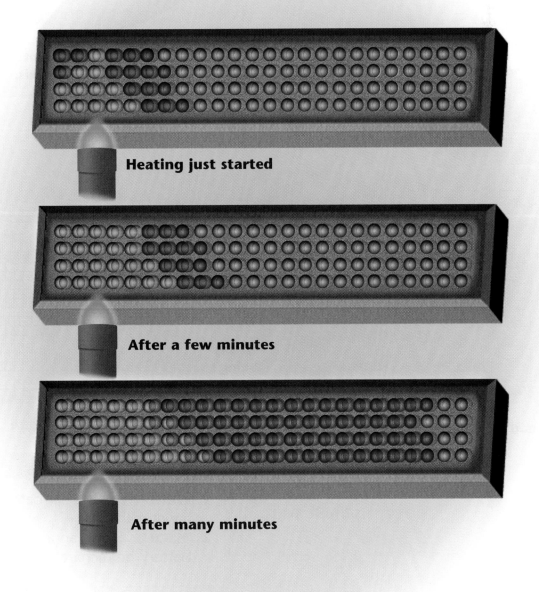

Heating just started

After a few minutes

After many minutes

How Do Wet Cell Batteries Work?

All cars have a battery to provide stored electricity. The electricity is needed to operate things like the radio, headlights, and tail lights. As the diagram shows, a car battery contains a sulfuric acid solution. For this reason it is called a **wet cell battery**. The chemical changes that produce electricity in a wet cell can be run backward. A running car can also supply electrons to its battery to recharge the battery for future use.

Many batteries contain dangerous chemicals.

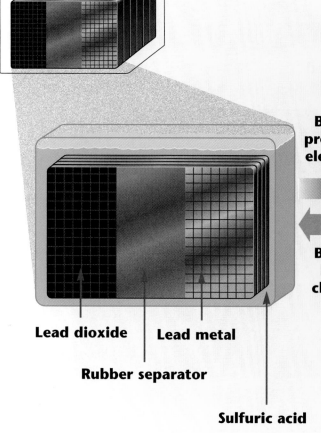

Lead dioxide

Lead metal

Rubber separator

Sulfuric acid

Battery producing electricity

Battery being charged

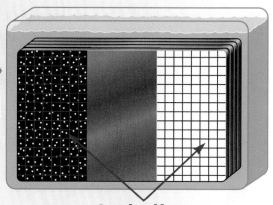

Lead sulfate

READING DIAGRAMS

1. **WRITE** Why is a car battery called a wet cell battery?
2. **DISCUSS** How can a wet cell car battery be recharged?

378

How Do Dry Cell Batteries Work?

Flashlight batteries use chemical changes different from wet cell batteries. In fact, flashlight batteries do not have a liquid inside, so they are called **dry cell batteries**. Look at the diagram to see how dry cell batteries produce electricity.

Energy comes in many forms. The air in your home is warmed by heat convection. However, it may be that without electricity, your heat won't go on. There is energy stored in batteries and energy stored in the food you eat. The Sun gives us light and heat as well. You depend on various forms of energy to live, move, and have a comfortable life.

The zinc in the can provides electrons by dissolving into the moist paste. The electrons flow through the circuit to the carbon rod.

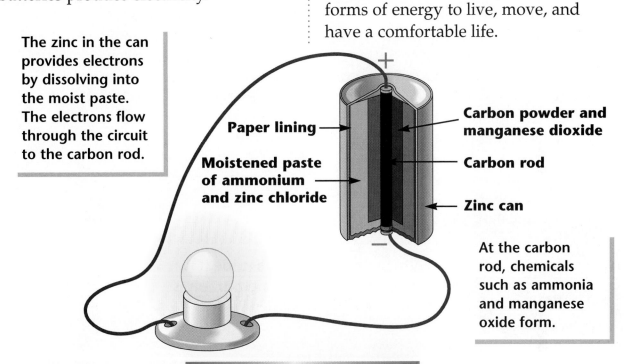

Paper lining

Moistened paste of ammonium and zinc chloride

Carbon powder and manganese dioxide

Carbon rod

Zinc can

At the carbon rod, chemicals such as ammonia and manganese oxide form.

REVIEW

1. Describe how a battery makes a light bulb glow. Mention the different forms energy takes.

2. Why is energy not a form of matter?

3. How does heat energy get from place to place?

4. **INFER** Insulating windows have two layers of glass with air sealed in between. Why is the layer of air important?

5. **CRITICAL THINKING** *Analyze* Two flashlights have the same kind of bulb. Yet one glows more dimly than the other. Can you suggest why?

WHY IT MATTERS THINK ABOUT IT
What kinds of energy do you use every day?

WHY IT MATTERS WRITE ABOUT IT
Write a paragraph about the kinds of energy you use on a weekend. Explain why these kinds of energy are important to you.

Cameras and Chemicals

Some people think photography is magic. Some even refuse to have their pictures taken. They think the pictures steal their souls.

Photography does seem like magic. You point a camera, click a shutter, and capture exactly how someone or something looks!

The science behind the magic is fairly simple. The film in a camera is sensitive to light. When exposed to light through a camera lens, the film reacts to the light. The film records what's dark and what's light. Later the film is treated with chemicals. With black-and-white film, what's been exposed to lots of light turns dark, and what's been exposed to less light stays light.

This film image is called a negative.

Next, light is shone through the negative onto light-sensitive paper. Then, the paper is treated with the same chemicals used to develop the film. This time the process is reversed, and a positive image appears on the paper. The click of the camera has frozen a moment in time.

DISCUSSION STARTER

1. What's a negative?

2. Describe how a photograph is developed..

1. Developer

2. Stop

3. Fixer

4. Water Rinse

To learn more about developing film, visit **www.mhschool.com/science** and enter the keyword DARKROOM.

*inter*NET
CONNECTION

380

SCIENCE WORDS

chemical change p.356

chemical reaction p.356

colloid p.346

conduction p.375

convection p.375

emulsion p.346

kinetic energy p.369

mixture p.340

physical change p.354

potential energy p.369

radiation p.375

solution p.344

USING SCIENCE WORDS

Number a paper from 1 to 10. Fill in 1 to 5 with words from the list above.

1. A(n) __?__ looks the same everywhere, even under a microscope.

2. Tiny droplets of fat spread through water form a(n) __?__.

3. In a(n) __?__ matter takes on a new form but not a new identity.

4. In a(n) __?__ two chemicals react to form a new substance.

5. Energy carried by light is __?__.

6–10. Pick five words from the list above that were not used in 1 to 5, and use each word in a sentence.

UNDERSTANDING SCIENCE IDEAS

11. Describe two ways heat energy can move from one place to another.

12. What is the difference between a mixture and a compound?

13. What is the difference between a physical change and a chemical change?

14. What is the difference between the energy of moving things and energy that is stored?

15. Describe two things that can happen during a chemical reaction.

USING IDEAS AND SKILLS

16. A certain material can be separated by physical changes. Can it be a single compound? Why or why not?

17. **READING SKILL: CAUSE AND EFFECT** What signs are there that baking bread is a chemical change?

18. Invent a way for the energy from a burning candle to turn a wheel. Draw and explain your invention.

19. **EXPERIMENT** A friend says he removed tarnish from a silver spoon by putting it in the bottom of an aluminum pot containing a hot baking-soda solution. What really removed the tarnish? Describe how you would perform experiments to find out.

20. **THINKING LIKE A SCIENTIST** You want the walls of an outdoor doghouse to keep heat in on cold days. What would you use as insulation? Explain.

PROBLEMS and PUZZLES

Lemon Wonders Work with a parent. Soak the tip of a toothpick in lemon juice. Use the soaked tip of the toothpick to write a word on paper. Let it dry. You can't see it. Have an adult place a hot electric iron on the paper and lift. Repeat until you see a change. What happens? Why?

UNIT 4 REVIEW

USING SCIENCE WORDS

Number a paper from 1 to 10. Beside each number write the word or words that best complete the sentence.

1. If you know the mass and volume of an object, you can compute its ___?___.

2. The smallest particle with the properties of an element is a(n) ___?___.

3. The smallest particle with the properties of a compound is a(n) ___?___.

4. The temperature at which a solid turns to liquid is its ___?___.

5. Solid, liquid, and gas are three ___?___.

6. Salt water is an example of a(n) ___?___.

7. An example of a(n) ___?___ is muddy water.

8. Raking a layer of leaves into a small pile is an example of a(n) ___?___.

9. Burning the pile of leaves is an example of a(n) ___?___.

10. Energy stored in a wound-up spring is an example of ___?___.

UNDERSTANDING SCIENCE IDEAS

Write 11–15. For each number write the letter for the best answer. You may wish to use the hints provided.

11. The density of a material may be measured in
    a. kg^2
    b. g/cm^3
    c. cm/s
    d. m/g^3
    (Hint: Read page 296.)

12. Which of the following is a liquid when at room temperature?
    a. oxygen
    b. butane
    c. mercury
    d. lead
    (Hint: Read pages 328–329.)

13. Which of the following is *not* a mixture?
    a. brass
    b. tea
    c. soap
    d. salt
    (Hint: Read page 341.)

14. Iron and oxygen can combine to form
    a. steel
    b. rust
    c. salt
    d. zinc
    (Hint: Read page 360.)

15. The energy produced by batteries comes from
    a. motion
    b. chemical reactions
    c. heat
    d. conduction
    (Hint: Read page 368.)

USING IDEAS AND SKILLS

16. Vegetable oil floats on water. Explain what that tells you about their densities.

17. Use the chart on page 296 to decide if a block of aluminum would float or sink in a bowl of mercury.

18. **MAKE A MODEL** Why do scientists use models to study atoms and molecules?

19. On a hot summer day, Mike the lineman strung a copper power line from one pole to the next. Tell why Mike made sure that the line sagged a little.

20. Describe two ways to separate mixtures.

21. Name three different kinds of mixtures, and give an example of each.

22. When water on your skin evaporates, it cools you off. Explain how this happens.

23. What happens when you mix baking soda and vinegar?

THINKING LIKE A SCIENTIST

24. **EXPERIMENT** In the experiment on page 361, one nail was called the *control nail.* Explain the importance of using a control in scientific experiments.

25. Copy the chart on page 371. Add a third column giving an example of each type of energy.

WRITING IN YOUR JOURNAL

SCIENCE IN YOUR LIFE
Name and describe five different mixtures you can observe on your way from home to school.

PRODUCT ADS
Whenever you use a cleaning material, you should always read the label carefully. Some kinds of cleaning materials should never be used together. Read the labels on several cleaning products, and identify warnings that refer to possible chemical reactions.

HOW SCIENTISTS WORK
Scientists use a variety of models to understand and explain the natural world. A formula such as H_2O is a model for water. Tell what the formula means. Give another example of a chemical formula, and tell what it means.

Design your own Experiment

Describe a way to find out whether pure water or salt water has a greater density. Check with your teacher before carrying out the experiment.

inter**NET** CONNECTION

For help in reviewing this unit, visit *www.mhschool.com/science*

PROBLEM SOLVING and PROJECTS

The $1,000 Prize

Can all types of matter exist as a solid, a liquid, or a gas? A wealthy chemist had his doubts. He offered a $1,000 prize for someone who could prove

- that the element iron could exist as both a liquid and a gas
- that the element oxygen could exist as both a liquid and a solid

Develop a plan for how you could win the $1,000 prize. Show the steps you would take to prove each statement. What difficulties would you face in trying to win the prize?

WIN $1,000!

if you can prove:

Boiling temperature for iron	-2450°C
Melting temperature for iron	-1530°C
Boiling temperature for oxygen	-219°C
Melting temperature for oxygen	-268°C

Fizz-ability

The makers of Fizzbery Super Fizz Soda are worried about bubble leakage—the tendency of bubbles to leak out of the bottle once it is open. How can bubble leakage be minimized? Should the soda be kept

- at warm temperatures?
- at cold temperatures?
- frozen? Or boiling?

Devise an experiment to test bubble leakage of Super Fizz Soda.

Predict your results. What would be the best way to prevent bubble leakage?

The Big O

A chemist ran electric current through water to show that it was made of two gases, oxygen and hydrogen. The only problem was—she didn't know which gas was which.

- Both gases were invisible.
- Both gases exploded when they were exposed to a spark.
- From the picture you can tell that one gas had twice the volume of the other.

- The gas on the left actually weighed more than the gas on the right.

Which gas is oxygen? How do you know that it is oxygen? How could you prove that it was oxygen? Explain.

Gas? Gas? **Electric current**

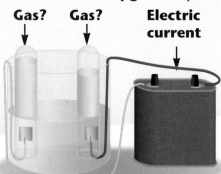

CHAPTER 9

EARTH, YOUR HOME

Mountains give you a pretty good view of Earth, your home. Why are mountains as tall as they are? Will they always be as tall? What are they made of?

Mountains are only one kind of feature of your home, Earth. In Chapter 9 you'll read more about your home.

 In Chapter 9 you will read for sequence of events.

WHY IT MATTERS

Earth provides the things needed to support life.

SCIENCE WORDS

solar system the Sun and the objects that are traveling around it

planet any of the nine objects that travel around the Sun and shine by reflecting its light

gravity a force of attraction, or pull, between any object and any other objects around it

inertia the tendency of a moving object to keep moving in a straight line

lithosphere the hard, outer layer of Earth, about 100 kilometers thick

crust the rocky surface that makes up the top of the lithosphere

resource any material that helps support life on Earth

hydrosphere Earth's water

Earth and Its Neighbors

If you could look at Earth from space, what would you see? The Sun, far in the distance, lights up Earth. Could you see Earth's clouds? How could you tell the water from the land?

Earth is not standing still in one spot. It is moving around the Sun in an almost circular path. A force holds Earth around the Sun. Why doesn't the force just pull Earth into the Sun?

EXPLORE

HYPOTHESIZE How does a force hold Earth around the Sun? What would happen if the force let go? Write a hypothesis in your *Science Journal*. Test your ideas.

Investigate How Earth and the Sun Are Held Together

Use a model to explore the force between the Sun and Earth.

MATERIALS

- clay
- 1 m of string
- scissors
- meterstick
- goggles
- *Science Journal*

PROCEDURES

SAFETY Wear goggles. Twirl the model close to the ground.

1. **MAKE A MODEL** Cut a 40-cm length of string. Wrap it around a small, round lump of clay in several directions. Tie the ends to make a tight knot. Measure 60 cm of string, and tie it to the string around the ball.

2. **OBSERVE** Spin the ball of clay slowly—just fast enough to keep the string tight and keep the ball off the ground. Keep the ball close to the ground. In your *Science Journal*, describe the path of the ball.

3. **EXPERIMENT** At one point while spinning, let the string go. What happens? In your *Science Journal*, describe the path of the ball of clay. Repeat until you get a clear picture of what happens.

CONCLUDE AND APPLY

1. **IDENTIFY** How did your model represent Earth and the Sun? What represented Earth? Where was the Sun located? How did you represent the force between them?

2. **INFER** Explain what happened when you let the string go. Why do you think this happened?

GOING FURTHER: Problem Solving

3. **USE VARIABLES** How would your results change if the mass of the clay was doubled? Tripled? How does the mass affect the pull on the string? Make a prediction. Try it.

How Are Earth and the Sun Held Together?

If you were traveling in a spaceship through space as fast as light, you would be passing stars. Perhaps in time you would approach one star in particular, the star you know as the Sun. If so you would be approaching your home address, the **solar system**. The solar system is the Sun and the objects that are traveling around it.

The objects around the Sun include nine **planets**. Planets are objects that travel around a star in a path. That path is called an *orbit*. Like the clay ball in the Explore Activity, the planets are held in orbit around the Sun. The planets do not give off light, as stars do. They reflect light from their star. Earth and the other planets reflect sunlight.

Can you find your home, Earth? It is the third planet from the Sun. Find its orbit, the third orbit shown around the Sun.

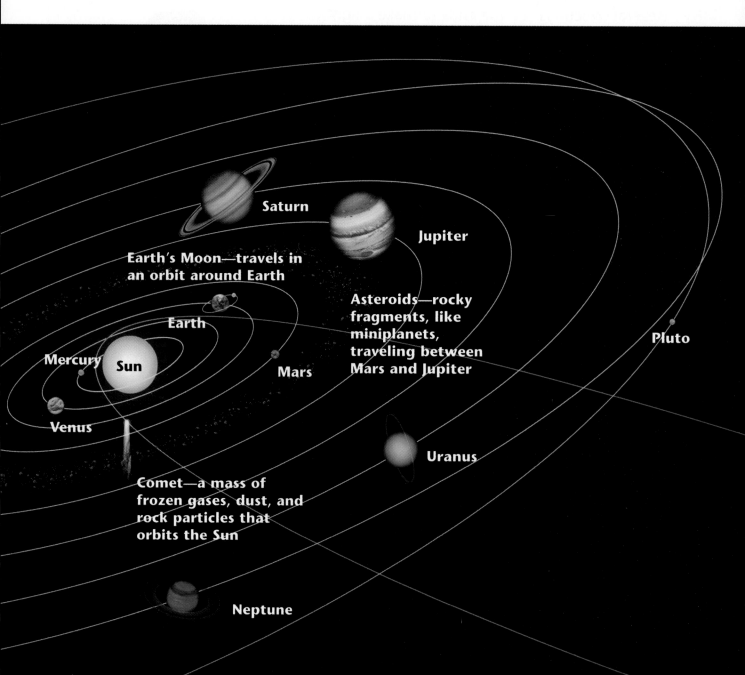

Saturn

Jupiter

Earth's Moon—travels in an orbit around Earth

Earth

Asteroids—rocky fragments, like miniplanets, traveling between Mars and Jupiter

Pluto

Mercury   Sun

Mars

Venus

Uranus

Comet—a mass of frozen gases, dust, and rock particles that orbits the Sun

Neptune

Orbit Times

HYPOTHESIZE What does the length of time for an orbit depend on? Write a hypothesis in your *Science Journal*. Test it.

Planet	Average Distance to the Sun (million km)	Year Time for complete orbit around the Sun (in Earth days)
Mercury	57.9	88 days
Venus	108.2	224 days
Earth	149.6	365 days
Mars	227.9	687 days
Jupiter	778.3	4,333 days
Saturn	1,427	10,759 days
Uranus	2,870	30,685 days
Neptune	4,497	60,188 days
Pluto	5,900	90,700 days

Brain Power

What is the farthest planet from the Sun? Is there only one answer? Explain.

MATERIALS

- several sheets of graph paper
- *Science Journal*

PROCEDURES

COMMUNICATE Use graph paper. Draw a bar graph to compare the revolution times for the planets. The vertical axis of the graph represents time. Decide how much time each square on the paper represents. The horizontal axis represents the planets. How many pieces of graph paper will you need? Write your description in your *Science Journal*.

CONCLUDE AND APPLY

1. **DRAW CONCLUSIONS** Based on your graph and the data table, what relationship can you find between the length of the year (time) and the planet's location in the solar system?

2. **REVISE** How could you change your graph to show the relationship even better? What might your new graph reveal?

The orbit of each planet is almost a circle. Each orbit is slightly oval. What effect does an orbit of this shape have on the distance from a planet to the Sun?

One complete trip of an object in its orbit around the Sun takes one *year*. A year is different from planet to planet. For Earth one year is 365.25 days. The table shows how long a year takes for each planet. The time is given in days as days are timed on Earth.

389

What Keeps the Planets in Orbit?

The clay ball in the Explore Activity was kept in orbit by holding the string. Earth travels around the Sun, but you won't find a string connecting them! What is it that holds Earth in its path around the Sun? What keeps Earth from flying off into space?

This question once puzzled scientists, too. They knew that everything in the solar system orbits the Sun. What holds it all together?

One scientist who lived about 300 years ago, Sir Isaac Newton, had some ideas to explain this. He described a "string" holding the Sun and a planet together. The string is an invisible force, which he called **gravity**. He described

gravity as a property of all matter. It is a force of attraction, or pull, between any object and any other objects around it.

Gravity depends on two measurements—mass and distance. The more matter, or mass, in an object, the greater the pull in the object's direction. The closer two objects are, the stronger the pull of gravity between them.

When Newton's ideas are applied to the world around us, we find that they can explain how most objects behave. In fact Newton extended his ideas to include all objects on Earth, in the solar system, and beyond. His ideas are called the Law of Universal Gravitation.

Sir Isaac Newton, 1642–1727, was an English mathematician and scientist. It is said that he thought of gravity when an apple dropped on his head.

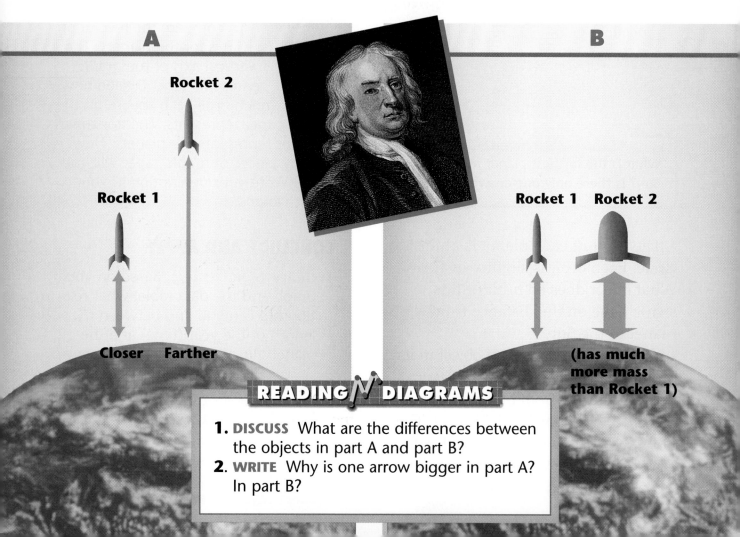

A

Rocket 2

Rocket 1

Closer   Farther

B

Rocket 1   Rocket 2

(has much more mass than Rocket 1)

READING IN DIAGRAMS

1. **DISCUSS** What are the differences between the objects in part A and part B?
2. **WRITE** Why is one arrow bigger in part A? In part B?

The Sun makes up more than 99 percent of the mass of the entire solar system. The Sun's mass is more than 1,000 times greater than Jupiter's and about 330,000 times greater than Earth's. How might the Sun's mass compare with the mass of Mercury? Of Venus?

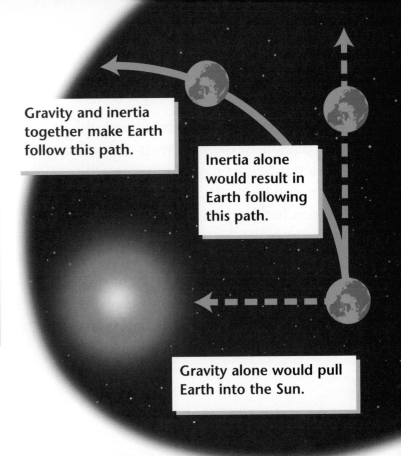

Gravity and inertia together make Earth follow this path.

Inertia alone would result in Earth following this path.

Gravity alone would pull Earth into the Sun.

Why Don't the Planets Fall into the Sun?

According to Newton's Law, there is a force of attraction between you and Earth. Earth pulls you. You pull Earth. When you stumble, why do you fall down? Why doesn't Earth fall up?

Compared to Earth you have a very small amount of mass. As a result your gravity is very weak. Earth's gravity, however, is very strong because Earth is so massive. Earth's pull is strong enough to make everything near it move in its direction, including you. That's why you fall "down" if you stumble.

The Sun has far more mass than Earth or any other planet. Since it is much more massive than Earth, its gravity is much stronger, too. The Sun's gravity holds all of the objects in the solar system together. Without gravity Earth and all of the other objects orbiting the Sun would go flying off into space.

However, gravity alone is not the only reason why the planets stay in their orbits. Gravity alone would pull Earth into the Sun, because the Sun is so massive. That doesn't happen because the planets are moving. The planets, as do all objects, have a property called **inertia** (i nûr'shə). Inertia is the tendency of a moving object to keep moving in a straight line.

In the Explore Activity, the ball flew off in a straight line when the string was let go. The planets, too, because of their inertia would move in straight lines without gravity. Gravity "steers" the planets in their oval paths around the Sun. It is gravity and inertia that keep the planets in their orbits.

How Does the Sun Light Up Earth?

The Sun does more than just hold the planets in their orbits in the solar system. It also provides them with light and warmth. The Sun is the reason for day and night. All planets spin, or *rotate*, like huge spinning tops. At any point in time, half of a planet is facing the Sun—it has daylight on that half. At the same time, half is facing away from the Sun—that half is in darkness, night.

As a planet rotates, places that are in darkness eventually turn to face the Sun and those in daylight eventually turn away. Each planet makes one complete spin in its day. Each planet has its own speed of turning. The length of a day (that is, one complete day-night cycle) is different for each planet.

How much light and warmth a planet receives depends on how far it is from the Sun. Light spreads out as it travels outward from the Sun. An area of 1 square meter on the planet Mercury receives much more energy than an area of 1 square meter on a farther planet—such as Pluto. That is why Mercury is much hotter than Pluto.

MATH LINK

LENGTH OF DAY

Planet	Day = time for complete spin (in Earth hours or days)
Mercury	59 days
Venus	243 days
Earth	24 hours
Mars	$24\frac{1}{2}$ hours
Jupiter	9 hours 56 minutes
Saturn	10 hours 40 minutes
Uranus	17 hours 14 minutes
Neptune	16 hours 6 minutes
Pluto	6.39 days

READING CHARTS

1. **WRITE** Make a list of planets in order from the shortest day to the longest day.
2. **DISCUSS** Is there a relationship between the length of a planet's day and its distance from the Sun? Explain your answer.

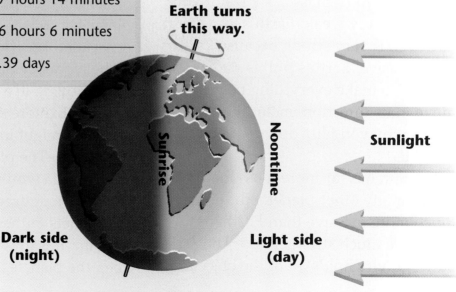

Earth turns this way.

Sunlight

Dark side (night)

Light side (day)

Sunrise

Noontime

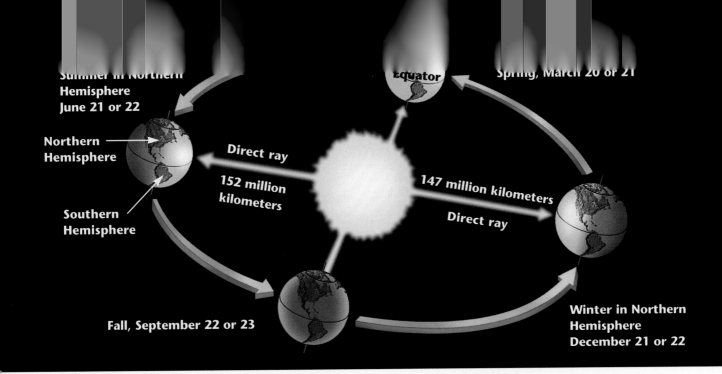

Summer in Northern Hemisphere June 21 or 22

Northern Hemisphere

Direct ray

152 million kilometers

Southern Hemisphere

Fall, September 22 or 23

Equator

Spring, March 20 or 21

147 million kilometers

Direct ray

Winter in Northern Hemisphere December 21 or 22

Why is Earth Special?

As the third planet from the Sun, Earth is at a location where it receives just the right amount of energy to provide living things with the warmth and light they need.

Different animals and plants live in different temperatures, in different climates, and at different heights above sea level on Earth.

Why are places generally cooler in winter than in summer?

Earth's orbit is like a slightly stretched circle—an oval. This shape brings Earth slightly closer to the Sun during part of the year and farther away during other parts of the year. In the Northern Hemisphere, Earth is actually slightly closer to the Sun during winter than during summer. Then what causes colder winters and warmer summers?

The answer is Earth's shape and tilt. Earth is tilted as it travels around the Sun. During the summer the Northern Hemisphere is tilted toward the Sun.

During the winter it is tilted away from the Sun. The sunlight reaching the Northern Hemisphere in the winter is more spread out. Temperatures are lower. In the Northern Hemisphere the midday summer Sun is higher in the sky. Temperatures are warmer.

The closer a place is to the equator, the less change there is in temperatures from season to season. Why? The midday Sun is high in the sky all year round.

Also, some surfaces warm up more than others when bathed in sunlight. Land heats up more than water. Dark soils heat up more than light-colored sands. As a result Earth ends up with a whole range of temperatures, which can support the many different kinds of life on Earth.

Brain Power

How do plants or animals adapt to living through cold winters and hot summers? Give some examples.

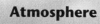
Atmosphere

Sea level

Lithosphere

Hydrosphere

Earth

How Else Does the Sun Affect Earth?

Is Earth a solid planet? Liquid? Gas? Earth is all of these. It has a solid surface layer, mostly covered by a layer of water, all surrounded by layers of gases. The Sun interacts with all of these layers of Earth.

• The **lithosphere** (lith′ə sfîr′) is the hard, outer layer of Earth, about 100 kilometers thick. The rocky surface that makes up the top of the lithosphere is the **crust**. The crust includes the continents and the ocean floors.

The crust has the soil and many other **resources**. Earth's resources are materials that help support life on Earth. Earth has high mountains, like the Rockies. It also has low valleys, like those of the ocean bottoms.

• The **hydrosphere** (hī′drə sfîr′) is Earth's water—trillions of liters of water. Earth's waters are another valuable resource. There is so much water that it covers most of the lithosphere. Most of this water is called the ocean. It is salty because of minerals that have been washed into

it over the ages. The hydrosphere also includes all of Earth's lakes, rivers, streams, underground water, and ice. Most of this is fresh water, which we use for drinking, cooking, and bathing.

However, the hydrosphere is very thin compared to the diameter of Earth. Use a basketball to model Earth. If you dip the ball in water, the water wetting its surface would represent the hydrosphere.

The hydrosphere acts as a big heat absorber. Water changes temperature slowly compared to land. The oceans keep temperatures on Earth from changing too drastically.

The Sun is continually interacting with the lithosphere and hydrosphere. Plants and other producers on Earth's surface are trapping the Sun's energy and producing food. They also produce the gas oxygen in the process.

Also, water in and on the ground evaporates as it absorbs the Sun's energy. Water from the oceans evaporates. Evaporation is part of the water cycle. The Sun's energy is the driving force of this cycle.

What Causes Weather?

Pictures of Earth taken from space show lots of white clouds swirling in the *atmosphere*. The atmosphere is not one, but many layers of gases that surround Earth. The atmosphere contains oxygen needed for living things on Earth. It also contains other gases that help protect Earth from forms of harmful energy from the Sun. These gases are more of Earth's precious resources.

Driven by the Sun's energy, the water cycle brings water into the atmosphere in the form of the gas water vapor. The water vapor condenses, or changes back into liquid. Clouds form as a result. Rain and snow fall from the clouds. The atmosphere carries the water all living things need far over the land as rain and snow. This is part of what we call Earth's weather changes. It also distributes water over the surface as needed by living things.

The Sun's heating of Earth's three layers results not only in a water cycle.

It drives Earth's weather, the day-to-day changes in the atmosphere at each place on Earth. The Sun is also responsible for Earth's climates, the overall pattern of temperatures and rain or snow that each area has.

Part of Earth's weather are the winds that move across the surface. In addition to day-to-day winds, the Sun's energy drives the major wind systems of the atmosphere. Because of Earth's round shape, the surface is heated unequally. The result is the global wind patterns, such as the prevailing westerlies that blow across much of North America.

These winds, in turn, blow across Earth's oceans and drive surface ocean currents. These currents are movements of surface water in huge circular patterns. As ocean currents flow along the edges of continents, they affect the land's climate. The California Current carries cold water along the West Coast of our country, helping it stay cool there. On the East Coast, the Gulf Stream keeps the climate warm.

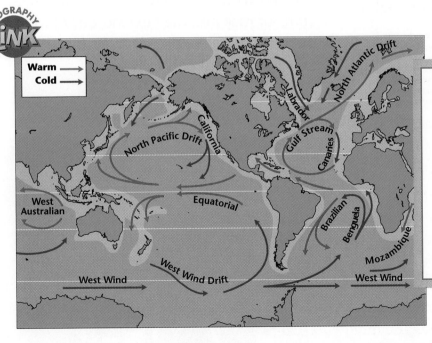

GEOGRAPHY LINK

Warm →
Cold →

READING N MAPS

1. **WRITE** In what direction is the Gulf Stream flowing? How does this direction help keep the East Coast warm?
2. **DISCUSS** In what direction is the California Current flowing? How does it help keep the West Coast warm?

What Is Earth's Closest Neighbor Like?

Earth is teeming with life and movement. You've seen how the Sun's energy helps produce seasons, day-to-day weather, and climates. You've seen the motion of Earth's surface currents.

With a telescope you can take a close look at Earth's nearest neighbor in the solar system. "Only" 400,000 kilometers from Earth, the Moon's surface does not look at all like Earth's surface. You won't see clouds or oceans. There are no hills covered with forests—in fact there are no signs of life at all.

The Moon has no hydrosphere. It has no atmosphere to speak of. There is no water to drink, no air to breathe. There is no weather. Without the atmosphere to trap heat and the hydrosphere to circulate it, temperatures change greatly during a Moon day. At midday on the Moon, the surface temperature climbs as high as 117°C, hotter than boiling water! During the lunar nighttime it drops to –193°C, cold enough to liquefy oxygen!

Earth's nearest neighbor looks nothing much like Earth.

The Moon has a lithosphere, a rocky surface. With a telescope you can see features of the surface—such as dark-colored regions called *maria* (mär'ē ə). *Maria* is Latin for "seas." In the past these areas were thought to be seas. They are really dry, flat land surrounded by mountains and ridges.

Much of the Moon's surface is covered with huge dents, called craters. Trails of rock and dust extend out from them. They reflect sunlight and look like rays coming out of the crater.

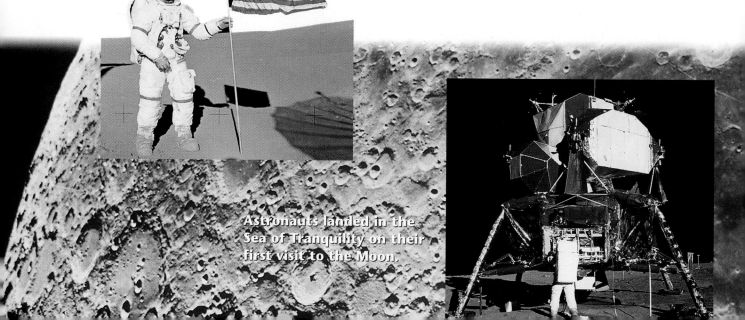

Astronauts landed in the Sea of Tranquility on their first visit to the Moon.

How Does the Moon Affect Earth?

The Moon is not a planet. It travels in an orbit around Earth. "Moon" light is actually "Sun" light. Your part of Earth is not facing the Sun at night. However, the Sun's light reaches the Moon, and the Moon bounces it toward Earth.

The Moon can darken the sky during the day in an event called a solar eclipse. The Moon moves in its orbit directly between the Sun and Earth. For a short period, it casts a shadow on places on Earth.

If you live along a coast, you can see one way the Moon affects Earth. You can see the tides come in and go out. Tides are the rising and falling levels of water. Tides result from the gravity between Earth, the Sun, and the Moon. Living things along coasts depend on the tides.

When astronauts first visited the Moon in 1969, they faced a tough problem. How do you survive in such a place? They had to bring all of the things they needed to stay alive all the way from Earth. *Apollo 11* carried with it on its long journey through space everything needed to support life.

Earth is the only member of the solar system that supports life as we know it.

At high tide many living things along the water's edge are underwater. At low tide, however, they are exposed to the air.

REVIEW

1. How would you state your address in space? Explain your answer.

2. How is gravity important for Earth?

3. How does the Sun affect life on Earth?

4. **DRAW CONCLUSIONS** Why is the Moon unlivable compared with Earth?

5. **CRITICAL THINKING** *Analyze* Would you weigh the same on all of the planets? Explain your answer.

WHY IT MATTERS THINK ABOUT IT
The Moon has only about one-sixth of the mass of Earth. That means it has one-sixth of Earth's gravity. What would it be like to carry out your daily activities on the Moon?

WHY IT MATTERS WRITE ABOUT IT
What would you need to bring along on a space mission to another planet? Explain your choices.

NATIONAL GEOGRAPHIC

World of SCIENCE

Searching FOR E.T.

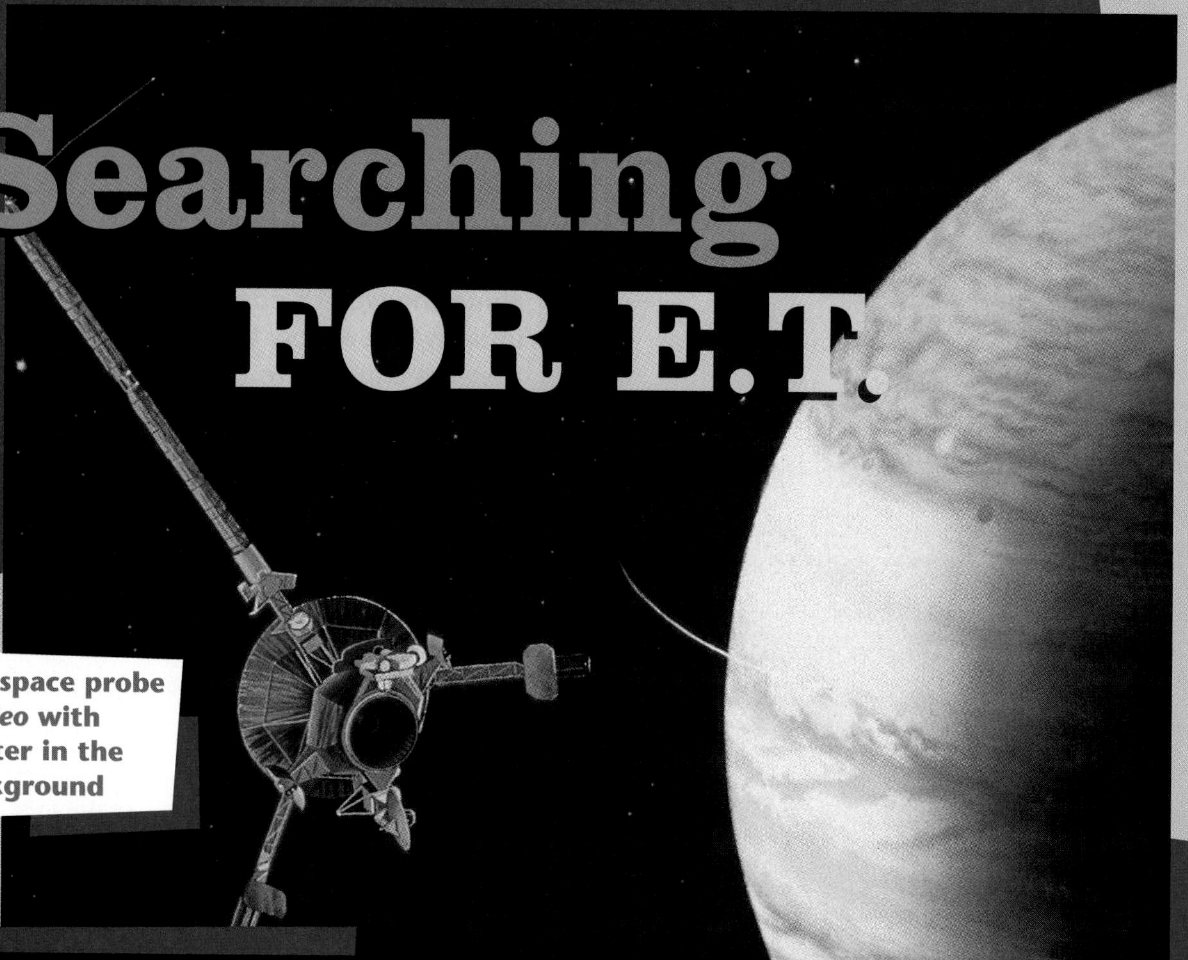

The space probe *Galileo* with Jupiter in the background

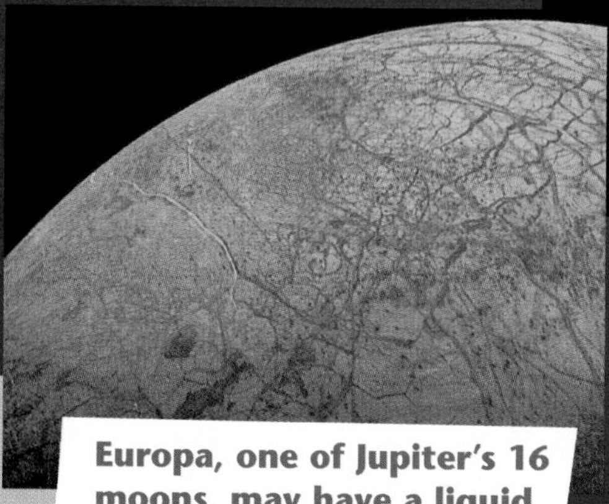

Europa, one of Jupiter's 16 moons, may have a liquid ocean that supports life.

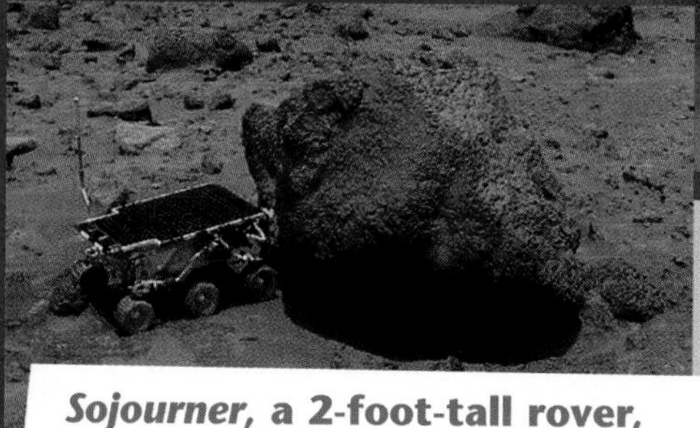

Sojourner, a 2-foot-tall rover, gathers data from Martian rocks during the 1997 Mars *Pathfinder* mission.

Could life exist anywhere else in our solar system? Life on Earth requires oxygen, water, sunlight, soil, gravity, and temperatures that are neither too hot nor too cold.

Do other planets meet those needs? Here's a summary of what NASA has learned from its unmanned probes. In 1974 and 1975, *Mariner 10* discovered there's no oxygen on Mercury. Its temperatures range from –173°C (–279°F) to 425°C (797°F).

In 1978 *Pioneer Venus 2* found that Venus's atmosphere of 97 percent carbon dioxide traps the Sun's heat. *Magellan* has orbited Venus since 1990, sending pictures of soil baked by temperatures that could melt lead!

Pathfinder found evidence in 1997 that Mars once had water. With temperatures between –21°C (–6°F) and –124°C (–191°F), could life exist there? On Earth algae live under Earth's polar ice caps, and tube worms live in very hot water near deep ocean vents.

The outer planets are made of gas, so they have no solid surface. However, in 1997 *Galileo* found that one of Jupiter's moons, Europa, was rocky, like Earth, and may have more water than Earth's oceans! The atmosphere on Titan, one of Saturn's moons, may be like Earth's was four billion years ago. In 2004 spacecraft will visit these moons.

Voyager 2 has discovered that conditions on Uranus and Neptune probably won't support life. Probes haven't yet reached Pluto, a "snowball" smaller than Earth's moon.

Discussion Starter

1 What does finding life near ocean vents or under polar caps on Earth have to do with finding life on other planets?

2 Do you think scientists will ever find human life on other planets in our solar system? Why or why not?

*inter*NET **CONNECTION** To learn more about space, visit **www.mhschool.com/science** and enter the keyword **CALLBACK.**

Topic
EARTH SCIENCE
2

WHY IT MATTERS

Changes in Earth's crust affect the lives of many people.

SCIENCE WORDS

fault a crack in the crust, whose sides show evidence of motion

geologist a scientist who studies Earth

magma hot, molten rock deep below Earth's surface

lava magma that reaches Earth's surface

weathering the breaking down of rocks into smaller pieces

erosion the picking up and carrying away of pieces of rock

deposition the dropping off of bits of eroded rock

meteorite a chunk of rock from space that strikes a surface (such as Earth or the Moon)

Earth's Changing Crust

What causes an earthquake? An earthquake seems to happen without warning. The ground shakes suddenly, often with enough power to damage objects on the surface.

Where do earthquakes happen? Earthquakes are common in places where the crust is "cracked." One such crack extends through much of the state of California. Why do you think earthquakes happen along this crack?

EXPLORE

HYPOTHESIZE What kind of motion causes an earthquake? Does it always cause destruction? Can it result in anything else? Write a hypothesis in your *Science Journal.* Test your ideas.

EXPLORE ACTIVITY

Design Your Own Experiment

WHAT MAKES THE CRUST MOVE?

PROCEDURES

1. MAKE A MODEL Work with a partner to model layers of rock. You may use books, clay, or other materials to represent rock layers. Build your model on wax paper. Include a "crack" down through the layers. Stack cubes on the top of the model to represent buildings and other surface features.

2. EXPERIMENT Find as many ways of moving the model as you can to show how the crust may move during an earthquake. What happens to the surface features as you move the model each way? Draw and describe each way in your *Science Journal.*

3. EXPERIMENT How can you show movement without causing any visible effect on the surface features?

CONCLUDE AND APPLY

1. COMPARE AND CONTRAST How many different ways could you move your model? How were they different?

2. CAUSE AND EFFECT How did each way you moved the model affect the surface features? How did each way change the positions of the layers? Explain.

3. CAUSE AND EFFECT How did you move the model without moving the surface features? Did the model change in any way? Explain.

GOING FURTHER: Problem Solving

4. EXPERIMENT How can you use your model to show how a mountain might rise up high above sea level? Explain and demonstrate.

401

Remains of ancient sea life are sometimes found in rock layers high up in mountains.

Fossils in mountain areas

Brain Power

How can remains of ancient sea life be found high above sea level? How can these remains be proof that the crust moves?

What Makes the Crust Move?

Earth's crust is constantly moving, if not in one place then in another. Sometimes it moves quickly enough to be seen and felt. People who have been through an earthquake tell of seeing the ground heave up and down like an ocean wave.

As the Explore Activity showed, earthquakes are related to cracks in the crust called **faults**. These faults may have formed from earlier earthquakes. Sometimes they form while the earthquake happens. During an earthquake the crust on either side, or on both sides, of a fault is in motion.

During an earthquake vibrations travel through the crust. The farther away people are from the earthquake, the harder it is for them to feel the vibrations. However, delicate devices called *seismographs* (sīz′mə grafs′) can record this motion at locations all around the crust.

Most of the time, however, the crust moves very slowly. Rocks can move slowly on either side of a fault over centuries. People only realize there is movement when something visibly changes position. Not all motion happens along faults, either. Often layers of the crust bend, such as you see here. Bending, like motion along a fault, may happen gradually over time.

To measure crust movement, *surveyors* (sər vā′ərz) measure *elevation*—how high a place is above sea level. They leave plaques called *bench marks* that tell the exact location and elevation of a place. When some bench marks are remeasured, they are found to have risen or sunk.

Geologists (jē ol′ə jists), scientists who study Earth, place sensitive devices all along faults, such as the San Andreas Fault in California. They hope that records of tiny movements can be used to predict an earthquake.

Below the Crust

The crust is Earth's hard surface. Compared to the distance to Earth's center, it is very thin. It is only about one-thousandth of Earth's thickness.

Under the crust is the mantle, Earth's thickest layer. The rock material here is solid. Yet, it can flow like a liquid—as putty can "flow" when you squeeze it between your hands. Below the mantle is Earth's core. It is in two parts, a liquid outer core and a solid inner core.

The rock material in the mantle is in motion, something like heated water in a pot. It rises and pushes against the bottom of the crust. This movement causes the thin, brittle crust at the surface to break into pieces, or *plates*. The plates themselves can move along Earth's surface. Earthquakes and the slow motions of the crust all result from moving plates.

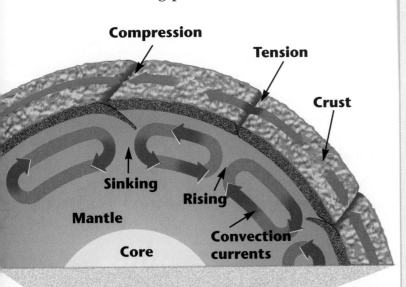

Compression

Tension

Crust

Sinking

Rising

Mantle

Convection currents

Core

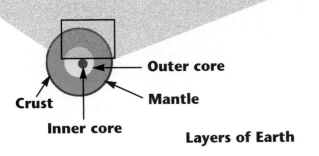

Outer core

Mantle

Crust

Inner core

Layers of Earth

Model of Earth

HYPOTHESIZE Can materials with different properties be used to make a solid Earth? Write a hypothesis in your *Science Journal*.

MATERIALS
- mashed ripe banana (in a plastic bag)
- peanut butter
- hazelnut
- graham cracker crumbs (in a plastic bag)
- wax paper
- *Science Journal*

PROCEDURES

⚠ SAFETY
Students who are allergic to peanuts should not do this activity!

1. **INFER** You will use four materials to make a model of Earth on wax paper. Each material is one of Earth's layers. Read step 2. Decide which material represents which layer. Decide how thick each layer needs to be.

2. **MAKE A MODEL** Wash your hands. Cover the nut with a layer of peanut butter. Put the covered nut in the bag of mashed banana so that banana covers it completely. Roll the result into the graham cracker crumbs on waxpaper.

CONCLUDE AND APPLY

1. **DRAW CONCLUSIONS** Why does each material represent a different layer?

2. How thick did you decide to make each layer? Explain your reasoning.

403

What Forces Act on the Crust?

What makes the crust move? As the plates of the crust move, they can collide. They can pull away from each other. They can also slide past each other. These movements cause three kinds of forces to act on the crust.

- *Tension* stretches or pulls apart the crust.

- *Compression* squeezes or pushes together the crust.

- *Shear* twists, tears, or pushes one part of the crust past another.

Each of these forces can cause a fault to form in the crust. Each can cause movement along a fault. These forces can also result in other kinds of motion in the crust.

As forces inside the Earth cause the crust to move upward, the land is built up. Compression can crumple rock layers into wavy folds. The mountains shown here formed when two pieces of crust crashed together.

The impact squeezed the crust, causing it to crumple into huge folds. Mountains made of crumpled and folded layers of rock are called *fold mountains*. The Appalachians, the Alps, and the Himalayas are all ranges of fold mountains.

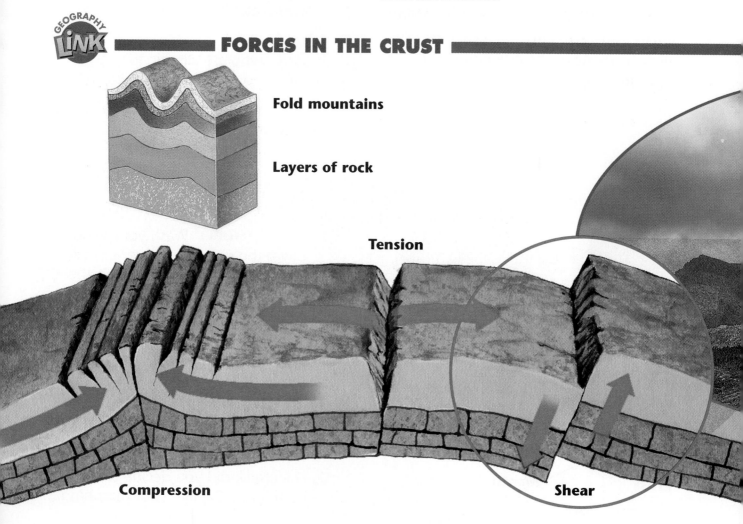

GEOGRAPHY LINK

FORCES IN THE CRUST

Fold mountains

Layers of rock

Tension

Compression

Shear

What Else Can Constructive Forces Do?

Tension and shear can also build up the crust. Mountains can be formed as the crust is pulled apart. How? Hot molten rock deep below Earth's surface, called **magma**, rises upward. If magma reaches the surface, it may flow out as **lava**.

Lava flows out or is hurled out when a volcano erupts. This volcano is building a new island off the coast of Iceland. Its lava is gushing up through a crack between two pieces of crust that are being pulled apart.

Surtsey, an island near Iceland, is forming from an undersea volcano.

Tension and shear also cause great blocks of crust to break apart cleanly and move along faults. Blocks of crust moving along a fault can form *fault-block mountains*. A vast region of fault-block mountains known as the Basin and Range Province blankets several western states (see map).

Fault-block mountains

Basin and Range Province

READING IN DIAGRAMS

1. **DISCUSS** How are fold mountains and fault-block mountains the same? How are they different?
2. **WRITE** Write a paragraph about how a volcano can become a new island.

What Other Forces Shape Earth's Surface?

While movements of the crust are building up Earth's surface, other forces are at work breaking it down. These processes are known as **weathering** (we<u>th</u>'ər ing) and **erosion** (i rō'zhən). Weathering is the breaking down of the materials of Earth's crust into smaller pieces. Erosion is the picking up and carrying away of the pieces. Weathering and erosion have been going on for billions of years! They both happen in many, many ways.

Weathering happens when the crust is exposed to water, air, and changes in temperature. How do these break down rocks?

Water can break down the crust in many ways. Water can dissolve some minerals right out of the crust. Moving water can make pieces of rock bang into each other. Small chips can break off the surface of the rock. This causes the rock to get smaller and rounder. The churning waters of a stream can wear down big pieces of rock into small rounded pebbles.

Wind is moving air. The wind blows sand and other broken bits of rock over Earth's surface. These particles also wear away rock.

Air also contains gases that react chemically to form new substances. Oxygen in air reacts with iron to form rust. Carbon dioxide and sulfur dioxide in air react with rain to form acids. These acids eat away at limestone rocks. The cavern seen here was once solid rock! Acid rainwater seeping through the rock dissolved part of it. It "ate away" a huge hole—the cavern!

Rounded pebbles near a churning river

This beautiful rock formation was carved by wind-blown sand.

Limestone cavern

What Does Temperature Do to Rocks?

If the temperature drops low enough, water can freeze. When water freezes it expands, or takes up more space. Water freezing in cracks in rocks expands against the rock. The force of the expanding water is so great that it can split the rock apart.

Changes in temperature also cause rock to expand and contract. A rock may be made of a number of different materials. Sometimes one part of a rock expands or contracts more than another part. This difference can cause one part of the rock to push or pull against another part of the rock. Some geologists think that this eventually can cause the rock to break.

This huge boulder was eventually broken apart by small amounts of water that seeped into cracks and froze.

Erosion

Erosion is the carrying away of pieces of weathered rock by gravity, water, wind, and ice. Piece by piece erosion can carry away a boulder, a hill, or even a whole mountain range!

The greatest agent of erosion is water. From the moment a drop of water falling from the sky first hits the ground, it erodes the land.

It may not seem like much, however, think of how many raindrops fall in a rainstorm. Altogether they can move a lot of soil.

Once water reaches the ground, it begins to flow downhill. Moving water can push and carry things along with it. Think of a raft full of people. How much do you think it weighs? What is moving all that weight along?

Water running downhill picks up pieces of rock and carries them downhill. The faster the water is moving, the bigger the pieces of rock it can move.

Brain Power

What if all of the topsoil in a region were washed away? How would the plants in the region be affected? How would this affect the animals in the region? The people living there?

What do you think happened to the ground under this house? Where do you think it went?

407

How Can Wind and Ice Erode Rock?

Wind is moving air. Wind can push things along with it, just like moving water. Yet air is less dense than water. Wind does not exert as hard a push as water moving at the same speed. Therefore, wind mostly erodes pieces of rock that are sand sized or smaller.

Ice also causes a lot of erosion. This glacier in Alaska is a moving river of ice. It may not move as quickly as water, but don't underestimate its power. When the ice of a glacier freezes onto rock and then the glacier moves downhill, the rock is torn right out of the ground. This glacier can carry chunks of rock bigger than your house with ease.

Glaciers also wear away the land as they flow over it. Place an ice cube in some sand for a minute or two. Then look at the bottom of the ice cube. What has become frozen into the bottom of the ice cube? Now rub the bottom of the ice cube on a bar of soap. What happens to the surface of the bar of soap?

Rocks of all sizes become frozen into the bottom of a glacier. As the glacier moves, the rock beneath it is scratched and worn down. Ten thousand years ago, a glacier covered New York City. Can you guess how the scratches in these rocks in Central Park were made?

The grooves on this rock in New York City were cut by a glacier millions of years ago.

The Margerie Glacier in Alaska

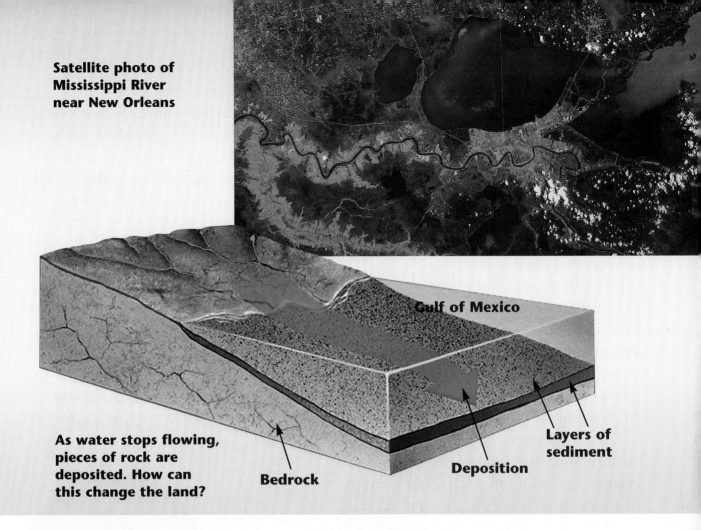

Satellite photo of Mississippi River near New Orleans

Gulf of Mexico

As water stops flowing, pieces of rock are deposited. How can this change the land?

Bedrock

Deposition

Layers of sediment

Where Do Eroded Rocks Go?

What happens to pieces of rock that are carried along by wind, moving ice, or moving water? A fast wind eventually slows down. A glacier stops moving and eventually melts at its front end and sides. All streams eventually slow down and end when they flow into a large body of water, such as a lake or ocean.

When water stops moving, it also stops carrying along bits and pieces of rock. The pieces of rock are dropped to the bottom of the stream, lake, or ocean. The dropping off of bits of eroded rock is called **deposition** (dep'ə zish'ən).

Deposition also takes place when glaciers melt and winds stop blowing. Layer by layer, pile after pile, bits and pieces of rock deposited by water, wind, and ice build up Earth's surface.

Very slowly deposition may fill up depressions, or basins, in Earth's surface. It can build up land along shorelines and at the end of rivers. Deposition does not seem as dramatic as colliding continents. However, the slow, steady work of deposition is one of the greatest constructive actions on Earth.

Brain Power

Look in your community for signs of change. Where do you see signs of weathering, erosion, or deposition?

How Is the Moon Different from Earth?

Earth's Moon, our nearest neighbor in space, is a far different place from Earth. There is no evidence of earthquakes as on Earth's crust. There are no erupting volcanoes. In fact there is no evidence of any of the kinds of motion that Earth's crust has.

Without air and water, there can be very little weathering or erosion. The Moon has almost no air or water. There are no streams, no glaciers, and no wind. The only weathering and erosion is due to the impact of rocks from space hitting the Moon's surface.

These rocks from space that strike a surface are called **meteorites**. Some craters formed by the impact of meteorites are big enough to be seen from Earth. Others are so tiny the entire crater is on a single mineral crystal.

Can meteorites also strike Earth's surface and produce craters? Yes! However, Earth's atmosphere protects its surface from many such impacts. Rocks from space "burn up" as they pass through Earth's atmosphere. The Moon has no atmosphere. How does that fact affect the Moon's surface?

Meteorite impacts shatter rocks on the Moon and also create a lot of heat. The heat melts the rock. Pieces of rock may melt together, and droplets and globs of molten rock can splatter outwards. Over time continual meteorite impacts break down the rock. The end result is a mixture of shattered pieces of rock, rock droplets, and melted-together bits of rock.

Meteorite impact has been recorded on the Moon's surface.

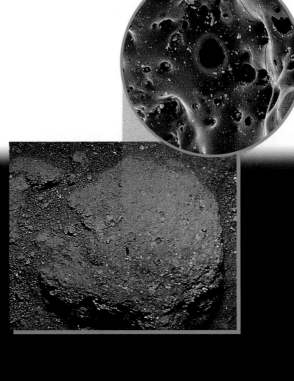

Do Other Planets Change?

As the solar system has been explored, evidence of surface changes and erosion has been found on other worlds. There are perhaps thousands of volcanoes on Venus. The largest volcano in the solar system is Mars's Olympus Mons. It is 24 kilometers (15 miles) high and 550 kilometers (34 miles) across.

Some of Jupiter's moons also show evidence of constructive and destructive forces. The *Voyager* and *Galileo* spacecraft even sent back pictures showing some of Io's volcanoes erupting! The moons Ganymede, Callisto, and Europa have water ice. The presence of water, organic compounds, and internal heat mean life may be possible on Europa.

This volcano was erupting on Jupiter's moon Io as the Voyager spacecraft flew by.

REVIEW

1. What are some types of evidence that show Earth's crust has moved?

2. What are three types of forces acting on Earth's crust?

3. How are earthquakes measured?

4. **COMPARE AND CONTRAST** What is the difference between weathering and erosion?

5. **CRITICAL THINKING** *Analyze* How do fault-block mountains compare to fold mountains?

WHY IT MATTERS THINK ABOUT IT
How do you think people can protect themselves if an earthquake happens?

WHY IT MATTERS WRITE ABOUT IT
How can people plan ahead to prepare for an earthquake or any other kind of force that can change the crust suddenly?

READING SKILL
Write a paragraph to explain the sequence of events involved when an earthquake occurs.

Waves of Erosion

Have you ever stood by the ocean and felt a wave pull the sand from under your feet? Waves constantly carry sand away from a beach, bit by bit. The sand is deposited elsewhere on the shoreline.

People who live by beaches can watch their "front yards" slowly disappear. Many beach homes are built on stilts. That puts the buildings above water during high tides and storms. However, if the sand supporting the stilts washes away, the houses fall!

If there are cliffs on a shoreline, the pounding waves can wear away the lowest parts. Eventually the cliffs collapse and fall into the water. Then waves slowly break the rocks into smaller pieces. In time the cliffs will become sand!

Stormy winter weather increases erosion. Fierce winds push the waves, giving them the strength to pick up and carry small stones. The stones pound cliffs along with the waves and help to break the rocks. The stronger

Waves can wear away the sand that supports a beachfront home.

A Closer Look

wind also pushes waves farther inland.
Some towns truck in sand to replace
what's lost. Other towns build
breakwaters close to shore. The stone
and concrete breakwaters reduce the
force of the waves before they reach
shore. An island or a sandbar close to
shore serves as a natural breakwater.

Nearly all sand and rock removed by
wave erosion is deposited elsewhere.
Only one percent is carried out to sea.

People sometimes build sea walls to try to protect the beaches behind the walls from pounding waves.

DISCUSSION STARTER

1. How does erosion build beaches?

2. How do waves erode a cliff?

To learn more about erosion, visit
www.mhschool.com/science and
enter the keyword BREAKDOWN.

*inter*NET
CONNECTION

413

Topic 3
EARTH SCIENCE

WHY IT MATTERS

Minerals are used in many different ways.

SCIENCE WORDS

mineral a solid material of Earth's crust with a definite composition

luster the way light bounces off a mineral's surface

streak the color of the powder left when a mineral is rubbed against a hard, rough surface

hardness how well a mineral resists scratching

cleavage the tendency of a mineral to break along flat surfaces

ore a mineral containing a useful substance

gem a mineral valued for being rare and beautiful

nonrenewable resource a resource that cannot be replaced within a short period of time or at all

Minerals of Earth's Crust

How many substances do you think make up Earth's solid surface, the crust? Would you believe about 2,000?

The substances that make up Earth's crust are minerals. Here are two of them. One is gold. The other looks like gold, but isn't. It's nicknamed "fool's gold." Many of the miners who went to California in the 1800s could not tell real gold from fool's gold. Which of the two do you think is real gold?

EXPLORE

HYPOTHESIZE How do you think people can tell minerals apart? Write a hypothesis in your *Science Journal.* Test your ideas.

Investigate How You Can Identify a Mineral

Compare properties of minerals to tell minerals apart.

PROCEDURES

1. COMMUNICATE Use tape and a marker to label each sample with a number. In your *Science Journal*, make a table with the column headings shown. Fill in numbers under "Mineral" to match your samples.

2. OBSERVE Use the table shown as a guide to collect data on each sample. Fill in the data in your table. Turn to the table on page 419 for more ideas to fill in "Other."

CONCLUDE AND APPLY

1. ANALYZE Use your data and the table below to identify your samples. Were you sure of all your samples? Explain.

2. MAKE DECISIONS Which observations were most helpful? Explain.

GOING FURTHER: Problem Solving

3. DRAW CONCLUSIONS How could you make a better Scratch (Hardness) test?

MATERIALS

- mineral samples
- clear tape
- red marker
- copper penny or wire
- streak plate
- porcelain tile
- hand lens
- mineral property table (page 419, or see *Science Journal*)
- nail
- *Science Journal*

Color = color of surface

Porcelain Plate Test = the color you see when you rub the sample gently on porcelain

Shiny Like a Metal = reflects light like a metal, such as aluminium foil or metal coins

Scratch (Hardness): Does it scratch copper? A piece of glass?

Other: Is it very dense? (Is a small piece heavy?) Has it got flat surfaces?

	Mineral	Color	Shiny Like a Metal (Yes/No)	Porcelain Plate Test	Scratch (Hardness)	Other
1.						
2.						

What Are Minerals?

What do diamond rings, talcum powder, and aluminum foil have in common? They are made from **minerals**. So are copper wire, teeth fillings, china dishes, and table salt.

With so many differences in minerals, what can they have in common? Minerals are solid materials of Earth's crust. Like all matter they are made of elements. Some minerals, like gold, silver, copper, and carbon, are made of one element. Most minerals are made of compounds, that is, two or more elements joined together.

Whether it is an element or a compound, each mineral has a definite chemical composition. Scientists can identify minerals by checking out the elements or compounds inside.

As minerals form, their atoms and molecules get into fixed patterns. These patterns cause minerals to form geometric shapes, called *crystals*. Different patterns form different crystal shapes. You can see the six main crystal shapes on these pages.

MATH LINK

Tetragonal crystal shape

The mineral chalcopyrite (kal′kə pī′rīt) is a compound made of the elements copper, iron, and sulfur. It is where much of our copper comes from. Copper is used for wire, coins, pots, and pans.

Cubic crystal shape

Hexagonal crystal shape

Rock salt, which is used to melt ice, is the mineral halite (hal′īt). It is a compound made of the elements sodium and chlorine.

The "lead" in a lead pencil is not the metal element lead at all. It is the mineral graphite (graf′īt), which is a form of the element carbon.

How Can You Identify a Mineral?

No two minerals are exactly alike. Each mineral has a different composition. Each has its own set of properties that you can use to tell them apart. Crystal shape is one property. However, telling the exact chemical composition of most minerals or their crystal shape isn't easy. This requires special instruments.

The Explore Activity introduced some simpler properties to use.

- The color of the outer surface of the mineral is the first thing you see. However, if a mineral is exposed to weather, it can become discolored.

Therefore, you should always observe color on a fresh surface. Color alone cannot be used to identify most minerals. Why not? Some minerals come in a variety of colors, and some colors are common to many minerals.

- **Luster** is the way light bounces off a mineral. Minerals with a metallic luster are shiny, like metals. Graphite has a metallic luster.

Minerals with a nonmetallic luster may look shiny or dull. Nonmetallic luster can be described as glassy, waxy, pearly, earthy, oily, or silky. Talc has a nonmetallic luster often described as oily.

Brain Power

1. Which minerals on these pages have metallic luster?
2. Which have nonmetallic luster?

Orthorhombic crystal shape

Topaz is a mineral used in many kinds of jewelry. It comes in many colors— pink, pale blue, and even yellow or white.

Monoclinic crystal shape

Talc is the mineral used in talcum powder. Talc comes in white and greenish colors.

The mineral kaolinite (kā'ə lə nīt') is used in china plates and ceramic objects. It comes in many colors—red, white, reddish brown, and even black.

Triclinic crystal shape

417

Hematite has a blackish color but a reddish streak.

Galena has three cleavage planes. It breaks into cubes.

Mica has one cleavage plane. It breaks into sheets.

MOH'S SCALE OF HARDNESS

Hardness	Sample Mineral	Tool
1	Talc	
2	Gypsum	
		Fingernail
3	Calcite	
		Copper penny/wire
4	Fluorite	
		Iron nail
5	Apatite	
		Glass plate
6	Feldspar	
		Steel file
7	Quartz	
		Streak plate
8	Topaz	
9	Corundum	
10	Diamond	

READING  CHARTS

1. **DISCUSS** Which mineral is the softest? The hardest?
2. **WRITE** Which minerals does a fingernail scratch? Which does a glass plate scratch?

How Can Rubbing and Scratching Help?

Here are three other ways to identify a mineral.

- **Streak** is the color of the powder left when a mineral is rubbed against a hard, rough surface. Rub it against a porcelain streak plate. The streak is always the same for a given mineral, even if the mineral varies in color.

The streak may not be the color of the outer surface of the mineral. Fool's gold, pyrite, is brassy yellow, but it has a greenish black streak. Gold has a yellow streak. You would need a streak plate to tell that the real gold on page 414 is on the right.

- **Hardness** is a measure of how well a mineral resists scratching. Soft minerals are easily scratched. Moh's Scale of Hardness is a numbered list of minerals. Talc, number 1, is the softest mineral. It can be scratched with your fingernail! Any item on the list, including the tools, can scratch something above it. You can use the tools to help find the hardness.

- The way a mineral breaks is also helpful. Some minerals have **cleavage**. This property is the tendency of a mineral to break along flat surfaces. Cleavage is described by the number of directions, or planes, the mineral breaks in.

Many minerals do not break smoothly. They are said to have *fracture*. Quartz, for example, shows jagged edges when it breaks.

Some minerals have special proper-ties that help you identify them. Magnatite, for example, is attracted by a magnet. Some minerals are very dense—such as gold, silver, and galena. Even a small sample feels quite heavy.

PROPERTIES OF MINERALS

MINERAL	COLOR(S)	LUSTER (Shiny as metals)	PORCELAIN PLATE TEST (Streak)	CLEAVAGE (Number)	HARDNESS (Tools Scratched by)	DENSITY (Compared with water)
Gypsum	colorless, gray, white, brown	no	white	yes—1	2 (all five tools)	2.3
Quartz	colorless, various colors	no	none	no	7 (none)	2.6
Pyrite	brassy, yellow	yes	greenish black	no	6 (steel file, streak plate)	5.0
Calcite	colorless, white, pale blue	no	colorless, white	yes—3 (cubes)	3 (all but fingernail)	2.7
Galena	steel gray	yes	gray to black	yes—3 (cubes)	2.5 (all but fingernail)	7.5
Feldspar	gray, green, yellow, white	no	colorless	yes—2	6 (steel file, streak plate)	2.5
Mica	colorless, silvery, black	no	white	yes—1 (thin sheets)	3 (all but fingernail)	3.0
Hornblende	green to black	no	gray to white	yes—2	5–6 (steel file, streak plate)	3.4
Bauxite	gray, red, brown, white	no	gray	no	1–3 (all but fingernail)	2.0–2.5
Chacopyrite	brassy to golden yellow	yes	greenish black	no	3.5–4 (glass, steel file, streak plate)	4.2
Hematite	black or red-brown	yes	red or red-brown	no	6 (steel file, streak plate)	5.3

A form of calcite shows double image because it refracts light twice as you look through it.

READING CHARTS

1. **WRITE** Which minerals would feel heaviest if you had equal-sized samples of all?
2. **DISCUSS** How is hornblende different from quartz? From feldspar? From mica?

The specks you see in this rock include minerals such as quartz, feldspar, hornblende, and mica. How would you tell them apart?

Quartz crystal

Granite quarry

How Do Minerals Form?

Where do you find minerals? The answer is simple—in the ground. Minerals make up the rocks of the crust. If you examine rocks with a hand lens, you can often find some of the most common rock-forming minerals in the rock.

How do minerals form? Many form when hot liquid rock, or magma, cools and hardens into a solid. Magma is very hot, and its molecules move very fast. When magma cools its molecules slow down and get closer together. Then they connect into a pattern, forming crystals. The longer it takes magma to cool, the more time the crystals have to grow, and the larger they get. The huge quartz crystal shown here formed in magma that cooled very slowly.

Some of the rarest minerals form deep within Earth. The temperatures are high at great depths. The weight of rocks overhead presses down on rocks below, like a huge pressure cooker. The heat and pressure produce minerals such as diamonds. Movements of Earth's crust then bring the minerals near the surface, where they can be mined.

Diamond

How Do Minerals Form in Water?

Crystals can form from the cooling of hot water. Water heated by magma inside Earth is rich in dissolved minerals. Hot water can hold more dissolved minerals than cold water. As the water cools, it is able to hold less dissolved minerals. The minerals that can no longer stay dissolved form crystals. These crystals then slowly settle to the bottom of the water.

Minerals can also form from evaporation. Ocean water contains many dissolved substances. As the ocean water evaporates, the substances that were dissolved form crystals. Common table salt is mined in areas that were once covered with salt water. The salt is a mineral, halite. It was left behind when an ancient sea evaporated.

The piles of brightly colored minerals in this hot spring form when the heated water cools as it is exposed to the air.

Growing Crystals PHYSICAL SCIENCE LINK

HYPOTHESIZE How can you watch crystals grow? Write a hypothesis in your *Science Journal.*

MATERIALS
- foam cup half-filled with hot water
- granulated table salt
- 2 plastic spoons
- crystal of rock salt
- string (about 15 cm)
- pencil
- *Science Journal*

PROCEDURES

Your teacher will put a cup of hot water onto a counter for you.

SAFETY Use a kitchen mitt if you need to hold or move the cup. Don't touch the hot water.

1. Gradually add small amounts of salt to the water. Stir. Keep adding and stirring until no more will dissolve.

2. Tie one end of the string to a crystal of rock salt. Tie the other end to a pencil. Lay the pencil across the cup so that the crystal hangs in the hot salt water without touching the sides or bottom.

3. **OBSERVE** Observe the setup for several days. In your *Science Journal,* record what you see.

CONCLUDE AND APPLY

COMPARE AND CONTRAST Did any crystals grow? If so, did they have many shapes or just one? Explain your answer. If not, how would you change what you did if you tried again?

421

What Are Minerals Used For?

Can you find minerals being used at home or school? Minerals are used to make many products, from steel to electric light bulbs.

Some of the most useful minerals are called **ores** (ôrz). An ore is a mineral that contains a useful substance. Ores contain enough useful substances to make it valuable to mine them.

For example, iron comes from the mineral hematite (hē′mə tīt′). Iron is used to make nails, buildings, and even ships. Aluminum comes from the mineral bauxite. It is used for food-wrap foil, soft-drink cans, and pie tins, just to name a few uses.

The iron and aluminum that come from these two ores are *metals*. Metals have many useful properties. Many of them conduct electricity and can be stretched into wires. The metal copper, for example, comes from a mineral ore. It is used to make electrical wires.

Aluminum is lightweight and strong. It shares these properties with another metal that comes from an ore, magnesium. These metals are ideal for use in building jets and spacecraft.

If you look in a jewelry store window, you'll probably see some minerals called **gems**. Gems are minerals that are valued for being rare and beautiful. You may have seen diamond rings. Rubies and sapphires are other gemstones.

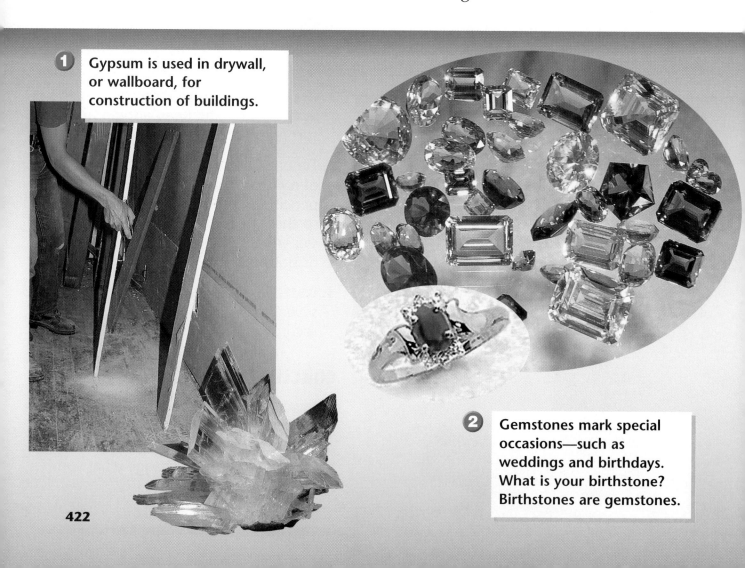

1 Gypsum is used in drywall, or wallboard, for construction of buildings.

2 Gemstones mark special occasions—such as weddings and birthdays. What is your birthstone? Birthstones are gemstones.

Do Minerals Last Forever?

A diamond ring may last centuries. However, Earth's supply of minerals is being used up.

Minerals are **nonrenewable resources**. They cannot be replaced, for example, as trees can be. They take so long to form that they cannot be replaced in your lifetime.

Because minerals are nonrenewable, they must be *conserved. To conserve* means "to use wisely or avoid waste." One way people can conserve minerals is by recycling them— finding ways to treat them and use them again. Researchers can also come up with substitutes to use in place of natural minerals. Many diamonds used in industry for cutting stone, for example, are not natural diamonds.

You use minerals all the time. Quartz is just one example. The most common kind of sand is bits of quartz. Quartz sand can be used to make concrete or glass.

Quartz contains the element silicon. This silicon can be removed and used to make computer chips. Quartz crystals, when a small electric current is added, vibrate and can keep time.

REVIEW

1. Which properties are most useful to identify a mineral—streak, color, luster? Explain your answer.

2. **IDENTIFY** What if you had two white samples of talc and gypsum? How would they be alike? How could you tell them apart in one step?

3. How does time affect crystals?

4. How useful are metallic ores? Give some ways you use one of them.

5. **CRITICAL THINKING** *Apply* How could you avoid the mistake that miners made, thinking fool's gold was real gold? What are all the observations you might make to tell them apart?

WHY IT MATTERS **THINK ABOUT IT**
Start with an empty room. As you decorate it, how might you be using minerals?

WHY IT MATTERS **WRITE ABOUT IT**
How many ways do you use glass in a typical day? How can you conserve glass? Other minerals?

MONUMENTS TO MINERALS

The hotel's paint is peeling, but that doesn't matter. The last guest checked out years ago. Nobody lives in this town anymore. It's just one more ghost town in America's West.

Ghost towns were once busy places. Most were built soon after silver, copper, gold, or other minerals were discovered nearby. The towns were like a monument honoring the minerals!

In the late 1800s, hopeful miners and their families rushed to live in these new towns. They left just as quickly when the mines closed.

Jerome, Arizona, was built in 1882 on the steep sides of Cleopatra Hill. The town wasn't far from some new copper and gold mines. By the 1920s Jerome had a population of 15,000. Over time gravity and poor construction caused the town to slide down the hill. Its Sliding Jail moved 70 meters (230 feet)!

Soon Jerome faced bigger problems. By 1945 the copper and gold were gone, so the mines closed. By 1995 Jerome had a population of about 560.

Most ghost towns end up like Copper Hill, Arizona. Set up in 1908, the town had 500 residents, shops, a school, and a hospital by 1925. By 1933 Copper Hill was completely deserted. Can you guess why?

Some ghost towns have been preserved for others to enjoy.

DISCUSSION STARTER

1. What attracted people to places that later became ghost towns?

2. What caused people to leave Jerome and other ghost towns?

To learn more about mining, visit *www.mhschool.com/science* and enter the keyword MINES.

*inter*NET CONNECTION

425

WHY IT MATTERS

It is important to know how to tell different kinds of rocks apart so we can get what we need from them.

Earth's Rocks and Soil

What do we walk on, sail over, climb, fly over, live in, and even sit on?

Rocks! Rocks make up the crust. Are all rocks alike? Is the granite shown here just like any other rocks? How can we use granite? Why bother digging it out of the crust?

EXPLORE

HYPOTHESIZE Are rocks all alike? Are they different? If so, how? Write a hypothesis in your *Science Journal.* How would you test your ideas?

SCIENCE WORDS

rock a naturally formed solid in the crust, made up of one or more minerals

igneous rock a rock formed when melted rock material cools and hardens

sedimentary rock a rock made of bits of matter joined together

fossil any remains or imprint of living things of the past

metamorphic rock a rock formed under heat and pressure from another kind of rock

humus decayed plant or animal material in soil

pollution adding any unnatural substances to Earth's land, water, or air

rock cycle rocks changing from one form into another in a never-ending series of processes

Design Your Own Experiment

HOW ARE ROCKS ALIKE AND DIFFERENT?

PROCEDURES

1. Use the tape to number each sample in a group of rocks.

2. CLASSIFY Find a way to sort the group into smaller groups. Determine what properties you will use. Group the rocks that share one or more properties. Record your results in your *Science Journal*.

3. COMPARE You might consider hardness, the ability to resist scratches. Your fingernail, the copper wire, and the edge of a streak plate are tools you might use. Scratch gently.

4. USE NUMBERS You might estimate the density of each sample. Use a balance to find the mass. Use a metric ruler to estimate the length, width, and height. **Length x width x height = volume**
Density = mass ÷ volume

MATERIALS

- samples of rocks
- clear tape
- red marker
- hand lens
- copper wire
- streak plate
- balance
- metric ruler
- calculator
- *Science Journal*

CONCLUDE AND APPLY

1. DRAW CONCLUSIONS How were you able to make smaller groups? Give supporting details from the notes you recorded.

2. ANALYZE Could you find more than one way to sort the rocks into groups? Give examples of how rocks from two different smaller groups may have a property in common.

3. COMMUNICATE Share your results with others. Compare your systems for sorting the rocks.

GOING FURTHER: Problem Solving

4. EXPERIMENT If you could not easily measure your samples, how could you find their volume?

5. INFER How might some properties that you observed make a sample useful?

How Are Rocks Alike and Different?

Rocks are mineral treasure chests. A **rock** is any naturally formed solid in the crust made up of one or more kinds of minerals. In the Explore Activity, a hand lens showed that you can often see mineral crystals in a rock. Sometimes the crystals are too small to see easily.

Look with a hand lens at a piece of granite. You can often find crystals of quartz (whitish), feldspar (pink), mica (black), and even hornblende (black).

Each mineral in a rock has its own streak, hardness, or crystal shape. A rock with several minerals may have a mixture of properties. For example, it may have both hard and soft minerals. It may make both light and dark streaks.

The most exact way to identify a rock is to name the minerals it contains. However, color, density, and the way the rock's surface feels, or its *texture*, are also identifying features. The texture comes from the size, shape, and arrangement of the mineral crystals or grains in a rock. Are the grains large (coarse) or small (fine)? Do they interlock, or can you see each clearly? Are they soft edged or jagged?

A rock's color, density, and texture result from how the rock was formed. Rocks are grouped into three types according to how they were formed. Here are rocks of the most common type.

Granite has a coarse texture. The crystals are large enough to be seen. It is a light-colored rock.

Gabbro (gab'rō) has a coarse texture, but it is dark colored.

Brain Power

How could you classify the rocks shown on these two pages? Show your results by making a table with two or three columns and rows. Use the properties as headings, and fill in the table with rock names.

Which Are Earth's Most Common Rocks?

All the rocks on these two pages were at one time deep below Earth's surface. There it is hot enough for some rocks to be melted, or molten. Molten rock material deep below the surface is called magma.

Magma is less dense than the material surrounding it, so it rises toward the surface. Before magma reaches the surface, however, it may cool and harden into solid rock. Rocks that form when melted rock material cools and hardens are called **igneous rocks**.

Often magma makes it all the way to the surface before hardening. Magma that reaches the surface is called *lava*. Exposed to the air above ground, lava, too, hardens and cools, forming igneous rocks.

Below ground magma cools slowly. Crystals take a long time to grow. They grow to large (coarse) sizes.

Above ground cooling is much quicker. Crystals are smaller. Lava may cool so quickly that no crystals have a chance to form. What results is obsidian, a solid piece of volcanic glass.

The granite and gabbro shown on the facing page formed below ground. They both have large mineral crystals. However, granite contains lighter-colored minerals than gabbro.

All the rocks on this page formed above ground. They have small crystals or no crystals at all. How do they differ in color?

The texture and color make a difference in how an igneous rock is used. If you were making a monument, like a big stone wall, to honor someone, which of these rocks might you choose?

Rhyolite (rī'ə līt') has a fine texture and is dark colored.

Obsidian (əb sid'ē ən) has no mineral grains and is dark colored.

Basalt (bə sôlt') has a fine texture and is dark colored.

429

How Can Bits and Pieces Make Rocks?

How do the rocks here compare with igneous rocks? These rocks are **sedimentary rocks**. Sedimentary rocks are made of small bits of matter joined together. These bits of matter, or sediments, may be bits of weathered rocks. They may be shells or other remains of living things. Long ago water, wind, and ice picked up sediment and carried it. Eventually they dropped the sediment in places where it collected into layers.

Most common sedimentary rocks are formed when sediment is compacted or cemented together. The weight of layer upon layer of sediment on top of each other compacts or squeezes sediment together.

Coarser sediments are cemented by bits of minerals that "glue" the sediments together. Water that contains dissolved minerals seeps between the coarse pieces of sediment. The water evaporates, and mineral crystals form. These crystals hold together the coarse sediment, turning it into a solid rock.

You can see the pieces of sediment that make up these rocks. These rocks are named by the size of the sediment they contain.

Some sedimentary rocks are made of crystals of minerals that were once dissolved in water. The crystals were left behind when the water evaporated. Halite, the rock salt that is used to melt snow and ice, is formed this way.

A type of limestone consists mostly of a mineral called calcite. The mineral was dissolved in ocean water. As the water evaporated in certain areas, the calcite was left behind as solid limestone.

Some sedimentary rocks are made of substances that were once part of, or made by, living things. Cemented-together shells form *coquina* (kō kē'nə). Coral skeletons form coral limestone.

Coquina

Sediment (Small to Large)	Rock
Clay	Shale
Silt	Siltstone
Sand	Sandstone
Gravel	Conglomerate

What Good Is a Clump of Bits and Pieces?

They may be just clumps of bits and pieces, but sedimentary rocks are very useful. Sandstone, for example, is used for buildings and trim. Limestone is used for buildings, trim, monuments, and even park benches. Shale is often broken into pieces that are mixed with other materials to make concrete and cement.

Sedimentary rocks are very useful in helping to piece together Earth's history. They often contain clues to life long ago, **fossils**. Fossils are the remains or imprints of living things of the past.

The remains of dead organisms were often covered with mud, sand, or other sediment. Sometimes a living thing left an imprint, such as a footprint, in soft mud. Over centuries of time, the sediment and the remains or imprint hardened into rock. Almost all fossils are found in sedimentary rocks. Why do you think fossils could not be found in an igneous rock?

A type of coal is a sedimentary rock. This coal is called bituminous (bī tü′mə nəs) coal, or soft coal. Earth's supplies of coal were formed millions of years ago from dead plants buried in ancient swamps and forests. Coal today is a source of energy, the energy that comes from those ancient forms of life.

Fossils

Limestone blocks

Bituminous coal lights quickly and provides much energy, but it burns with a lot of soot and yellow smoke.

How Can Rocks Get Baked into New Rocks?

Deep below Earth's surface, rocks can undergo great change. They are heated by the high temperatures at great depths. They are under pressure from the rocks lying above.

Great heat and pressure can change one rock into another rock. A rock formed under heat and pressure from another kind of rock is called a **metamorphic** (met'ə môr'fik) **rock**. In the process the original rock does not melt under heat and pressure. If it did it would become an igneous rock. Instead the original rock remains solid, but

- the mineral grains in the original rock may flatten and line up

- the minerals may change their identity; substances in a mineral may be exchanged with substances in surrounding minerals
- the minerals in the original rock may separate into layers of different densities

In each case the result is a rock different from the original.

Original Rock	Metamorphic Rock
Granite (igneous rock)	gneiss (nīs)
Shale (sedimentary rock)	slate
Sandstone (sedimentary rock)	quartzite
Limestone (sedimentary rock)	marble
Slate (metamorphic rock)	schist

Pressure

Limestone

Heat

Marble

Pressure

Granite

Heat

Gneiss

How Useful Are Makeovers?

Metamorphic rocks are "rock makeovers." In their remade form, these rocks have new properties that are very useful.

Slate, for example, breaks into thin sheets. The minerals in slate are so tightly packed together that water cannot seep through this rock. This makes slate useful as roofing shingles as well as stepping stones and outdoor floors.

Marble is often shiny. It often contains minerals that give it brilliant colors, from greenish to red. It is easy to carve. It's often a first choice for making statues, floors, countertops, and monuments.

One kind of coal is a metamorphic rock. It is called anthracite, or hard coal. Anthracite is formed from soft coal.

Anthracite, hard coal, burns cleaner and longer than soft coal, but does not provide as much energy.

THE STORY OF COAL

Millions of Years Ago					
300	280	220	150	10	Present
A forest swamp	Plants die and sink to the bottom.	A thick layer of peat, partly decayed plants, builds up.	The swamp dries up. Buried under layers of sediment, the peat changes to a sedimentary rock called lignite (lig'nit).	Buried by more and more layers of sediment, the lignite becomes more compacted. It forms bituminous coal.	Buried even deeper, bituminous coal is changed by great heat and pressure. It forms anthracite, a metamorphic rock.

Peat

Lignite

Bituminous (soft) coal (sedimentary rock)

Anthracite (hard) coal (metamorphic rock)

READING N DIAGRAMS

1. DISCUSS How is the position of the fuel layer changing from picture to picture?

2. WRITE How does this position affect what happens to the layer?

Skill: Defining Terms Based on Observations

DEFINING SOIL

Earth's crust is made up of rocks and minerals. However, to get to the rocks, you usually have to dig through layers of soil.

Soil looks different at different places. It has different properties. Soil can be sandy. It can be moist.

Just what is soil? Make some observations. Write a definition that fits your observations.

MATERIALS

- moist soil sample in plastic bag
- sand sample in plastic bag
- hand lens
- 2 cups
- 2 plastic spoons
- *Science Journal*

PROCEDURES

1. OBSERVE Use a hand lens to examine a sample of moist soil. What materials can you find? How do their sizes compare? Write a description in your *Science Journal*.

2. COMPARE Some soils are more like sand. How does a sample of sand compare with your moist soil sample?

3. USE VARIABLES Which sample absorbs water more quickly? Fill a cup halfway with sand and another with moist soil. Pour a spoonful of water in each at the same time.

4. EXPERIMENT Which absorbs more water? Make a prediction. Find a way to test your prediction.

5. EXPERIMENT Make any other observations. Look for other differences.

CONCLUDE AND APPLY

1. DRAW CONCLUSIONS Based on your observations, what is soil made up of?

2. DRAW CONCLUSIONS How may soils differ?

3. DEFINE Write a definition for *soil*. Take into account all your observations.

What Has Soil Got to Do with Rocks?

Under a hand lens, you can see that any soil shows that it is a mixture of many things. The main ingredient in soil is weathered rock. Soil may also contain water, air, bacteria, and *humus*. **Humus** is decayed plant or animal material.

Where does soil come from? A layer of solid rock weathers into chunks. The chunks weather into smaller pieces. Living things die and decay and form humus.

Gradually layers of soil, or soil horizons, develop. If you dig down through soil, you can see many layers and the solid rock, bedrock, beneath it. How do the horizons differ?

Soils differ in different locations. In polar deserts there is no A horizon at the top. However, grassland and forest soils can have very thick A horizons. Why do you think this is so? Some soils are very sandy. Why? How would they differ from soils in many farms?

Sometimes the materials in soil match the bedrock below it. Sometimes they do not match. Can you explain why?

Soil is Earth's greatest treasure. All rooted plants need soil to grow. Therefore, almost all living things depend on soil for food—and survival. One of the most important uses of soil is farming. All of the food you eat depends on soil.

SOIL HORIZONS

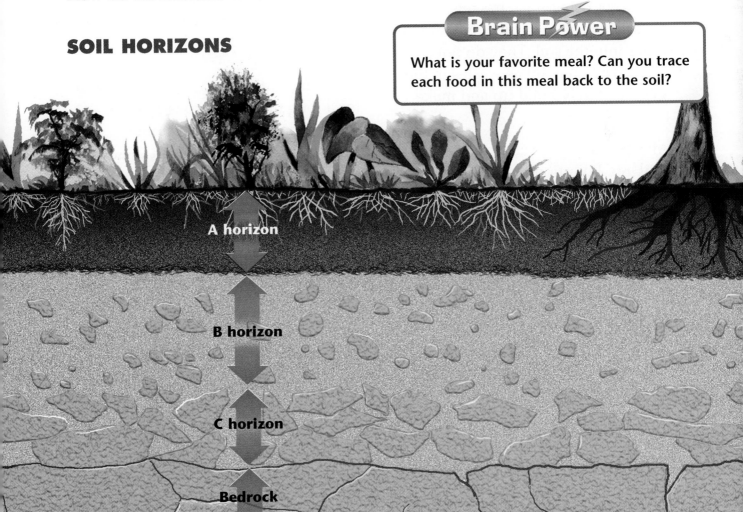

A horizon

B horizon

C horizon

Bedrock

Brain Power

What is your favorite meal? Can you trace each food in this meal back to the soil?

435

How Can People Ruin Soil?

People depend on soil. Would you believe people ruin and waste soil? That might include you! It may be people, in general, or industries—such as factories or farms. People often

- get rid of garbage and hazardous wastes by burying them in soil. Hazardous wastes are wastes that may be poisonous or cause diseases, such as cancer.

- spray chemicals on soil to kill unwanted animals and plants. These chemicals become a part of the soil.

- toss foam cups, plastic wrappers, and materials onto the ground, instead of using trash baskets. These materials may be carried by wind or water into the soil. They do not decay. They remain as wastes in the soil. They may build up and make the soil unusable.

All these materials add up to **pollution**. Pollution means adding any unnatural substances to Earth's land, water, or air. The substances are called *pollutants*. When people add pollution, we say they *pollute* soil, water, or air.

Not only do people pollute soil, but they often waste it, too. For example, soil needs plants. When plants die and decay, they add valuable substances back into the soil. When a crop is harvested, the plant bodies are removed. They do not decay and return nutrients back into the soil. Growing the same crop year after year uses up the nutrients in soil. Plants don't grow well in nutrient-poor soil.

Plant roots hold soil particles together. They protect soil from being blown or washed away by wind or water. If plants are removed or if weak, sickly plants are growing in an area, the soil is exposed to erosion by wind and rain.

Letting cattle graze in the same area for a long time also exposes soil. Cutting down forests for lumber exposes soil, too. As a result of any of these practices, soil that took centuries to form may be removed in weeks.

Each piece of garbage was thrown away by somebody. It takes people to make garbage. What are some ways to prevent this kind of pollution?

How Can People Protect the Soil?

Have you ever taken care of a pet? If so, what was it like? How did you have to protect your pet?

People also need to take care of soil. We have to protect it from being polluted and wasted. Farmers take care of soil by

- *adding fertilizers and humus.* After growing crops, farmers add these materials to replace minerals removed by crops.

- *rotating crops.* Each year farmers grow different crops. In this way the soil does not use up the same kinds of minerals year after year. Crops from one year may help replace minerals in the soil that are used up another year.

- *strip farming.* Many crops have stems spaced far apart. Rainwater can run off between the stems and wash soil away. In strip farming strips of tightly growing grasses are grown between more widely spaced crops. The grasses trap runoff and the soil it carries. The next year the position of the strips is switched.

- *contour plowing.* Farmers plow furrows across a slope rather than up and down a slope. Each furrow traps rainwater and keeps it from eroding the soil.

- *terracing.* A hillside is shaped into a series of steps. Runoff water and eroded soil get trapped on the steps. Planting rows of trees to block the wind prevents soil from being blown away.

What can you do to prevent soil from being polluted or wasted? Think about what you toss away as garbage. Is there any way to throw it away to make sure it does not simply end up in the soil? Is there any way to keep from throwing as much stuff away each day as you might?

Contour means "shape." How does contour plowing prevent water from running downhill?

By building terraces people in Bali have been able to farm steep hillsides.

How Do Rocks Get Made Over Again and Again?

Where do rocks and soil come from? Igneous rocks come from magma or lava. However, where did the magma and lava come from? Magma or lava, remember, is melted rock material.

Sedimentary rock is made of broken up pieces of rock. However, where did the pieces of rock come from?

You also learned that a rock had to exist in order to change into a metamorphic rock. Where do the existing rocks come from?

All rocks come from other rocks! Rocks are constantly changing from one rock into another. They change in a never-ending series of processes called the **rock cycle**. Part of this cycle is the weathering of rocks into bits and pieces—some of which may eventually become soil.

Rocks are constantly forming—one changing into another. However, any rock takes a really long time to form. When we dig up a deposit of sandstone or use up the coal in an area, it cannot be replaced. Rocks are a non–renewable resource.

Soil may take centuries to form. However, with care, people can prevent it from being wasted. Fertilizers and humus may replenish overused soil. In many ways soil is renewable—but only with care.

READING IN DIAGRAMS

1. **WRITE** Describe a way a sedimentary rock can become an igneous rock.
2. **DISCUSS** How might it become a metamorphic rock?
3. **DISCUSS** How might it become another sedimentary rock?

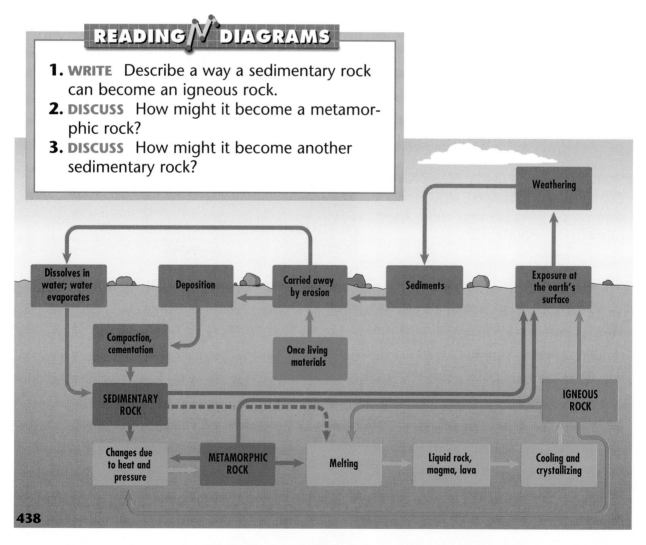

Can People Make Rocks?

The rock cycle diagram does not show how people get into the rock-making process.

Concrete is a rock material made out of water, sand, and chunks of gravel, held together with a binding mixture. The binding mixture is made of lime-stone and shale, crushed to a fine powder, mixed with gypsum and another mineral.

Some bathtubs are also made from a human-made rock. Porcelain is clay that has been heated to a high temperature and then cooled. It contains mostly the mineral kaolinite.

Bricks are another artificial rock. Made mostly of clay, they can be shaped while soft and then baked in an oven to rock hardness. How many other human-made rocks can you find?

Concrete is made of sand and gravel, mixed with powdered limestone and shale, minerals, and water. Where is concrete used in your neighborhood?

WHY IT MATTERS

It is important to be able to tell one type of rock from another. Just think of all the ways you use rocks. What would life be like without them? There would be no mountains to climb, no beaches to walk on. There would be no soil—so that means, no food, or forests, or fields. There would be no metals, because metals come from mineral ores that are found in rocks. There would be no bricks, no concrete, no buildings, no . . .

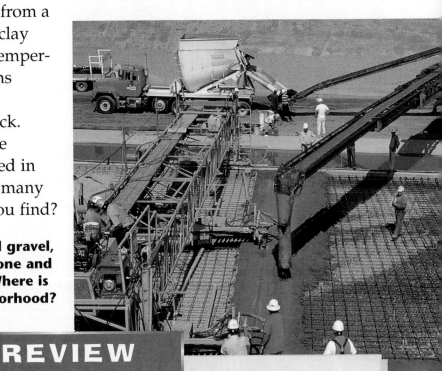

REVIEW

1. **DEFINE** How can you tell rocks apart? Why are they different to identify than minerals?

2. How can you tell igneous rocks apart?

3. You pick up a rock. How can you tell if it is a sedimentary rock?

4. How are soils alike? How are they different?

5. **CRITICAL THINKING** *Synthesize* How can an igneous rock become a metamorphic rock? Think of three different ways.

WHY IT MATTERS THINK ABOUT IT
How are rocks a part of your life?

WHY IT MATTERS WRITE ABOUT IT
How do you depend on soil, even if you don't live anywhere near a farm?

What if There Were No Electricity?

What if there were also no gas or oil deliveries? What would you do for energy? How would you get to school? Get the news of the day? Light your house? Cook your food? You'd probably learn to use different energy sources, like your ancestors did!

Electricity didn't come into use until the 1900s. What did people do before that? They burned wood or coal to make heat. They lit torches and candles to provide light. They cooked on wood-burning stoves or over logs in fireplaces. Town criers or storytellers told them the news of the day. People rode to town on horseback or in wagons.

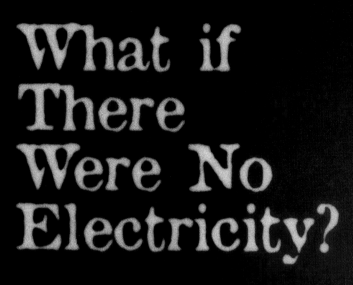

Science, Technology, and Society

In the 1970s America had an energy crisis. The country had become dependent on oil to provide its energy. Oil prices rose higher and higher, and then there was a shortage of oil. Americans had to cut down on their use of electricity. They did it by using some of the old sources their ancestors had used.

Stores couldn't keep coal- or wood-burning stoves in stock during the energy crisis. So many stoves were in use that in some places smoke hung over the town. This was in places that usually had very clean air, too!

Many people began carpooling or riding buses to save gas. Other people used human energy and walked or rode bikes to the store, school, or work. A few people even rode horses!

After a few years, the energy crisis was over. However, people still search for other energy sources because . . . what if it happens again!

DISCUSSION STARTER

1. If necessary how could your family use coal or wood instead of electricity?

2. What are some other ways you can save energy?

To learn more about alternate energy, visit *www.mhschool.com/science* and enter the keyword ALTERNATES.

SCIENCE WORDS

erosion p.406

fossil p.431

geologist p.402

hydrosphere p.394

igneous p.429

lithosphere p.394

metamorphic p.432

mineral p.416

ore p.422

planet p.388

pollution p.436

rock cycle p.438

sedimentary p.430

solar system p.388

USING SCIENCE WORDS

Number a paper from 1 to 10. Fill in 1 to 5 with words from the list above.

1. Rock that changes due to heat and pressure is ___?___ rock.

2. The oceans are part of Earth's ___?___.

3. The Sun and planets are part of the ___?___.

4. A scientist who studies Earth is called a(n) ___?___.

5. Earth is a(n) ___?___ that orbits the Sun.

6–10. Pick five words from the list above that were not used in 1 to 5, and use each in a sentence.

UNDERSTANDING SCIENCE IDEAS

11. Describe the difference in the way sedimentary and igneous rocks are formed.

12. Explain the difference between weathering and erosion.

13. Describe the rock cycle.

14. Describe two tests you can use to determine what minerals a rock is made of.

15. What is a fossil?

USING IDEAS AND SKILLS

16. **READING SKILL: CAUSE AND EFFECT** Why is it unlikely we will find life on other planets in our solar system?

17. Tension, compression, and shear affect rock differently. Is this true or false? Explain your answer.

18. What force keeps planets orbiting the Sun? What would happen if that force did not exist?

19. **DEFINE** You find a rock that is made up of different-colored layers. It seems to be made of different-sized grains. Some of it looks as though it is made of tiny seashells glued together. What type of rock is it?

20. **THINKING LIKE A SCIENTIST** Do you think wet or dry sand warms up faster in sunlight? Why? State and explain your hypothesis. Describe how you might test your idea.

PROBLEMS and PUZZLES

Not Just Dirt Where would you expect to find more living things, in soil from a desert or in soil from a forest? Explain your answer.

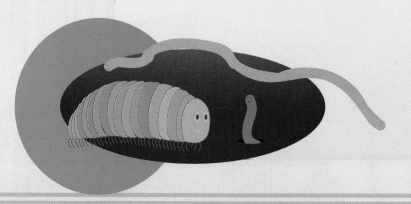

CHAPTER 10

EARTH'S AIR, WATER, AND ENERGY

You can't drink ocean water. However, water from the oceans is part of a cycle that produces clouds, rain, and water for Earth's land—freshwater.

The oceans also provide food, and, in some places, energy. Drilling into the ocean bottom in the Gulf of Mexico off the coast of Texas provides a rich source of oil.

How else does planet Earth provide materials that make life possible?

In Chapter 10 you will read in order to practice drawing conclusions.

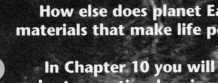

Topic 5
EARTH SCIENCE

WHY IT MATTERS

Air pollution affects everyone and everything.

SCIENCE WORDS

renewable resource a resource that can be replaced in a short period of time

ozone layer a layer of ozone gas in the atmosphere that screens out much of the Sun's UV rays

fossil fuel a fuel formed from the decay of ancient forms of life

smog a mixture of smoke and fog

acid rain moisture that falls to Earth after being mixed with wastes from burned fossil fuels

Earth's Atmosphere

Every day American cars burn about 200 million gallons of gasoline. How do you think this affects the land, air, and water?

How can the air be different from day to day? The air may seem clear and clean on some days. If you live in or near a big city, you may have days when the air seems smoky, or "hazy." Why?

EXPLORE

HYPOTHESIZE What kinds of pollutants are in the air that can make it look as it does in the picture? Write a hypothesis in your *Science Journal*. Test your ideas.

EXPLORE ACTIVITY

Investigate What Makes Air Dirty

Try to collect pollutants to analyze them.

PROCEDURES

1. Make square "frames" by taping together the corners of four cardboard strips. Make three frames, and label them A, B, and C. Tie a 30-cm string to a corner of each frame.

2. Stretch and attach three strips of tape across each frame, with all sticky sides facing the same way. Use a plastic knife to spread a thin coat of petroleum jelly across each sticky side.

3. PREDICT Hang the frames in different places to try to collect pollutants. Decide on places indoors or outdoors. Be sure to tell a parent or teacher where.

4. OBSERVE Observe each frame over four days. Note the weather and air condition each day in your *Science Journal*.

5. USE NUMBERS Then collect the frames. Observe the sticky sides with a hand lens and a metric ruler to compare particles.

MATERIALS

- 12 cardboard strips, about 12 cm long
- petroleum jelly
- plastic knife
- transparent tape
- string
- hand lens
- metric ruler
- marker
- *Science Journal*

CONCLUDE AND APPLY

1. INTERPRET DATA How did the frames change over time? How did the hand lens and ruler help you describe any pollution?

2. COMMUNICATE Present your data in a graph to show differences in amounts.

GOING FURTHER: Problem Solving

3. PLAN What kinds of pollutants would your frames not collect? How might you design a collector for them?

4. PLAN How might you extend this activity over different periods of time?

445

How Do Living Things Use Air?

Why couldn't humans live on a planet that does not have an atmosphere as on Earth? Every minute of every day you need air.

Air is a mixture of nitrogen, oxygen, and a few traces of other gases, including water vapor. This mixture is a vital resource. It supports and protects life on Earth in many ways.

Almost all organisms need air to live. Actually, they need oxygen, one of the gases that is in air. On land living things have structures that enable them to get oxygen directly from the air. Living things in water habitats take in oxygen that is dissolved in the water.

What is oxygen for? Living things take in oxygen for respiration. In this process oxygen is used to break down food so that energy can be gotten from it. As a result of this process, living things give off wastes, including the gas carbon dioxide.

Why doesn't the atmosphere fill up with carbon dioxide? Plants and other producers, living things that have the green substance chlorophyll, take in carbon dioxide. They use it for making food. In the presence of light, these organisms carry on the process called photosynthesis. In this process they make food and give off oxygen.

Producers range in size from green plants to one-celled algae. They replace oxygen in the atmosphere. This makes oxygen a naturally **renewable resource.** A renewable resource is one that can be replaced. It can be replaced in a short enough period of time, such as a human lifetime, to support life on Earth.

Brain Power

How do you take in oxygen? What are some structures that animals have to take in oxygen? How do plants take in oxygen?

HOW EARTH'S ATMOSPHERE SUPPORTS LIFE

LIFE LINK SCIENCE

One-celled algae of the oceans produce most of Earth's oxygen supply.

Oxygen

All living things take in oxygen for respiration. They give off carbon dioxide.

Producers take in carbon dioxide and produce food and oxygen.

Oxygen

Carbon dioxide

Carbon dioxide

How Does Air Protect?

The atmosphere also acts as a protective shield. It shields Earth's surface from harmful energy that comes from the Sun. The atmosphere helps screen out harmful radiation, such as X rays, gamma rays, and most ultraviolet rays (UV rays) from the Sun. About 30 kilometers above your head is a layer of gas called ozone (ō′zōn). This **ozone layer** screens out from 95 to 99 percent of the Sun's UV rays.

The atmosphere also shields Earth from rocks from space. The "shooting stars" you see on a clear night are not stars. They are rocks from space that burn up due to friction with the air as they speed through the atmosphere.

The atmosphere also protects life from extremes of temperature. Clouds block sunlight during the day. At night they keep much of the heat from

escaping into space, so that the planet does not "cool off." Whenever one part of the atmosphere gets hotter than another, the air moves or circulates in ways that spread the heat around.

Most of the air, about 70 percent, is nitrogen. Nitrogen is an important ingredient in food, namely proteins. How does it get into proteins? Nitrogen is taken from the air by certain kinds of bacteria. These bacteria change the nitrogen into a form that stays in the soil.

Plants use the changed form of nitrogen to make proteins. As living things eat the plants, nitrogen is passed along. It is returned to the air when living things die.

READING 𝒩 DIAGRAMS

1. **DISCUSS** Do you see any cycles in this picture? Cycles are continuous processes, where one thing happens after another over and over in the same order.
2. **WRITE** Explain any cycles you see.

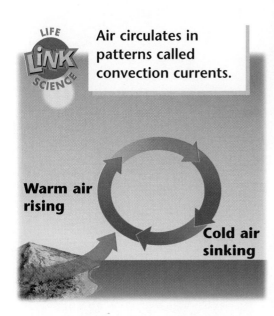

LIFE LINK SCIENCE

Air circulates in patterns called convection currents.

Warm air rising

Cold air sinking

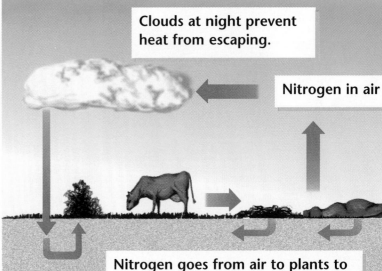

Clouds at night prevent heat from escaping.

Nitrogen in air

Nitrogen goes from air to plants to all living things. When living things die, nitrogen is returned to the air.

What Makes Air Dirty?

Many of the things we humans do add pollution to the air. The Explore Activity on page 445 showed a way to collect and observe solid pollutants. In addition to solids, there are harmful gases and liquids in the air. Where do they come from?

Many pollutants get into the air from burning **fossil fuels**. These fuels were formed from the decay of ancient forms of life. Fossil fuels include coal, oil, natural gas, and gasoline. Cars, buses, trucks, and planes burn these fuels, as do many homes and power plants. The wastes from burning these fuels add pollution to the air.

Burning trash adds smoke to the air. Dust comes from plowed fields. It comes from construction sites and from mines. Factories add chemical wastes to the air.

Other events also add to air pollution. Volcanoes erupt and shoot gases and particles into the air. Forest fires and grass fires can spread smoke over great distances

All these pollutants can build up into thick clouds, called **smog**. Smog is a mixture of smoke and fog. It forms when smoke and fumes collect in moist, calm air. Smog irritates the eyes, nose, and throat. People with breathing problems have died from heavy smog.

Smog hangs like a brown cloud over many cities. Why do you think it is most common in big coastal cities like Los Angeles?

Sometimes ozone can form in smog. High up in the atmosphere, remember, ozone protects Earth from UV radiation. However, at ground level this gas can make people sick.

1 Natural events can add to air pollution.

2 Industries produce wastes that add to air pollution.

3 How can a mask help at times when smog is very heavy?

How Can Rain Be Harmful?

What can destroy forests, kill animals and plants in lakes, and even eat away at buildings? Part of the answer comes from power plants that burn coal to produce energy. Another part comes from motor vehicles that burn gasoline.

Wastes that come from burning these fossil fuels travel into the air. In the air the wastes mix with moisture. They can form chemicals called acids in the moisture. The moisture with acids can eventually fall to Earth's surface as **acid rain**. This term includes all forms of precipitation—snow, hail, and sleet.

Acid rain can harm soil and water supplies. Some trees sicken and die if there is too much acid in the soil. Fish die in lakes whose waters contain too much acid. The acid weathers away statues and buildings. It can cause metal surfaces on cars to crumble.

(4) **Trees yellow and die due to acid rain.**

QUICK LAB

Acids

HYPOTHESIZE How can acid rain change a rock? Write a hypothesis in your *Science Journal*.

MATERIALS
- chalk
- limestone and other rock samples
- vinegar (a mild acid)
- plastic cups
- goggles
- plastic wrap
- rubber bands
- plastic knife
- *Science Journal*

PROCEDURES

 SAFETY Wear goggles.

1. **USE VARIABLES** Break a stick of chalk into smaller pieces. Place some small pieces in a plastic cup. Place each rock sample in its own cup. Slowly pour vinegar in each cup to cover each object.

2. **OBSERVE** Watch for any changes in the chalk and the rocks. Watch for several minutes and then at later times in the day. Record your observations in your *Science Journal*.

3. Cover each cup using plastic wrap and a rubber band to help keep the vinegar from evaporating.

CONCLUDE AND APPLY

1. **EXPLAIN** Vinegar is a mild acid. How did it change the chalk?

2. **COMPARE AND CONTRAST** Do all rocks change the same way? Explain based on your results.

449

How Can We Clean Up the Air?

Cleaning up the air is a job that takes all nations to work on. That is why the Congress of the United States passed laws to protect the air. It passed the Clean Air Act in 1967 and added more parts in 1970, 1977, and 1990.

There are a few common pollutants found all over the United States. The Clean Air Act has many programs designed to decrease air pollution. This list from a booklet called "Plain English Guide to the Clean Air Act" gives you some idea of its scope. Do you see a part that might affect you or your family?

Clean Air Resolutions

As a result of these laws, cars now have lowered the amounts of harmful wastes that are released. "Clean coal" methods were introduced to lower the amount of harmful wastes that result in acid rain. Power plants that burn coal can wash coal before burning it to remove sulfur. The sulfur can result in acid rain when the coal burns.

In 1970 the first Earth Day was celebrated. People were becoming very concerned about the health of planet Earth. That year the Environmental Protection Agency (EPA) was formed. The EPA is part of the United States government. It has the job of checking that laws are being followed. It investigates new dangers and offers solutions and guidelines.

Stop Damage Before It's Too Late

These photographs show "holes" in the ozone layer. The ozone layer, remember, is a layer high up in the atmosphere that protects Earth from harmful UV radiation. However, it seems we humans have poked holes in this layer. The holes are letting UV radiation through.

How did the holes get there? Scientists are not totally sure. Much evidence points to substances that people have been using a lot. These substances are called CFCs, which is short for chlorofluorocarbons (klôr′ō flur′ō kär′bənz). They are gases used in such things as refrigerators, freezers, and air conditioners. When the CFCs leak out from these appliances, they rise into the atmosphere. There they can affect the ozone layer.

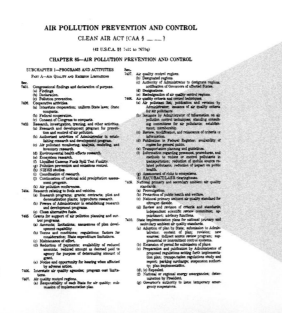

CFCs were also used in many aerosol spray cans. Spray paints, hair sprays, and even shaving foams released CFCs with each squeeze of the push button. Concern about the ozone layer changed that. In 1990 a group of representatives from around the world met in London. They signed an agreement to ban the use of CFCs worldwide in just ten years.

Aerosol spray cans now use substitutes. Just read the label on a spray can item and you can see for yourself.

These photographs show holes developing in the ozone layer.

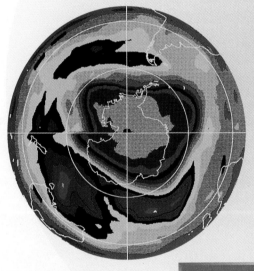

Air pollution harms trees, lakes, and buildings. It can also affect you directly. Air pollution can make people sick. It can make your eyes and nose feel like they are burning. It can make your throat feel itchy and irritated.

Laws help to protect the air. However, it takes people to save the air. The Clean Air Act can work only if people work together. For example, using less electricity can save fuel. Finding ways to cut down on using cars saves fuel, too. Cutting down on burning fuel lowers air pollution.

REVIEW

1. Why is air important to living things?

2. How does the atmosphere protect Earth?

3. How do people pollute the air?

4. **CAUSE AND EFFECT** What causes acid rain? How does acid rain affect land and water?

5. **CRITICAL THINKING** *Apply* How can using less electricity cut down on use of fossil fuels?

WHY IT MATTERS THINK ABOUT IT
How do you know when air is polluted?

WHY IT MATTERS WRITE ABOUT IT
How can you cut down on using electricity and fuel? Be specific. Think about things you, your family, and your friends can do.

451

PLANETARY WEATHER

What's the weather like on other planets, and should we care? Yes, knowing about the atmosphere on other planets tells us more about our whole solar system!

Over the years scientists have learned that Venus's atmosphere is 97 percent carbon dioxide. Venus is an example of the greenhouse effect. The layer of carbon dioxide traps the Sun's heat, making Venus's average temperature 460°C (860°F)!

Like Earth, Jupiter has storms. Ours begin when the Sun heats the atmosphere. On Jupiter, storms begin when bubbles of heat rise from its hot inner core. When it rains on Jupiter it rains liquid helium!

Venus has yellow clouds of sulfuric acid. Rain from these clouds is like acid rain on Earth, only worse.

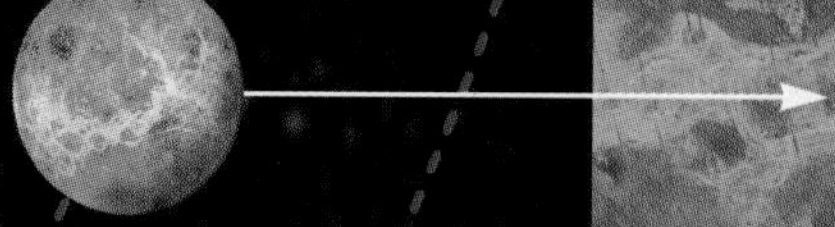

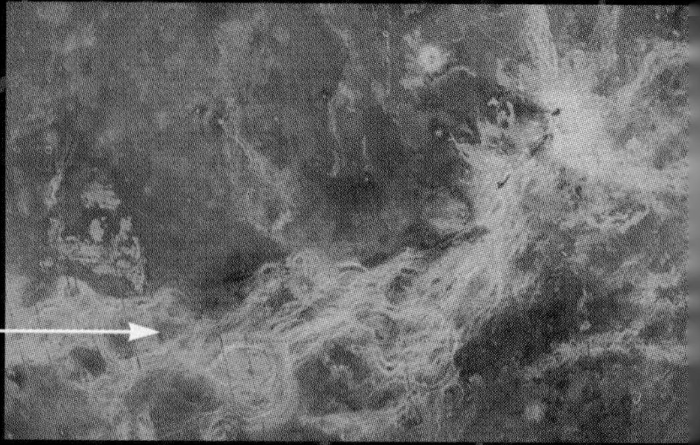

A Closer Look

One of Jupiter's storms, the Great Red Spot, began long before telescopes were invented. It's two or three times the size of Earth.

Saturn has three cloud layers—water clouds, ammonia clouds, and ammonia hydrosulfide clouds. Together they form . . . smog!

Venus, Jupiter, Saturn, Uranus, and Neptune have lightning, just as we do on Earth. The lightning is from electrical discharges.

Flashes on Jupiter may be 500 kilometers (310 miles) across!

Pluto has the greatest weather changes of all the planets. That's because its orbit is irregular. When Pluto's close to the Sun, the heat turns the frozen nitrogen on Pluto into a gas. This gives Pluto an atmosphere and weather to go with it. As Pluto moves farther from the Sun, the gas drifts away!

DISCUSSION STARTER

1. Why should the atmosphere on Venus be a warning to us on Earth?

2. What forms of weather do we share with other planets?

To learn more about weather on other planets, visit *www.mhschool.com/science* and enter the keyword CLIMATE.

*inter*NET
CONNECTION

WHY IT MATTERS

Everyone must help save water and keep it clean.

SCIENCE WORDS

desalination getting fresh water from seawater

water cycle the continuous movement of water between Earth's surface and the air, changing from liquid to gas to liquid

groundwater water that seeps into the ground into spaces between bits of rock and soil

water table the top of the water-filled spaces in the ground

aquifer an underground layer of rock or soil filled with water

spring a place where groundwater seeps out of the ground

well a hole dug below the water table that water seeps into

reservoir a storage area for freshwater supplies

Earth's Water Supply

On the average an American uses about 240 liters (64 gallons) of water a day. Where do we get all that water?

Over 70 percent of Earth's surface is covered with water. However, most of this is not fresh water but salt water in Earth's oceans. People don't use salt water for drinking or cleaning. Where does our fresh water come from then? How might we change salt water into fresh water?

EXPLORE

HYPOTHESIZE How can water with something dissolved in it be changed into fresh water? Write a hypothesis in your *Science Journal*. Test your ideas.

EXPLORE ACTIVITY

Investigate How to Make Salt Water Usable

Decide how the water cycle can make salt water fresh.

MATERIALS

- tea bag
- deep pan
- plastic cup
- saucer (or petri dish)
- large, clear bowl or container
- water
- *Science Journal*

PROCEDURES

1. MAKE A MODEL Keep a tea bag in a cup of water until the water is orange.

2. MAKE A MODEL Place a pan where there is strong light (sunlight, if possible). Pour some tea water into the saucer. Put the saucer in the pan. Cover the saucer with a large bowl.

3. OBSERVE Look at the bowl and pan several times during the day and the next day. Note any water you see on the bowl or in the pan. Write your observations in your *Science Journal*.

CONCLUDE AND APPLY

1. COMPARE AND CONTRAST How was the water that collected in the bowl or pan different from the tea water?

2. INFER What do you think caused the water to collect in the bowl and pan?

3. DRAW CONCLUSIONS How does this model represent what might happen to salt water, the water of Earth's oceans?

GOING FURTHER: Problem Solving

4. USE VARIABLES How long did it take for water to collect in the bowl and pan? How might this process be speeded up?

5. EVALUATE Do you think this model shows a useful way of turning ocean water into fresh water? Explain.

How Do We Use Earth's Oceans?

If all the water in Earth's hydrosphere was represented by 100 cents, not even 3 cents would represent fresh water. Over 97 cents would be salt water. Salt water is water in the oceans as well as saltwater lakes and inland seas.

Much of the salt in salt water is halite, common rock salt. Salt water has seven times more salt than a person can stand. A person cannot survive drinking it. However, Earth's oceans and inland seas are still useful for the resources they contain.

- **Seafood** What kinds of seafood do you eat? Why are these foods healthful? The oceans support many forms of life. The water has dissolved gases, oxygen, and carbon dioxide, as well as minerals. Plants and other producers of the sea are able to get sunlight so that they can make food. They become food for other forms of sea life, which become food for us.

- **Minerals** Almost everything dissolves in water, at least a little. A pail of seawater contains almost every known element. It contains more minerals than just rock salt.

Hot water bubbling out of underwater volcanoes is especially mineral rich. It leaves rich deposits of minerals on the sea floor. Nodules, or lumps, of minerals can be picked up from the sea floor. They contain manganese and iron. Metals such as tin and gold are also found on the sea floor.

- **Fossil fuels** Offshore rigs pump oil and natural gas from beneath the ocean floor in many places around the globe. This fuel is worth more than all other resources taken from the oceans.

MATH
LiNK

WATER IN THE HYDROSPHERE

Fresh water: 2.8%

Salt water: 97.2%

Lakes and streams: 0.01%

Surface water and groundwater: 0.6%

Ice caps and glaciers: 2.2%

Water vapor in atmosphere: 0.001%

READING N' GRAPHS

1. **WRITE** Order the items in the bar graph from greatest to least.
2. **DISCUSS** Where is most of Earth's fresh water found?

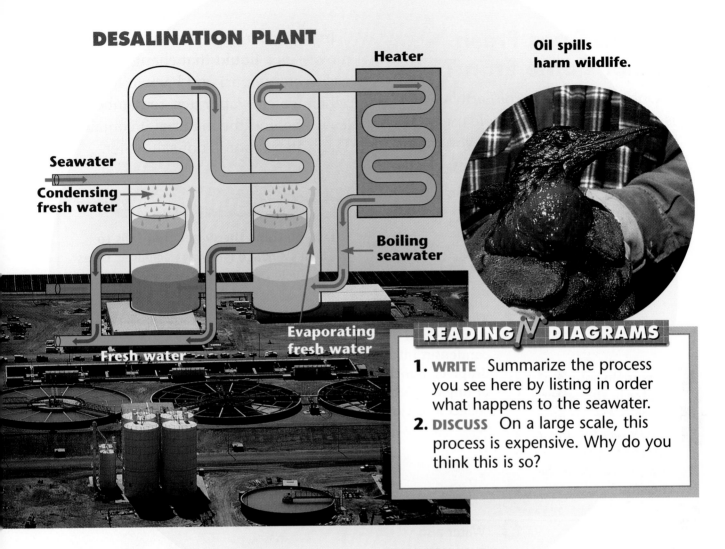

DESALINATION PLANT

Seawater

Condensing
fresh water

Heater

Boiling
seawater

Oil spills
harm wildlife.

Evaporating
fresh water

Fresh water

READING DIAGRAMS

1. **WRITE** Summarize the process you see here by listing in order what happens to the seawater.
2. **DISCUSS** On a large scale, this process is expensive. Why do you think this is so?

How Can We Make Salt Water Usable?

You can't drink seawater or use it to water plants. You need fresh water. Your fresh water comes mostly from freshwater lakes and rivers.

Some areas have very little fresh water available. The islands of Malta, for example, are surrounded by oceans. However, they have no permanent lakes or rivers. Over two-thirds of the water used by the people is gotten from seawater.

Getting fresh water from seawater takes a process called **desalination** (dē sal'ə nā'shən). The Explore Activity introduced this process.

Seawater contains dissolved rock salt and other materials. As water evaporates it leaves the dissolved materials behind. The liquid water that collects at the end of the process is free of dissolved materials.

What else is in seawater that can make it harmful? In the past barges loaded with garbage and poisonous wastes would sail out every day to dump their loads at sea. Sometimes accidents such as oil spills from tankers poured huge amounts of oil into the oceans.

Pollution in the ocean does not go away. It builds up. Eventually it can kill sea life. It ruins our seafood supplies in certain parts of the oceans.

Where Does Fresh Water Come From?

Only a tiny fraction of Earth's water is usable fresh water. People use so much fresh water each day, you might wonder why it doesn't run out. Fresh water doesn't run out because it is constantly renewed by the water cycle.

In the water cycle, water is on the move—as a liquid that changes to a gas (water vapor) and back to liquid. When water evaporates, remember, it leaves behind the material it contained. The water vapor is not salt water.

Brain Power

Do you think the water that falls to Earth's surface is always "clean"? Does this cycle provide water for every place on Earth? Explain your answers.

WATER CYCLE

③ Water vapor in the air cools and condenses into tiny droplets. Bunches of tiny droplets collect into clouds.

① The main source of water in the water cycle is the oceans. Every day trillions of liters of water evaporate from the oceans.

④ Water from clouds falls back to Earth's surface as precipitation. Rain and snow are the main sources of fresh water on land.

② Water also evaporates from rivers, lakes, and other sources on land. Plants give off water vapor as well.

Water vapor in the atmosphere

Ice caps and glaciers

Lakes and streams

Drainage basins

⑤ When water reaches the ground, three things happen to it. Some water seeps into the ground. Some runs downhill over the surface. Some evaporates back into the air.

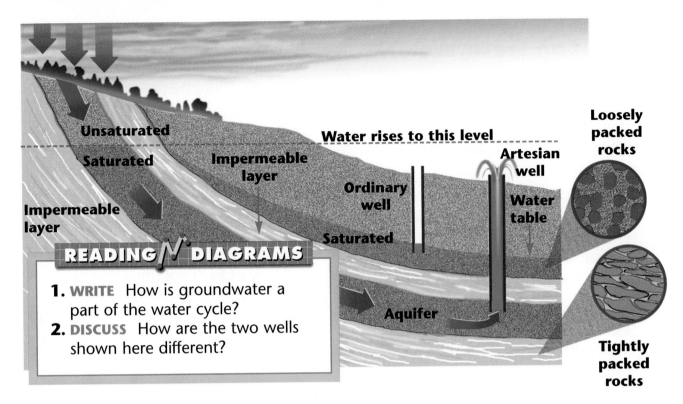

Unsaturated

Saturated

Impermeable layer

Impermeable layer

Water rises to this level

Ordinary well

Saturated

Artesian well

Water table

Loosely packed rocks

Aquifer

Tightly packed rocks

READING ⟋ DIAGRAMS

1. **WRITE** How is groundwater a part of the water cycle?
2. **DISCUSS** How are the two wells shown here different?

Where Rain and Snow Go

When water falls back to Earth, where does it go? Some water seeps into the ground. It becomes **groundwater**. Groundwater seeps into the spaces between bits of rock and soil. It seeps downward until it is blocked by a kind of rock that is so tightly packed that it has few spaces.

Then the water starts to back up and fill the spaces in the soil and rocks above. The top of the water-filled spaces is called the **water table**. If the water table reaches above the surface, a pond, a lake, or a stream forms.

Ponds and lakes are still bodies of water. They form where water fills up low-lying places. Streams, however, are flowing downhill. As they flow they join with other streams and become larger, a river. Eventually rivers reach the ocean or some other large bodies of water.

An underground layer of rock or soil that is filled with water is called an **aquifer** (ak′wə fər). Water can move through an aquifer for great distances.

Some groundwater seeps out of the ground in what is called a **spring**. Springs occur where the water table meets the surface. They can feed water into streams and lakes long after it stops raining.

Long ago people learned to tap into groundwater by digging **wells**. Wells are holes dug below the water table. The water seeps into the hole. In some wells people get the water out of the hole with pumps. Wells can also be dug deep into aquifers that are sandwiched between tightly packed layers of rock. Water spouts up in these wells because it is being squeezed by the rock layers.

Most supplies of fresh water for large towns and cities come from **reservoirs** (rez′ər vwärz′). Reservoirs are storage areas for freshwater supplies. They may be human-made or natural lakes or ponds. Pipelines transport the water from reservoirs.

How Can Fresh Water Be Polluted?

Oceans are polluted by people dumping wastes and spilling chemicals. Fresh water can be polluted, too, in many ways.

- **Precipitation** Rain or snow may pick up pollutants from the air. Some chemicals in the air make the rain turn into an acid. Acid rain harms living things and property.

- **Runoff water** Fresh water also gets polluted as it runs off over the land. Water that runs over dumped garbage can end up in streams and lakes. In some cases garbage is dumped into rivers.

- **Groundwater** As water soaks down through the soil, it can pick up chemicals, such as pesticides.

- **Industry** Water used by industry gets polluted as it is used. For example, water that is used to help produce paper is filled with fibers and chemicals.

- You pollute water, too. Every time you flush the toilet, take a bath, brush your teeth, or wash dishes or clothes, water is polluted with wastes. Where do you think this water ends up?

Because of local pollution, many families use water-treatment devices in their faucets. Some families have to use bottled water for cooking and drinking.

PURE

Glacier Water

Skill: Forming a Hypothesis

HOW DO WASTES FROM LAND GET INTO LAKES AND RIVERS?

In seeking an answer to a question, the first thing you might do is find out as much as possible. You make observations. You might look up information.

Next, you would think of an explanation for these observations. That explanation is a hypothesis. It may be stated as an "If . . . then" sentence. "If water runs over land where garbage is dumped, then . . ." Sometimes you can test a hypothesis by making and observing a model.

MATERIALS

- soil
- food color
- foam bits
- 2 deep pie pans
- 1 L (2 c) of water
- 2 textbooks
- *Science Journal*

PROCEDURES

1. FORM A HYPOTHESIS Write a hypothesis to answer the question above.

2. MAKE A MODEL Pack moist soil to fill one-half (one side) of one pie pan. As you pack the soil, add 10–20 drops of food color to the soil just below the surface. Sprinkle crumbled bits of foam over the top.

3. EXPERIMENT Use two books to tilt the pan with the soil side up. Place the lower edge of the soil-filled pan in the other pan. Pour water over the uppermost edge of the pan. In your *Science Journal*, describe what happens. Let your model stand for some time and observe it again.

CONCLUDE AND APPLY

1. EXPLAIN How does this model represent wastes on land?

2. DRAW CONCLUSIONS Based on the model, how do wastes from land get into water? Does the model support your hypothesis? Explain.

3. FORM A HYPOTHESIS How can some wastes be removed from water? Form a hypothesis, and test your ideas.

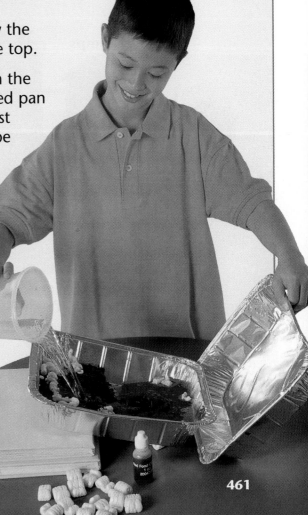

461

How Can We Solve Water Problems?

Can polluted water be cleaned up? Yes, it can be—in many ways. For example, the water cycle helps clean water. Remember that when water evaporates, it leaves behind materials it contained. The water vapor and eventually the rain that forms no longer contain those materials.

When water seeps into the ground, the ground acts as a fine screen, or filter. Most dirt particles in water are trapped, or filtered out, as water seeps down through the ground. As a result a well that is dug down deep in the ground collects water that has been filtered.

Freshwater supplies for large areas can be cleaned on a large scale. Follow the steps in the process.

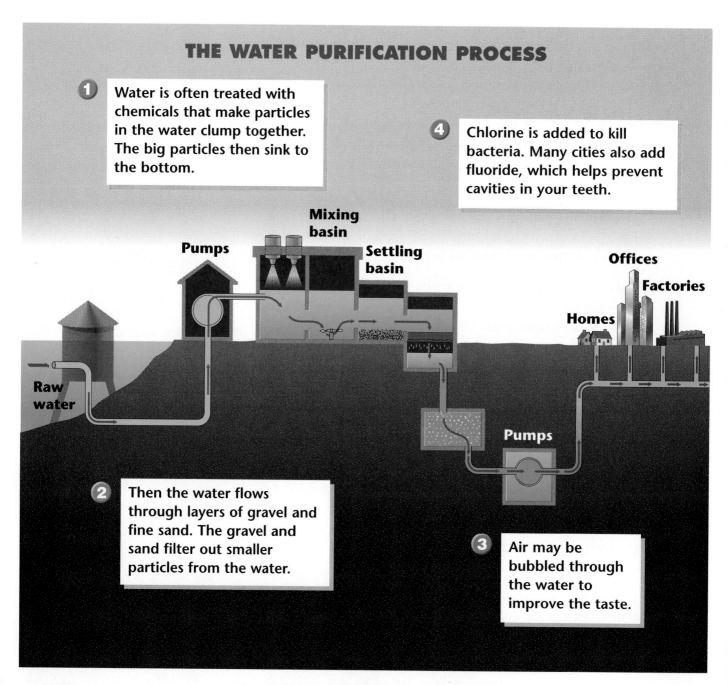

THE WATER PURIFICATION PROCESS

1 Water is often treated with chemicals that make particles in the water clump together. The big particles then sink to the bottom.

4 Chlorine is added to kill bacteria. Many cities also add fluoride, which helps prevent cavities in your teeth.

Pumps

Mixing basin

Settling basin

Offices

Factories

Homes

Raw water

2 Then the water flows through layers of gravel and fine sand. The gravel and sand filter out smaller particles from the water.

Pumps

3 Air may be bubbled through the water to improve the taste.

What Can You Do?

People waste fresh water more than they realize. Often water can be safely reused. At times when the rainfall is low, water supplies may be very low. You may live in a part of the country where water supplies are low much of the time. No matter where you live, saving and recycling water should be part of your daily routine.

DAILY USES OF WATER

Activity	Amount of Water Used
Flushing a toilet	16–24 liters
Washing dishes	32–40 liters
Taking a shower	80–120 liters
Taking a bath	120–160 liters

READING CHARTS

1. **REPRESENT** How could you make a graph to represent these numbers?
2. **WRITE** How does taking a shower help save water?

The United States Congress has passed laws such as the Safe Drinking Water Act and the Clean Water Act. These laws set standards for water purity. The Environmental Protection Agency (EPA) checks that these laws are being followed.

Laws are important. However, it takes people—like you—to help save water and keep it clean.

How does a sprinkler attached to a hydrant help save water?

REVIEW

1. How do you depend on the oceans, even if you don't live near one?

2. **HYPOTHESIZE** How does the Sun help provide you with freshwater supplies?

3. How do wastes get into ocean water? Fresh water?

4. How can freshwater supplies be cleaned up?

5. **CRITICAL THINKING** *Evaluate* How can you tell the amount of water wasted in a day by a leaky faucet? Find a way to tell without wasting any.

WHY IT MATTERS THINK ABOUT IT
How would you add to the table above to include other ways you use water? To include other ways water is used in your neighborhood or town?

WHY IT MATTERS WRITE ABOUT IT
How can you help keep water clean? How can you save water?

463

Water Works!

The people of San Antonio, Texas, get their water from one of Earth's great natural resources: the Edwards Aquifer. If too much water's taken from from the aquifer, however, the springs near San Antonio stop flowing. Then plants and animals that depend on the springs have no water source.

During dry periods very little water can be taken from the aquifer. "The city needs a water source that is reliable, even during droughts," says Ken Diehl of the San Antonio Water System (SAWS). He's a water recycling specialist in charge of treating sewer water so it can be used again!

Air force bases near San Antonio use recycled water to wash planes and water lawns.

First, mud and other solid material is removed from the water. Next, bacteria are used to kill harmful organisms. Then, the water is filtered. Chlorine is added to kill germs and is then removed. Finally, the cleaned water is pumped into the city's rivers.

In 1998 SAWS decided not to continue releasing all the recycled water into rivers. It began building a 125-kilometer (78-mile) pipeline to carry some recycled water to air force bases and businesses. Water for many activities, such as washing machinery, need not be as pure as drinking water.

Making a Difference

Using recycled water will reduce SAWS's use of the aquifer by up to 20 percent. Diehl says, "For every drop of recycled water used, one drop of water from Edwards Aquifer is saved. SAWS is taking a leadership role in wisely using its water resources."

DISCUSSION STARTER

1. What causes springs to stop flowing?

2. How does recycling water help the environment?

SAWS has been recycling the city's water since the 1930s. It cleans millions of gallons of water from San Antonio homes daily.

To learn more about waterworks, visit *www.mhschool.com/science* and enter the keyword WATERWORKS.

*inter*NET
CONNECTION

Topic 7
EARTH SCIENCE

WHY IT MATTERS

Conserving energy is everyone's responsibility.

SCIENCE WORDS

alternative energy source a source of energy other than the burning of a fossil fuel

geothermal energy Earth's internal energy

biomass energy from plant matter or animal waste

Energy Resources

How many hours a day do you use energy? What kinds do you use, and what do you use them for? Did you know that you are using energy all the time? How is that possible?

How many different ways are the people in this picture using energy?

EXPLORE

HYPOTHESIZE How many different ways do you use energy each day? How can you use less energy? Write a hypothesis in your *Science Journal*. Test your ideas.

Investigate How People Use Energy

Record all the ways you use energy in a day.

PROCEDURES

1. **COMMUNICATE** Make a list in your *Science Journal* of all the different *ways you use energy*. You might list cooking, heat or air conditioning, transportation, lighting, entertainment (TV, radio, CD player), computer, and so on.

2. **COMMUNICATE** Make a list of all the different *kinds of energy* you use in a day. Types of energy you might list include electricity (lights, TV), gasoline (riding in cars), gas (stove), wood (fireplace), oil (heat), solar energy.

3. **COLLECT DATA** Make a table listing all the kinds of energy you use in a day, how you use that energy, and how many hours you use each.

> ### MATERIALS
> - *Science Journal*

CONCLUDE AND APPLY

1. **ANALYZE** How many different ways do you use electricity each day? How many hours a day do you use electricity? What other sources of energy do you use? How many hours a day do you use each?

2. **INFER** Make a log to keep track of your energy use at home and at school. How can you use that information to help you make a plan to save energy?

3. **USE NUMBERS** If it costs you an average of ten cents an hour for the energy you use, how much would the energy you use cost each week? About how much would it cost each month?

GOING FURTHER: Apply

4. **HYPOTHESIZE** How can you use less electricity? How much money do you think you could save on energy use in a month? How would you go about testing your hypothesis?

How Do People Use Energy?

As the Explore Activity showed, you use a number of different energy sources each day. Where does the energy you use come from? Try tracing it back to its source. Many homes, schools, and businesses get heat by burning oil or natural gas. Some older buildings still burn coal for heat. Some homes burn wood for heat.

The heat in many other homes and businesses comes from electricity. So does the energy to run many common devices, such as lights, computers, radios, TVs, and washers. Some small devices such as flashlights and portable CD players get their electricity from batteries. Most of the other devices use electricity from a wall outlet. That electricity comes from a power plant. Electricity from that plant reaches your home through wires. However, the power plant makes electricity by using energy from burning fuels such as coal, oil, and natural gas.

It takes a lot of energy to move a car, bus, or train. Public and private transportation is one of the greatest uses of energy in today's world. Most vehicles get their energy from burning fuels such as gasoline or diesel oil. Others run on electricity, propane, or liquefied natural gas.

As you can see, most of the energy you use can be traced back to fossil fuels—coal, oil, or natural gas. These energy sources are burned in order to release energy.

Brain Power

How did people solve their energy problems in the past? Find out what sources of energy they used and how.

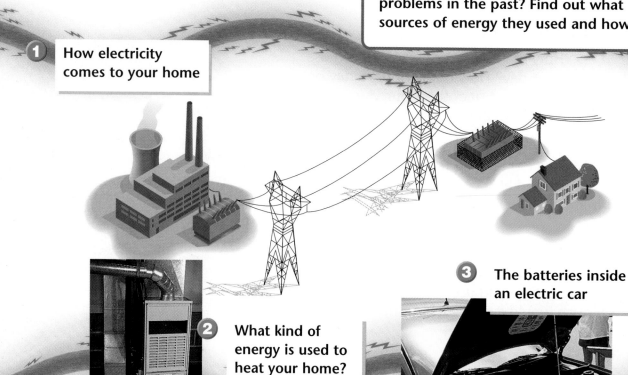

1 How electricity comes to your home

2 What kind of energy is used to heat your home?

3 The batteries inside an electric car

How Are Fossil Fuels Turned into Energy?

Heat from burning fossil fuels can be used directly to heat homes, schools, businesses, and factories.

The heat can also be used to generate electricity. The heat is used to boil water and turn it into steam. The steam is trapped, and pressure builds up. Then the steam is released. The steam is directed at a big, pinwheel-like turbine. When the steam hits the turbine, it causes it to spin. The spinning turbine turns a generator to make electricity.

All fuels have advantages and disadvantages. The advantage of using fossil fuels is that they contain a lot of energy. However, fossil fuels take millions of years to form. Once used they cannot be replaced fast enough for future use. Therefore, they are nonrenewable.

Burning a fossil fuel also gives off smoke, gases, and other by-products. These pollute the environment. That is why the search is on for other, cleaner fuels.

A cloud of smog

Where Do Fossil Fuels Come From?

Fossil fuels are the remains of once-living things. Coal formed from the remains of dead plants buried in ancient swamps and forests. Natural gas and oil formed from the remains of tiny ocean plants and animals. These sea creatures died and fell to the bottom of the ocean. There their bodies were buried by layers of sand and mud. As more and more layers covered these remains, pressure on them built up. Eventually, the layers of sediments turned into sedimentary rock. Over millions of years, the plant and animal remains changed into oil and natural gas.

Brain Power

To whom do Earth's energy resources belong? What should we do to try to conserve them?

HOW FOSSIL FUELS ARE FORMED

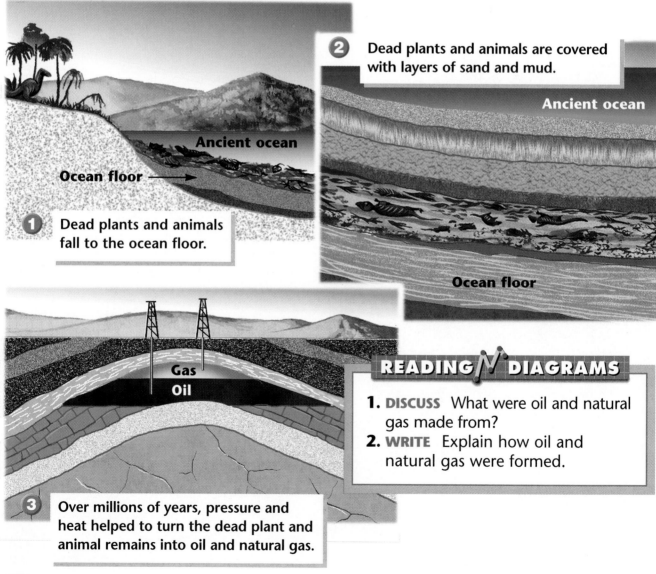

Ancient ocean

Ocean floor

1 Dead plants and animals fall to the ocean floor.

2 Dead plants and animals are covered with layers of sand and mud.

Ancient ocean

Ocean floor

Gas
Oil

3 Over millions of years, pressure and heat helped to turn the dead plant and animal remains into oil and natural gas.

READING DIAGRAMS

1. **DISCUSS** What were oil and natural gas made from?
2. **WRITE** Explain how oil and natural gas were formed.

How Much Energy Do We Have Left?

Our supplies of fossil fuels are limited, and fossil fuels are not a renewable energy source.

With the growth of industry, the demand for and use of energy also grows. The United States is the world's largest consumer of energy. The energy we use makes our lives easier. However, energy use pollutes the environment. It also speeds up the rate at which Earth's energy resources are used up.

If we continue to use fossil fuels at our present rate, we will run out of them. There are two possible solutions to this problem. One is to conserve our energy resources so that they will last longer. Another is to search for other sources of energy.

DID YOU KNOW?

The Sun is often called an inexhaustible source of energy. As far as you are concerned, it is. Yet even the Sun will run out of energy one day.

Astronomers estimate that the Sun will keep shining much the way it does today for "only" about another five billion years. What do you think will happen then?

QUICK LAB

Fuel Supply

MATH LINK

HYPOTHESIZE We are using fossil fuels at the rates shown in the table. How long will Earth's fossil fuel supply last? Write a hypothesis in your *Science Journal.* Test your ideas.

MATERIALS
- *Science Journal*

This table shows how fast we are using up oil and natural gas.

World Supply of Oil and Natural Gas (as of January 1, 1996)	
Oil	1,007 billion barrels (1,007,000,000,000)
Natural gas	4,900 trillion cubic feet

World Use of Oil and Natural Gas for 1995	
Oil	about 70 million barrels a day (70,000,000)
Natural gas	about 78 trillion cubic feet

PROCEDURES

1. **OBSERVE** Examine the data in the table.

2. **COMMUNICATE** Draw a graph showing how long the fossil fuels we know about will last at our current rate of use.

CONCLUDE AND APPLY

INFER Predict how long it will be until we run out of each type of fossil fuel.

What Other Sources of Energy Are There?

Sources of energy other than the burning of fossil fuels are called **alternative energy sources**. Here are some alternative energy sources.

Modern Waterwheels

Any whitewater rafter can tell you that running water has a lot of energy. That energy can be harnessed to do work using waterwheels. Running or falling water turns the wheel. The turning wheel spins an axle, which is attached to various machines to do work.

In a mill the axle turns a big stone that grinds up grain. In a sawmill it spins a blade to cut wood. In a *hydroelectric* (hī′drō i lek′trik) *plant*, running or falling water spins a generator to make electricity.

Harnessing the Wind

Have you ever watched a pinwheel spin in the wind? Wind, or moving air, can also spin a wheel. Holland is well known for its great windmills.

Earth's Furnace

The Earth's interior is very hot. The most common evidence of that heat is simply hot water or steam coming out of the ground. The water is heated below the surface in places where magma collects. Earth's internal heat is called **geothermal** (jē′ō thûr′məl) **energy**. Geothermal energy can be used to heat homes and produce electricity.

- Homes in Boise, Idaho, have been heated by hot springs since the 1890s.
- At *The Geysers* in California, steam drives turbines that generate electricity. The steam comes from underground water heated by geothermal energy.

2 The windmills in this array in California spin generators to make electricity.

1 A hydroelectric plant uses moving water to produce electricity.

3 Geothermal energy helps keep the country of Iceland warm.

How Can We Use Solar Energy?

Every day the Sun bathes Earth in energy. We usually think of that solar energy simply as sunlight. Plants harness the Sun's energy through photosynthesis to make chemical compounds rich in energy. When you burn wood, you are releasing energy that a tree absorbed from the Sun.

Sunlight also gives water the energy to evaporate and rise into the atmosphere. In this way the energy of running water can also be traced back to sunlight.

Today people are using new ways to harness the power of sunlight. One way is to trap or concentrate sunlight with the use of solar panels, or collectors. The trapped sunlight can be used to heat water or entire homes. Another way to use it is with solar cells. Solar cells are devices that convert sunlight into electric energy.

Tapping the Tide

Every day the tide causes the water level to rise and drop along the world's coastlines. Now imagine a big tank built just below the high-water level. The tide rises, and water fills the tank. When the tide drops, the water flows out of the tank. Add a water-wheel so the water flowing out of the tank spins the wheel. Now you have a spinning axle that can be used to do work. That's the idea behind this tidal power plant in Holland.

5 Tidal power plant in Holland

4 Solar houses use solar cells for electric energy and solar collectors for heat.

473

How Can We Conserve Energy?

Unfortunately alternative energy sources are not fully replacing fossil fuels. Therefore, we need to conserve these nonrenewable resources.

What does it mean to conserve our resources? It means we don't waste what we have and we use as little of what we have as possible. Take a typical house as an example. Better insulation of homes has cut United States' consumption of fuel oil almost in half. Newly designed bodies and engines have doubled the gasoline mileage of most cars. If we could cut our present consumption in half, our oil reserves would last twice as long! How can we do that?

One way is to use alternative energy sources such as water, wind, and solar energy. Every watt of electricity we get from a solar cell is one less watt we have to get by burning oil or coal.

How Else Stored Sunlight Is Used

You have learned that fossil fuels are the stored energy that came from once-living plants and animals. Fossil fuels are nonrenewable. However, there is renewable energy we can get from plant matter and animal wastes or other remains. It is called **biomass**. Plant material and animal wastes that might wind up as garbage can be processed to form fuel. This is done in waste-treatment plants. The treated wastes can then be burned. Special devices called scrubbers help prevent pollutants from entering the air when these wastes are burned. Solid wastes can also be digested by bacteria. The bacteria produce methane gas in the process. Methane gas can be used as fuel.

Corn and other grains, and even sugarcane, can also be turned into fuel. This fuel can be used to heat foods. It can also be mixed with gasoline to help run cars while saving gasoline supplies.

This car is powered by a special mixture that combines alcohol from biomass with gasoline.

Recycling

Another way to conserve energy is to recycle. Making things uses energy. If we can reuse a material, we save the energy needed to make it. For example, getting aluminum metal out of its ore takes a lot of electricity. If we recycled aluminum cans, some of the metal we needed would come from the cans rather than from ore. Can you think of other ways in which you could conserve energy?

You probably look forward to driving a car someday. Won't it be great to get around on your own? Well, think about this: Cars run on gasoline, and gasoline comes from oil. Remember the graph you did comparing known oil reserves with our current rate of use? If we don't conserve, will there be enough gas for your car? Will there be enough gas for your children's cars? Will there be enough gas for their children?

REVIEW

1. How do you use energy each day?

2. Why are coal, oil, and natural gas called "fossil" fuels?

3. How does the burning of fossil fuels pollute the environment?

4. **COMPARE AND CONTRAST** List five ways people can help to conserve fossil fuels. Which of these suggestions do you think would conserve the most fuel? Which of these suggestions do you think more people would be willing to try?

5. **CRITICAL THINKING** *Analyze* What alternatives do we have to using fossil fuels for energy? What are some of the advantages and some of the disadvantages of using these energy sources?

WHY IT MATTERS THINK ABOUT IT
Alternative sources of energy help us to conserve fossil fuels. What if your house was close to a stream or bathed in strong sunlight every day, or there was a hot spring in your neighborhood? How could you use an alternative energy source to save energy in your home?

WHY IT MATTERS WRITE ABOUT IT
Describe how you might use an alternative energy source to supply some of the energy needs for your home.

READING SKILL
Write a paragraph to explain what conclusions you would draw about relying less on fossil fuels.

Science, Technology, and Society

Nuclear... or Not?

Nuclear energy can be used to power a submarine, explode a bomb, or run a power plant. Today nuclear power costs about the same as coal power. Which is best to use?

Small amounts of uranium can run a nuclear power plant for years. Coal-fired plants use tons of coal daily, and someday we'll run out of coal.

Coal smoke adds to air pollution and global warming. Nuclear plants release only water vapor.

Both nuclear and coal plants can be damaged. In 1986 a nuclear plant in the Soviet Union exploded. Radioactive fallout spread all over northern Europe.

Coal-fired plants have burned down, but damage was limited to the plant.

Both nuclear and coal wastes have leaked. Nuclear wastes can be radioactive for thousands of years. Coal ash can contaminate water supplies.

DISCUSSION STARTER

1. What is a disadvantage of nuclear power? Of coal power?

2. Is nuclear or coal power better for the environment? Why?

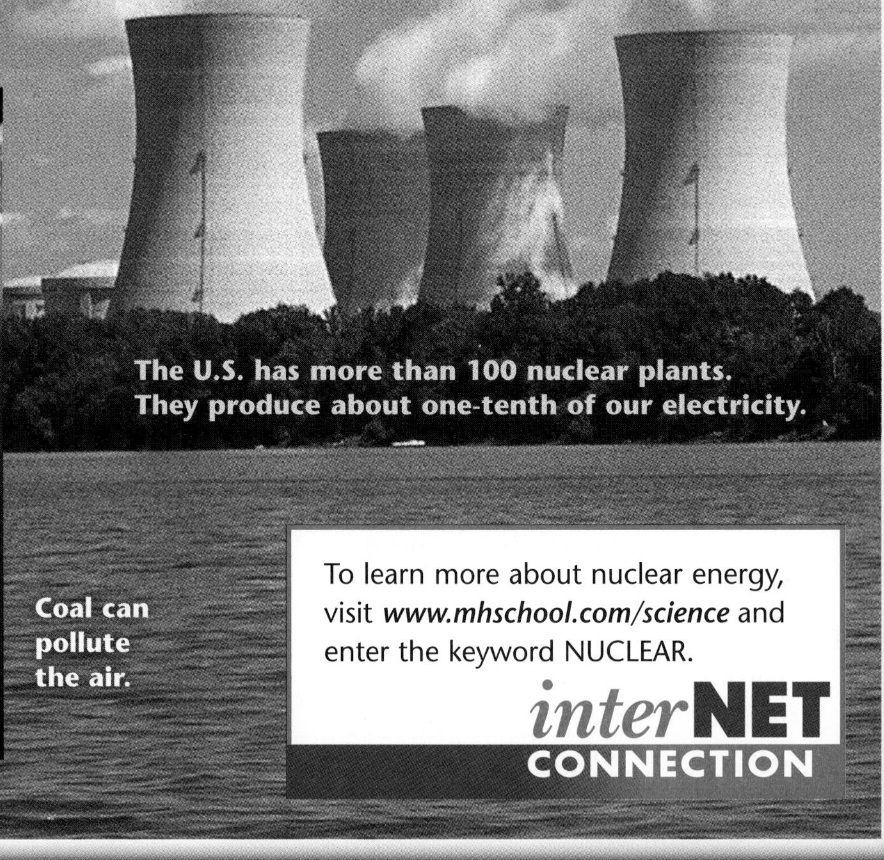

The U.S. has more than 100 nuclear plants. They produce about one-tenth of our electricity.

Coal can pollute the air.

To learn more about nuclear energy, visit *www.mhschool.com/science* and enter the keyword NUCLEAR.

*inter*NET
CONNECTION

SCIENCE WORDS

acid rain p.449   ozone layer p.447

biomass p.474   renewable p.446

desalination p.457   reservoir p.459

fossil fuel p.448   smog p.448

groundwater p.459   water table p.459

USING SCIENCE WORDS

Number a paper from 1 to 10. Fill in 1 to 5 with words from the list above.

1. Solar power is a(n) __?__ resource.

2. A renewable resource that gets energy from garbage is __?__.

3. A type of precipitation caused by air pollution is __?__.

4. Dangerous air pollution is called __?__.

5. Natural gas is a(n) __?__.

6–10. Pick five words from the list above that were not used in 1 to 5, and use each in a sentence.

UNDERSTANDING SCIENCE IDEAS

11. What is the difference between renewable and nonrenewable energy sources?

12. How were fossil fuels formed?

13. Where does geothermal energy come from?

14. What is the difference between fossil fuels and biomass?

15. Explain how to turn salt water into fresh water.

USING IDEAS AND SKILLS

16. How does smog form?

17. **READING SKILL: DRAW CONCLUSIONS** All electricity is made by burning fossil fuels. Is this true or false? Explain your answer.

18. Sunlight is free. However, solar energy is considered "too expensive" to use in the Northeast. How can something that is free be too expensive? Research the cost of various energy sources in your area.

19. **HYPOTHESIZE** Does rain remove pollutant particles from the air? Form a hypothesis. What could you do to test your hypothesis?

20. **THINKING LIKE A SCIENTIST** Does filtering water remove all impurities? Explain your answer. How would you prove your answer?

PROBLEMS and PUZZLES

Saving Soil How do growing plants help conserve soil? Grow some grass seeds in a tray. In a second tray, lay down some soil. Tilt both trays, and use a watering can to produce "rain" over them. Which tray loses more soil?

UNIT 5 REVIEW

USING SCIENCE WORDS

Number a paper from 1 to 10. Beside each number write the word or words that best complete the sentence.

1. The tendency of an object to move continually in a straight line is called ___?___.

2. All of Earth's water is collectively called the ___?___.

3. The breakdown of rocks into small pieces is called ___?___.

4. Streak, luster, hardness, and cleavage are properties of ___?___.

5. Marble, formed by the action of heat and pressure on limestone, is a(n) ___?___.

6. Oxygen that is given off by plants is an example of a(n) ___?___.

7. The gas that screens out UV (ultraviolet) rays from the Sun is ___?___.

8. Groundwater seeps out of the ground at places called ___?___.

9. Fresh water can be produced from seawater by a process called ___?___.

10. Energy from geysers is an example of ___?___.

UNDERSTANDING SCIENCE IDEAS

Write 11 to 15. For each number write the letter for the best answer. You may wish to use the hints provided.

11. The length of a day on a planet is always
    a. 24 hours
    b. one rotation of the planet
    c. dependent on its distance from the Sun
    d. the same for all planets
    (Hint: Read page 352.)

12. Which of the following can be scratched by glass?
    a. steel plate
    b. diamond
    c. chalk
    (Hint: Read page 418.)

13. Which of the following pollutes the air?
    a. sulfur
    b. calcium
    c. water
    d. oxygen
    (Hint: Read page 450.)

14. Most fresh water is found in
    a. groundwater
    b. ice caps and glaciers
    c. oceans
    d. lakes and streams
    (Hint: Read page 456.)

15. What fuel is used by most cars and trucks?
    a. natural gas
    b. electricity
    c. gasoline or diesel oil
    d. propane
    (Hint: Read page 468.)

USING IDEAS AND SKILLS

16. Why doesn't Earth fly away from the Sun in a straight line?

17. In what way is the Moon's gravity important?

18. How do we know that Earth's surface can move?

19. **DEFINE** How is hardness defined for minerals?

20. What are the two types of coal? How are they related?

21. Explain what a renewable resource is. Give an example.

22. How does burning coal cause acid rain?

23. Where does the fresh water found in glaciers and rivers come from?

THINKING LIKE A SCIENTIST

24. **HYPOTHESIZE** Explain why you might have to use a model to test a hypothesis.

25. Would a tidal power plant be able to produce electricity at all hours of the day? Explain.

WRITING IN YOUR JOURNAL

SCIENCE IN YOUR LIFE
Describe two ways you use water each day and two ways businesses or farms use water. Explain how these uses might pollute water.

PRODUCT ADS
More and more ads are appearing for electric cars (EVs) that run on electricity rather than gasoline. Why do you think companies are starting to make such cars?

HOW SCIENTISTS WORK
Scientists routinely organize information in tables and graphs. Use two examples from this unit to tell why this is useful.

Design your own Experiment

Form a hypothesis about how much garbage is produced in your school. Design an experiment to test your hypothesis. Think safety first. Review your experiment with your teacher before you attempt it.

inter**NET** CONNECTION

For help in reviewing this unit, visit *www.mhschool.com/science*

PROBLEMS and PUZZLES

Weathering Model

There are two types of weathering. Physical weathering is the grinding up of rocks into smaller pieces. Chemical weathering takes place when chemicals change or break down rocks.

Does physical weathering affect chemical weathering? Find out by filling two cups with water. Put a ground-up sugar cube in one cup and a whole cube in the other. Which type of sugar dissolves more quickly? Can you explain why?

Ground-up sugar cube **Whole sugar cube**

Garbage to the Moon

Each year each person in the United States creates a 15-foot-tall pile of garbage. If stacked end to end, could all of the garbage piles created by 260 million Americans reach the Moon? Could it reach the Sun? Use the data in the figure to find the answer. Explain how close or how far the garbage would reach.

Earth–Moon 240,000 miles

Earth–Sun 93,000,000 miles

Soil: A Close-Up View

Fill a tall glass jar one-third full with soil. Add water to make the jar two-thirds full. Add a capful of water softener, if available. Then analyze your soil.

1. Shake the mixture well. Then let it settle for 15 to 20 minutes, until layers form.

2. Which layer settles first? Second? Third? Hold a sheet of paper next to the jar. Draw each layer that you see.

3. Compare your soil to the soil shown in the diagram. Is your soil sandy, silty, or high in clay?

4. Which kind of soil do you think is best for growing plants? Plant some seeds, and see if you are right.

3 **Clay: The lightest, finest particles are clay. Some stay suspended in the water.**

2 **Silt: The silt layer is made of the small, heavy particles. Silt settles after the sand.**

1 **Sand: Sand settles first. The sand layer is made of the large, heavy particles.**

ECOSYSTEMS AROUND THE WORLD

CHAPTER 11

ECOSYSTEMS

The water around you, the air above you, the rocks and soil under your feet, and all living things around you make up your ecosystem. Living things in an ecosystem depend on each other and on the nonliving things around them. Animals, for example, depend on plants for food and for the oxygen plants make.

Do plants depend on animals? In Chapter 11 you will learn how animals provide materials needed for the plants to grow. How does this plant depend on animals?

In Chapter 11 you will have many opportunities to read diagrams for information.

Topic 7
LIFE SCIENCE

WHY IT MATTERS

Both living and nonliving things in an area interact with each other.

SCIENCE WORDS

ecosystem all the living and nonliving things in an area interacting with each other

ecology the study of how living things and their environment interact

abiotic factor a nonliving part of an ecosystem

biotic factor a living part of an ecosystem

population all the organisms of one species that live in an area at the same time

community all the populations living in an area

habitat the area in which an organism lives

niche the role an organism has in its ecosystem

Living Things and Their Environment

What do you need in order to survive? Your answers could include food, water, the right temperature, and a place to live.

What kinds of things do the animals and plants shown here need to survive? Where do you think they get these things?

EXPLORE

HYPOTHESIZE How do living things interact with each other and their environment? What do living things need in order to survive? Write a hypothesis in your *Science Journal*. How would you design a special environment to test your ideas?

Design Your Own Experiment

WHAT DO LIVING THINGS NEED TO SURVIVE?

PROCEDURES

1. For a water environment, add 4 cm (1.5 in.) of thoroughly washed sand or gravel to the jar. Fill the jar to about 4 cm (1.5 in.) from the top with water. Add a few floating plants, rooted plants with floating leaves, and submerged plants. Do not crowd the plants. Add two large or eight small water snails.

2. For a land environment, place a 2-cm (0.75-in.) layer of gravel on the bottom of the jar. Cover the gravel layer with a 5- to 7-cm (2- to 2.75-in.) layer of moistened soil. Add plants, and plant grass seeds. Add earthworms, sow bugs, and snails.

3. Place each jar in a lighted area but not in direct sunlight.

4. Cover each jar with its own lid or with a piece of plastic wrap. Record in your *Science Journal* how many and what kinds of living things you used.

5. **OBSERVE** Examine your jars every other day, and record your observations.

CONCLUDE AND APPLY

1. **INFER** What are the nonliving parts of your system? What are the living parts of your system?

2. **INFER** What do the living things need to survive? How do you know?

GOING FURTHER: Problem Solving

3. **EXPERIMENT** How could you design an environment that contains both land and water areas?

MATERIALS

- wide-mouthed, clear 3.8-L (1-gal) container with lid
- washed gravel
- pond water or aged tap water
- water plants such as *Elodea* or duckweed
- 2 large water snails or 8 small water snails
- soil
- small rocks
- grass seed and small plants
- 2 earthworms, 2 land snails, 4 sow bugs, or other small land animals that eat plants
- *Science Journal*

What Do Living Things Need to Survive?

What or whom do you interact with every day? Make a list. The Explore Activity showed how living things and nonliving things interact in an **ecosystem**. An ecosystem is all the living and nonliving things in an area interacting with each other. **Ecology** is the study of how all these things interact in order to survive.

Most ecosystems are much larger than a jar. Some, like the prairie ecosystem of North America, the deserts of Africa, and the rain forests of Brazil, cover large areas of a country or continent. Freshwater ecosystems cover less space than saltwater ecosystems. Saltwater ecosystems can cover entire oceans. It doesn't matter where they are or what they look like, all ecosystems have the same parts.

The nonliving parts of an ecosystem are the ecosystem's **abiotic** (ā'bī ot'ik) **factors**. All living things need certain nonliving things in order to survive. Abiotic factors include water, minerals, sunlight, air, climate, and soil.

All organisms need water. Their bodies are 50 to 95 percent water. The processes that keep living things alive— like photosynthesis and respiration— can only take place in the presence of water. Living things need minerals, such as calcium, iron, phosphorus, and nitrogen. Some living things, like plants and algae, need sunlight to make food. Animals need oxygen to produce the energy for their bodies. Plants and algae need carbon dioxide. The environment must also have the right temperature for organisms to survive.

Brain Power

What abiotic factors have recently changed where you live? How did the changes affect living things?

Abiotic factors in an ecosystem include light, water soil, temperature, air, and minerals.

EARTH LINK SCIENCE

What Do Living Things Contribute?

The right abiotic factors help make it possible for the *organisms*, or living things, in an ecosystem to survive. The living parts are animals, plants, fungi, protists, and bacteria. Mushrooms and molds are fungi. Protists include one-celled organisms. Microscopic bacteria live everywhere.

These organisms—animals, plants, fungi, protists, and bacteria—make up the **biotic** (bī ot′ik) **factors**, or living parts, of an ecosystem.

Each organism contributes something to the others in the ecosystem.

Plants and algae are called *producers*. They produce oxygen and food that animals need. Animals are *consumers*. Animals consume, or eat, plants or animals that eat plants. Animals also give off carbon dioxide that plants need to make food.

What do the fungi and bacteria contribute? They are a very important part of any ecosystem. Fungi and bacteria are *decomposers*. They *decompose*, or break down, dead plants and animals into useful things like minerals that enrich soil. Plants need these in order to grow.

Each of these kinds of organisms helps the others survive.

Biotic factors in an ecosystem include plants, animals, fungi, protists, and bacteria.

READING IN DIAGRAMS

1. **DISCUSS** How do these two diagrams differ? What does each diagram show?
2. **WRITE** Which of these two diagrams best shows the abiotic factors in the ecosystem? Explain your answer.

What Were the Prairies Like?

Long ago a "sea of wild grasses" covered North America from central Texas in the south to North Dakota in the north. These are America's prairie lands, the "range" of the famous song "Home on the Range."

Native Americans once hunted buffalo on prairie lands. Later, ranchers and farmers grazed cattle and planted crops such as corn and wheat.

Plants and animals of all kinds lived there. Many still do. Although most of the buffalo are gone, the cattle and the crops that provide much of our food are still there.

In Texas the Blackland Prairie stretches 483 kilometers (300 miles) from Austin in the south to Clarksville in the north. The Blacklands got their name from the rich black soil the early settlers found there. These settlers discovered that the summers were hot and long. However, there was enough rain to grow profitable crops, like cotton.

Before the land became farms and ranches, huge herds of buffalo grazed on the prairie grasses. Buffalo were not the prairie's only inhabitants. At least 50 different kinds of tall and short grasses provided food for plant-eating animals. Many kinds of wildflowers painted the landscape with beautiful colors. These wildflowers included purple cone-flowers, bluebells, yellow sunflowers, and golden dahlias. Near streams a traveler might come across oak, hickory, elm, or cedar trees.

Many kinds of animals and plants live in a prairie. A prairie is a region of tall grasses. It may be flat or hilly grassland.

What Animals Live in the Blacklands?

About 500 species, or different kinds, of animals still live on this prairie. The spotted chorus frog sings in the night near the streams and rivers. Rattle-snakes and lizards seek shelter under rocks.

Birds like pipits, longspurs, and horned larks, as well as 300 other kinds of birds, still live in the Blackland Prairie.

Raccoons, opossums, coyotes, white-tailed deer, and striped skunks live in the Blacklands. Cotton rats, white-footed mice, eastern cottontails, red bats, and bobcats live there, too.

Mountain lions, gray wolves, black bears, and jaguars used to come in search of prey. When people came and built towns, cities, and farms, the buffalo left. The animals that fed on the buffalo left, too. Some animals, however, came to the Blacklands from other places, and stayed. Armadillos arrived from Mexico as the Blacklands' climate warmed up over the past 150 years. Badgers invaded from northwestern Texas when their natural homes were cleared for development.

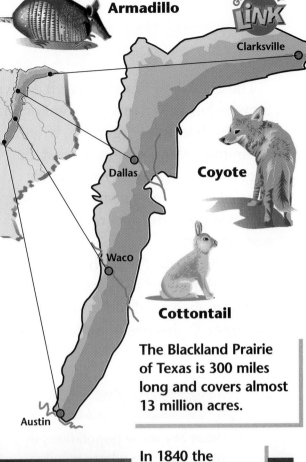

Armadillo

Clarksville

T E X A S

Dallas

Coyote

Waco

Cottontail

Rattlesnake

Austin

The Blackland Prairie of Texas is 300 miles long and covers almost 13 million acres.

In 1840 the Blackland Prairie was unspoiled territory. Today huge farms and cities, like Dallas, cover large parts of the Blackland Prairie.

READING MAPS

1. **DISCUSS** What large cities are on the Blackland Prairie?
2. **WRITE** Why do you think those cities are located where they are?

487

How Are the Living Things Organized?

The Blackland Prairie, like all ecosystems, is home to many different organisms. Each kind of organism, whether an animal, plant, fungus, protist, or bacterium, is a member of a single species. All the organisms of a species living in the same area make up a **population**.

The Blackland Prairie has populations of armadillos and badgers. It has little bluestem grass and Indian grass. It has elm trees. It also has pond algae, soil bacteria, and fungi.

Most people are satisfied with identifying the populations around them. Scientists want to know how populations interact. Scientists investigate the activities of animals, plants, fungi, protists, and bacteria in the ecosystem. They want to know which animals prey on others, which animals eat plants, and which insects eat crops. They are interested in how bacteria and fungi make the soil fertile. All these questions need to be answered to understand how an ecosystem stays healthy.

Scientists have to do more than study individual organisms in an ecosystem, or even individual populations in the ecosystem. They have to study the interactions of all the populations in an area. All the populations living in an area make up a **community**.

Brain Power

What are some populations in the ecosystem where you live? Why is it important to understand your ecosystem?

To understand what makes an ecosystem productive, scientists must study the interactions of different populations in the ecosystem's community of living things.

Where Do They Live? What Do They Do?

The place where a population lives is called its **habitat**. The chorus frog's habitat is in the scattered ponds of the Blacklands.

Each species in an ecosystem also has a role or place in the activities of its community. The role of an organism in the community is its **niche**.

A species' niche includes many factors. It includes what a species eats and what eats that species. It includes the kind of environment the species needs to live in. It even includes whether the species is active by day or night.

Scientists study the habitats and niches of organisms in a community. They do this to see if the community is healthy or in trouble. What would happen if farmers used powerful insecticides to kill pests on Blacklands crops? What might happen if these pesticides also killed some harmless ants?

Ants live in the same habitat as Texas horned lizards. Since the lizards eat ants, what happens to the ants may tell a lot about the future of the lizards. The relationship doesn't stop there. Birds of prey, such as hawks, feed on the lizards. What happens to the ants will also affect the lives of these birds.

The red bat's habitat is above the ground. During the day it hangs from tree branches like a red leaf. At night it streaks through the air looking for food. The habitat of the Texas horned lizard (below) is the dry soil of the Blackland Prairie.

Welcome to Texas!

Nonliving factors also affect organisms' lives. If conditions of an organism's niche change, it may have trouble surviving. If a drought hits the Blacklands, ponds may dry out. Chorus frogs reproduce in water, so a drought would mean fewer young frogs. This would also mean trouble for animals that feed on the frogs. However, it would increase the populations of organisms the frogs eat.

489

The eastern spadefoot toad can survive in a dry, hot habitat by burrowing into the soil and absorbing water through its skin.

How Do Organisms Survive Changes?

The world is a place of changes. One day the weather may be dry and cold. The next day it may be wet and warm. Heavy rains may drench the land one spring and summer. The next year's spring and summer may have cloudless skies day after day. This makes habitats change. A good habitat for a certain organism at one time may be a threatening one at another time. How do populations survive difficult times?

The Eastern Spadefoot Toad

The eastern spadefoot toad lives in the Blackland Prairie. This animal reproduces in water and needs water for its daily life. What happens if a drought strikes the Blacklands?

A close look at the toad's hind feet provided scientists with a clue to the answer. Its hind feet are shaped like little spades. They are adapted for digging. That's just what the spadefoot toad does when water is scarce. It digs into the ground and covers itself with soil. This toad can absorb water through its skin. There's a lot of clay in Blacklands soil, and clay holds water well. Usually there is some water in the soil, even though there may not be any water above it. The toad may be able to survive in the soil even during a drought.

Other animals may be adapted to changes in their habitats in different ways. A varied diet can be useful. Texas horned lizards eat mainly ants. They also eat other insects. If the ant population decreases, at least some lizards will survive. If the ant population increases, the lizards will have more food, and their population will increase.

American Bald Eagles

Many years ago there were bald eagles in the Blackland Prairie of Texas. Then they disappeared. A few have returned recently, especially around the lakes created by damming rivers. Why did the eagles disappear for a while?

On the next page, you can analyze data to discover one reason why bald eagles may have vanished from the skies above the Blackland Prairie.

SKILL BUILDER

Skill: Separating and Controlling Variables

VANISHING BALD EAGLES

The chart below shows the average number of bald eagle eggs that hatched in the wild during a 16-year period. It also shows the level of an insecticide in bald eagle eggs during the same period. What is the relationship between these two variables?

Bald Eagle Egg-Hatching Data

Year	1966	1967	1968	1969	1970	1971	1972*	1973	1974	1975	1976	1977	1978	1979	1980	1981
Average number of young hatched (per nest)	1.28	0.75	0.87	0.82	0.50	0.55	0.60	0.70	0.60	0.81	0.90	0.93	0.91	0.98	1.02	1.27
Insecticide in eggs (parts per million)	42	68	125	119	122	108	82	74	68	59	32	12	13	14	13	13

* pesticide banned

Variables are things that can change. In order to determine what caused the results of an experiment, you need to change one variable at a time. The variable that is changed is called the *independent variable.* A *dependent variable* is one that changes because of the independent variable.

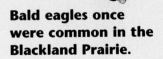

PROCEDURES

1. **INFER** What is the independent variable in the study? What is the dependent variable in the study?

2. **COMMUNICATE** Make a line graph showing the average number of young that hatched. Make another line graph showing the amount of insecticide in eggs.

Bald eagles once were common in the Blackland Prairie.

CONCLUDE AND APPLY

1. **INFER** Based on the graphs, what appears to be the relationship between the amount of insecticide in eggs and the number of young hatched?

2. **HYPOTHESIZE** Suggest a reason for the relationship.

491

What Is the Treasure of the Blackland Prairie?

Have you ever read about buried treasure? Unlike those stories the treasure of the Blackland Prairie is not buried underground. The treasure of the Blackland Prairie *is* the ground.

Prairie soils can often be identified by their dark brown to black *topsoil*. Topsoil is the top layer of soil. The dark color shows the presence of *humus*. Humus is partly decayed plant matter. The decay is produced by the Blacklands' tiniest organisms, bacteria and fungi.

The rich topsoil is full of minerals that prairie grasses and crops need. Two of the most important minerals are magnesium and calcium. Plants need magnesium in order to make chlorophyll molecules. Remember, chlorophyll is

Most of the Blackland Prairie has been changed into cropland. Should what's left of the natural Blacklands be preserved? Should some of the cultivated lands be turned back to nature? What price do we pay for answering either question with a yes or no?

what allows plants to use the Sun's energy to make food. Calcium is an important element of cell walls in plants.

The nutrients in certain prairie soils tend to stay near the surface. That's true because of the low yearly rainfall in prairies. There isn't enough water to carry the nutrients deep into the ground. Farmers take advantage of this by growing crops that have shallow roots, such as corn, wheat, cotton, and sorghum. Sorghum is a grain that is used to feed livestock.

What Grasses Grow on the Prairie Today?

Corn, wheat, and sorghum have something in common with the plants that grow naturally on the prairie. They are all classified as grasses!

Today most of the natural grasses that used to sway in the wind like ocean waves are gone from the Blackland Prairie. They have been replaced by "seas" of cultivated grasses. Is this a good thing?

In nature ecosystems tend to stay in balance. One population controls the number in another population. Communities help preserve and enrich the soil. Some organisms contribute to the health and well-being of others. This balance, however, can be upset by the actions of people. Cities are built on the land. Crops are cultivated. The land changes. Its natural inhabitants disappear. People gain certain things but lose others. It is important to make wise decisions when you think of changing an ecosystem. Otherwise you may lose more than you gain.

REVIEW

1. Describe the structure of an ecosystem.

2. What is the difference between a population and a community?

3. How does an animal's habitat relate to its niche?

4. 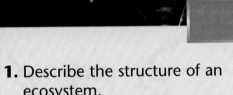 **USE VARIABLES** Give examples of how biotic and abiotic factors interact in an ecosystem.

5. **CRITICAL THINKING** *Apply* Identify changes caused by human activity in your ecosystem. Explain what was lost and what was gained. Evaluate the results.

WHY IT MATTERS THINK ABOUT IT
Give an example of how a change in one population can affect two other populations. Use real organisms in your example.

WHY IT MATTERS WRITE ABOUT IT
Write a fictional short story in which the theme is a changing ecosystem. Make sure the events in your story involve the lives or activities of people.

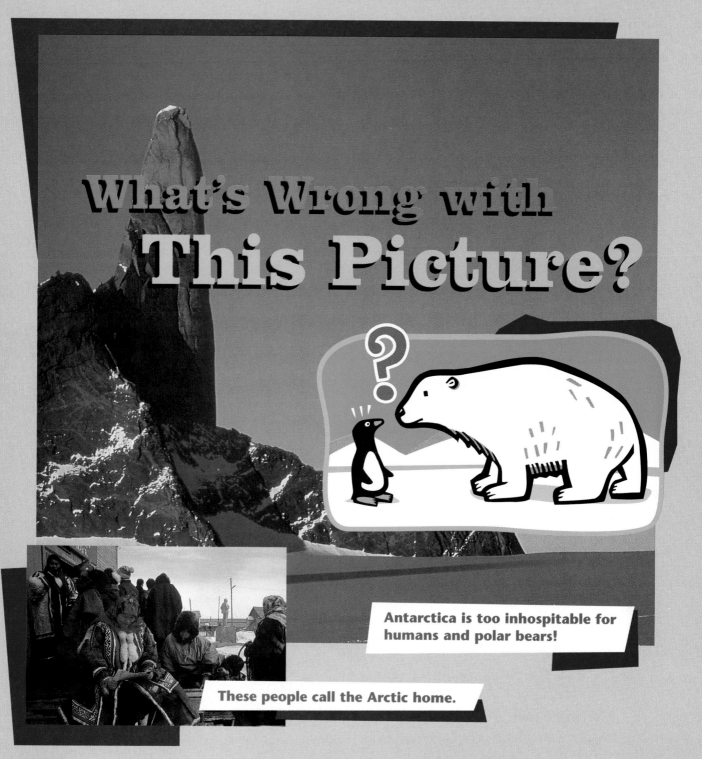

What's Wrong with This Picture?

Antarctica is too inhospitable for humans and polar bears!

These people call the Arctic home.

Geography Link

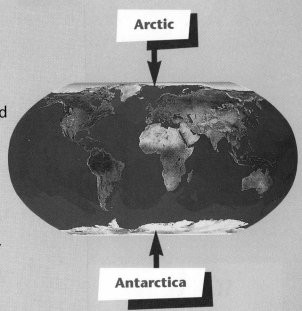

Arctic

Antarctica

A polar bear is looking for a meal. It spots a plump penguin. What happens next? Well . . . nothing. In real life a polar bear and penguin wouldn't meet in the wild. The penguin lives in Antarctica, and the polar bear lives in the Arctic. Both regions are covered with ice and snow most of the year, but there are big differences between them.

The Arctic, at the top of the world, is water surrounded by land. Antarctica, at the bottom of the world, is land surrounded by water. When it's winter in the Arctic, it's summer in Antarctica. Antarctica is the coldest place on Earth. Its lowest recorded temperature was –88°C (–126.4°F). The Arctic's lowest temperature was only –68°C (–94°F)!

More than 400 kinds of flowering plants are native to the Arctic. Mosses, lichens, grasses, herbs, and shrubs cover the area in warm months. Fewer plants can survive in Antarctica. Some 350 species live in small areas that are ice free, but only three of them are flowering plants.

The Arctic hosts polar bears, foxes, wolves, walruses, reindeer, and caribou. No land-based animals with backbones live full-time in Antarctica. Its largest animal is a fly called a midge! Other animals, like penguins and seals, visit in warmer months.

People are also more common in the Arctic than in Antarctica. Antarctica has no native peoples. Usually people stay in Antarctica only to study the region. With howling winds, frigid cold, and endless ice, Antarctica isn't most people's idea of a great place to live . . . or even to visit!

Discussion Starter

1 Why wouldn't you find polar bears and penguins in the same picture?

2 Compare and contrast the animals native to Antarctica with those native to the Arctic.

*inter*NET CONNECTION To learn more about the Arctic and Antarctica, visit **www.mhschool.com/science** and enter the keyword **POLES**.

SCIENCE WORDS

food chain the path of energy in food from one organism to another

food web the overlapping food chains in a community

herbivore an animal that eats plants

carnivore an animal that eats other animals

predator a living thing that hunts other living things for food

prey a living thing that is hunted for food

scavenger an animal that feeds on the remains of dead animals

omnivore an animal that eats both plants and animals

Food Chains and Food Webs

How do communities survive? Communities survive because their populations provide food for one another. In the Blackland Prairie of Texas, grasses and other green plants provide food for insects, such as grasshoppers, and mice. Lizards and birds eat the insects. Bullsnakes lie in wait for a mouse or bird. A snake, in turn, may become a meal for a sharp-eyed red-tailed hawk. What do you think might happen if a drought reduced the amount of grasses in the Blackland Prairie?

EXPLORE

HYPOTHESIZE How can changes in a population lead to changes in the ecosystem it lives in? What kinds of changes might these be? Write a hypothesis in your *Science Journal*. How might you test your ideas?

Investigate How Populations Interact

Use these cards to see what happens to a model ecosystem when changes occur in a population.

PROCEDURES

1. Cut out the cards representing the plants and animals in the ecosystem.

2. Label the top of your paper *Sunlight*.

3. Place the plant cards on the paper, and link each to the sunlight with tape and string.

4. Link each plant-eating animal to a plant card. Link each meat-eating animal to its food source. Only two animals can be attached to a food source. Record the links in your *Science Journal*.

5. Fire destroys half the plants. Remove four plant cards. Rearrange the animal cards. Remove animal cards if more than two animals link to any one food source. Record changes in your *Science Journal*.

CONCLUDE AND APPLY

1. OBSERVE What has happened to the plant eaters as a result of the fire? To the animal eaters?

2. ANALYZE Half of the plants that were lost in the fire grow back again. What happens to the animal populations?

3. EXPERIMENT Try adding or removing plant or animal cards. What happens to the rest of the populations?

GOING FURTHER: Apply

4. DRAW CONCLUSIONS If plants or prey become scarce, their predators may move to a new area. What will happen to the ecosystem the predators move into?

MATERIALS

- tape
- string
- Population Card Resource Master
- *Science Journal*

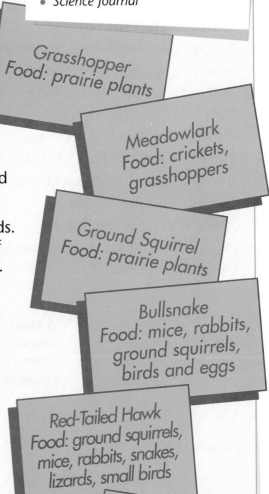

Grasshopper
Food: prairie plants

Meadowlark
Food: crickets, grasshoppers

Ground Squirrel
Food: prairie plants

Bullsnake
Food: mice, rabbits, ground squirrels, birds and eggs

Red-Tailed Hawk
Food: ground squirrels, mice, rabbits, snakes, lizards, small birds

Prairie Plants
Food: made from water, carbon dioxide, and sunlight

Coyote
Food: rabbits, ground squirrels, meadow mice, other rodents

How Do Populations Interact?

How important is a small change in a population? The Explore Activity showed that changes in one population can affect several other populations in the same ecosystem. Every population needs energy in order to survive. Where does that energy come from? The energy in an ecosystem comes from the Sun.

You can feel the Sun's energy as it warms your skin. A meadow mouse scurrying through a Blackland cornfield and a red-tailed hawk diving to snare the mouse can feel it, too. Neither of these animals can directly use the Sun's energy. However, they must have it to move, to breathe, to keep their hearts beating, and to stay alive.

The energy of the Sun is stored in food. The energy in the food is passed from one organism to another in a **food chain**. A food chain is the path energy takes from producers to consumers to decomposers.

On the prairie the first organisms in a food chain are plants. Plants capture the Sun's energy during photosynthesis. This energy is stored in the foods the plant makes for itself.

How Energy Is Passed On

What happens when a plant eater such as a grasshopper or mouse eats the plant? It takes in the energy-rich sugars. Some of the energy is released for the plant eater to use. Some of the energy is also stored in its tissues. Some is lost as heat.

A Texas horned lizard may snap up a grasshopper before a meadowlark can eat it. A bullsnake may compete with a badger for a mouse. Another organism may eat the bullsnake or badger.

The prairie food chain doesn't stop there. The red-tailed hawk flies high

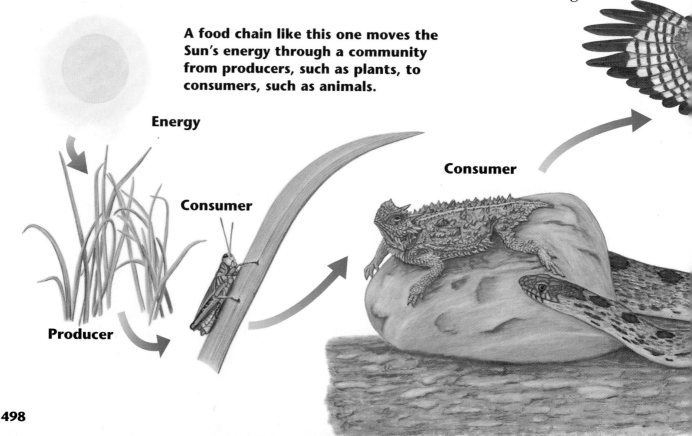

A food chain like this one moves the Sun's energy through a community from producers, such as plants, to consumers, such as animals.

Energy

Consumer

Consumer

Producer

in the air. In the prairie community, the hawk is one of the organisms at the top of the food chain. It eats snakes, mice, lizards, rabbits, and other birds.

The red-tailed hawk doesn't eat plant foods. However, because of the food chain, it gets some of the Sun's energy that was originally stored in them.

What happens when these plants and animals die? They become food for small organisms like crickets, worms, and ants. They are also a food source for microscopic organisms like bacteria.

READING 〽 DIAGRAMS

1. **DISCUSS** There are many food chains in a community. List some animals that, along with the red-tailed hawk, are at the top of prairie food chains.
2. **WRITE** Describe two or more food chains whose top link is the red-tailed hawk.

Consumer

Decomposers

QUICK LAB

Getting Food

HYPOTHESIZE What living things are in your community? Which are producers? Consumers? Write a hypothesis in your *Science Journal.*

MATERIALS
- pencil
- *Science Journal*

PROCEDURES

1. Take a walk outdoors around your home or school. Choose a community to study. Make a list of the living things you see. Don't include people or domestic animals like dogs, cats, and farm animals.

2. **CLASSIFY** Organize the organisms into two groups—those that can make their own food (producers) and those that cannot (consumers).

CONCLUDE AND APPLY

1. **CLASSIFY** Which organisms did you list as producers?

2. **CLASSIFY** Which organisms did you list as consumers?

3. **COMMUNICATE** Draw two or more food chains to show how energy moves through this community.

How Do Food Chains Become Food Webs?

How do organisms in a community compete? Plants compete for sunlight, water, and minerals. Animals compete for the plants and animals they eat.

This competition means that, in an ecosystem, many small food chains may overlap each other. A **food web** is the overlapping food chains. A food chain shows one population that eats or is eaten by another population. A food web shows how one population can be part of more than one food chain. It shows how each population in a community relates to all the other populations.

Producers

Food chains and food webs exist in all ecosystems. Yet wherever they are, they have certain things in common. They all have producers. The producers on land include grasses, trees, and all other organisms that use the Sun's energy to make their own food. In the oceans the main producers are algae.

Eating Producers

Organisms that cannot make their own food are *consumers*. Consumers get energy from the food made by other organisms. Consumers can be grouped according to the type of food they eat. **Herbivores** (hûr′bə vôrz′) eat producers. Both Earth's land and waters swarm with herbivores—animals that eat plants, algae, and other producers.

Eating Herbivores

Herbivores, in turn, are eaten by **carnivores** (kär′nə vôrz′)—animals that eat other animals. All cats, big and small, are carnivores. So are dogs, wolves, foxes, coyotes, and other sharp-toothed animals. The sea also has carnivores. The most frightening of these is the great white shark.

Land Food Web

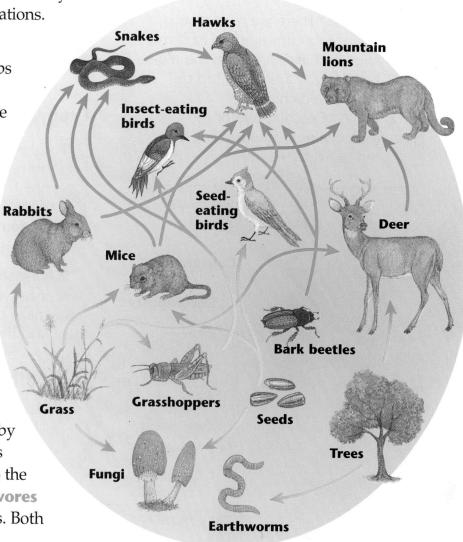

Marine Food Web

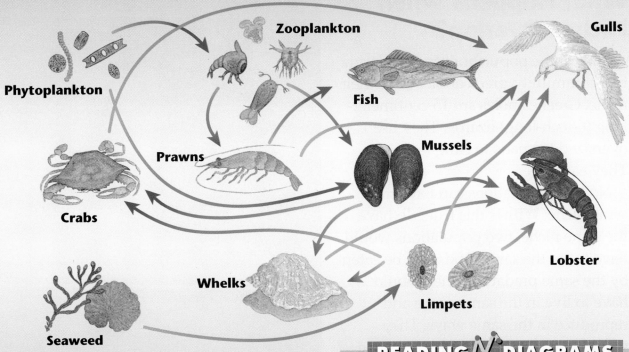

Phytoplankton · Zooplankton · Prawns · Fish · Mussels · Gulls · Crabs · Whelks · Seaweed · Limpets · Lobster

What Is a Predator?

Less fearsome sea dwellers also eat meat. Frolicking seals, playful dolphins, and gentle whales dine on fish, squid, and even penguins.

Living things that hunt other living things for food are **predators**. The hunted are called **prey**. The relationships between predators and prey are a key part of both food chains and food webs.

Yet not all meat eaters are predators. Some animals eat meat but don't hunt it. Such meat eaters are called **scavengers**. They feed on the remains of dead animals. Have you ever seen vultures circling a spot of land? Then you have seen scavengers. Crows are also scavengers. You might see them on a road, pecking on the body of an animal hit by a car.

The sea is home to many scavengers. One of these is the hagfish. It wanders the ocean floor in search of dead or

READING N DIAGRAMS

1. **DISCUSS** Which of these animals are predators? Which of these animals are prey?
2. **WRITE** Explain how scavengers differ from decomposers.

dying fish. Some tiny sea creatures also feed on the remains of dead sea animals.

When an animal eats both animals and plants, it is an **omnivore**. You're an omnivore. Bears are omnivores, too, eating things ranging from berries to salmon.

Every food chain and food web ends with *decomposers* such as worms, insects, bacteria, and fungi. These organisms break down dead matter into substances that can be used by producers. Decomposers break down dead organisms and wastes into simpler molecules. Some of these molecules are absorbed by the decomposers. Some of the molecules are returned to the soil.

What Happens when Niches Overlap?

Like all the populations in the Florida tree community, green anoles have their niche. Greene anoles are 15-centimeter-long (6-inch-long) lizards. They use oversized toe pads to cling to trees. They eat spiders.

No two populations can have the same niche. Why is this true? To have the same niche, two populations would have to eat the same foods and be eaten by the same predators. They would have to live in the same space and reproduce in the same ways. They would have to thrive under the same temperature, moisture, and light conditions. They would have to get the same

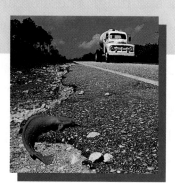

diseases and look and behave *exactly* alike. That is, they would have to be identical. Yet no two populations are identical. Therefore, no two populations have the same niche.

This does not mean that similar populations with different niches do not compete. They do. When two species are very similar, their niches may overlap. Sometimes the competition causes a population to change its niche. This is especially true when a very similar population invades the habitat of another population. This is what happened to Florida's green anole. It had to find another habitat.

The green anole (left), a native of the U.S. southeast, acquired a new niche when Cuban anoles (below) were introduced.

How Did the Anoles Deal with Competition?

HISTORY LINK

At one time green anoles could be spotted all over Florida, perched on the trunks of trees and the branches of bushes. They were adapted to this environment for a number of reasons. Their green color camouflaged them when they were among leaves. Their ability to turn brown did the same when they clung to tree trunks. This made them hard for predators to find.

Then a new and bigger species of anole arrived in Florida from the island of Cuba. Scientists don't know how it made the 144-kilometer (90-mile) trip. However, its size and, perhaps, other characteristics gave it an edge over the smaller green anole.

Soon the smaller green anole *seemed* to disappear, replaced by the Cuban anole. Was it really gone? If not, where could it be?

If you said high in the trees where the leaves were thickest and the green anoles could best hide, your thinking would make sense. It would also be right on target. That's where the scientists found the little green anole. It had found a new niche in its community, high up in the treetops.

How Is Energy Moved in a Community?

Plants capture energy from sunlight. When you eat a plant, how much of that energy the plant captured do you get? All organisms need energy to live. Producers get energy from the Sun. Consumers get it from the foods they eat. However, energy is lost as it passes from one organism to another in a food chain.

You can see the effect of this in the drawing of the energy pyramid on this page. An energy pyramid shows a number of things. It shows that there is less food at the top of the pyramid than at its base. It also shows that there are fewer organisms as you move from bottom to top.

Consumers get their energy from food. The less food there is, the less energy is available. Energy decreases from the base to the top of the pyramid.

In an Antarctic community, algae form the base. Algae are producers that store energy from the Sun.

Small fish that live in the icy waters eat some of these algae. The algae that are not eaten are lost to the community. Their energy is not passed up to the next level of the pyramid. Only some of the energy the fish get is passed up to the next level, too. The fish use some of the energy in swimming and other activities.

ENERGY PYRAMID FOR A LAND FOOD CHAIN

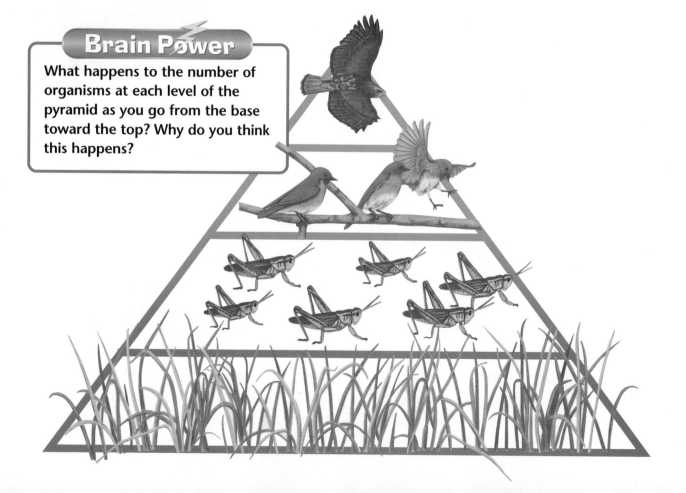

Brain Power

What happens to the number of organisms at each level of the pyramid as you go from the base toward the top? Why do you think this happens?

What Happens to the Energy?

The penguins dive for the small fish and eat as many as they can catch. Yet many fish get away. Nevertheless, the penguins have snared some energy-rich fish food. Some of the energy from the fish is stored in the penguins' tissues. Some of the energy is used to heat their bodies. A dip in the frigid water removes some of this heat from the penguins' bodies. Now they have less energy than they took in from the fish.

Rising from below, a leopard seal clamps its sharp teeth around a helpless penguin and eats it. Does this predator get all the energy that was originally in the algae the fish ate?

No. Energy has been lost at each level in the pyramid.

Kilogram for kilogram there are fewer fish than algae. There are fewer penguins than fish. There are fewer leopard seals than penguins. That's because there is less food and energy available at each higher level in the energy pyramid. The less food and energy there is, the fewer living things that can be supported.

How much energy is lost from one level of an energy pyramid to the next? Scientists have actually measured it. The startling figure is 90 percent! Of all the Sun's energy captured by the algae, the leopard seal gets only one-tenth of one percent.

ENERGY PYRAMID FOR AN OCEAN FOOD CHAIN

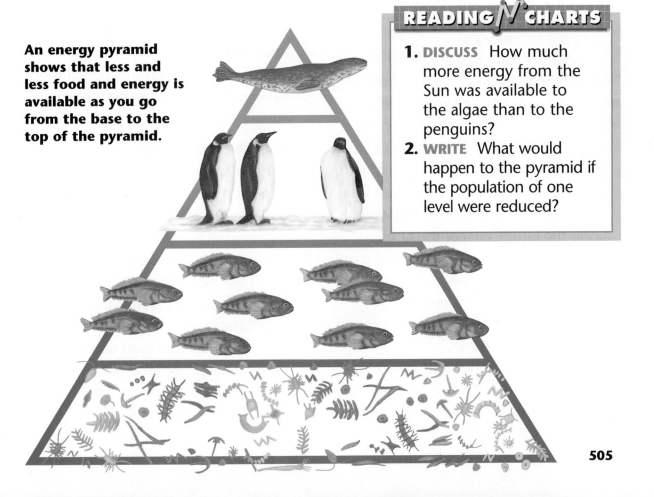

An energy pyramid shows that less and less food and energy is available as you go from the base to the top of the pyramid.

READING CHARTS

1. **DISCUSS** How much more energy from the Sun was available to the algae than to the penguins?
2. **WRITE** What would happen to the pyramid if the population of one level were reduced?

505

What Happens when There Is a Red Tide?

"Ocean Blooms on the Increase off Texas Coast" might not seem like a frightening headline. Yet to an ecologist, or even the average person, it means trouble.

The "blooms" refer to a sudden rapid increase in the population of microscopic sea organisms called *dinoflagilates*. These tiny algae are the producers at the bottom of the ocean food chain. They are a part of every ocean food web.

They are also the base of the ocean energy pyramid. They store the Sun's energy, which is passed up the pyramid. However, in the case of the blooming dinoflagilates, they also pass up poisons!

One dinoflagilate that does this belongs to a group of algae called fire algae. They get their name mainly because of their red color. When they bloom they can turn hundreds of square miles of ocean red. That's why a bloom of these organisms is called a red tide.

People who live close to the water along the Gulf Coast of the United States might get their first hint of a red tide when their throats and noses start to sting. This happens because the poisons produced by the fire algae can come in on sea breezes.

In the sea small fish and mussels feed on the algae. The algae's poison can kill the fish. This reduces the energy

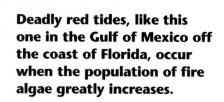

Deadly red tides, like this one in the Gulf of Mexico off the coast of Florida, occur when the population of fire algae greatly increases.

available to consumers higher up in the food chain. Fewer of these consumers can get enough energy to survive. The poison can also kill consumers higher on the food chain. In 1991 California pelicans began to die after eating anchovies that had eaten fire algae.

Dangers to People

People are also affected by red tides. A person who eats poisoned shellfish can become very sick. The shellfish themselves are not harmed. The poisons produced by fire algae seem to only affect the nervous systems of complex animals like fish, birds, and mammals.

What causes a red tide? What triggers a population explosion among poisonous fire algae? Scientists are trying to track down the answer. They've come up with some promising leads.

Clues?

One clue came from Hong Kong, across the Pacific Ocean. Between 1976 and 1986, the number of red tides increased from 2 a year to 18 a year. At the same time, the human population of Hong Kong went up six times. As the human population increased, so did the amount of fertilizers they used. Lots of the fertilizers were washed into the sea. The nutrients in the fertilizers fed the algae.

Could human activities cause red tides? When the Japanese government created rules that reduced ocean pollution, the number of red tides in the less polluted water was cut in half. The evidence seems to point to the conclusion that at least one cause of red tides is human activity.

If a food chain, food web, or energy pyramid changes, the result might affect humans. On farms a decrease in predators like insect-eating birds might lead to a population explosion of insects. If the insects are plant pests, crops may suffer, food prices may soar, and farmers may lose money.

If there were no predators to eat these insects, what might happen to the crops?

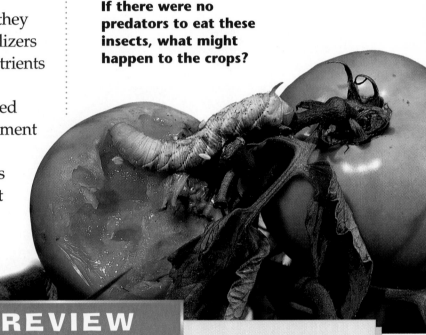

REVIEW

1. What is the original source of energy in an ecosystem?

2. Explain why it is, or is not, possible to have a food chain that has only a producer and a decomposer.

3. COMPARE AND CONTRAST What is the relationship between a food chain and a food web?

4. Choose a meat product you eat to construct a food chain that includes yourself as the final consumer.

5. CRITICAL THINKING *Analyze* Explain why there are fewer coyotes than mice in a prairie ecosystem.

WHY IT MATTERS THINK ABOUT IT
Think about a food web in your local ecosystem. What might happen if one of the plant populations died out?

WHY IT MATTERS WRITE ABOUT IT
Write a paragraph describing what might happen if the number of herbivores in your local ecosystem suddenly decreased.

BANKING ON SEEDS

Where do farmers get the corn seeds they plant each year? Before farmers knew about plant heredity, they just planted leftover seeds from the last year's crop. There were thousands of varieties of corn. Then farmers learned about hybrids.

Ears of corn from a hybrid all become ripe at the same time. They're the same size, so harvesting is easier. Today only six varieties make up 71 percent of all the corn grown in the United States.

Farmers can breed corn that thrives despite chemical pesticides and fertilizers. Many crops grow faster, produce more food, and store better.

That's the good news about farming. There's bad news, too. If farmers grow just one kind of plant, a disease or pest invasion can wipe out a whole crop.

That's what happened in Ireland during the 1840s. Almost every Irish farmer grew the same kind of potato. When a potato disease hit, it killed almost the entire Irish potato crop. There was a serious shortage of food, and many Irish people moved to the U.S.

If farmers grow only a few kinds of plants, other plants become extinct. Then animals that depend on a specific kind of plant die out as well.

As hybrids became more common, people became alarmed by the number of plant types dying out. Consequently seeds were collected from existing plants and placed in seed banks. The banks preserve the seeds from plants that otherwise might become extinct. Farmers have also been encouraged to grow more varied crops.

Social Studies Link

In a field of hybrids, all the corn looks the same.

DISCUSSION STARTER

1. How did hybrids change the way farmers farmed?

2. Why were seed banks started?

To learn more about seed banks, visit *www.mhschool.com/science* and enter the keyword BANKS.

*inter*NET
CONNECTION

Cycles of Life

In what order do you think the scenes on this page occurred? Could the scenes have happened in reverse order, too? Organisms require certain things to stay alive. Yet as they live, they use up these things. How can they, and the generations that follow them, continue to inhabit Earth?

WHY IT MATTERS

Animals play various roles in the water, carbon, and nitrogen cycles.

EXPLORE

HYPOTHESIZE How can we, and all living things, keep using water every day and not use it all up? Write a hypothesis in your *Science Journal*. How would you experiment to test your ideas?

SCIENCE WORDS

water cycle the continuous movement of water between Earth's surface and the air, changing from liquid to gas to liquid

carbon cycle the continuous transfer of carbon between the atmosphere and living things

nitrogen cycle the transfer of nitrogen from the atmosphere to plants and back to the atmosphere and directly into plants again

Investigate What Happens to Water

Use a model to see how water in the environment is recycled.

PROCEDURES

1. Place the dry paper towel, the dry soil, and the bowl of water in the plastic container. Close the container with the lid.

2. OBSERVE Place the container under a lamp or in direct sunlight. Observe every ten minutes for a class period. Record your observations in your *Science Journal*.

3. REPEAT Observe the container on the second day. Record your observations.

CONCLUDE AND APPLY

1. COMPARE AND CONTRAST What did you observe the first day? What did you observe the second day?

2. INFER What was the source of the water? What was the source of the energy that caused changes in the container?

GOING FURTHER: Apply

3. DRAW CONCLUSIONS What happened to the water?

4. INFER What parts of the water cycle does this model show?

MATERIALS

- plastic food container with clear cover
- small bowl or cup filled with water
- small tray filled with dry soil
- 4-cm-square (1.6-in.-square) piece of paper towel
- 100-W lamp (if available)
- *Science Journal*

What Happens to Water?

Does water get lost when it evaporates? The Explore Activity showed that water is not lost from an environment. It evaporates, condenses, and moves from one part of the environment to another. In other words the water is recycled.

This is what you saw happening in the photographs of the African water hole on page 510. The same thing happens on a much larger scale in nature. This process of naturally recycling water on Earth is called the water cycle. Here's how it works.

Condensation As the moist air rises hgher and higher, it cools. When cooled enough, water vapor condenses into tiny water droplets or changes from vapor to tiny ice crystals. If enough of them gather, they form a cloud. In clouds the droplets and ice crystals can grow larger and heavier. Water in the atmosphere represents only $\frac{1}{10,000}$ of Earth's water.

Flash flooding in an arroyo in Arizona

Condensation

Evaporation

OCEAN

Evaporation

MOUNTAINS

RIVER

DESERT

Collection Some of the water flows into streams, lakes, and rivers. Some of it soaks into the ground. This stored water is called *groundwater*. Lots of this water slowly finds its way back into Earth's oceans. The oceans contain more than 97 percent of the world's water.

READING DIAGRAMS

1. **DISCUSS** Explain the differences between evaporation, condensation, and precipitation.
2. **WRITE** What is the difference between runoff and groundwater?

Precipitation

Eventually the droplets or ice crystals become so large and heavy that they can no longer stay up in the air. They fall to Earth's surface as precipitation—rain, snow, sleet, or hail.

Snow in a cold, northern region of the world

Precipitation

Evaporation

Evaporation

Heat from the Sun is absorbed by oceans, seas, lakes, streams, ponds, puddles, and even dew. This heat energy makes the water evaporate and rise into the air. The Sun's energy also evaporates water that collects on the leaves of plants.

Runoff

On land some of the rain seeps into the ground. However, some of the water flows downhill across the surface instead. This water becomes *runoff*. Rapidly melting snow, sleet, or hail can also become runoff.

LAKE

FOREST AND FIELDS

Runoff

Transpiration

Transpiration

Transpiration

Living Things

Organisms are also part of the water cycle. Plants remove water from the soil. Some of this water returns to the atmosphere through the plants' leaves. Animals also take in water. Some of this water returns to the environment through the skin or during breathing. Some returns as waste products.

EARTH LINK SCIENCE

Plants play an important role in the water cycle.

513

This dead tree is being decomposed by fungi, shown here, and microscopic bacteria.

What Happens to a Dead Tree?

How can a dead tree help living things? A wind howls through the night in a forest. Suddenly the darkness is filled with the sounds of snapping branches as an old tree begins to topple. Down the tree falls. The ground shivers as the huge trunk crashes down. A few animals shriek. Then only the wind whistles in the night.

Yet other things are beginning to happen. The tree, which was once part of one food web, is becoming part of another food web.

Even though the tree is now dead, it is being turned into substances other organisms need to survive. Some of these organisms are other trees. The dead tree is providing elements for living trees. When these trees die, they will provide elements that other trees

need. The cycling of matter is continuous. How does this happen?

An old, fallen tree is made of wood, bark, and other dead tree tissue. That tissue holds all sorts of complex chemical substances. Most of the chemicals are too complex to be used by most other living things. They need to be broken down into simpler chemicals.

How Decomposers Help

They are organisms that recycle matter in dead organisms. They're called decomposers. Worms, crickets, cockroaches, bacteria, and fungi are decomposers. These organisms can break down dead wood and other dead plant parts into *carbon dioxide* and

Brain Power

How else might a dead tree help living things?

514

ammonia. All living plants need carbon dioxide in order to make sugars. Ammonia is a simple substance that contains the element *nitrogen*. Nitrogen is extremely important for plants. No plant can live or grow without nitrogen. All organisms need nitrogen in order to make proteins.

Fertilizers

Nitrogen is a chemical found in plant *fertilizers*. Fertilizers are substances used to add minerals to the soil. Some fertilizers are natural. These are decaying plants and animals, and animal wastes. Other fertilizers are made in factories. Both natural and artificial fertilizers contain nitrogen. The next time you go to a store that sells fertilizers, read the labels. You're sure to find nitrogen as one of the ingredients.

As you'll soon discover, like water, nitrogen and carbon have their own cycles in nature. Earth, like the setup in the Explore Activity, is a closed system. With the exception of energy, almost nothing gets out or gets in. It is recycled.

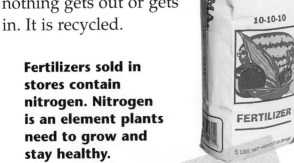

Fertilizers sold in stores contain nitrogen. Nitrogen is an element plants need to grow and stay healthy.

Guaranteed Analysis

Total Nitrogen (N) 10%
Available Phosphate (P₂O₅) 10%
Soluble Potash (K₂O) 10%
The Plant Foods used in Espoma Garden Food are Ammonium Sulfate, Triple Superphosphate and Potash. Also contained in Garden Food is the natural mineral limestone.

Food 10-10-10 is an agricultural

Soil Sample

HYPOTHESIZE How do nutrients get recycled in nature? Write a hypothesis in your *Science Journal*. Test it by examining a soil core.

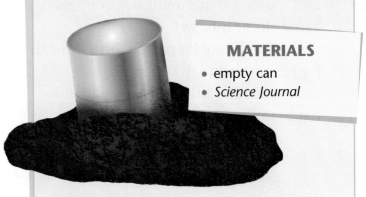

MATERIALS
- empty can
- *Science Journal*

PROCEDURES

▨▨▨ **SAFETY** Do not touch the sharp edges of the can.

1. Go to a wooded area in a park or other location near your school. Find a patch of soft, moist soil.

2. Press a can, open side down, into the soil to get a core sample. You might have to gently rotate the can so it cuts into the soil.

3. Carefully remove the core so it stays in one piece.

4. **OBSERVE** In your *Science Journal*, describe and draw the core.

CONCLUDE AND APPLY

1. **INFER** From top to bottom, what kind of matter does the core hold?

2. **INFER** In what order did the layers form?

3. **INFER** Which layer holds the most available nutrients? Explain.

515

How Is Carbon Recycled?

Sometimes simple activities can turn into a scientific investigation. Cooking a meal doesn't seem to have much in common with a scientific experiment. Yet what happens if a meal made of baked potatoes, steak, and toasted marshmallows is burned? What do you have?

The food may be ruined, but you can make an important scientific discovery. The burned food, which is made up of plant and animal products, is black and looks like charcoal. It contains the same black substance that makes up charcoal. That substance is *carbon*.

What scientific information is hidden in the ruined meal? One of the elements that make up all living things is carbon.

Nature recycles carbon, and it is used by all organisms. The recycling of this important substance is called the **carbon cycle**.

Nature recycles carbon in the carbon cycle. At the same time, oxygen is also being cycled through ecosystems.

Photosynthesis During photosynthesis plants use the carbon from carbon dioxide to make sugars, starches, and proteins.

Car exhaust

Decaying matter

Oil

Carbon Dioxide Carbon dioxide enters the air when plants and animals decay. It enters the air when animals breathe out. It enters the air when fossil fuels such as coal, oil, gasoline, and natural gas are burned. Forest fires also add carbon dioxide to the air.

READING 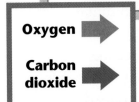 DIAGRAMS

1. **DISCUSS** When does carbon dioxide enter the air?
2. **WRITE** What happens to carbon when living things die?

Oxygen ➡

Carbon dioxide ➡

Oxygen

Carbon dioxide

Plants Plants take in carbon dioxide and give off oxygen, which animals use

Death, Decay, Storage When living things die, decay releases the carbon compounds in their bodies. Some of it is turned into carbon dioxide by decomposers. Over millions of years, some of it turns into fossil fuels.

Animals Animals eat plant sugars, starches, proteins, and other substances. The carbon in these substances is used by animals to make their own body chemicals.

How Is Nitrogen Recycled?

What do you need nitrogen for? When you eat meat, fish, cereal, or vegetables, you are taking in the nutrients that your body needs to make *proteins*. Proteins are a part of your muscles and many cell structures.

Among other things proteins are rich in the element nitrogen. You need nitrogen to make parts of your body, such as muscles, nerves, skin, bones, blood, and digestive juices.

If you know something about Earth science, you might say: "Who needs to eat protein to get nitrogen? The air is 78 percent nitrogen." That's true. However, animals and plants cannot use the nitrogen that is in the air. Animals get nitrogen by eating proteins. Plants get nitrogen by absorbing it from the soil. Some plants even get nitrogen with the help of a special group of bacteria.

The way nitrogen moves between the air, soil, plants, and animals is called the **nitrogen cycle**. Here's how it works.

Air Air is made up of about 78 percent nitrogen gas.

Nitrogen-Fixing Bacteria Some bacteria that grow on pea and bean roots give those plants the nitrogen they need. The bacteria turn nitrogen gas in the air to nitrogen-containing substances the plants can use to make their proteins.

Decomposers When the plant dies, decomposers in the soil break down the plant proteins. One product is the nitrogen-containing substance ammonia. Soil bacteria change ammonia into nitrites.

Ammonia

READING N DIAGRAMS

1. **DISCUSS** Compare the different ways various kinds of bacteria help in the nitrogen cycle.
2. **WRITE** How do pea and bean plants get the nitrogen they need?

Denitrifying Bacteria Some soil bacteria turn nitrates back into nitrogen gas.

Animals Animals eat plant proteins, or they eat other animals that eat plant proteins. Animal wastes contain nitrogen compounds.

Plants Plants absorb nitrates dissolved in water through their roots. The nitrogen is then used by the plant to make proteins.

Nitrogen compounds

Nitrites   **Nitrates**

Nitrites and ammonia

Bacteria Certain bacteria can use nitrogen from the air to make nitrogen-containing substances called *nitrites*. Other bacteria can turn nitrites into *nitrates*—another group of nitrogen-containing substances.

519

Why Recycle?

Have you ever seen a paper bag with a symbol that says "Printed on recycled paper"? Why is this important?

The environment provides the materials people use to make products. Sunlight is an *inexhaustible resource*. The Sun will last for millions, if not billions, of years. Other resources, however, are not inexhaustible. The paper to make books, magazines, newspapers, and containers comes from the wood in trees. Metals mined from the ground are used to make cars, ships, pots and pans, appliances, and many other things. Glass is made from sand. Plastics are made from chemicals in oil found deep underground.

Wood, metals, sand, and oil are called *raw materials*. Raw materials are the building blocks of products.

Many raw materials, such as oil and metals, are *nonrenewable resources*. Earth's oil was formed millions of years ago. There's a limited amount of it. When it's gone, it's gone forever.

Certain other resources, such as wood, are *renewable resources*. If trees are cut down for lumber and paper, more can be planted to replace them. Even so, trees take years to grow. Recycling paper and other wood products can help keep forests from being destroyed. This can also help keep the animals in them from losing their homes and, perhaps, facing extinction.

MATH LINK

This graph shows the percent of different materials in garbage thrown away each day by each person in the United States. Study the graph and answer the questions.

Percent vs. Material bar graph: Plastics, Food wastes, Yard wastes, Paper, Other, Metals, Glass

READING GRAPHS

1. **DISCUSS** Let's say there are 280,000,000 people in the United States. Each person throws away 1.8 kilograms (4 pounds) of garbage each day. How much garbage is thrown away by all the people each day?
2. **DISCUSS** How much of this is paper?
3. **WRITE** If a book has a mass of 2 kilograms (4.4 pounds), how many books would it take to make up the amount of paper thrown away?

How Are Recycled Products Used?

For all of these reasons, many people urge that we conserve raw materials by recycling them—just as nature recycles water, carbon, and nitrogen. Many communities have recycling programs. Glass products are collected in one set of bins, metal containers in another. Plastics are collected in still another. Papers are bundled up. Service stations save oil that is drained from car engines.

These materials are then sent to recycling centers. The manufacturers break them down into raw materials that can be used to make new products. What's the result? Less garbage piles up in our environment. Fewer raw materials are wasted. Less of Earth's valuable raw materials are used up.

The environment provides all the things you need. It provides food for you to eat, water for you to drink, and raw materials for the products you use. The environment will keep doing these things as long as we let it recycle the substances that make life possible and comfortable. People can either help or hinder this process.

REVIEW

1. By what process does water move from oceans, lakes, rivers, and streams into the air?

2. What organisms turn a dead tree into substances that can be used by living trees?

3. Describe three ways that carbon dioxide gets into the air.

4. **IDENTIFY** Name two substances that contain nitrogen.

5. **CRITICAL THINKING** *Apply* How can you and other people conserve trees?

WHY IT MATTERS THINK ABOUT IT
Why is it important to recycle cans, bottles, and paper?

WHY IT MATTERS WRITE ABOUT IT
Write a paragraph explaining the importance of using recycled materials.

READING SKILL
Look at the diagram on pages 516–517. Write a paragraph explaining what information you can get from reading this diagram.

The Human Touch

How do humans affect ecosystems? Sometimes in good ways, but other times humans can harm and change an ecosystem. Here are a few examples.

Thousands of years ago, people began irrigating crops, but not with fresh water. As irrigation water evaporated, it left salts behind. Over time the soil became poisoned. Crops that had once thrived in the fields stopped growing.

Today farmers use fertilizers containing nitrogen. Runoff carries the nitrogen into streams, lakes, and the ocean. Plants need some nitrogen to grow, but too much causes overgrowth. Water plants can grow so thick that they use up the oxygen and block the sunlight. Most water animals can't live in such conditions.

Gases in the exhausts from humans' cars are high in nitrogen compounds. So are gases from high-temperature burning in factories and power plants. The nitrogen pollutes the air and contributes to acid rain.

Acid rain can release poisonous aluminum compounds into the soil in forests. Trees begin to die. Living trees remove carbon from the air, while decaying or burnt trees release it.

When they burn fossil fuels, humans also increase the carbon dioxide in the air. Evidence suggests that this causes global warming—a rise in average air temperatures around the world.

Science, Technology, and Society

DISCUSSION STARTER

1. How have humans changed ecosystems?

2. What causes global warming?

Agricultural runoff has affected some fishing areas.

You can see the effects of acid rain on this forest.

To learn more about the consequences of human behavior, visit *www.mhschool.com/science* and enter the keyword PEOPLE.

*inter*NET
CONNECTION

SCIENCE WORDS

abiotic factor p.484   habitat p.489
biotic factor p.485   niche p.489
community p.488   population p.488
ecology p.484   predator p.501
ecosystem p.484   prey p.501

USING SCIENCE WORDS

Number a paper from 1 to 10. Fill in 1 to 5 with words from the list above.

1. Living things make up the ___?___ in an ecosystem.

2. Water is an example of a(n) ___?___.

3. A(n) ___?___ includes all the members of a single species in a certain place.

4. Corn, elms, and armadillos are part of the ___?___ of the prairie ecosystem.

5. The study of how living and nonliving things interact in the same place is called ___?___.

6–10. Pick five words from the list above that were not used in 1 to 5, and use each in a sentence.

UNDERSTANDING SCIENCE IDEAS

11. What is the difference between predators and prey?

12. Describe two ways food moves through a community.

13. What is the difference between biotic and abiotic factors?

14. Explain why carbon and nitrogen are always available to living things.

15. Describe the role of a vulture.

USING IDEAS AND SKILLS

16. What are two important characteristics of an energy pyramid?

17. What is the relationship between herbivores and carnivores?

18. **USE VARIABLES** Study the table below. Suggest a reason for the change in eagle population.

Ecosystem Changes

Year	Grasslands	Rabbits	Eagles
1960	26,418 km² (10,200 mi²)	101,000	1,050
1970	23,569 km² (9,100 mi²)	89,000	864
1980	21,238 km² (8,200 mi²)	78,000	782
1990	13,727 km² (5,300 mi²)	42,000	386
2000	13,313 km² (5,140 mi²)	41,900	378

19. **READING SKILL: READING DIAGRAMS** Examine the diagram on pages 512–513. How are condensation and evaporation related?

20. **THINKING LIKE A SCIENTIST** Plants need nitrogen, which is in the air. However, they can't take this nitrogen in. How do plants get nitrogen?

PROBLEMS and PUZZLES
Fire, Exit

SAFETY Wear goggles. Carbon dioxide is a useful fire extinguisher. Pour about $\frac{2}{3}$ cm ($\frac{1}{4}$ in.) of vinegar into a jar. Add a spoonful of baking soda to the vinegar. This mixture produces carbon dioxide gas, which causes bubbling. While the mixture is bubbling, use a pair of tongs to lower a lighted match into the glass. What happens?

CHAPTER 12

LIVING THINGS INTERACT

Penguins spend a lot of time in water catching fish, but they lay eggs and raise their young on land. They make nests in the grass or in a hollow dug in the bare ground. They make nests in large groups, or colonies, called rookeries. As many as a million birds can live together in one rookery.

How large can a population of penguins get? Why doesn't the population just grow and grow?

 In Chapter 12 summarize as you read. Write what each two pages are about before you move on to the next two.

WHY IT MATTERS

Organisms can help or hinder the survival of other organisms.

SCIENCE WORDS

limiting factor anything that controls the growth or survival of an organism or population

adaptation a characteristic that helps an organism survive in its environment

symbiosis a relationship between two kinds of organisms over time

mutualism a relationship between two kinds of organisms that benefits both

parasitism a relationship in which one kind of organism lives on or in another organism and may harm the organism

commensalism a relationship between two kinds of organisms that benefits one without harming the other

Surviving in Ecosystems

What affects the size of a population? Some forests are so thick with trees and shrubs that you would have a tough time hiking through them. Yet hiking through other forests would be as easy as walking down a country road or the street in front of your house. That's because these forests have few trees or shrubs. Why?

EXPLORE

HYPOTHESIZE What kinds of things do organisms need in their environment in order to survive? What happens when these things are limited or unavailable? Write a hypothesis in your *Science Journal*. Test your ideas.

Investigate What Controls the Growth of Populations

Experiment to see how light and water can affect the growth and survival of seeds.

PROCEDURES

1. Label the cartons 1 to 4. Fill carton 1 and 2 with dry potting soil. Fill cartons 3 and 4 with moistened potting soil. Fill the cartons to within 2 cm of the top.

2. Plant ten seeds in each carton, and cover the seeds with 0.5 cm of soil.

3. **USE VARIABLES** Place cartons 1 and 3 in a well-lighted area. Place cartons 2 and 4 in a dark place. Label the cartons to show if they are wet or dry and in the light or in the dark.

4. **OBSERVE** Examine the cartons each day for four days. Keep the soil moist in cartons 3 and 4. Record your observations in your *Science Journal.*

5. **COMPARE** Observe the plants for two weeks after they sprout. Continue to keep the soil moist in the cartons, and record your observations in your *Science Journal.*

CONCLUDE AND APPLY

1. **COMMUNICATE** How many seeds sprouted in each carton?

2. **OBSERVE** After two weeks how many plants in each carton were still living?

3. **IDENTIFY** What factor is needed for seeds to sprout? What is needed for bean plants to grow? What evidence do you have to support your answer?

GOING FURTHER: Problem Solving

4. **CAUSE AND EFFECT** Why did some seeds sprout and then die?

MATERIALS

- 4 small, clean milk cartons with the tops removed
- 40 pinto bean seeds that have been soaked overnight
- soil
- water
- *Science Journal*

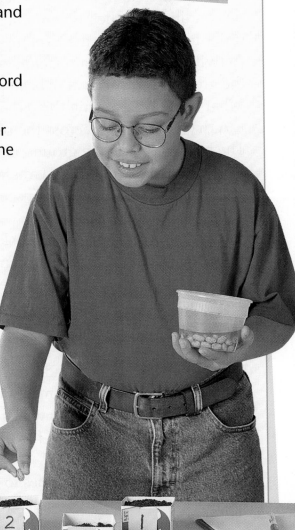

What Controls the Growth of Populations?

How much do living things depend on conditions in their environment in order to survive? As the Explore Activity showed, certain factors control the growth and survival of bean plants. What about other living things?

A dry wind howls across the prairie. The hot Sun bakes the ground below. No rain has fallen in days. Grasses have withered. Plant-eating insects have gone hungry.

High in the bright, cloudless sky, a hawk wheels one way and then another. Its sharp eyes sweep over the barren land below. An unsuspecting deer mouse scurries along the ground in search of an insect.

The mouse's tan fur blends in with the dusty soil, but its movement gives it away. The hawk tucks in its wings and dives like a falling rock. In a flash its talons grab the mouse.

Hidden in this story are clues to how the size of a population is limited.

Organisms like coyotes (above) and raccoons (left) compete with each other for resources such as food, water, and territory.

Anything that controls the growth or survival of a population is called a **limiting factor**.

Some limiting factors are nonliving. In the story the sunlight, wind, water, and temperature were nonliving limiting factors. They controlled the population of grasses on the prairie.

The grasses, insects, deer mice, and hawks were living limiting factors. The grasses had withered. There was less food for plant-eating insects, so the number of insects living in the prairie decreased. That meant there was less food for the insect-eating deer mice. The deer mouse population was also limited by the hawks, which are predators.

Brain Power

Identify a population in your area. What limiting factors affect this population? What is the role of each limiting factor?

How Do Predators Compete?

Predators are the hunters. The hunted are the prey. The number of predators in an ecosystem affects the number of prey. The number of prey in an ecosystem can also determine how many predators the ecosystem can support. If there were few hawks, the deer mouse population might stay steady or even rise. More hawks, however, mean fewer deer mice.

Hawks also compete with other predators, like coyotes and raccoons. Coyotes and raccoons hunt many animals, including small rodents like deer mice.

Coyotes and raccoons also compete with each other for food, water, and places to live, and for a territory. The population that wins such competitions is likely to grow.

Yet even a growing population faces problems. Its size will soon limit its growth. The organisms in the population will become crowded. They will have to compete with one another for food, water, and shelter. Some will die. Eventually there will be enough for the number of organisms that remain.

Overcrowding limits the growth of any population.

Playground Space

HYPOTHESIZE How much playground space does each student in your classroom have? Write a hypothesis in your *Science Journal*. Test it.

MATERIALS
- meterstick
- *Science Journal*

1. Working in groups use a meterstick to measure the length and width of your playground.

2. Multiply the length by the width to find the area in square meters.

3. Count the number of students in your class.

4. To find out how much space each student has, divide the area of the playground by the number of students.

CONCLUDE AND APPLY

1. **INFER** What would happen to the space each student had if the number of students doubled?

2. **INFER** Assume two other classes with the same number of students as yours used the playground at the same time as your class. What effect might this have on your class?

How Do Plants Survive in Harsh Environments?

Plants live almost everywhere on Earth. They live in deserts, where rain seldom falls. They live in the icy northland, where sunlight is weak and winters are long and frigid. They live on the floor of rain forests, where the Sun rarely shines and the soil has few nutrients.

Plants can survive in these conditions because they have developed special characteristics. Characteristics that help an organism survive in its environment are called **adaptations**.

One of the harshest areas for plant growth is a desert. What adaptations do desert plants have that allow them to live where less than 2 inches of rain falls each year? Most people in the United States live where that much rain might fall in a few hours.

The Sonoran Desert stretches from southern California to western Arizona. If you were to visit there, you would see the barrel cactus. The barrel cactus is very well adapted to desert conditions.

GEOGRAPHY LiNK

Sonoran Desert

The barrel cactus is adapted to the harsh conditions of the Sonoran Desert.

How Does the Barrel Cactus Survive?

The plant's roots are very shallow and grow only about 3 inches into the dry soil. There is an advantage to this. When rain does fall, the roots catch the rain and soak it up very quickly. However, during long dry spells, the fine ends of the roots fall off. What's the advantage? The lack of a fine network of root ends prevents water stored in the cactus from passing out into the soil.

The stem of the barrel cactus also helps it survive in the desert. It is folded and covered with needle-sharp spines. What are the advantages?

The stem stores water. The folds, which are deepest during dry spells, protect moist parts of the stem from hot, dry desert winds. Otherwise these winds would draw away water from the stem's surface. The spines keep away birds and small animals that try to get water from the stems of plants. If you have a small spiny cactus plant at home, you've probably learned two things—you don't have to water it often, and it is better not to touch it.

READING MAPS

WRITE Describe where in the United States the Sonoran Desert is.

531

How Do Different Kinds of Organisms Interact?

Different kinds of organisms interact with each other in a number of different ways. You have already seen that some organisms hunt others. Some organisms are predators. Some organisms are prey. You have also seen that different kinds of organisms may compete with each other for food or territory. Two different kinds of predators may hunt the same prey. However, there are also other kinds of relationships between different kinds of organisms. Some of these relationships are long lasting.

In nature a relationship between two kinds of organisms that lasts over a period of time is called **symbiosis**. There are different kinds of symbiosis. Sometimes both organisms benefit from the relationship. Sometimes one organism benefits while harming the other. Sometimes only one benefits, and the other is not affected. Let's take a closer look at each kind of symbiosis.

Mutualism

When a relationship between two kinds of organisms benefits both of them, it is called **mutualism**.

A strange-looking plant grows in the Mojave Desert of southern California. It's called a Joshua tree, or yucca plant.

When this tree's creamy flowers are in bloom, small gray shadows seem to dart from flower to flower. A more careful look reveals that the "shadows" are actually moths. These are yucca moths.

Yucca trees and yucca moths depend on each other for survival. Each helps the other reproduce.

Mojave Desert

How Do They Help Each Other?

Yucca moths cannot survive without yucca trees. The yucca trees would also quickly become extinct if the moths vanished. The yucca moths and the yucca trees benefit from each other and share a relationship of mutualism. How does this work?

At night a female yucca moth visits a yucca flower. Inside the flower the moth picks up pollen and rolls it up into a ball, which it holds gently in its mouth. Then the moth flutters over to another flower. There it makes a hole in the flower's ovary. The moth injects its eggs through the hole. Finally, it packs the sticky ball of pollen onto the flower's stigma. The stigma and ovary are female reproductive parts of a flower. Pollen holds male sex cells.

In protecting its eggs, the moth has also pollinated the yucca flower. The pollinated flower can then make seeds. Eventually some of the seeds will sprout into new yucca plants. This means yucca plants will continue to grow in the desert.

The moth's eggs and the tree's seeds develop at the same time. When the eggs hatch into larvae, the larvae will feed on some of the seeds. All this is happening inside the protective ovary wall. The larvae are not only getting needed food, they are also safe from predators.

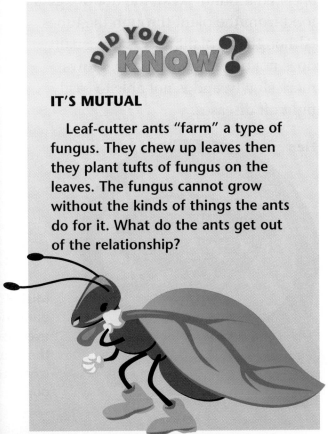

DID YOU KNOW?

IT'S MUTUAL

Leaf-cutter ants "farm" a type of fungus. They chew up leaves then they plant tufts of fungus on the leaves. The fungus cannot grow without the kinds of things the ants do for it. What do the ants get out of the relationship?

Parasitism

A relationship in which one kind of organism lives on or in another organism and may harm that organism is called **parasitism** (par′ə sī tiz′əm). The organisms that live on or in other organisms are called *parasites* (par′ə sīts′). The organisms they feed on are called *hosts*. The parasites benefit from the relationship. The hosts are harmed by it.

Fleas are parasites of dogs and cats. The dogs and cats are hosts of the fleas. The fleas live off the blood of these pets and give nothing back but itching and irritation. Plants also have parasites, which often are other plants.

The bright orange dodder plant has little chlorophyll. This means that it can't make enough food to live on. Instead it winds around a plant that can make its own food. The dodder then sends tubes into the stem of the plant it is coiled around. Next, the dodder gets food from the plant through the tubes. Although the plant it lives on usually does not die, it is weakened, grows more slowly, and is not able to easily fight off diseases.

The coiling dodder plant, which can't make enough of its own food, draws food from other plants.

Flea

Mistletoe is another parasitic plant. It is an evergreen that grows on the trunk or branches of trees such as hawthorn, poplar, fir, or apple.

Some tropical fish are protected from predators by the poison in an anemone's tentacles.

Orchids benefit from their position on the trunks of trees.

Commensalism

Few plants can grow on the floor of a rain forest. One reason is that the thick canopy above keeps light from reaching the ground. If plants could climb trees, they might overcome this. However, some plants, like orchids, attach themselves to the trunks of trees high above the rain forest floor. The orchids, which make their own food, don't take anything from the trees. They simply use the trees to get needed sunlight. This relationship where one organism benefits from another without harming or helping it is called **commensalism** (kə men'sə liz'əm).

Many animals also have this kind of relationship. There are certain tropical fish that live unharmed among the poisonous tentacles of sea anemones. The anemones provide safety for the fish. Yet the fish neither harm nor help the anemones.

When Changes Come, What Survives?

About 18,000 years ago, great sheets of ice moved deep into the center of what is now the United States. Vast ice sheets also covered much of Europe and parts of South America. Sea levels dropped as more and more water froze. New land was exposed. Earth was a cold place.

Slowly Earth began to warm up. The ice melted. Sea levels rose. Coastal land became flooded.

These kinds of changes have occurred no less than seven times during the past 700,000 years. Scientists call these cold periods *ice ages*.

Earth has also changed in other ways. Over millions of years, continents have moved north and south, east and west. Huge mountain-sized rocks have crashed into Earth. Volcanoes have poured gases and dust into the air.

Each of these events has had an effect on living things. Some have died out, or become extinct. Others have survived. Why did some of these creatures vanish, while others survived?

Even today volcanoes fill the air with ash, dust, and soot.

What Killed the Dinosaurs?

Let's travel back in time to a day about 65 million years ago. Fossil evidence indicates that dinosaurs shared the land with many other animals. These animals included frogs, snails, insects, turtles, snakes, and some small furry mammals. Plants of all kinds grew everywhere. The seas were full of organisms like fish, sea urchins, clams, and algae.

Then a meteorite up to 10 kilometers (6 miles) in diameter roared in from outer space. It weighed perhaps 200,000 tons. It streaked downward at 16 to 21 kilometers (10 to 13 miles) a second, crashing into Earth just north of Mexico's Yucatan Peninsula.

The impact created a tremendous explosion. It gouged out a crater 64 kilometers (40 miles) across and threw huge amounts of dust into the sky. The dust may have blanketed the sky for months, even years. Sunlight was probably blocked from reaching the ground.

Plants needing lots of sunlight may have died out. That means that the large plant-eating dinosaurs could not get enough food. They may have died out.

The large dinosaurs preying on plant eaters would have also died out. It may have been that every animal weighing more than about 121 kilograms (55 pounds) became extinct.

Yet many of the smaller animals could have survived. They needed less food to live. They could have moved more easily from habitat to habitat. They would no longer have been in competition with dinosaurs. They would have been free to grow in size and variety.

Possibly a world once ruled by dinosaurs became ruled by mammals. If not for such a catastrophe 65 million years ago, perhaps dinosaurs would still roam Earth today.

Scientific evidence suggests that about 65 million years ago, an asteroid from outer space may have struck Earth, killing off many animals and plants.

How Do People Change the Environment?

How do you affect your environment? About fifteen times a minute, you change the environment. That's the number of times you probably breathe in and out every 60 seconds. Each time you exhale, you add carbon dioxide and water to the air. Each time you inhale, you remove oxygen.

The amount of these substances you breathe in and out is small. Yet they change the environment around you and far away. That's because air circulates around Earth. Those molecules of carbon dioxide you exhaled might find their way into a local tree or a plant miles away. Oxygen that the plant gives off might be inhaled by an animal even farther from your home.

Although living thousands of miles from you, the woolly lemur (above) and the spot-billed toucanet (left) are affected by what you and other people do.

Eventually some of the air you exhaled might go though several cycles. In the process that air might also travel around the world.

Some of that air might find its way into a jaborandi (zha'bə ran'dē') tree in northern Brazil. Some of it might wind up in a periwinkle shrub in Madagascar. Madagascar is an island in the Indian Ocean off the east coast of Africa.

The plants use the carbon to build their stems, leaves, roots, and other parts. Some of these parts will be eaten by animals. They might be Madagascar's big-eyed woolly lemurs or Brazil's many-colored spot-billed toucanets. Each of these animals seeks food and shelter among the plants of its environment.

But there's more to the story. There's a chapter that could someday affect you or someone you know.

Why Are These Plants Important to People?

The jaborandi tree produces a chemical called *pilocarpine* (pī'lə kär'pēn'). Doctors use this chemical to treat an eye disease called glaucoma. Glaucoma can cause blindness if it is not treated. The Madagascar periwinkle produces a chemical called *vincristine* (vin kris'tēn'). Vincristine is used to treat a cancer called childhood *leukemia* (lü kē'mē ə). These plants are important for our health and survival. Many others are, too.

Many kinds of plants are endangered by human activities. When people pollute the air and water, they may harm other living things that depend on that air and water. People can interfere with an ecosystem by damming up rivers, using pesticides, or cutting down trees. Yet people can also find ways to improve the environment by cleaning up polluted air and water and by reducing future sources of pollution. They can plant trees to replace those that are cut down or are destroyed by forest fires. Each person has an effect. The lives of all organisms are affected by other living things— and by nonliving things—in their environment.

With every breath you take, you are changing not only your environment but the world's

REVIEW

1. Identify two biotic and two abiotic limiting factors.

2. **COMPARE AND CONTRAST** How is mutualism like commensalism? How is it different?

3. Identify an organism and its adaptation that helps it survive in its environment.

4. **CRITICAL THINKING** *Analyze* Several species of whales are threatened with extinction. Propose two hypotheses that might account for the threat.

WHY IT MATTERS THINK ABOUT IT How do you affect your environment? How does your community affect its environment?

WHY IT MATTERS WRITE ABOUT IT Make a list of ways you and your community affect your environment. Suggest what could be done to make things better.

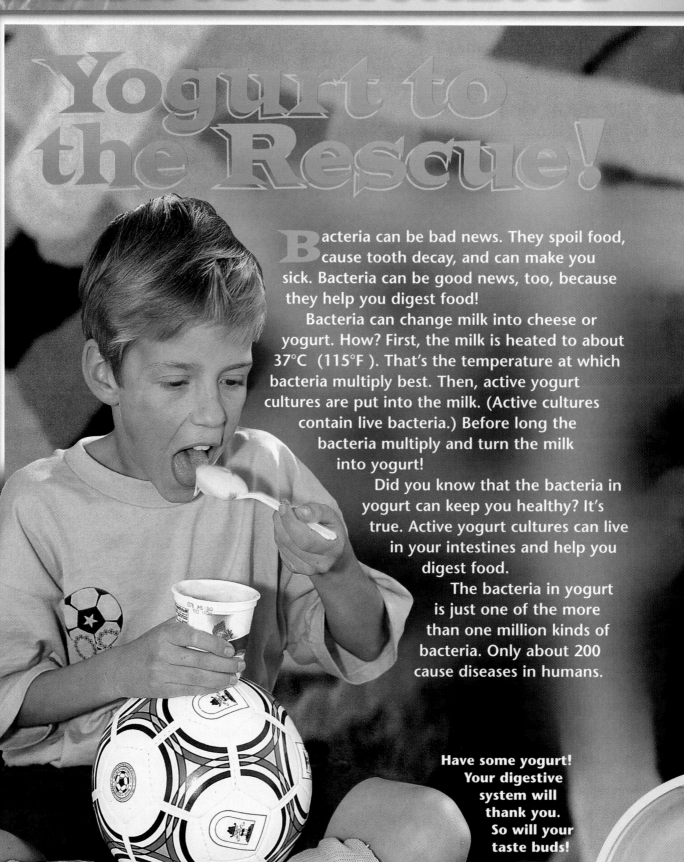

Yogurt to the Rescue!

Bacteria can be bad news. They spoil food, cause tooth decay, and can make you sick. Bacteria can be good news, too, because they help you digest food!

Bacteria can change milk into cheese or yogurt. How? First, the milk is heated to about 37°C (115°F). That's the temperature at which bacteria multiply best. Then, active yogurt cultures are put into the milk. (Active cultures contain live bacteria.) Before long the bacteria multiply and turn the milk into yogurt!

Did you know that the bacteria in yogurt can keep you healthy? It's true. Active yogurt cultures can live in your intestines and help you digest food.

The bacteria in yogurt is just one of the more than one million kinds of bacteria. Only about 200 cause diseases in humans.

Have some yogurt! Your digestive system will thank you. So will your taste buds!

Health Link

Antibiotics can kill bacteria that make people sick. Some antibiotics contain bacteria, too. Others are made from fungi.

However, antibiotics can kill useful bacteria in the body, too. When that happens you may have trouble digesting food. You may get stomach cramps or other problems. Let yogurt come to the rescue!

Live yogurt cultures move to the lining of your intestine. There they multiply and help restore your body's digestive balance. Therefore, if your doctor prescribes an antibiotic, pick up some yogurt, too!

DISCUSSION STARTER

1. What happens when active yogurt cultures are added to hot milk?

2. How can yogurt help if you're taking antibiotics?

To learn more about yogurt, visit *www.mhschool.com/science* and enter the keyword YOGURT.

*inter*NET
CONNECTION

WHY IT MATTERS

Climate and soil conditions affect where different populations live.

SCIENCE WORDS

biome one of Earth's large ecosystems, with its climate, soil, plants, and animals

taiga a cool, forest biome of conifers in the upper Northern Hemisphere

tundra a cold, tree-less biome of the far north, marked by spongy topsoil

desert a sandy or rocky biome, with little precipitation and little plant life

deciduous forest a forest biome with many kinds of trees that lose their leaves each autumn

tropical rain forest a hot, humid biome near the equator, with much rainfall and a wide variety of life

Places to Live Around the World

Where are you? In summer the Sun doesn't set here. In winter it never rises. Below the surface the soil is always frozen. Not much snow or rain falls. There are no tall trees.

Six thousand miles away, hot sunlight beats down. The air is dry as dust. The soil is sandy. You rarely see a tree. Where are you now?

Soil varies greatly and is a distinctive factor in each ecosystem. Soil content can determine what plants and animals can live there.

EXPLORE

HYPOTHESIZE Why is the soil in one kind of ecosystem different from the soil in another kind of ecosystem? What determines what the soil is like? Write a hypothesis in your *Science Journal.* Test your ideas.

Investigate Why Soil Is Important

Test sand and soil samples to see which have the most nutrients.

PROCEDURES

 **SAFETY** Wear goggles and an apron.

1. Place 1 tsp. of washed sand in a plastic cup.

2. **OBSERVE** Using the dropper add hydrogen peroxide to the sand, drop by drop. Count each drop. Bubbles will form as the hydrogen peroxide breaks down any decayed matter.

3. **COMMUNICATE** Record the number of drops you add until the bubbles stop forming in your *Science Journal*.

4. **EXPERIMENT** Perform steps 1–3 using the compost or soil.

CONCLUDE AND APPLY

1. **COMPARE AND CONTRAST** Which sample—soil or sand—gave off the most bubbles?

2. **INFER** Why was the sand used?

3. **INFER** Decayed materials in soil release their nutrients to form humus. The amount of humus in soil depends on the rate of decay and the rate at which plants absorb the nutrients. Which sample had the most humus?

GOING FURTHER: Apply

4. **EVALUATE** In which sample could you grow larger, healthier plants? Why?

MATERIALS

- washed sand
- compost, potting soil, or garden soil
- hydrogen peroxide
- 2 plastic cups
- 2 plastic spoons
- dropper
- goggles
- apron
- *Science Journal*

Why Is Soil Important?

Where would you rather try to grow plants—in sandy soil or in rich potting soil? As the Explore Activity showed, certain kinds of soil are better for growing plants than other kinds of soil are.

The land on Earth is divided into six major kinds of large ecosystems, called **biomes** (bī′ōmz). Each biome has its own kind of climate, soil, plants, and animals. Each biome can be found in different parts of the world. For example, a desert biome is found in North America. Another is found in Africa. Still another is found in South America. Others are found in Asia and Australia. The map shows where Earth's six biomes are located around our planet.

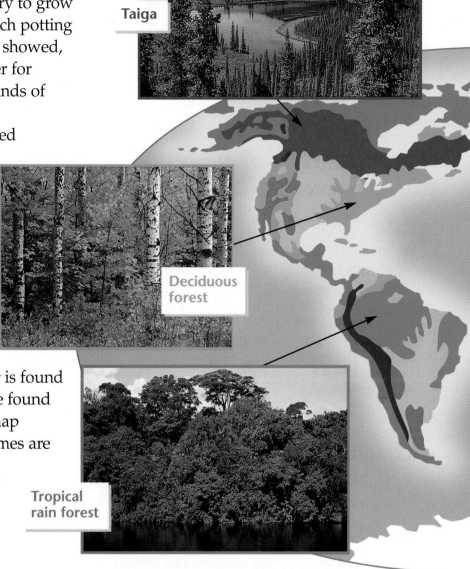

Taiga

Deciduous forest

Tropical rain forest

Desert

Location: Midlatitudes
Climate: Generally very hot days, cool nights; precipitation less than 10 inches a year
Soil: Poor in animal and plant decay products but rich in minerals
Plants: None to cacti, yuccas, scattered bunch grasses
Animals: Rodents, snakes, lizards, tortoises, insects, and some birds. The Sahara in Africa is home to camels, gazelles, antelopes, small foxes, snakes, lizards, gerbils, grasses, shrubs, and some trees.

Tundra

Location: High northern latitudes
Climate: Very cold, harsh, and long winters; short and cool summers; 10–25 centimeters (4–10 inches) of precipitation each year
Soil: Nutrient-poor, permafrost layer a few inches down
Plants: Grasses, wildflowers, mosses, small shrubs
Animals: Musk oxen, migrating caribou, arctic foxes, weasels, snowshoe hares, owls, hawks, various rodents, occasional polar bears

Grassland

Location: Midlatitudes, interiors of continents
Climate: Cool in winter, hot in summer; 10–30 inches of precipitation a year
Soil: Rich topsoil
Plants: Mostly grasses and small shrubs, some trees near sources of water
Animals: American grasslands include prairie dogs, foxes, small mammals, snakes, insects, various birds. African grasslands include elephants, lions, zebras, giraffes. What animals might live in Australia's grasslands?

Desert

Tundra

Grassland

READING N MAPS

1. **WRITE** Which kind of biome is most abundant?
2. **WRITE** Which is least abundant?

Deciduous Forest

Location: Midlatitudes
Climate: Relatively mild summers and winters, 76–127 centimeters (30–50 inches) of precipitation a year
Soil: Rich topsoil over clay
Plants: Hardwoods such as oaks, beeches, hickories, maples
Animals: Wolves, deer, bears, and a wide variety of small mammals, birds, amphibians, reptiles, and insects

Taiga

Location: Mid- to high latitudes
Climate: Very cold winters, cool summers; about 50 centimeters (20 inches) of precipitation a year
Soil: Acidic, mineral-poor, decayed pine and spruce needles on surface
Plants: Mostly spruce, fir, and other evergreens
Animals: Rodents, rabbits, lynx, sables, mink, caribou, bears, wolves

Tropical Rain Forest

Location: Near the equator
Climate: Hot all year round, 200–460 centimeters (80–180 inches) of rain a year
Soil: Nutrient-poor
Plants: Greatest diversity of any biome; vines, orchids, ferns, and a wide variety of trees
Animals: More species of insects, reptiles, and amphibians than any place else; monkeys, other small and large mammals, including in some places elephants, all sorts of colorful birds

545

What Has Happened to the Grasslands?

Why have so many grasslands become farmlands? As the name tells you, *grasslands* are biomes where grasses are the main plant life. They are areas where rainfall is irregular and not usually plentiful. Prairies, like the Blackland Prairie, are one kind of grassland.

Called the "bread baskets" of the world, few temperate grasslands look as they did years ago. *Temperate* means "mild." It refers to grasslands such as those in the United States and Ukraine. Today many of these grasslands are covered with crops such as wheat, corn, and oats.

However, large parts of the world's tropical grasslands still look much as they have for hundreds of years. Called *savannas* these lands stay warm all year round. Their soil is not as fertile as that of temperate grasslands. However, they get more rain—about 86–152 centimeters (34–60 inches) a year.

The most famous savanna covers the middle third of Africa. Here the dust rises as countless hoofed animals thunder across the land. There are more hoofed animals in savannas than anywhere else on Earth. Graceful zebras and giraffes live here. Wildebeests travel in awesome herds of tens of thousands. Antelopes run from sprinting cheetahs. In the heat of the afternoon, lions rest in the shade of a thorny acacia tree. Nearby hyenas prowl through the low grasses in search of dead or weak animals.

If you want to get a glimpse of a savanna while it still looks like this, you'd better do so soon. The land in savannas is being used more and more to graze domestic cattle. It won't be long until they replace the native animals, at least in unprotected parts of the savanna.

Where Are Evergreen Forests Found?

Evidence indicates that about 15,000 years ago, huge fingers of ice, called glaciers, inched down from Earth's arctic regions. The ice was hundreds of feet thick. As it moved southward like a giant white bulldozer, it gouged great chunks of land out of northern Europe, Asia, and North America.

Some of the sediment carried by the glaciers dammed up streams, forming ponds and lakes. More lakes formed when the ice began to pull back. Holes dug by the glaciers filled with fresh water. These are the lakes and ponds of a cool, forested biome called the **taiga** (tī'gə).

Taigas are mostly conifer forests. They spread out over 11 percent of Earth's land. They are located in the upper latitudes of the Northern Hemisphere—in Alaska, Canada, Norway, Sweden, Finland, and Russia.

If you visit the taiga in the summer, you may hear the pleasant songs of birds. Many different kinds migrate to the taiga in summer. However, they head for warmer regions in the fall. You might also hear the whining sound of chain saws. That's because the taiga is a major source of lumber and pulpwood. Much of the lumber is used for making houses for the world's growing population. The pulpwood is turned into paper products of all kinds, such as the pages of this book.

Thousands of years ago, moving sheets of ice dug away the land of the taiga. The dug-out land would become some of its lakes and ponds. Today these bodies of water are guarded by great stands of evergreen trees.

Where Is the Land of Frozen Earth?

Where is the ground frozen even in summer? Only 10–25 centimeters (4–10 inches) of rain fall here each year. Winters are long and icy cold. Summers are short and cool. Just a few inches below the surface, the ground is frozen all the time.

You can't find any plants taller than about 30 centimeters (12 inches). Yet you have no trouble spotting weasels, arctic foxes, snowshoe hares, hawks, musk oxen, and caribou. Near the coast you see a polar bear. When warmer weather comes, mosquitoes by the millions buzz through the air. There are snakes and frogs. Where are you?

You are in the far north. You're between the taiga and the polar ice sheets. It could be northern Alaska or northern Canada. It could be Greenland, or frigid parts of Europe or Asia. No matter which of these places

Among the large animals of the tundra is the caribou, a member of the deer family, and its predator, the 1,600-pound, nine-foot-long polar bear. Other tundra animals include weasels, arctic foxes, and snowshoe hares.

you are in, you are in the same biome. This cold biome of the far north is the **tundra**.

Why is it so cold? Even in summer the Sun's rays only strike the tundra at a low, glancing angle. The Sun melts ice in the top layer of the soil. Yet this water is kept from flowing downward by a layer of *permafrost*, or permanently frozen soil, underneath. The top layer of soil acts like a vast sponge for the melted ice.

Most tundra plants are wildflowers and grasses. The permafrost keeps large plants from developing the deep root systems they need. The growing season is very short—as little as 50 days in some places. The tundra soil is poor in nutrients, so the tundra cannot support large plants.

How Dry Is Dry?

Their names stir up thoughts of adventures in strange, dangerous places—Sahara, Gobi, Atacama. These are among the world's greatest **deserts**. A desert is a sandy or rocky biome, with little precipitation and little plant life.

Every continent has at least one desert. Africa has an enormous desert called the Sahara. Its sands dip down to the Atlantic Ocean in the west, the Mediterranean Sea to the north, and the Red Sea to the east. It is the largest desert on Earth, with an area of about 9,000,000 square kilometers (3,500,000 square miles). It is so large that it could cover all of the United States south of Canada. Picture those 48 states covered with sand and you get an idea of the size of the Sahara.

The Gobi Desert in China and Mongolia is the world's second largest desert. It is about 1,300,000 square kilometers (500,000 square miles). That's about twice the size of Texas.

In South America the Atacama Desert runs 968 kilometers (600 miles) from the southern tip of Peru down through Chile. It lies in between the Andes Mountains to the east and the Pacific Ocean in the west. The driest place on Earth is found in Arica, Chile. It averages only about $\frac{8}{100}$ centimeter ($\frac{3}{100}$) of rain a year. That's about the depth of six sheets of paper.

Few animals and plants live in deserts. Those that do are very hardy. They are well adapted to living in the desert.

To reach water the roots of the mesquite plant (above) have been known to grow more than 79 meters (260 feet) deep. That's the height of a 26-story building. Elf owls (left) build nests in cacti.

Where Is the Land of Falling Leaves?

When someone says, "I love the way the leaves change color in the fall," what biome is that person talking about? It's the **deciduous** (di sij'ü əs) **forest** biome. This is a forest biome with many trees that lose their leaves each year.

This is where broad-leaved trees grow. Each autumn the leaves turn yellow, orange, and red, painting the land with glorious colors. Then the leaves fall to the ground—which is what *deciduous* means—and decay. The dead leaves help make the soil rich and fertile.

Deciduous forests once covered most of the United States east of the Mississippi River and almost all of western Europe. Much has been cut down to make room for towns, cities, farms, and factories.

Many animals that once lived in deciduous forests still live on the land that was cleared for suburbs, farms, and towns. Chipmunks dart around bushes. Squirrels leap from branch to branch. Raccoons turn over trash cans. Skunks meander through the underbrush.

In some places deer have become a menace to drivers and gardeners alike. Birds like cardinals, robins, crows, and hawks, and insects such as bees still live in deciduous forests. Turn over a rock and you might discover a salamander or garter snake.

Many deciduous forests in the United States and Europe are now part of national parks or are in places where few people live. As long as they stay that way, people will be able to see the changing seasons.

The trees of a deciduous forest shed their leaves each autumn, painting the land yellow, orange, and red.

Although you'd probably not enjoy an encounter with this family, it's an important part of the deciduous forest biome.

Where Is It Hot and Humid?

In areas along and near Earth's equator are **tropical rain forests**. These biomes are hot and humid, with much rainfall. They support a wide variety of life.

The canopy of a tropical rain forest spreads like a huge umbrella. It is so thick that little sunlight ever reaches the ground. With little light few plants can grow on the ground. Most of the life is up high in the branches, where howling monkeys and purple orchids cling.

There are no tropical rain forests in North America or Europe. They are too far from the tropics. However, Central America, South America, India, Africa, Southeast Asia, Australia, and many Pacific Islands have rain forests. Each has its own kinds of plants and animals.

Millions of species of animals live in the world's tropical rain forests. Many species have yet to be discovered.

In Africa you might see a silverback gorilla or a troop of playful chimpanzees.

On the island of Borneo, you might see a red-haired, long-armed orangutan (ə rang'ù tan') swinging through the trees.

The world's most colorful birds—such as toucans (tü'kanz) and quetzals (ket sälz')—live in tropical rain forests. Giant snakes like the 9-meter-long (30-foot-long), 136-kilogram (300-pound) South American anaconda also live in tropical rain forests.

The anaconda, which lives in the South American rain forest, is the largest snake on the planet. The anaconda is a excellent swimmer. It often lurks in a river waiting to grab a mammal or bird.

The world's tropical rain forests have been victims of people's needs for lumber, farmland, and minerals. Fortunately, people are now replanting and restoring tropical rain forests. Still, some of their millions of undiscovered plant and animal species may become extinct before they are discovered.

Some of the most colorful birds on Earth, like this toucan live in tropical rain forests like those of South America.

Freshwater Communities

HYPOTHESIZE Do different organisms live in different locations in aquatic ecosystems? Write a hypothesis in your *Science Journal*. Test it.

MATERIALS

- dropper
- microscope slide
- coverslip
- microscope
- at least 3 samples of pond, lake, or stream water
- 3 or more plastic containers with lids
- *Science Journal*

PROCEDURES

1. Obtain samples of pond, lake, or stream water taken at different locations. CAUTION: Do not go beyond wading depth. Use a different container for each sample. Record the location each sample came from on the container.

2. **OBSERVE** Place a drop of water on a slide, and carefully place the coverslip over it. Examine the slide under a microscope.

3. **COMMUNICATE** Record the location of each sample and what you see. Use low and high power.

CONCLUDE AND APPLY

INTERPRET DATA What does this tell you about aquatic ecosystems?

What Are Water Ecosystems Like?

Temperature and precipitation differ among ecosystems on land. For Earth's watery ecosystems, the main difference is saltiness.

Lakes, streams, rivers, ponds, and certain marshes, swamps, and bogs tend to have little salt in them. They're all freshwater ecosystems. Oceans and seas are saltwater ecosystems.

In fresh water or salt water, organisms can be divided into three main categories. *Plankton* (plangk'tən) are organisms that float on the water. *Nekton* (nek'ton) are organisms that swim through the water. *Benthos* (ben'thos) are bottom-dwelling organisms.

Freshwater Organisms

Many plants live in the shallow waters of lakes, ponds, and other bodies of fresh water. If you were to wade here, you might get your feet tangled in cattails, bur reeds, wild rice, and arrowheads. You might also spot a frog, a turtle, or maybe a crayfish.

Farther out, where the water gets deeper, are microscopic plankton like algae and protozoa.

Look beneath the surface, and nekton come into view. There might be large trout or other game fish. All the way to the bottom, an aquatic worm might be burrowing into the mud.

What Lives in Salt Water?

More than 70 percent of Earth is covered by oceans and saltwater seas. Like the freshwater ecosystem, the marine, or ocean, ecosystem is divided into several sections.

The shallowest is the *intertidal zone*. There the ocean floor is covered and uncovered as the tide goes in and out. Crabs burrow into the sand so they won't be washed away. Mussels and barnacles attach themselves to rocks.

The open ocean is divided into two regions. The first region is up to 200 meters deep. In this upper region are many kinds of fish and whales. The world's largest animals—the 150-ton blue whales—live here. These giant whales eat only tiny shrimplike animals, called krill.

The lower region goes from 200 meters to the ocean bottom—perhaps $10\frac{1}{2}$ kilometers down. At depths greater than about 330 meters, there is no sunlight. It is completely black!

Photosynthetic organisms, like algae, can only live where there is sunlight. They are found in the intertidal zone and in waters up to about 100 meters deep. Many fantastic creatures live on the dark ocean bottom. Some of these fish "light up" like underwater fireflies. Other bottom-dwelling fish are blind. There are even bacteria that live in boiling water where fiery lava seeps out of the sea floor.

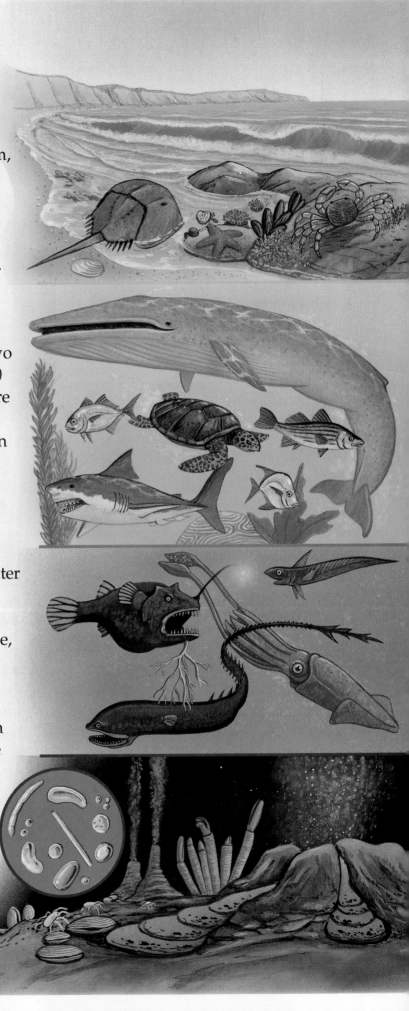

The types of animals you see in the ocean change as you go deeper.

Brain Power

How might the ocean ecosystem be affected if the whales died out? How might your own life be affected by the extinction of these whales?

What if the Great Whales Vanish?

People started hunting whales for their meat and oil at least 4,000 years ago. However, back then the oceans held so many whales that hunting didn't have much effect on their populations.

As the centuries passed, however, whale hunting increased. So did the technology of finding and killing these gentle mammals. By 1850 American whalers alone accounted for the killing of 10,000 a year. During the next decade, a Norwegian whaling captain invented a harpoon that contained a bomb, which would explode inside a whale. Few whales could escape such an attack.

Faster whaling vessels were built. During the first half of the 20th century, helicopters and small airplanes began to

Humpback whales form close family groups. They communicate by making a wide variety of sounds that can travel great distances in water.

be used to spot whales so that "catcher ships" could more easily track them down. Killing became more and more efficient. In 1962 alone 66,000 whales were killed. The whales could not reproduce fast enough to replace those that were being killed. Many species, like blue whales, humpbacks, bowheads, and right whales became threatened with extinction.

The whales were being used for human and animal food, oil for lamps, and fertilizer. However, there were other sources of such products. Recognizing this, and the danger to whale populations, the major whaling countries formed the International Whaling Commission (IWC) in 1946.

Can Whales Make a Comeback?

By the 1990s the IWC had succeeded in getting whaling countries to reduce or stop hunting threatened whales. Earlier, in 1971, the United States had banned its citizens from whaling for profit or even buying products made from whales. The only Americans allowed to kill whales are the Inuit Native Americans of Alaska, who hunt whales for their own food. They kill only a few whales a year.

Will the remaining whale populations survive, or are they too small to make a comeback? Will the eerie song of the humpback no longer be heard? Will the mighty blue whale vanish? No one is sure of the answers.

WHY IT MATTERS

The world's biomes remain undisturbed as long as their climates and the populations that live there remain basically unchanged. However, human and natural activities can change these factors. Changes in a biome can affect the kinds of plants that can grow there and the kinds of animals that can live there. It can also affect the lifestyles of the people who live there. It is important to know whether, how, and why these factors may be changing.

REVIEW

1. Describe the taiga biome in terms of its climate, soil, and nutrients.

2. **COMPARE AND CONTRAST** How do organisms found in desert and tundra biomes adapt to their environments?

3. Explain why few plants live on the floor of tropical rain forests.

4. Briefly describe the two types of aquatic ecosystems.

5. **CRITICAL THINKING** *Evaluate* Choose one biome, and explain how a change in its climate might affect its populations.

WHY IT MATTERS THINK ABOUT IT
How might a change in the biome you live in affect your way of life?

WHY IT MATTERS WRITE ABOUT IT
Write a paragraph explaining how your lifestyle might change if the biome where you live got warmer. What might happen if it got colder? What might happen if the amount of precipitation increased? What might happen if it decreased?

READING SKILL
Write a paragraph summarizing what this topic was about.

Are Rain Forests

Where would you be if you took a trip to the most famous ecosystem on Earth? You'd be in a tropical rain forest!

Rain forests are full of secrets because they're hard to get through and you can't see everything in them. More different kinds of organisms live in 1 square kilometer of a rain forest than in any other ecosystem!

Many plants and animals in the rain forests have never been seen or identified. Many could never survive outside the rain forests.

The greatest of Earth's rain forests is in the Amazon River Basin of South America. Each year about 13,000 square kilometers (5,019 square miles) of this rain forest are destroyed by burning or construction. The Amazon rain forest is at least 8,000 years old, but in 100 years it could be gone!

Worth Saving?

Green plants release oxygen in photosynthesis. Why are people destroying the rain forests? The human population around the Amazon is growing fast, and people need a place to live. Some people want to replace part of the rain forest with farms.

Most minerals in a rain forest are in the plants, not the soil. After trees are cleared for farms, the soil is rich for only a year or so. Then most of the nutrients are washed away by rain.

Parts of the rain forest are also rich in minerals, like gold. Some people want to clear the trees and build mines. Do you think they should?

DISCUSSION STARTER

1. How can there be unidentified animals and plants in the rain forest?

2. Why do some people want to destroy the rain forest?

■ Cleared forest land
■ Frontier forest today

The Amazon rain forest is about three-fourths the size of the United States.

To learn more about rain forests, visit *www.mhschool.com/science* and enter the keyword RAINFOREST.

*inter*NET
CONNECTION

WHY IT MATTERS

Ecosystems can change over time.

SCIENCE WORDS

ecological succession the gradual replacement of one community by another

pioneer species the first species living in an area

pioneer community the first community living in an area

climax community the final stage of succession in an area, unless a major change happens

How Ecosystems Change

Before May 18, 1980, the area around Mount Saint Helens in the state of Washington was decorated with beautiful groves of Douglas fir and western hemlock trees. Wildflowers sprouted from the soil. Animals of many kinds made their home here. Then the mountain exploded.

EXPLORE

HYPOTHESIZE Can different ecosystems affect each other when they change? How might an abandoned farm and a nearby forest affect each other? Write a hypothesis in your *Science Journal.* Test your ideas.

Investigate How Ecosystems Change

Compare what happened at Mount Saint Helens to what might happen to an abandoned farm at the edge of a forest.

MATERIALS
• *Science Journal*

PROCEDURES

1. OBSERVE Examine the photograph.

2. COMMUNICATE In your *Science Journal*, describe the two ecosystems that you see.

CONCLUDE AND APPLY

1. INFER How do the two ecosystems affect each other?

2. PREDICT If the land is not farmed for ten years, what would you expect the area to look like?

3. DRAW CONCLUSIONS How can one ecosystem be changed into another?

4. COMPARE AND CONTRAST Compare what you think will happen to the abandoned farm with what happened at Mount Saint Helens. In what ways would the changes in ecosystems be similar? In what ways would they be different?

GOING FURTHER: Apply

5. ANALYZE Think of another ecosystem that might be changed by nature. Think of another ecosystem that might be changed by humans. Describe how such ecosystems might continue to change over time.

How Do Ecosystems Change?

What happens when people abandon a city? Nature takes over. One example is the cities and temples of Angkor in Cambodia. They were built between 820 and about 1150. They are among the great wonders of the world. Many of their buildings still lie hidden under the vines and trees of the jungle. Yet it wasn't always that way. Once, hundreds of years ago, people cleared the land for their cities. Then about 600 years ago, the ancient cities were abandoned and the jungle crept over them.

Similar, if not so spectacular, changes happen everywhere on Earth. They can

After they were abandoned, the great cities of Angkor in Cambodia became covered by the jungle.

occur in your backyard. They can happen in an empty city lot or on one of its abandoned streets. They can occur in a suburb or on a farm. If given a chance, nature has a way of changing an ecosystem or producing a new one. How does nature change an abandoned farm's field into a flourishing forest?

From Farmland to Forest

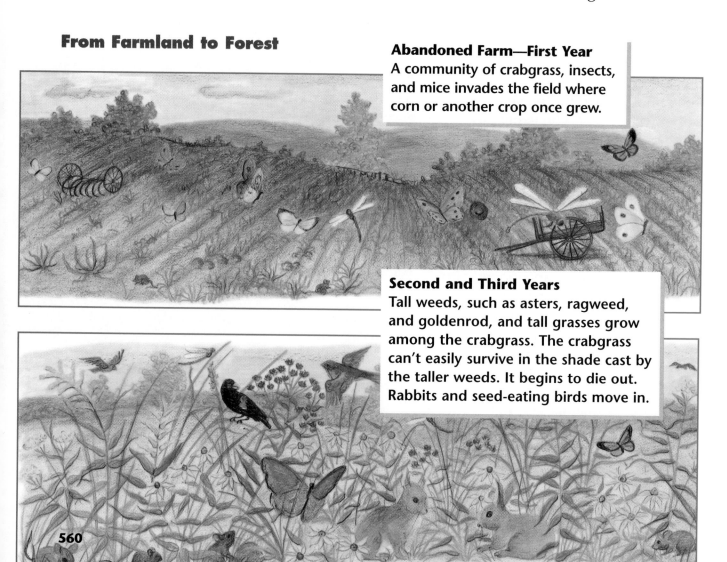

Abandoned Farm—First Year
A community of crabgrass, insects, and mice invades the field where corn or another crop once grew.

Second and Third Years
Tall weeds, such as asters, ragweed, and goldenrod, and tall grasses grow among the crabgrass. The crabgrass can't easily survive in the shade cast by the taller weeds. It begins to die out. Rabbits and seed-eating birds move in.

Four to Six Years Later

The hot, dry field of tall weeds provides a perfect environment for pine seeds to sprout. Pine trees begin to grow and shade the weeds, which begin to die out. More birds join the community, as do small mammals like opossums and skunks.

Twenty-Five Years Later

A pine forest has replaced the old farm field. Yet the number of new pine seedlings drops because they can't grow in the shade. Seeds of deciduous trees such as maple, hickory, and oak sprout and take root. Larger animals like raccoons and foxes begin to visit.

One Hundred Years Later

The forest is now mostly deciduous trees. These trees are the habitats of many different kinds of birds and small animals, such as squirrels. Deer, raccoons, and foxes also live in the forest.

How Do Communities Change?

The abandoned farm field you just read about gave way to short crabgrass, then tall grasses and shrubs. Later, pine trees, and finally, deciduous trees grew there. Scientists call the gradual replacement of one community by another **ecological succession**.

Ecological succession can begin in two different kinds of places. It can begin where a community already exists—such as in an abandoned farm field. Ecological succession in a place where a community already exists is called *secondary succession*.

Ecological succession can also happen where there are few, if any, living things. This is called *primary succession*. Primary succession can begin where communities were wiped out. Such places would include land swept clean by a volcanic eruption or forest fire. It can also begin where communities never existed before, such as on a new island that rises out of the sea.

How do you explore this kind of succession? Explore what happened to Mount Saint Helens in the state of Washington shortly after May 18, 1980.

Mount Saint Helens had just erupted. The blast from the volcano knocked down thousands of trees. To make matters worse, the whole area was covered knee-deep with hot volcanic ash and finely smashed up rock.

The landscape was different shades of gray as far as you could see. No spot of green greeted your eyes, not even a blade of grass. If you didn't know better, you might think you were on the Moon.

A year after Mount Saint Helens erupted, the rose-purple flowers of fireweed announced that life was returning to the destroyed land. Just four years after Mount Saint Helens erupted, seedlings of Douglas fir trees began to take root in the rubble of the volcano.

How Does Mount Saint Helens Change?

A year passes. You return to the slopes of Mount Saint Helens expecting to see unbroken stretches of rock and stumps of dead trees. However, something has happened in the year you were gone. Wind and rain have cleared some of the ash and dust, especially from steep slopes. The wind has also blown in some seeds and fruits from nearby forests. You see a scattering of rose-purple objects among the charred and fallen tree trunks. As you come closer, you recognize the objects. They are the flowers of a plant called fireweed. It gets its name from the fact that it is often the first plant to grow after a forest fire.

Scientists would call the fireweed a **pioneer species**. That's because it is the first species to be living in an otherwise lifeless area. You notice that the blooming of fireweed has attracted animals such as insects and an occasional insect-eating bird. A new community, called a **pioneer community**, is beginning to thrive around Mount Saint Helens.

You return in 1984 and almost step on a little green shoot. You bend down and take a closer look. The shoot has little needlelike leaves. You recognize it. It is the sprout of a Douglas fir tree. Its seed was probably blown here from a forest miles away.

Now you can picture the land around Mount Saint Helens 100 or 200 years in the future. It is covered with a dense forest of evergreens. The forest is much like the one that spread around it before that explosive day in 1980.

**Fir trees grow tall
11 years after the blast.**

What Makes Up Pioneer Communities?

Are the first organisms in a pioneer community always plants? In some places the answer is no. This is usually the case in newly formed fiery volcanic islands that rise from the sea. Here the pioneer community is usually made up of bacteria, fungi, and algae. Over many years these organisms slowly break down the volcanic rock into soil.

On a continent far away from an ocean, succession might be starting in a rocky field. Lichens, tiny organisms composed of algae and fungi, start to grow on a rock. The rock gradually crumbles over time into soil.

What happens when there is enough soil, and other conditions are right for plants to grow? A seed blown to the island by the wind or dropped by a passing bird will take root. The new plant, and others like it, will gradually spread over the land.

During their life cycles, plants will die and further enrich the soil. Perhaps a coconut will drift ashore. When it germinates its roots will find a good supply of nutrients. A coconut palm will spring up, and a new island paradise will be born.

What Is a Climax Community?

More years will pass—perhaps hundreds of them. The climate of the island will remain pretty much unchanged. Its community will grow. Its populations will become balanced and stable. Few new animals and plants will arrive. Few will leave. Ecological succession will slow down or stop altogether. A scientist visiting the island will see a **climax community**. It is a final stage of succession. This community will stay largely unchanged unless some major event occurs.

A PIONEER COMMUNITY

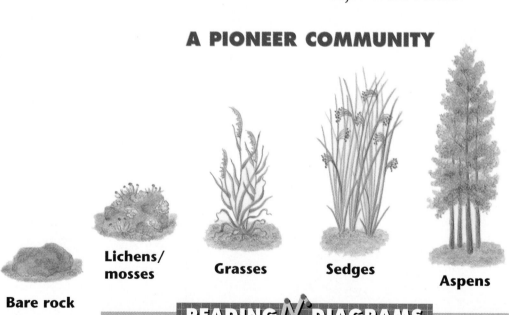

Bare rock   **Lichens/mosses**   **Grasses**   **Sedges**   **Aspens**   **Forest**

READING IN DIAGRAMS

REPRESENT Create a flow chart showing the changes from a pioneer community to a climax community.

What Kind of Event Could Change an Entire Ecosystem?

A hurricane may sweep across the island. The volcano that gave it birth might erupt again. People might come and build hotels or introduce new plants or animals. The climate might change. Then the processes of ecological succession would begin all over again. Another climax community would eventually develop. It might—or might not—be the same as the earlier climax community.

The volcano Kilauea erupting on the island of Hawaii

Predicting Succession

HYPOTHESIZE In what areas where you live do you think ecological succession may be taking place? Write a hypothesis in your *Science Journal*. Test it.

MATERIALS
• Science Journal

PROCEDURES

1. **OBSERVE** Identify an area near you where you think ecological succession is taking place.

2. **COMMUNICATE** Describe the area. List the evidence you have that indicates ecological succession is taking place.

CONCLUDE AND APPLY

1. **INFER** Do you think the succession will be primary or secondary? Explain.

2. **PREDICT** In what order do you think new species will colonize the area? Explain the reasons for your predictions.

3. **COMMUNICATE** Describe the climax community that you think will eventually live in the area. Give reasons for your conclusion.

What's Living on Surtsey?

In 1963 the island of Surtsey, near Iceland, was formed from a volcano. Between 1963 and 1996, at least 45 types of plants were seen growing there. Several kinds of birds, such as snow buntings, were also found raising their young on the island.

Flying insects have also been found there. Scientists expect that more types of plants and birds will live on Surtsey in the future.

Surtsey, a volcanic island, rose from the sea near Iceland in 1963.

By 1996 many plants and birds lived on Surtsey.

Damage caused by the Soufriere Hills volcano on the island of Montserrat

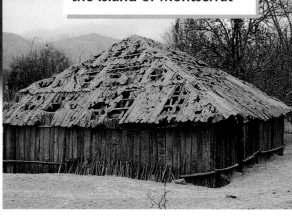

Brain Power

In the 1990s the erupting Soufriere Hills volcano on the island of Montserrat covered over much of the island. What do you think it is like there today? How would you find out if you are correct?

SKILL BUILDER

Skills: Interpreting Data and Inferring

COMPARING ECOSYSTEMS IN VOLCANIC AREAS

In this activity you will collect and interpret data about the ecosystems of two volcanic areas.

Data are different kinds of facts. They might include observations, measurements, calculations, and other kinds of information. Scientists collect data about an event to better understand what caused it, what it will cause, and how it will affect other events.

What do these data tell the scientist? The scientist first organizes the data in some way—perhaps a table, chart, or graph. The scientist then studies the organized data and interprets it. *Interpret* means "draw a conclusion." In this case you will draw a conclusion about what determines which plants will return to a volcanic area.

MATERIALS

- research books
- Internet
- *Science Journal*

PROCEDURES

1. Collect data on two volcanic areas, Mount Saint Helens and the Soufriere Hills volcano on the island of Montserrat or the active volcanoes of Hawaii. Organize the data in your *Science Journal.*

2. **COMMUNICATE** Describe the sequence of events that has taken place.

3. **INTERPRET DATA** Draw a conclusion about why certain plants return when they do.

CONCLUDE AND APPLY

1. **COMPARE** In what ways is succession in the two areas alike? In what ways is it different?

2. **INFER** Why is the succession in these two areas similar or different?

3. **INFER** What abiotic factors must you consider when drawing conclusions? What biotic factors must you consider?

Why Do Some Organisms Survive While Others Don't?

Our planet is changing all the time. Its continents move north and south, east and west. Climates change from hot to cold, cold to hot, wet to dry, or dry to wet. As these changes occur, populations and communities change with them.

Take, for example, the following mystery and its solution.

Clues

- Scientists gathering fossils in Italy make a discovery. About six million years ago, fish and other sea creatures disappeared from the Mediterranean Sea.

- Other fossils from a slightly later period reveal that horselike animals from Africa arrived in Europe.

- The fossil of an ancient African hippopotamus is found on an island in the middle of the Mediterranean.

- Fossil palm trees of the same age are dug up in Switzerland.

- Then there is another surprising discovery. Five-million-year-old fossils of fish turn up in the Mediterranean area.

Scientists study fossils to discover how the Mediterranean area changed.

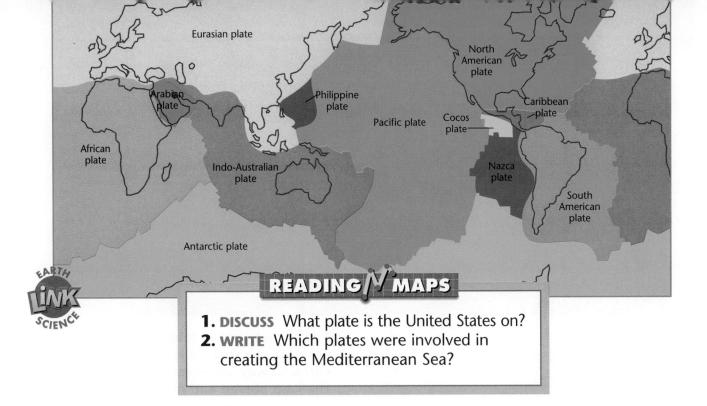

READING MAPS

1. **DISCUSS** What plate is the United States on?
2. **WRITE** Which plates were involved in creating the Mediterranean Sea?

6 million years ago

Present day

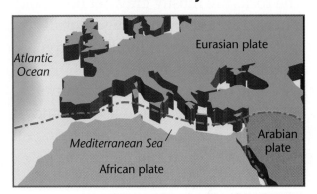

What could have gone on back then to have these clues make sense? Scientists have developed hypotheses. Here's one.

About six million years ago, the continents of Africa and Europe bumped into each other. Earth's crust is made up of moving plates—pieces of crust. Two plates—the African and the Eurasian—collided back then. This happened at what is now the Strait of Gibraltar. This collision created a natural dam between the Atlantic Ocean and the Mediterranean Sea.

Without a source of water from the ocean, the sea dried up in perhaps as little as 1,000 years. The Mediterranean Sea became a desert. The sea's fish and other marine life died out. Animals from Africa migrated across the desert to Europe. Palm trees sprouted in Switzerland.

Then about five million years ago, the dam began to crumble. A gigantic waterfall poured water into the desert. It carried many kinds of marine life from the Atlantic Ocean. The Mediterranean became a sea again.

Where Have All the Metals Gone?

The soil under your feet looks brown. The rocks are mostly gray. Yet both hold a treasure chest of glittering colorful metals—gold, silver, aluminum, iron, copper, and many more.

People use these metals in many ways. Gold is made into jewelry and coins. Silver is, too. Silver is also in photographic film and tableware.

Fly in an airplane. Ride in an automobile. Open a soft drink can. Squeeze a toothpaste tube. Marvel at fireworks. For all these things, you can thank aluminum. It's in each of these products.

Every large building, bridge, ship, train, and piece of machinery has iron in it—usually as part of steel.

Turn on your TV, your home's lights, a CD player. Electricity flowing through copper wires gets them going.

Clearly metals play an important part in our modern society. Yet we pay a price for them—and not only in money. Since metal-containing rocks

The easiest way to mine metals that are near the surface is to scrape the surface away. However, this leaves the land barren and often covered with dangerous chemicals.

are buried in the ground, we must change the ground to get at them. If the rocks are near the surface, we simply carve away huge areas of land. This is called surface mining, open-pit mining, or strip mining.

In the United States alone, about 2,331 square kilometers (900 square miles) of land has been cleared for mining. That's about three-fourths of the area of the entire state of Rhode Island.

The Problem Continues

That's not the end of the problem. Surface-mined land is loaded with substances that are harmful to living things. Rainwater flows easily over this kind of land and carries pollutants into nearby streams, rivers, and lakes. The wind picks up dust, which pollutes the air. In both cases, living things are harmed.

One Solution

We need metals. However, we don't need pollution and ugly landscapes. What can be done? Abandoned surface mines can be reclaimed. That means people can try to restore them as they once were. They can try to turn them into useful ecosystems after secondary succession takes place. This process is difficult and expensive. The restored soil may be poisonous to plants. Also there may not be fertile topsoil to put on the reclaimed land. Therefore, it may be difficult to grow plants there.

Another Solution

Yet maybe there's another solution. Cut down on the mining of metals. How? Reduce how much we use them. How do we do that? We do that by reusing and recycling. Those are the "3 Rs" of conservation—reduce, reuse, recycle.

The activities and health of all living things on Earth are intertwined. What happens to one living thing and one ecosystem usually affects other living things and other ecosystems. To control the effects of changes in ecosystems, people must first understand how they work.

REVIEW

1. Describe how an abandoned farm field becomes a deciduous forest.

2. Give an example of a pioneer community and a climax community.

3. **INTERPRET DATA/INFER** List the evidence that supports the conclusion that the Mediterranean Sea once dried up.

4. Explain how a volcanic eruption might affect an ecosystem.

5. **CRITICAL THINKING** *Apply* Write a regulation that would protect your community from a specific kind of pollution without causing hardships to people, such as business owners.

WHY IT MATTERS THINK ABOUT IT
What things do you do every day that can affect the ecosystem you live in?

WHY IT MATTERS WRITE ABOUT IT
Write a paragraph explaining what you can do to help preserve the ecosystem you live in.

Let It Burn!

Over a hundred different grasses and plants grow shoulder high on Bob and Mickey Burleson's Texas prairie. It looks just as it did when Europeans first came to this part of Texas, before they cut the native grasses and planted crops.

How did the Burlesons return their prairie to its original beauty? First, they plowed any existing plants under the soil. Then, they began to plant native Texas grasses and plants.

The Burlesons burn the plants every two years. The fire helps clear the ground so new plants can grow and creates ash to fertilize the soil. Some species of native plants also need fire in order to germinate. Fire helps the soil warm faster, giving the prairie a longer growing season.

Along Elm Creek in Texas, the Burlesons have restored 73 hectares (180 acres) to prairie land.

DISCUSSION STARTER

1. How did the Burlesons restore their prairie?

2. Why is burning the prairie important in maintaining it?

To learn more about prairies, visit *www.mhschool.com/science* and enter the keyword GRASSLANDS.

*inter*NET
CONNECTION

CHAPTER 12 REVIEW

USING SCIENCE WORDS

Number a paper from 1 to 10. Fill in 1 to 5 with words from the list above.

1. Part of the soil of the __?__ is frozen all year round.

2. The relationship of __?__ means that both populations benefit.

3. A relationship between two organisms in which one benefits while the other is harmed is called __?__.

4. The __?__ has many evergreen trees.

5. A(n) __?__ is made up of the first organisms to colonize an area.

6–10. **Pick five words from the list above that were not used in 1 to 5, and use each in a sentence.**

UNDERSTANDING SCIENCE IDEAS

11. Describe a major ancient event that affected the ability of organisms to survive in their environment.

12. What is the relationship between orchids and trees in a rain forest?

13. How does the structure of a cactus enable it to survive in the desert?

14. Give an example of a parasite.

15. How would you describe deserts, tropical rain forests, grasslands, and tundras?

USING IDEAS AND SKILLS

16. Compare and contrast freshwater and saltwater ecosystems.

17. Describe two examples of predator competition.

18. **READING SKILL: SUMMARIZING** Describe the process in which an abandoned farm becomes a deciduous forest.

19. **INTERPRET DATA/INFER** Write your interpretation of the data below.

Pond Populations and Acid Content

Acid	Yellow Perch	Brown Trout	Salamanders	Mayflies
High	23	6	2	0
Medium	28	11	7	2
Low	36	18	10	14

20. **THINKING LIKE A SCIENTIST** You discover that there are no fossils of dinosaurs above a certain layer of rock, but there are below it. The rock in that layer has more in common with rocks from space than in Earth rocks. Suggest how these two discoveries may be linked.

PROBLEMS and PUZZLES

Home Sweet Biome Collect data for the abiotic factors in your biome. What kind of organisms can be found in your biome? Where else does your kind of biome exist?

573

UNIT 6 REVIEW

USING SCIENCE WORDS

biotic factor p.485	nitrogen
climax	cycle p.518
community p.564	omnivore p.501
community p.488	parasitism p.534
desert p.549	pioneer
food chain p.498	species p.563
limiting	scavenger p.501
factor p.528	symbiosis p.532
niche p.489	tundra p.548

USING SCIENCE WORDS

Number a paper from 1 to 10. Beside each number write the word or words that best complete the sentence.

1. The role of a species in an ecosystem is called the species' __?__ .

2. The living parts of an ecosystem are known as __?__ .

3. Bears and people, which eat meat and plants, are both __?__ .

4. The path of the energy in food from an insect to the bird that eats it is called a(n) __?__.

5. Bacteria that grow in peas and bean roots play an important role in the __?__ .

6. The amount of available water can be a(n) __?__ of the size of a population.

7. Mutualism is a form of __?__ between two species.

8. The ground below the surface is always frozen in the biome called the __?__ .

9. The biome called the Sahara is a(n) __?__ .

10. The first living thing in an otherwise lifeless area is called a(n) __?__ .

UNDERSTANDING SCIENCE IDEAS

Write 11 to 15. For each number write the letter for the best answer. You may wish to use the hints provided.

11. All of the members of a species in an area make up a(n)
    a. community
    b. habitat
    c. abiotic factor
    d. population
    (Hint: Read page 488.)

12. Because elephants and rabbits eat only plants, they are both
    a. omnivores
    b. scavengers
    c. predators
    d. herbivores
    (Hint: Read page 500.)

13. A key ingredient in plant fertilizer is
    a. carbon
    b. nitrogen
    c. oxygen
    d. hydrogen
    (Hint: Read pages 514–515.)

14. Which biome has the most species of insects, reptiles, and amphibians?
    a. tropical rain forest
    b. deciduous forest
    c. taiga
    d. tundra
    (Hint: Read page 545.)

15. What is the best description of life on Mount Saint Helens today?
    a. no life, barren
    b. a pioneer community
    c. a climax community
    d. a deciduous forest
    (Hint: Read page 558.)

USING IDEAS AND SKILLS

16. List five abiotic things that plants and animals need.

17. Someone accidentally spills sugar next to an anthill. Describe what you think will happen to the ant population.

18. Explain why a seal in the food chain *algae → fish → penguin → seal* only gets about one-tenth of 1 percent of the algae's stored energy.

19. What material do decomposers convert dead trees into? What happens to the material?

20. Make a simplified diagram of the carbon cycle.

21. Why is the yucca moth *not* a parasite of the yucca tree?

22. What apparently killed the dinosaurs?

23. **USE VARIABLES** In many places there is an overpopulation of deer. What variable(s) do you think are responsible? How would you remedy this problem?

THINKING LIKE A SCIENTIST

24. **INTERPRET DATA/INFER** Look at the table on page 491. What happened to the amount of insecticide in bald eagle eggs between 1972 and 1977? Why do you think this happened?

25. What is the difference between primary succession and secondary succession?

WRITING IN YOUR JOURNAL

SCIENCE IN YOUR LIFE
List four things that limit the number of people that can live in your area. Why are these things limiting factors?

PRODUCT ADS
Advertisements for some products claim that the products are environmentally friendly. What does that mean? What are examples of products that are environmentally friendly and products that are not?

HOW SCIENTISTS WORK
Scientists make observations and gather data to learn about living things and how they interact. How do scientists obtain data? Give four examples from this unit.

Design your own Experiment

What pioneer species live in your area? Design an experiment to find out. Check with your teacher before carrying out the experiment.

inter**NET** CONNECTION

For help in reviewing this unit, visit *www.mhschool.com/science*

PROBLEMS and PUZZLES

Eco-Poems

Follow the directions below to write an eco-poem about an animal of your choice. On the first line, write the name of the animal. Follow the directions on each line after that. Use "The Frog" as your guide. Print your eco-poems on cards, and hang them from the ceiling.

> The Frog—
> Green like a lily pad
> Swimming fast, hopping, jumping
> Preying on flies, sticking out its long tongue
> Hiding underwater Among the leaves,
> Waiting.

1. **Name of animal**
2. **Color or shape**
3. **How it moves**
4. **What it eats**
5. **Habitats**
6. **What it often does**

School Community

Compare your school with a natural community. Instead of food your school community creates knowledge. Who are the producers of knowledge? The consumers? Does your school have primary and secondary consumers? What niches do different students, teachers, and other school workers fill? Draw a diagram to explain your knowledge community.

Biome Spinner Game

Play with two or more players. Take turns spinning the spinner. Name an animal or plant that lives in the biome that the spinner lands on. Score a point for each plant or animal you name. You may not use a plant or animal that has been used by another player.

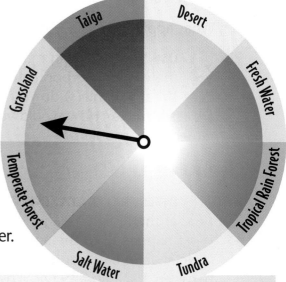

My Dog Has Fleas

To dogs, pests and parasites can be serious problems. What if two new parasites are released into the dog community? One is a flea that irritates the dog but causes no major damage to its body. The other is a worm that kills its dog hosts. Which parasite has a greater chance of becoming a long-term pest for dogs? Explain your answer.

CHAPTER 13
BLOOD
AND AIR

Do you ever receive mail? Think about how many people, buildings, and machines it takes to pick up and deliver mail to millions of homes and offices.

Your body is made up of more than 100 trillion living cells. To stay alive every cell needs nutrients and oxygen delivered to it all day, every day. Every cell also needs harmful wastes picked up and removed from your body.

No post office could do this much work. Do you know how your body does it?

 In Chapter 13 locate details as you read.

577

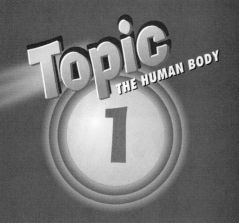
WHY IT MATTERS

Your body moves important materials to and from each of your cells.

SCIENCE WORDS

plasma the pale-yellow liquid part of blood that contains nutrients

hemoglobin a chemical that carries oxygen around in the body

platelet a cell fragment in blood that helps blood to form clots

artery a blood vessel that carries blood away from the heart

vein a blood vessel that carries blood toward the heart

capillary the smallest type of blood vessel, where materials are exchanged between blood and body cells

transfusion taking blood from one person and giving it to another person

antibody a protein in blood that helps the body find and destroy materials that may be harmful

A Blood System

A 35-year-old man goes to an eye doctor. She uses a light to look into his eyes and asks, "Do you eat hamburgers with french fries at fast food restaurants?"

He answers, "Yes."

Looking in the other eye, she asks, "How about pizza, soy sauce, and sausage?" Again the answer is yes.

The doctor says, "Your eyes are fine, but I want you to see another doctor for your heart."

EXPLORE

HYPOTHESIZE What do all the foods have in common? What do they have to do with his heart? Write a hypothesis in your *Science Journal*. Test your ideas.

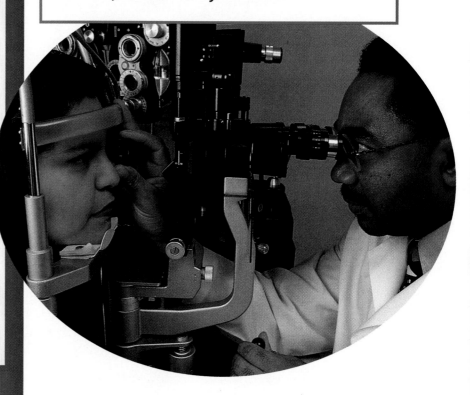

Investigate How Blood Travels

Examine the path blood takes through your heart.

PROCEDURES

■■■ **SAFETY** Use the scissors carefully!

1. MAKE A MODEL Draw an oval about the size of your fist on the paper. Cut it out. Cut the oval down the middle, and label it as shown.

2. Tape each piece of yarn to a white card. If *R* is the right side of the heart and *L* is the left side, trace the yarn and thread starting at *Out* on the *R* side. Sketch the model in your *Science Journal*.

3. COMPARE Tape the halves of the oval "heart" together. Does the path of the yarn and thread change?

CONCLUDE AND APPLY

1. SEQUENCE Assume blood flows through the yarn and the thread. Where does blood that enters the right side of the heart come from? Where does it go?

2. COMPARE AND CONTRAST Where does blood come from to enter the left side of the heart? Where does it go? How is this different from the right side?

GOING FURTHER: Problem Solving

3. DRAW CONCLUSIONS Why does the blood travel to the lungs? What do you think happens to the blood in the lungs?

MATERIALS

- sheet of paper
- scissors
- tape
- 5 cm (2 in.) of red yarn
- 5 cm of blue yarn
- four 5-cm-square white cards
- 10 cm (4 in.) of red yarn
- 10 cm of blue yarn
- two 10-cm pieces of black thread
- *Science Journal*

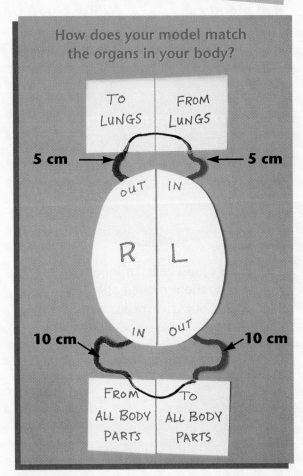

Tape the free ends of yarn to the proper parts of the model as shown. Label your oval as the above picture indicates.

How Does Blood Travel?

The Explore Activity showed that blood travels from all parts of your body to the heart. Then it is pumped to your lungs and back to the heart to be pumped out to the body again.

Blood is a mixture of liquid and cells. The pale-yellow liquid, called **plasma** (plaz′mə), is mostly water and contains nutrients. These nutrients include dissolved sugars, proteins, and gases.

Most cells in blood are red blood cells, which are shaped like a doughnut without the hole. They contain the chemical **hemoglobin** (hē′mə glō′bin), which carries oxygen around your body. Blood also contains germ-fighting white blood cells and **platelets** (plāt′lits). When you have a cut, platelets stop the bleeding by forming clots.

Blood travels through three kinds of blood vessels—**arteries** (är′tə rēz), **veins** (vānz), and **capillaries** (kap′ə ler′ēz). Arteries are blood vessels that carry blood away from your heart. Veins are blood vessels that carry blood back to your heart. Capillaries are where materials are exchanged between the blood and body cells.

Red blood cell   **White blood cell**

ARTERY

Blood vessels can range in size from large to very tiny. The largest vessels connect directly to your heart. The smallest arteries and veins connect to the smallest type of blood vessel, called a capillary.

Red blood cells' unique shape helps them move easily to carry out their tasks.

CAPILLARY

READING /N/ DIAGRAMS

DISCUSS How does blood flow change as blood moves from veins to capillaries?

Capillaries are too tiny to see without a microscope. Your red blood cells move through them in single file.

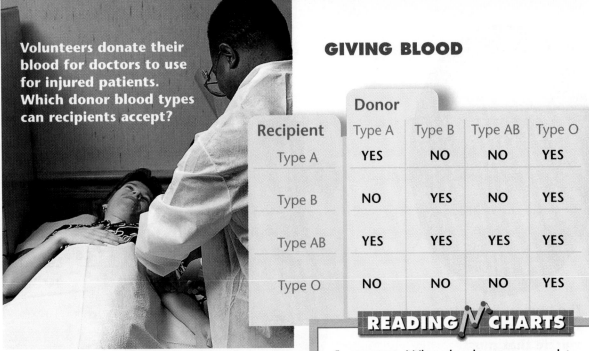

Volunteers donate their blood for doctors to use for injured patients. Which donor blood types can recipients accept?

Recipient	Donor			
	Type A	Type B	Type AB	Type O
Type A	YES	NO	NO	YES
Type B	NO	YES	NO	YES
Type AB	YES	YES	YES	YES
Type O	NO	NO	NO	YES

READING N CHARTS

1. **WRITE** Why do doctors need to know a patient's blood type before giving a transfusion?
2. **DISCUSS** If type O is the universal donor, which blood type would be the universal recipient?

What's Your Blood Type?

Have you ever read about injured people who needed **transfusions** (trans fū′zhənz)? A transfusion is blood taken from a healthy person and given to another person who needs it. The person giving the blood is the *donor*. The person receiving the blood is the *recipient*.

The first transfusions were done over 100 years ago. Some worked perfectly. Other times the transfused blood clumped, and the recipient died.

Scientists discovered two chemicals, called *antigens*, on the surface of red blood cells. They named the antigens A and B to distinguish between them.

People with only type A antigens in their blood have type A blood. People with only type B antigens have type B blood. AB blood contains both antigens. Blood without any A or B antigens is called type O blood.

Certain **antibodies** (an′ti bod′ēz) affect these chemical blood types. An antibody is a protein in blood that helps find and destroy harmful materials in the body.

Antibodies form clumps around unfamiliar antigens. For example, type A blood has antibodies to clump around blood cells with type B antigens.

Type O blood is special because it has no A or B antigens, so antibodies won't clump around it. This is why it is called the "universal donor" type.

Another chemical in blood cells is the Rh chemical. Blood with Rh chemical is called *Rh positive*. Blood without it is called *Rh negative*. Rh negative blood forms clumps around Rh positive blood. Doctors are very careful when mothers and babies have different blood types. They use special medicines to keep the two different blood types from clotting.

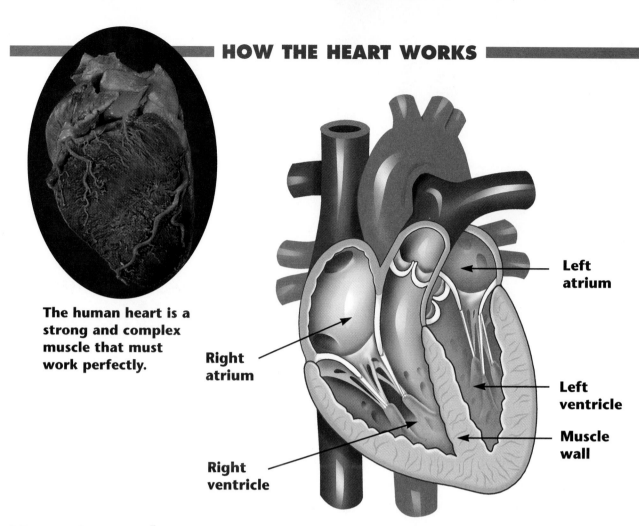

The human heart is a strong and complex muscle that must work perfectly.

Right atrium

Right ventricle

Left atrium

Left ventricle

Muscle wall

How Does the Heart Work?

Your heart constantly pumps blood to every part of your body. The Explore Activity showed how blood moves through the heart.

The heart is a muscle about the size of your fist, located in your rib cage.

The heart has two sides, a right side and a left side, separated by a thick muscular wall. Each side has two chambers for blood. The upper chamber is called the *atrium*. The lower chamber is called the *ventricle*. A one-way valve allows blood to move from the atrium to the ventricle.

Inside your heart special cells give off electrical signals without help from the

brain or nerves. The signals make heart muscle cells contract and relax. First each atrium squeezes, then each ventricle. Each contraction and relaxation makes one heart beat. Your heart beats 70 to 80 times a minute. That's more than one beat every second. The most your heart muscle ever rests is a split second. No other muscle can work that hard without tiring.

On the heart's right side, blood from your body enters the atrium from the largest vein in your body, called the *vena cava*. This blood lacks oxygen and must get rid of wastes it collected from cells in the body. It travels through the atrium to the ventricle and pulmonary artery.

Blood travels through each chamber of your heart.

TO THE LUNGS

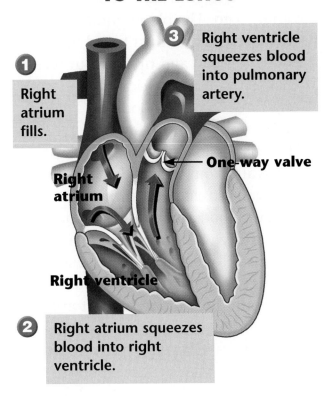

1 Right atrium fills.

3 Right ventricle squeezes blood into pulmonary artery.

Right atrium

One-way valve

Right ventricle

2 Right atrium squeezes blood into right ventricle.

FROM THE LUNGS

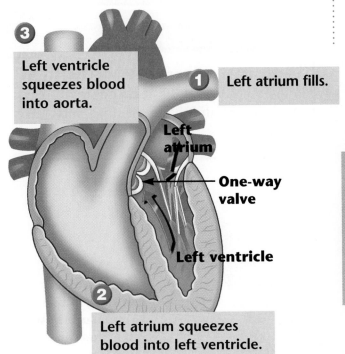

3 Left ventricle squeezes blood into aorta.

1 Left atrium fills.

Left atrium

One-way valve

Left ventricle

2 Left atrium squeezes blood into left ventricle.

How Do the Heart and Lungs Work Together?

The pulmonary artery carries blood into the lungs and branches into capillaries. Here the carbon dioxide leaves the blood to be exhaled by the lungs. Fresh oxygen from the lungs is attracted to the blood's hemoglobin. Hemoglobin carries oxygen around in the body, giving blood its bright red color.

The blood returns from the lungs to the heart through the pulmonary vein. The pulmonary vein conducts the blood into the left atrium. It flows to the left ventricle and out of the aorta.

The aorta is your largest artery. It carries blood full of oxygen into smaller and smaller arteries to reach every part of your body. As blood flows into the tiniest capillaries, it releases oxygen and other nutrients into the cells. Carbon dioxide and cell wastes enter the blood, giving it a blue-red color. Blood flows from the capillaries into larger and larger veins. Finally, the blood enters the vena cava again and flows into the right atrium.

READING N DIAGRAMS

1. **DISCUSS** What happens to the blood after it enters the right atrium? The left atrium?
2. **WRITE** When does blood flow to the lungs? From the lungs?

QUICK LAB

Squeeze Play

HYPOTHESIZE How easy is it for your heart to pump blood? What might it depend on? Write a hypothesis in your *Science Journal.*

MATERIALS

- empty plastic water bottle
- masking tape
- pushpin
- *Science Journal*

PROCEDURES

1. OBSERVE Squeeze the bottle with one hand, and feel how much air flows out with the other.

2. COMPARE Cover the opening with tape. Make a small hole in the tape with the pushpin. Squeeze. Does more or less air flow out? Is the bottle easier or harder to squeeze?

CONCLUDE AND APPLY

DRAW CONCLUSIONS
If your arteries start to narrow, will your heart work harder or less hard?

What Is Blood Pressure?

Every time your heart pumps, it squeezes blood out of your heart. The blood going to your lungs does not have far to go. The blood going through your aorta must travel to the top of your head and tips of your toes. To do that the left ventricle uses a strong force to push blood out. That force is your blood pressure.

The pushed blood presses on the artery walls from the inside. The elastic artery walls stretch and spring back to give your blood an extra push. You can feel an artery wall stretch by taking your pulse. To feel your pulse, place your fingers on the inside of your wrist. Count how many times it pulses in one minute.

Another way to gauge heart rate is by listening with a stethoscope. It sounds like "lub-dup, lub-dup, lub-dup." Can you guess what makes these sounds? It's not your blood or heart muscle. What's left?

Brain Power
MATH LINK

A marathon runner's resting pulse may be as low as 40 beats per minute. Why might an athlete's resting pulse be so low?

Athletes often use their pulse to measure how hard they are working.

How Do Blood Vessels Heal?

When you have a cut, blood pours out of the wound. Then the flow slows and soon stops. Bleeding stops because your blood clots.

Platelets help your blood to clot. They collect in a wound and stick to each other in a clump. Then proteins in your blood form a web of sticky threads. The threads and platelets trap red blood cells to form a clot that seals the wound. When the wound heals, the clot dissolves. If the clot does not dissolve, it can block the flow of blood in the blood vessels.

Germ-fighting white blood cells also rush to the wound. They attach to bacteria or viruses inside the wound. If the white cells in your blood don't destroy the germs, the white blood cells in your lymph vessels may.

Lymph vessels are similar to blood vessels. Instead of transporting blood, they collect *lymph*. Lymph is a straw-colored fluid surrounding the cells in your tissues. This fluid travels through lymph vessels that return the lymph to your blood.

Why don't the cells dry out as the lymph vessels collect fluid? More fluid leaks out of nearby capillaries to take its place.

Before returning to your blood, lymph passes through lymph nodes. Lymph nodes filter out harmful materials. They also produce white blood cells to fight infections. When you have a sore throat, you may feel swollen lymph nodes in your neck. They are a clue that your body is fighting germs that infected you.

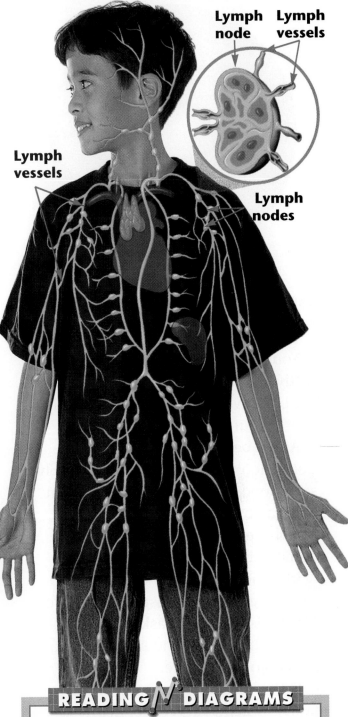

Lymph vessels run through your body to collect fluid and return it to the bloodstream.

Lymph node

Lymph vessels

Lymph vessels

Lymph nodes

READING N DIAGRAMS

1. **DISCUSS** Why do you think the lymph vessels are located where they are in your body?
2. **WRITE** How are the lymph vessels like blood vessels? How are they different?

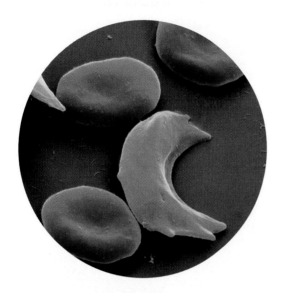

How Can You Help Your Heart?

You can see some blood vessels indirectly through your skin. A doctor can see blood vessels clearly and directly inside your eyes.

At the beginning of this topic, the doctor looked into the man's eyes. She saw blood vessels starting to thicken and narrow. These are signs of high blood pressure that can weaken and damage the arteries.

In some people very salty foods cause high blood pressure. Those were the foods the doctor asked about. Unhealthy weight and smoking also affect blood pressure.

Fatty foods can damage your circulatory system. Fats collect in arteries, limiting your blood flow. The arteries narrow, harden, and clog.

Worst of all a clot may form in a narrowed artery. Clots can stop the normal flow of blood and cause a heart attack.

By eating the right foods, exercising, and taking medicines, the man in the story can lower his blood pressure.

Other diseases are inherited. *Sickle cell anemia* occurs when people inherit genes with the sickle cell trait.

People who get this trait from only one parent do not develop this disease but can pass it on.

If a person gets this gene from both parents, sickle cell anemia develops. The person's red blood cells curve into a C shape, called a sickle. Sickle cells cannot move or absorb oxygen easily.

Sometimes sickle cells pile up in the blood vessels. The person feels pain from these blocked blood vessels.

Sickle cell anemia occurs mostly in people whose ancestors lived in tropical areas. Scientists learned that people in these areas need one copy of the gene to protect them from malaria.

Doctors today can test for this gene and are doing research to cure the disease.

Fatty foods damage arteries and make it hard for blood to pass.

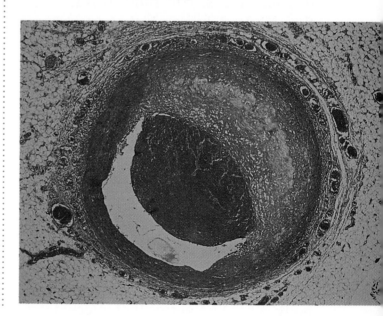

Understanding how blood travels through your body can help you take better care of your circulatory system. You now know that your cells need blood to provide essential oxygen and nutrients for them to use.

Knowing how blood travels helps you to understand how serious problems with your heart and blood vessels can be. If the circulatory system is not working well, it quickly affects every cell in your body. It is not enough to simply keep it from becoming damaged. You must be aware of how every part works together to make sure that it stays in top shape.

By eating right, exercising, and seeing your doctor regularly, you can strengthen and protect your circulatory system from harm.

Exercise encourages good blood flow in your body.

REVIEW

1. What are the three types of blood vessels your body uses to move blood in your body?

2. Name the four different blood types.

3. Describe the path blood takes through the heart.

4. MEASURE What is your resting pulse rate? How could you find out?

5. CRITICAL THINKING *Analyze* Why is the lymph system needed to keep your blood and cells healthy?

WHY IT MATTERS THINK ABOUT IT
Think about all of the places your blood travels to. What would happen to the rest of your body if part of your circulatory system were blocked?

WHY IT MATTERS WRITE ABOUT IT
What would make it easier for your blood to reach all of the cells in your body? What would make it more difficult? Write your ideas in your *Science Journal.*

READING SKILL
Look back at this topic. Locate the details you need, then write a paragraph to explain what the different parts of the blood do.

Sickle SICKNESS

If you have healthy red blood cells, you have lots of energy.

One child in four born to parents carrying the sickle cell gene (§) will have the disease.

Health Link

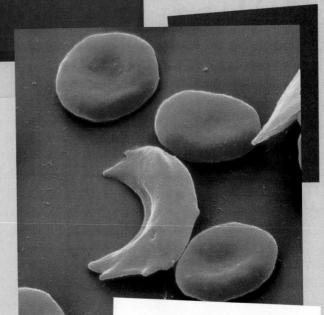

How do you feel today? If you're feeling energetic, you can probably thank your red blood cells. They're the cells that carry oxygen throughout your body. People who don't have enough red blood cells often feel tired and listless. Sickle cell anemia is a disease that affects the red blood cells. The disease makes the cells stiffen into hooklike, or sickle, shapes that can cause the cells to get stuck in small blood vessels. That blocks the flow of blood to parts of the body, causing pain. The affected red blood cells weaken and die. Without enough red blood cells, the person becomes anemic. That means he or she feels tired and weak.

Compare these normal red blood cells with the sickled cell.

Sickle cell anemia is inherited. To get the disease, a person must inherit a sickle cell gene from each parent. Many people carry one sickle cell gene. They're not affected by the disease. However, if two carriers have children, one in four of those children is likely to have the disease.

Sickle cell anemia is most common among people from Africa, the Mediterranean, the Caribbean, the Middle East, and India. More than 60,000 Americans now have the disease. About 2.5 million more carry the sickle cell gene.

People can take tests to find out whether they carry the sickle cell gene. This may help couples decide whether to have children. Tests can also identify newborns who have the disease.

Discussion Starter

1 Which body system does sickle cell anemia affect?

2 Can you get sickle cell anemia by sharing a soda with a person who has it? Why or why not?

*inter*NET CONNECTION To learn more about sickle cell anemia, visit **www.mhschool.com/science** and enter the keyword **SICKLE.**

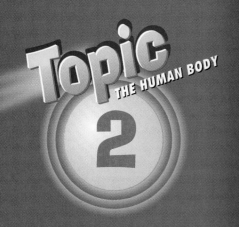

Topic 2
THE HUMAN BODY

WHY IT MATTERS

You need oxygen for all of your cells to use every day.

SCIENCE WORDS

respiration the process of obtaining and using oxygen in the body

diaphragm a sheet of muscle below the chest cavity that helps control breathing

trachea a stiff tube lined with cartilage that transports air between the throat and lungs

mucus a clear fluid that traps and prevents foreign particles from entering the body

cilia small hairlike structures that move small particles of dirt out of the respiratory system

diffusion the process by which a substance such as a gas moves from areas of high concentration to areas of low concentration

A Breathing System

What do the following have in common: coughing, sneezing, wheezing, yawning, laughing, speaking, smelling, and hiccupping? Why do climbers carry oxygen tanks to help them reach the tops of the world's highest mountains? Give up? Take a deep breath and try answering this: After you run as fast as you can for a short distance, why do you gasp for air when you stop running?

EXPLORE

HYPOTHESIZE Many things can make it easier or harder for you to breathe. What might affect your breathing? Write a hypothesis in your *Science Journal.* Test your ideas.

590

Investigate What Makes You Breathe

Use this experiment to learn what forces help you to breathe.

MATERIALS

- clear-plastic cup
- flexible plastic straw
- scissors
- pushpin
- small balloon
- large balloon
- 2 rubber bands
- clay
- *Science Journal*

PROCEDURES

SAFETY Use the scissors carefully!

1. Attach the opening of the small balloon to the end of the straw with a rubber band.

2. Make a hole at the bottom of the cup with the scissors or pushpin. Hold the cup upside down. Pull the open end of the straw through the hole so the balloon hangs inside the cup. Seal the cup hole around the straw with clay.

3. Tie the "neck" of the large balloon. Cut off the wide end. Stretch the balloon over the cup's open end. Secure it with a rubber band.

4. **OBSERVE** Pull down slowly on the stretched balloon. What happens to the balloon inside the cup? Push up on the stretched balloon. What happens inside the cup? Record your answers in your *Science Journal*.

CONCLUDE AND APPLY

1. **EVALUATE** Is there more or less space inside the cup when you pull down on the large balloon?

2. **IDENTIFY** When you pull the large balloon down, what fills the extra space in the cup?

GOING FURTHER: Problem Solving

3. **COMPARE** How is the air pressure in the balloon similar to the air pressure in your lungs? Write down what you think happens when you breathe air into your lungs.

HOW YOU BREATHE

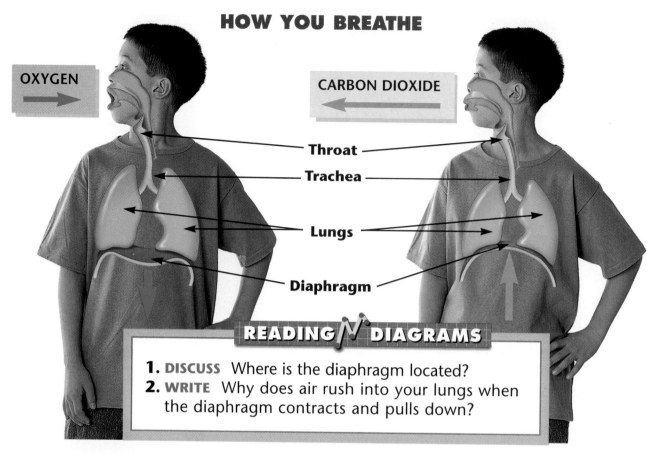

OXYGEN

CARBON DIOXIDE

Throat

Trachea

Lungs

Diaphragm

READING N DIAGRAMS

1. **DISCUSS** Where is the diaphragm located?
2. **WRITE** Why does air rush into your lungs when the diaphragm contracts and pulls down?

What Makes You Breathe?

The Explore Activity showed that changing the amount of space in a closed space changes the air pressure. Air rushes into empty spaces and rushes out when a space becomes smaller. What if the air did not move in and out?

Your cells can't live more than a few minutes without oxygen. They use it to turn food into energy. The process of obtaining and using oxygen in the body is called **respiration** (res'pə rā'shən).

Oxygen comes from air you breathe into your lungs. There's just one catch: The lungs are soft, spongy tissues that can't pull in air on their own. They need muscles to do the work of breathing.

Two main muscles control breathing. One is located between your ribs. The other is a dome-shaped

sheet of muscle called the **diaphragm** (dī'ə fram'). The diaphragm stretches below your chest cavity, under your lungs and above your abdomen.

To inhale, the diaphragm contracts and pulls down. Other muscles pull your ribs up and out. This creates more room in your chest. Air rushes into your lungs and fills the space.

To exhale, your diaphragm relaxes and returns to its dome shape. With less room inside your chest, the lungs get smaller and force air out.

Usually your diaphragm moves up and down smoothly. Sometimes the diaphragm jerks up and down causing hiccups. Laughing also makes your diaphragm move up and down more than usual.

The diaphragm causes you to inhale and exhale, but your respiratory system includes many other parts.

What Happens When You Breathe?

When you inhale, air is pulled into your nose or mouth. Nose hairs trap large dirt and dust particles, and your body warms the air.

Air travels down into the **trachea** (trā′kē ə), a stiff tube lined with cartilage that transports air between the throat and lungs. The trachea's cartilage rings keep it open for air to enter. When you eat, your epiglottis keeps food out of your trachea. Your voice box, or larynx, is located at the top of the trachea.

Your nose, throat, and trachea are lined with **mucus** (mū′kəs) and **cilia** (sil′ē ə). Mucus is a moist, sticky fluid that traps small particles. Cilia (singular, *cilium*) are small hairlike structures that move particles and

mucus along your throat. The mucus is swallowed, and your stomach acids destroy the particles it has collected.

In your chest the trachea divides into two bronchial tubes. One tube enters each of your lungs. Each tube branches into smaller tubes called bronchioles.

At the end of each bronchiole are tiny air sacs called *alveoli*. Alveoli look like very tiny grapes organized in clusters. Capillaries carrying blood from the heart surround them.

Your alveoli exchange carbon dioxide for oxygen by **diffusion** (di fū′zhən). In diffusion a substance such as a gas moves from areas of high concentration to areas of low concentration.

READING IN DIAGRAMS

1. **DISCUSS** How does the air you breathe get to your lungs?
2. **WRITE** What do alveoli do?

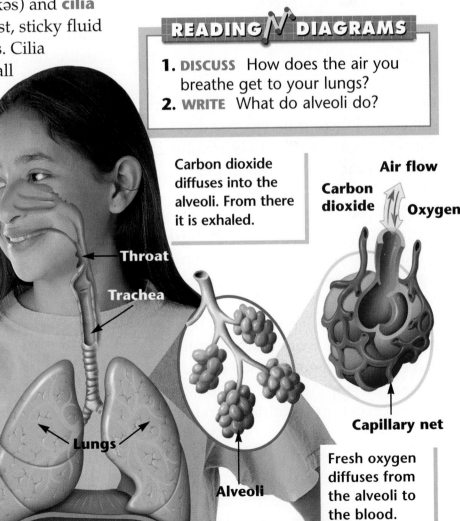

The air you breathe is about 21 percent oxygen.

The blood in the capillaries of your lungs has very little oxygen.

The blood has a higher concentration of carbon dioxide than the air.

Throat

Trachea

Lungs

Carbon dioxide diffuses into the alveoli. From there it is exhaled.

Air flow

Carbon dioxide

Oxygen

Capillary net

Alveoli

Fresh oxygen diffuses from the alveoli to the blood.

593

Can You Control Your Breathing?

Take a deep breath. Just now you controlled your breathing muscles by thinking about them. Even though you can control these muscles, you don't have to. Your brain controls breathing automatically by sensing carbon dioxide in your blood.

When you are tired, you may not breathe deeply enough. Carbon dioxide builds up in your blood. Your brain makes you take a deep breath, or yawn, to get rid of it.

When you run, your muscles need more oxygen to work hard. Your lungs can't take in oxygen quickly enough. When you stop running, you breathe hard to expel carbon dioxide and take in more oxygen.

If you visit mountainous places, you may feel tired, dizzy, or short of breath. The higher you go, the thinner the air gets. The gases in the air are more

Breathing hard is your body's way of recovering from hard work.

spread out. You breathe in less oxygen with each breath. Mountain climbers carry oxygen tanks with them to avoid these symptoms. Over a long period of time at high altitudes, the body makes more red blood cells to gather enough oxygen without breathing hard.

With so many people breathing in oxygen and using it up, why doesn't the supply run out? Why doesn't the air turn poisonous from all of the carbon dioxide being exhaled?

The reason these things don't happen is because plants and algae use carbon dioxide in photosynthesis. During photosynthesis plants use carbon dioxide and release oxygen into the air. This process is the reverse of how we use oxygen and carbon dioxide. Plants put carbon dioxide to use and provide more oxygen for us to use.

Brain Power

People sometimes yawn when they are not tired. Why do you think they do that?

What are some other ways plants help people?

SKILL BUILDER

Skill: Forming a Hypothesis and Measuring

HOW EXERCISE AFFECTS YOUR HEART AND LUNGS

A hypothesis is a reasonable, testable guess or statement about why something happens. It helps you design and learn from experiments. If the hypothesis is correct, the results will support it. If the hypothesis is wrong, you must rewrite it.

MATERIALS

- watch with a second hand
- *Science Journal*

1. **HYPOTHESIZE** In your *Science Journal*, write a hypothesis about how exercise affects your pulse and breathing rates.

2. **MEASURE** Place your index and middle fingers on the inside of your partner's wrist so you feel a pulse, or beat, on the artery. Count pulse rate for one minute. Have another student count how many times your partner breathes during the minute. Record the number of heart-beats as the resting pulse rate. Record the number of breaths as the resting breath rate.

3. **USE VARIABLES** Have your partner do jumping jacks for two minutes, then measure pulse and breathing rates for one minute. Record results.

4. **COMPARE** Wait two minutes, recount, and record both results.

CONCLUDE AND APPLY

1. **COMPARE** How much faster was the pulse rate after exercising? How much faster was the breathing rate?

2. **DRAW CONCLUSIONS** How does exercise affect the heart and the lungs?

3. **REVISE** Does this prove your hypoth-esis? If not, how can you change and test it?

What Can Harm Your Respiratory System?

Sometimes bacteria or viruses enter your respiratory system. Your nose may run as it makes excess mucus to trap germs. You cough and sneeze to expel germs. This is a normal process your body goes through to fight infection. Soon the immune system destroys the germs, and your system returns to normal.

Some people find breathing difficult even when they are not sick. Allergies and asthma can cause your airways to narrow. By spraying a mist of medicines into their lungs, people with asthma can breathe easier. People with allergies may take shots or pills to help them.

Respiratory problems can quickly become very serious. To keep your respiratory system healthy, exercise regularly and avoid smoking.

Exercise causes your heart and lungs to work hard for short periods of time. This work strengthens your heart and

Breathing hard during activity supplies your muscles with extra oxygen.

This athlete is using an inhaler for her asthma.

breathing muscles. A stronger heart circulates more blood when it pumps. Stronger breathing muscles take in more oxygen and release more carbon dioxide.

Smoking damages your respiratory system. You inhale tobacco smoke and the chemicals used to prepare the tobacco. Chemicals in burning tobacco paralyze cilia. They cannot sweep dirt and germs out of the nose, throat, and breathing tubes. These particles enter your lungs and irritate the soft tissues there. Your lungs begin to form a thick lining, which can build up and block your bronchial tubes.

Dangers of Smoking

Over time smoking destroys the air sacs in your lungs. Chemicals from smoke also cause cancers in the mouth, throat, and lungs. Many of these cancers are difficult to treat. Most cases of lung cancer cannot be cured.

WHY IT MATTERS

Understanding how your respiratory system works helps you keep it working at its best. You know how to strengthen and protect your lungs. By measuring your heart and breathing rates, you can learn how different activities affect your respiratory system. You will know when your respiratory system is working hard or being overworked.

By exercising and not smoking, you care for your throat, trachea, and lungs. Knowing about the complex actions of your respiratory system also helps you recognize problems with your breathing. If you ever have trouble breathing, tell an adult at once. You don't want anything to prevent your respiratory system from doing its job.

NATIONAL GEOGRAPHIC

FUNtastic Facts

Your lungs are like a pair of sponges full of millions of air sacs called alveoli. If you could flatten and spread out all the alveoli in the lungs of one adult, the air sacs would cover an area about one-third the size of a tennis court! How does smoking affect the alveoli?

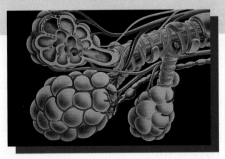

REVIEW

1. What parts of the respiratory system take air from outside of your body into your lungs?

2. What two gases are exchanged in your lungs?

3. What does asthma do to the body that makes it difficult for people to breathe?

4. **HYPOTHESIZE/MEASURE** Create a hypothesis about what you can do to strengthen your respiratory system. What data would you need to collect to prove your hypothesis?

5. **CRITICAL THINKING** *Analyze* What are some ways that people can improve the quality of the air they breathe?

WHY IT MATTERS THINK ABOUT IT
What did you learn about your respiratory system that will help you to take better care of it?

WHY IT MATTERS WRITE ABOUT IT
Write down some additional things that you think would harm your respiratory system. Write down ways you can avoid or change these things.

Asthma Attacks

Do you sneeze a lot when there's a lot of pollen or dust in the air? You may have an allergy. If you do your immune system will try to destroy the foreign substances you inhale.

In some people dust and pollen can trigger a serious asthma attack. Their bronchi and other airways swell up. The mucus that usually helps clean their lungs gets thicker and begins to block the airways. Muscles around their airways tighten until they're almost shut.

A mild asthma attack may cause only coughing, but a severe attack can trap air in the lungs. Air can't move in or out, making it impossible to take a deep breath. The person needs immediate medical help. Many asthma victims go to hospital emergency rooms for treatment.

Medicines can help to control asthma. Many people also carry bronchodilators. They contain medicine a person can

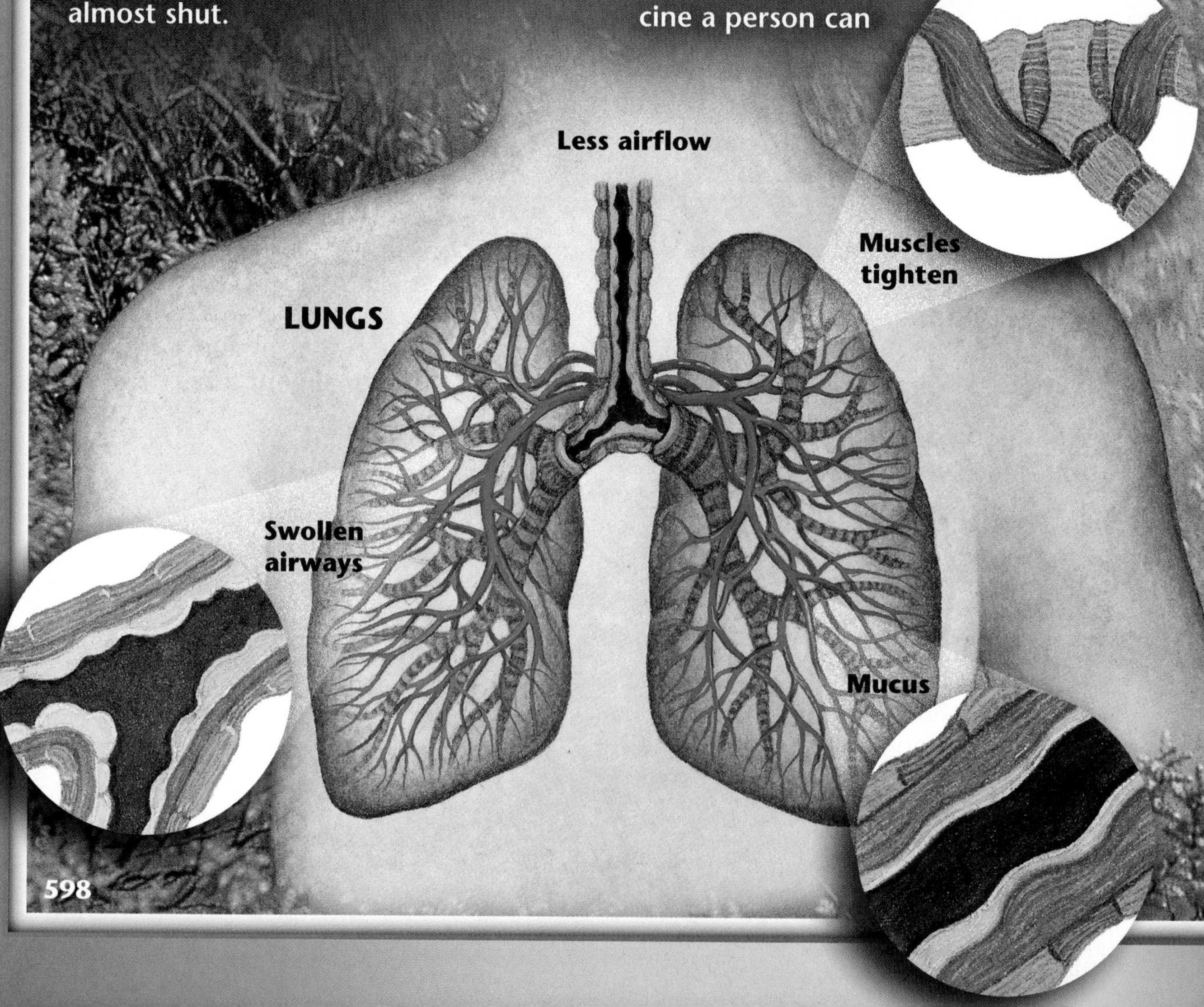

Less airflow

Muscles tighten

LUNGS

Swollen airways

Mucus

Health Link

inhale if an attack starts. The medicine helps open airways and relax muscles.

Not all asthma attacks are caused by allergies. For some people exercising too much or getting upset can trigger an attack. On a winter day, breathing very cold air can start an attack.

About three million kids in the United States have asthma. It can't be cured, but it can be controlled. Asthma patients learn to watch for warning signs, such as feeling out of breath, coughing, or wheezing as they breathe. People with asthma also know the importance of taking their medication.

DISCUSSION STARTER

1. How do allergies cause asthma?
2. How can people control asthma?

Having asthma doesn't rule out an active life. Jackie Joyner-Kersee won Olympic gold medals despite her asthma!

To learn more about asthma, visit *www.mhschool.com/science* and enter the keyword BREATHE.

*inter*NET
CONNECTION

SCIENCE WORDS

capillary p.580   plasma p.580

cilia p.593   platelet p.580

diaphragm p.592   respiration p.592

diffusion p.593   transfusion p.581

hemoglobin p.580   vein p.580

USING SCIENCE WORDS

Number a paper from 1 to 10. Fill in 1 to 5 with words from the list above.

1. The body obtains oxygen by ___?___.

2. Cell fragments that help to form clots are ___?___.

3. The tiniest blood vessels in the body are called ___?___.

4. A(n) ___?___ transfers blood between two people.

5. Gases move from one location to another by ___?___.

6–10. **Pick five words from the list above that were not used in 1 to 5, and use each in a sentence.**

UNDERSTANDING SCIENCE IDEAS

11. How does blood travel through the heart?

12. Describe how the diaphragm changes shape when you breathe.

13. Explain what role lymph vessels play in your body.

14. What can cause high blood pressure?

15. What proteins help the body find and destroy harmful proteins?

USING IDEAS AND SKILLS

16. At higher altitudes it becomes more difficult to breathe. Why does this happen, and how can your body adjust?

17. **READING SKILL: LOCATING DETAILS** The valves in the heart open in only one direction. Why is this important to your bloodstream?

18. The supply of oxygen in the air will run out because people are using it up. Is this true or false? Explain your answer.

19. **HYPOTHESIZE/MEASURE** What effect do you think high altitudes might have on athletes, such as runners or skiers? State your answer as a hypothesis, and suggest a way to test your idea.

20. **THINKING LIKE A SCIENTIST** Scientists try to learn if a disease is inherited or comes from behaviors, like smoking. What are some ways you could find this out? Write out your suggestions.

PROBLEMS and PUZZLES

Thump Thump Is your heart the most active muscle in your body? To find out fill a bucket with 4 liters of water. Using a $\frac{1}{2}$-cup measuring cup, transfer all 4 liters of water to a second bucket in one minute. That is about the rate at which the heart pumps blood. At that rate how soon would your other muscles tire?

CHAPTER 14
USING
FOOD AND
STAYING
FIT

Soon it will be time for another Olympics competition. Athletes from around the world will compete. Some will be only a few years older than you are.

Could you cross the finish line at the Olympics one day? That depends on how talented you are, how much you practice, and how much support you have. It also takes knowing how your body works so you can make it work at its best. When do you think your body works at its best?

In Chapter 14 you will read to find the main idea.

601

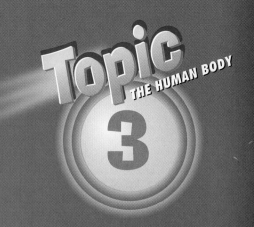

WHY IT MATTERS

Your body prepares food for your cells to use and eliminates the waste products left over.

SCIENCE WORDS

digestion the process of breaking food down into simpler substances for the body to use

enzyme a chemical that breaks down food into simple pieces that cells can use

bile a greenish-yellow fluid produced by the liver to digest fats

villus a tiny fingerlike projection in the small intestine that absorbs digested food

urea a substance formed from waste material in the liver and excreted in urine

excretion the process of removing waste products from the body

nephron a structure in the kidney that filters blood

A Food System

Every day people buy food to eat. A lot of what they buy and cook ends up in the trash.

Think about it. Foods come in boxes, bottles, trays, and bags. Some are recycled; the rest are tossed out.

Before cooking, fats, bones, seeds, peels, and other parts are removed from food. After the meal uneaten food is either saved or disposed of. Where do all of these wastes go?

EXPLORE

HYPOTHESIZE Every day your body uses some of the food you eat and turns some of it into waste. What does your body keep? How does it get rid of wastes? Write a hypothesis in your *Science Journal.*

Design Your Own Experiment

WHAT ARE SOME WAYS TO SORT MATERIALS?

PROCEDURES

SAFETY Use the scissors carefully!

1. Cut open the tea bag. Pour the tea leaves into the cup of water. Add pepper and cloves. Stir.

2. Open the coffee filter, and hold it over the bowl. Hold the tea strainer above the open filter.

3. Slowly pour the contents of the cup through the strainer and into the filter.

4. **OBSERVE** What is left in the strainer? What is left in the filter? Lift the filter. What is in the bowl? Record your observations in your *Science Journal.*

MATERIALS

- tea bag
- cup half-filled with water
- tea strainer or medium-sized strainer
- ground pepper
- cloves
- coffee filter
- plastic bowl
- scissors
- spoon
- *Science Journal*

CONCLUDE AND APPLY

1. **COMMUNICATE** What was in the strainer at the end of the activity? What was not present in the bowl at all?

2. **EXPLAIN** Why did the filtering system work? Why can some materials pass through while others cannot?

GOING FURTHER: Problem Solving

3. **DRAW CONCLUSIONS** How could your body use a system like this to separate solids from a liquid? Would this remove wastes effectively? Why or why not?

4. **EXPERIMENT** Design your own filtering experiment. Try placing different materials in different liquids, then filtering them out. Try other materials as filters. Answer Conclude and Apply questions 1 and 2 for your experiment.

What Are Some Ways to Sort Materials?

The Explore Activity showed that solid materials in a liquid can be sorted by size. Materials that are too large for the filter are trapped. Your body gets rid of some wastes in a similar way.

Many of these wastes come from the food you eat. Before getting rid of these wastes, the body separates out the useful nutrients. **Digestion** (di jes′chən) is the process of breaking down food into simple substances your body can use.

Digestion begins in the mouth when you chew your food. Chewing breaks the large pieces into smaller pieces. Chewing also moistens food with *saliva*, which contains digestive **enzymes** (en′zīmz). An enzyme is a chemical that breaks down food into simple pieces that cells can use. Saliva is produced in the *salivary glands*.

When you swallow, the food travels down a tube called the *esophagus* to your stomach. In the stomach food is mixed with gastric juice. Gastric juice contains acids and more enzymes to break down the proteins in your food.

The stomach walls contract to churn the food into a thick liquid. After a few hours, this liquid enters the *small intestine*.

In the small intestine, more digestive juices work on the food. Your *pancreas* makes a juice that breaks down proteins and changes starch to sugar. Other digestive juices come from your *liver*.

THE DIGESTIVE SYSTEM

Teeth →

Salivary glands

← Esophagus

Liver

Stomach

Pancreas

Large intestine

Small intestine

← Anus

READING DIAGRAMS

1. **DISCUSS** What happens to food after it leaves the stomach?
2. **WRITE** Describe what happens to the food you eat as it travels from your mouth to your stomach.

604

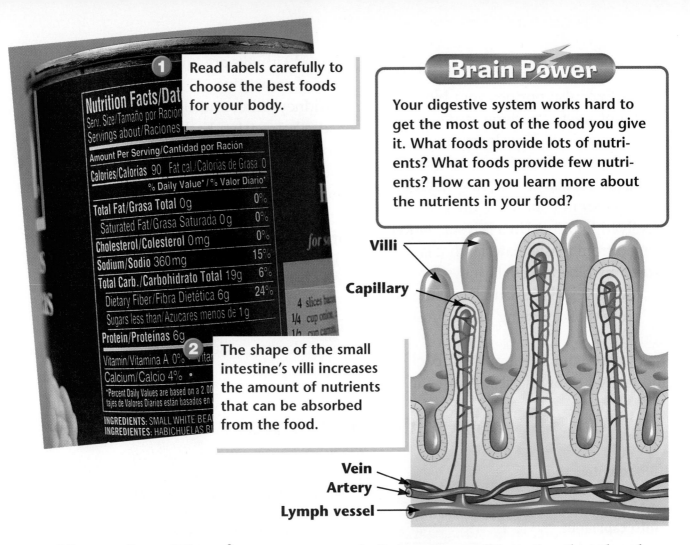

1 Read labels carefully to choose the best foods for your body.

Nutrition Facts/Dat...
Serv. Size/Tamaño por Ración
Servings about/Raciones...

Amount Per Serving/Cantidad por Ración
Calories/Calorías 90 Fat cal./Calorías de Grasa 0
% Daily Value*/% Valor Diario*

Total Fat/Grasa Total 0g	0%
Saturated Fat/Grasa Saturada 0g	0%
Cholesterol/Colesterol 0mg	0%
Sodium/Sodio 360mg	15%
Total Carb./Carbohidrato Total 19g	6%
Dietary Fiber/Fibra Dietética 6g	24%
Sugars less than/Azucares menos de 1g	
Protein/Proteínas 6g	

Vitamin/Vitamina A 0% • Vit...
Calcium/Calcio 4% •

*Percent Daily Values are based on a 2,00...
tajes de Valores Diarios están basados en u...

INGREDIENTS: SMALL WHITE BEA...
INGREDIENTES: HABICHUELAS BI...

4 slices bac...
1/4 cup onin...
1/2 cup carr...

2 The shape of the small intestine's villi increases the amount of nutrients that can be absorbed from the food.

Your digestive system works hard to get the most out of the food you give it. What foods provide lots of nutrients? What foods provide few nutrients? How can you learn more about the nutrients in your food?

Villi

Capillary

Vein

Artery

Lymph vessel

How Are Nutrients Absorbed?

The liver is the largest organ inside your body and has many jobs to do. One job is to produce **bile** (bīl). Bile is a greenish-yellow fluid produced by the liver to digest fats. Bile helps with the digestion process in your small intestine.

Bile, pancreatic juices, and other intestinal juices break down most of the remaining foods. When all of the food is chemically broken into nutrients, digestion is complete.

Now the nutrients must be absorbed. The walls of the small intestine are lined with **villi** (vil'ī) (singular, *villus*). Villi are tiny fingerlike projections lining the small intestine that absorb digested food.

The villi are filled with capillaries. Digested food passes through the villi and capillaries to enter the bloodstream. The blood transports nutrients to every part of your body.

Not all food can be digested and changed into nutrients. Undigested food and excess water go from the small intestine to the *large intestine*.

Your body absorbs the water from the large intestine. The remaining solid, undigested food travels through the large intestine. Bacteria in the large intestine break down the solid wastes. At the end of the large intestine, these wastes exit your body through the *anus*.

605

How Do Kidneys Work?

Your liver also purifies your blood. It filters out wastes, bacteria, drugs, and certain chemicals. Your liver converts these waste products into **urea** (yủ rē′ə). As a pure substance, urea is a white powder, but in your body, urea is dissolved in urine. Urea is a substance formed from waste material that is carried by blood to the kidneys for **excretion** (ek skrē′shən). Excretion is the process of removing waste products from the body.

Put your hands around your back and feel your lowest ribs. Your bean-shaped kidneys are under them on each side of your spine.

Kidneys filter and clean blood of urea and other wastes. Each kidney contains more than one million **nephrons** (nef′ronz). Nephrons are structures in the kidneys that filter blood.

Blood enters your kidneys through arteries. It travels to capillaries to be cleaned by the nephrons. The cleaned blood leaves through veins. The wastes collect in your kidneys as liquid urine. The urine flows down *ureters* to a muscular bag called the *bladder*.

HOW YOUR KIDNEYS WORK

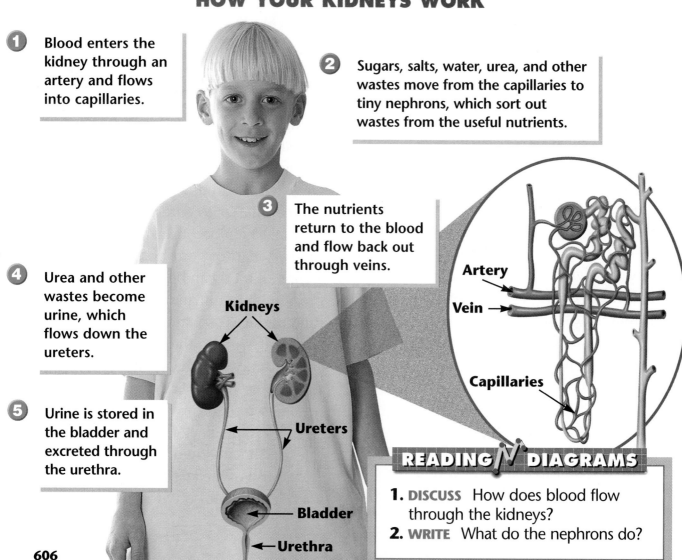

1 Blood enters the kidney through an artery and flows into capillaries.

2 Sugars, salts, water, urea, and other wastes move from the capillaries to tiny nephrons, which sort out wastes from the useful nutrients.

3 The nutrients return to the blood and flow back out through veins.

4 Urea and other wastes become urine, which flows down the ureters.

5 Urine is stored in the bladder and excreted through the urethra.

Kidneys

Ureters

Bladder

Urethra

Artery

Vein

Capillaries

READING N DIAGRAMS

1. DISCUSS How does blood flow through the kidneys?

2. WRITE What do the nephrons do?

Skill: Making a Model

HOW YOUR KIDNEYS WORK

A simple way to understand how kidneys and nephrons work is to make a model. Models can help us understand how things work. You can use very simple materials and familiar objects to represent complex systems. This model will show the sorting process of your excretory system.

MATERIALS

- plastic bag
- 5 red beans
- 5 white beans
- 5 rice grains
- 10 pennies
- *Science Journal*

PROCEDURES

1. MAKE A MODEL In this activity the bag stands for your blood, the red beans for urea, the white beans for sugars, the rice for salts, and the pennies for water. Place the beans, rice, and pennies in the bag. Record in your *Science Journal* what this represents.

2. Pour the contents of the bag on your desk to show materials moving from the blood to the nephrons.

3. Put all of the white beans back in the bag representing your blood. What does this illustrate?

4. Put four rice grains back in the bag to represent most of the salts.

5. Show that nearly all of the water returns to your blood by putting nine of the pennies back in the bag.

6. OBSERVE Record what is left on your desk.

CONCLUDE AND APPLY

1. EXPLAIN What items were left in step 6? What happens to these items in your body? What would happen if none of the materials in step 2 moved back into your blood?

2. PREDICT What would happen if none of the items ever left the blood? How could this harm your body?

GOING FURTHER: Apply

3. ANALYZE Many medicines are removed by your kidneys very quickly. How could you represent this in your model?

HOW YOU SWEAT

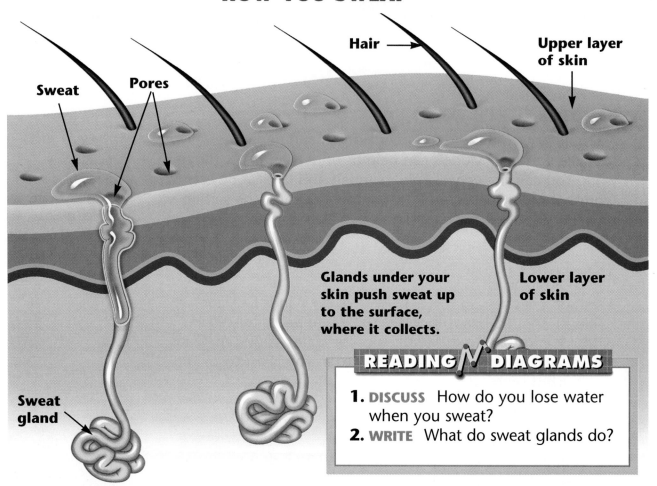

Sweat

Pores

Hair

Upper layer of skin

Glands under your skin push sweat up to the surface, where it collects.

Lower layer of skin

Sweat gland

READING DIAGRAMS

1. **DISCUSS** How do you lose water when you sweat?
2. **WRITE** What do sweat glands do?

What Is Sweat?

You already know how your body gets rid of carbon dioxide through exhaling. You also know how it gets rid of wastes from food. Your lungs, kidneys, and large intestine all take part in excretion.

Your skin also takes part in excretion when you sweat. Glands in the inner part, or *dermis*, of your skin produce sweat.

Sweat is mostly water. If a drop of sweat has ever rolled onto your tongue, you know it contains more than water. Sweat tastes salty because it contains mineral salts the body doesn't need. There is also a tiny amount of urea in your sweat.

Sweat is excreted by your sweat glands onto the outer layer of your skin. On your skin's surface, it changes by evaporation from liquid water to gaseous water vapor. This change takes place in part because of your body heat. When you use body heat to evaporate the sweat, you feel cooler. On hot days or when you exercise, you sweat more to keep your body from overheating.

When the water in sweat evaporates, it leaves the mineral salts and urea behind on your skin. These salts can build up over time, causing body odor, blocking your pores, and irritating your skin. Washing the skin regularly removes the solid materials left behind by sweat.

It is important to replace the water your body loses every day.

What Do You Need Water For?

Every time your heart beats, more blood flows into your kidneys. Over and over again, your kidneys filter and clean all of the blood in your body. Each time, water is used to transport the waste materials out.

Your kidneys perform a very difficult balancing act. Kidneys are responsible for balancing the amount of salt and water inside the body.

Your body is about two-thirds water. There is water inside and outside of your cells, in your blood, and in your lymph. Without water you could not cool down by sweating or remove wastes from your body.

You take in water every time you eat or drink. Cells make water during respiration. You lose water when you exhale and when you sweat. Water is also present in urine and solid food wastes.

It's up to your kidneys to balance the amount of water you lose with the amount you take in. When you sweat a lot on hot days, your body loses more water than usual. Your kidneys balance this by making less urine. If you drink more than usual, your kidneys will increase the amount of urine produced.

Drinking 6 to 8 glasses of water a day helps your kidneys do their job. With the right amount of water, kidneys can keep wastes moving out of your body. The water is also used by your blood, lymph, and cells. Without water your body struggles to carry out its work with limited resources. Make sure your body has enough water to do its work.

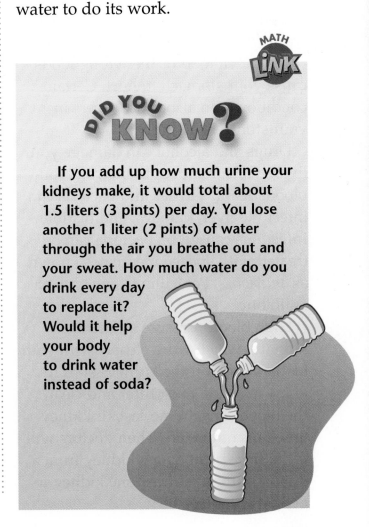

MATH LINK

DID YOU KNOW?

If you add up how much urine your kidneys make, it would total about 1.5 liters (3 pints) per day. You lose another 1 liter (2 pints) of water through the air you breathe out and your sweat. How much water do you drink every day to replace it? Would it help your body to drink water instead of soda?

Washing your face removes salt and urea left behind from sweat.

What Can You Do?

You depend on your excretory system. If the wastes are not removed or your body must remove too much waste, you become sick.

Too much food or the wrong foods cause your stomach to hurt. Certain conditions can also cause ulcers in your stomach.

Drugs and alcohol can damage your liver, which removes them from your bloodstream. Viruses and bacteria can infect the liver, kidneys, and bladder. Infections caused by bacteria can be treated with special medicines known as *antibiotics.* Penicillin is one type of antibiotic.

High blood pressure strains the kidneys, which work closely with your blood vessels. If the kidneys start to fail, a machine must filter and clean the blood. In extreme cases a kidney may fail completely. Then doctors will try to transplant a new kidney from a donor. Without at least one kidney, a person will die.

Many of these problems are preventable with proper nutrition. Foods with fiber help your large intestine excrete solid wastes. Drinking water makes your kidneys' job easier. Water and juices can keep your bladder healthy, too.

Washing your skin daily removes salts and other wastes left behind by sweat. It will keep your skin from becoming clogged and irritated.

Why Body Wastes Are Important

Why is it important for doctors to know what wastes your body is getting rid of? The wastes your body excretes can also indicate if you are sick. For example, doctors can detect *diabetes* by examining your urine. Diabetes is a condition in which the body's sugar levels are too high. Too much sugar in the urine may mean that not enough is staying in the body. Doctors can also test for other nutrients, bacteria, and types of cells in your urine.

Knowing how your body separates useful materials from wasteful materials helps you to take care of it.

Even things you may not think about can help your body. Chewing food well helps your esophagus and stomach. Drinking liquids provides water for your kidneys to use. Avoiding drugs and alcohol keeps your liver from working harder to remove wastes from your blood.

Now you know how hard your body works to remove wastes. You can help it by watching what you eat and by drinking plenty of water. You also know more about how your doctor can help you if you have problems with your digestion or excretory system.

REVIEW

1. Where are solid food wastes stored in your digestive system before they are excreted?

2. What is the waste material produced in your kidneys called?

3. Where is urine stored before leaving the body?

4. **MAKE A MODEL** How do exercise and weather affect how you feel when you sweat? How would you design a model to illustrate this?

5. **CRITICAL THINKING** *Apply* When your doctor prescribes medicines for you to take, what happens to the medicines in your body? How does your excretory system affect how often you must take more?

WHY IT MATTERS **THINK ABOUT IT**

What are some of the ways your diet affects your digestive and excretory systems? What would happen if you ate less food than normal? What if you ate too much?

WHY IT MATTERS **WRITE ABOUT IT**

Write down what you can do to take better care of your digestive system.

READING SKILL

Write a paragraph explaining the main idea of this topic.

Your Chemical Factory

Did you ever think of your liver as a storage chest? It is . . . sort of. Every minute about 10 percent of your blood is traveling through your liver. The blood brings the energy, vitamins, and minerals it picked up from food you've digested. The liver stores the vitamins and minerals until you need them!

A human liver weighs 3 to 4 pounds. As the blood moves through, the liver changes the blood's chemistry. That's why a liver is called a chemical factory! This important organ has more than 500 vital functions.

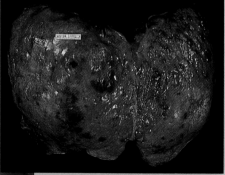

Alcohol can damage the liver. That's why it's best to say no to drinking!

It treats alcohol, steroids, and other drugs as poisons.

A Closer Look

It makes $\frac{1}{2}$ to 1 liter (1 to 2 pints) of greenish-yellow bile per day to store in the gallbladder. Bile helps you digest fats.

It filters wastes, poisons, bacteria, and other foreign substances out of the blood.

It helps you fight disease.

It produces the protein that allows your blood to clot. Without it you could bleed to death from a small cut!

It changes sugar in the bloodstream into starch and stores it. When your body needs energy, the liver changes the starch back into sugar.

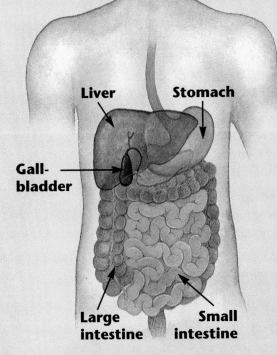

Liver

Stomach

Gall-bladder

Large intestine

Small intestine

Humans can live only about five days without a liver. If it isn't too badly damaged, a liver repairs itself—if only 10 percent of the liver is left after an operation, it grows back to full size!

DISCUSSION STARTER

1. How does the liver help the body handle wastes?

2. How does the liver help you feel energetic?

To learn more about your liver, visit **www.mhschool.com/science** and enter the keyword LIVER.

inter**NET**
CONNECTION

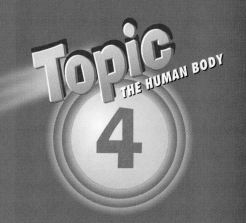

SCIENCE WORDS

physical fitness the condition in which your body is healthy and works the best it can

aerobic exercise a brisk and constant physical activity that increases the supply of oxygen to the muscles

balanced diet a diet, maintained over time, that includes a variety of foods providing nutrition in moderate amounts

food group one of the groups made up of foods that contain similar amounts of important nutrients

Fitness

The next time you watch a sport, keep your eye on the athletes. How long do they play without stopping? When they stop, how many athletes huff and puff to catch their breath?

Do any athletes look so tired you think they can't keep playing? Do any seem so full of energy that they could go on and on? Through exercise and practice, athletes can train their bodies to be physically fit.

EXPLORE

HYPOTHESIZE Being physically fit means your body is working at its best. Do you know what makes a body physically fit? How fit do you think your body is? Write your ideas in your *Science Journal*.

Investigate What Fitness Is

Explore skills needed for fitness.

MATERIALS
- *Science Journal*

PROCEDURES

1. **OBSERVE** Look at the photographs of the athletes on this page.

2. **COMMUNICATE** In each picture identify which body parts are being exercised. In your *Science Journal*, describe what you think is the most important skill or ability needed to do each activity.

CONCLUDE AND APPLY

1. **COMPARE** How are the skills you identified different from each other? Are the skills different for each activity? Do some skills and abilities usually go together?

2. **EVALUATE** Everyone has certain skills and abilities. How do top athletes use their skills and abilities to succeed? What type of training is involved in different activities? How much time do you think top athletes spend each week practicing these skills? Why do you think most top athletes train for years in order to master their sports?

GOING FURTHER: Apply

3. **ANALYZE** In your *Science Journal*, record some of your own skills and abilities. Think of activities that would help you use those skills.

615

There are many different ways to get aerobic exercise.

What Is Fitness?

The Explore Activity showed that skills and abilities help people to do all kinds of activities. Some require athletes to be physically fit.

Physical fitness (fiz′i kəl fit′nəs) is the condition in which your body is healthy and works the best it can. It involves working your skeletal muscles, bones, joints, heart, and respiratory system.

You control your skeletal muscles by thinking. Your brain sends electrical messages along nerves to make your muscles contract. The muscles pull on the bones they are attached to. When the electrical messages stop, your muscles return to their original size and position.

The more you use a muscle, the stronger it becomes. Even when relaxed, toned muscles stay slightly contracted.

Your muscles need energy to work and grow. The energy comes mainly from food combined with oxygen.

Taking your pulse at rest lets you know how hard your heart works even before you exercise.

616

As you exercise or become more active, your breathing rate increases to provide this oxygen. Your heart pumps faster to speed oxygen to your muscles.

In time your lungs will take in more air with each breath. Your heart will pump more blood with each beat. They do more work with less effort.

Brisk and constant physical activity that increases the supply of oxygen to the muscles is called **aerobic exercise** (â rō′bik ek′sər sīz′). Aerobic exercises include swimming, jogging, and biking.

Brain Power

How can you exercise your muscles, bones, joints, heart, and lungs? Would you need one activity or several?

Improving Physical Fitness

Aerobic exercises improve your physical fitness if you do them three to five times a week for about half an hour without stopping.

Stretching your muscles helps you gain flexibility to bend and move more easily. As you exercise more, your endurance lets you stay active longer without tiring.

As your muscles become stronger, you lift, pull, and push with more force. Your bones grow thicker and stronger. The energy your muscles use also forces your body to store less fat.

You can move and change position quickly without losing your balance. You can also react faster. Your body parts will work together to be coordinated and responsive.

QUICK LAB

Hit the Target

HYPOTHESIZE Your heart rate indicates if you are exercising hard enough. How can you monitor your heart during exercise? Write a hypothesis in your *Science Journal*.

MATERIALS
- watch with a second hand
- *Science Journal*

1. To improve your heart and lungs, you must reach your target rate during exercise. To find your target rate, subtract your age from 220.

2. Multiply the result first by 0.7 and then by 0.8. Write the numbers down. Your target rate is between those two numbers.

3. **COMPARE** Take your pulse for one minute. Record the number. Take your pulse again after exercising for one minute. Record the new number.

4. **DRAW CONCLUSIONS** How close is your heart rate after exercising to your target rate? Were you exercising hard enough to help your heart? Were you exercising long enough? How can your resting pulse tell you if your heart is getting stronger over time?

Can Food Help You Stay Fit?

There is more to fitness than exercise. Without a healthy diet, your body cannot work at its best.

One of the best sources of energy is in the sugars and starches of fruits, vegetables, and whole grains.

Your muscles are made of proteins. To keep them strong, you need food rich in proteins, such as meat, beans, and nuts. Your body breaks down food proteins into building blocks used for growth and repair.

Your body also needs some stored fat for energy. However, too much fat can harm your heart and blood vessels.

Most people get enough fat in the food they eat every day.

Muscles and bones also need vitamins and minerals to stay strong and do their jobs.

To make sure your body has these ingredients, eat a **balanced diet** (bal'ənsd di'it). This means a diet, maintained over time, that includes a variety of foods providing nutrition in moderate amounts.

A balanced diet includes all major **food groups** (füd grüps). Each group contains foods with similar amounts of important nutrients. The Food Guide Pyramid indicates how many servings of each group you need each day.

THE FOOD GUIDE PYRAMID

The Food Guide Pyramid makes it easy to remember to eat a balanced diet. Remember that you also need to drink enough water—about eight large glasses a day.

READING CHARTS

1. **DISCUSS** Is your diet balanced?
2. **WRITE** Describe healthful menus for a breakfast, a lunch, and a dinner.

Fats, Oils, and Sweets
Use sparingly

Milk, Yogurt, and Cheese Group
2–3 Servings

Meat, Poultry, Fish, Dry Beans, Eggs, and Nuts Group
2–3 Servings

Vegetable Group
3–5 Servings

Fruit Group
2–4 Servings

Bread, Cereal, Rice, and Pasta Group
6–11 Servings

How Can You Stay Safe?

To help prevent sports injuries, you should always warm up by bending and stretching. After your workout, bend and stretch to cool down. Your heart and breathing rates will slowly return to normal as you cool off.

You can also reduce injuries by learning the right way to perform exercises and sports moves. Ask your teacher or a coach. Find out if you need safety equipment, such as a helmet, kneepads, elbow pads, wrist guards, or goggles. Knowing sports safety can also prevent you from harming someone else.

Never ignore your body's signals. If you feel pain or can't breathe, your body is telling you to slow down and stop exercising.

Proper diet and exercise are part of a healthy lifestyle. They ensure that your body can do all of the activities you want it to do.

A stronger, healthier body will be able to do more for you now. As you grow older, proper diet and exercise will help your body stay strong, toned, and in shape.

REVIEW

1. What type of exercise strengthens your heart and lungs?

2. How can you determine your target heart rate for exercising?

3. How can you find out how much food from each group should be eaten every day?

4. **DRAW CONCLUSIONS** If you exercise regularly, your heart and lungs will get stronger. How will this affect your resting heart rate?

5. **CRITICAL THINKING** *Apply* What might happen if you don't get a balanced diet? How can people who can't eat certain foods make sure they still get enough nutrients?

WHY IT MATTERS THINK ABOUT IT
Why would athletes need to understand how their bodies work? Would this information help them to form good habits?

WHY IT MATTERS WRITE ABOUT IT
Write some practical ways you can use this information. How can your diet more closely match the Food Guide Pyramid? How can you get enough exercise each week?

Summer Sports Safety

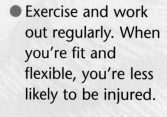

Want to enjoy the summer without getting hurt? Follow these tips!

- Warm up and stretch before you play any sport. Stretch again afterward.

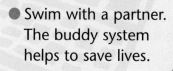

- Swim with a partner. The buddy system helps to save lives.

- Drink lots of fluids, especially when it's hot and humid.

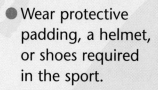

- Wear protective padding, a helmet, or shoes required in the sport.

- Exercise and work out regularly. When you're fit and flexible, you're less likely to be injured.

- Eat balanced meals. Calcium, phosphorus, and vitamin D help build strong bones. Muscles need protein, carbohydrates, magnesium, and other minerals and vitamins.

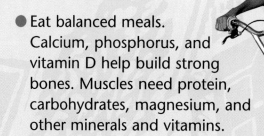

- Take some time to just kick back and relax!

- Follow the rules of each sport.

DISCUSSION STARTER

1. Which tip is most likely to keep you safe? Why?

2. Which tip do you think most kids ignore? Why?

To learn more about safety, visit *www.mhschool.com/science* and enter the keyword SAFE.

*inter*NET
CONNECTION

SCIENCE WORDS

aerobic
   exercise p.617
balanced
   diet p.618
bile p.605
digestion p.604

enzyme p.604
excretion p.606
food group p.618
nephron p.606
urea p.606
villus p.605

USING SCIENCE WORDS

Number a paper from 1 to 10. Fill in 1 to 5 with words from the list above.

1. Brisk activity is ___?___.

2. A diet that includes a variety of nutritious foods is a(n) ___?___.

3. Chemicals that break down food into pieces cells can use are called ___?___.

4. Digested food is absorbed in the small intestine by ___?___.

5. The liver forms ___?___.

6–10. Pick five words from the list above that were not used in 1 to 5, and use each in a sentence.

UNDERSTANDING SCIENCE IDEAS

11. Where does digestion start in the body?

12. How does exercise affect the amount of water your body needs?

13. How can you be sure to get a balanced diet every day?

14. Explain how the liver participates in both your digestion and excretion systems.

15. Describe the role your kidneys play in excretion.

USING IDEAS AND SKILLS

16. Regular exercise improves your physical fitness. What parts of the body might be involved in exercise?

17. People can survive without food longer than they can survive without water. Is this true of false? Explain your answer.

18. **READING SKILL: FINDING THE MAIN IDEA** Digested food is changed physically by the teeth and chemically by enzymes. Explain why both changes must happen.

19. **MAKE A MODEL** How could you build a model to show the effects of exercise on different parts of the body?

20. **THINKING LIKE A SCIENTIST** Many people do not eat enough nutritious food every day. Suggest some reasons for this. Suggest ways to encourage people to eat healthier diets. How can you find out if your suggestions will work?

PROBLEMS and PUZZLES

Break Down How does bile break down fat? To find out pour some olive oil into a test tube. Then, add an equal amount of water. Next, use a clean medicine dropper to add five drops of liquid detergent to one of the test tubes. The olive oil represents fat, so which substance represents bile? How does it act on the olive oil?

USING SCIENCE WORDS

aerobic
  exercise p.617
artery p.580
balanced diet p.618
bile p.605
cilia p.593
food group p.618

mucus p.593
nephron p.606
plasma p.580
trachea p.593
vein p.580
villus p.605

USING SCIENCE WORDS

Number a paper from 1 to 10. Beside each number write the word or words that best complete the sentence.

1. The liquid part of blood that contains nutrients is the ___?___.

2. Blood vessels that carry blood away from the heart are ___?___.

3. Air travels to the lungs through the ___?___.

4. The hairlike structures that push dust and mucus along the throat are ___?___.

5. Dust entering your nose when you breathe is trapped by a liquid called ___?___.

6. Digested foods are absorbed in the small intestine by ___?___.

7. The structures in the kidney that filter blood are ___?___.

8. Jogging is a kind of ___?___.

9. Good nutrition is the result of a(n) ___?___.

10. Dairy products make up a(n) ___?___.

UNDERSTANDING SCIENCE IDEAS

Write 11 to 15. For each number write the letter for the best answer. You may wish to use the hints provided.

11. The function of lymph nodes is to
    a. filter blood
    b. filter lymph
    c. make blood clot
    d. add oxygen to lymph
    (Hint: Read page 585.)

12. The blood vessels that exchange materials with cells are
    a. villi
    b. veins
    c. capillaries
    d. arteries
    (Hint: Read page 580.)

13. Why might you feel dizzy on a mountaintop?
    a. There isn't enough oxygen.
    b. There aren't enough plants.
    c. The Sun is bright.
    d. It is cold.
    (Hint: Read page 594.)

14. The functions of the liver include
    a. digesting food
    b. cleaning blood
    c. making vitamins
    d. making urea
    (Hint: Read page 606.)

15. How many daily servings of fruit and vegetables does the Food and Drug Administration recommend?
    a. two
    b. three
    c. four
    d. five
    (Hint: Read pages 618.)

USING IDEAS AND SKILLS

16. Sketch a red blood cell. Tell why the shape is important.

17. Since there are four donor blood types and two Rh blood types, how many combined types are there in all? List them.

18. **COMMUNICATE** Explain what happens at the alveoli of the lungs.

19. What is the purpose of a yawn?

20. What is the purpose of a sneeze?

21. Where does bile come from, and what does it do?

22. How do nutrients from the small intestine get into blood?

23. Why is aerobic exercise generally good for people?

THINKING LIKE A SCIENTIST

24. **PREDICT** Imagine that a person from a city located on a mountain travels down to a city in a valley. How might the person's breathing be affected? Why?

25. When and why do you sweat?

WRITING IN YOUR JOURNAL

SCIENCE IN YOUR LIFE
Tell why it is important for you to drink six to eight glasses of water every day.

PRODUCT ADS
Describe two or three TV ads for fast foods. Do any of them explain why these foods are nutritious? If so, give examples.

HOW SCIENTISTS WORK
In this unit you learned that with the discovery of different blood types, scientists were able to answer the question of why some blood transfusions don't work. What other questions about the human body do you think scientists might be asking today?

Design your own Experiment

Does holding your breath affect your heart rate? Determine a way to see if your heart rate is changed by holding your breath for short periods of time, such as 15 seconds, 30 seconds, and 45 seconds. Check with your teacher before carrying out the experiment.

*inter***NET** **CONNECTION**

For help in reviewing this unit, visit *www.mhschool.com/science*

PROBLEMS and PUZZLES

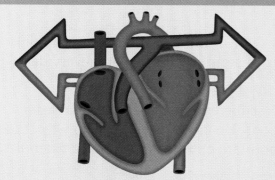

The Heart Is a Lonely Road

Imagine the circulatory system is a highway and you are a blood cell traveling through it. What kinds of road signs do you see in the heart? Trace the picture shown, and provide road signs for it. Your signs might include such words as *One Way, To the Lungs, Body, Entering Left Atrium, Turn Ahead, Left Turn Only,* and so on. Explain why you chose each sign.

Storing Oxygen

Your body is able to store food for the future. For example, you can go hours, even days, without eating. Does your body have the same ability to store oxygen? Explain.

How would your oxygen-storing ability compare with that of a whale? Imagine that you could increase the human body's ability to store oxygen. What kind of body structure can you imagine that could accomplish this? Make a design for an oxygen-storing structure in the body.

The Great Kidney Debate

People with damaged kidneys can live better lives with a kidney transplant. Where should kidneys come from? Organize a debate to address the following questions.

- Should kidneys be taken from animals such as baboons to help people?

- Most kidneys come from healthy people who are killed in road accidents. Should all drivers be required to carry a kidney donor card?

- Kidney transplants are expensive. Should wealthy people be able to spend extra money to get the kidney that they need?

- Who should get kidneys? Should the young be favored over the old, or should kidneys be distributed on a first come, first served basis?

- People have two kidneys. Should they be allowed to sell one kidney? Should selling kidneys be against the law?

REFERENCE SECTION

DIAGRAM BUILDERS

Building the Water Cycle

A cycle is a number of events or processes that happen in a given order over and over again. For example, Monday follows Sunday, Tuesday follows Monday, and so on, over and over again. Every drop of water is part of the water cycle. The water cycle is the continuous movement of water between Earth's surface and the air. **What happens to water in this cycle?**

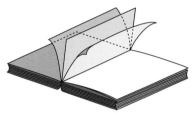

BASE

To find out, look at the diagram on the facing page. You can see many processes all happening at the same time. You can study this cycle one process at a time by lifting up all the plastic overlays (1, 2, 3). Look at the page beneath, the base. **What sources of water do you see? What source of energy do you see?**

OVERLAY 1

1 Now drop overlay 1 onto the base.
What happens to liquid water? Why?

OVERLAY 2

2 Now drop overlay 2 onto overlay 1.
What process follows those shown on the first overlay? What happens to the water?

OVERLAY 3

3 Now drop overlay 3 onto overlay 2.
What processes complete the cycle?

SUMMARIZE

What can happen to a drop of water that is in the ground, in the leaf of a plant, or at the surface of a body of water?

BASE: Start with water on and in the ground.

DIAGRAM BUILDERS
Activities

1 Make a Diagram

What cycles can you describe that take place over a week, a month, or a year? Make a diagram to show how the parts of the cycles are arranged.

2 Write About a Main Idea

Does a cycle have a beginning? An end? Write out your idea. Use the Water Cycle diagram to support your idea.

3 Make a Model

Use art materials, natural materials, and any other supplies to make a model of the water cycle. How might you make a working model that shows at least some of the processes of the cycle?

REFERENCE SECTION

HANDBOOK

The temperature is 77 degrees Fahrenheit.

That is the same as 25 degrees Celsius.

Water boils at 212 degrees Fahrenheit.

Water freezes at 0 degrees Celsius.

I weigh 85 pounds.

That baseball bat weighs 32 ounces.

32 ounces is the same as 2 pounds.

The mass of the bat is 907 grams.

This classroom is 10 meters wide and 20 meters long.

That means the area is 200 square meters.

This bottle of juice has a volume of 1 liter.

That is a little more than 1 quart.

She can walk 20 meters in 5 seconds.

That means her speed is 4 meters per second.

Table of Measurements

SI (INTERNATIONAL SYSTEM) OF UNITS

Temperature

Water freezes at 0°C and boils at 100°C.

Length and Distance

1,000 meters = 1 kilometer
100 centimeters = 1 meter
10 millimeters = 1 centimeter

Volume

1,000 milliliters = 1 liter
1 cubic centimeter = 1 milliliter

Mass

1,000 grams = 1 kilogram

ENGLISH SYSTEM OF UNITS

Temperature

Water freezes at 32°F and boils at 212°F.

Length and Distance

5,280 feet = 1 mile
3 feet = 1 yard
12 inches = 1 foot

Volume of Fluids

4 quarts = 1 gallon
2 pints = 1 quart
2 cups = 1 pint
8 fluid ounces = 1 cup

Weight

2,000 pounds = 1 ton
16 ounces = 1 pound

In the Classroom

The most important part of doing any experiment is doing it safely. You can be safe by paying attention to your teacher and doing your work carefully. Here are some other ways to stay safe while you do experiments.

Before the Experiment

■ Read all of the directions. Make sure you understand them. When you see be sure to follow the safety rule.

■ Listen to your teacher for special safety directions. If you don't understand something, ask for help.

During the Experiment

■ Wear safety goggles when your teacher tells you to wear them and whenever you see .

■ Wear a safety apron if you work with anything messy or anything that might spill.

■ If you spill something, wipe it up right away or ask your teacher for help.

■ Tell your teacher if something breaks. If glass breaks do not clean it up yourself.

■ Keep your hair and clothes away from open flames. Tie back long hair and roll up long sleeves.

■ Be careful around a hot plate. Know when it is on and when it is off. Remember that the plate stays hot for a few minutes after you turn it off.

■ Keep your hands dry around electrical equipment.

■ Don't eat or drink anything during the experiment.

After the Experiment

■ Put equipment back the way your teacher tells you.

■ Dispose of things the way your teacher tells you.

■ Clean up your work area and wash your hands.

In the Field

- Always be accompanied by a trusted adult—like your teacher or a parent or guardian.
- Never touch animals or plants without the adult's approval. The animal might bite. The plant might be poison ivy or another dangerous plant.

Responsibility

Acting safely is one way to be responsible. You can also be responsible by treating animals, the environment, and each other with respect in the class and in the field.

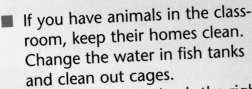

Treat Living Things with Respect

- If you have animals in the classroom, keep their homes clean. Change the water in fish tanks and clean out cages.
- Feed classroom animals the right amount of food.
- Give your classroom animals enough space.
- When you observe animals, don't hurt them or disturb their homes.
- Find a way to care for animals while school is on vacation.

Treat the Environment with Respect

- Do not pick flowers.
- Do not litter, including gum and food.
- If you see litter, ask your teacher if you can pick it up.
- Recycle materials used in experiments. Ask your teacher what materials can be recycled instead of thrown away. These might include plastics, aluminum, and newspapers.

Treat Each Other with Respect

- Use materials carefully around others so that people don't get hurt or get stains on their clothes.
- Be careful not to bump people when they are doing experiments. Do not disturb or damage their experiments.
- If you see that people are having trouble with an experiment, help them.

Use a Hand Lens

You use a hand lens to magnify an object, or make the object look larger. With a hand lens, you can see details that would be hard to see without the hand lens.

Magnify a Piece of Cereal

1. Place a piece of your favorite cereal on a flat surface. Look at the cereal carefully. Draw a picture of it.
2. Look at the cereal through the large lens of a hand lens. Move the lens toward or away from the cereal until it looks larger and in focus. Draw a picture of the cereal as you see it through the hand lens. Fill in details that you did not see before.
3. Look at the cereal through the smaller lens, which will magnify the cereal even more. If you notice more details, add them to your drawing.
4. Repeat this activity using objects you are studying in science. It might be a rock, some soil, or a seed.

Observe Seeds in a Petri Dish

Can you observe a seed as it sprouts? You can if it's in a petri dish. A petri dish is a shallow, clear, round dish with a cover.

1. Line the sides and bottom of a petri dish with a double layer of filter paper or paper towel. You may have to cut the paper to make it fit.
2. Sprinkle water on the paper to wet it.
3. Place three or four radish seeds on the wet paper in different areas of the dish. Put the lid on the dish, and keep it in a warm place.
4. Observe the seeds every day for a week. Use a hand lens to look for a tiny root pushing through the seed. Record how long it takes each seed to sprout.

Use a Microscope

Hand lenses make objects look several times larger. A microscope, however, can magnify an object to look hundreds of times larger.

Examine Salt Grains

1. Look at the drawing to learn the different parts of your microscope.
2. Place the microscope on a flat surface. Always carry a microscope with both hands. Hold the arm with one hand, and put your other hand beneath the base.
3. Move the mirror so that it reflects light up toward the stage. Never point the mirror directly at the Sun or a bright light.
4. Place a few grains of salt on the slide. Put the slide under the stage clips. Be sure that the salt grains you are going to examine are over the hole in the stage.
5. Look through the eyepiece. Turn the focusing knob slowly until the salt grains come into focus.
6. Draw what the grains look like through the microscope.
7. Look at other objects through the microscope. Try a piece of leaf, a human hair, or a pencil mark.

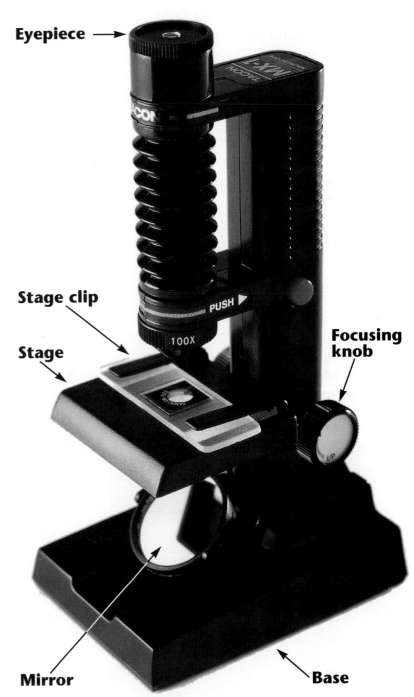

Eyepiece →

Stage clip

Focusing knob

Stage

Mirror

Base

HANDBOOK

Use a Collecting Net

You can use a collecting net to catch insects and observe them. You can try catching an insect in midair, but you might have better luck waiting for it to land on a plant. Put the net over the whole plant. Then you can place the insect in a jar with holes in the lid.

Use a Compass

You use a compass to find directions. A compass is a small, thin magnet that swings freely, like a spinner in a board game. One end of the magnet always points north. This end is the magnet's north pole. How does a compass work?

1. Place the compass on a surface that is not made of magnetic material, such as a wooden table or a sidewalk.

2. Find the magnet's north pole. The north pole is marked in some way, usually with a color or an arrowhead.
3. Notice the letters *N*, *E*, *S*, and *W* on the compass. These letters stand for the directions north, east, south, and west. When the magnet stops swinging, turn the compass so that the *N* lines up with the north pole of the magnet.
4. Face to the north. Then face to the east, to the south, and to the west.
5. Repeat this activity by holding the compass in your hand and then at different places indoors and outdoors.

Use a Telescope

You make most observations for science class during the day. Some things are observed best at night—like the Moon and the stars.

You can observe the Moon and the stars simply by looking up into a clear night sky. However, it's hard to see much detail on the Moon, such as craters and mountains. Also you can see only a tiny fraction of the stars and other objects that are actually in the sky. A telescope improves those observations.

A telescope uses lenses or mirrors to gather light and magnify objects. You can see much greater detail of the Moon's surface with a telescope than with just your eyes. A telescope gathers light better than your eyes can. With a telescope you can see stars that are too

faint to see with just your eyes. See for yourself how a telescope can improve your observations.

1. Look at the Moon in the night sky, and draw a picture of what you see. Draw as many details as you can.
2. Point a telescope toward the Moon. Look through the eyepiece of the telescope. Move the telescope until you see the Moon. Turn the knob until the Moon comes into focus.

3. Draw a picture of what you see, including as many details as you can. Compare your two pictures.
4. Find the brightest star in the sky. Notice if there are any other stars near it.
5. Point a telescope toward the bright star. Look through the eyepiece and turn the knob until the stars come into focus. Move the telescope until you find the bright star.
6. Can you see stars through the telescope that you cannot see with just your eyes?

Objective lens

Eyepiece lens
Focusing knob

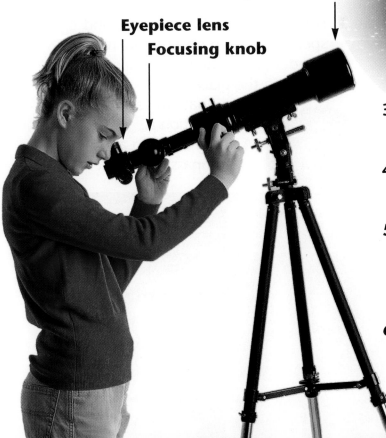

Use a Camera, Tape Recorder, Map, and Compass

Tape Recorder

You can record observations on a tape recorder. This is sometimes better than writing notes because, with a tape recorder, you can record your observations at the exact time you are making them. Later you can listen to the tape and write down your observations.

Camera

You can use a camera to record what you observe in nature. When taking photographs keep these tips in mind.

1. Hold the camera steady. Gently press the shutter button so that you do not jerk the camera.
2. Try to take pictures with the Sun at your back. Then your pictures will be bright and clear.
3. Don't get too close to the subject. Without a special lens, the picture could turn out blurry.
4. Be patient. If you are taking a picture of an animal, you may have to wait for the animal to appear.

Use a Map and a Compass

When you are busy observing nature, it might be easy to get lost. You can use a map of the area and a compass to find your way. Here are some tips.

1. Lightly mark on the map your starting place. It might be the place where the bus parked.
2. Always know where you are on the map compared to your starting place. Watch for landmarks on the map, such as a river, a pond, trails, or buildings.
3. Use the map and compass to find special places to observe, such as a pond. Look at the map to see what direction the place is from you. Hold the compass to see where that direction is.
4. Use your map and compass with a friend.

Length

Find Length with a Ruler

1. Look at this section of a ruler. Each centimeter is divided into 10 millimeters. How long is the paper clip?
2. The length of the paper clip is 3 centimeters plus 2 millimeters. You can write this length as 3.2 centimeters.
3. Place the ruler on your desk. Lay a pencil against the ruler so that one end of the pencil lines up with the left edge of the ruler. Record the length of the pencil.
4. Trade your pencil with a classmate. Measure and record the length of each other's pencil. Compare your answers.

1 centimeter = 10 millimeters

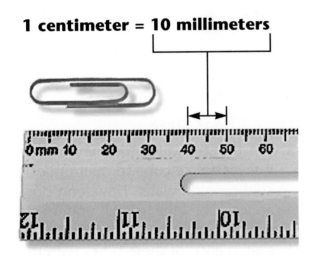

Find Length with a Meterstick

1. Line up the meterstick with the left edge of the chalkboard. Make a chalk mark on the board at the right end of the meterstick.
2. Move the meterstick so that the left edge lines up with the chalk mark. Keep the stick level. Make another mark on the board at the right end of the meterstick.
3. Continue to move the meterstick and make chalk marks until the meterstick meets or overlaps the right edge of the board.
4. Record the length of the chalkboard in centimeters by adding all the measurements you've made. Remember, a meterstick has 100 centimeters.

Measuring Area

Area is the amount of surface something covers. To find the area of a rectangle, multiply the rectangle's length by its width. For example, the rectangle here is 3 centimeters long and 2 centimeters wide. Its area is 3 cm x 2 cm = 6 square centimeters. You write the area as 6 cm².

1. Find the area of your science book. Measure the book's length to the nearest centimeter. Measure its width.
2. Multiply the book's length by its width. Remember to put the answer in cm².

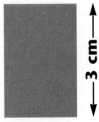

3 cm

◄ 2 cm ►

Time

You use timing devices to measure how long something takes to happen. Some timing devices you use in science are a clock with a second hand and a stopwatch. Which one is more accurate?

Comparing a Clock and Stopwatch

1. Look at a clock with a second hand. The second hand is the hand that you can see moving. It measures seconds.

2. Get an egg timer with falling sand or some device like a wind-up toy that runs down after a certain length of time. When the second hand of the clock points to 12, tell your partner to start the egg timer. Watch the clock while the sand in the egg timer is falling.

3. When the sand stops falling, count how many seconds it took. Record this measurement. Repeat the activity, and compare the two measurements.

4. Switch roles with your partner.

5. Look at a stopwatch. Click the button on the top right. This starts the time. Click the button again. This stops the time. Click the button on the top left. This sets the stopwatch back to zero. Notice that the stopwatch tells time in minutes, seconds, and hundredths of a second.

6. Repeat the activity in steps 1–3, using the stopwatch instead of a clock. Make sure the stopwatch is set to zero. Click the top right button to start timing the reading. Click it again when the sand stops falling. Make sure you and your partner time each other twice.

0 minutes
25 seconds
75 hundredths of a second

More About Time

1. Use the stopwatch to time how long it takes an ice cube to melt under cold running water. How long does an ice cube take to melt under warm running water?

2. Match each of these times with the action you think took that amount of time.

a. 0:00:14:55
b. 0:24:39:45
c. 2:10:23:00

1. A Little League baseball game
2. Saying the Pledge of Allegiance
3. Recess

HANDBOOK

Volume

Volume is the amount of space something takes up. If you've ever helped bake a cake or do other cooking, you might have measured the volume of water, vegetable oil, or melted butter. In science you usually measure the volume of liquids by using beakers and graduated cylinders. These containers are marked in milliliters (mL).

Measure the Volume of a Liquid

1. Look at the beaker and at the graduated cylinder. The beaker has marks for each 25 mL up to 200 mL. The graduated cylinder has marks for each 1 mL up to 100 mL.

2. The surface of the water in the graduated cylinder curves up at the sides. You measure the volume by reading the height of the water at the flat part. What is the volume of water in the graduated cylinder? How much water is in the beaker? They both contain 75 mL of water.

3. Pour 50 mL of water from a pitcher into a graduated cylinder. The water should be at the 50-mL mark on the graduated cylinder. If you go over the mark, pour a little water back into the pitcher.

4. Pour the 50 mL of water into a beaker.

5. Repeat steps 3 and 4 using 30 mL, 45 mL, and 25 mL of water.

6. Measure the volume of water you have in the beaker. Do you have about the same amount of water as your classmates?

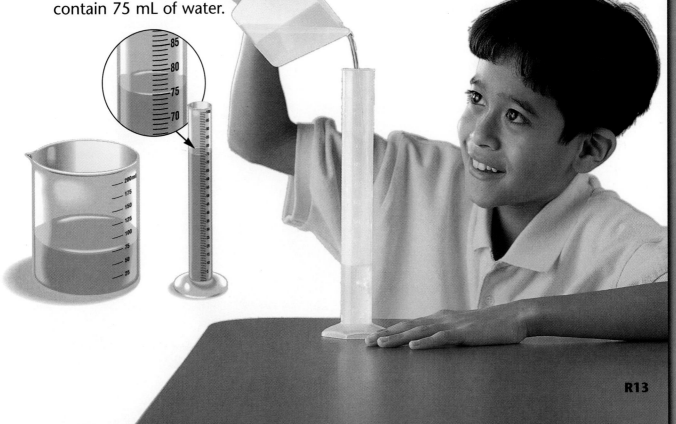

Mass

Mass is the amount of matter an object has. You use a balance to measure mass. To find the mass of an object, you balance it with objects whose masses you know. Let's find the mass of a box of crayons.

Measure the Mass of a Box of Crayons

1. Place the balance on a flat, level surface. Check that the two pans are empty and clean.

2. Make sure the empty pans are balanced with each other. The pointer should point to the middle mark. If it does not, move the slider a little to the right or left to balance the pans.

3. Gently place a box of crayons on the left pan. This pan will drop lower.

4. Add masses to the right pan until the pans are balanced.

5. Add the numbers on the masses that are in the right pan. The total is the mass of the box of crayons, in grams. Record this number. After the number write a *g* for "grams."

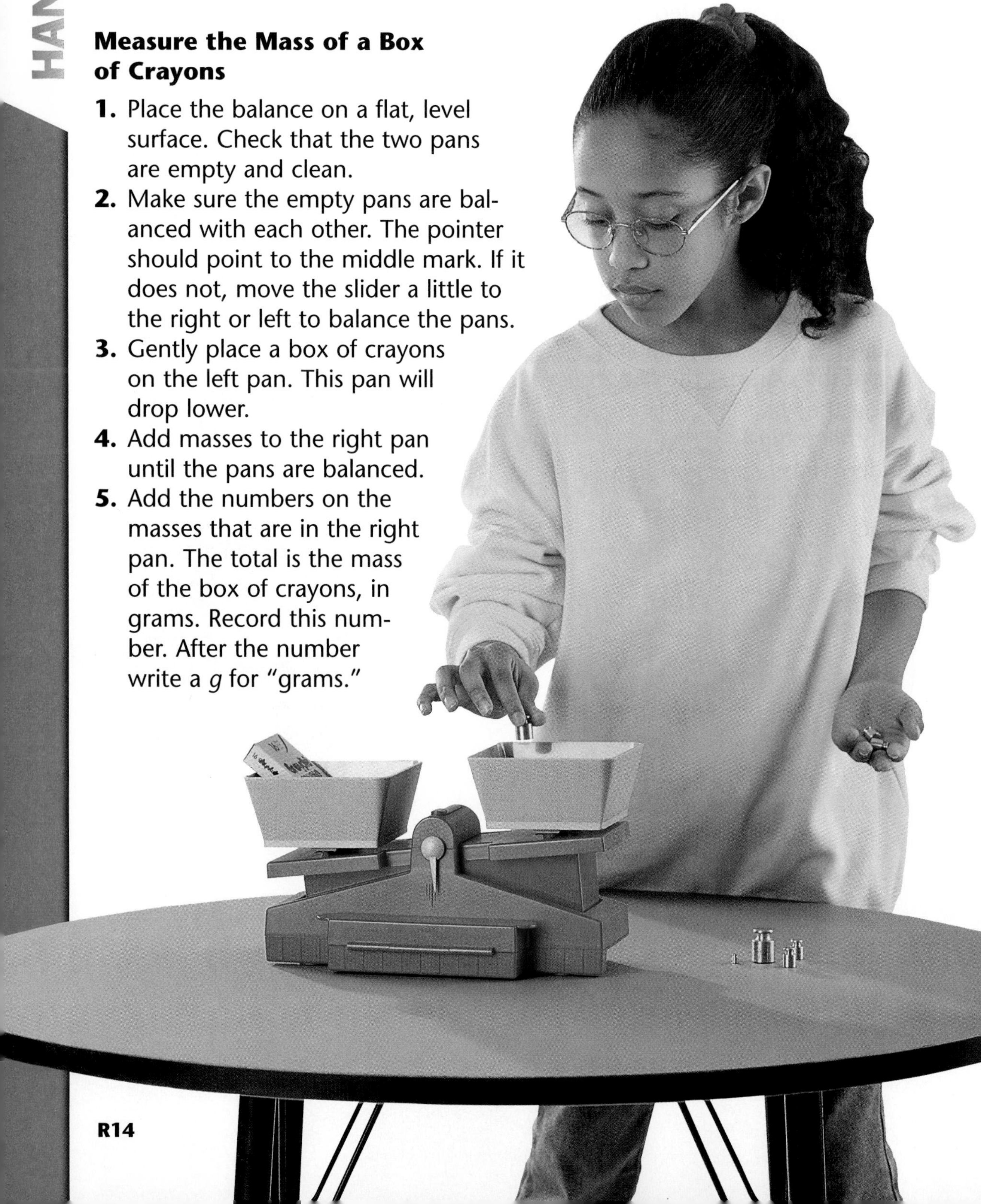

Predict the Mass of More Crayons

1. Leave the box of crayons and the masses on the balance.

2. Get two more crayons. If you put them in the pan with the box of crayons, what do you think the mass of all the crayons will be? Record what you predict the total mass will be.

3. Check your prediction. Gently place the two crayons in the left pan. Add masses to the right pan until the pans are balanced.

4. Add the numbers on the masses as you did before. Record this number. How close is it to your prediction?

More About Mass

What was the mass of all your crayons? It was probably less than 100 grams. What would happen if you replaced the crayons with a pineapple? You may not have enough masses to balance the pineapple. It has a mass of about 1,000 grams. That's the same as 1 kilogram because *kilo* means "1,000."

1. How many kilograms do all these masses add up to?

2. Which of these objects have a mass greater than 1 kilogram?
   a. large dog
   b. robin
   c. desktop computer
   d. calculator
   e. whole watermelon

Weight/Force

You use a spring scale to measure weight. An object has weight because the force of gravity pulls down on the object. Therefore, weight is a force. Weight is measured in newtons (N) like all forces.

Measure the Weight of an Object

1. Look at your spring scale to see how many newtons it measures. See how the measurements are divided. The spring scale shown here measures up to 5 N. It has a mark for every 0.1 N.

2. Hold the spring scale by the top loop. Put the object to be measured on the bottom hook. If the object will not stay on the hook, place it in a net bag. Then hang the bag from the hook.

3. Let go of the object slowly. It will pull down on a spring inside the scale. The spring is connected to a pointer. The pointer on the spring scale shown here is a small bar.

4. Wait for the pointer to stop moving. Read the number of newtons next to the pointer. This is the object's weight. The mug in the picture weighs 4 N.

More About Spring Scales

You probably weigh yourself by standing on a bathroom scale. This is a spring scale. The force of your body stretches a spring inside the scale. The dial on the scale is probably marked in pounds—the English unit of weight. One pound is equal to about 4.5 newtons.

Here are some other spring scales you may have seen.

Temperature

You use a thermometer to measure temperature—how hot or cold something is. A thermometer is made of a thin tube with colored liquid inside. When the liquid gets warmer, it expands and moves up the tube. When the liquid gets cooler, it contracts and moves down the tube. You may have seen most temperatures measured in degrees Fahrenheit (°F). Scientists measure temperature in degrees Celsius (°C).

°F   **°C**

Water boils →

Room temperature

Water freezes

Read a Thermometer

1. Look at the thermometer shown here. It has two scales—a Fahrenheit scale and a Celsius scale. Every 20 degrees on the Fahrenheit scale has a number. Every 10 degrees on the Celsius scale has a number.

2. What is the temperature shown on the thermometer? At what temperature does water freeze? Give your answers in °F and in °C.

What Is Convection?

1. Fill a large beaker about two-thirds full of cool water. Find the temperature of the water by holding a thermometer in the water. Do not let the bulb at the bottom of the thermometer touch the sides or bottom of the beaker.

2. Keep the thermometer in the water until the liquid in the tube stops moving—about a minute. Read and record the temperature in °C.

3. Sprinkle a little fish food on the surface of the water in the beaker. Do not knock the beaker, and most of the food will stay on top.

4. Carefully place the beaker on a hot plate. A hot plate is a small electric stove. Plug in the hot plate, and turn the control knob to a middle setting.

5. After a minute measure the temperature of water near the bottom of the beaker. At the same time, a classmate should measure the temperature of water near the top of the beaker. Record these temperatures. Is water near the bottom of the beaker heating up faster than near the top?

6. As the water heats up, notice what happens to the fish food. How do you know that warmer water at the bottom of the beaker rises and cooler water at the top sinks?

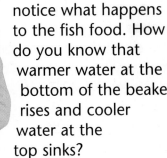

R17

Weather

What information is included in a weather report? You might think of temperature, cloud cover, wind speed, amount of rainfall, and so on. Various instruments are used to measure these parts of the weather. Some of them are shown here.

Barometer

A barometer measures air pressure. Most barometers are like the one shown here. It contains a flat metal can with most of the air removed. When air pressure increases (rises), the air pushes more on the can. A pointer that is attached to the can moves toward a higher number on the scale. When air pressure decreases (falls), the air pushes less on the can. The pointer moves toward a lower number on the scale.

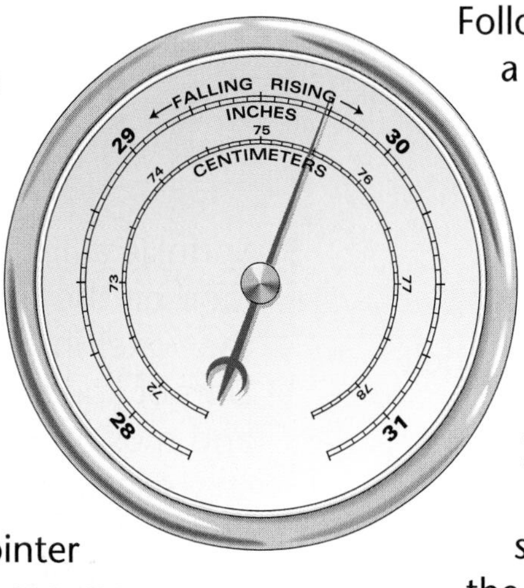

29.73 inches ➔

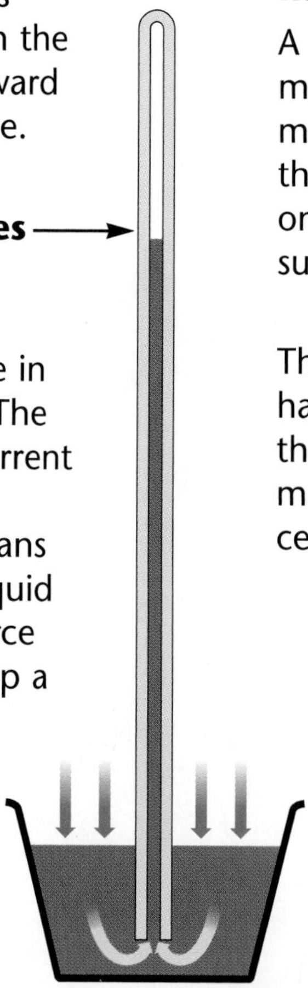

Notice that the barometer above measures air pressure in inches and in centimeters. The long arrow points to the current air pressure, which is 29.73 inches of mercury. That means the air pushing down on liquid mercury in a dish would force the mercury 29.73 inches up a tube, as the drawing shows. What is the air pressure in centimeters?

Follow these steps when you use a barometer.

1. Look at the current air pressure reading marked by the long arrow.

2. Turn the knob on the front of the barometer so the short arrow points to the current pressure reading.

3. Check the barometer several times a day to see if the pressure is rising, falling, or staying the same.

Rain Gauge

A rain gauge measures how much rain falls. This instrument is simply a container that collects water. It has one or more scales for measuring the amount of rain.

The rain gauge shown here has been collecting rain throughout the day. How much rain fell in inches? In centimeters?

Weather Vane

A weather vane measures wind direction. A weather vane is basically an arrow that is free to spin on a pole. Wind pushes on the widest part of the arrow—the tail—so that the arrow points to the direction that the wind is coming from. Letters on the weather vane show directions. If the vane doesn't have letters, you can tell direction with a compass. What direction is the wind coming from in the picture?

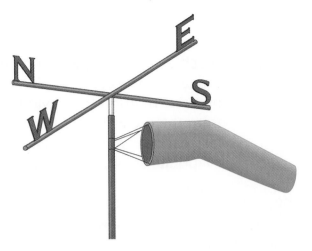

Windsock

A windsock also measures wind direction. You may have seen windsocks at airports. Windsocks are usually large and bright orange so that pilots can easily see which way the wind is blowing. The large opening of the windsock faces the wind. The narrow part of the windsock points in the direction that the wind is blowing. Which way is the wind blowing in the picture?

Anemometer

An anemometer measures wind speed. It is usually made of three shallow cones, or cups, that spin on an axle. The wind makes the cups and axle spin. The axle is attached to a dial that indicates wind speed. The faster the wind blows, the faster the cups turn.

Cycles

Much of what happens in nature happens in cycles. A cycle is a process that keeps repeating itself. For example, the movement of water through the environment is a cycle. Water evaporates from the ground, rises into the air, condenses into clouds, and falls back to Earth as rain or snow. Once on the ground, it might evaporate again, and the cycle continues.

The drawings below illustrate other natural cycles. See if you can describe each cycle shown.

Think about some cycles in your own life—things that you do over and over again on a regular basis. Describe a daily cycle from your experience. Describe a weekly cycle from your experience.

HANDBOOK

Make Graphs to Organize Data

When you do an experiment in science, you collect information. To find out what your information means, you can organize it into graphs. There are many kinds of graphs.

Circle Graphs

A circle graph is helpful to show how a complete set of data is divided into parts. The circle graph here shows how water is used in the United States. What is the single largest use of water?

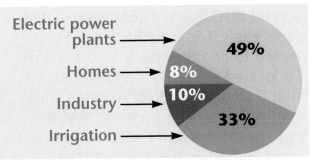

Electric power plants → 49%

Homes → 8%

Industry → 10%

Irrigation → 33%

Bar Graphs

A bar graph uses bars to show information. For example, what if you do an experiment by wrapping wire around a nail and connecting the ends of the wire to a battery? The nail then becomes a magnet that can pick up paper clips. The graph shows that the more you wrap the wire around the nail, the more paper clips it picks up.

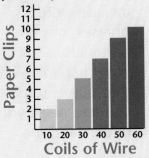

How many paper clips did the nail with 20 coils pick up? With 50 coils?

Line Graphs

A line graph shows information by connecting dots plotted on the graph. For example, what if you are growing a plant? Every week you measure how high the plant has grown. The line graph below organizes the measurements you collected so that you can easily compare them.

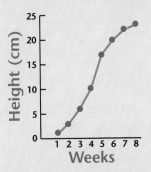

1. Between which two weeks did the plant grow most

2. When did plant growth begin to level off?

Make a Graph

What if you collect information about how much water your family uses each day?

Activity	Water Used (L)
Drinking	10
Showering	180
Bathing	240
Brushing teeth	80
Washing dishes	140
Washing hands	30
Washing clothes	280
Flushing toilet	90

Decide what type of graph would best organize such data. Collect the information and make your graph. Compare it with those of classmates.

Make Maps to Show Information

Locate Places

A map is a drawing that shows an area from above. Most maps have coordinates—numbers and letters along the top and side. Coordinates help you find places easily. For example, what if you wanted to find the library on the map? It is located at B4. Place a finger on the letter B along the side of the map, and another finger on the number 4 at the top. Then move your fingers straight across and down the map until they meet. The library is located where the coordinates B and 4 meet, or very nearby.

1. What color building is located at F6?
2. The hospital is located three blocks north and two blocks east of the library. What are its coordinates?
3. Make a map of an area in your community. It might be a park, or the area between your home and school. Include coordinates. Use a compass to find north, and mark north on your map. Exchange maps with classmates, and answer each other's questions.

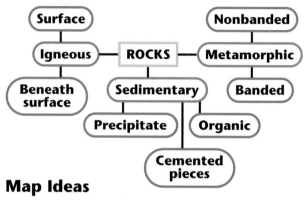

Map Ideas

The map shows how places are connected to each other. Idea maps, on the other hand, show how ideas are connected to each other. Idea maps help you organize information about a topic.

The idea map below connects ideas about rocks. This map shows that there are three major types of rock—igneous, sedimentary, and metamorphic. Connections to each rock type provide further information. For example, this map reminds you that igneous rocks are classified into those that form at Earth's surface and far beneath it.

Make an idea map about a topic you are learning in science. Your map can include words, phrases, or even sentences. Arrange your map in a way that makes sense to you and helps you understand the ideas.

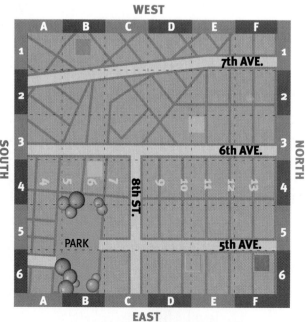

Make Tables and Charts to Organize Information

Tables help you organize data during experiments. Most tables have columns that run up and down, and rows that run across. The columns and rows have headings that tell you what kind of data goes in each part of the table.

A Sample Table

What if you are going to do an experiment to find out how long different kinds of seeds take to sprout? Before you begin the experiment, you should set up your table. Follow these steps.

1. In this experiment you will plant 20 radish seeds, 20 bean seeds, and 20 corn seeds. Your table must show how many radish seeds, bean seeds, and corn seeds sprouted on days 1, 2, 3, 4, and 5.

Make a Table

Now what if you are going to do an experiment to find out how temperature affects the sprouting of seeds? You will plant 20 bean seeds in each of two trays. You will keep each tray at a different temperature, as shown below, and observe the trays for seven days. Make a table you can use for this experiment.

Make a Chart

A chart is simply a table with pictures as well as words to label the rows or columns.

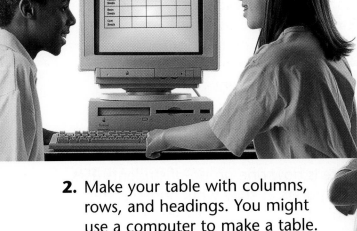

2. Make your table with columns, rows, and headings. You might use a computer to make a table. Some computer programs let you build a table with just the click of a mouse. You can delete or add columns and rows if you need to.
3. Give your table a title. Your table could look like the one here.

Computer

A computer has many uses. The Internet connects your computer to many other computers around the world, so you can collect all kinds of information. You can use a computer to show this information and write reports. Best of all you can use a computer to explore, discover, and learn.

You can also get information from CD-ROMs. They are computer disks that can hold large amounts of information. You can fit a whole encyclopedia on one CD-ROM.

Use Computers for a Project

Here is how one group of students uses computers as they work on a weather project.

1. The students use instruments to measure temperature, wind speed, wind direction, and other parts of the weather. They input this information, or data, into the computer. The students keep the data in a table. This helps them compare the data from one day to the next.

2. The teacher finds out that another group of students in a town 200 kilometers to the west is also doing a weather project. The two groups use the Internet to talk to each other and share data. When a storm happens in the town to the west, that group tells the other group that it's coming their way.

3. The students want to find out more. They decide to stay on the Internet and send questions to a local TV weather forecaster. She has a Web site and answers questions from students every day.

4. Meanwhile some students go to the library to gather more information from a CD-ROM disk. The CD-ROM has an encyclopedia that includes movie clips with sound. The clips give examples of different kinds of storms.

5. The students have kept all their information in a folder called Weather Project. Now they use that information to write a report about the weather. On the computer they can move around paragraphs, add words, take out words, put in diagrams, and draw their own weather maps. Then they print the report in color.

Calculator

Sometimes after you make measurements, you have to analyze your data to see what it means. This might involve doing calculations with your data. A calculator helps you do time-consuming calculations.

Find an Average

The table shows the lengths of a group of unshelled peanuts. What is the average length of the peanuts? You can use a calculator to help you find out.

Peanut	Length (mm)
1	32
2	29
3	30
4	31
5	33
6	26
7	28
8	27
9	29
10	29
11	32
12	31
13	23
14	36
15	31

1. Make sure the calculator is on. Press the **ON** key.
2. Add the numbers. To add a series of numbers, enter the first number and press **+**. Repeat until you enter the last number. Then press **=**. Your total should be 447.
3. While entering so many numbers, it's easy to make a mistake and hit the wrong key. If you make a mistake, you can correct it by pressing the clear entry key, **CE**. Then continue entering the rest of the numbers.
4. Look at the list of lengths, and estimate what you think the average length is. Find the average length of the peanuts by dividing your total by the number of peanuts. If 447 is displayed, press **÷** **1** **5** **=**. How close was your estimate to the actual average?

GLOSSARY

This Glossary will help you to pronounce and understand the meanings of the Science Words introduced in this book. The page number at the end of the definition tells where the word appears.

A

abiotic factor (ā′bī ot′ik fak′tər) A nonliving part of an ecosystem. (p. 485)

absorption (əb sôrp′shən) The disappearance of a sound wave into a surface. (p. 220)

acid rain (as′id rān) Moisture that falls to Earth after being mixed with wastes from burned fossil fuels. (p. 449)

adaptation (ad′əp tā′shən) A characteristic that enables a living thing to survive in its environment. (pp. 86, 530)

aerial root (âr′ē əl rüt) A root that never touches the ground but can take in moisture from the air. (p. 20)

aerobic exercise (â rō′bik ek′sər sīz′) A brisk and constant physical activity that increases the supply of oxygen to the muscles. (p. 616)

aerosol (âr′ə sôl′) A type of colloid in which liquid drops or solid particles are spread throughout a gas. (p. 346)

air mass (âr mas) A large region of the atmosphere where the air has similar properties throughout. (p. 150)

air pressure (âr presh′ər) The force put on a given area by the weight of the air above it. (p. 105)

alternation of generations (ôl′tər nā′shən uv jen′ə rā′shənz) The process in which off-spring are reproduced sexually, their offspring are reproduced asexually, and so on. (p. 49)

alternative energy source (ôl tûr′nə tiv en′ər jē sôrs) A source of energy other than the burning of a fossil fuel. (p. 472)

alveoli (al vē′ə lī′) *n. pl., sing.* **alveolus** (-ləs) Clusters of air sacs at the end of each bronchiole. (p. 593)

ammonia (ə mōn′yə) A simple substance that contains the element nitrogen. (p. 514)

anemometer (an′ə mom′i tər) A device that measures wind speed. (p. 142)

angiosperm (an′jē ə spûrm′) A seed plant that produces flowers. *See* **gymnosperm**. (p. 58)

antibody (an′ti bod′ē) A protein in blood that helps the body find and destroy materials that may be harmful. (p. 581)

antigen (an′ti jən) Either of two chemicals on the surfaces of type A or type B blood cells that limit their usefulness in providing blood transfusions. (p. 581)

aquifer (ak′wə fər) An underground layer of rock or soil filled with water. (p. 459)

artery (är′tə rē) A blood vessel that carries blood away from the heart. (p. 580)

asexual reproduction (a sek′shü əl rē′prō duk′shən) The production of a new organism from only one cell. (p. 50)

atmosphere (at′məs fîr′) The blanket of gases that surrounds Earth. (pp. 104, 395)

PRONUNCIATION KEY

The following symbols are used throughout the McGraw-Hill Science 2000 Glossaries.

a	at	e	end	o	hot	u	up	hw	white	ə	about
ā	ape	ē	me	ō	old	ū	use	ng	song		taken
ä	far	i	it	ô	fork	ü	rule	th	thin		pencil
âr	care	ī	ice	oi	oil	u̇	pull	th	this		lemon
		îr	pierce	ou	out	ûr	turn	zh	measure		circus

′ = *primary accent; shows which syllable takes the main stress, such as* **kil** *in* **kilogram** (kil′ə gram′)
′ = *secondary accent; shows which syllables take the lighter stresses, such as* **gram** *in* **kilogram**

GLOSSARY

atom (at′əm) The smallest unit of an element that retains the properties of that element. *See* molecule. (p. 312)

auditory nerve (ô′di tôr′e nûrv) The nerve that passes vibrations in the ear on to the brain, which interprets the vibrations as sound. (p. 199)

B

bacterium (bak tîr′ē əm) *sing., n., pl.* **bacteria** (-ē ə) A member of either of two kingdoms of one-celled living things that have no nucleus, or center, in their cell body. (p. 13)

balanced diet (bal′ənst dī′it) A diet, maintained over time, that includes a variety of foods providing nutrition in moderate amounts. (p. 618)

barometer (bə rom′i tər) A device for measuring air pressure. (p. 106)

Beaufort scale (bō′fərt skāl) A system for measuring wind speed by observing its effect on the surface of the sea, using a scale of 0 (low) to 12 (high) for each effect. (p. 143)

bench mark (bench märk) A plaque telling the exact location and elevation of a place. (p. 403)

benthos (ben′thos) Organisms that live on the bottom in aquatic ecosystems. (p. 552)

bile (bīl) A greenish-yellow fluid produced by the liver to digest fats. (p. 605)

bioluminescence (bī′o lü′mə nes′əns) Cool light produced by living organisms. (p. 237)

biomass (bī′ō mas′) Energy from plant matter or animal waste. (p. 474)

biome (bī′ōm) One of Earth's large ecosystems, with its own kind of climate, soil, plants, and animals. (p. 544)

biotic factor (bī ot′ik fak′tər) A living part of an ecosystem. (p. 484)

bladder (blad′ər) A muscular bag that collects urine produced by the kidneys. (p. 606)

boiling point (boil′ing point) The particular temperature for each substance at which it changes state from a liquid to a gas. (p. 325)

bronchial tubes (brong′kē əl tübz) The two tubes that connect the trachea to each of your lungs. (p. 593)

bronchioles (brong′kē olz) Smaller passages of the bronchial tubes that branch throughout the lungs. (p. 593)

buoyancy (boi′ən sē) The upward push of a liquid on an object placed in it. (p. 298)

C

cambium (kam′bē əm) The layer in plants that separates the xylem from the phloem. (p. 20)

camouflage (kam′ə fläzh′) An animal's use of its appearance to protect itself against predators. (p. 89)

capillary (kap′ə ler′ē) The smallest type of blood vessel, where materials are exchanged between blood and body cells. (p. 580)

carbon cycle (kär′bən sī′kəl) The continuous exchange of carbon dioxide and oxygen among living things. (p. 516)

carbon dioxide (kär′bən dī ok′sīd) A compound needed by all living plants to make sugars. (p. 514)

carnivore (kär′nə vôr′) An animal that eats another animal. (p. 500)

chemical change (kem′i kəl chānj) A change of matter that occurs when atoms link together in a new way, creating a new substance different from the original substances. (p. 356)

chemical reaction (kem′i kəl rē ak′shən) Another name for chemical change. (p. 356)

chlorofluorocarbons (CFCs) (klôr′ō flür′ō kär′bənz) Gases used in such things as refrigerators, freezers, and air conditioners. CFCs may make "holes" in the ozone layer. (p. 451)

chlorophyll (klôr′ə fil′) A green chemical in plant cells that allows plants to use the Sun's energy for making food. (p. 4)

chloroplast (klôr′ə plast′) The part of a plant cell containing chlorophyll, the green substance that enables the plant to produce food. (p. 32)

cilia (sil′ē ə) Small hairlike structures that move small particles of dirt out of the respiratory system. (p. 593)

cirrus cloud (sir′əs kloud) A high-altitude cloud with a featherlike shape, made of ice crystals. (p. 122)

classification (klas′ə fi kā′shən) The science of finding patterns among living things. (p. 5)

classify (klas'ə fī') To place materials that share properties together in groups. (p. 301)

cleavage (klē'vij) The tendency of a mineral to break along flat surfaces. (p. 418)

climate (klī'mit) The average weather pattern of a region. (p. 178)

climatic zone (klī mat'ik zōn) A region that has similar weather patterns based on temperature, precipitation, wind, distance from a coast, mountain ranges, ocean currents, and vegetation. (p. 178)

climax community (klī'maks kə mū'ni tē) The final stage of succession in an area, unless a major change happens. (p. 564)

cold front (kōld frunt) A front where cold air moves in under a warm front. (p. 152)

colloid (kol'oid) A special type of mixture in which the particles of one material are scattered through another and block the passage of light without settling out. (p. 346)

commensalism (kə men'sə liz'əm) A relationship between two kinds of organisms that benefits one without harming the other. (p. 535)

community (kə mū'ni tē) All the populations living in an area. (p. 488)

complete flower (kəm plēt' flou'ər) A flower that has petals, stamens, and pistils. (p. 70)

compound (kom'pound) Any substance that is formed by the chemical combination of two or more elements and acts like a single substance. (p. 310)

compression (kəm presh'ən) 1. The part of a sound wave where molecules are crowded together. (p. 198) 2. A movement of plates that presses together or squeezes Earth's crust. (p. 404)

concave lens (kon kāv' lenz) A lens that curves inward (is thicker at the edges than at the middle) and spreads light rays apart, making images appear smaller. (p. 254)

concave mirror (kon kāv' mir'ər) A mirror that curves in on the shiny side. (p. 242)

condensation (kon'den sā'shən) The changing of a gas into a liquid. (p. 115)

conduct (v., kən dukt') To allow heat to pass through easily. (p. 300)

conduction (kən duk'shən) The passing of heat through a material while the material itself stays in place. (p. 375)

conifer (kon'ə fər) Any of a group of gymnosperms that produce seeds in cones and have needlelike leaves. (p. 59)

consumer (kən sü'mər) Any animal that eats plants or eats other plant-eating animals. (p. 485)

contour plowing (kon'tür plou'ing) Preventing erosion by plowing across rather than up and down a slope. (p. 437)

contract (v., kən trakt') To shrink, as when a material gets cooler. (p. 331)

convection (kən vek'shən) The flow of heat through a material, causing hot parts to rise and cooler parts to sink. (p. 375)

convection cell (kən vek'shən sel) A circular pattern of air rising, air sinking, and wind. (p. 136)

convex lens (kon veks' lenz) A lens that curves outward (is thicker at the middle than at the edges) and brings light together, making images appear larger. (p. 254)

convex mirror (kon veks' mir'ər) A mirror that curves out on the shiny side. (p. 242)

core (kôr) The center of Earth, lying below the mantle. (p. 403)

Coriolis effect (kôr'ē ō'lis i fekt') The curving of the path of a moving object caused by Earth's rotation. (p. 138)

cortex (kôr'teks) The layer of tissue just inside the epidermis of a plant's roots and stems. (p. 20)

cotyledon (ko'tə lē'dən) A tiny leaflike structure inside the seed of an angiosperm. (p. 62)

PRONUNCIATION KEY

a **at**; ā **ape**; ä **far**; âr **care**; e **end**; ē **me**; i **it**; ī **ice**; îr **pierce**; o **hot**; ō **old**; ô **fork**; oi **oil**; ou **out**; u **up**; ū **use**; ü **rule**; ù **pull**; ûr **turn**; hw **white**; ng **song**; th **thin**; <u>th</u> **this**; zh **measure**; ə **about, taken, pencil, lemon, circus**

GLOSSARY

crop rotation (krop rō tā'shən) Growing different crops each year so that the soil does not use up the same kinds of minerals year after year. (p. 437)

cross-pollination (krôs'pol'ə nā'shən) The transfer of pollen from one flower to another. (p. 72)

crust (krust) The rocky surface that makes up the top of the lithosphere and includes the continents and the ocean floor. (p. 394)

crystal (kris'təl) The geometric shape a mineral forms when its atoms and molecules get into fixed patterns. (p. 416)

cumulus cloud (kū'myə ləs kloud) A puffy cloud that appears to rise up from a flat bottom. (p. 122)

cycad (sī'kad) One of the evergreen gymnosperms that resemble palms and have seed-bearing cones. (p. 59)

D

decibel (dB) (des'ə bel') A unit that measures loudness. (p. 210)

deciduous (di sij'ü əs) Said of a plant that loses its leaves each fall. *See* **evergreen**. (p. 59)

deciduous forest (di sij'ü əs fôr'ist) A forest biome with many kinds of trees that lose their leaves each autumn. (p. 550)

decomposer (dē'kəm pō'zər) Any of the fungi or bacteria that break down dead plants and animals into useful things like minerals and rich soil. (p. 485)

density (den'si tē) A measure of how tightly packed the matter in an object is. (p. 295)

deposition (dep'ə zish'ən) The dropping off of bits of eroded rock. (p. 409)

desalination (dē sal'ə nā'shən) Getting fresh water from seawater. (p. 457)

desert (dez'ərt) A sandy or rocky biome with little precipitation and little plant life. (p. 549)

diaphragm (dī'ə fram') A sheet of muscle below the chest cavity that controls breathing. (p. 592)

dicot (dī'kot') An angiosperm with two cotyledons in each seed. *See* **monocot**. (p. 62)

diffusion (di fū'zhən) The process by which a substance such as a gas moves from areas of high concentration to areas of low concentration. (p. 593)

digestion (di jes'chən) The process of breaking food down into simpler substances for the body to use. (p. 604)

Doppler effect (dop'lər i fekt') The change in frequency (and pitch) as a source of sound moves toward or away from you. (p. 225)

downdraft (doun'draft') A downward rush of air caused by the falling of rain during a thunderstorm. (p. 162)

dry cell battery (drī sel bat'ər ē) A battery that produces electricity but has no liquid inside it. (p. 379)

E

echo (e'kō) A reflected sound wave. (p. 222)

echolocation (ek'ō lō kā'shən) Finding an object by using reflected sound. (p. 224)

ecological succession (ek'ə loj'i kəl sək sesh'ən) The gradual replacement of one community by another. (p. 562)

ecology (ē kol'ə jē) The study of how living things and their environment interact. (p. 484)

ecosystem (ek'ō sis'təm) All the living and nonliving things in an area and their interactions with each other. (p. 484)

electromagnetic spectrum (i lek'trō mag net'ik spek'trəm) All the wavelengths of visible and invisible light in order, from short (gamma rays) to long (radio). (p. 277)

electromagnetism (i lek'trō mag'ni tiz'əm) The production of magnetism by electricity (and the production of electricity by magnets). (p. 276)

electron (i lek'tron) A particle in the space outside the nucleus of an atom that carries one unit of negative electric charge. (p. 313)

element (el'ə mənt) Pure substances that cannot be broken down into any simpler substances. (p. 308)

elevation (el'ə vā'shən) How high a place is above sea level. (p. 403)

embryo (em'brē ō') The immature plant inside a seed. (p. 74)

emulsion (i mul′shən) A type of colloid in which one liquid is spread through another. (p. 346)

enzyme (en′zīm) A chemical that breaks down food into simple pieces that cells can use. (p. 604)

epidermis (ep′i dûr′mis) An outermost layer of such plant parts as roots and leaves. (p. 20)

epiglottis (ep′i glot′is) A cartilage flap above the trachea that keeps food from entering the lungs. (p. 593)

erosion (i rō′zhən) Picking up and carrying away pieces of rocks. (p. 407)

esophagus (i sof′ə gəs) The tube that connects the mouth to the stomach. (p. 604)

evaporation (i vap′ə rā′shən) The changing of a liquid into a gas. (pp. 112, 325)

evergreen (ev′ər grēn′) Seed of a gymnosperm that keeps its leaves for at least a few years. *See* **deciduous**. (p. 59)

excretion (ek skrē′shən) The process of removing waste products from the body. (p. 606)

expand (ek spand′) To spread out, as when a material gets hotter. (p. 331)

F

fault (fôlt) A crack in the crust whose sides show evidence of motion. (p. 402)

fault-block mountain (fôlt blok moun′tən) A mountain formed by blocks of Earth's crust moving along a fault. (p. 405)

fertilization (fûr′tə lə zā′shən) The joining of a female sex cell and a male sex cell into one cell, a fertilized egg. (pp. 50, 73)

fertilizer (fûr′tə līz′ər) Nitrogen-containing substances used to make soil better for growing plants. (p. 515)

fibrous root (fī′brəs rüt) One of the many hairy branching roots that some plants have. (p. 20)

foam (fōm) A type of colloid in which a gas is spread throughout a liquid. (p. 347)

fog (fôg) A cloud that forms at ground level. (p. 123)

food chain (füd chān) The path of the energy in food from one organism to another. (p. 498)

food cycle (füd sī′kəl) The continual reuse of substances needed to survive as they are passed along from one organism to the next. (p. 514)

food group (füd grüp) One of the groups made up of foods that contain similar amounts of important nutrients. (p. 618)

food web (füd web) The overlapping food chains in an ecosystem. (p. 500)

fossil (fos′əl) Any remains or imprint of living things of the past. (p. 431)

fossil fuel (fos′əl fū′əl) A fuel formed from the decay of ancient forms of life. (p. 448)

freezing point (frēz′ing point) Another name for melting point when a substance changes state from a liquid to a solid. (p. 325)

frequency (frē′kwən sē) The number of times an object vibrates per second. (p. 209)

frond (frond) The leaf of a fern. (p. 49)

front (frunt) A boundary between air masses with different temperatures. (p. 151)

fruit (früt) The ripened ovary of a flowering seed plant. (p. 75)

fundamental frequency (fun′də men′təl frē′kwən sē) The lowest frequency at which an object vibrates. (p. 226)

fungi (fun′jī) *pl. n., sing.* **fungus** (fung′gəs) Members of a kingdom that contains one-celled and many-celled living things that absorb food from their environment. (p. 11)

G

gel (jel) A type of colloid in which a solid is spread throughout a liquid. (p. 347)

gem (jem) A mineral valued for being rare and beautiful. (p. 422)

PRONUNCIATION KEY

a at; ā ape; ä far; âr care; e end; ē me; i it; ī ice; îr pierce; o hot; ō old; ô fork; oi oil; ou out; u up; ū use; ü rule; u̇ pull; ûr turn; hw white; ng song; th thin; th this; zh measure; ə about, taken, pencil, lemon, circus

GLOSSARY

geologist (jē ol′ə jist) A scientist who studies Earth. (p. 403)

geothermal energy (jē′ō thûr′məl en′ər jē) Earth's internal energy. (p. 472)

germination (jûr′mə nā′shən) The sprouting of a seed into a new plant. (p. 75)

ginkgo (ging′kō) *n., pl.* **ginkgoes** A large gymnosperm with fan-shaped leaves. (p. 59)

gnetophyte (ne′tō fīt′) One of the gymnosperms that are closely related to flowering plants and live in both deserts and the tropics. (p. 59)

grassland (gras′land′) A biome where grasses, not trees, are the main plant life. Prairies are one kind of grassland region. (p. 546)

gravitropism (grav′ī trō′pi′zəm) The response of a plant to gravity. (p. 84)

gravity (grav′i tē) A force of attraction, or pull, between any object and any other objects around it. Gravity is a property of all matter. (p. 390)

greenhouse effect (grēn′hous′ i fekt′) The ability of the atmosphere to let in sunlight but not to let heat escape. (p. 183)

groundwater (ground wô′tər) Water that seeps into the ground into spaces between bits of rock and soil. (pp. 126, 459)

gymnosperm (jim′nə spûrm′) A seed plant that does not produce flowers. *See* **angiosperm**. (p. 58)

H

habitat (hab′i tat′) The place where a population lives. (p. 489)

hail (hāl) Pellets made of ice and snow. (p. 125)

hardness (härd′nis) How well a mineral resists scratching. (p. 418)

hemoglobin (hē′mə glō′bin) A chemical that carries oxygen around in the body. (p. 580)

herbivore (hûr′bə vôr′) An animal that eats plants, algae, and other producers. (p. 500)

hertz (Hz) (hûrts) A unit for measuring frequency. One hertz (Hz) equals a frequency of one vibration per second. (p. 209)

high-pressure system (hī′ presh′ər sis′təm) A pattern surrounding a high-pressure center, from which winds blow outward. In the Northern Hemisphere, these winds curve to the right in a clockwise pattern. (p. 140)

humidity (hū mid′i tē) The amount of water vapor in the air. (p. 112)

humus (hū′məs) Decayed plant or animal material in soil. (p. 435)

hurricane (hûr′i kān′) A very large, swirling storm with very low pressure at the center. (p. 166)

hydrocarbon (hī′drə kär′bən) Any of the large group of compounds made solely from hydrogen and carbon atoms. (p. 318)

hydroelectric plant (hī′drō i lek′trik plant) A factory where running or falling water spins a generator to make electricity. (p. 472)

hydrosphere (hī′drə sfîr′) Earth's water, whether found in continents and oceans, and includes the fresh water in ice, lakes, rivers, and underground water. (p. 394)

hydrotropism (hī drot′rə piz′əm) The response of a plant to a nearby source of water. (p. 85)

hyperthermia (hī′pər thûr′mē ə) The overheating of the body that can be caused by overexposure in a hot, dry climate. (p. 186)

hypothesis (hī poth′ə sis) A guess or if . . . *then* statement that can be answered clearly in an experiment. (p. 35)

I–K

igneous rock (ig′nē əs rok) A rock formed when melted rock material cools and hardens. (p. 428)

image (im′ij) A "picture" of the light source that light rays make in bouncing off a polished, shiny surface. (p. 242)

imperfect flower (im pûr′fikt flou′ər) A flower with either a stamen or a pistil, but not both. (p. 70)

incomplete flower (in′kəm plēt′ flou′ər) A flower that lacks petals or stamens or pistils. (p. 70)

inertia (i nûr′shə) The tendency of a moving object to keep moving in a straight line. (p. 391)

insolation (in'sə lā'shən) The amount of the Sun's energy that reaches Earth at a given time and place. *Insolation* is short for *in*coming *sol*ar *rad*i*ation*. (p. 100)

insulate (in'sə lāt') To prevent heat from passing through. (p. 300)

intertidal zone (in'tər tī'dəl zōn) The shallowest section of the marine, or ocean, ecosystem, where the ocean floor is covered and uncovered as the tide goes in and out. (p. 553)

isobar (i'sə bär') A line on a weather map connecting places with equal air pressure. (p. 140)

kinetic energy (ki net'ik en'ər jē) The energy of any moving object. (p. 369)

L

land breeze (land brēz) Wind that blows from land to sea. (p. 137)

larynx (lar'ingks) The voice box, located at the upper end of the trachea. (p. 593)

laser (lā'zər) A device that produces a thin stream of light of just a few close wavelengths. (p. 282)

lava (lä'və) Magma that reaches Earth's surface. (p. 405)

law of reflection (lô uv ri flek'shən) The angle between an incoming light ray and a surface equals the angle between the reflected light ray and the surface. (p. 241)

lightning (līt'ning) One of the huge electric sparks that leap from clouds to the ground in thunderstorms. (p. 162)

light ray (līt rā) A straight-line beam of light as it travels outward from its source. (p. 239)

limiting factor (lim'ə ting fak'tər) Anything that controls the growth or survival of a population. (p. 528)

lithosphere (lith'ə sfîr') The hard, outer layer of Earth, about 100 kilometers thick. (p. 394)

long-day plant (lông'dā plant) Plants that bloom when there is much more daylight than darkness. (p. 86)

low-pressure system (lō'presh'ər sis'təm) A pattern surrounding a low-pressure center, in which winds blow in toward the center. In the Northern Hemisphere, these winds blow to the right in a counterclockwise pattern. (p. 140)

luster (lus'tər) The way light bounces off a mineral's surface. (p. 417)

M

magma (mag'mə) Hot, molten rock deep below Earth's surface. (p. 405)

mantle (man'təl) The thickest layer of Earth, lying just under the crust. (p. 403)

mass (mas) A measure of the amount of matter in an object. (p. 292)

matter (ma'tər) Anything that has mass and takes up space. (p. 198)

melting point (melt'ing point) The particular temperature for each substance at which it changes state from a solid to a liquid. (p. 325)

membrane (mem'brān) A thin envelope surrounding the nucleus of a cell. (p. 12)

metamorphic rock (met'ə môr'fik rok) A rock formed under heat and pressure from another kind of rock. (p. 432)

meteorite (mē'tē ə rīt') A chunk of rock from space that strikes a surface (such as Earth or the Moon). (p. 410)

mimicry (mim'i krē) An animal's use of its appearance to look like a different, unpleasant animal as a protection against predators. (p. 89)

mineral (min'ər əl) A solid material of Earth's crust with a definite composition. (p. 416)

mixture (miks'chər) A physical combination of two or more substances that are blended together without forming new substances. (p. 340)

molecule (mol'ə kūl') The smallest piece that matter can be broken into without changing the kind of matter; a group of more than one atom joined together that acts like a single particle. *See* **atom.** (pp. 198, 316)

PRONUNCIATION KEY

a **a**t; ā **a**pe; ä f**a**r; âr c**a**re; e **e**nd; ē m**e**; i **i**t; ī **i**ce; îr p**ie**rce; o h**o**t; ō **o**ld; ô f**o**rk; oi **o**il; ou **o**ut; u **u**p; ū **u**se; ü r**u**le; ù p**u**ll; ûr t**u**rn; hw **wh**ite; ng so**ng**; th **th**in; <u>th</u> **th**is; zh mea**s**ure; ə **a**bout, tak**e**n, penc**i**l, lem**o**n, circ**u**s

monocot (mon′ə kot′) An angiosperm with one cotyledon in each seed. *See* **dicot**. (p. 62)

mountain breeze (moun′tən brēz) A cool night wind that blows down a mountain slope to replace the warmer air in the valley. (p. 137)

mucus (mū′kəs) A clear fluid that traps and prevents foreign particles from entering the body. (p. 593)

mutualism (mū′chü ə liz′əm) A relationship between two kinds of organisms that benefits both. (p. 532)

N

nekton (nek′ton) Organisms that swim through the water in aquatic ecosystems. (p. 552)

nephron (nef′ron) A structure in the kidney that filters blood. (p. 606)

neutron (nü′tron) A particle in the nucleus of an atom that has no net electric charge. (p. 313)

NEXRAD (neks′rad′) A new form of Doppler radar that is used to track storms. The word stands for *NEXt generation of weather RADar*. (p. 173)

niche (nich) The role an organism has in its ecosystem. (p. 489)

nitrogen (nī′trə jən) An element that plants need to grow and stay healthy, and that all organisms need to make proteins. (p. 515)

nitrogen cycle (nī′trə jən sī′kəl) The continuous trapping of nitrogen gas into compounds in the soil and its return to the air. (p. 518)

nonrenewable resource (non′ri nü′ə bəl rē′sôrs′) A resource that cannot be replaced within a short period of time or at all. (p. 423)

nonvascular (non vas′kyə lər) Containing no plant tissue through which water and food move. (p. 7)

nucleus (nü′klē əs) **1.** A dense, dark structure inside the cell. (p. 12) **2.** One of the airborne dust particles around which water molecules condense as droplets or ice crystals before falling as precipitation. (p. 123)

O

occluded front (ə klüd′id frunt) A front formed where a warm front and cold front meet. (p. 152)

omnivore (om′nə vôr′) An animal that eats both plants and animals. (p. 501)

opaque (ō pāk′) Completely blocking light from passing through it. (p. 250)

orbit (ôr′bit) The path of a planet traveling around a star. (p. 388)

ore (ôr) A mineral containing a useful substance. (p. 422)

ovary (ō′və rē) A structure containing egg cells. (p. 72)

overtone (ō′vər tōn′) One of a series of pitches that blend to give a sound its quality. (p. 226)

ozone layer (ō′zōn lā′ər) A layer of ozone gas in the atmosphere that screens out much of the Sun's UV (ultraviolet) rays. (p. 447)

P

parasite (par′ə sīt′) An angiosperm that lives off other plants. It cannot live on its own because it has little or no chlorophyll. (p. 60)

parasitism (par′ə sī tiz′əm) A relationship in which one kind of organism lives on and may harm another. (p. 534)

perfect flower (pûr′fikt flou′ər) A flower with both male and female parts, that is, both a stamen and a pistil. (p. 70)

periodic table (pîr′ē od′ik tā′bəl) A table in which the elements are arranged in groups with similar properties. (p. 315)

phloem (flō′em) The tissue through which food from the leaves moves down through the rest of a plant. (p. 20)

photon (fō′ton) The tiny bundles of energy by means of which light travels. (p. 277)

photoperiodism (fō′tō pîr′ē ə diz′əm) The flowering response of a plant to changing periods of daylight and darkness. (p. 86)

photosynthesis (fō′tə sin′thə sis) The food-making process in green plants that uses sunlight. (p. 32)

phototropism (fō tot′rə piz′əm) The response of a plant to changes in light. (p. 84)

phylum (fī′ləm) *sing. n., pl.* **phyla** (-lə) One of the large groups in the animal kingdom. (p. 10)

physical change (fiz′i kəl chānj) A change of matter in size, shape, or state without any change in identity. (p. 354)

physical fitness (fiz′i kəl fit′nis) The condition in which your body is healthy and works the best it can. (p. 616)

pioneer community (pī′ə nîr′ kə mū′ni tē) The first community thriving in a once lifeless area. (p. 564)

pioneer species (pī′ə nîr′ spē′shēz) The first species living in an otherwise lifeless area. (p. 563)

pitch (pich) How high or low a sound is. (p. 208)

planet (plan′it) Any of the nine objects that travel around the Sun and shine by reflecting its light. (p. 388)

plankton (plangk′tən) Organisms that float on the water in aquatic ecosystems. (p. 552)

plant behavior (plant bi hāv′yər) The response of plants to conditions in their environments. (p. 82)

plasma (plaz′mə) The pale-yellow liquid part of blood that contains nutrients. (p. 580)

plate (plāt) One of the pieces of Earth's crust that has been broken by upward pressure from the mantle. (p. 403)

platelet (plāt′lit) A cell fragment in blood that helps blood to form clots. (p. 580)

polarization (pō′lər ə zā′shən) Allowing light vibrations to pass through in only one direction. (p. 251)

pollen (pol′ən) Dustlike grains in the flower of a plant that contain its male sex cells. (p. 64)

pollination (pol′ə nā′shən) The transfer of a pollen grain to the egg-producing part of a plant. (p. 72)

pollutant (pə lü′tənt) An unnatural substance added to Earth's land, water, or air. (p. 436)

pollution (pə lü′shən) Adding any unnatural substances to Earth's land, water, or air. (p. 436)

polymer (pol′ə mər) Any plastic, such as polyethylene, that is made of hydrocarbon molecules with very long chains of atoms. (p. 318)

population (pop′yə lā′shən) All the members of one species in an area. (p. 488)

potential energy (pə ten′shəl en′ər jē) Stored energy. (p. 369)

precipitation (pri sip′i tā′shən) Any form of water particles that falls from the atmosphere and reaches the ground. (p. 124)

predator (pred′ə tər) A living thing that hunts other living things for food. (p. 501)

prey (prā) A living thing that is hunted for food. (p. 501)

primary color (prī′mer′ē kul′ər) Red, green, or blue. Mixing these colors can produce all the colors of the spectrum. (p. 266)

primary pigment (prī′mer′ē pig′mənt) Magenta, cyan, or yellow. Materials with any of these colors absorb one primary color of light and reflect the other two. (p. 268)

prism (priz′əm) A cut piece of clear glass (or plastic) with two opposite sides in the shape of a triangle or other geometric shape. (p. 264)

producer (prə dü′sər) Any of the plants and algae that produce oxygen and food that animals need. (p. 485)

product (prod′ukt) A new substance produced by a chemical change. (p. 356)

property (prop′ər tē) A characteristic of matter. (p. 292)

prop root (prop rüt) One of the roots that grow out of a plant's stemlike main roots and helps prop up the plant. (p. 20)

protective coloration (prə tek′tiv kul′ə rā′shən) An animal's blending in with its background to protect itself against predators. (p. 89)

protist (prō′tist) A member of a kingdom that contains one-celled and many-celled living things, some that make food and some that hunt for food. (p. 12)

PRONUNCIATION KEY

a at; ā ape; ä far; âr care; e end; ē me; i it; ī ice; îr pierce; o hot; ō old; ô fork; oi oil; ou out; u up; ū use; ü rule; ů pull; ûr turn; hw white; ng song; th thin; <u>th</u> this; zh measure; ə about, taken, pencil, lemon, circus

proton (prō'ton) A particle in the nucleus of an atom that carries one unit of positive electric charge. (p. 313)

Q-R

quality (kwol'i tē) The difference you hear between two sounds of the same loudness and pitch. (p. 226)

radiation (rā'dē a'shən) The giving off of infrared rays through space. (p. 375)

radiative balance (rā'dē ā'tiv bal'əns) A balance between energy lost and energy gained. (p. 182)

rarefaction (râr'ə fak'shən) The part of a sound wave where molecules are spread apart. (p. 198)

reactant (rē ak'tənt) An original substance at the beginning of a chemical reaction. (p. 356)

reflection (ri flek'shən) The bouncing of a sound wave off a surface. (p. 220)

refraction (ri frak'shən) The bending of light rays as they pass from one substance into another. (p. 252)

relative humidity (rel'ə tiv hū mid'i tē) A comparison between the actual amount of water vapor in the air and the amount the air can hold at a given temperature. (p. 114)

renewable resource (ri nü'ə bəl rē'sôrs') A resource that can be replaced in a short period of time. (p. 446)

reservoir (rez'ər vwär') A storage area for freshwater supplies. (p. 459)

resource (rē'sôrs') Any material that helps support life on Earth. (p. 386)

respiration (res'pə rā'shən) 1. The process of obtaining and using oxygen in the body. (p. 592) 2. The release of energy in plants from food (sugar). (p. 33)

response (ri spons') What a living thing does as a result of a stimulus. (p. 84)

rhizoid (ri'zoid) One of the hairlike fibers that anchors a moss to the soil and takes in water from the soil. (p. 46)

rhizome (ri'zōm) The underground stem of a fern. (p. 49)

rock (rok) A naturally formed solid in the crust made up of one or more minerals. (p. 428)

rock cycle (rok sī'kəl) Rocks changing from one form into another in a never-ending series of processes. (p. 438)

root cap (rüt kap) A thin covering made up of cells that protect the root tip of a plant as it grows into the soil. (p. 20)

runoff (run'ôf) Precipitation that falls into rivers and streams. (p. 126)

S

scavenger (skav'ən jər) A meat-eating animal that feeds on the remains of dead animals. (p. 501)

sea breeze (sē brēz) Wind that blows from sea to land. (p. 137)

sedimentary rock (sed'ə men'tə rē rok) A rock made of bits of matter joined together. (p. 430)

seed (sēd) An undeveloped plant with stored food sealed in a protective covering. (p. 58)

seed coat (sēd kōt) The outer covering of a seed. (p. 74)

seed dispersal (sēd di spûr'səl) The movement of a seed from the flower to a place where it can sprout. (p. 75)

self-pollination (self'pol'ə nā'shən) The transfer of pollen from an anther to a stigma in the same plant. (p. 72)

sexual reproduction (sek'shü əl rē'prō duk'shən) The production of a new organism from a female sex cell and a male sex cell. (p. 50)

shear (shîr) A movement of plates that twists, tears, or pushes one part of Earth's crust past another. (p. 404)

short-day plant (shôrt'dā plant) Plants that bloom when there is more darkness and less daylight. (p. 86)

sickle cell anemia (sik'əl sel ə nē'mē ə) An inherited blood disease in which the red blood cells curve into a C shape and cannot move or absorb oxygen easily. (p. 586)

smog (smog) A mixture of smoke and fog. (p. 448)

solar system (sō'lər sis'təm) The Sun and the objects that are traveling around it. (p. 388)

solution (sə lü′shən) A mixture of substances that are blended so completely that the mixture looks the same everywhere, even under a microscope. (p. 344)

sound wave (sound wāv) A vibration that spreads away from a vibrating object. (p. 198)

spectrum (spek′trəm) A band of colors produced when light goes through a prism. (p. 264)

spore (spôr) Cells in seedless plants that grow into new organisms. (p. 46)

spring (spring) A place where groundwater seeps out of the ground. (p. 459)

states of matter (stāts uv mat′ər) One of the three forms that matter can take—solid, liquid, or gas. (p. 324)

stationary front (stā′shə ner ē frunt) An unmoving front where a cold air mass and a warm air mass meet. (p. 153)

statistical forecasting (stə tis′ti kəl fôr′kas′ting) Predicting weather by using past weather records, based on the chances of a pattern repeating itself. (p. 156)

stimulus (stim′yə ləs), *sing.*, *pl.* **stimuli** (-lī) Something in the environment that causes a living thing to react. (p. 84)

stomata (stō′mə tə) *pl. n., sing.* **stoma** Pores in the bottom of leaves that open and close to let in air or give off water vapor. (p. 25)

storm surge (stôrm sûrj) A great rise of the sea along a shore caused by low-pressure clouds. (p. 168)

stratus cloud (strā′təs kloud) A cloud that forms in a blanketlike layer. (p. 122)

streak (strēk) The color of the powder left when a mineral is rubbed against a hard, rough surface. (p. 418)

strip farming (strip fär′ming) Trapping runoff by alternating tightly growing grasses with more widely spaced plants. (p. 437)

surveyor (sər vā′ər) A specialist who makes accurate measurements of Earth's crust. (p. 403)

suspension (sə spen′shən) Mixtures in which suspended particles can easily be seen. (p. 345)

symbiosis (sim′bi ō′sis) A relationship between two kinds of organisms over time. (p. 532)

synoptic weather map (si nop′tik weth′ər map) A type of map showing a summary of the weather using station models. (p. 156)

T

taiga (tī′gə) A cool, forest biome of conifers in the upper Northern Hemisphere. (p. 547)

taproot (tap′rüt′) A root that has few hairy branches and grows deep into the ground. (p. 20)

tension (ten′shən) A movement of plates that stretches or pulls apart Earth's crust. (p. 404)

terracing (ter′is ing) Shaping hillsides into steps so that runoff and eroded soil get trapped on the steps. (p. 437)

thunder (thun′dər) The noise caused by lightning-heated air during a thunderstorm. (p. 162)

thunderhead (thun′dər hed′) A cumulonimbus cloud in which a thunderstorm forms. (p. 162)

thunderstorm (thun′dər stôrm′) The most common severe storm, formed in cumulonimbus clouds. (p. 162)

tidal power plant (tī′dəl pou′ər plant) A factory where the flow of tidewater is used to make electricity. (p. 473)

tissue (tish′ü) A group of similar cells that work together at the same job. (p. 5)

tornado (tôr nā′dō) A violent whirling wind that moves across the ground in a narrow path. (p. 164)

trachea (trā′kē ə) A stiff tube lined with cartilage that transports air between the throat and lungs. (p. 593)

trade winds (trād windz) A belt of winds around Earth moving from high pressure zones toward the low pressure at the equator. (p. 139)

PRONUNCIATION KEY

a **at**; ā **ape**; ä **far**; âr **care**; e **end**; ē **me**; i **it**; ī **ice**; îr **pierce**; o **hot**; ō **old**; ô **fork**; oi **oil**; ou **out**; u **up**; ū **use**; ü **rule**; ù **pull**; ûr **turn**; hw **white**; ng **song**; th **thin**; th **this**; zh **measure**; ə **about**, **taken**, **pencil**, **lemon**, **circus**

GLOSSARY

transfusion (trans fū′zhən) Taking blood from one person and giving it to another person. (p. 581)

translucent (trans lü′sənt) Letting only some light through, so that objects on the other side appear blurry. (p. 250)

transparent (trans pâr′ənt) Letting all light through, so that objects on the other side can be seen clearly. (p. 250)

transpiration (tran′spə rā′shən) The loss of water through a plant's leaves, which draws water up through the plant to replace it. (pp. 25, 113)

tropical rain forest (trop′i kəl rān fôr′ist) A hot, humid biome near the equator, with much rainfall and a wide variety of life. (p. 551)

tropism (trō′piz′əm) A growth response of a plant toward or away from a stimulus. (p. 84)

troposphere (trop′ə sfîr′) The layer of the atmosphere closest to Earth's surface. (p. 104)

tundra (tun′drə) A cold, treeless biome of the far north, marked by spongy topsoil. (p. 548)

U

ultrasonic (ul′trə son′ik) Said of a sound with a frequency too high to be heard by humans. (p. 209)

updraft (up′draft′) An upward rush of heated air during a thunderstorm. (p. 162)

urea (yu̇ rē′ə) A substance formed from waste material in the liver and excreted in urine. (p. 606)

ureter (yu̇ rē′tər) One of two long, narrow tubes that carry urine from the kidneys to the bladder. (p. 606)

urethra (yu̇ rē′thrə) The tube through which urine passes from the body. (p. 606)

V

vacuum (vak′ū əm) A space through which sound waves cannot travel because it contains no matter. (p. 274)

valley breeze (val′ē brēz) A cool wind that blows up a mountain slope and replaces the slope's rising Sun-warmed air. (p. 137)

variable (vâr′ē ə bəl) One of the changes in a situation that may affect the outcome of an experiment. (p. 35)

vascular (vas′kyə lər) Containing plant tissue through which water moves up and food moves down. (p. 7)

vein (vān) A blood vessel that carries blood toward the heart. (p. 580)

vibration (vī brā′shən) A back-and-forth motion. (p. 196)

villus (vil′əs) n., pl. **villi** (vil′ī) One of many tiny fingerlike projections in the small intestine that absorb digested food. (p. 605)

volume (vol′ūm) A measure of how much space an object takes up. (p. 292)

W–X

warm front (wôrm frunt) A front where warm air moves in over a cold front. (p. 152)

water cycle (wô′tər sī′kəl) The continuous movement of water between Earth's surface and the air, changing from liquid to gas to liquid. (pp. 127, 458, 512)

waterspout (wô′tər spout′) A tornado that forms over water. (p. 165)

water table (wô′tər tā′bəl) The top of the water-filled spaces in the ground. (p. 459)

water vapor (wô′tər vā′pər) Water in the form of a gas. (p. 112)

weather (we<u>th</u>′ər) What the lower atmosphere is like at any given place and time. (p. 106)

weathering (we<u>th</u>′ər ing) Breaking down rocks into smaller pieces. (p. 407)

weight (wāt) The force of gravity between Earth and an object. (p. 293)

well (wel) A hole dug below the water table that water seeps into. (p. 459)

wet cell battery (wet sel bat′ə rē) A battery that uses a chemical solution to produce electricity. (p. 378)

wind (wind) Air that moves horizontally. (p. 136)

wind vane (wind vān) A device that indicates wind direction. (p. 142)

xylem (zī′ləm) The tissue through which water and minerals move up through a plant. (p. 20)

INDEX

*Indicates an activity related to this topic.

*Indicates an activity related to this topic.

*Indicates an activity related to this topic.

INDEX

X

*Indicates an activity related to this topic.

CREDITS

Cover: ©Paul & Lindamarie Ambrose/FPG

Maps: Geosystems

Transvision: Richard Hutchings (photography, TP1); Guy Porfirio (illustration)

Illustrations: Denny Bond: pp. 33, 518; Ka Botzis: pp. 500-501, 598, 612-613; Dan Clifford: p. 512; Barbara Cousins: pp. 239, 242-244, 254, 299, 580, 582-583, 605, 608, 618; Marie Dauenheimer: pp. 4, 5; Drew-Brook-Cormack: pp. 116, 123; John Edwards: pp. 224, 239, 242-244, 254, 293, 296, 299, 388; Peter Fasolino: pp. 333, 346; Robert Frank: pp. 516, 536; Thomas Gagliano: pp. 134-135, 137; Greg Harris: pp. 151, 181, 553; Virge Kask: pp. 10, 70, 72-74, 76-77, 498, 504-505; George Kelvin: pp. 24, 32, 35, 50-52, 83, 85-86, 93, 276, 394, 403-404, 409, 433, 435, 446-447, 458-459, 470; Katie Lee: pp. 32, 54, 484-485, 560-561, 564; Tom Leonard: pp. 199, 256-257; Rebecca Merrilees: pp. 20-23, 37-38, 49; Dave Merrill: pp. 395, 405, 487, 531-532; Mowry Graphics: pp. 126, 150, 185, 553; Steve Oh: pp. 585, 592, 593, 604, 606; Saul Rosenbaum: pp. 96, 102-103, 114, 125, 136, 152, 162-163, 165, 183, 253, 274-275; Wendy Smith: pp. 6, 8-9, 60, 62, 268; Steve Stankiewicz: pp. 114, 138, 148-149, 156, 161, 165, 169, 174, 185, 228, 235, 240, 247, 255, 260, 261, 266, 270-271, 282, 284, 326, 332, 334, 342, 350, 368, 371, 373, 378-380, 416-417, 438, 457, 462, 468, 544, 556, 569, R13, R15, R18-R20; Art Thompson: pp. 100, 140, 166, 178, 180, 188, 295, 299, 341-343, 348, 392-393.

Photography Credits: All photographs are by Richard Hutchings Photography except as noted below:

TOC: iii: images copyright ©1998 PhotoDisc, Inc. iv: NASA/Digital Stock. v: Digital Stock. vi: ©Cabisco/VU. vii: NASA/Digital Stock. viii: ©John D. Cunningham/VU. ix: Ken Eward/Science Source/Photo Researchers, Inc. S2, S3: ©David M. Sanders; S4: *t.r.* J.A. Kraulis/Masterfile; *b.r.* Antman/The Image Works; *bkmk.* Tom & Pat Leeson/Photo Researchers, Inc. S5: David Mager. S6: *t.l., t.m.* Michael P. Gadomski/Photo Researchers, Inc.; *t.r.* Gregory K. Scott/Photo Researchers, Inc.; *b.l.* Michael Quintonings/National Geographic Society; *b.m.* Richard Megna/Fundamental Photographs; *b.r.* Paul Silverman/Fundamental Photographs. S7: Culver Pictures. S9: Gary Braasch/Woodfin Camp & Assoc. S10: *b.l.* Michael Quintonings/National Geographic Society; S11: Linde Waidhofer/Liaison International. S12: *l.* Jan Halaska/Photo Researchers, Inc. S14: *t.m.* Richard Hutchings/PhotoEdit; *b.m.* Polecat. S15: Joyce Photographics/Photo Researchers, Inc. S16: *t.r.* Ken N. Johns/Photo Researchers, Inc.; *b.* Sandra Baker/Liaison International. S17: Courtesy Tree Musketeers. **Unit 1** 1: *bkgnd.* Zig Leszcynski/Animals Animals; *inset* Bryan Reinhart/Masterfile. 2: *l.* Allsport/Rick Stewart; *r.* Jerry Wachter/Photo Researchers, Inc. 4: Peter Miller/Photo Researchers, Inc. 5: ©Dick Thomas/VU. 7: ©Jeff J. Daly/VU. 11: *l.* ©Veronika Burmeister/VU; *m.* ©Doug Sokell/VU; *r.* R.M. Meadows/Peter Arnold, Inc. 12: *t.l.* Patrick W. Grace/Science Source/Photo Researchers, Inc.; *b.l.* Gilbert S. Grant/Photo Researchers, Inc.; *l.m.* ©Veronika Burmeister/VU; *r.* ©R. Kessel-G. Shih/VU; *r.m.* ©Cabisco/VU. 13: *t.l.* Phil Degginger/Color-Pic; *b.l.* ©R. Robinson/VU; *t.r.* Blair Seitz/Photo Researchers, Inc.; *b.r.* ©VU. 14: *l.* ©Arthur R. Hill/VU; *r.* ©R.F. Ashley/VU. 16: *l.* Dr. Dennis Kunkel/PhotoTake; *r.* Gregory Ochocki/Photo Researchers, Inc. 17: D.P. Wilson/Eric & David Hosking/Photo Researchers, Inc. 18: *m.l.* ©George Herben/VU; *m.r.* ©Ken Lucas/VU; *b.r.* ©Arthur Morris/VU. 25: G. Buttner/OKAPIA/Photo Researchers, Inc. 26: *l.* ©David S. Addison/VU; *r.* ©Tim Hauf/VU. 27: James R. Holland/National Geographic Society. 28: *bkgnd.* J.C. Teyssier/Publiphoto/Photo Researchers, Inc.; *b.* Tom & Pat Leeson/Photo Researchers, Inc. 30: *l., r.* images copyright ©1998 PhotoDisc, Inc.; *m.* Michael P. Gadomski/Photo Researchers, Inc. 34: ©John Gerlach/VU. 36: ©Jack M. Bostrack/VU. 39: Gerry Ellis/ENP Photography. 40: *bkgnd.* ©Doug Sokell/VU; *b.* Michael P. Gadomski/Photo Researchers, Inc. 41: *t.* ©Ned Therrien/VU; *b.* ©David M. Philips/VU. 42: images copyright ©1998 PhotoDisc, Inc. 43: *bkgnd.* ©TSM/David D. Keaton; *inset* ©TSM/Charles Krebs. 44: ©Tim Hauf/VU. 46: *l.* ©Doug Sokell/VU; *m.* ©John Trager/VU. 47: *l.* ©Bill Beatty/VU; *r.* ©David Sieren/VU; *t.r.* ©Fritz Polking/VU; *b.r.* ©E.F. Anderson/VU. 48: *l.* Dan Suzio/Photo Researchers, Inc. 49: ©David Sieren/VU. 52: ©Dick Keen/VU. 53: George Haling/Photo Researchers, Inc. 56: *l.* Bonnie Sue/Photo Researchers, Inc.; *r.* Peter Skinner/Photo Researchers, Inc. 58: *l.* ©Jim Hughes/VU; *m.* ©VU; *r.* ©Gerald & Buff Corsi/VU. 59: *t.* ©E. Webber/VU; *b.l.* ©John N. Trager/VU; *b.r.* V.P. Weinland/Photo Researchers, Inc. 60: *t.* ©V. McMillan/VU; *b.* ©TSM/Dick Keen. 61: *t.* ©E.F. Anderson/VU; *b.* ©Bud Nielsen/VU. 63: *t.* ©Mark S. Skalny/VU; *b.* ©Arthur R. Hill/VU. 64: *l.* ©John Gerlach/VU; *r.* Jerome Wexler/Photo Researchers, Inc. 65: Alan & Linda Detrick/Photo Researchers, Inc. 66: *bkgnd.* Richard R. Hansen/Photo Researchers, Inc.; Dennis Fagan/Lady Bird Johnson Wildflower Center. 68: *t.* Dr. Jeremy Burgess/Photo Researchers, Inc.; *b.* Gunter Ziesler/Peter Arnold, Inc. 71: *t.* ©Derrick Ditchburn/VU; *m.* ©Doug Sokell/VU; *b.* Adam Jones/Photo Researchers, Inc. 74: R.C. Carpenter/Photo Researchers, Inc. 75: *l.* ©Inga Spence/VU; *m.* ©Ken Wagner/VU; *r.* ©Stephen J. Lang/VU. 79: Kenneth W. Fink/Photo Researchers, Inc. 80: *bkgnd.* Runk/Schoenberger/Grant Heilman Photography, Inc; *t.* Bill Gillette/Stock, Boston; *b.* Jeff Greenberg/PhotoEdit. 81: Emil Muench/Photo Researchers, Inc. 82: *l.* George & Judy Manna/Photo Researchers, Inc.; *r.* ©Mack Henley/VU. 84: ©David Newman/VU. 85: ©R. Calentine/VU. 87: ©Dick Keen/VU. 88: *t.* ©Parke H. John, Jr./VU; *b.* ©Bill Beatty/VU. 89: *b.l.* Steve Kaufman/Peter Arnold, Inc.; *t, b.r.* ©Stan W. Elems/VU. 90: *l.* ©Joe McDonald/VU; *m.* ©Arthur Morris/VU; *r.* ©Barbara Gerlach/VU. 91: Richard T. Nowitz/Corbis. 92: *bkgnd.* Brock May/Photo Researchers, Inc.; *t.* Joel Sartore/Grant Heilman Photography, Inc. **Unit 2** 97: *bkgnd.* ©Paul Chesley/TSI; *inset* images copyright ©1998 PhotoDisc, Inc. 98: *t.* ©Francis/Donna Caldwell/VU; *b.* ©Joe McDonald/VU. 106: *l., m.* Runk/Schoenberger/Grant Heilman Photography, Inc; *r.* Yoav Levy/Photo Researchers, Inc. 107: David Waitz. 108: Jay Smith/High and Wild Mt. Guides. 109: NASA/Corbis. 110: SuperStock. 112: Amy C. Etra/PhotoEdit. 115: Tony Freeman/PhotoEdit. 120: ©John Cunningham/VU. 122: *t.* ©A.J. Copley/VU; *m.* ©Henry W. Robison/VU; *b.* ©Mark A. Schneider/VU. 124: *l.* ©D. Cavagnaro/VU; *m.l.* ©W. Banaszewski/VU; *m.r.* ©Mark E. Gibson/VU; *r.* Layne Kennedy/Corbis. 125: Peter Turnley/Corbis. 128: Runk/Schoenberger/Grant Heilman Photography, Inc. 129: ©TSM/Aaron Rezney. 130: *bkgnd.* Digital Stock. 131: Sean Sexton Collection/Corbis. 132: David G. Houser/Corbis. 136: Superstock. 137: ©TSM/Torleif Svensson. 139: NASA. 142: *t.l.* ©Deneve Feigh Bunde/VU; *t.r.* ©Tom Edwards/VU; *b.l.* ©Mark E. Gibson/VU; *b.r.* ©Science VU. 144: *bkgnd.* Carl Purcell/Photo Researchers, Inc. 145: Tiziana and Gianni Baldizzone/Corbis. 147: *bkgnd.* ©Ed Degginger/Bruce Coleman, Inc./PNI; *inset* ©Gene Moore/PhotoTake/PNI. 148: images copyright ©1998 PhotoDisc, Inc. 154: *m.* NASA; *b.l., b.r.* ©1998 AccuWeather, Inc. 155: ©1998 AccuWeather, Inc. 157: ©TSM/David Stoecklei. 158: *b. bkgnd.* NASA; *t.l.* Paul Seheult/Eye Ubiquitous/Corbis; *t.r.* images copyright ©1998 PhotoDisc, Inc.; *b.r.* Corbis-Bettmann. 159: *t.l.* National Weather Service/AP/Wide World; *t.r.* NASA/AP/Wide World. 160: ©VU. 163: ©Nada Pencik/VU. 165: ©Gene Moore/PhotoTake. 167: ©Science VU. 168: Carlos Guerrero. 169: *bkgnd.* ©Marc Epstein/VU; *inset* ©Mark A. Schneider/VU. 170: *bkgnd.* ©R.F. Meyers/VU. 172: *t.* Keith Kent/Peter Arnold, Inc. 173: Carlos Guerrero. 176: *t.l.* ©TSM/Carlos Humberto; *t.r.* ©Martin G. Miller/VU; *b.l.* ©TSM/Strauss/Curtis; *b.r.* ©TSM/Torleif Svensson. 184: *l.* ©Science VU; *r.* ©VU. 185: Steve Kaufman/Peter Arnold, Inc. 186: *t.* ©Don Smetzer/TSI; *b.* Jeff Greenberg/PhotoEdit. 187: Abraham Hondius/Bridgeman Art Library Intl. Ltd. **Unit 3** 193: Ezio Geneletti/The Image Bank. 194: ©TSM/Photri. 196: Daemmrich/The Image Works. 197: ©Artville LLC 1997. 198: Macmillan/McGraw-Hill School Division. 200: ©Ken Fisher/TSI. 201: ©TSM/Norbert Wu. 203: ©TSM/Ed Bock. 204: *l.* National Geographic photographer Chris Johns; *r.* Michael A. Hampshire. 205: H. Edward Kim. 206: S. Tanaka/The Picture Cube. 208: ©Artville LLC 1997; *inset* images copyright ©1998 PhotoDisc, Inc. 209: Tim Davis/Photo Researchers, Inc. 210: *r.* Michael Krasowitz/FPG. 211: George Hall/Corbis. 213: ©TSM/Tibor Bognar. 214: images copyright ©1998 PhotoDisc, Inc. 215: Dr. Jeremy Burgess/Photo Researchers, Inc. 216: Brenda Tharp/Photo Researchers, Inc. 218: Gary Gold/Gamma-Liaison. 220: Allsport/Brian Bahr. 221: *l.* ©Marty Loken/TSI; *r.* Museum der Stadt, Vienna, Austria/Superstock. 222: *l.* Macmillan/McGraw-Hill School Division; *r.* ©TSM/John M. Roberts. 223: Wolfgang Kaehler/Corbis. 226: Joseph Schuyler/Stock, Boston. 227: Luc Novovitch/Gamma-Liaison. 231: *bkgnd.* Carr Clifton. 232: ©John Elk/TSI. 234: *t.* ©Arthur Morris/VU; *b.* Robert Holmgren/Peter Arnold, Inc. 235: ©TSM/Pete Saloutos. 236: *l.* ©Barb Gerlach/VU; *m.* ©Rich Treptow/VU; *r.* ©C.P. George/VU. 237: *t.* ©Science VU; *m.* ©Jeff Daly/VU; *b.r.* ©Cabisco/VU. 239: Barry B. Luokkala/Carnegie Mellon University. 242, 243: Roger Ressmeyer/Corbis. 244: Cesar Llacuna. 245: ©Yoav Levy/PhotoTake. 246: *bkgnd.* Wolfgang Kaehler/Corbis; *l.* Science Photo Library/Photo Researchers, Inc.; *r.* North Wind. 247: *l.* The Queens Borough Public Library, Long Island Division, Latimer Family Papers; *r.* Hall of Electricital History, Schenectady Museum, Schenectady, New York. 248: Kevin Fleming/Corbis. 250: *t.* ©Science VU. 251: *r.* ©Jeff Greenberg/VU. 252: *t.* ©Bill Beatty/VU. 258: ©James Webb/PhotoTake. 259: Bob Rowan/Progressive Images/Corbis. 267: Macmillan/McGraw-Hill School Division. 269: Allsport/Mike Powell. 272: ©Science VU. 276: Corbis-Bettmann. 278: *l.* Joseph Sohm/ChromoSohm, Inc./Corbis; *r.* ©Mark E. Gibson/VU. 279: *b.* ©Science VU; *t.* images copyright ©1998 PhotoDisc, Inc. 280: Macmillan/McGraw-Hill School Division. 281: *t.* Dr. Mony de Leon/Peter Arnold, Inc.; *b.* ©John D. Cunningham/VU. 282: ©Science VU. 283: Macmillan/McGraw-Hill School Division. 284: *bkgnd.* Hulton-Deutsch Collection/Corbis. **Unit 4** 289: *bkgnd.* ©Yoav Levy/PhotoTake; *inset* images copyright ©1998 PhotoDisc. 290: Jonathon Blair/Corbis. 297: *t.l.* Klaus Guldbrandsen/Science Photo Library/Photo Researchers, Inc.; *t.r.* George Bernard/Photo Researchers, Inc.; *m.l.* The Purcell Team/Corbis; *m.r.* Vaughan Fleming/Science Photo Library/Photo Researchers, Inc.; *b.l.* Buddy Mays/Corbis; *b.r.* Wolfgang Kaehler/Corbis. 299: Walter Meayers Edwards. 300: *t.* Ed Degginger/Color-Pic, Inc.; *m., b.* Phil Degginger/Color-Pic, Inc. 302: *t.* IBM Research/Peter Arnold, Inc.; *b.* ©National Railway of Japan/PhotoTake. 303: images copyright ©1998 PhotoDisc, Inc. 304, 305: Stephen Frink/Southern Stock/PNI. 306: NASA. 308: *t.* Lowell Georgia/Photo Researchers, Inc.; *b.* Rich Treptow/Photo Researchers, Inc. 309: *t.l.* ©Science/VU; *t.r., m., b.l., b.r.,* Charles D. Winters/Photo Researchers, Inc.; *m.l.* Russ Lappa/Science Source/Photo Researchers, Inc. 310: *t.l.* Runk/Schoenberger/Grant Heilman Photography, Inc.; *f.b.r.* ©Bill Beatty/VU; *b.m.* ©Yoav Levy/PhotoTake; *b.l. & b.r.* images copyright ©1998 PhotoDisc, Inc. 311: David Taylor/Photo Researchers, Inc. 312: *t.* IBM Research/Peter Arnold, Inc.; *b.* ©Science VU/BMRL. 314: *f.t.l., f.t.r.* E.R. Degginger/Color-Pic, Inc.; *t.l.* George Bernard/Photo Researchers, Inc.; *t.m., t.r.* Klaus Guldbrandsen/Photo Researchers, Inc.; *m.* Rich Treptow/Photo Researchers, Inc.; *b.l.* Charles D. Winters/Photo Researchers, Inc.; *b.r.* Russ Lappa/Photo Researchers, Inc. 318: *t.l.* Christine Coscioni/CO2, Inc; *t.r.* Leonard Lessin/Peter Arnold, Inc.; *b.l.* ©API/VU. 319: Christine Coscioni/CO2, Inc. 320: *l.* ©Gilbert L. Twiest/VU; *r.* Joe Sohm/Chromosohm/Stock, Boston. 321: images copyright ©1998 PhotoDisc, Inc. 322: ©Javier Domingo/PhotoTake. 324: *l.* Gordon Wiltsie/Peter Arnold, Inc.; *m.* Clyde H. Smith/Peter Arnold, Inc.; *r.* Jeff & Alexa Henry/Peter Arnold, Inc. 325: Cesar Llacuna. 328: *t.* ©Jakub Jasinski/VU; *b.l.* ©Kjell B. Sandved/VU; *b.r.* Darrell Gulin/Corbis. 330: *t.l.* ©Carolina Biological Supply/PhotoTake; *t.r.* Cesar Llacuna; *m.* Christine L. Coscioni/CO2, Inc; *b.* Charles D. Winters/Photo Researchers, Inc. 332: *t.* ©TSM/Mugshots; *b.* ©TSM/Chris Rogers. 333: Richard Choy/Peter Arnold, Inc. 334: Rod Plack/Photo Researchers, Inc. 337: ©TSM/Mark M. Lawrence. 338: *l.* Mark Marten/Science Source/Photo Researchers, Inc.; *r.* Alex S. MacLean/Peter Arnold, Inc. 340: *r.* Jacana/Photo

R48

PERIODIC TABLE OF THE ELEMENTS

	1						

Atomic Number
(number of protons) ——— 1

Symbol ——— **H**

Element ——— Hydrogen

State of Matter

1 **H** Hydrogen							

3 **Li** Lithium	4 **Be** Beryllium

11 **Na** Sodium	12 **Mg** Magnesium

		3	**4**	**5**	**6**	**7**	**8**	**9**

4

19 **K** Potassium	20 **Ca** Calcium	21 **Sc** Scandium	22 **Ti** Titanium	23 **V** Vanadium	24 **Cr** Chromium	25 **Mn** Manganese	26 **Fe** Iron	27 **Co** Cobalt

5

37 **Rb** Rubidium	38 **Sr** Strontium	39 **Y** Yttrium	40 **Zr** Zirconium	41 **Nb** Niobium	42 **Mo** Molybdenum	43 **Tc** Technetium	44 **Ru** Ruthenium	45 **Rh** Rhodium

6

55 **Cs** Cesium	56 **Ba** Barium	57 **La** Lanthanum	72 **Hf** Hafnium	73 **Ta** Tantalum	74 **W** Tungsten	75 **Re** Rhenium	76 **Os** Osmium	77 **Ir** Iridium

7

87 **Fr** Francium	88 **Ra** Radium	89 **Ac** Actinium	104 **Rf** Rutherfordium	105 **Db** Dubnium	106 **Sg** Seaborgium	107 **Bh** Bohrium	108 **Hs** Hassium	109 **Mt** Meitnerium

**The Most
Reactive
Metals**

Lanthanide Series

58 **Ce** Cerium	59 **Pr** Praseodymium	60 **Nd** Neodymium	61 **Pm** Promethium	62 **Sm** Samarium	63 **Eu** Europium

Actinide Series

90 **Th** Thorium	91 **Pa** Protactinium	92 **U** Uranium	93 **Np** Neptunium	94 **Pu** Plutonium	95 **Am** Americium